W9-ALW-030

PANAMA

1st Edition

by David Dudenhoefer

**Where to Stay and Eat
for All Budgets**

**Must-See Sights
and Local Secrets**

Ratings You Can Trust

Fodor's Travel Publications   New York, Toronto, London, Sydney, Auckland
www.fodors.com

FODOR'S PANAMA
Editor: Heidi Leigh Johansen (lead project editor), Kelly Kealy, Kelly Lack, Josh McIlvain, Adam Taplin

Editorial Production: Linda K. Schmidt
Editorial Contributors: David Dudenhoefer, with help from Nicholas Gill (Outdoor & Learning Vacations), and Victoria Patience (Essentials)
Maps & Illustrations: David Lindroth, *cartographer;* Bob Blake and Rebecca Baer, *map editors*
Design: Fabrizio LaRocca, *creative director;* Guido Caroti, Siobhan O'Hare, *art directors;* Tina Malaney, Chie Ushio, Ann McBride, *designers;* Melanie Marin, *senior picture editor;* Moon Sun Kim, *cover designer*
Cover Photo (Bocas del Toro Island): Tyler Stableford/The Image Bank/Getty Images
Production/Manufacturing: Matthew Struble

COPYRIGHT
Copyright © 2008 by Fodor's Travel, a division of Random House, Inc.

Fodor's is a registered trademark of Random House, Inc.

All rights reserved. Published in the United States by Fodor's Travel, a division of Random House, Inc., and simultaneously in Canada by Random House of Canada, Limited, Toronto. Distributed by Random House, Inc., New York.

No maps, illustrations, or other portions of this book may be reproduced in any form without written permission from the publisher.

1st Edition

ISBN 978-1-4000-1926-7

ISSN 1940-8811

SPECIAL SALES
This book is available at special discounts for bulk purchases for sales promotions or premiums. Special editions, including personalized covers, excerpts of existing books, and corporate imprints, can be created in large quantities for special needs. For more information, write to Special Markets/Premium Sales, 1745 Broadway, MD 6-2, New York, New York 10019, or e-mail specialmarkets@randomhouse.com.

AN IMPORTANT TIP & AN INVITATION
Although all prices, opening times, and other details in this book are based on information supplied to us at press time, changes occur all the time in the travel world, and Fodor's cannot accept responsibility for facts that become outdated or for inadvertent errors or omissions. So **always confirm information when it matters,** especially if you're making a detour to visit a specific place. Your experiences—positive and negative— matter to us. If we have missed or misstated something, **please write to us.** We follow up on all suggestions. Contact the Panama editor at editors@fodors.com or c/o Fodor's at 1745 Broadway, New York, NY 10019.

PRINTED IN THE UNITED STATES OF AMERICA
10 9 8 7 6 5 4 3 2 1

Be a Fodor's Correspondent

Your opinion matters. It matters to us. It matters to your fellow Fodor's travelers, too. And we'd like to hear it. In fact, we need to hear it.

When you share your experiences and opinions, you become an active member of the Fodor's community. That means we'll not only use your feedback to make our books better, but we'll publish your names and comments whenever possible. Throughout our guides, look for "Word of Mouth," excerpts of your unvarnished feedback.

Here's how you can help improve Fodor's for all of us.

Tell us when we're right. We rely on local writers to give you an insider's perspective. But our writers and staff editors—who are the best in the business—depend on you. Your positive feedback is a vote to renew our recommendations for the next edition.

Tell us when we're wrong. We're proud that we update most of our guides every year. But we're not perfect. Things change. Hotels cut services. Museums change hours. Charming cafés lose charm. If our writer didn't quite capture the essence of a place, tell us how you'd do it differently. If any of our descriptions are inaccurate or inadequate, we'll incorporate your changes in the next edition and will correct factual errors at fodors.com immediately.

Tell us what to include. You probably have had fantastic travel experiences that aren't yet in Fodor's. Why not share them with a community of like-minded travelers? Maybe you chanced upon a beach or bistro or B&B that you don't want to keep to yourself. Tell us why we should include it. And share your discoveries and experiences with everyone directly at fodors.com. Your input may lead us to add a new listing or highlight a place we cover with a "Highly Recommended" star or with our highest rating, "Fodor's Choice."

Give us your opinion instantly at our feedback center at www.fodors.com/feedback. You may also e-mail editors@fodors.com with the subject line "Panama Editor." Or send your nominations, comments, and complaints by mail to Panama Editor, Fodor's, 1745 Broadway, New York, NY 10019.

You and travelers like you are the heart of the Fodor's community. Make our community richer by sharing your experiences. Be a Fodor's correspondent.

Buen viaje!

Tim Jarrell, Publisher

CONTENTS

ABOUT THIS BOOK

Our Ratings

Sometimes you find terrific travel experiences and sometimes they just find you. But usually the burden is on you to select the right combination of experiences. That's where our ratings come in.

As travelers we've all discovered a place so wonderful that its worthiness is obvious. And sometimes that place is so unique that superlatives don't do it justice: you just have to be there to know. These sights, properties, and experiences get our highest rating, **Fodor's Choice**, indicated by orange stars throughout this book.

Black stars highlight sights and properties we deem **Highly Recommended**, places that our writers, editors, and readers praise again and again for consistency and excellence.

By default, there's another category: any place we include in this book is by definition worth your time, unless we say otherwise. And we will.

Disagree with any of our choices? Care to nominate a place or suggest that we rate one more highly? Visit our feedback center at www.fodors.com/feedback.

Budget Well

Hotel and restaurant price categories from ¢ to $$$$ are defined in the opening pages of each chapter. For attractions, we always give standard adult admission fees; reductions are usually available for children, students, and senior citizens. Want to pay with plastic? **AE, D, DC, MC, V** following restaurant and hotel listings indicate whether American Express, Discover, Diners Club, MasterCard, and Visa are accepted.

Restaurants

Unless we state otherwise, restaurants are open for lunch and dinner daily. We mention dress only when there's a specific requirement and reservations only when they're essential or not accepted—it's always best to book ahead.

Hotels

Hotels have private bath, phone, TV, and air-conditioning and operate on the European Plan (aka EP, meaning without meals), unless we specify that they use the Continental Plan (CP, with a Continental breakfast), Breakfast Plan (BP, with a full breakfast), or Modified American Plan (MAP, with breakfast and dinner) or are all-inclusive (AI, including all meals and most activities). We always list facilities but not whether you'll be charged an extra fee to use them.

Many Listings

★	Fodor's Choice
★	Highly recommended
✉	Physical address
✛	Directions
⌂	Mailing address
☎	Telephone
🖷	Fax
⊕	On the Web
✍	E-mail
💷	Admission fee
☉	Open/closed times
Ⓜ	Metro stations
▭	Credit cards

Hotels & Restaurants

🏨	Hotel
⤻	Number of rooms
⚭	Facilities
ⵜⵔ	Meal plans
✕	Restaurant
⤢	Reservations
⤡	Smoking
ⵜⵔ	BYOB
✕🏨	Hotel with restaurant that warrants a visit

Outdoors

🏌	Golf
⛺	Camping

Other

☾	Family-friendly
⇨	See also
✉	Branch address
☞	Take note

WHEN TO GO

Most people head to Panama during the dry season, usually from December to May, but your choice depends on your interests. Bird-watching is best from October to March, when northern migrants boost the native population. In fact, it's easier to see all wildlife during the dry months, because the forest foliage thins. The fishing is best from January to March, though Pacific sailfish run from April to July, and there are plenty of fish biting from July to January. The surf is best from June to December in the Pacific, whereas the Caribbean gets more waves between November and March, and some swells in July and August. The best months for white-water rafting and kayaking are June to December, when you have half a dozen rivers to choose from, but Panama's two best can be navigated from June to March. Scuba diving varies according to the region. The Caribbean's best diving conditions are between August and November, though March and April can also be good. The Gulf of Panama and Azuero Peninsula have better visibility from June to December, but the trade winds make the sea progressively colder and more murky there from December through to May. Those winds have less of an impact on the Gulf of Chiriquí and Isla de Coiba, where the diving is best from December to July, after which large swells can decrease visibility and complicate diving.

Panama City is a fun place to visit any time of year, but the dry months are nicest. Jazz fans will want to be there in late January, when the city celebrates its annual jazz festival, but travelers interested in folk music and dance can track down a folk festival in the Azuero Peninsula just about any time of year. Hotels often fill up between Christmas and Easter, and it's especially hard to find a room outside Panama City when Panamanians go on vacation—around New Year's, Carnaval week, and Easter week. The holidays are bad times to go to the beach, but they hardly affect Kuna Yala and the Darién.

Climate

Panama is an unmistakably tropical country, where the temperature fluctuates between 70°F and 90°F year-round, and humidity is usually about eighty percent. The country experiences two seasons: dry, from late December to May, and rainy from early May to December. January through April are the sunniest months for most of the country, with the exception of Bocas del Toro province, which gets plenty of rain in December and January. The sunniest months in Bocas del Toro are March, September, and October. The Darién gets more rain than the central and western provinces, and has a slightly shorter dry season. The mountain valleys of Boquete, Bambito, and Cerro Punta experience strong winds, mist, and low temperatures from December to mid-February, making March and April the nicest months there. Panama experiences a partial dry season in July and August, when it can go days without raining. You can count on downpours just about every afternoon in May, June, October, and November, when it sometimes rains for days on end.

Forecasts Weather Channel Connection (☎ *900/932–8437, 95¢ per minute* ⊕ *www.weather.com*).

WHAT'S WHERE

PANAMA CITY	Panama City is an obligatory stop, and a surprisingly pleasant hub for exploring the country, since international flights arrive here, and daily domestic flights, ferries, and buses depart from here. It is a vibrant and diverse metropolis with excellent dining, lodging, and nightlife, and an abundance of day-trip options. The brick streets and balconies of the Casco Viejo old quarter evoke southern France, but the skyline of the new city looks more like that of Chicago. The restaurants and marinas of the Calzada de Amador feel like Miami, but next to them is the unmistakable Panama Canal, and nearby is a rain forest where you can see monkeys, sloths, and tropical birds.
THE CANAL & CENTRAL PANAMA	Between them, the Panama Canal and Central Panama have everything from jungle-lined waterways to gorgeous beaches and misty mountain forests. This region holds an array of landscapes and attractions in a relatively small area, much of which can be explored on day trips from Panama City. It also has overnight options in wild and beautiful places where you may wake up to parrot squawks or the sound of waves washing against the shore. The Panama Canal is the region's biggest attraction, literally, and it can be admired from half a dozen vantage points or navigated on day trips that cost a fraction of what a cruise does. Nearby, several national parks shelter exuberant forests, Caribbean coral reefs, indigenous villages, colonial fortresses, dozens of idyllic islands, and the splendid mountain scenery of El Valle de Antón. This region also holds some of the country's best bird-watching, river rafting, hiking, golf, kayaking, fishing, horseback riding, and scuba diving.
THE AZUERO PENINSULA & VERAGUAS	The country's cultural cradle, home to ageless towns and colorful folk festivals, this region also has some of Panama's best surf and scuba diving. Few foreigners make it here, but those who do are rewarded by rich folklore, colonial churches, remote beaches, and varied marine life. Playa Venado and Playa Santa Catalina have some of Panama's best surf, whereas Isla de Coiba has some of the best diving in the eastern Pacific, and the more accessible Isla Iguana is comparably impressive.

CHIRIQUÍ PROVINCE	The western province of Chiriquí stretches from the peaks of the Talamanca Mountains southward to the islands that lie in the Golfo de Chiriquí, comprising everything from cloud forest to coral reefs, and white-water rivers to white-sand beaches. World-class surfing, river rafting, sportfishing, bird-watching, skin diving, and hiking make Chiriquí a destination meant for lovers of the great outdoors. But the refreshing climate and breathtaking scenery of its mountain valleys also make them excellent places to hang out and admire the hummingbirds, boulder-strewn rivers, and frequent rainbows. Some of the country's best lodges and restaurants take advantage of the province's scenery and provide comfortable access to its diverse flora and fauna.
BOCAS DEL TORO ARCHIPELAGO	The Bocas del Toro Archipelago holds an impressive mix of beaches, jungle, idyllic cays, and coral reefs. The archipelago's dozens of islands are surrounded by turquoise waters and lined with pristine strands that provide access to great skin diving or surfing, according to the season. The provincial capital of Bocas del Toro is a funky Caribbean town where boats and bicycles outnumber cars, hotels are perched over the water on pilings, and the dinner selection ranges from lobster fettuccine to chicken curry. Beyond it are countless acres of coral, indigenous villages, pristine beaches, and ecolodges where you may see a monkey from your porch, or a manta ray.
KUNA YALA (SAN BLAS) AND THE DARIÉN	The eastern provinces of Kuna Yala and the Darién are Panama at its wildest, where every trip is an adventure. Kuna Yala, home of the Kuna Indians, is known for the San Blas Islands, with their immaculate beaches and vibrant coral reefs. Since all hotels there are Kuna owned and lie near villages, a trip includes ample exposure to their indigenous culture. The Darién is known for its wildlife, which includes many species found nowhere else in the country, but it is also holds dozens of Emberá and Wounaan Indian villages, some of which accommodate visitors. The Darién also has the country's best sportfishing, and one of the world's top fishing lodges.

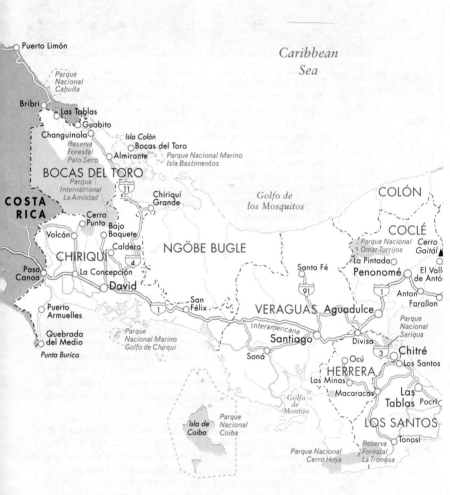

Caribbean
Sea

Puerto Limón

Parque
Nacional
Cahuita

Bribri
Las Tablas
Guabito
Changuinola
Isla Colón
Reserva
Forestal
Palo Seco
Bocas del Toro
Almirante
Parque Nacional Marino
Isla Bastimentos

BOCAS DEL TORO
Parque
Internacional
La Amistad

COSTA
RICA

Chiriquí
Grande

Golfo de
los Mosquitos

COLÓN

COCLÉ

Cerro
Punto
Bajo
Boquete
Volcán
Caldera

NGÖBE BUGLE

Parque Nacional
Omar Torrijos
Cerro
Gaitál

CHIRIQUÍ

Santa Fé
La Pintada
Penonomé

El Vall
de Antó

Paso
Canoa
La Concepción
David

San
Félix

VERAGUAS
Aguadulce
1
Anton
Farallon

Puerto
Armuelles

Interamericana
Santiago
Divisa

Parque
Nacional
Sariqua

Quebrada
del Medio
Punta Burica

Parque Nacional Marino
Golfo de Chiriquí

Soná

Ocú
HERRERA
Las Minas
Macaracas
Chitré
Los Santos

Las
Tablas
Pocrí

Golfo
de
Montijo

Isla de
Coiba
Parque
Nacional
Coiba

LOS SANTOS

Parque Nacional
Cerro Hoya
Reserva
Forestal
La Tronosa
Tonosí

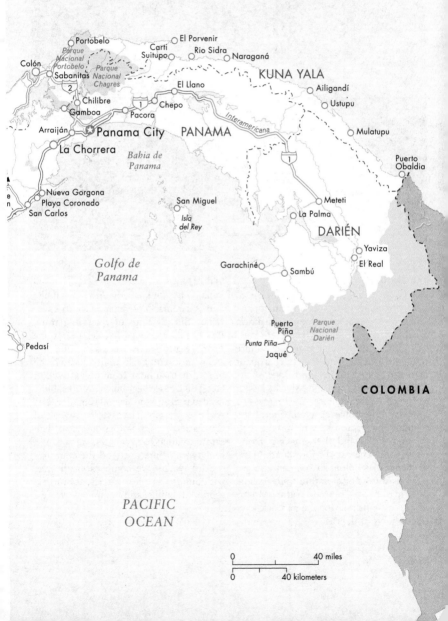

Panama

Portobelo
Parque Nacional Portobelo
Colón
Sabanitas
2
Chilibre
Gamboa
Arraiján
Panama City
La Chorrera

Parque Nacional Chagres

El Porvenir
Cartí Suitupo
Río Sidra
Naraganá

KUNA YALA

El Llano
Chepo
Pacora
1

PANAMA

Interamericana

Ailigandí
Ustupu

Mulatupu

Bahía de Panama

1

Puerto Obaldía

Nueva Gorgona
Playa Coronado
San Carlos

San Miguel

Isla del Rey

Meteti

La Palma

DARIÉN

Yaviza
El Real

Garachiné
Sambú

Golfo de Panama

Puerto Piña
Punta Piña
Jaqué

Parque Nacional Darién

COLOMBIA

Pedasí

PACIFIC OCEAN

0   40 miles
0   40 kilometers

QUINTESSENTIAL PANAMA

The Big Ditch

A century has passed since its completion, but the Panama Canal remains an impressive feat of engineering, not to mention a simply inspiring sight. There are various spots from which you can admire the "Big Ditch," and watching a giant cargo ship float under the Bridge of the Americas or slide into a massive lock is an unforgettable experience. The best way to appreciate it, however, is on one of the regular transit tours, which take you through locks and the canal's narrowest stretch. The canal's forests are home to plenty of wildlife, so you can also get onto its waters on a nature tour, such as the trip to Barro Colorado Nature Monument, or by fishing for the peacock bass that inhabit its depths.

Wild Things

Panama has an amazing array of wildlife and is a remarkably easy place to experience the diversity of tropical nature. Its capital, Panama City, lies near some of the world's most accessible rain forest, with several parks that you can reach in less than an hour from downtown. In fact, you can see keel-billed toucans, blue-headed parrots, and several simian species within city limits. The eastern province of the Darién is even wilder, home to such rare animals as harpy eagles, jaguars, and four types of macaw. And the country's coastal waters are comparably diverse, with hundreds of fish species, sea turtles, spotted dolphins, and humpback whales.

Idyllic Isles

Panamanian waters hold more than 1,600 islands, ranging from vast Isla del Rey to tiny cays topped with a few palm trees, like the castaway isles depicted in comics. The closest islands to Panama City are historic Isla Taboga, and Isla Contadora, a mere 20-minute flight away from the city, which has a dozen beaches and nearby isles that were featured on "Survivor Pearl Islands." To the northeast are the San Blas Islands, home of the fascinating Kuna Indians, with white-sand cays ringed by coral reefs. The Bocas del Toro Archipelago, to the west, has comparable island scenery and marine life, and better accommodations. Less accessible Isla Iguana, Isla de Coiba, and the private archipelago of Islas Secas have some of the best diving in the eastern Pacific, plus great beaches. To leave Panama without visiting at least one island would be criminal; actually you could feasibly spend your entire trip island hopping.

Cultural Cornucopia

Panama is a human rainbow. Though the indigenous peoples represent only six percent of the population, the country's Kuna, Emberá, Wounaan, and Ngöbe-Buglé Indians have fascinating traditions that they happily share with visitors. The folk music and dances of the Latino majority are on display at colorful rural festivals and several Panama City venues all year long. Meanwhile, the country's European, African, Middle Eastern, and Asian immigrants ensure that you'll find a rich variety of cuisines and interesting neighborhoods to explore just about everywhere you go.

IF YOU LIKE

Adventure Sports

The options for enjoying Panama's great outdoors range from hiking through the cloud forest to paddling down a white-water river. The country's world-class fishing, surfing, diving, and bird-watching draw plenty of people focused on just one activity, but Panama is also a great destination for travelers who want to dabble in several adventure sports.

Rafting. The Chagres and Chiriquí Viejo Rivers have exciting white-water rafting routes that pass through pristine rain forest. From June to December they are complemented by half a dozen smaller rivers near Boquete.

Hiking. Panama's hiking options range from short walks into the rain forest near Panama City to longer hikes though the mountains above El Valle de Antón, Boquete, or Cerro Punta, to a two-week trek through the jungles of the Darién.

Surfing. With dozens of surf spots on two oceans, Panama has waves most of the year. Expert-only reef breaks are the norm, but a handful of beach breaks are good for neophytes too. Try Playa Venado, Playa Santa Catalina, Morro Negrito, Bocas del Toro, and Isla Grande.

Kayaking. Sit-on-top kayaks are available at many lodges for exploring reefs and mangroves, but serious kayakers can join tours by the outfitter Xtrop to paddle the lower Chagres River, the Panama Canal's Pacific entrance, or the San Blas Islands.

Horseback Riding. Equestrian tours can take you through the mountain forests of Cerro Azul, El Valle de Antón, Boquete, Volcán, or Cerro Punta, the tropical dry forests of the Azuero Peninsula, or the rain forest of Bocas del Toro.

History

The site of the first Spanish colony on the American mainland, Panama has remnants of five centuries of European influence, including ancient fortresses, a dozen colonial churches, and indigenous cultures that have hardly changed since Columbus sailed down the country's coast.

Panama Viejo. The ruins of Panama's first city—founded almost five centuries ago, and sacked by the pirate Henry Morgan in 1671—evoke the nation's start as a trade center.

Casco Viejo. Panama City's historic quarter holds an enchanting mix of colonial churches, abandoned monasteries, 19th-century buildings, and timeless plazas that are perfect for a drink, or meal.

Portobelo. Together with nearby Fuerte San Lorenzo, these colonial fortresses hemmed by jungle and perched over aquamarine waters are stunning reminders of the days when pirates cruised the Caribbean in search of booty.

The Azuero Peninsula. With their colonial churches, timeless plazas, and adobe homes, the Azuero Peninsula's older towns are time capsules where the past comes alive during religious holidays and folk festivals.

The Canal. The Panama Canal's creation only a century ago was a historic event that is celebrated by displays in the visitor center at Miraflores Locks and murals in the Canal Administration Building.

Nature Lodges

With more than 960 bird species, 9,000 kinds of flowering plants, and such rare animals as tapirs and ocelots, Panama is a great place for nature lovers. And there's no better way to experience that wildlife

than a stay at a nature lodge, where you can bird-watch from your porch or bed.

Cana Field Station. Nestled in Parque Nacional Darién, this remote and rustic lodge is surrounded by jungle that is home to more than 400 bird species and an array of other wildlife, making it the best place in Panama to see animals.

Canopy Tower. This refurbished radar station in Parque Nacional Soberanía has good bird-watching from the restaurant, the rooftop deck, and every room. Expert guides and daily hikes help guests see as much as possible, whereas the property's sister Canopy Lodge, in El Valle de Antón, provides more comfort in a gorgeous setting.

Sierra Llorona. Surrounded by a 500-acre private nature reserve traversed by miles of trails, this small, affordable lodge has more than 200 bird species, various types of monkeys, and other wildlife on the property.

Finca Lerida. Rooms on this coffee farm at the edge of Parque Nacional Volcán Barú are very near a cloud forest where guests regularly see resplendent quetzals, emerald toucanets, and hundreds of other birds.

La Loma Jungle Lodge. With just three open-air bungalows inside the rain forest on Isla Bastamentos, in Bocas del Toro, this intimate lodge provides constant exposure to nature.

Los Quetzales Lodge. Cabins inside the cloud forest here feature amazing views and bird-watching, whereas guests at the main lodge can choose from hikes in two national parks.

Diving

With two oceans, 1,600 islands, and countless acres of coral, Panama is a world-class dive destination. Its Caribbean reefs and wrecks are adorned with dozens of sponge and coral species, and a mind-boggling array of fish and invertebrates, but the Pacific has the country's most spectacular dives, with schools of big fish, manta rays, sharks, and other marine creatures.

Isla de Coiba. Protected within a vast national park, Coiba is surrounded by the country's best diving, with immense reefs, submerged pinnacles, and legions of fish. Explore it on a one-week dive cruises or shorter trips from Play Santa Catalina.

Isla Iguana. An inexpensive alternative to Coiba, this protected island off the coast of the Azuero Peninsula is encircled by a 100-acre coral reef inhabited by more than 350 fish species.

Islas Secas. This remote archipelago in the Gulf of Chiriquí has extensive reefs teeming with marine life that can be explored from the exclusive resort on the islands, or on day trips from Boca Chica.

Bocas del Toro. With plenty of coral reefs and several dive shops, this popular Caribbean archipelago is perfect for scuba divers and snorkeling enthusiasts alike.

Kuna Yala. Though scuba diving is prohibited in Kuna Yala, the province holds impressive reefs, especially at the Cayos Holandeses, which can be visited on cruises with San Blas Sailing.

The Canal. Scuba Panama offers a unique dive in the Panama Canal, where steam shovels and trains used to dig it lie submerged in the murky depths.

National Parks & Activities

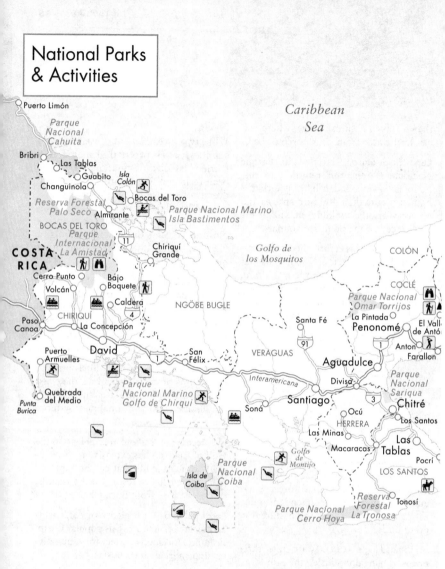

Puerto Limón

Parque Nacional Cahuita

Caribbean Sea

Bribri

Las Tablas

Guabito

Changuinola

Isla Colón

Bocas del Toro

Reserva Forestal Palo Seco

Almirante

Parque Nacional Marino Isla Bastimentos

BOCAS DEL TORO

Parque Internacional La Amistad

COSTA RICA

Chiriquí Grande

Golfo de los Mosquitos

COLÓN

Cerro Punto

Volcán

Bajo Boquete

Caldera

NGÖBE BUGLE

COCLÉ

Parque Nacional Omar Torrijos

La Pintada

Penonomé

El Valle de Antó

CHIRIQUÍ

4

Santa Fé

Paso Canoa

La Concepción

91

Antón

Farallon

David

San Félix

VERAGUAS

Aguadulce

1

Puerto Armuelles

Parque Nacional Marino Golfo de Chiriquí

Interamericana

Divisa

Parque Nacional Sariqua

3

Quebrada del Medio

Santiago

Chitré

Punta Burica

Soná

Ocú

HERRERA

Los Santos

Las Minas

Las Tablas

Isla de Coiba

Parque Nacional Coiba

Golfo de Montijo

Macaracas

LOS SANTOS

Pocrí

Parque Nacional Cerro Hoya

Reserva Forestal La Tronosa

Tonosí

0   40 miles

0   40 kilometers

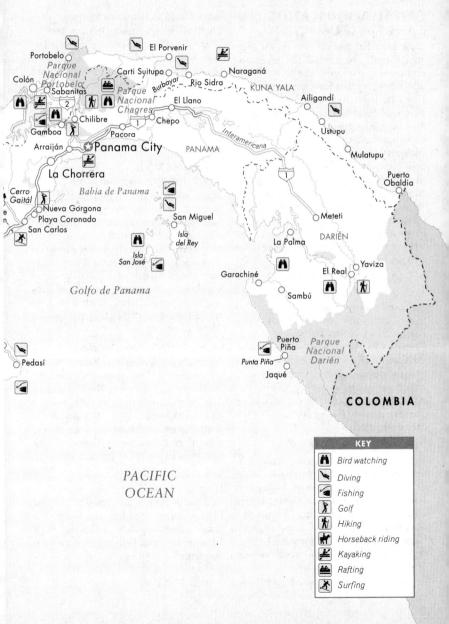

Portobelo

Parque Nacional Portobelo

Colón
Sabanitas

2

Chilibre

Gamboa

Arraiján

Pacora

★ Panama City

La Chorrera

Cerro Gaitál

Bahía de Panamá

Nueva Gorgona
Playa Coronado
San Carlos

Golfo de Panamá

Pedasí

PACIFIC OCEAN

El Porvenir

Carti Suitupo

Burbayar

Parque Nacional Chagres

El Llano

Chepo

Río Sidra

Naraganá

KUNA YALA

Ailigandí

Interamericana

PANAMA

1

San Miguel

Isla del Rey

Isla San José

Meteti

La Palma

DARIÉN

El Real

Garachiné

Sambú

Yaviza

Ustupu

Mulatupu

Puerto Obaldia

Puerto Piña

Punta Piña

Parque Nacional Darién

Jaqué

COLOMBIA

KEY	
	Bird watching
	Diving
	Fishing
	Golf
	Hiking
	Horseback riding
	Kayaking
	Rafting
	Surfing

GREAT ITINERARIES

CANAL AND ISLANDS
2 Days: Panama City & Canal

Take a partial transit tour of the Panama Canal, then spend the afternoon and evening exploring the Casco Viejo, which has several good restaurants. Start Day 2 bird-watching in the rain forest of Parque Natural Metropolitano or Parque National Soberanía, then check out city sights such as the Museo Antropológico, Esclusas Miraflores, Mi Pueblito, or Balboa. Calzada de Amador is a great place for sunset cocktails or dinner. **Logistics:** Most companies can book canal transit tours, and several offer bird-watching tours in nearby parks. Taxis are an easy way to get around town, where most trips cost $2–$5, or you can hire a cab for $10 per hour.

Day 1: Railway and Caribbean

Take the train to Colón and spend the day exploring the Caribbean coast, fortresses, rain forest, or beaches of Portobelo or San Lorenzo before returning to Panama City. You can also overnight on the Caribbean side, but you'll need more time for travel on Day 2. **Logistics:** Several companies offer day tours that pick you up at the train station in Colón, or you can take a bus to Colón 2000, and rent a car or hire a cab.

Days 3 and 4: Hills and Forests

Head to El Valle de Antón for bird-watching, hiking, biking, or horseback riding; or combine a night at Sierra Llorona or Burbayar with a visit to an Emberá Indian village. **Logistics:** The Sierra Llorona and Burbayar lodges provide transport; renting a car is the best option for El Valley de Antón, which is a two-hour drive west of Panama City.

Days 5 and 6: Island Adventures

Fly to Isla Contadora or Isla San José, or boat to Isla Taboga, and top off your trip with sun, sea, and sand. Sportfishing or diving are good choices for more active travelers here. **Logistics:** From Panama City there are two daily flights to Isla Contadora, one flight to Isla San José most days, and two or three daily ferries to Isla Taboga.

ADVENTURE
Day 1: Panama City and Canal

Start the day in the rain forest of Parque Natural Metropolitano, or Parque National Soberanía. Explore the Casco Viejo in the afternoon, then kayak on the Panama Canal at sunset, before dining on the causeway. **Logistics:** Several companies offer tours to the parks; Xtrop offers kayaking on the canal. Taxis are an easy way to get around town, where most trips cost $2–$5, and you can hire a cab for $10 per hour.

Day 2: Parque Nacional Chagres

Spend Day 2 driving into Parque Nacional Chagres and paddling down the class III–IV rapids of the upper Río Chagres, or head up the lower stretch of that river to an Emberá Indian village. **Logistics:** Aventuras Panama runs rafting trips on the Chagres from June to April; several tour operators have trips to Emberá villages.

Day 3: Kuna Yala

Fly to Kuna Yala for a day of snorkeling, beach time, and a visit to a Kuna Indian village, spending the night in a Kuna lodge. **Logistics:** Flights to Kuna Yala depart from Panama City at 6 AM and return at 6:40 AM.

Days 4 to 7: Western Wonders

Fly to David, in Chiriquí, where you can spend three nights in Boquete, Cerro Punta, and Boca Chica, or Islas Secas. The western province's outdoor options include cloud-forest hikes, bird-watching, horseback riding, mountain biking, a canopy tour, diving, kayaking, rafting, and sportfishing. **Logistics:** There are several daily flights between Panama City and David, where you can rent a car, bus, or taxi to Chiriquí's attractions, which are 1–2 hours away.

WILD PANAMA

Days 1 and 2: Canal, Forest & City

Take a partial transit tour of the Panama Canal, then spend the afternoon in the Casco Viejo and the Calzada de Amador. Or take the day tour to Barro Colorado on Gatún Lake. Start Day 2 in the rain forest of Parque Natural Metropolitano or Parque National Soberanía, then have lunch at Esclusas Miraflores or on the Calzada. Fly to David in the afternoon and sleep in Boquete. **Logistics:** Most companies offer canal transits and morning trips to the rain-forest parks. Only the Smithsonian Tropical Research Institute runs tours to Barro Colorado. Taxis are an easy way to get around town, where most trips cost $2–$5, and you can hire a cab for $10 per hour. You can rent a car in David, or bus, or taxi to Boquete, which is an hour away.

Days 3 to 6: Chiriquí Highlands

Bird-watch at Finca Lerida and other areas in Boquete, which has plenty of hiking trails, horseback riding, river rafting, and a canopy tour. Spend at least one night in Bambito, or Cerro Punta, which also have great forests and birds. **Logistics:** Chiriquí is easily explored by car, though buses make regular trips to Boquete and Cerro Punta, and there are taxis everywhere.

Days 7 and 8: Bocas del Toro

Fly, or taxi, to Bocas del Toro and spend two days bird-watching, diving, beach combing, or visiting an Indian village. **Logistics:** There are early morning flights from David to Bocas del Toro, but you can also take a taxi to Almirante—bird-watching in Lago Fortuna on the way—where water taxis depart for the islands. Most transportation in Bocas del Toro is by boat.

Day 9: Panama City

Fly to Panama City and spend the afternoon exploring the nearby rain forest, enjoy a late lunch at Gamboa, or hit city sights. **Logistics:** There are several daily flights from Bocas del Toro to Panama City.

Days 10 to 13: The Darién

Fly to the Darién for an extended stay at the Cana Field Station, Punta Patiño, or an Emberá Indian village. You may see macaws, harpy eagles, and other rare animals in the province's forest. **Logistics:** Ancón Expeditions arranges charter flights to Cana, whereas Air Panama has twice-weekly flights to La Palma, where you can catch a boat to Punta Patiño and Indian villages.

Day 14: Panama City

Spend your last afternoon in Panama City exploring city sights, shopping, or in a nearby forest. **Logistics:** Taxis are an easy way to get around town.

ON THE CALENDAR

		New Year's, Carnaval, and Holy Week are the holidays that have Panamanians flocking to the beaches and mountains, and folk festivals take place nearly every month on the Azuero Peninsula. Check the Panama Tourism Bureau's Web site (⊕*www.visitpanama.com*) for exact dates.
DRY SEASON	Jan.	The **Panama Jazz Festival** (⊕*www.panamajazzfestival.com*) brings together international and local artists for a concert series in Panama City's historic Casco Viejo in late January.
	Late Feb.–early Mar.	**Carnaval** is celebrated throughout Panama, but the most spectacular parades take place in Panama City and Las Tablas, on the Azuero Peninsula.
	Mar.	The **Festival de la Caña** *(Sugarcane Festival)* (☎974–4532) is held in the rum-producing town of Pesé, southwest of Chitré, on the Azuero Peninsula, with folk music, dancing, and heavy drinking during a weekend in early March.
	Apr.	The **Desfile Mil Polleras** *(Thousand Polleras Parade)* (☎526–7000 ⊕*www.milpolleras.pa*) takes place in downtown Panama City on the last Sunday in April. It features lots of folk music floats, and women in *polleras* (embroidered dresses).
WET SEASON	Late May–early June	**Corpus Christi** is a colorful celebration in La Villa de Los Santos and nearby towns, featuring dances by *los diablitos* (little devils), groups of men in red and black costumes and elaborate papier-mâché masks.
	June	The **Festival de Manito,** one of the country's most important folk festivals, is held in the tiny town of Ocú, in the heart of the Azuero Peninsula, during the last week in June.
	July	The **Festival de la Pollera** is celebrated in the town of Las Tablas, on the Azuero Peninsula, July 20–23, with folk music, dancing, a parade, and plenty of women in *polleras*.
	Aug.	The **Fundación de Panama la Vieja** (☎226–8915 ⊕*www.panamaviejo.org*) celebrates the founding of Panama Viejo with a ceremony and folk dances in the ruins on August 15.
	Sept.	The **Festival Nacional de la Mejorana** (⊕*www.festivalnacionaldelamejorana.com*), held during the third week of September in tiny Gauraré, on the Azuero Peninsula, is dedicated to folk music played on a tiny guitar called *la mejorana*.
	Nov.	The **Día de la Independencia** celebrates the country's independence from Spain in 1821 with parades and drumming.

Panama City

WORD OF MOUTH

"It's undoubtedly the *best* kept secret on Earth! I'm talking about Panama in general and Panama City (the capital) in particular. On a clear day, as the aircraft makes its final approach, passengers on their first trip to Panama City stare in disbelief at the sight of gleaming skyscrapers unfolding below."

–Eloy A. Haughton

By David
Dudenhoefer

PANAMA CITY IS AN INCREDIBLY diverse and hospitable place, with an assortment of urban and natural environments to please just about any taste. Founded nearly five centuries ago, the city is steeped in history, yet much of it is remarkably modern. The baroque facades of the city's old quarter appear frozen in time, while the area around Punta Paitilla (Paitilla Point) is positively vaulting into the 21st century, with gleaming skyscrapers towering over the waterfront.

The city can feel schizophrenic, changing personality as you move from one neighborhood to another. That could be said of many a metropolis, but Panama City's diversity is disproportionate to its size. Though its metropolitan area has just over 1 million inhabitants, Panama City is home to races, religions, and cultures from around the world, reflected in its various Christian churches and synagogues, plus a mosque and a Hindu temple—not to mention its many restaurants. Whereas the high-rises of Punta Paitilla and the Area Bancária (banking district) create a skyline more impressive than that of Miami, the brick streets and balconies of the Casco Viejo evoke the French Quarter of New Orleans. The tree-lined boulevards of Balboa—built by the U.S. government between 1905 and 1920—are a pleasant mixture of early-20th-century American architecture and exuberant tropical vegetation. The islands reached by the nearby Calzada Amador (Amador Causeway)—a man-made causeway that stretches 2 mi into the Pacific—have brand-new bars and restaurants, plus a yacht-packed marina. The best part? All these neighborhoods lie within 15 minutes of one another.

The city's proximity to tropical nature is astounding, with significant patches of forest protected within city limits on Cerro Ancón (Ancón Hill) and in Parque Metropolitano, and the national parks of Camino de Cruces and Soberanía just to the northwest of town. You could spend a morning hiking through the rain forest of the Parque Metropolitano to see parrots and toucans, then watch pelicans dive into the sea while sipping a sunset drink at one of Amador Causeway's restaurants. There are plenty of spots in and around the city that offer views of the ocean or the Panama Canal, and those views include massive ships anchored offshore or plying the interoceanic waterway.

An impressive array of restaurants, an abundance of shops and handicraft markets, and a vibrant nightlife scene round out Panama City's charm. This is good news for travelers, since the city is Panama's transportation hub, which makes overnights here unavoidable. All international flights arrive at Panama City's Tocumen Airport (airport code PTY), which is 25 km (16 mi) east of the city; domestic flights and buses depart from the neighborhood of Albrook, just west of downtown. ⚠ **The city can also serve as a base for an array of day trips, including Panama Canal transit tours, a boat ride to Isla Taboga, a trip on the Panama Canal Railway, a day at the colonial fortresses of Portobelo, or hikes through various rain-forest reserves.**

The downside of Panama City is that its colorful contrasts include all the ugly aspects of urban life in the developing world. It has its fair share of slums, including several around must-see Casco Viejo. Traffic

TOP REASONS TO GO

1

THE PANAMA CANAL

With a length of 50 mi, the inter-oceanic canal is literally Panama's biggest attraction. Whatever your reasons for traveling to Panama, the canal is simply a must-see; there are half a dozen spots in or near the capital from which to admire it. The Calzada Amador, the Balboa Yacht Club, the scenic overlook on the east side of the Bridge of the Americas, and the visitor center at Miraflores Locks all offer impressive vistas of the "big ditch," which you can experience more closely on a transit tour or on one of the nature tours of Gatún Lake.

CASCO VIEJO

The balconies, brick streets, and quiet plazas of the historic Casco Viejo have a European air, and the neighborhood's ancient churches and monasteries stand as testimony to the country's rich colonial history. After decades of neglect, the old quarter is finally undergoing a renaissance. The neighborhood also has some of the city's nicest restaurants and bars, which makes it a must-visit, even if only for dinner followed by a stroll and a cocktail.

RAIN FORESTS

Panama City lies near some of the most accessible rain forests in the world, with jungle trails a short drive from most hotels. Parque Natural Metropolitano, within the city limits, is home to more than 200 bird species. Within Parque Nacional Soberanía, and the highland forests of Cerro Azul and Altos de Campana, live such animals as the keel-billed toucan and howler monkey.

THE CALZADA AMADOR

The Amador Causeway provides a great escape from the cement and traffic of downtown Panama City. Stretching 2 mi (3 km) into the Pacific to connect three islands to the mainland, the Causeway has panoramic views of the city's skyline, the canal's Pacific entrance, and the Bay of Panama, as well as an excellent selection of restaurants, bars, and diversions—all of them cooled by ocean breezes.

DAY TRIPS

Panama City is the perfect base for day trips into the wild that can leave you sweaty, muddy, or sunburned, but get you back to your hotel in time to clean up for a delicious three-course meal. In addition to boat trips on the Panama Canal, or wildlife watching on Gatún Lake, you can hike into the forests of various national parks. Parque Nacional Chagres holds Emberá Indian villages and white-water rafting, and day trips to the island of Isla Taboga or the Caribbean fortresses of Portobelo combine history with beach time. All in all, there are enough day-trip options to keep you busy for a week.

can be downright terrible, and the ocean along its coast is very polluted. Brand-new SUVs waiting at stoplights are solicited by people selling oranges and car accessories. The city has a high unemployment rate, and crime can be a problem in some neighborhoods. Be sure to use your common sense and be careful where you walk around, especially at night. The city as a whole, though, is quite safe, especially the downtown area, where you'll find its bustling hotels, restaurants, and bars.

ORIENTATION & PLANNING

ORIENTATION

Panama City is a sprawling urban area, stretching for 10 km (6 mi) along the Bahía de Panamá (Bay of Panama) on the Pacific Coast and several miles into the sultry hinterland. The good thing for visitors is that most of its attractions and accommodations are within a few miles of one another in the city's southwest corner, near the Panama Canal's Pacific entrance. The eastern edge of the canal's entrance—because Panama snakes west to east, the canal runs north from the Pacific to the Atlantic—is defined by the former American Canal Zone, which includes the Calzada Amador (the breakwater connecting several islands to the mainland), and the neighborhoods of Balboa, Ancón, and Albrook. To the east of Balboa stands Cerro Ancón, a forested hill topped by a massive Panamanian flag that is a landmark visible from most of the city. To the east of Cerro Ancón is the busy Avenida de los Mártires, which was once on the border between the Canal Zone and Panama City. To the east of that former border lie the slums of Chorrillo and Santa Ana, both of which should be avoided; the Plaza Cinco de Mayo (where the country's congress is located); and the Avenida Central pedestrian mall, which runs southeastward into the historic Casco Viejo.

Avenida Balboa, one of the city's main east-west routes, runs along the Bay of Panama between the Casco Viejo and modern Paitilla Point. It is lined by an attractive waterfront promenade called the malecón, in the middle of which is a small park with a monument to Balboa. The neighborhood along its western half is a bit sketchy, so you should only stroll the malecón to the east of the Balboa monument. Avenida Balboa ends at Punta Paitilla, with its Multicentro shopping mall, skyscrapers, and private hospitals. There it branches into the Corredor Sur, an expressway to the international airport, and the inland Vía Israel, which eventually turns into Avenida Cincuentanario, and leads to the ruins of Panamá Viejo.

The main eastbound street to the north of Avenida Balboa is Avenida Justo Arosemena, which runs east from Plaza Cinco de Mayo and flows into Calle 50 (Cincuenta) (also called Calle Nicanor de Obarrio). The main westbound route is Vía España, a busy boulevard lined with banks and shopping centers that curves south to become the Avenida Central, which in turn becomes a pedestrian mall at Plaza Cinco de Mayo, after which it curves eastward to become the main avenue in the Casco Viejo.

PLANNING

WHEN TO GO

Because Panama City has the country's only international airport and is the transportation hub for domestic flights and buses, you may return here several times during your trip. This means you can explore the capital bit by bit over the course of your stay in the country.

Unlike the rest of the country, Panama City hardly has a low season, since the bulk of its visitors are business travelers. Most tourists head here during the dry season, from December to May; this is when the city's hotels are packed. Carnaval, in mid-February, is a fun time to be in the capital, since that long weekend is celebrated with parades and lots of partying. The city is fairly quiet during Easter week, on the other hand, since businesses close from Thursday to Easter Sunday and every resident who can leaves town. The Mil Polleras parade, held on the last Sunday of April, is a celebration worth catching, with lots of folk music and women in *polleras,* elaborately embroidered dresses. November 3 and 28 are independence days, from Colombia and Spain respectively: they are noisy dates to be in town, since every high school has a drum corps that marches in the parades. In fact, late October and November is a noisy time of year, because those drummers spend much of it practicing for the big parades.

May, June, and September through November are the rainiest months in Panama City, though most of that rain falls in the afternoon or evening. The rains let up a bit in July and August, which is a good time to visit, since you have to share the place with fewer tourists than during the dry season.

GETTING AROUND

Panama City is a confusing place to drive, but, thankfully, taxis and buses are abundant and inexpensive. If you navigate the city using a map, keep in mind that many streets change names from one neighborhood to the next. To add to the confusion, street corners often lack signs, and, outside of the former Canal Zone, what few street numbers exist on buildings tend to be random. So do as the locals do, and steer yourself by major landmarks, such as Plaza Cinco de Mayo, Vía España, or hotels and shopping centers.

Taxis are the easiest way to get around town, and they are usually dirt-cheap. They don't have meters, but the city is divided into zones, with the flat fare for one person being $1, to which they add a quarter each time you cross into another zone, plus 25 cents for each additional person. A short trip, such as between the Casco Viejo and Area Bancária, should cost about $2 for two people, whereas a trip to the Calzada Amador should cost $3 to $5. A taxi to Tocumen International Airport costs between $15 and $20. Taxis that wait outside hotels are more expensive, but the car should be nice, and the driver is likely to speak English.

If you really want to experience the local ways, hop onto one of the city buses, which run along the main east-west routes, with their destinations painted on their windshields. The fare is a quarter, which you pay as you get off the bus. Even if you don't ride in one, you may at least want to take a picture, since they tend to display wildly colorful airbrush artwork.

Between 11 AM and 3 PM the heat is oppressive, so serious strolling should be limited to the morning and evening hours. Much of the city is safe for walking, even in the evening, especially Vía España, El Cangrejo, the Area Bancária, and Paitilla, where most of the city's hotels and restaurants are located. The Casco Viejo and Avenida Central pedestrian mall are safe by day, but after dark you'll want to limit your wandering to the area around Plaza Bolívar and Plaza Francia, which is where all the restaurants and bars are. ■TIP➔ **Areas that should be avoided at all hours are El Chorillo and Santa Ana, just west of the Casco Viejo; the southwestern half of Caledonia, including the Avenida Balboa west of the Balboa Monument; and Curundú, just to the west of Caledonia.**

WHAT TO DO

STROLL THROUGH HISTORY
Learn about Panama's rich past by visiting the museum and ruins of Panama Viejo, then head to the Casco Viejo, the city that replaced it. Another history lesson awaits you on the other side of Ancón Hill, where murals commemorating the canal's construction adorn the Panama Canal Administration Building's rotunda.

COMMUTE
Tired of looking at the Pacific? Hop onto the Panama Railway's early morning commuter service, and you'll be on the Caribbean in an hour, having marveled at the beauty of the canal and surrounding forest along the way. You can then hire a car in Colón and spend the day exploring the Spanish fortresses and beaches of Portobelo.

NAVIGATE THE DITCH
It's hard not to be impressed by the sight of a massive cargo ship floating under the Bridge of the Americas, or sliding into a lock as 700-ton doors close behind it, but to experience fully the wonder of the Panama Canal, spend a morning, or a day, navigating it on one of several boats that offer canal transit tours.

GET YOUR SHOP ON
Whether you're in the market for a new camera or indigenous handicrafts, Panama City's abundant stores, markets, and shopping malls offer more bargains than you can shake a credit card at. Many Latin Americans are drawn to Panama by its cheap imported goods, but the city also has hundreds of handicraft vendors hawking colorful *molas* (patchwork fabric pictures), woven baskets, bags, and jewelry.

PARTY PANAMA-STYLE
Whether you prefer listening to Latin jazz in the old quarter, sipping a martini while a DJ spins downtown, barhopping on Calle Uruguay, or savoring a beer by the marina on the Calzada Amador, Panama City has nightlife options to fit your every mood. The city has folk-dancing shows, salsa concerts, Latin dance classes, massive casinos with sports bars, and an ample supply of strip clubs.

1

RESTAURANTS & CUISINE

Don't plan on losing weight in Panama City. There are simply too many good restaurants, and a cuisine selection that pretty much spans the globe, from Indian and Italian to Lebanese and Panamanian (of all things!). The city has some inventive chefs who do an excellent job of combining local ingredients with farther-flung culinary traditions; the results make for some remarkable dining at reasonable prices.

The seafood tends to be quite fresh, which shouldn't come as a surprise, since the word "Panama" means "abundance of fish," and it's relatively inexpensive, with the exception of lobster and crab. Pastas and pizzas are also affordable, but the best beef is imported from the United States, and can be more expensive. A typical entrée at an expensive restaurant runs about $15, whereas a main dish at a less expensive eatery averages around $7. It's customary to tip at least 10%, but some restaurants automatically add a 10% *servicio* charge, so be sure to have a good look at the check. Service can be slow, especially in the more economical restaurants, and it's rarely delivered with a smile.

Many restaurants close Sundays. Reservations are required only at the best restaurants. Jackets and ties aren't necessary, but don't wear shorts and sandals unless the restaurant is outdoors.

ABOUT THE HOTELS

Panama City has an extensive selection of hotels, yet there is often a shortage of rooms at everything but the budget levels, which means you'll want to reserve well ahead of time, especially for the December–May dry season. If you travel off-season, or reserve through the Web sites of the big hotels, you should be able to get rooms for considerably less than the rack rate. The city's best hotels are quite nice, and varied enough in what they offer to suit most tastes, but some can suffer from poor service. Nevertheless, travelers on a budget can find a variety of comfortable accommodations for less than $100, including hotels with swimming pools and Internet. All hotels listed in this chapter have private bathrooms with hot water, air-conditioning, telephone, and cable TV.

PAYING

The accepted currency is the U.S. dollar, which is often called the balboa, in reference to the long defunct national currency. Credit cards are widely accepted and ATM machines are all over, including in the lobbies of large hotels and at gas stations and supermarkets.

WHAT IT COSTS IN U.S. DOLLARS					
	¢	$	$$	$$$	$$$$
RESTAURANTS	under $5	$5–$10	$10–$15	$15–$20	over $22
HOTELS	under $50	$50–$100	$100–$160	$160–$220	over $220

Restaurant prices are per person for a main course at dinner. Hotel prices are for two people in a standard double room, excluding service and 10% tax.

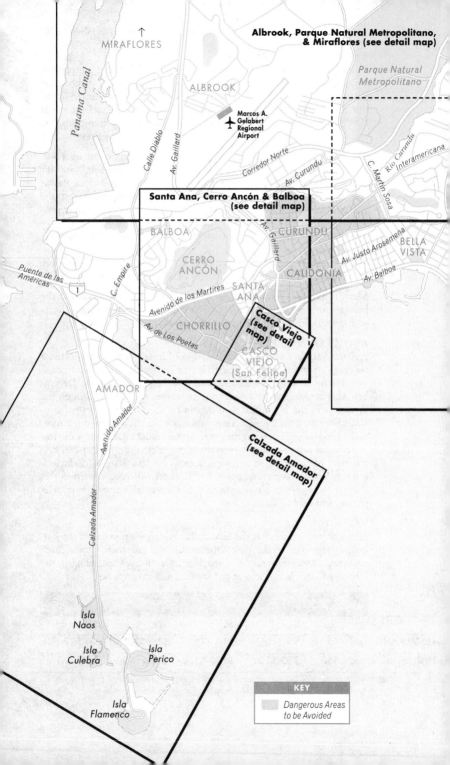

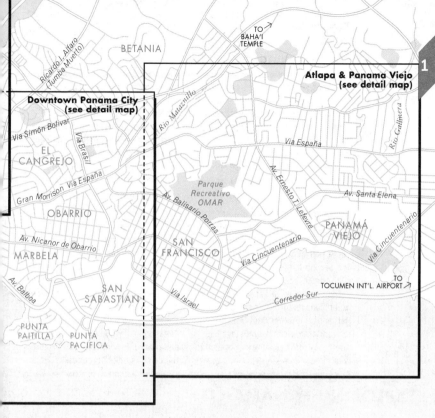

BETANIA

TO →
BAHA'I
TEMPLE

**Atlapa & Panama Viejo
(see detail map)**

1

Ricardo J. Alfaro
(Tumba Muerto)

**Downtown Panama City
(see detail map)**

Río Matasnillo

Via Simón Bolívar

EL
CANGREJO

Via Brasil

Via España

Río Gallinera

Av. Ernesto T. Lefevre

Av. Santa Elena

Gran Morrison Via España

Parque
Recreativo
OMAR

Av. Balisario Porras

OBARRIO

PANAMÁ
VIEJO

Via Cincuentenario

Av. Nicanor de Obarrio

SAN
FRANCISCO

Via Cincuentenario

MARBELA

Av. Balboa

SAN
SABASTIAN

Via Israel

Corredor Sur

TO
TOCUMEN INT'L. AIRPORT ↗

PUNTA
PAITILLA

PUNTA
PACIFICA

Bahía de Panama

0 ——————— 1/2 mile
0 ——————— 1/2 kilometer

*PACIFIC
OCEAN*

Panama City

The Panamanians

CLOSE UP

You won't spend long in Panama City before realizing that it is home to an extremely varied populace. Thanks to the canal and the country's commercial importance, immigrants flock here from around the world. A walk through one of the city's busy streets will prove just how diverse its residents are.

The majority of Panamanians are mestizo, which refers to the mixture of European and native Panamanian blood that began with the conquest. The second-largest group of residents is of African descent, some of whose ancestors arrived in Panama as slaves, others whose ancestors came from Barbados and other Caribbean islands to work on the canal, and stayed. About 10% of the country's population is of direct European descent, a group that includes descendants of Spanish conquistadors, seamen who have settled here, and former American "Zonians" who stayed on when the canal became Panamanian. The capital is also home to significant numbers of Sephardic and Ashkenazi Jews, Arabs from various nations, Chinese, and East Indians, who together control much of the city's retail and wholesale sectors.

Descendants of the original Panamanians, on the other hand, represent only 6% of the national population, and most of them live in *comarcas*, or indigenous territories. There are plenty of native Panamanians working in the city, though; you're bound to spot Kuna women, who sell their *molas* and other handicrafts as you explore the capital's neighborhoods.

EXPLORING PANAMA CITY

CASCO VIEJO

Panama City's charming historic quarter is known as the Casco Viejo, (pronounced CAS-coh Bee-EH-hoh), which translates as "old shell." It's spread over a small point in the city's southeast corner, where timeless streets and plazas are complemented by views of a modern skyline and the Bahía de Panamá. The Casco Viejo's narrow brick streets, wrought-iron balconies, and intricate cornices evoke visions of Panama's glorious history as a major trade center. A stroll here offers opportunities to admire a beautiful mix of Spanish colonial, neoclassical, and art nouveau architecture. And though most of its buildings are in a lamentable state of neglect, and the neighborhood is predominantly poor, it is a lively and colorful place, where soccer balls bounce off the walls of 300-year-old churches and radios blare Latin music.

While it's hardly the safest neighborhood in Panama City, Casco Viejo really shouldn't be missed. The streets tend to be busy on weekdays and weekend afternoons, when government workers and Panamanians head here in large numbers, and the area is always patrolled by tourism police, who work out of a station behind the Teatro Nacional. Take basic travelers' precautions, and don't wander around after dark.

EXPLORING TIPS

Panama City is a pretty hassle-free place to explore on your own: many people speak English, the U.S. dollar is legal tender, and there are ATMs, restaurants, pharmacies, shops, and taxis just about everywhere. You can explore some areas on foot, though distances between neighborhoods make public transportation necessary for many trips. If you ever feel uneasy about a location or situation and there aren't any police around, just flag down a taxi, which are abundant and widely considered to be safe. If you have a medical problem, go to Hospital Punta Pacífica, the best private clinic in the city. It also has a dental clinic.

It's best to get rolling early, take a long break around lunch (when the weather is hottest), and head back into the street when the heat begins to subside. If you're here during the rainy season, you can expect downpours every afternoon: the best thing to do when it starts to pour is find a restaurant and have a cup of coffee or a drink. Rest your feet until the deluge subsides, which is usually within 20 minutes. Keep in mind that most, though not all, museums are closed on Monday. The most convenient COTEL, or post office, is on the lower floor of the Plaza Concordia mall, on Vía España. Farmacia Arrocha has a dozen large pharmacies scattered around the city, and the ones near the big hotels are open 24 hours. ⚠ **The folks at the IPAT tourism information office on the corner of Vía España and Calle Ricardo Arias can answer basic questions.**

National police ☏ *104.* **Fire department** ☏ *103.* **Ambulance** *Hospital Punta Pacífica* ☏ *204–8180.*

COTEL (post office) ✉ *Plaza Concordia No. 121, Vía España El Cangrejo* ☏ *512-6232.* **IPAT Tourist Information Offices** ✉ *Vía España and Calle Ricardo Arias, El Cangrejo* ☏ *269-8011.* **Farmacia Arrocha** ✉ *Calle 49 Este at Vía Esaña Area Bancária* ☏ *223–4505* ✉ *Av. Balboa Punta Paitilla* ☏ *264–9044.* **Hospital Punta Pacífica** (✉ *Boulevard Pacífica y Vía Punta Darién Punta Pacífica* ☏ *204–8000.*

TIMING & PRECAUTIONS

The Casco Viejo is best explored on foot, though due to the intensity of the tropical heat, you should do your walking either first thing in the morning or late in the afternoon. Three o'clock in the afternoon is a great time to stroll around, when you can enjoy the evening light at Plaza Francia, have a drink on Plaza Bolívar, then dine at a nearby restaurant. Give yourself at least 2½ hours to tour this neighborhood, and more if you plan to shop and explore all the museums. Unfortunately, the area's museums have very little information in English.

Casco Viejo is predominantly poor, but it isn't as dangerous as it looks. Nevertheless, precautions should be taken: leave jewelry and valuables in your hotel safe, don't bring or show heaps of money, and be discreet with camera or video equipment. The crime problem is not so much in Casco Viejo but in the adjacent neighborhoods, so you shouldn't stray from the areas covered in the walking tour. At night you'll want to limit your wandering to the area around Plaza Francia, Plaza Bolívar, and Plaza Catedral.

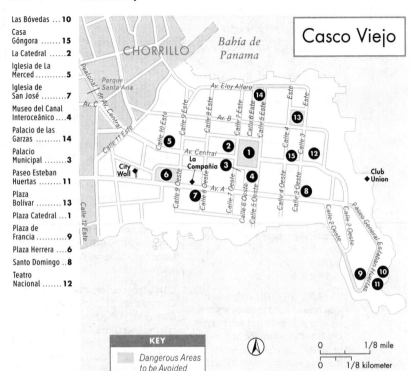

WHAT TO SEE

❿ **Las Bóvedas.** The arched chambers in the wall on the eastern side of Plaza Francia, which originally formed part of the city's battlements, served various purposes during the colonial era, from storage chambers to dungeons. Dating from the late 1600s, when the city was relocated to what is now Casco Viejo, the Bóvedas were abandoned for centuries. In the 1980s the Panama Tourist Board initiated the renovation of the cells, two of which house a sad, musty art gallery managed by the Instituto Nacional de Cultura. Three cells hold a French restaurant called Las Bóvedas, which also has tables on the plaza where you can enjoy drinks in the afternoon and live jazz on Friday nights. ⊠*Plaza Francia, Calle 1, Casco Viejo* ☎*501–4034* ⊠*Free.*

⓯ **Casa Góngora.** Built by Captain Pablo Góngora in the late 18th century, this Spanish colonial house was restored by the mayor's office at the beginning the 21st century to serve as a cultural center. It usually has an art exhibit, and is worth popping into just to admire the restored architecture and woodwork. Free jazz concerts are on offer on Wednesday nights at 8 PM; check ahead, as there's occasionally a Friday night concert as well. ⊠*Calle 9 and Av. Central Casco Viejo* ☎*506–5836* ⊠*Free* ☉*Tues.–Sun. 10–6.*

A BIT OF HISTORY

In 1519, Panama City became the first city that the Spanish founded on the Pacific Coast of the Americas, and its Pacific orientation coupled with its location on a narrow isthmus led to a prosperous future. Only a decade earlier, Vasco Nuñez de Balboa had discovered a new ocean he'd dubbed "Pacific." Exploration of the Pacific Ocean was fairly limited, but in 1532 Francisco Pizarro sailed south to what is now Peru and conquered the Inca Empire, which had a treasure trove of gold and silver and a network of productive mines.

En route to Spain, Pizarro brought his plunder to Panama, and the former fishing village quickly gained prominence in the Spanish colonies. South American gold and silver was shipped to what is now called Panamá Viejo (Old Panama), from where it was carried across the isthmus on mule trains and river boats, and then loaded onto galleons for the trip across the Atlantic. Those same galleons carried European goods for the southern colonies, which crossed the isthmus in the other direction. Panama City grew rich, with cobblestone streets, mansions, and churches with altars covered in stolen gold, but that wealth soon attracted the attention of pirates. In 1671 the city was attacked and completely destroyed by the English pirate Henry Morgan. (Hence the ruins of Panamá Viejo.) Two years later the city relocated to a small peninsula, now Casco Viejo, which was deemed easier to defend. Though it was fortified, the Spanish monarchy changed the shipping route, sending its gold through the Strait of Magellan instead.

With the departure of the Spanish fleet many merchants abandoned the city, which slipped into a prolonged depression. The colonies won their independence from Spain in 1821, and Panama became a province of Colombia, but nothing improved until the 1850s. In response to the California gold rush, an American company built a railroad across the isthmus as part of a steamship route between the eastern and western costs of the United States that was used between 1855 and 1869. The enterprise was not only a boon to Panama's economy, it also marked the first of several waves of immigration of foreign laborers, which included the city's first Chinese immigrants. The inauguration of the U.S. Transcontinental Railroad in 1869 made the Panama route obsolete, and the city again slipped into a depression, but was revived in 1880 by the French, led by Ferdinand de Lesseps, who orchestrated the first attempt to build an interoceanic canal. Though de Lesseps's efforts failed within a decade, they had a lasting effect on the city's Casco Viejo, which the French completely refurbished.

Modern Panama City's development began with the arrival of the United States, which helped the country gain independence from Colombia, then demanded a 10-mi-wide slice of the isthmus. The Canal Zone was an American colony fenced off for most of the 20th century, but in accordance with the Panama Canal treaties, signed by Jimmy Carter and Omar Torrijos in 1977, it has since reverted to Panamanian control. The inauguration of the canal in 1914 led to the birth of a significant service sector in Panama City, which has only expanded of late.

Indigenous Panama

Though the guardians of Panama's original cultures represent a mere 6% of the country's population, they are a very visible minority, which is in no small part due to their spectacular native dress. You don't need to spend long exploring Panama City to see Kuna Indian women in traditional costume, and, if you pay attention, you may also spot Ngöbe women in their colorful, flowing dresses. Though Panama has seven indigenous ethnicities, most of the country's Indians belong to three groups—the Kuna, Emberá-Wounaan, and Ngöbe-Buglé—each of which has its distinctive native dress, language, customs, and cultures. You'll notice their varied handicrafts in markets and shops across the city, and photos or murals of Indians adorn many a wall in the capital. That's because Panama celebrates its indigenous cultures more than many nations, and the government has taken care to treat its indigenous citizens better than the regional norm.

An important example of that treatment is the existence of *comarcas*—autonomous indigenous territories—that are administered by each of the major ethnic groups. These isolated territories are for the most part difficult to visit; the exception is the Comarca Kuna Yala, which is served by daily flights from the capital. The comarcas retain much of their forests, which the Indians conserve, to extract the raw materials for their homes, utensils, tools, medicines, and food. A trip to one of these communities will take you into primeval Panama, past stretches of tropical forest and over crystalline waters that hold coral reefs.

The Kuna are Panama's most famous indigenous people, thanks to their

tradition of receiving tourists, and the colorful traditional dress of Kuna women, which includes beautiful hand-stitched *molas* (patchwork pictures). The Kunas own some of the most spectacular real estate in Central America—a vast province called the Comarca Kuna Yala, or "Land of the Kuna." That comarca includes the Seranía de San Blas, a long mountain chain covered with jungle that has kept the Kuna isolated for centuries, and approximately 365 San Blas Islands, most of which are paradises in miniature: uninhabited cays of ivory sand and coconut palms. The turquoise sea that surrounds these idyllic isles holds countless acres of coral reef—home to a wealth of marine life—so snorkeling is practically an obligatory part of any trip there. And thanks to the existence of more than a dozen rustic lodges that offer tours of the villages, it is the easiest comarca to visit.

Panama's largest indigenous group is the **Ngöbe-Buglé**, who were once called the Guaymí. The Ngöbe-Buglé consist of two groups on the Pacific and Atlantic slopes of the Talamanca Mountain Range, in the western provinces of Chiriquí and Bocas del Toro. Unlike the Kuna and Emberá Wounaan, who live in relatively compact villages, the Ngöbe-Buglé tend live on farms, which means their communities lack a town center. They are most easily visited in Bocas del Toro, which has a couple of accessible communities on Isla Bastimentos, and Ngöbe families living in the towns of Bocas and Carenero. Plenty of Ngöbe-Buglé live outside the comarca, in agricultural communities such as Cerro Punta, Boquete, and Cerro Azul. You'll find traditional Ngöbe dresses, jute bags, and bead work for sale at craft

markets and stores around the country. Also look out for the **chaquiras,** a decorative ornament worn originally by Guaymi warriors during celebrations, now produced and sold to travelers as a keepsake.

Panama's third major indigenous group consists of two related tribes, the **Emberá and Wounaan,** who share two comarcas in the eastern Darién province. Collectively known as the Chocó Indians, after the region of northwest Colombia where most of their people live, these two tribes have similar languages and live in villages scattered along the larger rivers of eastern Panama. The traditional dress of both the Wounaan and Emberá is a loincloth for men and a brightly colored skirt for women, to which they add jewelry and body paint. Their beautiful handicrafts include baskets woven from palm and chunga fibers, *cocobolo* wood carvings, and sculpted and painted seeds of the *tagua* palm. Because

the government relocated several villages to what is now Parque Nacional Chagres in the 1970s, when their land was inundated by the Bayano hydroelectric project, it is possible to visit an Emberá village on a day trip from Panama City. Those communities, however, have had a lot of contact with modern society, so for a more authentic Emberá experience, you'll want to head to Bayano Lake or the remote jungles of the Darién.

② La Catedral *(Catedral de Nuestra Señora de la Asunción)*. Built between 1688 and 1796, Panama City's stately cathedral survived an earthquake almost one hundred years later. The interior is rather bleak, but for the marble altar, made in 1884, beautiful stained glass, and a few religious paintings. The stone facade, flanked by painted bell towers, is quite impressive, especially when lit at night, with its many niches filled with small statues. The bell towers are decorated with mother-of-pearl from the Pearl Islands, and the bells in the left tower were salvaged from the city's first cathedral, in Panamá Viejo. ⊠ *Av. Central and Calle 7, Casco Viejo* ☏ *No phone* ☉ *Opens for masses.*

⑤ Iglesia de La Merced *(Mercy Church)*. One of the oldest structures in the Casco Viejo, La Merced's timeworn, baroque facade was actually removed from a church of the same name in Panamá Viejo and reconstructed here, stone by stone, in 1680. Flanked by white bell towers and tiny chapels that are now abandoned, it's a charming sight, especially in late-afternoon light. The interior was destroyed by fires and rebuilt in the early 20th century, when some bad decisions were made, such covering massive cement pillars with bathroom tiles. ⊠ *Calle 9 and Av. Central, Casco Viejo* ☏ *No phone* ☉ *Opens for masses.*

⑦ Iglesia de San José *(Saint Joseph's Church)*. This church is an exact rep-
★ lica of the temple of the same name in Panamá Viejo. It is the sanctuary of the country's famous golden altar, the most valuable object to survive pirate Henry Morgan's razing of the old city. According to legend, a wily priest painted the altar with mud to discourage its theft. Not only did Morgan refrain from pilfering it, but the priest even managed to extract a donation from the pirate. The ornate baroque altar is made of carved mahogany covered with gold leaf. It is the only real attraction of the small church, though it does have several other wooden altars and a couple of lovely stained-glass windows. ⊠ *Av. A at Calle 8, Casco Viejo* ☏ *No phone* ☑ *Free* ☉ *Daily 8–4.*

④ Museo del Canal Interoceánico *(Interoceanic Canal Museum)*. Once the only museum dedicated to the Panama Canal, the Museo del Canal Interoceánico has been put to shame by the visitors' center at Miraflores Locks. The museum is packed with artifacts, paintings, photographs, and videos about the Panama Canal, but, unfortunately, the information is only in Spanish. There are English-speaking guides available, but you must call the day before to reserve one. Though the building was constructed in 1875 to be the Gran Hotel, it soon became the offices of the Compagnie Universelle du Canal Interoceanique, the French company that made the first attempt to a dig a canal in Panama. After that effort went bust, the building became government property, and before being converted to a museum in the 1990s was the central post office. ⊠ *Plaza Catedral, Casco Viejo* ☏ *228–6231* ☑ *$2, children $.75, tour guide $5* ☉ *Tues.–Sun. 9–5.*

⑭ Palacio de las Garzas *(Palacio Presidential)*. The neoclassical lines of the
★ stunning, white presidential palace stand out against the Casco Viejo's skyline. Originally built in the 17th century by an official of the Spanish crown, the palace was a customs house for a while, and passed through

various mutations before being renovated to its current shape in 1922, under the administration of Belisario Porras. President Porras also started the tradition of keeping pet herons, or egrets, in the fountain of the building's front courtyard, which led to its popular name: "Palace of the Egrets." Because the building houses the president's offices and is surrounded by ministries, security is tight in the area, though nothing compared to the White House. During the day the guards may let you peek into the palace's Moorish foyer at its avian inhabitants, two great egrets and two African cranes. ⊠ *Av. Alfaro, 2 blocks north of Plaza Mayor, Casco Viejo.*

❸ Palacio Municipal *(City Hall).* The city council now meets in this stately white building, but it was originally built, in 1910, as the seat of the country's legislature (which grew too large for it and moved to its current home on Plaza Cinco de Mayo). It replaced a colonial palace that had stood at the same spot for nearly three centuries. On the third floor is the **Museo de la Historia de Panamá,** which traces the country's history from the explorations of Christopher Columbus to the present day. ⚠ **As with the Museo del Canal Interoceánico, next door, the history museum's information is all in Spanish, but the admission is low enough that it is worth paying just to have a look inside the building.** ⊠ *Plaza Catedral, Casco Viejo* ☎ *228–6231* ✍ *$1* ☾ *Weekdays 8–4.*

⓫ Paseo Esteban Huertas. This promenade built atop the old city's outer
★ wall is named for one of Panama's independence leaders. It stretches around the eastern edge of the point at the Casco Viejo's southern tip. From the Paseo you can admire views of the Bay of Panama, the Amador Causeway, the Bridge of the Americas, the tenements of El Chorrillo, and ships awaiting passage through the canal. As it passes behind the Instituto Nacional de Cultura, the Paseo is shaded by a bougainvillea canopy where Kuna women sell handicrafts and couples cuddle on the benches. It's amazing to see the modern skyline across the bay: the new city viewed from the old city. ⊠ *Plaza Francia, between the stairway at the back of the plaza and Calle 1, Casco Viejo* ☎ *No phone* ✍ *Free* ☾ *Always.*

⓭ Plaza Bolívar. A small plaza surrounded by 19th-century architecture,
Fodor's Choice this is one of the Casco Viejo's most pleasant spots, especially at night,
★ when people gather at its various cafés for drinks and dinner. It's centered around a monument to the Venezuelan general Simón Bolívar, the "Liberator of Latin America," with decorative friezes marking events of his life and an Andean condor perched above him. In 1926 Bolívar organized a meeting of independence with leaders from all over Latin America in the Franciscan monastery in front of the plaza, which in the end, he was unable to attend. The hall in which the meeting took place, next to the Iglesia de San Francisco, holds a small museum called **Salón Bolívar** (⊠ *Calle 3, Plaza Bolívar, Casco Viejo* ☎ *228–9594* ✍ *$1* ☾ *Tues.–Sat. 9–4*). The original San Francisco Church was destroyed by fire in the 18th century, and restored twice in the 20th century. The church is only open for mass on Sunday evening, and the former monastery is now occupied by a Catholic school. Across the plaza from it, on the corner of Avenida B and Calle 4, is the smaller church, the

Iglesia de San Philip Neri, which was undergoing restoration work at press time. The Hotel Colombia, across the street from it, was one of the country's best when it opened its doors in 1937, but it fell into neglect during the late 20th century until it was renovated in the '90s and converted to luxury apartments. The restaurant on the ground floor is a good spot for a drink or snack. ⊠ *Av. B between Calles 3 and 4, Casco Viejo.*

❶ Plaza Catedral. The city's main square is also known as Plaza Mayor and ★ Plaza de la Independencia, since the country's independence from both Spain and Colombia were celebrated here. Busts of Panama's founding fathers are scattered around the plaza, at the center of which is a large gazebo. The plaza is surrounded by historic buildings such as the Palacio Municipal, the Museo del Canal Interoceánico, and the Hotel Central, which once held the city's best accommodations, but is now abandoned, awaiting renovation. Plaza Catedral is shaded by some large *tabebuia* trees, which are ablaze with pink blossoms during the dry months, when the plaza is sometimes the site of weekend concerts. ⊠ *Av. Central between Calle 5 and 7, Casco Viejo.*

❾ Plaza de Francia. Designed by Leonardo de Villanueva, this walled plaza ☾ at the southern tip of the Casco Viejo peninsula is dedicated to the Fodor'sChoice French effort to build the canal, and the thousands who perished in ★ the process. An obelisk towers over the monument at the end of the plaza, where a dozen marble plaques recount the arduous task. Busts of Ferdinand de Lesseps and his lieutenants gaze across the plaza at the French Embassy—the large baby-blue building to the north of it. Next to them is a bust of Dr. Carlos Finlay, a Cuban physician who later discovered that yellow fever, which killed thousands during the French effort, originated from a mosquito bite—information that prompted the American campaign to eradicate mosquitoes from the area before they began digging. The plaza itself is a pleasant spot shaded by poinciana trees, which carry bright-orange blossoms during the rainy months. At the front of the plaza is a statue of Pablo Arosemena, one of Panama's founding fathers and one of its first presidents. The infamous dungeons of Las Bóvedas line one side of the plaza, and next door stands a large white building that was once the city's main courthouse but now houses the Instituto Nacional de Cultura *(National Culture Institute).* ⊠ *Bottom of Av. Central, near the tip, Casco Viejo.*

❻ Plaza Herrera. This large plaza a block off the Avenida Central has seen much better days, as is apparent from the faded facades of the buildings that surround it. At the center of the plaza is a statue of local hero General Tomás Herrera looking rather regal on horseback. Herrera fought in South America's wars for independence from Spain and later led Panama's first attempt to gain independence from Colombia, in 1840. The plaza lies next to a poorer section of the city, but you ought to cross it and have a look at the remaining chunk of the ancient wall that once enclosed the Casco Viejo, called the Boularte de la Mano de Tigre (Tiger's Hand Bulwark), which stands just west of the plaza. ⊠ *Av. A and Calle 9, Casco Viejo.*

DAY-TRIPPING FROM THE CAPITAL

Panama City is the perfect base for an array of half- and full-day trips; enough, even, to fill a week or more. All of these excursions are to areas covered in The Canal and Central Panama chapter, and many of them can also be overnight trips. There are about a dozen day-trip options for exploring the canal and surrounding rain forest, which is protected within several national parks that you can explore on your own, or with a guide on a bird-watching or hiking tour. The canal is best experienced on a transit tour, which takes you through the series of locks and Gailard Cut, but you can also get onto the water on one of several nature tours on Lago Gatún. One of the best nature tours on Gatún Lake is the Smithsonian Tropical Research Institutes' day tour to the island of **Barro Colorado** (⇨ *Barro Colorado Nature Monument in The Canal & Central Panama chapter),* one of the world's oldest nature reserves, which is an excellent place to see wildlife. A 30- to 40-minute drive, taxi ride, or bus trip northwest from Panama City will bring you to trails that wind into the forests of **Parque Nacional Soberanía,** a vast rain-forest reserve that is home to more than 400 bird species and an array of mammals that ranges from timid tapirs to tiny tamarins. At **Gamboa,** which lies between the park and the canal, it is easy spot wildlife on the grounds of the Gamboa Rainforest Resort, which has a rain-forest tram and an excellent restaurant, Los Lagartos, on the Chagres River, which is the perfect spot for lunch amidst nature (⇨ *Parque Nacional Soberanía, or Gamboa, in The Canal & Central Panama chapter).*

For a fascinating day trip, ride the **Panama Canal Railway** through the forests and lakes that line the canal to the Caribbean port of Colón, and spend the day exploring either the rain forests around the colonial fort of **San Lorenzo** or the colonial fortresses, beaches, and forest of **Portobelo,** a trip that can be done independently or on a tour (⇨ *Panama Canal Railway, San Lorenzo, and Portobelo in The Canal & Central Panama chapter).* There are several options for exploring nearby **Parque Nacional Chagres,** which include hiking in Cerro Azul, white-water rafting on the Chagres River, or a trip to one of several Emberá Indian communities within the park (⇨ *Parque Nacional Chagres in The Canal & Central Panama chapter).*

The beaches of the Central Pacific Coast can be visited on day trips, but note that most of them require a good deal of driving, which is why many Panamanians head to the nearby island of **Isla Taboga** on weekends. Historic Isla Taboga is a great day trip, since it has a small but lovely beach, and the boat trip there, which passes dozens of moored ships, is quicker and more pleasant than driving to the coastal beaches. (⇨ *Isla Taboga in The Canal & Central Panama chapter). For a real treat, consider* **Isla Contadora,** one of the Pearl Islands, because it has more and nicer beaches than Taboga. It is usually visited on overnight trips, but since there are flights to the island most mornings and afternoons you could easily visit it on a day trip (⇨ *Isla Taboga in The Canal & Central Panama chapter).*

8 **Santo Domingo.** A catastrophic fire ruined this 17th-century church and Dominican monastery centuries ago. What's left at the entrance is the Arco Chato, or flat arch, a relatively precarious structure that served as proof that the country was not subject to earthquakes, tipping the scales in favor of Panama over Nicaragua for the construction of the transoceanic canal. The arch finally collapsed in 2003, without the help of an earthquake, but the city fathers considered it such an important landmark that they had it rebuilt. Next to the ruins is a newer church of Santo Domingo that holds the **Museo de Arte Religioso Colonial,** an extensive collection of colonial religious art that includes some 16th- and 17th-century Spanish works that survived the sacking of Panamá Viejo by Henry Morgan. Its collection of religious paintings, statues, and a 16th-century altar decorated in gold leaf are well worth the price of admission. ⊠ *Av. A at Calle 3, Casco Viejo* ☎ *228–2897* ✉ *$1* ⊘ *Mon.–Sat. 8–4.*

NEED A BREAK?

Exploring Casco Viejo's narrow streets can be a hot and exhausting affair, which makes the gourmet ice-cream shop of **Gran Clement** (⊠ *Av. Central and Calle 3* ☎ *228–0737*) an almost obligatory stop. Located in the ground floor of a restored mansion one block west of the Policía de Turismo station, the shop serves a wide assortment of ice creams including ginger, coconut, passion fruit, and mango. Gran Clement is also open at night, and until 11 PM on weekends.

12 **Teatro Nacional** *(National Theater).* The interior of this theater is truly posh, with ceiling murals, gold balconies, and glittering chandeliers—a little bit of Europe in the heart of old Panama City. After serving as a convent and, later, an army barracks, the building was remodeled by Italian architect Genaro Ruggieri in 1908. Paintings inside by Panamanian artist Roberto Lewis depict Panama's history via Greek mythology. Check the local papers so see whether the national symphony orchestra is playing here while you're in town, as attending a concert is the best way to experience the building. ⊠ *Av. B and Calle 3, Casco Viejo* ☎ *262–3525* ⊘ *Mon.–Fri. 8–4.*

SANTA ANA, CERRO ANCÓN & BALBOA

For the better part of the 20th century, the area to the west of Casco Viejo held the border between the American Canal Zone and Panama City proper, and it continues to be an area of stark contrasts. The busy Avenida de Los Mártires (which separates the neighborhoods of El Chorrillo and Santa Ana from Cerro Ancón (Ancón Hill) was once lined with a chain link fence, and the martyrs it was named for were Panamanian students killed during demonstrations against American control of the zone in 1964. To the west of that busy avenue, which leads to the Bridge of the Americas and the other side of the Canal, rises the verdure and stately buildings of the former Canal Zone, whereas the area to the east of it is dominated by slums. Aside from Casco Viejo, the only areas to the east of that avenue that are worth visiting are Santa Ana's **Avenida Central** pedestrian mall and the area around **Plaza**

TALE OF TWO CITIES

1

For the better part of the 20th century, this city was actually two cities—one American and one Panamanian—separated by walls and fences. When the newly created nation of Panama ceded a strip of its territory to the United States for the construction of the canal, a border was drawn along the edge of what was then the tiny capital. As that city grew, it soon found itself squeezed between the American Canal Zone and the Pacific Ocean, which led to a cramped urban core that sprawled eastward and suffered serious traffic problems. The Americans, on the other hand, had more than enough room; the U.S. government built orderly towns and military bases where tropical trees shaded sidewalks and vast expanses of rain forest were left intact. To house the thousands of laborers who flocked to the country to build the canal, the Americans built hundreds of wooden tenement houses on the Panamanian side of the border; though they have been largely replaced by cement buildings, most remain slums to this day.

Though the fences were dismantled following the signing of the Panama Canal Treaties in 1977, the border remains quite visible to this day in areas such as the Avenida de los Mártires, where the greenery and stately buildings of Cerro Ancón stand to the west and the crowded streets and buildings of Chorrillo and Santa Ana lie to the east. Since the last American properties were handed over to Panama on January 31, 1999, the country has begun integrating the former Canal Zone into the city, building new roads and allowing some development, but strict zoning will likely ensure that the former Canal Zone retains its green areas and distinctive ambience.

Cinco de Mayo, at the pedestrian mall's northern end. A few blocks to the east of Plaza Cinco de Mayo is the **Museo Afroantillano,** but since it's in a rather sketchy neighborhood, you may want to take a taxi there. Another option is to cross the Avenida de los Mártires near Plaza Cinco de Mayo, just south of the Palacio Legislativo, and explore the eastern side of Cerro Ancón, where you'll find the **Museo de Arte Contemporáneo,** a block to your left, and the offices of the **Smithsonian Tropical Research Institute** perched on a ridge to your right. **Mi Pueblito** is several blocks south of the Museo de Arte—you may want to take a taxi there. Also cab it to **Balboa,** which lies to the west of Cerro Ancón, about a mile over the hill from the Museo de Arte. There you'll want to be sure to visit the **Edificio de la Administració del Canal** (Panama Canal Administration Building), which overlooks Balboa from a ridge.

TIMING & PRECAUTIONS

As with most of Panama City, you are better off exploring these areas in the morning, or late afternoon, since the middle of the day is simply too hot for hoofing it. There is no reason to visit any of these areas at night. Whereas Balboa and Cerro Ancón are perfectly safe, you'll want to avoid the neighborhoods that flank the Avenida Central pedestrian mall and to the north and east of Plaza Cinco de Mayo.

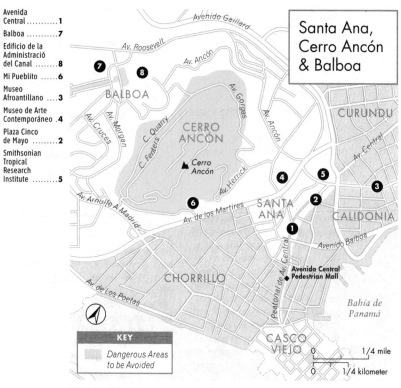

WHAT TO SEE

7 **Balboa.** The heart of the former Canal Zone is quite a switch from the rest of Panama City, with its wide tree-shaded lawns and stately old buildings. It sometimes feels like a bit of a ghost town, especially after you spend time on the busy streets of Panama City proper, but it's an enjoyable, green area. You may spot toucans and *agoutis* (large jungle rodents) near the Panama Canal Administration Building; the Fridays restaurant behind the Balboa Yacht Club has a front-row view of the canal and Bridge of the Americas. Balboa also has Panama City's biggest handicraft market, in the former gym of the local YMCA, called the **Centro Artesanal Antiguo YMCA** (⊠*Av. Arnulfo Arias and Av. Amador, Balboa* ☎*211–0100*).

8 **Edificio de la Administració del Canal** *(Panama Canal Administration*
★ *Building)*. Well worth a stop is this impressive structure set atop a ridge with a dramatic view of Balboa and the canal—a site chosen by the canal's chief engineer, George W Goethals. The building, designed by New York architect Austin W. Lord, was inaugurated in 1914, one month before the SS *Ancon* became the first ship to navigate the canal. Since it holds the offices of the people in charge of running the canal, most of the building is off-limits to tourists, but you can enter its lovely rotunda and admire the historic murals of the canal's construction. The

murals were painted by William B. Van Ingen, who also created murals for the U.S. Library of Congress and the Philadelphia Mint. They're quite dramatic, and capture the monumental nature of the canal's construction in a style that is part Norman Rockwell, part Frederic Edwin Church. The rotunda also houses busts of the three canal visionaries: Spain's King Carlos V, who first pondered the possibility in the 16th century; the Frenchman Ferdinand de Lesseps, who led the first attempt to dig it; and President Theodore Roosevelt, who launched the successful construction effort. The doors at the back of the rotunda are locked, but if you walk around the building you'll be treated to a view of the neat lawns and tree-lined boulevards of Balboa. ✉ *Calle Gorgas, Balboa* ☎ *272–7602* ⊙ *Daily 8–5.*

❻ Mi Pueblito. It might seem touristy, but this hillside re-creation of rural Panama is worth a stop, especially if you won't be traveling to other parts of the country. The main attraction is a small replica of a 19th-century rural town square, similar to those in many Azuero Peninsula towns, such as Parita. The collection of faux-adobe buildings is actually quite picturesque, and the plaza comes to life on Sunday afternoons (2 PM), when it becomes the stage for a free folk-dance performance. You can also visit the traditional Panamanian restaurant on the plaza; the small museum dedicated to the *pollera* (an intricately stitched dress); and the obligatory souvenir shops. Next door is a re-creation of a Caribbean town that bears some resemblance to Bocas de Toro. On Saturday evenings Kuna dancers perform for tips in a tiny reproduction of a Kuna Indian village above it. A trail through the forest leads to the re-creation of typical Emberá Indian home. ✉ *Off Av. de los Mártires and Calle Jorge Wilbert, Cerro Ancón* ☎ *228–9785* 💲 *$2* ⊙ *Tues.–Sun. 9–9.*

❸ Museo Afroantillano. *(Afro-Antillean Museum).* Three blocks northeast of Plaza Cinco de Mayo, in the midst of a rough neighborhood, stands a simple wooden museum dedicated to the tens of thousands of West Indian workers who supplied the bulk of the labor for the canal's construction. The West Indians, mostly Barbadians and Jamaican, did the toughest, most dangerous jobs, but were paid in silver, while the Americans were paid in gold. A disproportionate number of them died during canal construction; the survivors and their descendents have made important contributions to Panamanian culture. The museum has period furniture and historic photos. ⚠ **You'll want to take a taxi here; consider asking the taxi to wait for you while you visit the museum.** ✉ *Av. Justo Arosemena and Calle 24 Este, Santa Ana* ☎ *262–5348* 💲 *$1* ⊙ *Tues.–Sat. 8:30–3:30.*

❹ Museo de Arte Contemporáneo. Panama's modern art museum, housed in a two-story white building on the edge of Cerro Ancón, is managed by a local foundation. Though the country isn't known for its modern art, it does have some excellent painters, some of whose work is in the museum's permanent collections. The museum also hosts temporary exhibitions for local artists, some better than others. ✉ *Calle San Blas and Av. de los Mártires, Cerro Ancón* ☎ *262–8012* 💲 *$2* ⊙ *Tues.–Sun. 9–5, Thurs. 9–9.*

② **Plaza Cinco de Mayo.** A tiny expanse on north end of the Avenida Central pedestrian mall, this plaza has several notable landmarks nearby. To the northeast of the plaza stands a large brown building that was once a train station, and later housed the country's anthropological museum, which was recently moved to a new home near the Parque Metropolitano. Just behind it on Avenida 4 Sur is a small handicraft market called the **Mercado de Buhonería** that few people visit, so you can score some good deals there. One the other side of the Avenida Central, behind a large monument, is the **Palacio Legislativo** *(Legislative Palace)*, Panama's Congress, which does not accept visitors. Across Calle 9 de Enero from the Palacio Legislativo is the Saca Bus Station, where buses depart for Miraflores Locks and Gamboa. The areas to the north and east of the Plaza should be avoided. Plan to arrive at and leave Plaza Cinco de Mayo in a taxi or bus. ⊠ *Av. Central, Santa Ana.*

> ### AVENIDA CENTRAL
>
> The city's Central Avenue is closed to traffic for about half of a mile between Casco Viejo and Plaza Cinco de Mayo; the resulting pedestrian mall is a great place for people-watching and shopping. The bigger stores that line it sell some clothing items for as little as $1. Smaller stores employ aggressive salesmen who stand in front clapping and coaxing passersby inside. Though the pedestrian mall is busy and well patrolled by police, the side streets head into neighborhoods that you should avoid.

⑤ **Smithsonian Tropical Research Institute.** Spread over a ridge on the north side of Cerro Ancón and lined by trees, the home office of the Smithsonian Tropical Research Institute (STRI), known as the Earl S. Tupper Center, has offices, meeting halls, a large library, a bookstore, and a café. A branch of the Washington, D.C.–based Smithsonian Institution, the STRI has half a dozen research stations in Panama, the most famous of which is on Barro Colorado Island. The institute also coordinates scientific studies in various other tropical countries. Most people head to the Tupper Center to pay for their tour to Barro Colorado Island or to shop at the bookstore, which has an excellent selection of natural history titles, as well as souvenirs. The library, which has an extensive collection of literature on the tropics, is open to the general public, Panamanian and foreign. ⊠ *Av. Roosevelt, Cerro Ancón* ☎ *228–6231* ⊗ *Mon.–Fri. 10–4:30.*

OFF THE BEATEN PATH The rain forest that covers most of Cerro Ancón is a remarkably vibrant natural oasis in the midst of the city. The best area to see wildlife is on the trails to the **Cerro Ancón Summit,** (⊠ *Quarry Heights, 400 meters south of ANCON, Cerro Ancón*) which is topped by radio towers and a giant Panamanian flag. The best way to ascend the hill is on a trail that starts high on its western slope, in the luxuriant residential neighborhood of Quarry Heights, above Balboa. Turn right at the offices of ANCON, Panama's biggest environmental group, and continue past several apartment buildings and the B&B La Estancia until you come upon a stairway on your left, which is the trailhead. The hike takes about 20 minutes each way, and is best done early in the morning or late in the afternoon, when you are likely to see animals such as the keel-billed toucan, squirrel cuckoo, and Geoffrey's tamarind—Panama's smallest simian. If you have a taxi drop you off at the trailhead (ask the driver to take you to the "Oficinas de ANCON" in Quarry Heights), you can hike down the other side of the hill to Mi Pueblito, where you should be able to flag a cab.

CALZADA AMADOR

The Calzada Amador (Amador Causeway) is the place to go when you tire of the city's cement and traffic jams. The sprawling views and refreshing breezes coming off the ocean seem a world apart from the hustle and bustle of Panama City, yet this oasis is less than 20 minutes from most downtown hotels. Located directly to the southeast of Balboa, the Calzada was originally constructed as a breakwater, when the canal's builders were looking for places to deposit the trainloads of debris that the digging produced. The resulting causeway, which is topped with a palm-lined road and promenade, stretches almost 2 mi (3 km) into the Pacific Ocean to connect the mainland to three islands: **Isla Naos, Isla Perico, and Isla Flamenco.** The causeway and islands have views of the canal's Pacific entrance, the city's gleaming skyline, Isla Taboga, and the dozens of ships that anchor offshore on any given day. Flocks of pelicans and magnificent frigate birds can often be seen on the forested islands. Long a popular destination for Panamanians, the Calzada has become busier than ever in recent years thanks to the construction of several shopping centers with dozens of bars and restaurants on the islands. The city's residents flock here on Sundays and holidays, when traffic on the two-lane road creeps along and the promenade fills with joggers, bikers, and roller skaters.

TIMING & PRECAUTIONS

The Calzada Amador is a great spot to visit at just about any time of day, as long as it isn't raining, but the late afternoon is especially delightful, when you can watch the sunset illuminate the city's skyline. The restaurants on the islands serve lunch and dinner, some of them until quite late, and the bars on Isla Perico rock till the pre-dawn hours on weekends. During the day, be sure to use sunscreen and a hat, since sunburn is the biggest danger here. There are a couple of small beaches on Isla Naos, but swimming in the ocean is not recommended until the government completes Panama City's sewage system.

WHAT TO SEE

The mainland of Amador, a former U.S. Army base in the midst of slow redevelopment, is a rather desolate area with an abundance of parking lots and rundown military housing. Toward its southern tip stands the ornate Figali Convention Center, the site of occasional conventions and concerts, next to which is a hotel and condominium development. To the south of the convention center is a large open-air restaurant called Las Pencas, where you can rent bicycles, tandems, tricycles, and other pedal-powered vehicles for cruising on the nearby causeway.

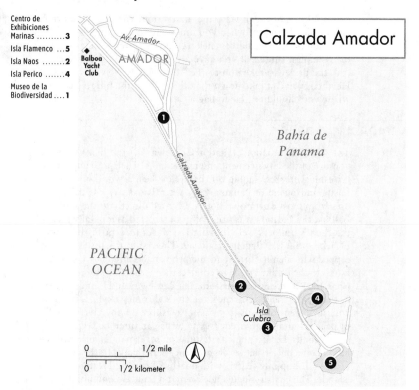

The triangle of land where the Causeway begins is the site of the **Museo de la Biodiversidad** (Museum of Biodiversity). Also called Panama: Bridge of Life, the museum was designed by the American architect Frank O. Gehry, famous for the Guggenheim Museum in Bilbao, Spain, and the pavilion at Chicago's Millennium Park. The museum is currently under construction, but should be open by 2009. It will feature exhibits about the remarkable biodiversity of Panama's forests and oceans, as well as the isthmus's role as a biological bridge between North and South America. In the meantime, you can stop by the construction site and have a look at Gehry's model and work in progress.

The first island that you'll reach on the causeway, **Isla Naos,** is dominated by the marine research laboratories of the Smithsonian Tropical Research Institute (STRI). On the far side of the island are various restaurants, a large marina, which is where you catch the ferry to Isla Taboga, and the STRI Marine Exhibition Center on Punta Culebra. The dirt road that leads to the marina and Punta Culebra is on the right just in front of Mi Ranchito, one of the Causeway's most popular restaurants, which has a high thatch roof. Just south of Mi Ranchito is a small strip mall with several bars and restaurants, one of which has a swimming pool that costs just a few dollars to use.

③ ☼ Though it doesn't compare to the aquariums of other major cities, the **Centro de Exhibiciones Marinas** *(Marine Exhibition Center)* is worth a stop. It was created by the scientists and educators at the STRI, and is located on a lovely, undeveloped point with examples of several ecosystems: beach, mangrove forest, rocky coast, and tropical forest. A series of signs leads visitors on a self-guided tour. There are several small tanks with fish and sea turtles, as well as pools with sea stars, sea cucumbers, and other marine creatures that kids can handle. The spyglasses are great for watching ships on the adjacent canal. ⚠ **Be sure to go out to the lookout on the end of the rocky point.** ✉ *Punta Culebra, Isla Naos, Calzada Amador* ☎ *212–8793* 💲 *$2, children 50¢* ⊙ *Tues.–Fri. 1–5, weekends 10–6.*

> **WILD BUSES**
>
> Panama City's buses are a sight to behold, even if you don't ride in one. They are all privately owned Blue Bird school buses, which are short on legroom and can be hot and stuffy, but what they lack in comfort, they make up for in pizzazz. Most of them have snazzy air-brush paint jobs, featuring lightning bolts, flames, cartoon characters, women's names, or a portrait of a famous person— usually a Latin American singer or *telenovela* (soap opera) star.

④ The second island on the causeway, **Isla Perico**, is a popular nightspot, since its long strip mall, Brisas de Amador, holds an array of restaurants and bars, including **El Tambor de la Alegria** (✉ *Brisas del Amador, Calzada de Amador* ☎ *314–3360*), which features a nightly folk-dancing spectacle. The restaurants have terraces that face the canal's Pacific entrance, so you can watch the ships passing. The bars in Brisas de Amador are the causeway's most popular nightspots, so on weekends that mall stays busy until the wee hours. ✉ *Calzada Amador.*

⑤ The Amador Causeway ends at **Isla Flamenco**, which has two shopping centers and an assortment of restaurants. The Flamenco Marina is a popular mooring spot for yachts and fishing boats; it's the disembarkation point for cruise-ship passengers, most of whom board tour buses. Several restaurants and bars overlook the marina, which also has a great view of the city's skyline, making it a popular destination night and day. ✉ *Calzada Amador.*

NEED A BREAK? Behind Las Pencas Restaurant, on the mainland at the entrance to Calzada Amador, **Bicicletas Moses** (☎ *211–2579* ⊙ *Daily 8–8*) rents an array of bikes, including kids' sizes. One hour costs $2 to $8.50, depending on the bike you choose.

ALBROOK, PARQUE NATURAL METROPOLITANO & MIRAFLORES

The area to the north of Balboa, which was also part of the American Canal Zone, has undergone considerable development since being handed over. The former U.S. Army airfield of Albrook is now Panama City's domestic airport, Aeropuerto Marcos A. Gelabert; next to that are Albrook Mall and the city's impressive bus terminal, the Terminal

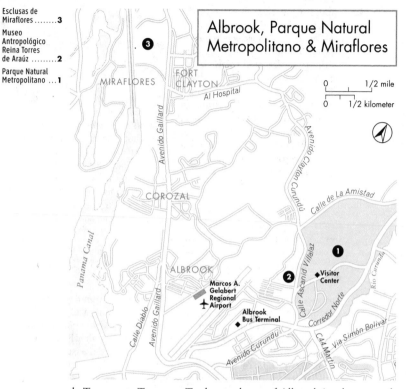

Albrook, Parque Natural
Metropolitano & Miraflores

de Transporte Terrestre. To the northeast of Albrook is a large swath of rain forest protected within **Parque Natural Metropolitano,** which is home to more than 227 bird species. To the west of the park is the country's anthropological museum, **Museo Antropológico Reina Torres de Araúz.** The former military bases and canal-worker housing to the north of Albrook have gotten some new shopping centers, but remain largely the same as they were during the American tenure, though many people have expanded and modified their homes. The former army base of Clayton is now called the Ciudad del Saber, or City of Knowledge; many of its buildings are occupied by international organizations. Across the road are the first set of locks on the Pacific side of the canal, the **Esclusas de Miraflores** (Miraflores Locks), an area that is much more visitor-friendly than it was when the canal was U.S. property. The Panamanian administration has built a state-of-the-art visitor center and museum, making it among the most popular places to visit in Panama City. From there the road follows the canal northwest through the rain forest of Soberanía National Park to the small canal port and community of Gamboa, where it ends.

TIMING & PRECAUTIONS

You should visit Parque Natural Metropolitano as early in the day as you can, or late in the afternoon, since those are the times when birds and other animals are most active. Bring insect repellent with you, stay on the trails, and watch your footing, since there are poisonous snakes in these areas. You could visit the Museo Antropológico immediately afterward, or anytime before 4 PM, except Monday, when the museum is closed. The visitor center at Miraflores Locks is open seven days a week; it's air-conditioned, so it is one of the few places in Panama City that you can comfortably visit in the late morning or early afternoon. ⚠ Though the visitor center closes at 5 PM, the restaurant on its second floor is open until 10:30; it's a fun place to dine, as the canal is actually busier at night than during the day.

WHAT TO SEE

❸ ☻

Fodor'sChoice
★

Esclusas de Miraflores (*Miraflores Locks*). The four-story visitor center next to these double locks provides a front-row view of massive ships passing through the lock chambers. It also houses an excellent museum about the canal's history, engineering, daily operations, and environmental demands. Because most of the canal lies at 85 feet above sea level, each ship that passes through has to be raised to that level with three locks as they enter it, and brought back to sea level with three locks on the other end. Miraflores has two levels of locks, which move vessels between Pacific sea level and Miraflores Lake, a man-made stretch of water between Miraflores Locks and the Pedro Miguel Locks. Due to the proximity to Panama City, these locks have long been the preferred place to visit the canal, but the visitor center has made it even more popular.

There are observation decks on the ground and fourth floors of the massive cement building, from which you can watch vessels move through the locks as a bilingual narrator explains the process and provides information about each ship, including the toll they paid to use the canal. The museum contains an excellent combination of historic relics, photographs, videos, models, and even a simulator of a ship passing through the locks. There is also a gift shop, a snack bar, and a restaurant on the second floor called Restaurante Miraflores, which has an excellent view and a decent, though pricey, kitchen. ⊠ *Road to Gamboa, across from Ciudad del Saber, Clayton* ☎ *276–8325* 💲 *$8, children $5; deck only $5, children $3* ☉ *Daily 9–5.*

❷ Museo Antropológico Reina Torres de Araúz (*Reina Torres de Araúz Anthropological Museum*). After decades of being on display in a former railway station, the government's collection of pre-Columbian artifacts is now housed in a spacious building just down the road from the Parque Natural Metropolitano visitor center. The museum is named for Panama's pioneering anthropologist, Reina Torres de Araúz, who first opened this and half a dozen other museums in the country, and it includes a display on her life's work. The museum's main exhibits feature artifacts from various cultures dating back thousands of years. Its relatively small collection consists of stone statues, painted ceramics, and gold jewelry, including exquisite bells, and pendants in the shape of frogs, eagles, and other creatures. There is also information about the country's pre-Columbian inhabitants and current indigenous groups. ⊠*Av. Ascanio Villalaz, next to Esso station, Altos de Curundú* ☎*232–7485* 🎫*$2* ⊙*Tues.–Fri. 9–4, weekends 10–5.*

❶ **Parque Natural Metropolitano** (*Metropolitan Natural Park*). A mere 10-
☺ minute drive from downtown, this 655-acre expanse of protected wil-
★ derness is an excellent and remarkably convenient place to experience the flora and fauna of Panama's tropical rain forest. Its forest is home to 227 bird species ranging from migrant Baltimore orioles to keel-billed toucans. Five well-marked trails, covering a total of about 5.3 km (3 mi), range from a climb to the park's highest point to a fairly flat loop. On any given morning of hiking you may spot such spectacular birds as a gray-headed chachalaca, a collared aracari, a mealy parrot, or a red-legged honeycreeper. The park is also home to 45 mammal species, so keep an eye out for a sloth hanging from a branch or a dark brown agouti, which is a large jungle rodent. Keep your ears perked for tamarins, tiny monkeys that sound like birds.

There is a visitor center near the southern end of the park, next to El Roble and Los Caobas trails, where the nonprofit organization that administers the park collects the admission fee and sells cold drinks, snacks, and nature books. ⚠ **This is the best place to begin your exploration of the park, since they can give you a simple map; El Roble and Los Caobas connect to form an easy loop through the forest behind the visitor center.**

Across the street from the visitor center is a shorter loop called Sendero Los Momótides. Serious hikers may want to explore the Mono Titi and La Cieneguita trails, which head into the forest from the road about 1 km north of the visitor center, and connect to each other to form a loop through the park's most precipitous terrain. The Smithsonian Tropical Research Institute (STRI) has a construction crane in the middle of the forest near the Mono Titi trail that is used to study life in the forest canopy, which is where the greatest diversity of flora and fauna is found. El Roble connects with La Cieneguita, so you can hike the northern loop and then continue through the forest to the visitor center; the total distance of that hike is 3½ km (2 mi).

If you reach the park in a taxi, you may want to have them pick you up a few hours later; otherwise you could flag a cab down on the road that runs through the middle of the park, Avenida Juan Pablo II, which is fairly busy. Be sure to bring water, insect repellent, and binoculars, and be careful where you put your feet and hands, since the park does have poisonous snakes, biting insects, and spiny plants. ⊠*Av. Juan Pablo II, Altos de Curundú* ☎*232–5552* ⊕*www.parquemetropolitano.org* 🎫*$2, children 50¢* ⊙*Daily 6–6.*

OFF THE
BEATEN
PATH

Perched atop a forested hill 11 km (7 mi) north of the city is **Baha'i House of Worship** (⊠*Transístmica, near Centro Comercial Milla Ocho Las Cumbres* 🎫*Free* ⊙*Daily 10–6*) one of the world's seven Baha'i temples. The Baha'i believe that all the world's religions are separate manifestations of a single religious process, which culminated with the appearance of their founder, Bahà'u'llàh, who preached about a new global society. Most Baha'i temples are in Asia. Panama's temple is simple but also quite lovely, with a white dome surrounded by tropical foliage (from the air, it resembles a giant egg). It was designed by the British architect Peter Tillotson. It is open to everyone for prayer, meditation, and subdued exploring. Men should wear long pants, and women long pants or long skirts.

DOWNTOWN PANAMA CITY

The area northeast of the old city, stretching from the neighborhoods of El Cangrejo to Punta Paitilla, is where you'll find most of the city's office towers, banks, hotels, restaurants, and shops. As Panama City's economy grew and diversified during the 20th century, those who had money abandoned Casco Viejo and built homes in new neighborhoods to the northeast; apartment buildings and office towers soon followed. Many of Panama City's best hotels and restaurants are clustered in **El Cangrejo,** which lies just west of busy **Vía España** and is dominated by **El Panamá,** the city's original luxury hotel, which covers a small hill there. Just to the east of El Cangrejo is the **Area Bancária** (Banking Area), which stretches southeast from to Calle 50 (Calle Nicanor de Obarrio), another of the city's main arteries. A few hotels and a good selection of restaurants are scattered though the Area Bancária, amidst the gleaming towers of international banks. A few blocks to the southeast of Calle 50 is **Avenida Balboa,** another of the city's major thoroughfares, which curves along the coast between the Casco Viejo and Punta Paitilla. Between Calle 50 and Avenida Balboa you'll find the neighborhoods of Bella Vista and Marbella, which hold an interesting mix of tree-lined streets, apartment towers, aging mansions, and modern shopping centers. Just to the east of Marbella is Punta Paitilla, a small point that is packed with skyscrapers.

TIMING & PRECAUTIONS

The downtown area is very safe to explore, although you should be careful crossing its main streets, especially during rush hour. Avenida Balboa is best strolled in the morning or evening; it skirts some rough neighborhoods to the west of the Balboa Monument, so stick to the stretch between the Monument and Punta Paitilla.

WHAT TO SEE

➋ **Area Bancária** *(Banking Area).* Narrow streets shaded by leafy tropical trees make the city's financial district a pleasant area to explore, especially at night, when it is cooler, and there is little traffic. Together with El Cangrejo, which lies across the Vía España from it, the Area Bancária holds a critical mass of hotels, restaurants, and other services that make it an almost obligatory stop for travelers. You'll find the city's highest concentration of bars and restaurants, however, in the area around **Calle Uruguay** *(Calle 48),* just to the south of the Area Bancária, between Calle 50 *(Nicanor de Obarrio)* and Avenida Balboa. Panama City's busiest area on weekend nights, Calle Uruguay is a fun place to head any night but Sunday, and is within walking distance of most hotels. ⊠*Between Vía España and Calle 50*

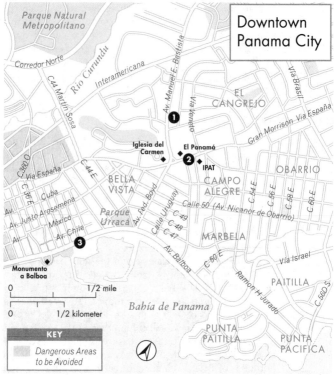

Downtown
Panama City

❸ **Avenida Balboa.** One of the city's main attractions, this busy waterfront
★ boulevard is lined with palm trees and a shiny mosaic wall, and features
great views of the Bay of Panama and Casco Viejo. The sidewalk that
runs along the bay, known as the *malecón,* is a popular strolling and
jogging route. To the west of the Miramar towers and the Yacht Club
is a small park holding a monument to Vasco Nuñez de Balboa, who,
after trudging through the rain forests of the Darién in 1501 became
the first European to set eyes on the Pacific Ocean. That gleaming white
Monumento a Balboa is topped by a steel sculpture of the conquistador gazing out at the Pacific. The statue was a gift to the Panamanian
people from Spain's King Alfonso XIII in 1924. Do most of your walking to the east of the Monumento: if you can do it around high tide,
all the better. Unfortunately, the big problem with the malecón is that
Panama City's raw sewage pours into the bay from a series of pipes just
below it, which is especially noxious when the tide is out. The government is finally building the city's long-overdue sewage system, which
will take years to complete, but there are also plans to demolish the
malecón and move the monument to a new location deeper in the bay,
on a landfill that would include a highway and parks, called the *Cinta
Costera.* ⊠*Av. Balboa, Marbella.*

NO SWIMMING!

Viewed at night, the Bay of Panama looks very romantic; by day, however, you'll notice that the water is extremely murky. All it takes is a quick stroll (and, if you dare, a quick sniff) at low tide along the malecón—the waterfront promenade on Avenida Balboa—to understand the extent of the city's sewage-treatment problems: for centuries, the capital's raw sewage has been dumped directly into the ocean. Add to that neighboring municipalities such as San Miguel and Pedregal, and you've got nearly one million toilet owners polluting this bay. It's amazing that there are still any fish along the coast, but there are plenty, as the flocks of pelicans attest. The only good news is that the government has finally started to fix the problem, thanks in no small part to Mayor Juan Carlos Navarro. The cost of modernizing the city's sewage system and building treatment plants has been calculated at more than $350 million; it may take years to finish the job. Our fingers are crossed that it'll happen in an organized and speedy manner.

② **Vía España.** An extension of the Avenida Central, this busy one-way street is lined with shopping centers and office towers for the better part of a mile. Long an important commercial strip, the Vía España's star has faded a bit in recent years, due to the opening of several big malls in other neighborhoods. Nevertheless, it remains one of the city's busiest streets, and since it pretty much bisects the main hotel and restaurant district, you may risk your life crossing it. Thankfully, there is a pedestrian bridge just to the north of **Vía Veneto,** a crowded side street that runs west from Vía España to an array of hotels, restaurants, and shops. Several blocks to the southwest, where Vía España intersects with Avenida Federico Boyd, stands the pale and conspicuous **Iglesia del Carmen,** a Gothic-style church with high spires built in 1947. To the south of that church, the Vía España quickly loses its glitz.

ATLAPA & PANAMA VIEJO

The coast to the east of Punta Paitilla has a growing supply of condominium towers, but just behind them lie residential neighborhoods where houses and smaller apartments are still the norm. The area only has two spot of interest to travelers: **ATLAPA,** the city's original convention center, and the ruins of **Panama Viejo,** which was the original city. That historic site consists of little other than a museum and a collection of stone walls, but it provides a vague idea of what the colonial city looked like and how its inhabitants lived.

TIMING & PRECAUTIONS

As with any outdoor attraction in often-sweltering Panama City, it's best to visit Panama Viejo first thing in the morning or later in the afternoon, though you need to get to the museum by 4 PM. Though the ruins are patrolled by tourism police on mountain bikes, the surrounding neighborhoods are less tourist-friendly, so don't wander too far from the main road—Vía Cincuentenaria—and the Plaza Mayor.

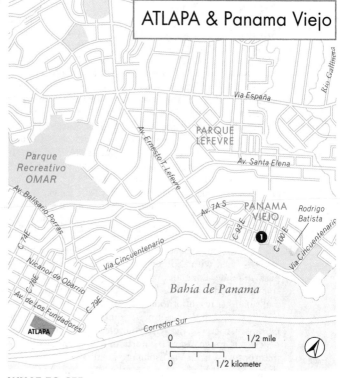

ATLAPA & Panama Viejo

WHAT TO SEE

1 **Panama Viejo** *(also called Panama la Vieja; Old Panama).* Crumbling ruins are all that's left of Old Panama, the country's first major Spanish settlement, which was destroyed by pirate Henry Morgan in 1671. Start your visit at the **Centro de Visitantes** (Visitor Center) (⊠ *Vía Cincuentenaria, 2 km east of ATLAPA* ☎ *226–1757* ⌑ *$6, children $3* ⊙ *Daily 9–5*)—a large building on the right as you enter Panama Viejo on Vía Cincentenaria, which is how most people get there. From ATLAPA, that street heads inland for 2 km through a residential neighborhood before arriving at the ruins, which are on the coast. Once you see the ocean again, look for the two-story visitor center on your right. It holds a large museum that chronicles the site's evolution from an indigenous village to one of the wealthiest cities in the western hemisphere. Works on display include indigenous pottery made centuries before the arrival of the Spanish, relics of the colonial era, and a model of what the city looked like shortly before Morgan's attack. Keep that model in mind as you explore the site, since you need a good dose of imagination to evoke the city that was once home to between 7,000 and 10,000 people from the rubble that remains of it. Panama Viejo is part of all city tours, which can be a good way to visit the site, if you get a knowledgeable guide. There are also sometimes guides at the Plaza Mayor who provide free information in Spanish.

Panama Viejo was founded in 1519 by the conquistador Pedroarias Dávila. Built on the site of an indigenous village that had existed for centuries, the city soon became a busy colonial outpost. Expeditions to explore the Pacific coast of South America left from here. When Francisco Pizarro conquered the Inca empire, the copious gold and silver he stole arrived in Panama Viejo, where it was loaded onto mules and taken across the isthmus to Spain-bound ships. For the next 150 years Panama Viejo was a vital link between Spain and the gold and silver mines of South America. Year after year, ships came and went; mule trains carried precious metals to Panama's Caribbean coast and returned with Spanish goods bound for the southern colonies. The city's merchants, royal envoys, and priests accumulated enough gold to make a pirate drool. At the time of Morgan's attack, Panama Viejo had a handful of convents and churches, one hospital, markets, and luxurious mansions. The fires started during the pirate attack reduced much of the city to ashes within days.

The paucity of the remaining ruins is not due entirely to the pirates' looting and burning: the Spanish spent years dismantling buildings after they decided to rebuild their city, now known as Casco Viejo, on the peninsula to the southwest, which was deemed easier to defend against attack. The Spanish carried everything that could be moved to the new city, including the stone blocks that are today the walls of the city's current cathedral and the facade of the Iglesia de la Merced.

From the visitor center you need to cross the street to reach the main ruins, which you can walk through to the east to what was once the city's Plaza Mayor, which is dominated by a stone tower. The collections of walls that you'll pass on your way to the Plaza Mayor are all that remain of several convents, the bishop's palace, and the San Juan de Dios Hospital. The Plaza Mayor is approximately 1 km from the visitor center, so you may want to drive, or take a cab, instead of walking through the ruins, especially between 11 AM and 3 PM. Vía Cincuentenaria curves to the left in front of what was once the city's **Plaza Mayor** *(Main Plaza)*, a simple cobbled square backed by a stone tower that is the only part of Panamá Viejo that has undergone any significant renovation. You will either need to show the ticket you were given at the visitor center, or buy a ticket to enter the plaza. Climb the metal staircase inside the Torre de la Catedral *(Cathedral Tower)*—the former bell tower of Panama's original cathedral—for a view of the surrounding ruins. The structure just south of the tower was once the city hall; walls to the north and east are all that remains of homes, a church, and a convent. The extensive ruins are shaded by tropical trees, which attract plenty of birds, so the nature and scenery are as much of an attraction as the ancient walls. Just to the south of the Plaza Mayor is the **Mercado de Artesanía** *(Craft Market)*, where dozens of independent vendors sell their wares from tiny shops and stands. ⌂ *Av. Cincuentenario, about 3 km (2 mi) east of ATLAPA, Panamá Viejo* ☎ *226–8915* ⊕ *www.panamaviejo.org* 🎟 *Plaza Mayor $4, children $2; Plaza Mayor and visitor center $6, children $3* ⊙ *Daily 9–5.*

Morgan's Fury

The countless pounds of gold and silver that crossed Panama in the 16th to 17th centuries made it the target of many a buccaneer, but none of them stole as much, or caused as much damage, as the legendary Henry Morgan. In 1668 the Welsh privateer captured Panama's Caribbean port of Portobelo and held it until the Spanish paid him a hefty ransom, which came in addition to what he had already plundered there. Though that adventure and previous piracy made Morgan a rich man, he still coveted the big prize—Panama Viejo, a target most Caribbean corsairs considered too remote to capture.

In 1671 Morgan assembled an army of some 1,500 men of various nationalities and sailed to Panama's Caribbean coast with 36 vessels. He began by attacking Fort San Lorenzo, which guarded the mouth of the Chagres River from a high promontory; despite its imposing location, he managed to capture it with little trouble. From there he and his team traveled upriver in smaller boats and marched through the jungle on the Camino de Cruces to Panamá Viejo, where his troops managed to defeat a Spanish infantry of comparable strength by attacking the unfortified city from two sides. What ensued were days of looting and pillaging that resulted in a fire that consumed much of the city's buildings. Morgan and his men took everything of value that they could find, even torturing people to learn where they'd hidden their money. They did miss out on one treasure, though: the famous golden altar that now sits in the Casco Viejo's Iglesia de San José. Legend has it that a clever priest covered the altar with mud to disguise it before the pirates arrived. Morgan and his men needed 200 mules to carry their booty back to his boats on the Chagres River. When they reached Fort San Lorenzo, they rested before sailing to Jamaica, but story goes that Morgan slipped off in the night with the lion's share of the booty. Upon arriving in Jamaica, the pirate was informed that he had violated a peace treaty recently signed by England and Spain, and he was shipped to London. He was able to convince the English authorities that he hadn't heard about the treaty, and he received no punishment greater than having to give the state its share of his booty. Two years later Morgan was knighted, and the following year he was appointed Lieutenant Governor of Jamaica. He spent the rest of his years living quite comfortably on that Caribbean island, dabbling in politics, and as might be expected of a former pirate, drinking inordinate amounts of rum.

WHERE TO EAT

It's not quite New York or London, but Panama City's restaurant scene is pretty impressive for a city of its size. Panamanians like to eat out, and enough of them have incomes that allow for regular dining on the town, which has resulted in a growing cadre of excellent restaurants. The city is also quite cosmopolitan, which means the cuisine selection can take you right around the globe. Many of the best restaurants are clustered in parts of the Casco Viejo, El Cangrejo, and Area Bancária, the last two of which happen to be where most of the best hotels are. The area around Calle Uruguay, just south of the banking district, has

1

a number of good restaurants, though it is better known for its bar scene. Java junkies will rejoice over the fact that you can get a good cup of coffee just about anywhere here; even the inexpensive restaurants usually grind their own beans and make every cup to order with espresso machines.

CASCO VIEJO

The old quarter has some of Panama City's best restaurants, and the ambience is spectacular to boot. The only problem is that it is relatively far from the hotels, so you'll have to take a taxi there and back. The good news is that from most hotels the ride is quick and inexpensive. And because the evening is a great time to explore that charming area and hang out on Plaza Bolívar, you may want to dine there several nights. The neighborhood's restaurants are definitely worth the trip.

$$–$$$$
Fodor's Choice
★ ✕**S'cena.** One of Panama's most popular restaurants, S'cena sits above one of the city's most popular bars, Platea, which makes it a busy spot on weekend nights. The city's hip and affluent flock here for Mediterranean classics such as paella and original dishes such as *langosta en salsa mediterranea* (lobster in almond sauce), *filet a los tres hongos* (filet mignon with portobello, shiitake, and cremini mushrooms), and *atún rojo* (grilled tuna marinated in a cherry-soy sauce). It occupies the second floor of a restored colonial-era building, with patches of the stone walls exposed in spots and historic photos and paintings by local artists hanging on the plastered stretches. S'cena's location between Plaza Francia and Plaza Bolívar makes it a good spot to have lunch before, or dinner after, exploring the Casco Viejo. It is also well worth the taxi trip, and if you have a late dinner there on a Thursday or Saturday, you can step downstairs afterward for the live music. ☒ *Calle 1, Casco Viejo* ☏ *228–4011* ▭ *MC, V* ☾ *Closed Sun.*

$–$$$
★ ✕**Mostaza.** Nestled in a restored colonial building across the street from the ruins of Santo Domingo, Mostaza offers a cozy and delicious dining experience in the heart of the historic quarter. Start with a drink on the plaza in front of Santo Domingo, then move into one of the two narrow dining rooms, one of which has a centuries-old exposed stone wall. The Argentine and Panamanian owners are usually in the kitchen, preparing an eclectic mix of local seafood and meat dishes that range from *lenguado* (sole) in a mushroom sauce to pork tenderloin in a *maracuya* (passion fruit) sauce. They offer some inventive fresh pastas, such as seafood ravioli in a vodka salmon sauce, and *langostinos* (prawns) sautéed with Gran Marnier, but meat lovers will want to try the classic Argentine *bife de chorizo* (a thick cut of tenderloin) with *chimichuri*, an olive oil, garlic, and parsley sauce. ☒ *Av. A and Calle 3, Casco Viejo* ☏ *228–3341* ▭ *AE, MC, V* ☾ *Closed Mon. No lunch weekends.*

$$
Fodor's Choice
★ ✕**Café René.** After managing Manolo Caracol for years, René opened his own place, while following Manolo's popular formula of offering a set menu that changes daily and consists of about a dozen items served in five or six courses. The difference is a more intimate setting, more Caribbean influence in the cuisine, and the fact that René is almost always there, making sure his guests are happy. The small restaurant is in a historic building on the northwest corner of Plaza Catedral, with

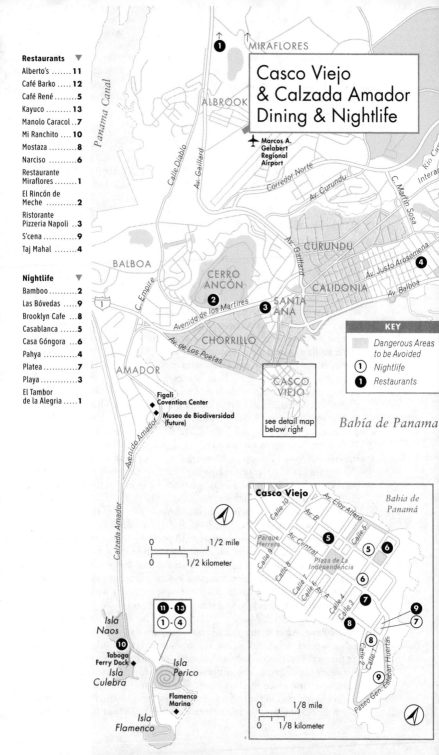

Casco Viejo & Calzada Amador Dining & Nightlife

Restaurants ▼

Alberto's **11**
Café Barko **12**
Café René **5**
Kayuco **13**
Manolo Caracol ..**7**
Mi Ranchito **10**
Mostaza **8**
Narciso **6**
Restaurante
Miraflores **1**
El Rincón de
Meche **2**
Ristorante
Pizzeria Napoli ..**3**
S'cena **9**
Taj Mahal **4**

Nightlife ▼

Bamboo **2**
Las Bóvedas **9**
Brooklyn Cafe ...**8**
Casablanca **5**
Casa Góngora ...**6**
Pahya **4**
Platea **7**
Playa **3**
El Tambor
de la Alegria **1**

MIRAFLORES

Panama Canal

ALBROOK

Calle Diablo

Av. Gaillard

✈ Marcos A.
Gelabert
Regional
Airport

Corredor Norte

Av. Curundu

C. Martín Sosa

Río Curu

Interan

CURUNDU

BALBOA

C. Empire

Av. Gaillard

CERRO
ANCÓN

Avenida de los Martires

CALIDONIA

SANTA
ANA

Av. Justo Arosemena

Av. Balboa

1

Av. de Los Poetas

CHORRILLO

KEY

*Dangerous Areas
to be Avoided*

① *Nightlife*

❶ *Restaurants*

AMADOR

Figali
Covention Center

Museo de Biodiversidad
(future)

CASCO
VIEJO

see detail map
below right

Bahía de Panama

Avenido Amado

Calzada Amador

0 ————— 1/2 mile
0 ————— 1/2 kilometer

Isla
Naos

11 · **13**
① · ④

Isla
Culebra

Taboga
Ferry Dock ♦

Isla
Perico

Flamenco
Marina ♦

Isla
Flamenco

Casco Viejo

*Bahía de
Panamá*

Calle 10

Av. Eloy Alfaro

Av. B

Calle 9

Parque
Herrera

Av. Central

Calle 6

Calle 8

Plaza de La
Independéncia

5

Calle 7

Calle 6 Av. A

Av. Central

⑤

⑥

⑥

7

Calle 4

Calle 3

8

Calle 2

Calle 1

⑧

⑨

⑨

⑦

Paseo Gen. Esteban Huertas

0 ————— 1/8 mile
0 ————— 1/8 kilometer

a high ceiling and white walls that are invariably decorated with the work of a local artist. There are also several tables on the sidewalk with cathedral views. The dining experience is a sort of culinary journey, in which fresh dishes appear every time you complete a course, and you happily chew your way forward, toward a light dessert. Simpler, inexpensive lunches are an alternative to René's seemingly endless dinners. ⊠ *Plaza Catedral, Calle Pedro J. Sossa, Casco Viejo* ☎ *262–3487* ⊟ *MC, V* ☉ *Closed Mon.*

$$ ✕ **Manolo Caracol.** Owned by Spaniard Manolo Maduño and named ★ after one of his country's great flamenco singers, this restaurant-cum-art gallery in a restored colonial building behind the Teatro Nacional is dedicated to the joy of dining and the art of cooking. Each night they offer only one set menu consisting of 10 to 12 items served in five or six courses. All you need to do is choose your beverage—perhaps a beer or a Spanish wine—and wait for the succession of succulent surprises that the waiters will deliver as you scrape each plate clean. Meals tend to be strong on seafood, but there are always a couple of meat dishes. Manolo's is for people who like to eat big, so if you're a light eater you should head elsewhere, or come for lunch. With its tin buckets of fresh fruit, eclectic shrine to the Virgin Mary, and ancient, whitewashed walls hung with modern art, it's a charming spot to spend a few hours, especially when Manolo is there working the crowd. However, it can get noisy on weekend nights, when it can be hard to carry on a conversation. ⊠ *Av. Central and Calle 3, Casco Viejo* ☎ *228-4640* ⊟ *No credit cards.*

$–$$ ✕ **Narciso.** Together with its sister restaurant, Ego, Narciso has tables ★ . on Plaza Bolívar, overlooking the Iglesia de San Francisco's illuminated facade, which makes it one of Panama City's most charming dinner spots. If you can't handle the heat, though, you can always move into one of the dim dining rooms in the historic building across the street. Narciso's cuisine is predominantly Italian, but with Latin American influences, such as stuffed ravioli with a spicy Peruvian chicken stew called *ají de gallina*. The menu is mostly fresh pastas, with a few seafood and meat dishes. You can also order off of the menu from Ego, the restaurant next door, which serves a mix of seafood carpaccios, Peruvian *ceviches* (fish cooked with lime juice), and *mini brochettas*: try the breaded pork option with sesame seeds and tamarind sauce. Those *tapas* and the gorgeous setting make this a good spot for a cocktails and appetizers even if you dine elsewhere. ⊠ *Calle 3 on Plaza Bolívar, Casco Viejo* ☎ *262–2045* ⊟ *AE, MC, V* ☉ *Closed Sun.*

SANTA ANA, CERRO ANCÓN & BALBOA

Most of the restaurants in this area are low-budget cafeterias and fast-food outlets, though there are a couple of good lunch spots here that can be a convenient option for a meal while sightseeing.

¢–$ ✕ **El Rincón de Meche.** Overlooking the picture-perfect church and plaza of **Mi Pueblito**, this typical Panamanian restaurant occupies a copy of a turn-of-the-century adobe building, with beamed ceilings and colorful Carnaval masks hanging on the walls. The only anachronisms are the ceiling fans, the stereo playing Panamanian folk music, and the sound of traffic on nearby Avenida de los Mártires. Nevertheless, the setting is quite pleasant, and they serve an ample menu of typical Panamanian fare, from *arroz con pollo* (rice with chicken) to *cazuela de mariscos* (seafood stew). The views from tables on the covered terrace and second-floor porch are quite nice, if you can live without the ceiling fans. It's a good spot to be on Sunday afternoons, when there is a free folk-dancing performance on the plaza. ⊠ *Mi Pueblito, Cerro Ancón* ☎ *314–1427* ▭ *MC, V* ◷ *Closed Mon.*

¢–$ ✕ **Ristorante Pizzeria Napoli.** If you're in the area of the **Avenida Central** pedestrian mall or **Plaza Cinco de Mayo** around lunchtime, and you want to grab a quick, inexpensive pizza, pop into this historic restaurant down the street from the Avenida de los Mártires. It hasn't been redecorated since it opened in 1962, nor have the prices changed a lot—a small pepperoni pizza is just $3. The various pasta, meat, and seafood dishes won't run you a whole lot more, but pizza is the best bet here. ⊠ *Calle Estudiante, across from Instituto Nacional, Santa Ana* ☎ *263–8799* ▭ *V* ◷ *Closed Tues.*

CALZADA AMADOR

The great thing about eating on the Amador Causeway is that you usually get an ocean view with your meal. A great place for lunch, the Causeway is also a popular dinner destination, and its restaurants tend to serve food pretty late.

$–$$$$ ✕ **Alberto's.** The best tables here are across the drive from the main res-
★   taurant, overlooking the Flamenco Marina and the city skyline beyond, but they are also the first ones to fill up. The other options are to sit on the large covered terrace, cooled by ceiling fans, or in the air-conditioned dining room. The food here is the best on the Causeway, but the service can be leisurely, especially if you sit by the marina. The menu has something for everyone, though seafood is definitely your best bet. You can start with a *duo de mar* (corvina and lobster in béchamel sauce), or a *mero* (grouper) carpaccio, and move on to a pizza, salmon ravioli in a creamy tomato sauce, *corvina al cartucho* (sea bass and julienne vegetables broiled in tinfoil), or *langostinos provencal* (prawns sautéed in with fine herbs and tomatoes). You may want to walk around the island a few times before visiting their Italian ice-cream shop. ⊠ *Edificio Fuerte Amador, Isla Flamenco, Calzada Amador* ✑ *Apdo. 11531–081, El Dorado* ☎ *314–1134* ▭ *AE, MC, V.*

$$–$$$ ✕ **Café Barko.** The correct spelling is *barco,* but "boats" are a common theme at this large restaurant in the Flamenco Shopping Plaza, with one room that is designed to resemble the deck of a Spanish galleon. The nicest place to sit is on the front deck under a thatch roof, in the middle of which is the trunk of a *gumbo-limbo* tree. Unfortunately, a parking lot takes up most of the view. The specialties are from the surrounding sea, such as grilled fresh tuna topped with sesame seeds and bean sprouts, and *pulpo al coco isleño* (octopus in a ginger and coconut sauce). You can also feast on paella, steaks, and burgers. The wine list has nearly 90 vintages from around the world. On Thursday nights there's a free folk-dancing show (reserve a table ahead). ⊠ *Isla Flamenco, Calzada Amador* ☎ *314–0000* ▭ *MC, V.*

1

$-$$ ✕ **Mi Ranchito.** Topped by a giant thatch roof that has become an Ama-
⏱ ★   dor Causeway landmark, this popular restaurant is almost an obligatory stop, if only for a drink, for its excellent view of the city skyline.
It is also one of the best places in town for Panamanian food, such as
carimañolas (fried yucca dumplings stuffed with ground beef), *camarones a la criolla* (shrimp in a tomato and onion sauce), and *pescado
entero* (a whole fried small snapper). Our favorite is *corvina al ajillo*
(sea bass smothered in a garlic sauce), though a hungry party of two
can't go wrong with a *mixto de mariscos al ajillo,* which is mix of seafood sautéed in the same sauce. They also serve great *batidos* (frozen
fruit drinks) made from papaya, melon, and *piña* (pineapple). At night
you can enjoy the live music, often traditional Panamanian; follow
suit when those around you switch from batidos to rum. ⊠*Isla Naos,
Calzada Amador* ☎*228–0116* ⊟*AE, MC, V.*

¢–$ ✕ **Kayuco.** This collection of simple tables shaded by umbrellas at the
⏱   edge of the Flamenco Marina is the place to go for inexpensive seafood
or a cold drink with a view. The food is basic but good—the Panamanian version of bar food—with dishes such as *ceviche,* chicken fingers,
whole fried snapper, all served with *yuca* (fried cassava root) or *patacones* (plantain slices that have been fried and smashed). The relaxed
atmosphere and low prices are a winning combination, and the place
is usually packed. The proximity to the water and lovely view of the
Panama City skyline are best enjoyed at sunset. ⊠*Isla Flamenco, Calzada de Amador* ☎*314–1988* ⊟*MC, V.*

ALBROOK, PARQUE METROPOLITANO & MIRAFLORES
Though Albrook has a few restaurants, there's only one place worth
making the trip out to this area for a meal, and that is the restaurant in
the Miraflores Visitor's Center, which offers an incomparable view of
massive ships sliding through the locks to complement its menu.

$$–$$$$ ✕ **Restaurante Miraflores.** The big attractions here, literally, are the
★   ships that make their careful way through the locks directly in front
of the restaurant. Located on the second floor of the visitor center at
Miraflores Locks, this eatery has glass walls that take advantage of its
unique view. A fascinating sight by day, the locks are perhaps more
impressive at night, when the area is well lighted at its busiest. The
restaurant is run by the Hotel El Panamá, which has a good reputa-
tion, though the kitchen definitely plays second fiddle to the view. The
eclectic menu runs the gamut from "Caribe scallops" (deep fried in a
coconut batter), "San Blas Islands Crab" (king crab mixed with peach
palm and served in its shell), to rabbit in a mustard sauce. It isn't cheap,
and you can expect to pay $10 for a taxi back to your hotel, but the
setting is incomparable. ⊠*Miraflores Visitor Center, 2nd fl., Clayton*
☎*232–3120* ⊟*AE, MC, V.*

DOWNTOWN PANAMA CITY
This area is safe to walk around, and many of its restaurants are within
walking distance of the big hotels. Not only does the downtown area
have the highest concentration of restaurants, it also has the greatest
variety of cuisines and prices. There are also plenty of bars for a pre-
dinner cocktail.

$$–$$$$ ✕**Angel Restaurante.** The most elegant of the city's Spanish restaurants, Angel has a dining room decorated with antiques and original art, as well as a few photos of the owner receiving awards for his cooking. The cuisine is Spanish with some French influence, with dishes such as *cordero chilidrón* (lamb sautéed in tomato sauce) and *conejo deshuesado* (rabbit in a garlic sauce). It's located on quiet, tree-lined Vía Argentina, a short walk from most El Cangrejo hotels. ⊠ *Vía Argentina No. 6868, El Cangrejo* ☎*263–6411* ▭*AE, MC, V* ☽*Closed Sun.*

$$–$$$$ ✕**Eurasia.** One of the city's most attractive restaurants, Eurasia has
Fodor'sChoice several dining rooms with high ceilings and walls hung with paintings
★ by Latin American artists. It occupies the second floor of an elegant former home surrounded by condominium towers, and has a small tropical garden in back that seems a world apart from the traffic of nearby Avenida Balboa. Owners Gloria and Kim Chu offer a soothing ambience and an innovative mix of Asian and French cuisine, with dishes that range from veal chops in a mushroom sauce to duck in a pineapple-plum sauce. They also have some enticing seafood creations, such as prawns in a tamarind and coconut sauce, sea bass with Chinese parsley and pumpkin puree, and grouper in seafood tomato sauce au gratin. You'll walk by a well-stocked pastry table as you enter the dining room, which should inspire you save room for dessert. Three-course executive lunches are a good deal, and an excellent excuse to take a break from the heat and hustle of the surrounding city. ⊠*Calle 48, just east of Parque Urraca, Bella Vista* ✆*Apdo. 6-4396, El Dorado* ☎*264–7859* ▭*AE, MC, V.*

$$–$$$$ ✕**Fusion.** The central dining area of this trendy restaurant in the Decap-
★ olis Hotel looks like something out of a Hollywood adventure movie, dominated by a 20-foot bust reminiscent of the statues on Easter Island. If that's a bit too much for you, look for a table in one of the other dining nooks, where the artistic decor includes giant vases and a wall of TVs broadcasting simultaneous images. The menu matches the atmosphere with originality, and is true to the restaurant's name in its inventive mix of Continental, Asian, and Latin American cuisines. You can start your dinner with the likes of spring rolls with a sweet chili sauce or saffron-cream-spiked seared scallops, then dive into some shrimp and vegetables in a coconut curry, lamb chops with a sweet and spicy sauce, or grouper and shrimp ravioli. ⊠*In Hotel Decapolis, Av. Balboa next to Multicentro, Paitilla* ☎*215–5000* ▭*AE, MC, V.*

$$–$$$$ ✕**Gauchos.** This Argentine restaurant in a Spanish-style house on Calle Uruguay is for serious carnivores who like their steaks big, tender, and juicy. The meat is flown in from the United States, but the cuts are mostly Argentine, such as the *bife de chorizo,* a thick sirloin cut, or the *filete en trozo,* a 16-ounce slice of filet mignon. They are served with *chimichuri* (olive oil, garlic, and parsley), whereas salads and sides, such as a baked potato, are à la carte. They also serve *corvina, langostinos,* and a dozen salads, but the attraction here is the beef. Big windows surround the kitchen, so you can watch them slap slabs of meat onto the grill, or you can admire the cow hides, black-and-white photos, and paintings of *gauchos* (Argentine cowboys) that adorn the

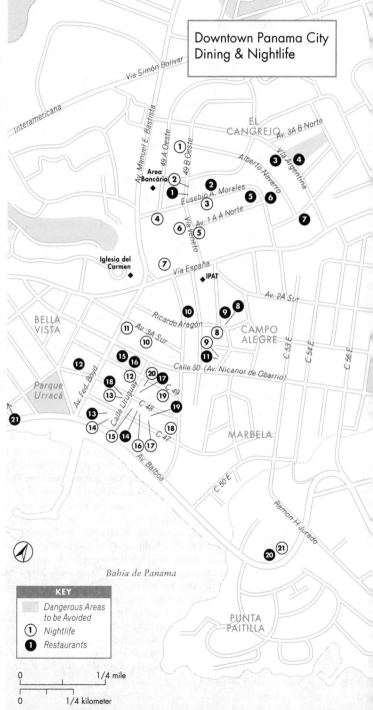

Restaurants ▼

1985 .... **2**
Angel
Restaurante **3**
Beirut **8**
Caffé Pomodoro . **1**
Costa Azul **10**
Eurasia **12**
Fusion **20**
Gauchos **17**
Habibi's
Fusion Café **18**
Limoncillo **14**
Machu Picchu **5**
Madame Chang **19**
Market **13**
Matsuei **6**
La Posta **16**
Restaurante
La Mexicanita .. **15**
Restaurante El
Patio Mexicano ..**7**
Restaurante
Vegetariano
Mireya **9**
Taj Mahal **21**
Ten Bistro **11**
El Trapiche **4**

Nightlife ▼

Azucar **20**
Bamboleo **18**
BLG **12**
La Bodeguita .. **14**
Decapolis
Martini Bar **21**
Greenhouse ... **15**
Habibi's **13**
Istmo Brew Pub .**3**
Manolo's **5**
Marriott Casino ..**8**
Mystik **17**
El Panamá
Casino **4**
El Panamá
Social Club **7**
Pavo Real **9**
Pizza Piola **10**
Sahara **16**
La Terraza **1**
Las Tinajas ....
Urbano Bar **19**
Veneto Casino ...**6**
The Wine Bar **2**

Downtown Panama City
Dining & Nightlife

EL CANGREJO

Via Simón Bolívar

Interamericana

Av. Manuel E. Batista

49 A Oeste

49 B Oeste

Av. 3A B Norte

Alberto Navarro

Via Argentina

Area
Bancária

Eusebio A. Morales

Av. 1 A A Norte

Via Veneto

Iglesia del
Carmen

Via España

IPAT

Av. 2A Sur

Ricardo Aragón

**CAMPO
ALEGRE**

C. 53 E

C. 54 E

C. 56 E

**BELLA
VISTA**

Av. 3A Sur

Calle 50 (Av. Nicanor de Obarrio)

Parque
Urracá

Av. Fed. Boyd

Calle Uruguay

C. 49

C. 48

C. 47

MARBELA

Av. Balboa

C. 50 E

Ramon H. Jurado

Bahía de Panama

**PUNTA
PAITILLA**

KEY

Dangerous Areas
to be Avoided
① Nightlife
❶ Restaurants

0 — 1/4 mile

0 — 1/4 kilometer

walls. ⊠*Calle Uruguay and Calle 48, Bella Vista* ☎*263–4469* ☰*AE, MC, V.*

$$–$$$$ ✕**La Posta.** The ambience in this elegant, refurbished house just off
Fodor'sChoice   Calle Uruguay is classic Caribbean, with ceiling fans spinning over the
★   cane chairs, white tablecloths, colorful tile floors, potted palms, and an
abundance of young waiters in white *guayaberas* (traditional pocketed
tops). There is usually Cuban music playing, and the shiny, hardwood
bar stretching down one end of the dining room is the perfect place
to sip a *mojito*. La Posta is the work of New York restaurateur David
Henesy, who ran the popular La Vitrola in Cartagena, Colombia, for
years before opening what has become one of Panama City's hottest
restaurants. His menu is an innovative mix of Latin American flavors
with a bit of European flair thrown in for good measure. Starters range
from a Peruvian *tiradito de salmon* (marinated fish in a yellow chili
sauce) to Panamanian *carimañolas* (mashed cassava dumplings) stuffed
with organic lamb. For the main course, consider *mero encebollado*
(baked grouper topped with onions and red peppers), or *chuletón de
cerdo* (thick pork chop baked in a wood oven with a spicy topping).
There's a small selection of gourmet pizzas and some tasty pastas.
Reserve a table in the back, overlooking the small, tropical garden.
⊠*Calle 49 and Calle Uruguay, Marbella* ⊕*Apdo. 0832-0833, W. T.
C.* ☎*269–1076* ☰*AE, MC, V.*

$$–$$$$ ✕**Ten Bistro.** This trendy, eclectic bistro in the ground floor of the Hotel
Fodor'sChoice   De Ville is owned by Chef Fabién Migny, one of the founders of Eur-
★   asia. Ten's menu is similar to Eurasia's in its blending of French and
Asian traditions, but the decor is something completely different. The
rounded white walls, orange lights, abundant candles, and bird-of-
paradise flowers suspended over the tables in giant test tubes, together
with the beat of the house music, provide a very 21st-century ambience. You may start with saffron crab soup in a puff pastry, or dip some
prawn spring rolls into a tropical sauce. The main fare ranges from
grouper poached in coconut milk to beef tenderloin Indochine—with
Chinese mushrooms and mustard leaves, served with potato tempura.
The name refers to the fact that many main courses cost just $10,
though some dishes are considerably more expensive. The desserts are
decadent, so be sure to save room. ⊠*Hotel De Ville, Calle Beatriz
Miranda, Area Bancária* ⊕*Apdo. 0832-0172 W.T.C.* ☎*213–8250*
☰*MC, V* ☉*Closed Sun.*

$–$$$$ ✕**Madame Chang.** The city's most elegant Chinese restaurant, Madame
★   Chang has forgone the traditional red and gold of its competitors for
a peach and beige decor. The long dining room is decorated with Ori-
ental art. There really is a Madame Chang—Sui Mee Chang—though
her children run the restaurant now. They serve traditional Mandarin
cuisine (with a few exceptions), and local ingredients such as *róbalo*
(snook) steamed with ginger and green onions, or *corvina* with mustard
leaves. You can also sink your teeth into Peking-style barbecued pork
ribs, and roast duck. Visiting celebrities often dine here—apparently,
Mel Gibson was amazed to find such good Chinese food in Panama. Of
course, he might have been drinking. ⊠*Calle 48, Bella Vista* ☎*269–
1313* ☰*AE, MC, V.*

1

$–$$$$ ✕ **Market.** This casual steak house on busy Calle Uruguay, with cement floors and a corrugated metal roof, is an appropriate place to sink your teeth into a cheeseburger or a rib-eye steak. They serve only Omaha beef here, which isn't cheap, nor is it very exotic for American travelers, but if you've got to have a burger, this is the place to go. They also offer such American classics as a cobb salad and sides of macaroni and cheese, which are no doubt novelties for their predominantly Panamanian clientele. For something more exciting, try a Cajun-rubbed sirloin or salmon maître d'hôtel. They have an extensive wine selection. ✉ *Calle Uruguay and Calle 47, Bella Vista* ☎ *226–9401* ⊟ *MC, V* ✷ *Closed Sun.*

$$–$$$ ✕ **Limoncillo.** Hip and innovative Limoncillo (Spanish for "Little Lime") is the work of Jennifer Spector and Clara Icaza, a celebrated chef who melds Mediterranean, African, and Latin American traditions. Located half a block east of Calle Uruguay, the small restaurant has a modern, mellow ambience, with moody lighting and original art on the walls. Though Limoncillo's star may have faded a bit since it burst into Panama City's restaurant scene in 1999, the menu remains quite impressive. Clara's creations include the likes of grilled chicken with a Moroccan spice rub served with vegetable couscous, beef tenderloin stuffed with basil and chipotle peppers in a roasted garlic sauce, and three-mushroom risotto. ✉ *Calle 47 edificio 17, Bella Vista* ☎ *262–8788* ⊟ *AE, MC, V.*

$$–$$$ ✕ **1985.** Named for the year it opened, this restaurant holds the strange distinction of occupying the only building in Panama City that resembles a Swiss chalet. The owner, chef Willie Dingelman, trained in Lausanne then moved to Panama on a lark three decades ago, only to end up developing a small restaurant and wine-importing empire. The menu is consequently complemented by an excellent wine cellar. Dingelman's original Swiss restaurant, called the Rincón Suizo, used to be next door, but is now a dining room in the back of 1985—two menus under one roof. The decor is a bit of this and a bit of that, with a cluttered collection of chairs and couches in the long entrance, but people come here for the consistently good food at reasonable prices. Come hungry for cordon bleu, chicken tarragon, lobster, tenderloin in green peppercorn sauce, raclette, bratwurst, or *Zürcher Geschnetzeltes* (veal chunks in a mushroom cream sauce). It is no coincidence that the large parking lot is often full on weeknights. ✉ *Calle Eusebio A. Morales, just east of Hotel Las Vegas, El Cangrejo* ☎ *263–8541* ⊟ *AE, MC, V.*

$–$$$ ✕ **Matsuei.** Panama City's original Japanese restaurant, Matsuei has been operated and owned by the Matsufuji family for three decades, who have maintained a loyal clientele in the face of burgeoning competition. The small restaurant has a very traditional feel, with simple pine tables and chairs separated by *shoji* screens, but the roll selection is quite innovative. It may be too innovative, considering such inventions as the "rasta roll," and the "rock & roll." Nonetheless, they have rolls for every taste, and the sushi and sashimi are very fresh. They also serve an array of hot dishes such as tempuras, teriyaki, and teppanyaki. ✉ *Av. Eusebio A. Morales 12-A, El Cangrejo* ☎ *264–9562* ⊟ *AE, DC, MC, V.*

$–$$$ ✗**Restaurante El Patio Mexicano.** This place is a feast for the eyes. Every surface seems to be painted a different bright color, and the walls are decorated with a collection of Mexican handicrafts that includes sombreros, angels, wooden statues, tin stars, ceramic suns, and a small collection of *calacas* (skeleton statues made for the Day of the Dead). Owners Juan Manuel and Laura Uribe, who hail from Guadalajara, have assembled what amounts to a museum of Mexican handicrafts, and their menu is a comparable celebration of the country's varied cuisine. While they do a great job with the standard fajitas, enchiladas, and tacos, they earn kudos for dishes such as *estofado de puerco* (pork in a spicy sauce), *mole poblano* (chicken in a chili-chocolate sauce), *langostinos mayab* (prawns in a cheese sauce), and the hearty *mujer dormido* (sleeping woman), which includes a marinated steak, a quesadilla, and rice and beans. ⊠*Calle Guatemala and Calle Alberto Navarro, El Cangrejo* Ⓓ*Apdo. 6-3035, El Dorado* ☎*263–5684* ▭*AE, MC, V* ☺*Closed Mon.*

$–$$$ ✗**Taj Mahal.** You wouldn't expect it from the exterior, but walking through the door of this refurbished house is liking stepping onto the set of a Bollywood movie. The Technicolor columns, arches, and table settings, Mughal art, and bhangra music may inspire you to show off your Indian dance moves. If you don't have any Indian dance moves, you might pick a few up during dinner, since there is usually a Bollywood musical playing on the big plasma TV on the back wall. The ambience is the work of a Canadian of Punjabi descent, though the tandoori chef came straight from the old country. The food may not always be as spectacular as the decor, but is usually quite yummy. They serve an extensive tandoori selection, an array of curries, including plenty of vegetable dishes, biryanis, and even a few Indo-Chinese specialties. ⊠*Calle 42 No. 27½, across from El Viejo Pipo, Bella Vista* ☎*225–7844* ▭*MC, V* ☺*Closed Mon.*

$–$$ ✗**Machu Picchu.** This popular Peruvian restaurant named after that country's famous Inca ruins occupies an unassuming house a short walk from the hotels of El Cangrejo. Its relatively small dining room, decorated with paintings of Peruvian landscapes and colorful woven tablecloths, is often packed with Panamanians at night. The food they come for is traditional Peruvian, with a few inventions by Chef Aristóteles Breña, such as *corvina Hiroshima* (sea bass in a shrimp, bell pepper, ginger sauce) and *langostinos gratinados* (prawns au gratin). You can't go wrong with such Peruvian classics as *ceviche, ají de gallina* (chicken in a chili-cream sauce), *seco de res* (Peruvian stewed beef), and *sudado de mero* (grouper in a spicy soup). Be careful how you apply their *ají* hot sauce; it's practically caustic. ⊠*Calle Eusebio A Morales No. 16, El Cangrejo* ☎*264–9308* ▭*AE, MC, V.*

¢–$$$ ✗**Habibi's Fusion Cafe.** Habibi's menu has a Middle Eastern core, but it draws from other Mediterranean and global influences. They serve good falafel and shish kebabs, but also offer pizzas, pastas, *arañitas* (breaded baby octopuses), and even Cajun chicken. The dining room bears some semblance to a sultan's tent, with its white ceiling canopy, whereas the bar is very modern and cozy, with hardwoods, armchairs, and giant windows. The large, covered terrace is a happening spot on weekend nights, when it sits at the epicenter of the Calle Uruguay party scene. ⊠ *Calle Uruguay and Calle 48, Bella Vista* ☎264–3647 ⊟ *AE, MC, V.*

¢–$$$ ✕**El Trapiche.** El Trapiche is one of the best places for traditional Panamanian food, thanks to its convenient location and the quality of its cuisine. The menu includes all the local favorites, from *ropa vieja* (stewed beef) to *cazuelo de mariscos* (seafood stew) and *sancocho* (chicken soup). They serve inexpensive set lunches, and a typical Panamanian breakfasts, which include *bistec encebollado* (skirt steak smothered in onions), *tortillas* (deep-fried corn patties), and *carimañolas* (fried yucca dumplings stuffed with ground beef). The decor is appropriately folksy, with a terra-cotta floor, Carnaval masks and other handicrafts hanging on the walls, and a barrel-tile awning over the front terrace, at the end of which is the old *trapiche* (traditional sugarcane press) for which the place is named. ⊠ *Vía Argentina, 2 blocks off Vía España, El Cangrejo* ☎269–4353 ⊟ *AE, MC, V.*

$–$$ ✕**Costa Azul.** A bit of an institution, this large, 24-hour restaurant half a block south of the Vía España is where locals head for a good meal at a reasonable price. The decor in the large, bright restaurant is functional, and the service can be slow when it's busy, but the terrace in front is a good place for people-watching. The menu ranges from Panamanian classics such as *bistec a la criolla* (steak in a tomato sauce) to Spanish dishes such as *corvina a la vasca* (sea bass in a shrimp and clam sauce). An extensive list of daily specials printed on a piece of paper inserted into the menu is usually the best bet, both in terms of price and freshness. They also make about 40 different *emparedados* (sandwiches), including the classic *Cubano* which has salami, ham, roast beef, cheese, and toppings. ⊠ *Calle Ricardo Arias, between Hotel Continental and Marriott, Area Bancária* ☎269–0409.

¢–$$ ✕**Beirut.** The interior of this Lebanese restaurant goes a bit overboard,
★ with faux-stone columns and murals of Roman ruins, but the food is consistently good, and the waitstaff is attentive. The extensive menu goes beyond the Middle East to include dishes such as grilled salmon and pizzas, but the best bets are the Lebanese dishes, which include an array of starters such as *falafel* (fried garbanzo balls), *baba ghanoush* (roasted eggplant), and a dozen salads that can make for an inexpensive, light meal. Be sure to order some fresh flat bread to go with your meal. There is usually Arabic music playing, and there is a collection of hookahs for smoking in the back room, or on the patio, which is a nice place to eat at night, as long as it isn't full of hookah smokers. They also have a restaurant on the Amador Causeway. ⊠ *Calles 52 and Ricardo Arias, across from Marriott Hotel, Area Bancária* ☎214–3815 ⊟ *AE, MC, V.*

¢–$$ ✕**Caffé Pomodoro.** The best thing about this popular Italian restaurant
Fodor's Choice in the Hotel Las Vegas is the large interior patio, with its tropical trees,
★ potted plants, and palms decorated with swirling Christmas lights. At breakfast and lunch it feels like a jungle oasis in the heart of the city, with birds singing in the branches above. The food is a close second, with eight varieties of homemade pastas served with a dozen different sauces, a variety of broiled meat and seafood dishes, personal pizzas,

and focaccia sandwiches, all at very reasonable prices. For dessert, choose from homemade ice cream, chocolate cheesecake, tiramisu, and other treats. They often have a guitarist at dinnertime, and the Wine Bar next door has acoustic Latin music until late. ⊠ *Vía Veneto and Calle Eusebio A. Morales, El Cangrejo* ✆*Apdo. 0834-963, Plaza Concordia* ☎*269–5836* ▭*MC, V.*

¢–$ ✕**Restaurante La Mexicanita.** This unassuming Mexican eatery in a former home on busy Calle 50 is a mom-and-pop place that has pretty much had the same staff, menu, and to a certain degree, clientele, for years. They make their own tortillas and chips, whip up guacamole to order, and offer a fairly standard lineup of Tex-Mex entrees that include soft tacos, enchiladas, burritos, tostadas, and a combo platter called the "Especial La Mexicanita." Wash it down with a Mexican beer, margarita, or *horchata* (a sweet, cinnamony drink). The ambience is "nothin' fancy," limited to a few posters of Mexican destinations on the walls. ⊠*Calle 50, just west of Calle Uruguay, Area Bancária* ☎*213–8952* ▭*AE, MC, V* ☾*Closed Mon.*

¢   ✕**Restaurante Vegetariano Mireya.** Panama City's original vegetarian restaurant, Mireya is a popular lunch spot with bank and office workers looking for an inexpensive alternative to the grease and meat that dominate the Panamanian diet. The stainless-steel cafeteria line holds a remarkably varied selection of dishes that usually includes lasagna, soy meat in sauces, and mixed vegetables. You'll need to use your imagination for some of the dishes, such as soy *chuletas* (pork chops), or *mondongo* (tripe). There is a small salad bar, and a good selection of fresh fruit drinks, healthy desserts, yogurt, and pastries. You can eat at one of the cast-metal tables in the air-conditioned dining room or on the terrace overlooking busy Calle Ricardo Arias. ⊠*Calle Ricardo Arias, across the street from Hotel Marriott, Area Bancária* ☎*269–1876* ▭*No credit cards* ☾*No dinner.*

ATLAPA & PANAMA VIEJO

Though slightly out of the way from most hotels, the following eateries are good alternatives to dining at the Sheraton, and convenient spots for a meal either just before or after visiting Panama Viejo.

$–$$$$ ✕**Golden Unicorn.** Hidden on the fourth floor of the Evergreen Build-
★   ing, down the street from the Sheraton Hotel, this popular spot has a spacious dining room decorated in gold and brown, with walls of windows that provide views of the ATLAPA Convention Center and the ocean beyond it. A Cantonese restaurant that serves some Mandarin and Szechuan dishes, the Golden Unicorn is popular with Chinese families, who gather around its large round tables and order enough dishes to fill the lazy Susan. The menu is as long as a novella, and is written in Spanish and Chinese, which can be a challenge. You can't go wrong with dishes such as *robalo al vapor con salsa de frijol negro* (steamed snook in a black bean sauce), *pollo salteado con setas* (sautéed chicken and seta mushrooms), *pato salteado con piña y gingibre* (sautéed duck with pineapple and ginger), *langostinos Yau-Pao* (prawns with mini vegetables), or spicy Szechuan shrimp (*camarones*). They also serve

dim sum, the traditional Chinese breakfast, starting at 8 A.M. ⊠*Edificio Evergreen, 4th floor, ATLAPA* ☎*226–3838* ▭*AE, MC, V.*

$–$$$ ✕**Parrillada Jimmy.** Jimmy is Greek, but there is very little Greek food on
★ the menu. If he'd opened his restaurant in Chicago instead of Panama City, it would no doubt be called Jimmy's Grill. Its big draws are such local favorites as sizzling steaks, chicken, prawns, or octopus served with a green salad and baked potato or fries. You can also get a good *corvina al ajillo* (sea bass scampi), or *sancocho* (Panamanian chicken soup with tropical tubers). It's a big place, with lots of windows, red-tile floors, and a large terrace overlooking busy Vía Cincuentenaria, but it still manages to get packed on weekends. ⊠ *Vía Cincuentenaria, behind ATLAPA Convention Center, ATLAPA* ✉*Apdo. 0816-04699, Panama City* ☎*226–1870* ▭*AE, MC, V.*

WHERE TO STAY

Panama City has a good hotel selection, with plenty of variety for tastes and budgets. There are various large hotels scattered around the city, but the majority of the upper- and middle-range hotels are clustered in El Cangrejo and parts of the Area Bancária. There are also some decent budget hotels to the southwest of there, between Bella Vista and the northern end of Calidonia. For a quieter alternative, head to the Cerro Ancón and Amador. Demand has outpaced supply in recent years, so reserve your room well ahead of time, especially if your trip is during high season.

CASCO VIEJO

For the moment, the only lodging options in the Casco Viejo are budget hotels fit only for backpackers, and apartment rentals, which are an excellent option for those who want to experience life in the city's colorful historic quarter.

SANTA ANA, CERRO ANCÓN & BALBOA

$$ ▦**Country Inn & Suites Panama Canal.** The homey lobby of this American
★ chain hotel, with its fireplace and checkered arm chairs, more resembles rural Pennsylvania than Panama, but historic photos of the canal's construction adorn the hallways, and the view from the pool and guest rooms of the Big Ditch's Pacific entrance is unmistakable. This is the only hotel with a Panama Canal view, which, together with the peace and quiet that comes with its out-of-town location, is the reason to stay here. The rooms are standard size with tile floors, colorful quilts, and sliding-glass doors that open onto a balcony. There is, however, a big difference between the various views, so be sure to pay the extra money for a view of the canal or you'll end up contemplating the hotel's parking lot. The canal view is partially obstructed by a large tree on the right side of the hotel, so get into a room in the left, or south wing, preferably one with a number between 300 and 313, or 200 and 215. It's a short drive to downtown, and minutes to the restaurants, nightlife, and ocean views of the Calzada Amador. **Pros: great canal view, peaceful, good rates. Cons: far from downtown, "garden views" dis-**

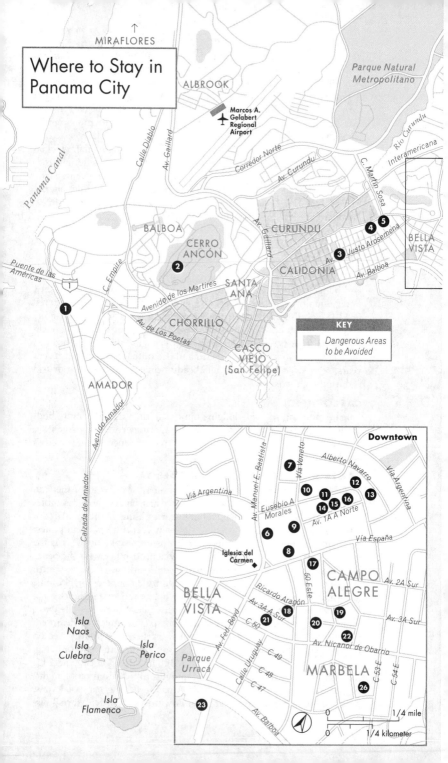

Where to Stay in Panama City

MIRAFLORES ↑

ALBROOK

Marcos A.
Gelabert
Regional
Airport

Parque Natural
Metropolitano

Panama Canal

Calle Diablo

Av. Gaillard

Corredor Norte

Av. Curundu

Río Curundu

Interamericana

C. Martín Sosa

BALBOA

CERRO
ANCÓN

❷

CURUNDU

❹ ❺

BELLA
VISTA

Av. Gaillard

Av. Justo Arosemena ❸

CALIDONIA

Puente de las
Américas

C. Empire

SANTA
ANA

Av. Balboa

Avenido de los Martires

❶

CHORRILLO

Av. de Los Poetas

CASCO
VIEJO
(San Felipe)

KEY

*Dangerous Areas
to be Avoided*

AMADOR

Avenido Amador

Calzada de Amador

Isla
Naos

Isla
Culebra

Isla
Perico

Parque
Urracá

Isla
Flamenco

Downtown

Av. Manuel E. Bastista

Vía Veneto

Alberto Navarro

Vía Argentina

❼

Vía Argentina

❿ ⓫ ⓬

⓭

Eusebio A.
Morales

⓮ ⓯ ⓰

❻ ❾

Av. 1A A Norte

❽

Vía España

Iglesia del
Carmen

⓱

CAMPO
ALEGRE

Av. 2A Sur

BELLA
VISTA

Ricardo Aragón

60 Este

⓲

Av. 3A A Sur

C. 50

㉑

⓳

Av. 3A Sur

Av. Fed. Boyd

⓴

㉒

Calle Uruguay

C. 49

Av. Nicanor de Obarrio

C. 48

MARBELA

C. 53 E

C. 54 E

C. 47

㉖

Parque
Urracá

㉓

Av. Balboa

0   1/4 mile

0   1/4 kilometer

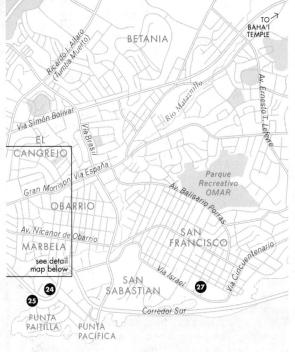

Bahía de Panama

*PACIFIC
OCEAN*

| 0 | | 1/2 mile |
| 0 | | 1/2 kilometer |

appointing. ⊠*Calles Amador and Pelicáno, Balboa* ☎*211–4500, 888/201–1746 in the U.S.* ⊕*www.countryinns.com/panamacanalpan* ⤳*101 rooms, 58 suites* ☐*In-room: safe, refrigerator (some), Wi-Fi. In-hotel: restaurant, room service, tennis court, pool, gym, bicycles, laundry facilities, public Wi-Fi, airport shuttle, parking (no fee), no-smoking rooms* ⊟*AE, MC, V* ⦿*BP.*

$ 📷⊞ **La Estancia.** One of the city's only

Fodor's Choice   bed-and-breakfasts, La Estancia is

★   the perfect spot for nature lovers, or anyone who wants to avoid the noise and crowds downtown, since

> ### FOR LONGER STAYS
>
> Half a dozen fully equipped apartments in beautifully restored Casco Viejo buildings can be rented through **Casco Viejo Living** (☎*6602–0590 vielkaquezada@yahoo.com*), a small rental service run by Vielka Quezada. She can set you up with a two-bedroom apartment at $250, or a shared rental of a two-bedroom apartment for $125. Rentals include breakfast and daily maid service.

it sits at the edge of the forest that covers the top of Ancón Hill (Cerro Ancón). The breakfast area and common lounges include long balconies that overlook a strip of forest where you might see tamarins, tanagers, and toucans. The trail to the summit of Cerro Ancón starts just up the road, so it is the perfect spot from which to make that hike first thing in the morning. The owners, Gustavo and Tammy Liu, have a small travel agency; they can set up day trips, or tours of the country, but are also happy to offer friendly advice. The tile-floor rooms are small and simple. Because the hotel used to be an apartment building for the U.S. Army, the bathrooms of a few rooms are across the hall. There are also two suites that are full apartments with kitchens and balconies (these are the only rooms with TVs). Most guests hang out in the common areas, where complimentary Continental breakfasts are served, and which have wicker furniture, balconies, Wi-Fi, and a self-service bar. **Pros: quiet, surrounded by nature, friendly, helpful owners and staff. Cons: rooms small, some bathrooms separate from rooms.** ⊠*Quarry Heights, Casa No. 35; 50 yards south of ANCON office, Cerro Ancón* ⦿*Apdo. 0832-01705 W.T.C.* ☎*314–1417* ⊕*www.bedandbreakfastpanama.com* ⤳*10 rooms, 2 suites* ☐*In-room: no TV (some), kitchen (some). In-hotel: no elevator, public Wi-Fi, parking (no fee) no-smoking rooms* ⊟*MC, V* ⦿*CP.*

DOWNTOWN PANAMA CITY

Panama City's critical mass of accommodations is found in this amalgam of neighborhoods that extends from El Cangrejo to Punta Paitilla. Many of them are found near the intersection of Vía España and Vía Veneto, the heart of El Cangrejo. Several are scattered through the Area Bancária, the city's financial district, just to the east of El Cangrejo, and a few more are on the coast, near where Avenida Balboa terminates at Punta Paitilla. This area is safe for walking and is sprinkled with restaurants, nightlife, shops, and other diversions.

$$$$ ✕⊞ **The Bristol.** Designed with an English manor in mind, the Bristol is

★   gorgeous and classy, much like a European boutique hotel. Its selling points include a convenient location in the Area Bancária, personalized service, and attention to detail. This carries through to the rooms, with high ceilings, handsome hardwood furniture, original artwork adorning the walls, and a marble bathroom. The beds are sumptuous. Services include a 24-hour concierge, room service, and coffee or tea delivered with your wake-up call. There is a gorgeous bar downstairs with polished hardwoods and windows overlooking lush atriums. The restaurant next door, Las Barandas, is run by one of the country's most famous chefs, Couquita, whose nouveau Panamanian menu includes Asian and European touches. **Pros: excellent service, good location, good restaurant. Cons: expensive, no pool.** ⊠ *Av. Aquilino de la Guardia, between Calle 50 and Vía España, Area Bancária* ☎ *507/265–7844, 800/323–7500 in the U.S.* ⊕ *www.thebristol.com* ⊄ *44 rooms, 12 suites* ⊘ *In-room: safe, DVD, Wi-Fi. In-hotel: restaurants, room service, bar, gym, concierge, laundry service, airport shuttle, parking (no fee), no-smoking rooms* ⊟ *AE, MC, V* ⦿ *BP.*

$$$$ ⬚**Crowne Plaza.** Though it doesn't have a lot of personality, this large hotel has a good location and bright, spacious rooms. There is nothing about the rooms that would indicate that you are in Panama, aside from the view of such nearby landmarks as the Iglesia del Carmen and the Hotel El Panamá, but they are comfortable and well equipped. The bar and restaurant, just off the lobby, are a bit cramped, without a window between them, but there are plenty of other bars, restaurants, and casinos within walking distance. The hotel also has small pool in the corner of a deck off the fourth floor, near which is a small gym. The rack rate here is among the city's highest, but you can expect to pay a fraction of it at any time but the peak holidays. Check the hotel's Web site for special rates. **Pros: good location, friendly staff, free airport shuttle. Cons: slightly noisy, small pool, public areas small.** ⊠ *Av. Manuel Espinosa Batista and Vía España, El Cangrejo* ☎ *206–5555* ⊕ *www.cppanama.com* ⊄ *114 rooms, 36 suites* ⊘ *In-room: safe, Wi-Fi. In-hotel: restaurant, room service, bar, pool, gym, laundry service, executive floor, airport shuttle, parking (no fee), no-smoking rooms.* ⊟ *AE, DC, MC, V* ⦿ *BP.*

$$$$ ⬚**InterContinental Miramar.** No hotel in Panama City can top the Mira-
★ mar's view. Every room in this 25-story tower on the waterfront ends in a wall of windows with views of the Bay of Panama, the skyscrapers of nearby Punta Paitilla, the Casco Viejo, and the islands of the Amador Causeway. It is just as spectacular at night, when the lights of dozens of ships anchored offshore shine against the sea. The higher the floor, the more breathtaking the view. Once you pry your eyes from that panorama, you'll see that the rooms themselves are nicely decorated in earth tones, with hints of art nouveau in the wooden furniture and antique prints of tropical flora on the wall. The top five floors hold executive rooms and suites, which share a lounge and a small pool on the 21st floor. George W. Bush once stayed in the Royal Suite. There is a bar on the fifth floor, and a spacious restaurant near the lobby that serves a finger-licking complimentary breakfast buffet. It overlooks a large pool with a bridge, islands, tropical gardens, and artificial waterfall, surrounded by plenty of spots to soak up the sun. Step out onto

Avenida Balboa, one of the city's most beautiful streets, and you can or stroll down to the Balboa monument or to the shopping, restaurants, and nightlife of nearby Calle Uruguay and Punta Paitilla. **Pros: amazing view, good location, great pool. Cons: expensive.** ✉ *Miramar Plaza, Av. Balboa at Av. Federico Boyd, Bella Vista* ⊡ *Apdo. 816-2009* ☎ *206–8888* ⊕ *www.miramarpanama.com* ✈ *181 rooms, 4 suites* ⊘ *In-room: safe, Wi-Fi. In-hotel: restaurant, room service, bar, pool, tennis court, concierge, laundry service, executive floors, airport shuttle, parking (no fee), no-smoking rooms* ⊟ *AE, MC, V* ⦿ *BP.*

$$$$ 🏨 **Panama Marriott Hotel.** Enter the ground floor of this sleek, 20-story
Fodor'sChoice tower in the heart of the banking district and you'll find yourself in
★ an immaculate, airy lobby with high arches, marble floors, and leafy plants. The spacious rooms are equally attractive, with high ceilings, a hardwood desk, a couch and table, TV hidden in a cabinet, and a marble bathroom. The big windows have either impressive views of the sea through the office-tower jungle, or disappointing views of the skyscraper next door. The top-four executive floors share a lounge where complimentary breakfast and cocktail hour are served. There is a full-service gym and a small pool area hemmed by tropical foliage on the second floor. The expansive lobby has all the services of a small village: a large restaurant that specializes in buffets, an elegant lobby bar, airline and car-rental offices, a business center, a gift shop, a café, and a sports bar that serves a damn good burger. There's even a two-story casino next door, and the tree-lined streets that surround the hotel hold plenty more bars and restaurants. **Pros: good location, friendly staff, spacious rooms, some great views. Cons: small pool, some obstructed views.** ✉ *Calle 52 and Calle Ricardo Arias, Area Bancária* ⊡ *Apdo. 832-0498, W. T. C.* ☎ *210–9100, 888/236–2427 in the U.S.* ⊕ *www.marriott.com* ✈ *290 rooms, 4 suites* ⊘ *In-room: safe, Ethernet. In-hotel: restaurants, room service, bars, pool, gym, laundry service, concierge, executive floors, public Wi-Fi, airport shuttle, parking (no fee), no-smoking rooms* ⊟ *AE, MC, V* ⦿ *EP.*

$$$ ✗🏨 **DeVille.** One of the city's few boutique hotels, the DeVille has a
★ British ambience, despite its French name and restaurant, and is considerably less expensive than the competition in that category. It feels like a businessperson's hotel, for lack of a pool and other facilities, but plenty of travelers stay here. Rooms are elegant, if a bit dark, since some of them overlook the wall of a nearby building. They have an eclectic mix of elegant Asian- and French-style furnishings, and the beds are heaped with fluffy goose-down pillows and have Egyptian cotton sheets. Bathrooms have Italian marble and roomy showers. Large desks with broadband Internet connection, the small business center behind the lobby, and a largely peaceful atmosphere make this a good choice if you've work to do. The restaurant, 10 Bistro, is one of the city's best, serving innovative French-Asian fusion cuisine. **Pros: handsome rooms, good location, great restaurant. Cons: no pool or gym.** ✉ *Av. Beatriz Cabal, near Calle 50 Este, Area Bancária* ☎ *206–3100* ⊕ *www.devillehotel.com.pa* ✈ *33 rooms* ⊘ *In-room: safe, Ethernet. In-hotel: restaurant, bar, concierge, laundry service, public Wi-Fi, parking (no fee)* ⊟ *AE, MC, V* ⦿ *BP.*

$$$ El Panamá. Panama's first luxury hotel, the venerable Panamá once hosted every VIP who passed through town. Its star has since faded, and its design is a bit dated, but the expansive complex covering a small hill behind the Vía España is well maintained and quite pleasant. The spacious, open-air lobby has a very tropical feel, with polished floors, wicker furniture, and potted palms. Behind it lies a large pool surrounded by a wide deck, palm trees, gardens, and an open-air restaurant. Standard rooms in a nine-story building are big enough to play handball in—if it weren't for the queen beds, large desks, and other furniture—and their picture windows provide views of the banking district. "Cabañas" in two-story buildings along the pool area are brighter, slightly quieter rooms just steps away from the water, which makes them a good option for families. The open-air, poolside grill is a pleasant spot for dinner, but there are plenty of other dining, nightlife, and shopping options a short walk from the hotel. The hotel's location in the heart of busy El Cangrejo is a big part of the attraction, whereas the in-house shopping arcade and airline counters add to the convenience. **Pros: big pool, big rooms, good location. Cons: some traffic noise, spotty service.** ⊠ *Vía España and Vía Veneto, El Cangrejo* ☎*216–9000* ⊕*www.elpanama.com* ⇝*113 rooms, 17 suites* ☖*In-room: safe, Wi-Fi. In-hotel: 2 restaurants, room service, bars, pool, laundry service, concierge, parking (no fee), no-smoking rooms.* ▤*AE, MC, V* ⦙◎⦙*BP.*

$$$ Radisson Decapolis. Some hotels were clearly designed for business travelers, but this ultramodern, 29-story high-rise is a party hotel. Consider the fact that that guests are given a $20 voucher for the hotel's bars upon check-in, and that the lobby borders a large lounge that is often packed with people sipping martinis to the pulsating beat of house music. There are a business center and executive floors, but the ambience is definitely more conducive to relaxing and partying. The rooms are quite mod, with white-tile floors, splashes of bright green and orange, giant photos, and walls of windows with city views. Rooms on the west side of the building have knockout ocean views through the skyscrapers; those on the east side overlook cement. The hotel's trendy restaurant, Fusion, serves an eclectic menu in what may be the city's wildest ambience: round windows on the high ceiling allow guests to look up into the hotel's pool. An elevated walkway connects the hotel's lobby with the Multicentro shopping mall, which has a large casino, movie theater, and Hard Rock Cafe. **Pros: hip, some great views, good restaurant, near shops and entertainment. Cons: some mediocre views, small pool.** ⊠*Av. Balboa, next to Multicentro, Paitilla* ⦅*Apdo. 0833-0293* ☎*215–5000, 888/201-1718 in the U.S.* ⊟*215–5715* ⊕*www. radisson.com/panamacitypan* ⇝*240 rooms* ☖*In-room: safe, refrigerator, Wi-Fi. In-hotel: 2 restaurants, room service, bars, pool, gym, spa, laundry service, concierge, public Wi-Fi, airport shuttle, parking (no fee), no-smoking rooms* ▤*AE, MC, V* ⦙◎⦙*BP.*

Fodor'sChoice ★

$$$ Riande Continental. Renovation and expansion have added a touch of pizzazz to this hotel, one of the city's older luxury accommodations, but it didn't completely strip it of kitsch. The rambling, wood-paneled lobby has shops and a small, rounded bar that holds the pieces of a giant Wurlitzer organ that was played each evening for decades, but has thankfully been retired. It overlooks a courtyard with a small, round pool that turns into a fountain at night. The hotel is a 14-story, L-shaped building on busy Vía España, which means street noise can be a problem, but it is within walking distance of an array of shops, restaurants, and offices. Be sure to get a room with a pool view, to avoid the traffic symphony. The bright rooms are conservatively furnished, with a small desk, table, and chairs; they're decorated with prints of an English fox hunt, of all things. There's a business center, a 24-hour casino, a coffee shop, and an upscale restaurant, Divas, which serves something called "fashion cuisine," and is decorated with posters of stars such as J Lo and Britney Spears. Yum? **Pros: central location, friendly staff. Cons: street noise, average rooms.** ⊠ *Vía España and Calle Ricardo Arias, El Cangrejo* ☎*263–9999* ⊕*www.hotelesriande. com* ⇋*317 rooms, 44 suites* ⬧*In-room: safe, Wi-Fi. In-hotel: 2 restaurants, room service, bar, pool, gym, laundry service, parking (no fee), no-smoking rooms* ⊟*AE, MC, V* ⦿|*BP.*

$$$ 🏨 **Sheraton Four Points.** This comfortable hotel around the corner from busy Calle 53 is located near Punta Paitilla in Panama's World Trade Center. Its small, curved lobby has a shiny marble floor and a sunken bar in the corner with a large saltwater aquarium and live piano music most evenings. In the mezzanine is a business center and a small sports bar-restaurant that serves a mix of Panamanian and international dishes. Above it are a spa, gym, pool, and tennis court. The bright rooms are carpeted and tastefully decorated with a hardwood desk, a couch and coffee table, and paintings by Panamanian artists. **Pros: attractive, friendly staff, near shopping mall. Cons: away from most restaurants and nightlife.** ⊠ *Calle 53 and Av. 5 B Sur, World Trade Center, Marbella* ☎*265–3636, 800/368–7764 in the U.S.* ⊕*www. starwoodhotels.com* ⇋*112 rooms, 16 suites* ⬧*In-room: safe, Wi-Fi. In-hotel: restaurant, room service, bar, tennis court, pool, gym, spa, laundry services, concierge, airport shuttle, parking (no fee), no-smoking rooms* ⊟*AE, MC, V* ⦿|*BP.*

$$$ ✕🏨 **Veneto Hotel & Casino.** The Veneto's massive marquee, plastered with flashing colored lights, is Panama City's answer to Las Vegas. Since opening a few years ago, it has become the epicenter of El Cangrejo's vibrant nightlife; on weekends its large entrance is a place of constant movement, as Panamanians and tourists flock to its popular casino and bars. The hotel is consequently a great place for people who like to party, and it's probably not the atmosphere that families and nature lovers are looking for. Nevertheless, the guest rooms, which are on floors 8 to 17, are surprisingly staid, and could well be another hotel entirely, if you didn't have to walk through the lobby to get to them. Those spacious, elegant rooms are carpeted, with either two queens or a king-size bed, a marble-topped desk and dresser, and a large marble bathroom. They are well equipped, and have large windows with good views, especially those on the south side of the building, which glimpse the sea between office towers. The large pool and nearby spa and gym are also relatively quiet, and the hotel has a small business center and an executive floor. The vast lobby is elegant, except for the escalators

1

that lead up to the even bigger casino; it has an attractive lobby bar, a gift shop, an Italian restaurant, and a steak house, though you'll eat better at many of the restaurants in the surrounding neighborhood. **Pros: centrally located, hopping casino, good views. Cons: lobby may be too busy for some.** ⊠ *Vía Veneto and Av. Eusebio A. Morales, El Cangrejo* ☎*340–8888, 800/531–2034 in the U.S.* ⊕*www.venetocasino.com* ➪*300 rooms, 26 suites* ⋄*In-room: safe, Wi-Fi. In-hotel: 2 restaurants, room service, bars, pool, gym, spa, laundry service, concierge, executive floor, public Wi-Fi, airport shuttle, parking (no fee), no-smoking rooms* ⊟*MC, V* ℩◎❙*EP.*

$–$$ ▦**The Executive.** This well-situated hotel is perfect for a business traveler on a budget, or any traveler looking for a good deal. Its 15 stories of carpeted rooms offer less space than the luxury hotels, and they have a very '60s feel, but they are comfortable, equipped with one or two queen beds, and all the amenities the big guys offer, for less. Rooms have small balconies, and the hotel is perched on a hill, which gives it a great view of the city and sea beyond, but because of a design flaw, most rooms face the other direction. Each room has a large desk and Internet access. There's also a large business center and an exercise room on the roof. The tiny pool next to the lobby is quite possibly Panama City's smallest. The lobby bar and 24-hour coffee shop have a tropical feel, with wicker furniture and bright colors; the coffee shop is a popular Sunday breakfast spot with locals. **Pros: convenience and connection. Cons: small pool and not a ton of ambience.** ⊠ *Calle 52 and Calle Aquilino de la Guardia, Area Bancária* ☎*265–8011* ⊕*www.executivehotel-panama.com* ➪*96 rooms* ⋄*In-room: safe, refrigerator, Ethernet. In-hotel: restaurant, room service, bar, pool, gym, laundry service, concierge, public Wi-Fi, airport shuttle, parking (no fee), no-smoking rooms* ⊟*AE, MC, V* ℩◎❙*BP.*

$ ▦**Best Western La Huacas Hotel and Suites.** Rooms in this former apart-
★ ment building are spacious and anything but bland, thanks to their bright colors and murals depicting tropical wildlife. But this hotel's greatest assets are its location on a quiet side street just blocks away from El Cangrejo's busy Vía Veneto and its reasonable rates. The bright, comfortable rooms have kitchenettes with breakfast bar separated from the bedrooms by a half wall, high ceilings, and smallish bathrooms with interesting mosaic or stone showers. Some rooms have balconies, but because the building is squeezed between two apartment towers, only those in front have a decent view. A complimentary breakfast buffet is served in Café Bijauas, a colorful restaurant behind the hotel that also serves inexpensive lunch specials and a mix of Panamanian and continental cuisine. **Pros: big rooms, great location, friendly staff. Cons: no pool, no gym.** ⊠ *Calle 49, 1½ blocks north of Salsa's Bar & Grill, El Cangrejo* ⊕*Apdo. 0819-12496* ☎*213–2222, 800/780–2734 in the U.S.* ⊕*www.lashuacas.com* ➪*32 rooms* ⋄*In-room: kitchen, refrigerator, Wi-Fi. In-hotel: restaurant, laundry service, parking (no fee), no-smoking rooms* ⊟*AE, MC, V* ℩◎❙*BP.*

$ ▦**Coral Suites.** Like the other small "suite" hotels in El Cangrejo, Coral
★ Suites is a good deal, offering tiny apartments with many of the same amenities you get at the luxury hotels for about half the price. It is

similar to Suites Ambassador next door, but has smaller rooms. The hotel's rooms have tile floors and are well furnished, with a pullout bed in the sofa, a small bathroom, and all the necessary appliances. There is a small, blue-tile pool on the roof, an exercise room, and laundry facilities. The location on quiet Calle D near the restaurants and nightlife of El Cangrejo is a big part of the attraction of this economical hotel. The rates drop for stays longer than a week. **Pros: affordable, lots of amenities, great location. Cons: pool is small.** ⊠ *Calle D, half a block east of Vía Veneto, El Cangrejo* ☎ *269–2727* ⊕ *www.coral-suites.net* ↝ *62 rooms* ⚒ *In-room: safe, kitchen, refrigerator, Wi-Fi. In-hotel: pool, gym, laundry facilities, parking (no fee), no-smoking rooms* ☰ *AE, MC, V* ⫘ *EP.*

$ ☷ **Hotel Roma Plaza.** Located on busy Avenida Justo Arosemena, one block south of historic Parque Belisario Porras, which is surrounded by government buildings, the Roma is away from the main hotel and restaurant areas, but is closer to the Casco Viejo, Balboa, and the Amador Causeway. It is pretty self-sufficient, with a small shop, the 24-hour Rainforest Café, travel services, exercise room, and a rooftop pool. The rooms aren't going to win any decorating awards, but they are clean, with shiny white-tile floors. Those in front are quite bright, but can be noisy by day, though things quiet down at night. They have some interior rooms that are much quieter, but they lack windows, which can be disconcerting. The rooftop pool has a nice view of the bay and Casco Viejo. **Pros: good value, pool, restaurant. Cons: far from most hotels and restaurants.** ⊠ *Av. Justo Arosemena and Calle 33, Bella Vista* ☎ *227–3844* ⊕ *www.hotelromaplaza.com* ↝ *133 rooms* ⚒ *In-hotel: restaurant, room service, pool, laundry service, public Internet, parking (no fee), no-smoking rooms* ☰ *AE, MC, V* ⫘ *BP.*

$ ☷ **Las Vegas Hotel Suites.** El Cangrejo's original "suite" hotel is in the process of slow renovation, with some rooms stuck in the 1970s and others boasting new tile floors and furniture. Despite the work-in-progress feel, it is a good deal, especially for families or for long stays. The hotel has spacious studios with one or two queen beds and suites that have separate bedrooms, full kitchens, and a dining-living area. They have a free Internet access, laundry facilities, a small exercise room, and a covered deck on the roof with a great view, but no swimming pool. The popular Italian restaurant in the hotel's garden courtyard is a charming spot for a meal or drink, and it is mere steps away from of El Cangrejo's varied nightlife and dining options. The problem is that it sits at a busy intersection, and the street noise disturbs the peace and quiet of the day, and well into the night on weekends. **Pros: central location, spacious rooms, great restaurant. Cons: noisy, some rooms timeworn, no pool.** ⊠ *Vía Veneto and Calle Eusebio A. Morales, El Cangrejo* ☎ *300–2020* ⊕ *www.lasvegaspanama.com* ↝ *50 suites, 30 studios* ⚒ *In-room: kitchen (some), Wi-Fi. In-hotel: restaurant, bar, gym, laundry facilities, public Wi-Fi, airport shuttle, parking (no fee), no-smoking rooms* ☰ *AE, MC, V* ⫘ *EP.*

$ ☷ **Plaza Paitilla Inn.** Standing amidst the condominiums of Paitilla Point,
★   this round, 19-story tower was no doubt a giant when it opened in the 1970s, but it is now a bit of a dwarf in Panama City's increasingly

RELAX!

1

Travelers are all too often tempted to *go, go, go*, but it's important to remember why we go on vacation—to relax. And the professionals at the country's abundant spas are trained to help you do just that. Spas at most Panama City hotels are open to nonguests; there are also spas near some of the country's beaches and in the mountains, so you'll have plenty of opportunities to rejuvenate during your travels.

City Spas One of Panama City's best spas is located on the fourth floor of the **Radisson Decapolis** (✉ *Av. Balboa, next to Multicentro, Paitilla* ☎ *215–5000* ⊕ *www.radisson.com/ panamacitypan*). If the treatments there don't leave you sufficiently relaxed, you can always top them off with a martini at the hotel's trendy lobby bar. The flashy **Veneto Hotel & Casino** (✉ *Vía Veneto and Av. Eusebio A. Morales El Cangrejo* ☎ *340–8888* ⊕ *www.venetocasino. com*), on busy Vía Veneto, may seem like the last place you'd go to escape the hustle and bustle, but the large spa on the hotel's eighth floor is actually a very tranquil spot. The **Sheraton Panama** (✉ *Vía Israel and Calle 77, San Francisco* ☎ *305– 5100* ⊕ *www.sheratonpanama.com. pa*), next to the ALTAPA convention center on the east end of town, has a small but pleasant spa next to its swimming pool. The serene **Sheraton Four Points** (✉ *World Trade Center, Paitilla* ☎ *265–3636* ⊕ *www. starwoodhotels.com*) has a small spa. The most economical massage can be had at **Cayena Spa** (✉ *Vía Veneto, Edificio Montecarlo. Morales El Cangrejo* ☎ *340–8888*), in the heart of El Cangrejo, which also offers beauty treatments.

Country Spas The **Intercontinental Playa Bonita Resort and Spa** (✉ *Playa Kobbe* ☎ *211–8600* ⊕ *www.playabonitapanama.com*), on the beach 8 km (5 mi) from Panama City, has a large spa offering an array of treatments for guests. The **Gamboa Rainforest Resort** (✉ *Gamboa* ☎ *314–9000* ⊕ *www. gamboaresort.com*) has a complete spa just steps away from the jungle. **Los Mandarinos** (✉ *El Valle de Antón* ☎ *983–6645* ⊕ *www.lacasa- delourdes.com*) is an attractive hotel and spa at the edge of the forest El Valle de Antón, offering a long list of treatments that range from massages to anti-aging therapies. **La Posada Ecológica del Cerro la Vieja** (✉ *Chiguirí Arriba* ☎ *983– 8900* ⊕ *www.posadaecologica.com*), an ecolodge in the mountains 30 km north of Penonomé, has a small, inexpensive spa with a wonderful forest view. In the western mountain town of Boquete, the historic **Panamonte Inn** (✉ *Boquete* ☎ *720– 1324* ⊕ *www.panamonteinnandspa. com*) has a spa that offers massage and various beauty treatments. There is a small spa in the mountain town of Cerro Punta at **Los Quetzales Lodge** (✉ *Cerro Punta* ☎ *771–2291* ⊕ *www.playabonitapanama.com*) that has a spa offering massage and various beauty treatments. **Esthetic Island Relax** (✉ *Calle 10, Av. G, Bocas del Toro* ☎ *6688–4303*) is a small spa near the beaches and coral reefs of Bocas del Toro that provides various massages and skin treatments.

vertical skyline. Still, when you're on one of its upper floors peering across the bay, you feel like you're on top of the world. About half the rooms in this hotel have gorgeous views of the tower-lined Bay of Panama, Casco Viejo, and the Causeway. The views aren't quite as spectacular as those of the nearby Hotel Miramar, but they are a fraction of the price. The carpeted, wedge-shaped rooms have curved walls of windows but rather small bathrooms. Though they've been recently refurbished, they could have come up with something better than the gold-trimmed wood furniture. Each room has a small desk, an armchair and table, and most of the same appliances that the luxury hotels offer. The only Internet access is in the business center. The circular pool has an ocean view. The hotel is on a quiet street just steps away from Avenida Balboa, various restaurants, and the Multicentro shopping mall. The refurbishers missed some parts of the lobby and grounds, which show their age, and you'll want to take meals other than breakfast elsewhere, but the ocean views from the upper floors here are priceless, and the rates quite reasonable. **Pros: half of the rooms have great views, low rates, quiet neighborhood. Cons: half of the rooms have mediocre views, some areas dog-eared.** ⊠ *Vía Italia at Av. Balboa, Punta Paitilla* ⌂ *Apdo. 0816-06579, Zona 5* ☎ *208–0600* ⊕ *www.plazapaitillainn.com* ⟳ *255 rooms* ⚬ *In-room: safe. In-hotel: restaurant, rooms service, bar, pool, laundry service, parking (no fee), no-smoking rooms* ⊟ *AE, MC, V* ⦿ *EP.*

$ ⛏ **Sevilla Suites.** This is one of several midrange hotels in El Cangrejo that offer many of the same amenities as the luxury hotels on a smaller scale. Sevilla Suites' rooms are well-stocked kitchenettes, with lots of amenities, but are slightly smaller than the nearby competition, and they're on a street that is pretty busy on weekdays. While all rooms have shiny tile floors, kitchenettes, tables, chairs, and couches, the standard "Junior Suites" are a bit cramped. "Executive suites" have separate bedrooms, and a sofa with a foldout bed, which makes them well worth the extra $10. There is a small pool, exercise room, and laundry room on the roof. Rates include a Continental breakfast and free wireless Internet, and they drop for stays of one week or more. **Pros: lots of amenities, good location. Cons: spotty service.** ⊠ *Av. Eusebio Morales, east of Las Vegas, El Cangrejo* ☎ *213–0016* ⊕ *www.sevillasuites.com* ⟳ *44 rooms* ⚬ *In-room: safe, kitchen, refrigerator, DVD (some), Wi-Fi. In-hotel: pool, gym, laundry facilities, parking (no fee), no-smoking rooms* ⊟ *AE, MC, V* ⦿ *CP.*

$ ⛏ **Suites Ambassador.** Most rooms in this small, friendly hotel are
★   extremely spacious, with a bedroom and a separate living room with a kitchenette, a couch, and a table with chairs for meals. They are actually small apartments, and the management will add beds for families. Rooms this size cost much more elsewhere, and the Ambassador is conveniently located on one of El Cangrejo's quieter streets, a short walk away from a dozen restaurants and the hustle and bustle of Vía Veneto. They also have some "studios," with the kitchenette and bed packed into one large room, but those aren't much cheaper than the suites, so they're hardly a bargain. There is a small pool and sundeck on the roof, a workout room, and coin laundry. Internet access is free, as

is the Continental breakfast they serve in a small lounge off the lobby, next to which is a room with computers for guest use. They cater to long-term guests with discounted weekly rates. **Pros: big suites, great location, friendly staff, lots of amenities. Cons: pool is small.** ⊠*Calle D, half a block east of Vía Veneto, El Cangrejo* ⌂*Apdo. 0816-01662* ☎*263–7274* ⊕*www.suitesambassador.com.pa* ⇆*31 suites, 8 studios* ⌖*In-room: safe, kitchen, refrigerator, Wi-Fi. In-hotel: pool, gym, laundry facilities, public Internet, parking (no fee), no-smoking rooms* ⊟*AE, MC, V* ¶Ο¶*CP.*

¢–$ 🏨**Hotel El Parador.** A relatively new addition to El Cangrejo's ample hotel selection, El Parador offers comfortable, though basic, rooms in an excellent location—this is the place for travelers on a tight budget. Its smallish rooms are well furnished and have tiny, curved balconies with views of the surrounding apartment buildings and restaurants. The view from the swimming pool and deck atop this seven-story building is impressive—a full skyscraper panorama with glimpses of the sea. There is a small restaurant next to the lobby that offers room service, but you can get better food nearby, since the hotel is surrounded by good restaurants, and is a short walk from both Vía España and Vía Veneto. The Parador is popular with Panamanians, because it's a bargain, but the service is mediocre, and if the receptionist smiles, consider yourself lucky. Still, it's often full. **Pros: central location, pool, inexpensive. Cons: small rooms, indifferent staff, busy street.** ⊠*Calle Eusebio A. Morales, across from Martin Fierro, El Cangrejo* ☎*214–4586* ⊕*www.hotelparadorpanama.com* ⇆*85 rooms* ⌖*In-hotel: restaurant, room service, pool, laundry service, public Internet, parking (no fee), no-smoking rooms* ⊟*AE, MC, V* ¶Ο¶*EP.*

¢–$ 🏨**Marbella.** The attraction of this small hotel on tranquil Calle D, in the heart of El Cangrejo, it that it offers clean, affordable rooms in one of the nicest areas of the city, steps away from an array of restaurants, nightlife, shops, and services. The rooms are nothing special, slightly cramped, but comfortable with either one queen bed or a double plus a single, and such basic amenities as a small TV (cable), telephone, and a tiny desk. The brightest ones are at the front of the building. They have a tiny "business center" that offers Internet access, and a small restaurant. **Pros: great location, quiet, inexpensive. Cons: small rooms, indifferent staff, no pool.** ⊠*Calle D, half a block east of Vía Veneto, El Cangrejo* ☎*263–2220* ⊕*www.hmarbella.com* ⇆*84 rooms* ⌖*In-hotel: restaurant, room service, laundry service, public Internet, parking (no fee), no-smoking rooms* ⊟*AE, MC, V* ¶Ο¶*EP.*

¢–$ 🏨**Tower House Suites.** Located on a quiet side street in the banking district, this yellow cement tower has an attractive, though hot, open-air lobby, and a pool that is larger than those of some of the city's most expensive hotels. The rooms are much bigger than most in this price range, with separate areas that hold tables and chairs and a single bed. They could use a fresh coat of paint and more diligent cleaning, but the place is a bargain. Through some architectural error, rooms here overlook the apartment buildings across the street, whereas they would have ocean views if the hotel were oriented in the other direction. Junior suites, at the end of each floor, have partial ocean views, cross ventilation, and kitchenettes for a few dollars more than standards. Complimentary breakfast is served in a large restaurant off the lobby, and the restaurants and nightlife of the Area Bancária and Calle Uruguay are within walking distance. **Pros: inexpensive, good location, big pool. Cons: timeworn rooms.** ⊠ *Calle 51 No. 36, Area Bancária* ☎ *269–2244* 🖷 *269–2869* ⤵ *36 rooms and 6 junior suites* ⟁ *In-room: refrigerator (some), In-hotel: restaurant, pool, public Internet, parking (no fee) no-smoking rooms* ⊟ *AE, MC, V* ⦿ *BP.*

¢ 🏨 **Hotel California.** This place on the Vía España, a short hike from the restaurants of El Cangrejo and the Area Bancária, has long been popular with budget travelers thanks to its spacious, bright, and clean rooms. It is usually full. It also has a problem: it lies on busy Vía España, which means it is quite noisy by day. Rooms in back are quieter—ask for a room with a number ending in 1, 2, 3, or 4—but there's no complete escape from the honking. As the night wears on, things get quieter. The hotel has an exercise room, and a small restaurant that serves acceptable lunch specials. It is a short hike, or taxi trip, from the ample restaurant and nightlife selections of El Cangrejo, the Area Bancária, or Calle Uruguay. **Pros: crisp, cheap and clean. Cons: busy and noisy during the day.** ⊠ *Vía España and Calle 43 E, Bella Vista* ☎ *263–7736* ⊕ *www.hotelcaliforniapanama.com* ⤵ *60 rooms* ⟁ *In-hotel: restaurant, bar, laundry service, public Wi-Fi* ⊟ *MC, V* ⦿ *EP.*

¢ 🏨 **Hotel Costa Inn.** This budget hotel is away from the main restaurant and bar areas, but it offers some good perks. Among its attractions are a rooftop pool and sundeck with an ocean view, free pick-up at the domestic airport or bus station, free daily shuttles to the international airport, mini-refrigerators in most rooms, and free wireless Internet access. Its main problem is its location on busy Avenida Peru, one of the city's main bus routes, which means it can be noisy during the day. Be sure to get a room in the back of the building, preferably on the fourth or fifth floor. Rooms vary in size and design, but most have pastel walls, tiled floors, and small bathrooms. Suites, which cost $20 more, are bigger, and have more amenities—rooms 509 and 508 are the best ones, since they have ocean views. There's a small restaurant, a bar, and a tour company on the ground floor. The pool deck is a good place for a sunset cocktail. **Pros: friendly staff, pool, lots of freebies. Cons: noisy, mediocre rooms.** ⊠ *Av. Peru and Calle 39, Bella Vista* ☎ *227–1522* ⤵ *99 rooms* ⟁ *In-room: Wi-Fi. In-hotel: restaurant, room service, bar, pool, laundry service, public Internet, airport shuttle, parking (no fee), no-smoking rooms* ⊟ *AE, MC, V* ⦿ *CP.*

¢ 🏨 **Hotel Milan.** With surprisingly inexpensive rooms near some of the
★ best restaurants in El Cangrejo, the Hotel Milan is one of the city's best options for budget travelers. The rooms are nothing to write home about, but they are as big and well equipped as hotels that charge twice as much. The hotel is consequently often full. They have either a queen bed, or a double and a single, and some have small tables and chairs, whereas others have a sofa. Spacious suites have a king-size bed and a bathtub, and cost just $10 more. There is a restaurant and free Internet access downstairs, and it is a short walk from both Vía

España and Vía Veneto. **Pros: good location, inexpensive. Cons: no pool, indifferent staff.** ⊠ *Calle Eusebio A. Morales No. 31, El Cangrejo* ☎ *263–6130* ♺ *53 rooms* ⚿ *In-room: safe. In-hotel: restaurant, room service, laundry service, public Internet, parking (no fee), no-smoking rooms* ☐*MC, V* ⦿*EP.*

SAN FRANCISCO

The predominantly residential neighborhood of San Francisco holds a decent supply of restaurants and one large hotel, the Sheraton, which is next door to the ATLAPA Convention Center.

$$$
☾
Fodor'sChoice
★

🏨 **Sheraton Panama.** One of the city's original luxury hotels, the Sheraton has had various names over the years, and has hosted numerous heads of state, including King Juan Carlos of Spain, and Fidel Castro, who apparently went to the laundry to shake hands with the workers. It is now one of many luxury hotels, but remains one of the best, in no small part thanks to the spaciousness of its public areas. The lobby is designed to resemble a colonial courtyard, surrounded by wooden balconies, with a central fountain and exuberant orchid displays. It spills into a gallery of shops with an excellent café. The pool area is also quite expansive, with gardens and tall coconut palms. The nearby health club is one of the city's best, and overlooking the pool is a 24-hour restaurant, next to which is the Italian restaurant Il Crostini. Guest rooms are quite chic but on the dark side, with stained-wood furniture, marble-top tables, and lots of beige and brown in the carpet and walls. There is nothing about them that is terribly Panamanian, but they are well equipped, with large desks, three phones, and a plasma TV screen perched on the wall. The executive floor has a lounge with great view of the ocean, where complimentary breakfast is served. **Pros: spacious, quiet, nice pool, friendly staff, quick trip to the airport. Cons: far from many attractions, low showers.** ⊠ *Vía Israel and Calle 77, next to ALTAPA convention center, San Francisco* ✉ *Apdo. 0819-05896* ☎ *305–5100, 800/325-3535 in the U.S.* ⊕ *www.sheratonpanama. pa* ♺ *342 rooms, 19 suites* ⚿ *In-room: safe, Wi-Fi. In-hotel: 2 restaurants, room service, bar, tennis courts, pool, gym, spa, laundry service, concierge, executive floor, public Wi-Fi, airport shuttle, parking (no fee), no-smoking rooms* ☐*AE, MC, V* ⦿*EP.*

NIGHTLIFE & THE ARTS

There is plenty to do in Panama City once the sun sets, though it is much more of a party town than a cradle of the arts. Because it is so hot by day, the night is an especially inviting time to explore the city. The entertainment and nightlife centers are Casco Viejo, Calzada Amador, El Cangrejo, and the Calle Uruguay area. The entertainment tends more toward high culture in Casco Viejo, which holds the National Theater and several jazz venues, while the scene in the other areas is more about casinos, dining, and dancing the night away.

THE ARTS

Panama may be a commercial center, but its arts scene is lacking. There are a few small theaters downtown, and occasional dance or classical music performances in Casco Viejo. The most popular arts attractions for tourists are the folk-dancing performances offered by several restaurants, and jazz or Latin music played at various bars and nightclubs. The Teatro Nacional hosts occasional concerts and performances by local and international artists that can be a wonderful way to experience that historic venue. For information on concerts, plays, and other performances, check out the listings in the free tourist newspaper called *The Visitor* or the IPAT Web site (⊕ *www.visitpanama.com*).

FOLK DANCING

Panamanians love their folk dancing, which forms an important part of regional festivals and other major celebrations. The typical folk dances have their roots in popular Spanish dances of the 18th century, but there are also African and indigenous influences in the dances performed on certain holidays or in certain regions. The country's major indigenous groups also have their dances, though they are quite simple compared to the African and Spanish traditions. You can enjoy a free folk-dancing performance at **Mi Pueblito** on Sunday afternoons, around 2 PM, which makes it a good place to head for lunch. A group of young Kuna dancers performs for tips in front of the nearby reproduction of a Kuna village on Saturdays and Sundays around 4 PM.

Several restaurants in the capital offer folk-dancing performances with dinner that combine the country's varied dance traditions. **Las Tinajas** (⊠ *Calle 51 No. 22, near Av. Federico Boyd, Area Bancária* ☎ 269–3840) is an attractive Panamanian restaurant that offers the city's original folk-dancing show at a convenient location in the banking district every Tuesday, Thursday, Friday, and Saturday night. The hour-long show starts at 9 PM and costs $5—plus you need to consume $10 of food and drink. You should reserve several days ahead of time, and get there early to choose a good table, since the stage is at the center of the room and not all tables have great views. **El Tambor de la Alegria** (⊠ *Brisas del Amador, Calzada Amador* ☎ 314–3360) is a newer place on the second floor of the Brisas de Amador shopping center, on Isla Perico, near the end of the Amador Causeway, that serves traditional Panamanian food and offers a dance show that relates the country's history. Shows are Tuesday through Saturday at 9 PM and cost $10, with no minimum consumption at the restaurant. This is the only performance offered on Wednesday night, and it is a big show on an elevated stage, though it's a bit schmaltzy. The restaurant is not attractive, but the food is good. **Café Barko** (⊠ *Isla Flamenco, Calzada Amador* ☎ 314–0000) is a good seafood restaurant in the shopping center at the back of Isla Flamenco, at the end of the Amador Causeway, which offers a free folk-dancing show with dinner on Thursday nights.

JAZZ

Panama has long had a jazz scene, especially in the Caribbean port of Colón, but its best musicians have always moved abroad. The city's prodigal son is Danilo Pérez, a celebrated pianist who has played with the best, and lives in the States. Other notable Panamanian jazz musicians have included saxophonist Maurice Smith, who played with everyone from Charlie Mingus to Dizzy Gillespie, and pianist Victor Boa. Some very good musicians live in the city, though some of them have to play salsa and other popular genres to survive. Jazz fans do, however, have several opportunities per week to hear good music in the city. **Casa Góngora** (⊠ *Calle 9 and Av. Central, Casco Viejo* ☎*506–5836*), a small cultural center in the Casco Viejo, offers free jazz concerts Wednesday nights at 7 PM, though sometimes the music is a Latin genre such as bolero or trova. The bar at the French restaurant **Las Bóvedas** (⊠*Plaza Francia, Casco Viejo* ☎*228–8068*) has live jazz from the Colón tradition on Friday nights. It is a mellower atmosphere than the Latin vibe at nearby Platea, and they play early, starting around 7 PM. **Platea** (⊠*Calle 1, in front of the old Club Union, Casco Viejo* ☎*228–4011*), the Casco Viejo's most popular night spot, offers Latin jazz on Thursday nights with great ambience in the ground floor of a restored colonial building. The best time for jazz fans to visit the city is late January, during the Panama Jazz Festival, which features concerts by international stars in the beautiful Casco Viejo. For information on the next festival, check the Web site (⊕*www.panamajazzfestival.com*).

THEATER

Panama City has a small theater scene, but since most plays are in Spanish, they tend to be of little interest to tourists. There is, however, one group that performs plays in English, and attending a play in Panama is a lot cheaper than Broadway; tickets usually cost $10. **The Ancón Theater Guild** (☎*212–0060* ⊕*www.ancontheater.com*), which has been producing plays for more than 50 years, presents comedies and the occasional drama in English on Friday and Saturday nights at 8 PM in the Ancón Theater, next to the PTJ on Cerro Ancón. **Teatro La Cuadra** (⊠*Calle D, near Vía Argentina, El Cangrejo* ☎*214–3695* ⊕*www. teatroquadra.com*) is the city's best venue for Spanish-language theater, and is conveniently located in El Cangrejo.

NIGHTLIFE

Panama City is a party town, no doubt about it. The city's after-dark offerings range from a quiet drink on historic Plaza Bolívar, to dancing till dawn at one of the clubs on Calle Uruguay, with plenty of options in between. While there are bars everywhere, nightlife is concentrated in the Casco Viejo, Calzada Amador, El Cangrejo, and Calle Uruguay, though there are also a few nice spots in the Area Bancária and near Punta Paitilla.

While the Casco Viejo has several spots for quiet drinks, the neighborhood's most popular club, Platea, rocks till the wee hours on weekends. The Calzada Amador offers something for everything, from a quiet

CLOSE UP

Panama, Musica

Considering that Panama has long been a crossroads for people and goods, it's hardly surprising that the country is home to an array of musical styles. While traveling here, you are likely to hear such Panamanian music as *pindín* and *cantadera*, as well as such internationally popular genres as *salsa, merengue, soca,* and *reggaeton.* Commerce and immigration have long connected Panama to musical traditions from far-flung places. Witness the resulting musical mélange for yourself by surfing the radio in the capital, spending an evening at one of the city's dance clubs, or simply by walking up and down the streets catching snatches of music that seep out of homes and apartments.

Panama's current musical panorama has its roots in the mixing of Spanish, African, and indigenous traditions centuries ago, which resulted in the development of the country's folk music. Panamanian musicians have also excelled in genres from other countries, such as jazz, calypso, and salsa. However, most Panamanians are especially fond of the country's home-grown music, namely *cantadera, mejorana, música foclórica,* and *pindín.*

Mejorana is a Panamanian music that was developed on the Azuero Peninsula and can now be heard mostly at folk festivals and cultural celebrations. It is played on five-string guitar called the *mejoranera,* and usually accompanies folk dancing. *Cantadera* is a popular music form evocative of flamenco; it consists of an improvisational exchange between a guitarist and singer, with a consistent rhythm. The guitarist performs a simple chord progression punctuated by more complex melodic improvisations called *torrentes,* and the singer accompanies him with a series of *décimas,* traditional ten-lined poems that often have comic endings.

Folk dances are accompanied by what is simply called *música foclórica,* or folk music, which is similar to the *vallenato* of Colombia, a country of which Panama was a part for nearly a century. That rhythmic music is performed by groups with an accordion, different types of drums, and a *churuca*—a serrated gourd or metal cylinder that is scraped with a stick. During the twentieth century *música foclórica* gave birth to a more popular form known as *pindín:* a lyric-driven, danceable music in which the accordion is accompanied by an electric guitar and bass, and the percussion includes a drum set. Pindín is the music that many rural Panamanians party, dance, and live to, but it's also popular in the city, where you're likely to hear it in taxis, bars, and restaurants and can try dancing to it yourself. Pindín has its share of well-known stars, such as Dorindo Cárdenas, Victor Vergara, and the siblings Samy y Sandra Sandoval.

In Panama City pindín has traditionally shared the airwaves with salsa and other Caribbean dance music. A child of the Cuban *son,* salsa was largely developed in New York during the 1960s and '70s, but it has been popular in Panama from day one. The country has produced some excellent salsa musicians, the most famous of whom is singer and composer Ruben Blades, who is currently Panama's minister of tourism. He has also acted in dozens of Hollywood movies and TV shows, is known for using salsa to tell stories or to address social and political issues. His most popular

song, "Pedro Navaja," about a criminal, is based on the song "Mack the Knife" and is one of the greatest hits in the history of salsa.

Panama also has a strong tradition of jazz, especially in the Caribbean port of Colón, where big bands reigned in the 1940s and '50s. The country has produced some excellent jazz musicians, among them pianist Victor Boa, singer Barbara Wilson, and pianist Danilo Pérez. Pérez was instrumental in the creation of the Panama Jazz Festival (⊕ www.panamajazzfestival. com), a weeklong celebration that brings together international and local musicians in late January.

The thousands of Afro-Caribbean workers who settled in Panama after completion of the canal made the country home to Antillean music, such as *mento, calypso,* and *soca.* The Afro-Caribbean connection has more recently resulted in Panamanian versions of *reggaeton,* the Latin American response to Jamaican dance-hall, which mutated out of reggae in the 1980s as a response to American rap music. Panama has produced a few international reggaeton stars over the years, among them El General and Nando Boom, and for better or worse, reggaeton could well replace both pindín and salsa as Panama's most popular music.

beer and a snack to throbbing techno bars that could be in Fort Lauderdale, all of it surrounded by lovely ocean views. The streets around Calle Uruguay are packed on weekends, when a predominantly young crowd fills its abundant bars and dance clubs, but it also has a few spots for a quiet drink. There are a few night spots in the Area Bancária, whereas across the Vía España, in El Cangrejo, the options range from massive casinos to street-side cafés perfect for people-watching. The big attraction in Paitilla is the martini lounge in the Hotel Decapolis, but the area also has various other late-night spots.

There are half a dozen strip clubs, locally called "nightclubs," scattered between the Area Bancária and El Cangrejo. They have traditionally catered to business travelers, but are becoming a bit of a tourist attraction in their own right. Prostitution is legal in Panama, but streetwalking is not, so the world's oldest profession is based in the city's nightclubs and massage parlors. Those places all advertise in the free tourist publications *The Visitor* and *Focus Panama*.

BARS & MUSIC

CASCO VIEJO **Ego** (⊠ *Calle 3 on Plaza Bolívar, Casco Viejo* ☎262–2045) is a tapas
Fodor's Choice restaurant with tables on Plaza Bolívar, most of which overlook the
★ illuminated facade of the Iglesia de San Francisco, making it one of the city's most romantic spots for a drink. **Casablanca** (⊠ *Calle 4 on Plaza Bolívar, Casco Viejo* ☎212–0040), on the ground floor of the old Hotel Colombi, has tables on beautiful Plaza Bolívar, which is a great spot for a quiet drink and conversation. **Las Bóvedas** (⊠ *Plaza Francia, Casco Viejo* ☎228–5068), the French restaurant on Plaza Francia, has tables on the plaza and a bar inside one of the Bóvedas that features live jazz on Friday nights. **Brooklyn Cafe** (⊠ *Calle 1 and Av. A, Casco Viejo* ☎211–0961), between Plaza Francia and Platea, is a pleasant spot for a quiet drink.

EL CANGREJO **The Wine Bar** (⊠ *Calle Eusebio Morales east of Vía Veneto, El Cangrejo* ☎265–4701), located in the ground floor of the Las Vegas Hotel Suites, has live, mellow Latin music most nights, mostly duos or one musician, and serves good pizza and other snacks till late. **Istmo Brew Pub** (⊠ *Calle Eusebio Morales east of Vía Veneto, El Cangrejo* ☎265–5077), across the street from the Las Vegas Hotel Suites, serves several home brews, as well as the city's best selection of imported beers. It's a popular spot, with seating out front and inside, pool tables, a bar, and pop music blasting. Sample the beers before ordering a house brew. **La Terraza** (⊠ *Vía Veneto, half a block north of Calle Eusebio Morales, El Cangrejo* ☎264–5822) is an open-air bar cooled by ceiling fans that is a popular watering hole for expat gringos and Panamanians alike. They serve burgers and other bar food, play rock music, and sometimes have live bands. **Manolo's** (⊠ *Vía Veneto and Calle D, El Cangrejo* ☎264–5822) is a café and restaurant on busy Vía Veneto with a wraparound terrace cooled by ceiling fans that is a great place for people-watching, a quiet drink, or a late-night snack.

AREA **Pizza Piola** (⊠ *Calle 51, half a block up from The Bristol, Area Bancária*
BANCÁRIA ☎263–4668) is a small Argentine restaurant that offers tango nights

on Thursdays, which start with a class at 8 PM, and Argentine folk dancing on Friday nights, on a small terrace in front. **Pavo Real** (⊠ *Calle 51, near Calle Ricardo Arias, Area Bancária* ☎ *269–0504*) is an attractive British-style pub on a quiet street around the corner from the Marriott's casino. It has a pool table, serves fish-and-chips and other bar food, and has live music, mostly rock, on weekends. It can be a good place to meet other English speakers.

CALLE
URUGUAY

Sahara (⊠ *Calle 48 and Calle Uruguay, Bella Vista* ☎ *214–8284*) is a massive bar with seating on a front terrace or inside, where there are a couple pool tables. They sometimes have live rock bands, and reggae nights on Wednesdays. **Urbano Bar** (⊠ *Calle 48, above Palms restaurant, Bella Vista* ☎ *265–7256*), located on the second floor above trendy Palms restaurant, near Calle Uruguay, is an otherworldly nightspot that is utterly 21st century. Think George Jetson on LSD. The **Greenhouse** (⊠ *Calle Uruguay between Calles 47 and 48, Bella Vista* ☎ *269–6846*) is one of the few places in the Calle Uruguay area where you can get a quiet drink on weekends. Seating is amidst the foliage on the front patio, or inside the low-lit bar. They also serve a good selection of sandwiches and wraps. **Habibi's** (⊠ *Calle 48 and Calle Uruguay, Bella Vista* ☎ *264–3647*) is mainly a restaurant, but its covered terrace is also a great spot for a late-night drink on weekends, since it sits at the center of the Calle Uruguay action. They also serve food till late.

PUNTA
PAITILLA
★

Decapolis Martini Bar (⊠ *Av. Balboa next to Multicentro, Paitilla* ☎ *215–5000*), a large lounge located in the chic Hotel Decapolis, is a very hot spot, with DJs spinning house music and martinis being consumed in dangerous quantities.

CALZADA
AMADOR
★

Bamboo (⊠ *South of Brisas del Amador shopping center, Calzada Amador* ☎ *314–3337*), an open-air bar under a giant thatched roof, is one of the most popular spots on the Calzada Amador, with a young crowd squeezing in to try and converse above the loud music on weekend nights. **Kayuco** (⊠ *Isla Flamenco, Calzada Amador* ☎ *314–1998*) is a popular open-air bar and restaurant overlooking the marina on Isla Flamenco, with a great view of the city's skyline. It's one of the only spots on the causeway for a drink by the water, and they serve fried seafood and other snacks into the wee hours.

CASINOS

Gambling is a popular pastime in Panama City, and there are casinos all over the place, ranging from fancy to seedy. The nicest by far are located in, or next to, the city's big hotels, namely the Marriott, Veneto, and Panamá, but few of the people who frequent them are guests. Panama City has a lot of gambling addicts.

The **Veneto Hotel & Casino** (⊠ *Vía Veneto and Calle Eusebio Morales, El Cangrejo* ☎ *340–8888*) has the city's biggest and most popular casino, which includes a sports bar, craps and poker, and a sea of slot machines. Expect music, and young Panamanians who simply come to party. **El Panamá** (⊠ *Vía Veneto and Calle Eusebio Morales, El Cangrejo* ☎ *215–9000*) has a large Fiesta Casino behind it that is popular with Panamanians. It includes a Salsas Sports Bar and a restaurant, and often has live music. The **Marriott** (✉ *Calle 52 and Calle Ricardo Arias, Area Bancária* ☎ *210–9100*) has a two-story casino next door that is quite popular with locals. It often has live music, and sometimes hosts concerts by the country's most popular groups.

DANCE CLUBS

The city's dance clubs play a broad mix of music, including American pop, salsa, merengue, reggaeton and the popular Panamanian music called *pindín*. Cover charges run between $3 and $10, and sometimes include a drink.

CASCO VIEJO
Fodor's Choice
★

Platea (✉ *Calle 1, in front of the old Club Union, Casco Viejo* ☎ *228–4011*), the popular bar underneath S'cena restaurant, may not have much of a dance floor, but they book hot salsa bands and are packed most Friday and Saturday nights, when people dance in the aisles or wherever else there's room. The bartenders and waiters, dressed in black with Panama hats, are part of the show, as they juggle bottles and dance while delivering mojitos and cuba libres.

EL CANGREJO
★

El Panamá Social Club (✉ *Vía Veneto and Calle Eusebio Morales, El Cangrejo* ☎ *215–9000*), the Hotel Panamá's dance club was once one of the city's premier nightspots, but its star has faded. The good thing is that there is now plenty of room on the dance floor, and they don't charge a cover. The attractive bar has live bands on weekends, and salsa dancing classes on Thursday at 8 PM that are a great introduction to those Latin dance steps; they cost $8. They also have a tango presentation and class on Wednesday nights at 8 PM that costs $5.

CALLE
URUGUAY
★

Mystik (✉ *Calle 47 east of Calle Uruguay, Bella Vista* ☎ *380–0550*), a dark and modern club with stools and couches surrounding a small dance floor, is the current hot spot with the city's college-age set. They spin a good mix of modern Latin, Jamaican, American, and European music, and charge a $10 cover on weekends. **La Bodeguita** (✉ *Calle Uruguay, half a block north of Av. Balboa, Bella Vista* ☎ *213–2153*), inspired by the famous Havana bar of the same name, sometimes has live bands, and always has Cuban or another Latin music playing. It gets packed on weekends, when it closes around 5 AM. **Bamboleo** (✉ *Calle 48, 1 block east of Calle Uruguay, Bella Vista* ☎ *390–5905*) is a popular dance club with an unreasonably small dance floor. It specializes in Latin music—salsa, merengue, reggaeton, and Panama's popular pindín. **BLG** (✉ *Calle 49 and Calle Uruguay, Bella Vista* ☎ *265–1624*) plays a mix of house, pop, and Latin music for a predominantly gay clientele. **Azucar** (✉ *Calle 49 and Calle Uruguay, Bella Vista* ☎ *302–7806*) is a Latin dance club that tends to get busy late—after 4 AM—when the other bars around Calle Uruguay start closing.

CALZADA
AMADOR
★

Playa (✉ *South end of Brisas del Amador shopping center, Calzada Amador* ☎ *314–3372*) is a vast open-air dance club and lounge with low couches and half beds, and a small swimming pool with cement tables and benches in it, for dancers who overheat. They charge a $5 cover on weekends. **Pahya** (✉ *Brisas del Amador shopping center, Calzada Amador* ☎ *314–3366*) is a fairly popular, modern dance club where they play a lot of reggaeton, as well as other Latin and pop music.

SHOPPING

Panama City has more shopping options than you can shake a credit card at. Because of the country's role as an international port, manufactured goods from all over the world are cheaper in Panama than just about anywhere else in the hemisphere, and merchants from South and Central America regularly travel here to shop, though they tend to do their business in the Colón Free Zone. Even people who go to Panama on vacation end up filling the old suitcase with new toys, but American tourists will find that the U.S. megastores often beat the local prices for cameras and other electronic goods—plus the stores back home are more convenient in terms of warranties. Clothing, on the other hand, is dirt-cheap in Panama. The Avenida Central pedestrian mall is lined with massive clothing stores that sell imported shirts and blouses for as little as a few dollars, though most of the styles cater to Latin American tastes. Busy Vía Veneto, in El Cangrejo, has several decent souvenir and T-shirt shops. The city also has several modern malls, where the selection ranges from the cheap stuff to name brands.

Panama also produces some lovely handicrafts. The famous Panama hat is misnamed since it originated in Ecuador, but it has been associated with Panama since Teddy Roosevelt was photographed wearing one when he traveled to the country to check on canal construction. Panama does, however, produce some handwoven hats, mostly in the provinces around the Azuero Peninsula, though they are stiffer than the Panama hat, and have dark brown patterns woven into them. Panamanian hats and imported Panama hats are available at souvenir shops and handicraft markets around the city.

The most popular Panamanian handicraft is the *mola,* a fabric picture sewn by Kuna Indian women and worn on their blouses as part of their traditional dress. They are lovely framed, and the Kuna also incorporate them into shirts, blouses, bags, and other items. The Kuna are also known for their bead bracelets and necklaces, as well as simple jewelry made from seeds and shells. The Emberá and Wounaan Indians also make some fine handicrafts. The men carve animal figures out of dark *cocobolo* wood and the seed of a rain-forest palm called *tagua,* which is known as "vegetal ivory." The women weave attractive rattan baskets, bowls, and platters, which can take weeks to complete, and are consequently expensive. The Ngwöbe-Bugle Indians are known for their colorful dresses and jute shoulder bags, which can serve as shopping bags or purses. They also create intricate bead necklaces called *chakiras.*

HANDICRAFT MARKETS

Even if you're not interested in buying, take a walk around one of the city's various handicraft markets, all of which are open daily 9–6. The rows of stalls filled with native handicrafts are great places to browse and learn a bit about the local cultures. The city's biggest and nicest craft market occupies what was once the gym of the Balboa YMCA, which is why it is called the **Centro Artesanal Antiguo YMCA** (⊠ *Av. Arnulfo Arias and Av. Amador, Balboa* ☎ *211–0100*). The spacious building holds dozens of stands, each with a different owner and selection. Wares range from kitsch to native handicrafts, and include molas sewn into bags, shirts, glasses cases, and pot holders, plus embroidered blouses, jewelry, handwoven hats, and plenty of work by the Emberá and Wounaan Indians of the Darién province. A good place to shop for molas is the **Centro Municipal de Artesanias Panameñas** (⊠ *Av. Arnulfo Arias, three blocks up from old YMCA, Balboa* ☎*211–3924*), a small market where most of the stands are owned by Kuna women, who are often sewing molas as they wait for customers. They also sell bead necklaces called *chaquiras,* bags, hammocks, dresses, framed butterflies, T-shirts, and other souvenirs.

The **Mercado de Artesanía de Panamá Viejo** (⊠ *Vía Cincuentenaria, Panama Viejo* ☎*No phone*), next to the old cathedral tower at Panamá Viejo, is a two-story cement building packed with small shops and stalls selling everything for indigenous handicrafts—many shop owners are Indians—to woven hats, Carnaval masks, and other works of mestizo artisans in the country's interior. A number of Kuna families have simple stalls on the second floor, which is a good place to shop for *molas.* Masks, hammocks, and other handicrafts tend to be relatively inexpensive at the **Mercado de Buhonería** (⊠ *Av. 4 at Av. B, Santa Ana* ☎*No phone*), a small market behind the old train station, just east of Plaza Cinco de Mayo, that receives few visitors. If you visit the Avenida Central pedestrian mall, you should definitely stop by here.

HANDICRAFT SHOPS

Though the selections are never as impressive as those of the handicraft markets, the city's handicraft shops tend to have more convenient locations. **Galería Arte Indígena** (⊠ *Calle 1, No. 844, Casco Viejo* ☎*228–9557*), just down the street from Plaza Francia, has an extensive selection of indigenous handicrafts, such as Emberá baskets, animal figures carved from *tagua* palm seeds, decorated gourds, hammocks, Panama hats (imported from Ecuador), and T-shirts. **Flory Saltzman Molas** (⊠ *Vía Veneto, by entrance to Hotel El Panamá, El Cangrejo* ☎*223–6963*) has the country's biggest *mola* collection—thousands of those colorful creations divided by theme and quality, and stacked to the ceiling. Flory's daughter Lynne is usually there in the afternoons, and she is happy to explain the significance of the designs and their role in Kuna culture. The quality of their collection varies greatly, and the good ones tend to cost considerably more than the Kuna vendors charge on the streets or in the markets.

JEWELRY

Most of Panama's jewelry shops specialize in flashy, gold-plated stuff that you could pick up in any major city, but there are a few shops worth checking out. **Reprosa** (⊠ *Av. A and Calle 4, Art Deco Building, Casco Viejo* ☎*271–0033* ⊠ *Av. Samuel Lewis and Calle 54, Obarrio* ☎*269–0457*) sells elegant jewelry based on reproductions of pre-Columbian gold pieces and Spanish coins, as well as interesting modern designs in silver and high-quality indigenous *chakira* beadwork, *cocobolo* wood carvings, paintings, and the obligatory *molas.* They have a shop in Obarrio, which is near El Cangrejo and the Area Bancária, and one in the heart of the Casco Viejo that closes Monday. The **Museo de la Esmeralda** (⊠ *Calle Pedro J. Sossa on Plaza Catedral, Casco Viejo* ☎ *262–1665*) is a small, cheesy museum about emerald mining that is an excuse to get people in to look at their emerald jewelry. It is owned by a Colombian company that has its own mines and factories, so the quality and prices are good, but the designs aren't going to win any awards.

MALLS

Panama City has several modern shopping malls and the more traditional Avenida Central. The **Avenida Central pedestrian mall** (⊠ *Between Plaza Santa Ana and Plaza Cinco de Mayo, Santa Ana*) is lined with shops selling imported electronics, jewelry, fabrics, and clothing. A stroll down this busy street can be quite entertaining, even if you don't buy anything. **Multicentro** (⊠ *Av. Balboa, Punta Paitilla* ☎ *208–2500*), a modern, four-story mall, holds dozens of shops, as well as a movie theater, food court, and casino at a convenient location across from Punta Paitilla. **Multiplaza** (⊠ *Vía Israel, San Francisco* ☎ *302–5380*) is a large mall just east of Punta Paitilla that has dozens of shops, a movie theater, and a food court. **Albrook Mall** (⊠ *In front of Terminal de Buses, Albrook* ☎ *303–6333*) is the people's mall, with more discount stores than the malls downtown. That, combined with its convenient location between the city's massive bus terminal and Albrook Airport, makes it the busiest mall.

SOUVENIR SHOPS

La Ronda (⊠ *Calle 1 and Plaza Francia, Casco Viejo* ☎ *211–1001*) is an attractive little shop in a historic building near Plaza Francia that sells a mix of handicrafts and souvenirs: *molas,* Carnaval masks, wood carvings, paintings, Panama hats, and assorted knickknacks. **Aizaga** (⊠ *Vía Veneto, El Cangrejo* ☎ *399–9012*) sells a mix of Panamanian and Ecuadorean souvenirs, including an ample selection of Panama hats, from a convenient location on Busy Vía Veneto.

SPORTS & THE OUTDOORS

Thanks to its proximity to forest, canal, and ocean, Panama City offers plenty of options for enjoying the outdoors, which include hiking in the world's largest chunk of urban rain forest, biking down the causeway, navigating the Panama Canal, and white-water rafting in the jungle.

BEACHES

Because of the silt that the Panama Canal dumps into the ocean and the sewage from Panama City, the beaches near the city are not recommended for swimming. The closest beach is **Playa Bonita** (Playa Kobbe), 8 km (5 mi) southwest of the city, on the other side of the canal. It is the site of the massive, expensive Intercontinental Playa Bonita Resort, and the only option there for nonguests is to have lunch at the hotel's beachfront restaurant, Pelicano, though you need to reserve the day before, and you can't use the pool *(⇨ Isla Taboga in Canal and Central Panama chapter).* **Playa Veracruz,** located 16 km (10 mi) southwest of the city, is a wide, gray public beach lined with a few open-air restaurants where you can get an inexpensive beer and fish lunch. The clearest water near Panama City is found on **Isla Taboga,** a 60-minute ferry ride from the Calzada Amador, which is a popular day trip *(⇨ Isla Taboga in Canal and Central Panama chapter).* Some of the country's nicest Pacific beaches are on **Isla Contadora,** a 20-minute flight from the city, which is usually visited as an overnight trip but is an easy day trip because there are flights to the island in the morning and afternoon *(⇨ Isla Contadora in Canal and Central Panama chapter).*

BIKING

Though there are several good mountain-biking routes near the city, none of the tour operators currently offers bike tours. You can, however, rent bikes near the beginning of the Calzada Amador, which is a wonderful, easy ride on a sidewalk out to the islands. If you're feeling energetic, you could explore nearby Balboa and Cerro Ancón by bike; both are safe, and Cerro Ancón has plenty of shade. Be careful, however, not to take Avenida Arnulfo Arias past the busy Avenida de los Mártires, across which are the slums of Chorrillo.

Fodor'sChoice **Eco Circuitos Panama** (⊠ *Country Inn & Suites, Calles Amador and*
★ *Pelicáno, Balboa* ☎ *314–0068* ⊕ *www.ecocircuitos.com*) rents mountain bikes at their office in the Country Inn & Suites Panama Canal, which is equidistant from Balboa and the Amador Causeway. **Bicicletas Moses** (⊠ *Behind Las Pencas, entrance to Calzada Amador* ☎ *211–2579* ⊗ *Daily 8–8*) rents an array of bikes for riding on the causeway.

BIRD-WATCHING

Panama City has world-class bird-watching as close as the **Parque Nacional Metropolitano,** which is home to more than 200 avian species and is less than 15 minutes from most hotels. There are several spots in nearby **Parque Nacional Soberanía,** which has more than 400 bird species, all within 40 minutes of downtown, including **Pipeline Road,** where the Panama Audubon Society has held several world-record Christmas bird counts *(⇨ Parque Nacional Soberanía in Canal and Central Panama chapter).* Unless you're an expert, you're best off going with an experienced birding guide. Several local tour companies can set you up with a private guide, or can book you onto an existing trip, which is less expensive. You may need to call several companies to find a trip for your dates, though.

Fodor'sChoice **Ancon Expeditions** (⊠ *Calle Elvira Mendez, Edificio El Dorado No. 3,*
★ *Area Bancária* ☎ *269–9415* ⊕ *www.anconexpeditions.com*) has excellent birding guides, and offers day tours to the main protected areas near the capital, including exploration of the forest canopy of Parque Metropolitano using a modified construction crane, and a great boat trip on Gatún Lake. **Advantage Panama** (⊠ *Llanos de Curundú No. 2006, Curundú* ☎ *6676–2466* ⊕ *www.advantagepanama.com*) is a small nature tourism company that offers early-morning tours of Parque Metropolitana and day trips to Parque Nacional Soberanía. They can also arrange custom trips to other areas, and are reasonably priced. **Eco Circuitos Panama** (⊠ *Country Inn & Suites, Calles Amador and Pelicáno, Balboa* ☎ *314–0068* ⊕ *www.ecocircuitos.com*) offers several half- and full-day birding trips out of the capital. The **Panama**

Audubon Society (✉ *Casa #2006-B, Altos de Curundú* ☎*232–5977* ⊕*www.panamaaudubon.org*) runs occasional, inexpensive bird walks and overnight excursions that require a bit of self-sufficiency, but can be a great way to meet locals.

Pesantez Tours (✉ *Plaza Balboa officina #2, Punta Paitilla* ☎*223–5374* ⊕*www.pesantez-tours.com*), one of the country's biggest tour operators, offers a half-day bird-watching trip to Parque Nacional Soberanía.

Panoramic Panama (✉ *Quarry Heights, casa #35, Cerro Ancón* ☎*314–1417* ⊕*www.panoramicpanama.com*) is a small company that can set up customized birding trips.

The **Smithsonian Tropical Research Institute (STRI)** (✉ *Tupper Center, Av. Roosevelt, Cerro Ancón* ☎*212-8951* ⊕*www.stri.org*) offers full-day trips to Barro Colorado Island that combine bird-watching with general information on tropical ecology, but which usually need to be booked well ahead of time.

CANAL TOURS

While the canal is impressive when admired from any of the city's various viewing points, there's nothing quite like getting onto the water and navigating it amidst the giant cargo ships. People spend thousands of dollars on cruises that include a canal crossing, but you can have the same experience for $100–$160, and spend the night in a spacious hotel room. Two companies offer partial transit tours, which travel through the canal's Pacific locks and Gailard Cut, and occasional full transits, which take you from one ocean to the other. All transits are accompanied by an expert bilingual guide. Full transits include a Continental breakfast and a simple lunch. Partial transits travel between the islands at the end of the Amador Causeway and the port of Gamboa, on Gatún Lake, a trip that lasts 4–5 hours. They take place every Saturday during the low season, and Thursday, Friday, and Saturday from January through April. Full transits take place once or twice a month and last 8–9 hours. Either trip is an unforgettable experience, fit for travelers of all ages.

Canal Bay Tours (✉ *Bahia Balboa Building, next to Nunciatura Punta Paitilla* ☎*209–2009* ⊕*www.canalandbaytours.com*) offers partial and full transit tours on one of two ships: the 115-foot *Fantasia del Mar,* which has air-conditioned cabins and a large upper deck, and the 85-foot *Isla Morada,* which has one large covered deck. Partial transits cost $99 for adults and $45 for children; full transits, $145 adults and $55 children. **Pacific Marine Tours** (✉ *Villa Porras and Calle Belén, No. 106, San Francisco* ☎*226–8417* ⊕*www.pmatours.net*) runs canal transits on the 119-foot *Pacific Queen,* a comfortable ship with air-conditioned cabins and two large decks. Partial transits cost $105 for adults and $55 for children; full transits, $165 adults and $65 children.

GOLF

The **Summit Golf Resort** (✉20 km [12 mi] northwest of town on road to Gamboa ☎232–4653 ⊕www.summitgolfpanama.com) has an 18-hole, par-72 championship course designed by Jeff Myers that is hemmed by the rain forest of Camino de Cruces National Park. It's just 30 minutes from most hotels, and the course is open to nonmembers. Greens fees are $120 on weekdays and $150 on weekends, golf cart included, and club rentals cost $15–$45, according to the quality.

HIKING

The hiking options in and around Panama range from the 40-minute trek to the top of Cerro Ancón to more demanding expeditions into the vast lowland forest of Parque Nacional Soberanía and the mountains of Parque Nacional Altos de Campana. The **Parque Natural Metropolitano** has five well-marked trails covering a total of about 3 mi, which range from flat stretches to a steep road up to a viewpoint. **Parque Nacional Soberanía** has several trails ranging from the historic **Camino de Cruces** to the shorter **Sendero el Charco,** which is on the right after Summit Botanical Gardens and Zoo (⇨ Parque Nacional Soberanía in Canal and Central Panama chapter). The mountains of Cerro Azul and Parque Nacional Altos de Campana, which lie less than an hour to the east and west of the city respectively, also have hiking trails as well as panoramic views, and some flora and fauna different from what you'll see in the lowland forests around the city (⇨ Cerro Azul, or Parque Nacional Altos de Campana in Canal and Central Panama chapter).

Advantage Panama (✉Llanos de Curundú No. 2006, Curundúp ☎6676–2466 ⊕www.advantagepanama.com) can arrange custom tours for hiking enthusiasts. **Eco Circuitos Panama** (✉Country Inn & Suites, Calles Amador and Pelicáno, Balboa ☎314–0068 ⊕www.eco-circuitos.com) offers hiking tours to Parque Metropolitano and Parque Nacional Soberanía. **Futura Travel** (✉Centro Comercial Camino de Cruces, El Dorado ☎360–2030 ⊕www.extremepanama.com) runs a hiking tour to the summit of Cerro de La Cruz in Parque Nacional Altos de Campana.

HORSEBACK RIDING

Margo Tours (✉Calle 50, next to Farmacia Arrocha, San Francisco ☎302–0390 ⊕www.margotours.com) offers half-day horseback-riding tours through the pastures and forest of the Haras Orillac Ranch, in the mountains of Cerro Azul, just 40 minutes east of downtown.

SPORTFISHING

The Bay of Panama has good sportfishing, but the best fishing is around and beyond the Pearl Islands, which are best fished out of **Isla Contadora** or **Isla San José,** each of which is a short flight from the city (⇨ Isla Contadora or Isla San José in Canal and Central Panama chapter). Day charters are available out of Panama City, and usually head to the area around Isla Otoque and Isla Bono, which are about 90 minutes southwest of the city. You have a chance of hooking mackerel, jack, tuna, roosterfish, or wahoo in that area (billfish are less common there than in other parts of the country). A closer, less expensive option is light-tackle fishing for snook and peacock bass in **Gatún Lake,** the vast man-made lake in the middle of the Panama Canal. The lake is full of South American peacock bass, which fight like a smallmouth bass, but can reach 8–10 pounds *(⇨ Lago Gatún in Canal and Central Panama chapter).*

Panama Canal Fishing (☎315–1905 or 6699–0507 ⊕*www.panama-canalfishing.com*) is the premier operator for freshwater fishing on Gatún Lake. It runs fishing charters for serious anglers and families on a Hurricane Fundeck with two swivel chairs on the bow, and usually hooks 20 or 30 fish per day. Trips also include wildlife observation and views of giant ships on the canal. An all-inclusive day of fishing for two to four people costs $260. **Panama Fishing and Catching** (☎6622–0212 or 6505–9553 ⊕*www.panamafishingandcatching.com*) offers bass and snook fishing on Gatún Lake ($400); snook, snapper and tarpon fishing on the Bayano River ($400); inshore fishing along the coast and nearby islands ($400–$650); and deep-sea fishing charters in the Bay of Panama ($1,000–$1,800), with rates varying according to boat size and destinations. **Las Perlas Fishing and Tours** (⊠ *Isla Contadora* ☎6689–4916) runs deep-sea fishing charters out of Contadora, which is an easy day trip (20-minute flight). **Margo Tours** (⊠ *Villa Porras and Calle Belén, No. 106, San Francisco* ☎226–8417 ⊕*www.pma-tours.net*) offers a one-week tour that combines bass fishing on Gatún Lake with a day of ocean fishing with sightseeing in Panama City. **Pacific Marine Tours** (⊠ *Villa Porras and Calle Belén, No. 106, San Francisco* ☎226–8417 ⊕*www.pmatours.net*) can arrange deep-sea fishing charters in the Bay of Panama. **Panama Johnny Tours** (☎264–8230 ⊕*www.panamajohnny.com*) can arrange deep-sea fishing charters on a 31-foot Silverton ($1,200 per day), or bass fishing on Gatún Lake in a Nitro Bass Tracker ($250 for one or two people).

WHITE-WATER RAFTING

Aventuras Panama (⊠*Calle El Parcial 1½ blks west of Transístmica, Edif. Celma Of. 3* ☎260–0044 ⊕*www.aventuraspanama.com*) runs white-water rafting trips on the **Chagres River (Class II–III),** which flows through the rain forests of Chagres National Park *(⇨ Parque Nacional Chagres in Canal and Central Panama chapter).* The full-day trip requires no previous rafting experience and provides access to impressive tropical nature. It begins with a long drive down rough dirt roads into the heart of the national park, where you begin a five-hour river trip that includes a picnic lunch, and ends at Madden Lake. The trip is available from May to late March; it lasts 11–12 hours and costs $175 per person. Also on offer is a shorter, more exhilarating trip on the **Mamoní River (Class III–IV),** which flows through an agricultural area and includes a portage around a waterfall. That trip is available from May to March, and takes about 10 hours, about half of which is spent on the river, and costs $125.

PANAMA CITY ESSENTIALS

TRANSPORTATION

BY AIR

Panama City's airport, Aeropuerto Internacional de Tocumen (PTY), 26 km (13 mi) northeast of Panama City, is the gateway into the country. All U.S. carriers, and the Panamanian airline Copa, fly direct to Panama City. Domestic flights leave from Albrook Airport (Aeropuerto Marcos a Gelabert), which is located just a few miles west of downtown.

Airports **Aeropuerto Internacional de Tocumen** (⊠ *Corredor Norte, 26 km [15 mi] northeast of the city* ☎ *238–2600*). **Aeropuerto Marcos a Gelabert (Albrook Airport)** (⊠ *Av Gaillard, Albrook* ☎ *315–0241*).

Airlines Panama has two domestic airlines, which fly out of Aeropuerto Marcos a Gelabert to most of the same destinations for the same prices—between $70 and $150 round-trip—which vary according to the destination.

Aeroperlas (⊠ *Aeropuerto Marcos A. Gelabert, Albrook* ☎ *315–7500* ⊕ *www. aeroperlas.com*) flies to approximately 20 destinations in the country, with several flights daily to the more popular cities. The country's original domestic carrier, it forms part of the regional conglomerate Grupo Taca. The company emphasizes pilot training and safety.

Air Panama (⊠ *Aeropuerto Marcos a Gelabert, Albrook* ☎ *316–9000* ⊕ *www. flyairpanama.com*) is the country's newest domestic airline, and consequently has its newest fleet. It flies to about two dozen destinations in Panama, and to San José, Costa Rica. **Copa** (☎ *507/227–5000 in Panama* ⊕ *www.copaair.com*) is a Continental Airlines partner that flies throughout Central America and to the United States.

BY BUS

If you don't mind the heat and cramped seating, the local buses (converted Blue Bird school buses) are a cheap (25¢) way to get around the city. Most have wild paint jobs, and each bus has its destination and route painted broadly across the windshield. The word to remember when you want to get off is *parada* (stop). You pay your fare as you get off. All buses pass by the massive Terminal de Buses in Albrook, where you can catch buses to almost everywhere else in the city and the country. Buses to the Miraflores Locks, Summit Zoo, and Gamboa leave hourly from the SACA terminal, one block north of Plaza Cinco de Mayo.

BY CAR

Driving a car in Panama City is not an undertaking for the meek, but renting a car can be an excellent way to explore the surrounding countryside. Rentals usually cost $40–$50 per day, whereas four-wheel-drive vehicles cost $60–$70. All the big car-rental companies have one or more offices in the city, and at the airports.

Car-Rental Agencies Avis ☎*238–4056.* **Budget** ☎*263-8777.* **Dollar** ☎*270-0355.* **Hertz** ☎*260-2111.* **National** ☎*265-3333.* **Thrifty** ☎*204-9555.*

BY TAXI

Taxis in Panama are all independently owned, tend to be smaller cars, and don't have meters. The city is divided into zones, the flat fare for one person being $1, to which they add a quarter each time you cross into another zone, plus a quarter for each additional person. Fares also increase 20% after 10 PM. A short trip should cost about $1.50 for two people, whereas a trip to the domestic airport in Albrook or the Calzada Amador can run $3–$5, and the trip to Tocumen International Airport should cost $20. Tips are not expected. You will be charged double, or several times the standard rate, by the taxi drivers who wait outside hotels, but their cars are usually standard size, and drivers are likely to speak some English. Flagging a cab in the street is widely considered to be safe. If you're alone, you may be expected to share a taxi, a common practice in Panama, as is sitting in the passenger seat next to the driver.

CONTACTS & RESOURCES

EMERGENCIES

One of the advantages of Panama City is that in the unlikely event that you suffer an accident or medical emergency, the police are relatively efficient, and there are good hospitals nearby. You are always better off having a local call the police or an ambulance, since they can communicate your location to the operator more easily than you can.

Emergency Services National police (☎*104*). **Fire department** (☎*103*). **Ambulance** (*Hospital Punta Pacífica* ☎*204–8108*).

Hospitals Hospital Punta Pacífica (✉*Boulevard Pacífica y Vía Punta Darién, Punta Pacífica* ☎*204–8000*), affiliated with Johns Hopkins Medicine International, is the country's newest and best hospital, with 24-hour emergency and ambulance service and a medical tourism program. **Centro Medico Paitilla** (✉*Calle 53 and Av. Balboa, Punta Paitilla* ☎*265-8800*) is a large, well-respected hospital and clinic with 24-hour emergency service and a complete out-patient clinic for consultations during the week.

Pharmacies Farmacia Arrocha (✉*Calle 49 Este at Vía España, Area Bancária* ☎*223–4505* ✉*Av. Balboa, Punta Paitilla* ☎*264-9044* ✉*Calle 50, San Francisco* ☎*270-0722*) is the country's biggest pharmacy chain, with stores near most of the big hotels that stay open 24/7.

INTERNET

Internet access is easy in Panama City. Most hotels have either wireless or cable broadband connections. Midrange and budget hotels provide guests with free Internet access, however the luxury hotels tend to charge $10–$15 per day for it. Most hotels that don't have Wi-Fi have one or two computers with high-speed Internet connections for guest use, and in most neighborhoods there is an Internet café every block or two that charges $1 per hour.

MAIL & SHIPPING

Small *correos* (post offices), officially called **COTEL** in Panama, are scattered all over the city. They are open Monday–Friday 7 to 5:30 and Saturday 7–4:30. It costs 35¢ to mail a letter to the United States and 45¢ to Europe. Postcards cost 25¢ to the United States and 35¢ to Europe. Mail tends to take a week to reach U.S. destinations and two weeks to reach Europe. If you need to receive mail in Panama, you can have it addressed to your name and *entrega general* at any COTEL outlet, though you are better off using the P.O. Box of a hotel you frequent or American Express's mail service if you are a member. The courier services Federal Express and DHL have dozens of drop-off boxes scattered around the city, and can pick packages up, or drop them off, at any hotel.

Courier Services FedEx (⊠ *Edificio Globus, Av. Samuel Lewis and Calle 55, Obarrio* ☎ *800–1122*). **DHL** (⊠ *Av. Samuel Lewis, Obarrio* ☎ *272–3400*).

Post Office The most convenient post office for travelers is located on the ground floor of the Plaza Concordia shopping mall, on Vía España near El Cangejo: **Cotel** (⊠ *Plaza Concordia #121, Vía España, El Cangejo* ☎ *512-6232*).

MONEY MATTERS

The U.S. dollar replaced Panama's national currency, the balboa, half a century ago, but Panamanians still call dollars "balboas." Panama does, however, mint its own coins, which are the same size as U.S. coins but have different portraits on them. Prices of most things are considerably lower in Panama than in the United States or Europe. A cup of coffee can cost 50¢ to $1.50, according to where you order it, and a beer costs $1–$2 at most bars.

ATMS Cash machines aren't as ubiquitous in Panama City as they are in Miami or New York, but almost. You can find ATMs in the lobbies of the biggest hotels, gas stations with convenience stores, pharmacies, supermarkets, and the city's abundant banks. Banks that have a lot of ATMs scattered around the city include BAC and Banistmo. Debit cards and credit cards from U.S., Canadian, and European banks should work in all Panamanian ATMs, but there is often an additional charge for international transactions, usually 1%.

SAFETY

Most of the city is safe for walking, even at night, especially Vía España, El Cangrejo, the Area Bancária, and Paitilla, where the bulk of the city's hotels and restaurants are located. The Casco Viejo and Avenida Central pedestrian mall are safe by day, but after dark you should limit your wandering to the area around Plaza Bolívar and Plaza Francia, which is where all the restaurants and bars are. Even during the day you should lock your fancy jewelry and watch, passport, and most of your credit cards and cash into your hotel safe before heading to the Casco Viejo, just to be on the safe side. Areas that should be avoided at all times are El Chorillo, which lies immediately to the west of the Casco Viejo, and all of Santa Ana aside from the Avenida Central and Plaza Cinco de Mayo area. At night you should travel to and from the Casco Viejo only by taxi or rental car, but by day walking there from Plaza Cinco de Mayo on Avenida Central is fine. Keep out of the

VACATION EDUCATION

Travelers who want to take home more than just photos and souvenirs have the option of learning or brushing up on their Spanish while in Panama. A handful of small schools cater to travelers and foreign residents with Spanish-language-instruction options that range from one-month courses to private tutors, either in Panama City or the popular destinations of western Panama.

SpanishPanama.com (✉ *Calle G, off Vía Argentina, behind El Trapiche, El Cangrejo* ☎ *213–3121* ⊕ *www. spanishpanama.com*) offers inexpensive group classes and one-on-one instruction at your hotel, restaurants, while sightseeing, or at their conveniently located center.

ILISA (✉ *Calle Gonzalo Crance, Edificio 8, Clayton* ☎ *317–1011* ⊕ *www.ilisa.com/panama*), a Costa Rican Spanish school that has expanded into Panama, has an institute in the Ciudad del Saber, near Miraflores Locks, a good distance from downtown but quite close to the rain forest.

Spanish by the Sea (✉ *Entrega General, Bocas del Toro* ☎ *757–9518* ⊕ *www.spanishbythesea.com*) offers classes in the town of Bocas del Toro and at its sister school, **Spanish by the River,** in the mountain town of Boquete (☎ *720–3456*), in Chiriquí.

southwestern half of Caledonia, including the Avenida Balboa west of the Balboa Monument; and Curundú, which lies to the northwest of Caledonia. You don't need a map or a Geiger counter to realize when you're headed into a bad neighborhood, though some areas look more dangerous than they actually are. If you're on foot and feel any apprehension about where you've ended up, flag down the first taxi, even if it has another passenger in it, and go someplace you know is safe.

TOURS

Fodor'sChoice ★ Panama City has a plethora of tour companies, all of which offer tours of the city, canal, and nearby parks, but not all of them have guides of the same caliber, and few have true naturalist guides. The premier ecotourism company is **Ancón Expeditions,** but the comparable **Ecocircuitos** also has good guides and environmentally friendly policies. One of the oldest companies is **Pesantez Tours,** which has some good naturalist guides but concentrates on more traditional tours. The problems with such established companies is that their best guides are often reserved by the top U.S. companies, which hire them to run their Panama tours, so independent tourists may end up with newer, less experienced guides. Smaller, newer companies that can often provide a more customized service include **Panoramic Panama** and **Advantage Panama,** which specializes and bird-watching and nature. Other established tour operators that offer some unique day trips are **Margo Tours, Futura Travel,** and **Aventuras Panama,** a white-water outfitter that also offers hiking, and visits to Emberá Indian communities in Chagres National Park.

Tour Companies Advantage Panama (✉ *Llanos de Curundú No. 2006, Curundú* ☎ *6676–2466* ⊕ *www.advantagepanama.com*). **Ancón Expeditions** (✉ *Calle*

Elvira Mendez, Edificio El Dorado No. 3, Area Bancária ☎269–9415 ⊕www.
anconexpeditions.com). **Aventuras Panama** (✉*Calle El Parcial ,1½ blks west of
Transístmica, Edif. Celma Of. 3, El Dorado* ☎260–0044 ⊕www.aventuraspanama.
com).* **Eco Circuitos Panama** (✉*Country Inn & Suites, Calles Amador and Pelicáno,
Balboa* ☎314–0068 ⊕www.ecocircuitos.com).* **Futura Travel** (✉*Centro Comercial
Camino de Cruces, El Dorado* ☎360–2030 ⊕www.extremepanama.com).* **Margo
Tours** (✉*Calle 50, next to Farmacia Arrocha, San Francisco* ☎302–0390 ⊕www.
margotours.com).* **Panoramic Panama** (✉*Quarry Heights, casa #35, Cerro Ancón*
☎314–1417 ⊕www.panoramicpanama.com).* **Pesantez Tours** (✉*Plaza Balboa
officina #2, Punta Paitilla* ☎223–5374 ⊕www.pesantez-tours.com).*

VISITOR INFORMATION

The **Instituto Panameño de Turismo** (*IPAT* ✉*Calle Ricardo Arias, across
from Hotel Continental, Area Bancária* ☎269–8011 *or* 526–7000
⊕*www.visitpanama.com*) has a decent Web page and a small information office, together with the Policía de Turismo, at Vía España and
Calle Ricardo Arias, where they answer basic questions and hand out
brochures.

The Canal & Central Panama

WORD OF MOUTH

"As we reached the outskirts of Portobelo after about 2.5 hours we saw the first of an old fortress, covered in jungle vines at the edge of the blue Caribbean . . . how cool is that!"

–Faithie

"Isla Contadora is absolutely beautiful. The beaches of the Pearl Islands, as you must see the surrounding islands, are pristine just like in Survivor: Pearl Islands."

–Rodraad

By David
Dudenhoefer

THE PANAMA CANAL BISECTS THE country just to the west of Panama City, which enjoys excellent views of the monumental waterway. Between the canal and the rain forest that covers its islands, banks, and adjacent national parks, there is enough to see and do to fill several days. Central Panama stretches out from the canal across three provinces and into two oceans to comprise everything from the mountains of the Cordillera Central, to the west, to the jungles around Bayano Lake east of the canal, and from the coral reefs of the Caribbean coast in the north to the beaches of the Pearl Islands in the Bahía de Panamá (Bay of Panama) in the south. Much of the region can be visited on day trips from Panama City, but the hotels in gorgeous natural settings outside the city will make you want to do some overnights. You could easily limit your entire vacation to Central Panama; the region holds most of the nation's history and nearly all the things that draw people to the country—beaches, reefs, islands, mountains, rain forests, native cultures, and, of course, the Panama Canal. Within hours of Panama City, in many cases a fraction of an hour, you can enjoy bird-watching, sportfishing, hiking, golf, skin diving, white-water rafting, horseback riding, whale-watching, or lazing on a palm-lined beach.

The Panama Canal can be explored from Panama City, Gamboa, or Colón, and its attractions range from the wildlife of Barro Colorado Island to the feisty peacock bass that abound in Gatún Lake. The coast on either side of the canal's Caribbean entrance offers the remains of colonial fortresses hemmed by jungle, half a dozen beaches, and mile upon mile of coral reef, most of it between 90 minutes and three hours from Panama City. The mountains to the east of the canal hold flora and fauna that you won't find in the forests that flank it, as well indigenous Emberá villages and a white-water rafting route on the Chagres River. The Pacific islands offer idyllic beaches, a little history, good sportfishing, decent dive sites, and seasonal whale-watching, all within an hour of the capital by boat or plane. The coast to the southwest of Panama City also has some nice beaches, whereas the nearby highland refuge of El Valle presents exuberant landscapes populated by a multitude of birds and an ample selection of outdoor activities.

ORIENTATION & PLANNING

ORIENTATION

Central Panama is basically everything within a three-hour drive from Panama City, plus the islands to the southeast (within an hour of the city by boat or plane). Most of the region's attractions can be visited on day trips from the capital, but a few spots require overnights. Calle Omar Torrijos leads north from Panama City's Balboa neighborhood to the canal's Pacific locks, Summit, and Gamboa. The Corredor Norte connects to the Transísmica, which leads to Sabanitas—where the road east to Portobelo and Isla Grande begins—and Colón. The Corredor Sur, which begins near Panama City's Punta Paitilla, flows into the eastbound Carretera Interamericana (Inter-American Highway, or CA1)

TOP REASONS TO GO

THE PANAMA CANAL

More than just a sight worth admiring, the Panama Canal is a waterway to be explored. The most popular way to do so is by taking the weekly transit tours that ply its waters between the Calzada Amador (Amador Causeway) and Gamboa. You can get a different perspective on one of the nature or fishing tours available out of Gamboa, or by staying at the Meliá resort, near Colón.

THE RAIN FOREST

Central Panama has some of the most accessible rain forest in the world, with roads, trails, and waterways leading into wilderness that's home to hundreds of bird species and other animals. Tropical nature can be experienced to the fullest in the forests along the canal, in the mountains to the east and west of it, or along the Caribbean coast.

THE OCEANS

With the Caribbean and Pacific just 50 mi apart at the canal, you can bathe or skin dive in two oceans on the same day. The Caribbean coast has miles of coral reef, whereas the Pacific islands lie near good fishing, dive spots, and seasonal whale-watching.

THE ISLANDS

Panama's best beaches are on its islands, and Central Panama has isles where the sand is lined by coconut palms or thick jungle. These range from funky Isla Grande, a short boat ride from the Caribbean coast, to historic Isla Taboga, to the uninhabited isles of the Pearl Archipelago, where several seasons of *Survivor* were based.

THE MOUNTAINS

The hills of Central Panama are considerably lower than those in the country's western provinces, but they still provide a refreshing respite from the lowland heat, and their lush forests are home to hundreds of bird species.

just before Tocumen Airport, near which left turns lead to Cerro Azul. The westbound Carretera Interamericana is reached by taking Avenida de los Mártires over the Bridge of the Americas, near which left turns lead to Kobbe and Veracruz beaches. After that, it becomes a two-lane highway heading west around Chorrera and over the mountains to the Central Pacific beaches and El Valle de Antón, one to two hours from the city by car. The Pacific islands of Islas Taboga, Contadora, and San José are reached by daily ferries or flights.

PLANNING

WHEN TO GO

Most of the canal and Central Pacific sites lie within 30 minutes to two hours of Panama City, so if you're based there, plenty of attractions can be visited on a spare morning or afternoon; others are amenable to spending an extra night or two. The best time to explore the area is the December to May dry season, or when rains let up in July and August. Note that Panamanians generally travel between Christmas and New Year's, during the weekend of Carnaval in mid-February, or during

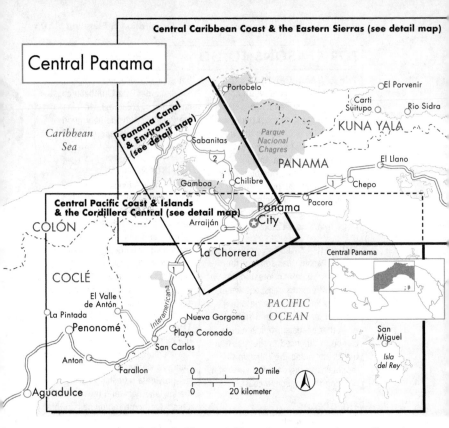

Map labels:

Central Caribbean Coast & the Eastern Sierras (see detail map)

Central Panama

Panama Canal & Environs (see detail map)

Central Pacific Coast & Islands & the Cordillera Central (see detail map)

Caribbean Sea

Portobelo

El Porvenir

Carti Suitupo

Rio Sidra

KUNA YALA

Sabanitas

Parque Nacional Chagres

PANAMA

El Llano

Gamboa

Chilibre

Chepo

COLÓN

Pacora

Arraiján

Panama City

La Chorrera

Central Panama

COCLÉ

El Valle de Antón

La Pintada

Penonomé

Nueva Gorgona

PACIFIC OCEAN

San Miguel

Playa Coronado

Anton

San Carlos

Isla del Rey

Farallon

Aguadulce

Interamericana

0   20 mile
0   20 kilometer

Easter week; hotels fill up quickly at these times, and you will need to reserve rooms well in advance. Colorful Congo dances are performed in Portobelo for New Year's, Carnaval, and the Festival de Diablos y Congos (which takes place shortly after Carnaval).

GETTING AROUND

You can visit most of the Central Pacific's sites on your own, but you have to join tours to do the canal transit, trips on Gatún Lake, tours of the indigenous communities, and white-water rafting in Chagres National Park. You can reach Summit, Parque Nacional Soberanía, and Gamboa by bus or taxi, but you should rent a car to explore more distant areas such as the Cerro Azul and most Pacific beaches. Tours or hotel transfers are available to most of those areas. Portobelo, Isla Grande, and El Valle de Antón are easy to reach on public buses, but you'll get there quicker in a car. The Panama Canal Railway is an interesting trip, but the downside is getting dumped in a dangerous part of Colón, which is why most people take the train as part of a tour that meets them at the Colón train station and takes them to nearby sites.

Of the Pacific islands, Isla Taboga can be reached by taking a 60-minute ferry, Isla Contadora and Isla San José by taking short flights from Albrook Airport.

A BIT OF HISTORY

Nearly all Panama's history took place here in Central Panama, a region sometimes a mere 50 mi across. This was a vital link between Spain and its mineral-rich South American colonies; for centuries, Andean gold and silver crossed the isthmus via mule on a jungle road called the Camino Real. After successive pirate attacks on the Caribbean port Nombre de Dios, the Spanish moved port to safer Portobelo, and the new Camino de las Cruces was built. But further pirate attacks forced Spain to ship around Cape Horn instead and Panama was eventually absorbed as a province of Colombia.

In 1849, tens of thousands of would-be millionaires joined the California Gold Rush. Before the Transcontinental Railroad sped up land travel across the United States, most people traveled to California by sea, first via Nicaragua's San Juan River and later through Panama. The American-built Panama Railroad, inaugurated in 1855, ran between Panama City and the new port Aspinwall (now Colón). After the U.S. rail route started service in 1869, though, the Panama Railroad's heyday and the region's importance both hit a downturn.

But within a decade Fernando de Lesseps, of Suez Canal fame, acquired the rights from Colombia to dig an interoceanic canal here. His French company started work in 1882, but fund mismanagement and disease caused the barely begun project to be abandoned in 1889. The Cementerio Francés, a small graveyard on the road to Gamboa, commemorates the 20,000 French workers lost, and you can still see part of their effort to the west of the Gatún Locks.

When Colombia rejected a proposal by the United States to finish the job, President Theodore Roosevelt helped foment an independence movement, complete with U.S. battleship backup, that helped the Panamanians declare independence in 1903. A new treaty ceded a 10-mi-wide strip of land to the Americans, where the Canal would be constructed, and gave the U.S. military the right to intervene whenever U.S. interests were threatened.

For the next six decades the Canal Zone was an affluent guarded enclave ensuring American influence in the region. But by the middle of the 20th century, protests became frequent, one resulting in several student deaths. In the 1970s Panamanian General Omar Torrijos launched a successful international campaign to get the United States to negotiate, and the subsequent Torrijos-Carter treaties of 1977 mapped out the ultimate transfer of the Canal to Panama on December 31, 1999 (though not before the United States invaded in 1989 to firm up a democracy).

Since the handover, the Panamanian government has facilitated private investment, such as Panama Railway rehabilitation and the construction of hotels and housing, while maintaining forests and historic structures. The autonomous Panama Canal Authority is currently preparing for construction of a third set of locks, which will allow larger ships to transit the canal and launch a new era for the country and international shipping.

WHAT TO DO

WATCH THAT WILDLIFE Hundreds of bird species, mischievous monkeys, smiling crocodiles, and delicate blue morpho butterflies await. The list of wildlife you might encounter in this region's wilderness is impressive, and nowhere is it easier to explore a tropical rain forest; don't miss the opportunity.

CRUISE THAT CANAL Taking a Panama Canal transit tour should be near the top of your to-do list. A five-hour partial transit takes you under the Bridge of the Americas, through several locks, and down Gaillard Cut for about $100, a fraction of what you'd pay for a Panama Canal cruise.

VISIT THE EMBERÁ If you don't travel to the Darién or Kuna Yala, try to visit an Emberá Indian village in Chagres National Park or on Bayano Lake for a fascinating glimpse of Panama's rich indigenous heritage.

EXPLORE THE MOUNTAINS The mountains to the east and west of the canal offer different natural experiences than the region's lowland jungles, and they can be explored on foot, on horseback, by bike, or in a river raft.

RESTAURANTS & CUISINE

Though Central Panama's restaurant selection is neither as impressive nor as varied as Panama City's, the region has some excellent dining options, which include charming spots and impressive scenery. Rather than unforgettable food, you're likely to enjoy good food in unforgettable settings, which include the ocean views on the Caribbean coast and Pacific Islands, and Chagres River views in Gamboa.

ABOUT THE HOTELS

The accommodations in Central Panama range from basic cement rooms to wonderful bungalows in stunning natural surroundings. The region includes some world-class nature lodges, where you can wake up to a full-service resort surrounded by rain forest, all-inclusive beach resorts where the bars stay open well past midnight, or homey B&Bs a short walk from the beach or forest. Even in the cheapest hotels you can expect a private bathroom and air-conditioning. ■TIP→ **You can save a bundle (sometimes upwards of $100) at some of the more expensive hotels and resorts by booking via their Web sites, especially for midweek or off-season stays.**

PAYING

The accepted currency is the U.S. dollar, which is often called the balboa, in reference to the long defunct national currency. Credit cards are widely accepted and ATM machines are all over, including the lobbies of large hotels and at gas stations and supermarkets.

WHAT IT COSTS					
	¢	$	$$	$$$	$$$$
RESTAURANTS	under $5	$5–$10	$10–$15	$15–$20	over $20
HOTELS	under $50	$50–$100	$100–$160	$160–$220	over $220

Restaurant prices are per person for a main course at dinner. Hotel prices are for two people in a standard double room, excluding service and 10% tax.

THE PANAMA CANAL & ENVIRONS

The Panama Canal stretches 80 km (50 mi) across one of the narrowest parts of the isthmus to connect the Pacific Ocean and the Caribbean Sea. For much of that route it's bordered by tropical wilderness. About half of the waterway is made up of Lago Gatún (Gatún Lake), an enormous artificial lake created by damming the Río Chagres (Chagres River). In addition to forming an integral part of the waterway, the lake is notable for its sportfishing and for the wildlife of its islands and the surrounding mainland.

As much an attraction as the canal itself are the forests that line it, which for decades were protected within the Canal Zone, a 10-mi-wide strip of land that was U.S. property until the Carter-Torrijos treaties took effect. The Panamanian government has turned most of the former Canal Zone forests into national parks, whereas most of the former U.S. infrastructure, including the Summit golf course and most buildings, has been privatized. Some of the former U.S. communities have become part of Panama City, while others, such as Gamboa, stand apart. The national parks have become increasingly important tourist attractions, and trails into the wilderness of Parque Nacional Soberanía and Monumento Natural Barro Colorado make the former Canal Zone one of the best places in the world to visit a tropical rain forest.

THE PANAMA CANAL

Panama's biggest attraction and most famous landmark, the Panama Canal stretches 80 km (50 mi) from the edge of Panama City to the Caribbean port of Colón, and a paved road follows its route between the islands of the Amador Causeway and the inland port of Gamboa. The most interesting spot for viewing the canal is the visitor center at the Miraflores Locks (⇨ Esclusas de Miraflores *in* Chapter 1). North of Miraflores the road to Gamboa heads inland but still passes a couple of spots with canal vistas, namely the Pedro Miguel Locks and the one-way bridge over the Chagres River. The bridge (and Gamboa in general) offers front-row views of the big ships as they pass though the canal; it's one of the waterway's narrowest spots. The Panama Canal Railway train to Colón continues north from Gamboa past other vantage points, which is much of that trip's draw. Two other spots with impressive views are the monument erected by the country's Chinese community on the Bridge of the Americas' western side, and the Esclusas de Gatún (Gatún Locks), 10 km (6 mi) south of Colón. But nothing matches the experience of getting out onto the water, which can be done on a canal transit tour (⇨ Canal Transits, *below*) or on a nature tour or fishing trip on Gatún Lake (⇨ Gamboa, *below*).

TO & FROM

Since the Panama Canal runs along the western edge of Panama City, there are various spots within the metropolitan area from which to admire it (⇨ Chapter 1). A taxi should charge $8–$10 to Miraflores Locks and $15–$20 to Gamboa. Buses to Gamboa depart from the

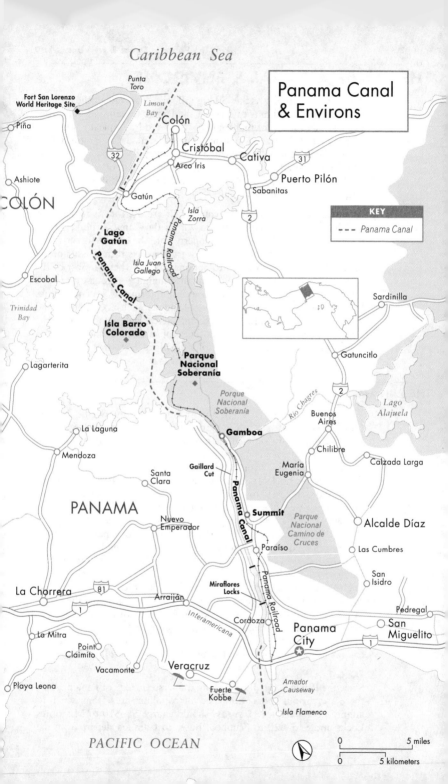

Panama Canal & Environs

KEY
- - - Panama Canal

Caribbean Sea

Punta Toro
Fort San Lorenzo World Heritage Site
Piña
Ashiote
COLÓN
Limon Bay
Colón
Cristóbal
Cativa
Puerto Pilón
Sabanitas
32
Gatún
Arco Iris
31
Isla Zorra
Lago Gatún
Isla Juan Gallego
Panama Railroad
2
Escobal
Panama Canal
Sardinilla
Trinidad Bay
Isla Barro Colorado
Gatuncitlo
Lagarterita
Parque Nacional Soberanía
Porque Nacional Soberanía
Río Chagres
2
Lago Alajuela
La Laguna
Buenos Aires
Mendoza
Gamboa
Chilibre
Calzada Larga
Santa Clara
Gaillard Cut
María Eugenia
PANAMA
Nuevo Emperador
Panama Canal
Summit
Parque Nacional Camino de Cruces
Alcalde Díaz
Paraíso
Las Cumbres
San Isidro
La Chorrera
81
Arraiján
Miraflores Locks
Panama Railroad
Pedregal
1
Interamericana
Cordoza
San Miguelito
La Mitra
Point Claimito
Vacamonte
Veracruz
Panama City
1
Amador Causeway
Playa Leona
Fuerte Kobbe
Isla Flamenco

PACIFIC OCEAN

0   5 miles
0   5 kilometers

SACSA station near Plaza Cinco de Mayo about every hour (⇨ Gamboa, *below*) and can drop you off at Miraflores Locks.

SUMMIT

20 km (12 mi) northwest of Panama City.

A short drive from the city, past Camino de Cruces National Park, this former American enclave consists of a golf course and a combination botanical garden and zoo. The course at **Summit Golf & Resort** (⇨ *below*) was created by the U.S. government in 1930 for canal workers and military personnel, but was redesigned by Jeffery Myers in 1999 and is now a private club that's open to tourists.

About a mile northwest of Summit Golf & Resort is **Parque Natural Summit** *(Jardín Botánico Summit, or Summit Botanical Garden)*, a large garden and zoo surrounded by the rain forest. Started in 1923 as a U.S. government project to reproduce tropical plants with economic potential, it evolved into a botanical garden and a zoo in the 1960s. The gardens and surrounding forest hold thousands of species, but the focus is on about 150 species of ornamental, fruit, and hardwood trees from around the world that were once raised here. These range from coffee and cinnamon to the more unusual candle tree and cannonball tree. The zoo is home to 40 native animal species, most of them in cages that are depressingly small, though a few have decent quarters. Stars include jaguars, ocelots, all six of the country's monkey species, several macaw species, and the harpy eagle, Panama's national bird. A neat thing about Summit is that most of the animals exhibited in the zoo are also found in the surrounding forest, so you may spot parrots, toucans, and agoutis (large rodents) not only in cages, but in the wild as well. ⊠ *22 km (13 mi) northwest of downtown on road to Gamboa* ☎ *232–4854* ⊕ *www.summitpanama.org* ☜ *$1* ⊙ *Daily 9–5.*

SPORTS & THE OUTDOORS

The **Summit Golf & Resort** (⊠ *20 km [12 mi] northwest of town on road to Gamboa* ☎ *232–4653* ⊕ *www.summitgolfpanama.com*) has an 18-hole, par-72 championship course designed by Jeff Myers that is hemmed by the rain forest of Camino de Cruces National Park. It is just 30 minutes from most hotels, and the course is open to nonmembers. Greens fees are $120 on weekdays and $150 on weekends, golf cart included. Club rentals are $15–$45, depending on quality.

TO & FROM AND LOGISTICS

Summit is an easy drive from Panama City. Follow the signs from Avenida Balboa or Avenida Central to Albrook, veer right at the traffic circle, and follow the Gailard road 20 km (12 mi) to the Summit Golf & Resort entrance on the right. Less than a mile after that, turn left onto the road to Gamboa (after passing under a railroad bridge), and look for the Parque Natural Summit on your right. A taxi from Panama City should charge $10–$15 to drop you there. SACSA buses leave from the station two blocks east of Plaza Cinco de Mayo every hour or so on weekdays and every two hours on weekends.

Building the Panama Canal

Nearly a century after its completion, the Panama Canal remains an impressive feat of engineering. It took the U.S. government more than a decade and $352 million to dig the "Big Ditch," but its inauguration was the culmination of a human drama that spanned centuries, and claimed, or changed, tens of thousands of lives. As early as 1524, King Carlos V of Spain envisioned an interoceanic canal, and he had Panama surveyed for routes where it might be dug, though it soon became clear that the task was too great to attempt. It wasn't until the 1880s that the French tried to make that dream a reality, but the job turned out to be tougher than they'd imagined. The Frenchman Fernando de Lesseps, who'd recently overseen construction of the Suez Canal, intended to build a sea-level canal similar to the Suez, which would have been almost impossible given the mountain range running through Panama. But a different obstacle thwarted the French enterprise: Panama's swampy, tropical environment. Nearly 20,000 workers died of tropical diseases during the French attempt, which together with mismanagement of funds drove the project bankrupt by 1889.

The United States, whose canal-building enterprise was spearheaded by President Theodore Roosevelt, purchased the French rights for $40 million, and went to work in 1904. Based on recent advances in medical knowledge, the Americans began their canal effort with a sanitation campaign led by Dr. William Gorgas that included draining of swamps and puddles, construction of potable water systems, and other efforts to combat disease. Another improvement over the French strategy was the decision to build locks and create a lake 85 feet above sea level. A corps of engineers led by John F. Stevens and George Goethals oversaw the biggest construction effort since the building of the Great Wall of China, as tens of thousands of laborers were brought in from the Caribbean islands, Asia, and Europe to supplement the local workforce. While the Americans were paid with gold, those laborers were paid with silver and lived in crowded wooden tenements. Some 6,000 workers lost their lives to disease and accidents during the American effort, which, when added to deaths during the French attempt, is more than 500 lives lost for each mile of canal.

The most difficult and dangerous stretch of the canal to complete was Gaillard Cut, named for Colonel David Gaillard, the engineer in charge of digging through the rocky continental divide. Thousands of workers spent seven years blasting and digging through that natural barrier, which consumed most of the 61 million pounds of dynamite detonated during canal construction. The countless tons of rock removed from Gailard Cut were used to build the Amador Causeway and to fill in swamps that line much of the coast of what is now Panama City.

Canal construction resulted in numerous records and engineering innovations. One of the biggest tasks was the damming of the Chagres River with the Gatún Dam, a massive earthen wall 1½ mi long and nearly a mile thick. It was the largest dam in the world when built, and the reservoir it created, Gatún Lake, was the largest man-made lake. The six sets of locks, which work like liquid elevators that raise and lower ships the 85 feet between Gatún Lake and the sea, were major engineering feats. Each lock chamber is 1,000 feet long and 110 feet wide—measurements that have governed shipbuilding ever since—and water flows in and out of them by gravity, so there are no pumps. At the time of their construction, the Gatún Locks, which hold six chambers, were the largest cement structure ever built. It took four years to complete that massive structure, using mammoth forms into which concrete was poured from six-ton buckets. Between the locks and sea walls, canal construction actually caused a global cement shortage.

When the SS *Ancon* became the first ship to transit the Panama Canal on August 15, 1914, it was the culmination of a colossal effort, but work continued after that, as Gaillard Cut was widened, the lake was constantly dredged, and the locks maintained. That digging along Gaillard Cut is now more intense than ever, as Panama works toward construction of a third set of locks. As the canal approaches its 100th birthday, it remains an innovative and vital link in the global economy, and a monument to the ingenuity and industriousness of the people who built it.

CANAL FACTS

■ More than 14,000 vessels under the flags of some 70 countries use the canal each year.

■ A boat traveling from New York to San Francisco saves 7,872 mi by using the Panama Canal instead of going around Cape Horn.

■ Most ships take 8–10 hours to traverse the canal, but the U.S. Navy hydrofoil *Pegasus* has the record for the fastest transit at 2 hours and 41 minutes.

■ Each of the canal's locks is 1,000 feet long and 110 feet wide, dimensions that have governed shipbuilding since the canal's completion in 1914. The massive Panamax ships that move most cargo through the canal are designed to carry as much as possible while still fitting into the locks.

■ For each large ship that passes through the canal, 52 million gallons of fresh water are used by six locks, and more than one billion gallons of water flow from the canal into the sea every day. (It's a good thing the canal was built in a rain forest.)

■ The highest toll for Panama Canal passage was $249,165.00, paid by the container ship *Maersk Dellys* on May 30, 2006, though that record may have been broken by the time you read this.

■ The lowest toll on record was the $0.36 paid by Richard Halliburton, who swam the canal in 1928. Halliburton's record is safe for posterity, since tolls have risen considerably since then.

CANAL TRANSITS

While the canal is impressive when admired from any of Panama City's various viewing points, there's nothing quite like getting onto the water and navigating it amidst the giant cargo ships. People spend thousands of dollars on cruises that include a canal crossing, but you can have the same experience for $100–$200 and be free to spend the night in a spacious hotel room. Two companies offer partial transit tours, which travel through the canal's Pacific locks and Gailard Cut, and full transits, which take you from one ocean to the other. All transits are accompanied by an expert guide who tells a bit of the canal's history, and include a continental breakfast, and, on full transits, a cold box lunch. Partial transits travel between the island marinas on the Amador Causeway and the port of Gamboa, on Gatún Lake, a trip that lasts four to five hours. They take place every Saturday May–December, and on Thursday, Friday, and Saturday January–April. Full transits take place once or twice a month and last eight or nine hours. Either trip is an unforgettable experience, suitable for travelers of all ages.

Canal Bay Tours (⊠ *Bahia Balboa Building, next to Nunciatura, Punta Paitilla* ☎ *209–2009* ⊕ *www.canalandbaytours.com*) offers partial and full transit tours on one of two ships: the 115-foot *Fantasia del Mar*, which has air-conditioned cabins and a large upper deck, and the 85-foot *Isla Morada*, which has one large covered deck. Partial transits are $99, full transits are $145. **Pacific Marine Tours** (⊠ *Villa Porras and Calle Belén, no. 106, San Francisco* ☎ *226–8417* ⊕ *www.pmatours.net*) runs canal transits on the 119-foot *Pacific Queen*, a comfortable ship with air-conditioned cabins and two large decks. Partial transits are $105, full transits are $165.

PARQUE NACIONAL SOBERANÍA (SOBERANÍA NATIONAL PARK)

Park entrance 25 km (15 mi) northwest of Panama City.

★ One of the planet's most accessible rain forest reserves, **Parque Nacional Soberanía** comprises 19,341 hectares (48,000 acres) of lowland rain forest along the canal's eastern edge that is home to everything from howler monkeys to chestnut-mandible toucans. Long preserved as part of the U.S. Canal Zone, Soberanía was declared a national park after being returned to Panama, as part of an effort to protect the canal's watershed. Trails into its wilderness can be reached by public bus, taxi, or by driving the mere 25 km (15 mi) from downtown Panama City. Those trails wind past the trunks and buttress roots of massive kapok and strangler fig trees, and the twisted stalks of lianas dangling from their high branches. Though visitors can expect to see only a small sampling of its wildlife, the park is home to more than 500 bird species and more than 100 different mammals, including such endangered species as the elusive jaguar and the ocelot.

If you hike some of the park's trails (⇨ Hiking, *below*), you run a good chance of seeing white-faced capuchin monkeys, tamandua anteaters, raccoonlike coatis, or large rodents called agouti. You may also see

2

iridescent blue morpho butterflies, green iguanas, leafcutter ants, and other interesting critters. On any given morning here you might see dozens of spectacular birds, such as red-lored parrots, collared aracaris, volacious trogons, and purple-throated fruit crows. From November to April the native bird population is augmented by the dozens of migrant species that winter in the park, among them the scarlet tanager, Kentucky warbler, and Louisiana water thrush. It is the combination of native and migrant bird species, plus the ocean birds along the nearby canal, that have enabled the Panama Audubon Society to set the Christmas bird count world record for two decades straight. ⊠ *Ranger station on Carretera Gamboa, 25 km (15 mi) northwest of Panama City* 🕾 *Free* ⊙ *Daily 8–5.*

WHERE TO STAY

$$$ 🖹 **Canopy Tower Ecolodge.** Occupying a former U.S. Army radar tower
★ topped by a giant yellow ball, the Canopy Tower is perched on Semaphore Hill in the heart of Soberanía National Park, where it affords an amazing view of the rain forest. The innovative lodge is dedicated to serious bird-watchers and nature lovers with views of the forest canopy from every room, and daily guided hikes. Rooms are small and basic, with cement floors, painted metal walls, ceiling fans, and tiny bathrooms, but they have big windows with views of the lower canopy—they are on the third floor—where there are often birds flitting about. Amenities such as air-conditioning have been forgone as part of the lodge's commitment to keeping its environmental impact as low as possible. Suites are roomier, with hammocks and decent-sized bathrooms, but people tend to spend most of their time in the forest or on the fourth floor, which holds a dining room and a lounge with a small natural-history library, and has walls of windows that let you look right into the forest canopy. The best view is from the rooftop deck, just above the forest canopy, where you can watch birds and climbing animals and see portions of the canal and of Panama City's skyline. Three meals and one nature tour per day are included in the price. **Pros: Constant exposure to nature, excellent guides, good food. Cons: Basic rooms, lots of stairs, expensive.** ⊠ *Carretera Gamboa, 25 km (15 mi) northwest of Panama City* 🖃 *Apdo. 0832-2701, W.T.C.* 🕾 *264–5720, 800/930–3397 in the U.S.* ⊕ *www.canopytower.com* 🛏 *10 rooms, 2 suites* 🖧 *In-room: no a/c, no phone. In-hotel: restaurant, no elevator, airport shuttle, no-smoking rooms* ⊟ *AE, MC, V* 🍽 *FAP.*

SPORTS & THE OUTDOORS

BIRD-   Soberanía has world-class bird-watching, especially from November to
WATCHING   April, when the northern migrants boost the local population. Unless
Fodor'sChoice   you're an expert, though, you're really better off joining a tour or hir-
★   ing a guide through one of Panama City's nature-tour operators. Guests at the **Canopy Tower Ecolodge** (⇨ *above*) enjoy almost nonstop birding and daily tours led by the lodge's resident guides. **Ancon Expeditions** (🕾 *269–9415* ⊕ *www.anconexpeditions.com*) has excellent guides that can take you bird-watching on Pipeline Road or on Gatún Lake. **Advantage Panama** (🕾 *6676–2466* ⊕ *www.advantagepanama.com*) has a day trip to Soberanía that combines a forest hike with a boat trip on Gatún

CLOSE UP

Interoceanic Jungle

An almost continuous belt of forest stretches between the Pacific Ocean and the Caribbean Sea in Central Panama, where separate swaths of wilderness extend to the northwest and north of Panama City. That invaluable tropical nature is sequestered within a half-dozen national parks and other protected areas that are home to more than half of the country's bird species, five kinds of monkeys, the world's largest rodent (the capybara), and such endangered animals as the jaguar, tapir, and harpy eagle. One reason for the diversity is that though the interoceanic wilderness is relatively continuous, it is by no means homogenous, since the altitudes in the region range from sea level to more than 3,000 feet, and it rains twice as much per year in some of the Caribbean forests as it does in the forests near Panama City, less than 50 mi away. The combination of varied weather and topography provides niches for an amazing diversity of flora and fauna for such a small area.

Aside from the canal area, the only other place in Panama, or Central America, where the forest cover

stretches from the Pacific to the Caribbean is in remote Darién Province, which is difficult and expensive to explore. But there are dozens of places and ways that you can explore the varied tropical wilderness of the canal area, ranging from an early morning bird-watching tour in the forests near Panama City to a one-week hiking expedition on the route of the historic Camino Real, offered by Ancon Expeditions (⇨ Hiking *in* Parque Nacional Chagres, *below*).

You can take a taxi or bus to Parque Nacional Soberanía and hike one of its trails; take one of several boat tours to the islands and forested shores of Gatún Lake; drive an hour to the mountain forests of Cerro Azul or Sierra Llorona; take a day trip to Barro Colorado, San Lorenzo, or Portobelo; raft down the Chagres River; or zip through forests of Soberanía on the Panama Canal Railway. But experiencing the flora and fauna can also be as effortless as looking out the window at nature lodges such as the Canopy Tower, Gamboa Rainforest Resort, and Sierra Llorona Lodge.

Lake. **Eco Circuitos Panama** (☎314–0068 ⊕*www.ecocircuitos.com*) has a Soberanía birding tour that starts with a hike and ends with a boat trip. **Pesantez Tours** (☎223–5374 ⊕*www.pesantez-tours.com*) runs a half-day tour to Soberanía.

HIKING   Soberanía's natural treasures can be discovered along miles and miles of trails and roads, whereas the western edge of the park can be explored on boat tours through local companies. The park also protects a significant portion of the old **Camino de Cruces,** a cobbled road built by the Spanish that connected old Panama City with a small port on the Chagres River, near modern-day Gamboa. It's more than 10 km (6 mi) long, and intersects with the Plantation Road before reaching the river, but you don't have to hike far to find cobbled patches that were restored a couple of decades ago.

The **Plantation Road** is a dirt road that heads east into the forest from the road to Gamboa for about 4 mi, to where it connects to the

Camino de Cruces. That wide trail follows a creek called the Río Chico Masambi, and is a great place to see waterbirds and forest birds. Two kilometers (1 mi) past the entrance to the Canopy Tower is the **Sendero el Charco** (Pool Footpath), which forms a loop through the forest to the east of the road to Gamboa. The *charco* (pool) refers to a man-made pond near the beginning of the trail that was created by damming a stream. The trail follows that stream part of the way, which means you may spot waterbirds such as tiger herons in addition to such forest birds as toucans and chachalacas. It is one of the park's most popular trails because it's a loop, it's short (less than a kilometer), and it's flat enough to be an easy hike.

The park's most famous trail is the **Camino del Oleoducto** (Pipeline Road), a paved road that follows an oil pipeline for 17 km (11 mi) into the forest parallel to the canal. One of the country's premier bird-watching spots, it is here that the Panama Audubon Society has had record-breaking Christmas bird counts year after year. The Pipeline Road is a great place to see trogons (five species have been logged there), motmots, forest falcons, and other bird species as well as monkeys, tamandua anteaters, and agoutis. You can hike on your own, but you'll see and learn more of you take a bird-watching tour.

TO & FROM AND LOGISTICS
Soberanía is an easy drive from Panama City and is reached by following the same route for Summit and Gamboa. Shortly after the Summit Golf Resort the road passes under the railroad and comes to an intersection where a left turn will put you on the road to Gamboa and most of the park's trails. If you want to hike the Camino Cruces trail you should head straight at that intersection, toward Chilibre, and drive 6 km (3½ mi) to a parking area with picnic tables on your left, behind which is the trail. Turn left for the Plantation Road, which is on the right 3 km (1½ mi) past the Parque Natural Summit, at the entrance to the Canopy Tower. The dirt Plantation Road heads left from that entrance road almost immediately. The Sendero Los Charcos is on the right 2 km after the Plantation Road. The Pipeline Road begins in Gamboa, at the end of the main road, past the dredging division and town. A taxi should charge $15–$20 to drop you off at any of these trails. All but the Camino de Cruces trail can be reached via SACSA buses to Gamboa, which depart every hour or 90 minutes and will stop wherever you ask.

GAMBOA

32 km (20 mi) northwest of Panama City.

Though it lies a mere 40 minutes from downtown Panama City, the tiny community of Gamboa feels remote, no doubt due to the fact that it is surrounded by exuberant tropical nature. Its location on the north bank of the flooded Chagres River, nestled between the Panama Canal and rain forest of Soberanía National Park, makes Gamboa a world-class bird-watching destination, and the departure point for boat trips on the Lago Gatún. It is also a great place to stroll, have lunch amid

CRAZY WEATHER

Because Panama lies just north of the equator, the temperature tends to swing between warm and torrid, with the exception of the western mountains where it can actually get cold at night. In any region, though, there's more temperature variation in a day than through the course of a year. The temperature in the lowlands tends to be slightly cool at daybreak, miserable at noon, and bearable again once the sun starts to set, whether it's December or July. The only seasons are rainy (May– December) and dry (January–April). But the rainy season is not constant, since it rains considerably less in July and August. There is also plenty of regional variation, with much more rain falling along the Caribbean side of the country than the Pacific, and the Bocas del Toro area hardly following the rainy and dry season scenario. In fact, though they are a mere 50 mi apart, Colón gets nearly twice as much rain as Panama City, though most of it falls at night.

nature, or kick back and admire the impressive tropical scenery. It is home to a massive nature resort that offers enough diversions to fill several days, but Gamboa's proximity to the capital also makes it a convenient day trip from Panama City.

The town of Gamboa was built by Uncle Sam in the early 20th century to house workers at the Panama Canal dredging division, which is based here. The town's tiny port is full of canal maintenance equipment, but it's also the point of departure for the daily boat to Barro Colorado Island and for Pacific-bound partial canal transits. Private yachts sometimes spend a night near the port on the way through the canal, and a simple marina on the other side of the Chagres River holds the boats of local fishermen and tour companies that take groups onto the canal for wildlife-watching along the forest's edge.

Over the years, biologists and bird-watchers have come to realize that Gamboa's combination of forests and wetlands make it home to an inordinate diversity of birds. The Panama Audubon Society has set world records for Christmas bird counts year after year on the **Camino del Oleoducto** (Pipleine Road), which heads into Parque Nacional Soberanía on the northwest end of town. That trail is the main destination for day visitors, but you can also see plenty of wildlife from the roads around town and the banks of the Chagres River.

The massive **Gamboa Rainforest Resort** (⇨ *below*), just east of town, is spread over a ridge with a panoramic view of the Chagres River. The resort has a 340-acre forest reserve which is contiguous with Soberanía National Park, within which is an aerial tram, a small orchid collection, a butterfly farm, an aquarium, and a serpentarium. The resort also has its own marina on the Chagres River; near it is the riverside restaurant Los Lagartos, which is a great spot for lunch and wildlife-watching even if you don't stay at the hotel. The resort's owner even convinced a small community of Emberá Indians who were living in nearby Chagres National Park to rebuild their village across the Chagres River from the hotel, where they now receive tourists. The Gamboa Rainforest Resort has its own tour company, **Gamboa Tours** (☎314–9000), which offers a day tour to nonguests that includes the aerial tram, a wildlife-watching tour on Lago Gatún and Monkey Island, and lunch, for $90.

WHERE TO STAY & EAT

$-$$ ✗**Los Lagartos.** Built out over the
★ Chagres River, this open-air restaurant at the Gamboa Rainforest Resort is a great place to see turtles, fish, crocodiles, and waterfowl feeding in the hyacinth-laden water. If you travel with binoculars, you'll definitely want to bring them here, so that you can watch wildlife while you wait for your lunch. A small buffet is frequently available, but the à la carte selection is usually a better deal, with choices such as peacock bass in a mustard sauce, grouper topped with an avocado sauce and cheese, or the hearty, spicy fisherman's stew. Lighter items include Caesar salad, hamburgers, and quesadillas. It isn't Panama's best food, but it's good, and the view of the forest-hemmed Chagres River populated with grebes, jacanas, and mangrove swallows is worth the trip out here even if you have only a cup of tea. ✉*Carretera Gamboa, right after bridge over Chagres River* ☎*314–9000* ✆*Apdo. 0816-02009, Panama City* ▤*AE, MC, V* ⊘*Closed Mon.*

$$-$$$$ ✗▣**Gamboa Rainforest Resort.** The panorama of the forested Chagres
♻ River valley through the lobby windows here is so captivating that it
★ takes you a while to notice the bright, airy lobby itself; life-size crane sculptures hang overhead and a stream cascades through a three-story tropical atrium, flowing into a swimming pool below. Spacious rooms have wicker furniture, hammocks, and tropical-flower bedspreads, but it's the balcony views that make them special. Junior suites, with two additional queen beds in a loft, work well for families. Garden views are disappointing—stick with rooms with numbers in the 100s. The historic "villas" cost considerably less, but they lack the view and suffer severe mildew problems. Activities include bird-watching, the aerial tram, a boat trip to Monkey Island, kayaking, and fishing. Both restaurants serve good food with a great view—El Corotu offers buffets and à la carte; the more upscale Chagres River View serves three-course prix-fixe dinners for $35. **Pros: Amazing views, wildlife, ample facilities and diversions. Cons: Massive, expensive, guides are mediocre.** ✉*Carretera Gamboa, 32 km (19 mi) northwest of Panama City* ☎*314–9000, 877/800–1690 in the U.S.* ᵫ*314–9020* ⊕*www.gamboaresort.com* ✆*Apdo. 0816-02009, Panama City* ⇱*160 rooms, 4 suites, 48 villas* △*In-room: safe, Ethernet. In-hotel: 2 restaurants, room service, bars, tennis courts, pool, gym, spa, water sports, laundry service, concierge, public Wi-Fi, no-smoking rooms* ▤*AE, MC, V* ⦿*BP.*

WORD OF MOUTH

The [Gamboa Rainforest Resort] is a lovely setting and you'll get to experience a bit of the rain forest as well. There are some wonderful trails right near the tram ride that follow along the river, and monkeys will be crashing through the trees all around you . . . great fun.

–ojoy

NIGHTLIFE & THE ARTS

The **Discoteca Capybara** (☎314–9000), in the basement of the Gamboa Rainforest Resort, opens on Friday and Saturday night. Those who prefer a quiet drink head for the **Monkey Bar,** behind the reception area in the lobby.

SPORTS & THE OUTDOORS

BIRD-WATCHING All the big nature tour operators offer bird-watching tours on Pipeline Road (⇨ Parque Nacional Soberanía, *above*).

Guests at the Gamboa Rainforest Resort can book a morning of bird-watching on nearby Pipeline Road with **Gamboa Tours** (☎314–9000 Ext. 8158 ⊕ *www.gamboatours.com*), which will have them in the national park by 7 AM.

HIKING **Gamboa Tours** (☎314–9000 Ext. 8158 ⊕ *www.gamboatours.com*) has a three-hour hiking tour on the historic Camino de Cruces, which ends on the other side of the Chagres River from the Gamboa Rainforest Resort—it's an excellent trip for seeing wildlife.

SPORTFISHING Gatún Lake is full of peacock bass, and also has snook and tarpon, adding up to excellent sportfishing. Charters depart from Gamboa's two marinas, and anglers may hook as many as 20 or 30 peacock bass before returning in the afternoon. **Panama Canal Fishing** (☎315–1905 or 6699–0507 ⊕ *www.panamacanalfishing.com*) is the best operator for fishing on Gatún Lake. An all-inclusive day of fishing on the Hurricane Fundeck with swivel chairs on the bow costs $260. **Gamboa Tours** (☎314–9000 Ext. 8158 ⊕ *www.gamboatours.com*) offers full-day bass-fishing charters for up to three people for $263.

TO & FROM AND LOGISTICS

Gamboa is an easy 40-minute drive from Panama City. Follow the signs from Avenida Balboa or Avenida Central to Albrook, veer right at the traffic circle and follow that road north, into the forest. Shortly after driving under a railroad bridge, turn left and stay on that road all the way to the one-way bridge over the Chagres River. Turn right just after the bridge for the Rainforest Resort and Los Lagartos restaurant, or continue straight ahead for the Pipeline Road. A taxi from Panama City should charge $15–$20 to drop you off here. SACSA buses depart from the station two blocks east of Plaza Cinco de Mayo in Panama City approximately every hour from 5 AM to 6:30 PM weekdays and approximately every two hours on weekends.

LAGO GATÚN (GATÚN LAKE)

Covering about 163 square mi, an area about the size of the island nation Barbados, Gatún Lake extends northwest from Parque Nacional Soberanía to the locks of Gatún, just south of Colón. The lake was created when the U.S. government dammed the Chagres River, between 1907 and 1910, so that boats could cross the isthmus at 85 feet above sea level. By creating the lake, the United States saved decades of digging that a sea-level canal would have required. It took several years for the rain to fill the convoluted valleys, turning hilltops into islands

THE HARPY EAGLE

The harpy eagle, Panama's national bird, is an impressive creature, with a beak the size of a jackknife, talons as long as a grizzly bear's claws, and a plumed crest evoking the war bonnet of an Indian chief. It is one of the world's largest and most powerful raptors, with a wingspan of almost 6½ feet, and can tear a full-grown monkey out of a treetop with one swoop. Since pre-Columbian times the bird has maintained a mythical stature among the region's indigenous peoples, and you can see gold eagle figures displayed at the anthropological museum in Panama City. But because it is perched at the top of a food chain in an endangered ecosystem, the harpy is threatened in most of its range.

The harpy (*Harpia harpyja*) was once common from southeast Mexico to northern Argentina, but hunting and deforestation have practically wiped the species out north of Panama, and are steadily reducing its numbers in South America. Panama still has a significant number of harpies—hundreds, perhaps—thanks to the work of conservation groups and governmental protection of vast expanses of rain forest. Harpies require large areas of forest to survive because their prey is relatively scarce; accordingly, deforestation hits them hard. They also have a low reproductive rate, mating only once every two years, when they build a life-raft-size nest atop a large *kapok* or *quipo* tree—the tallest trees in the rain forest—and spend the next year raising one chick. The U.S. conservation group Peregrine Fund (www. peregrinefund.org) is working to save the harpy eagle in Panama by breeding captive birds on loan from zoos—they remove eggs so that the females lay more—then releasing young birds into the wild. The organization also runs an educational program for people in rural communities where the raptors live.

Panama is one of the countries where you are most likely to see the elusive harpy eagle. They are most common in the eastern Darién Province, but have been spotted in Soberanía, Chagres, and other central parks. If you are lucky enough to encounter a perched harpy, you may be able to get pretty close, because the birds generally don't fear people and are curious, which unfortunately works to the advantage of poachers. One place you are guaranteed to spot a harpy eagle is Parque Natural Summit, the botanical garden and zoo north of Panama City, which has captive birds and an excellent display about them.

and killing much forest (some trunks still tower over the water nearly a century later). When it was completed, Gatún Lake was the largest man-made lake in the world. The canal route winds through its northern half, past several forest-covered islands (the largest is Barro Colorado, one of the world's first biological reserves). To the north of Barro Colorado are the Islas Brujas and Islas Tigres, which together hold a primate refuge—visitors aren't allowed. The lake itself is home to crocodiles, manatees, and peacock bass, a species introduced from South America and popular with fishermen. Fishing charters for bass, snook, and tarpon are out of Gamboa (⇨ *above*).

TO & FROM AND LOGISTICS

Aside from seeing the entire canal on a complete transit tour, you can see a bit of the lake during the boat trip to Barro Colorado, or on one of the nature tours or sportfishing charters that leave from the marinas at Gamboa and the Meliá Resort, near Colón. You can also see parts of it from the Panama Railway.

ISLA BARRO COLORADO

55 km (34 mi) northwest of Panama City, in the Panama Canal.

The island of Barro Colorado in Lago Gatún is a former hilltop that became an island when the Río Chagres was dammed during construction of the Panama Canal. It covers 1,500 hectares (3,700 acres) of virgin rain forest and forms part of the Barro Colorado Nature Monument, which includes five peninsulas on the mainland, and protects an area several times that size. The reserve is home for more than 400 species of birds, 225 ant species, and 122 mammal species, including collared peccaries, ocelots, coatis, and five kinds of monkeys. Its forest has 1,200 plant species—more than are found in all of Europe—ranging from delicate orchids to massive strangler fig trees.

In 1923 the island was declared a biological reserve and a tropical research station was built there; it is now the oldest such facility in the world. The island is administered by the Smithsonian Tropical Research Institute (STRI), which facilitates research by 200 or so visiting scientists and students per year, and runs several weekly educational tours. Those tours are not only one of the most informative introductions to tropical ecology you can get in Panama, they are excellent opportunities to see wildlife; after decades of living in a protected area full of scientists the animals are hardly afraid of people.

Barro Colorado can be visited on full-day tours run by the **Smithsonian Tropical Research Institute (STRI)** (⊠ *Av. Roosevelt, Cerro Ancón, Panama City* ☎ *212-8951* ⊕ *www.stri.org*) every Tuesday, Wednesday, Friday, Saturday, and Sunday. The $70 tour is well worth the money, since the English-speaking guides do an excellent job of pointing out flora and fauna and explaining the rain forest's complex ecology. Lunch in the research station's cafeteria and boat transportation to and from Gamboa are included. Tours tend to fill up months ahead, so fill out the form on the STRI Web site and reserve your trip as early as possible. Reservations that haven't been paid for a week before the tour will be canceled; to join one at the last minute, it's worth calling Tamara Castillo at the STRI office and asking whether there is space on a tour (there often is). In this case, you have to pay at least one day in advance. Bring your passport, tour receipt, bottled water, binoculars, and a poncho or raincoat (May–December). Wear long pants, hiking shoes, and socks to protect against chiggers. Be in decent shape, since the tour includes several hours of hiking on trails that are steep in places and can be slippery; children under 10 are not allowed. You can reserve and pay for tours at the STRI's Tupper Center in Panama City weekdays from 8 to 2.

THE PANAMA RAILWAY

The one-hour trip on the **Panama Railway** (✉ *Av. Omar Torrijos, Corozal, Panama City* ☎ *317–6070* ⊕ *www.panarail.com*) from Corozal, just north of Albrook, to the Caribbean city of Colón, offers an interesting perspective on the rain forests of Soberanía National Park and the wetlands along Gatún Lake. The railway primarily moves freight, but it has a commuter service on weekdays that departs from Panama City at 7:15 AM (returning from Colón at 5:15 PM), and costs $22 each way. Tourists ride in an air-conditioned car with curved windows on the roof that let you see the foliage overhead. The best views are from the left side of the train, and though the train moves too fast to see much wildlife, you may spot toucans, herons, and black snail kites flying over the lake. The downside: the trip passes a garbage dump and industrial zone near the end, and leaves you just outside the slums of Colón at 8:15 AM, which is why you may want to take the trip as part of a tour that picks you up in Colón and takes you to either San Lorenzo or Portobelo. It is possible to do the trip on your own, in which case you should board one of the shuttle vans that await the train in Colón and have them take you to the Colón 2000 (pronounced coh-*loan* dose-*mill*) cruise-ship port, where you can pick up a rental car and drive to Portobelo, or hire a taxi for the day ($80–$100). The trains leave promptly, and it is complicated to prepurchase tickets, so get to the station by 7 AM to buy your tickets.

The original Panama Railway was built in the 1850s in response to the 1849 California gold rush, since it was a safer and quicker way for people to travel between the East and West coasts of the United States than risking the trip through Indian country. That railroad took five years to build and cost $6.5 million, but it transported millions of passengers and more than $700 million worth of gold from California during the next decade. When the U.S. government began work on the Panama Canal it moved the railway to its current route, when parts of the original route were flooded. The railway was given to the government of Panama in the 1980s, and in 1998 a consortium of American companies signed a 50-year concession to operate it, completely refurbishing it and connecting it to new container ports on either side of the canal. Transporting containers between ships in the two oceans is now the railway's main activity.

TO & FROM AND LOGISTICS

Barro Colorado can only be visited on tours run by the Smithsonian Tropical Research Institute (⇨ *above*). Tours leave from the STRI pier in Gamboa at 7 AM on weekdays and 7:45 on weekends. The pier is down a gravel road on the left after the dredging division, and is best reached from Panama City by taxi ($15–$20).

THE CENTRAL CARIBBEAN COAST

Coral reefs, rain forests, colonial ruins, and a predominant Afro-Caribbean culture make Panama's Caribbean coast a fascinating place to visit. People from Panama City head to the Costa Arriba, the coast northeast of Colón, to enjoy its beaches and feast on fresh lobster, conch, or king crab. Scuba divers flock to Portobelo, a colonial town guarded by ancient fortresses and surrounded by rain forest, but the diving is even better to the northeast of there. The bird-watching is excellent around the colonial fortress of San Lorenzo and on Sierra Llorona, but is also quite good at Portobelo.

COLÓN

79 km (49 mi) northwest of Panama City.

The provincial capital of Colón, beside the canal's Atlantic entrance, has clearly seen better days, as the architecture of its older buildings attests. Its predominantly Afro-Caribbean population has long had a vibrant musical scene, and in the late 19th and early 20th centuries Colón was a relatively prosperous town. But it spent the second half of the 20th century in steady decay, and things have only gotten worse in the 21st century. For the most part, the city is a giant slum, with unemployment at 15% to 20% and crime on the rise.

⚠ Travelers who explore Colón on foot are simply asking to be mugged, and the route between the train station and the bus terminal is especially notorious; do all your traveling in a taxi or rental car. If you do the Panama Railway trip on your own without a tour company, take one of the shuttle vans to the Colón 2000 (pronounced coh-*loan* dose-*mill*) cruise-ship terminal, where you can rent a car or hire a taxi to see the sights near town. The Espinar neighborhood 10 km (6 mi) to the south, in the former U.S. Canal Zone, is a tranquil area that holds the Meliá Hotel and can serve as a base to visit Gatún Locks, San Lorenzo, and Portobelo.

Many South American merchants go to Colón to shop at the **Zona Libre,** which handles about $6 million worth of wholesale and retail sales per year. Northern visitors likely won't be wowed by the prices, and won't recognize the brand names here. It is also downright ugly. Two blocks from the Zona Libre is the city's cruise-ship port, **Colón 2000,** which is basically a two-story strip mall next to the dock where ships tie up and passengers load onto buses for day trips. It has a supermarket, restaurants, two rental-car offices, and English-speaking taxi drivers who can take you on sightseeing excursions ($70–$100 for a full day).

Twelve kilometers (7 mi) south of Colón are the **Esclusas de Gatún** *(Gatún Locks),* a triple lock complex that's nearly a mile long and raises and lowers ships the 85 feet between sea level and Gatún Lake. There's a small viewing platform at the locks and a simple visitor center that's nothing compared to the center at Miraflores Locks. However, the sheer magnitude of the Gatún Locks is impressive, especially when packed with ships. You have to cross the locks on a swinging bridge to

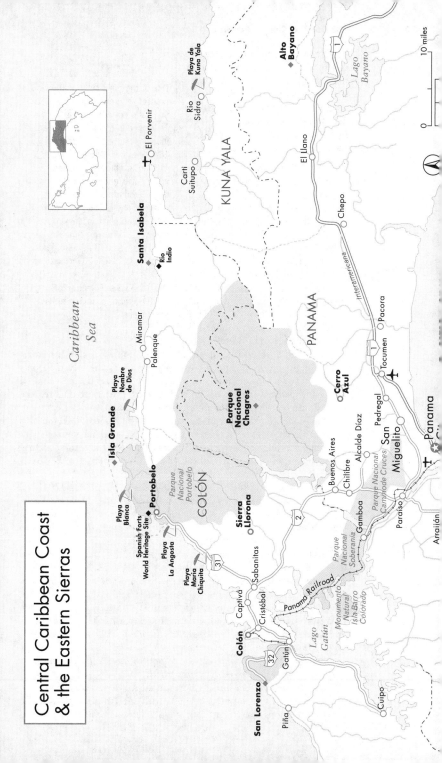

Central Caribbean Coast & the Eastern Sierras

Caribbean Sea

Playa de Kuna Yala

Alto Bayano

Lago Bayano

10 miles

El Porvenir

Rio Sidra

Carti Suitupo

KUNA YALA

El Llano

Santa Isabela

Rio Indio

Chepo

Miramar

Palenque

PANAMA

Interamericana

Pacora

Playa Nombre de Dios

Parque Nacional Chagres

Cerro Azul

Tocumen

Isla Grande

Parque Nacional Portobelo

Buenos Aires

Alcalde Diaz

Pedregal

San Miguelito

Playa Blanca

Portobelo

COLÓN

Chilibre

Spanish Forts World Heritage Site

Playa La Angosta

Sierra Llorona

Gamboa

Parque Nacional Camino de Cruces

Paraíso

Playa Maria Chiquita

31

2

Parque Nacional Soberanía

Panama City

Sabanitas

Captivá

Panama Railroad

Monumento Natural Isla Barro Colorado

Arraiján

Cristóbal

Colón

Lago Gatún

32

Gatún

Piña

San Lorenzo

Cuipo

get to San Lorenzo and the **Represa Gatún** *(Gatún Dam),* which holds the water in Gatún Lake. At 1½ mi long, it was the largest dam in the world when it was built, a title it held for several decades. Get there by taking the first left after crossing the locks.

WHERE TO STAY

$$$ **Meliá Panama Canal.** Perched on a lush peninsula 10 km (6 mi) south of Colón, overlooking Lago Gatún, the Meliá occupies buildings that were once the School of the Americas, a controversial U.S. training academy for Latin American military officers. It now promotes nothing more insidious than sportfishing, bird-watching, or lounging by the pool, which is surrounded by a lawn hemmed by tropical foliage. The hotel's interior is grand, with an Old Spain motif, handsome wooden furniture, stained-glass windows, and a four-story atrium in the lobby. Rooms have picture windows, large bathrooms with tubs, and are decorated with hand-painted tiles. A casino and business center are on-site. The steak house has views of the illuminated jungle and often offers poolside barbecues. If you get a discount rate on the resort's Web site, this can be a decent base for a night or two, but the hotel has management problems, so don't expect four-star service. Pros: Quiet, safe, natural environment, outdoor diversions. Cons: Erratic service, grounds overrun with cruise-ship passengers. ⊠*End of Calle Principal, Res. Espinar* ☎*470–1100, 888/956–3542 in the U.S. and Canada* 🖷*470–1200* ⊕*www.solmelia.com* 🖀*310 rooms* ⌂*In-room: safe, Wi-Fi. In-hotel: 2 restaurants, bars, tennis courts, pool, gym, water sports, no elevator, laundry service, concierge, public Internet, airport shuttle, parking (no fee), no-smoking rooms* ▭*MC, V* ⦿*BP.*

¢ **Harbor Inn.** In the Canal Zone neighborhood of Espinar, Harbor Inn offers safety, tranquillity, and access to good bird-watching at a low price. Its rooms are pretty basic, with tile floors and small desks. The restaurant serves fish, burgers, and other light fare; you can eat at the nearby Meliá hotel, too, which also offers various tours of Gatún Lake. Pros: Inexpensive, quiet, natural area. Cons: Mediocre rooms and restaurant. ⊠*Calle Principal, Res. Espinar* ☎*470–0639* 🖷*470–0641* ⊕*www.harborinnpanama.com* 🖀*24 rooms* ⌂*In-room: Wi-Fi. In-hotel: restaurant, bar, no elevator, laundry service, public Internet, parking (no fee), no-smoking rooms* ▭*AE, MC, V* ⦿*CP.*

¢ **Hotel Washington.** The historic hotel on the northwest corner of town is a reminder of Colón's glorious past, with enough peeling paint and tacky renovations to confirm that the glory days are long gone. Opened

---

CONGO DANCING

One of the main cultural attractions of the Central Caribbean Coast are **congos,** dances developed in escaped-slave communities of the 15th through 18th centuries. One is a parody of Spanish officials marching while devils and witch doctors dance around them; the music is thoroughly African. Common on the patron saints' days of many coastal towns, congo is most prominent in Portobelo on January 31, March 20, or during a festival shortly after Carnaval. The Panama Tourist Bureau (IPAT) Web site (www.visitpanama.com) has exact dates.

in 1913, the Washington was once one of the country's best hotels; it's now one of its best deals, with bright, renovated rooms at budget rates. Be sure to get one with a view of the ocean and ships awaiting a canal passage. The façade's ornate and the lobby elegant, but the ample grounds are shabby (though they do have a swimming pool and tennis courts), food and service are mediocre, and it's dangerous outside the grounds. **Pros: Historic, ocean views, inexpensive. Cons: Indifferent service, mediocre food, dangerous neighborhood.** ⊠ *Calle 1 and Paseo Washington* ☎*441–7133* 🖷*441–7397* ⊕*www.newwashingtonhotel. com* ⌫*124 rooms* ⌂*In-hotel: restaurants, bar, room service, tennis courts, pool, laundry service, public Internet, parking (no fee), no-smoking rooms* ☰*AE, DC, MC, V* ⊙|*EP.*

SPORTS & THE OUTDOORS

SPORTFISHING The **Meliá Panama Canal hotel** (⊠ *Calle Principal, Res. Espinar* ☎*470–1100*) runs inexpensive fishing tours ($35) on Gatún Lake that are open to nonguests. The fishing gear is basic, but they can pretty much guarantee you'll catch some peacock bass. They also offer bird-watching and night tours on the lake for a minimum of four people.

TO & FROM

The easiest way to get to Colón is to take the Panama Canal Railway commuter train that departs from Panama City at 7:15 AM and returns at 5:15 PM. If you start your railway journey in Colón, you will need to purchase tickets from the conductor. Buses depart from Panama City's Albrook Terminal de Buses every 20 minutes, and the trip takes 90 minutes to two hours. Get directly into a taxi upon arrival at either the train or bus station; both are in unsafe neighborhoods. It usually takes 90 minutes to drive to Colón from Panama City. Take the Corredor Norte to the Transístmica, a slow-moving two-lane road. If you are headed for the Meliá hotel, Gatún Locks, or San Lorenzo, bypass Colón and turn left at the Super 99, or the Centro Comercial Cuatro Altos, about 8 km (5 mi) before Colón, and follow the signs to Residencial Espinar for the hotel, and Esclusas de Gatún for the locks.

Contacts Budget ⊠ *Colón 2000* 🖷*441–7161.* **Hertz** ⊠ *Colón 2000* 🖷*441–3272.* **Panama Canal Railway** 🖷*317–6070.* **Terminal de Bus de Colón** ⊠*Av. Balboa and Calle Terminal* 🖷*441–4044.*

SAN LORENZO PROTECTED AREA

40 km (25 mi) west of Colón.

For information about San Lorenzo's park, fort, tours and accommodations, visit www.achiotecoturismo.com and www.sanlorenzo.org.pa.

Perched on a cliff overlooking the mouth of the Chagres River are the ruins of the ancient Spanish **Fuerte San Lorenzo** *(San Lorenzo Fort)*, destroyed by pirate Henry Morgan in 1671. The Spaniards built Fort San Lorenzo in 1595 in an effort to protect the South American gold they were shipping down the Chagres River, which was first carried along the Camino de Cruces from Panamá Viejo. The gold was then shipped up the coast to the fortified city of Portobelo, where it was stored until the Spanish armada arrived to carry it to Spain. The fortress's commanding position and abundant cannons weren't enough of a deterrent for Morgan, whose men managed to shoot flaming arrows into the fort, causing a fire that set off stored gunpowder and forced the Spanish troops to surrender. Morgan then led his men up the river and across the isthmus to sack Panamá Viejo.

In the 1980s UNESCO restored the fort to its current condition, which is pretty sparse—it hardly compares to the extensive colonial ruins of Portobelo. Nevertheless, the setting is gorgeous, and the view from that promontory of the blue-green Caribbean, the coast, and the vast jungle behind it is breathtaking. Be careful walking around the edge outside the fort; there are some treacherous precipices. *⊠23 km (14 mi) northwest of Gatún Locks ☎No phone ✉Free ⊙Daily 8–4.*

The wilderness just behind the fortress is part of **Parque Nacional San Lorenzo,** a 23,843-acre (9,653-hectare) protected area that includes rain forest, wetlands, rivers, and coastline. For decades this was the U.S. Army's jungle training area, where tens of thousands of troops trained for warfare in the tropics. The army used parts of the park as a bombing range, and there may still be unexploded ordnance in its interior, though far from the roads and fortress. Today the park is the haunt of bird-watchers, who hope to focus their binoculars on some of the more than 400 bird species. Mammalian residents include spider monkeys, armadillos, tamarins, and coatis. The lush forest here gets nearly twice as much rain as Panama City, and it doesn't lose as much of its foliage during the dry season. Most of that rain falls at night, so mornings are often sunny, even during the rainy season.

The most famous bird-watching area in Parque Nacional San Lorenzo is the **Achiote Road** *(Camino a Achiote)* , which is about 25 km (15 mi) south of the fort. To reach it, turn left after crossing the locks and drive 15 km (9 mi) south. Members of the Panama Audubon Society once counted 340 bird species in one day on the Achiote Road during their Christmas bird count. Anchiote is an excellent place to observe the massive hawk and vulture migration in October and March. The community of Achiote, about 4 km (2½ mi) northwest of the park on the Achiote road, has trained birding guides and a visitor center with rustic accommodations. *⊠15 km (9 mi) west of Gatún Locks ☎6664–2339 ⊕www.sanlorenzo.org.pa ✉Free ⊙Daily 8–4.*

SPORTS & THE OUTDOORS

BIRD-
WATCHING
The tour operator at the **Meliá Panama Canal hotel** (*⊠Calle Principal, Residencial Espinar, Colón* ☎470–1100) runs half-day trips to San Lorenzo. Panama City–based operator **Ancon Expeditions** (☎269–9415 ⊕www.anconexpeditions.com) can send you to Colón on the train, pick you up at the station, and drive you straight to San Lorenzo for bird-watching and exploring the fortress. **Advantage Panama** (☎6676–2466 ⊕www.advantagepanama.com), in Panama City, runs a full-day tour to San Lorenzo with the option of returning by train.

TO & FROM AND LOGISTICS

It usually takes two hours to drive to San Lorenzo from Panama City, and 40 minutes from Colón, if it doesn't take too long to cross the Gatún Locks. Follow directions for Colón, but turn left at the Centro Comercial Cuatro Altos, 8 km (5 mi) before Colón, and follow the signs to Esclusas de Gatún. After crossing the locks, veer right and drive 12 km (7 mi) to Fort Sherman. Turn left onto a dirt road after the entrance to Fort Sherman and drive another 11 km (6 mi) to the fort. The Achiote Road is reached by turning left after crossing the locks and driving 12 km (7 mi)—over the Gatún Dam—to the second road on the right. The town of Achiote is 10 km (6 mi) up that dirt road.

PORTOBELO

99 km (62 mi) north of Panama City; 48 km (30 mi) northeast of Colón.

★ Portobelo is an odd mix of colonial fortresses, clear waters, lushly forested hills, and an ugly little town of cement-block houses crowded higgledy-piggledy amid the ancient walls. It holds some of Panama's most interesting colonial ruins, with rusty cannons still lying in wait for an enemy assault, and is a UNESCO World Heritage Site, together with San Lorenzo. Depending on your timing, you can also see congo dancing or the annual Festival del Cristo Negro (Black Christ Festival, ⇨*below*). Between the turquoise sea, jungle, coral reefs (great for scuba diving or snorkeling), and beaches, you may feel like a castaway.

Once the sister city of Panamá Viejo, Portobelo was an affluent trading center during the 17th century, when countless tons of Spanish treasure passed through its customs house, and shiploads of European goods were unloaded on their way to South America. Portobelo received its name, "beautiful port" in Italian, from Christopher Columbus who anchored in the bay in 1502 on his fourth and final voyage to the Americas. The Spaniards moved their Atlantic port in Panama from Nombre de Dios to Portobelo in 1597, since the deep bay was deemed an easier place to defend against pirates, who had raided Nombre de Dios repeatedly. During the next two centuries Portobelo was one of the most important ports in the Caribbean. Gold from South America was stored here after crossing the isthmus via the Camino de Cruces and Chagres River, awaiting semi-annual *ferias,* or trade fairs, in which a fleet of galleons and merchant ships loaded with European goods arrived for several weeks of business and revelry before sailing home laden with gold and silver. That wealth attracted pirates, who repeatedly attacked Portobelo, despite the Spanish fortresses flanking the entrance to the bay and a larger fortress near the customs house. After a century and a half of attacks, Spain began shipping its South American gold around Cape Horn in 1740, marking the end of Portobelo's ferias, and turning the town into an insignificant Caribbean port. What remains today is a mix of historic and tacky, twentieth-century structures surrounded by spectacular natural scenery that looks much the same as it did in Columbus's day.

You can explore Portobelo's historic sites in a couple of hours, which leaves plenty of time for outdoor diversions. Several beaches in the area are worth visiting, half a dozen diving and snorkeling spots are nearby, and the bird-watching is good, too.

The forested hills that rise up behind the bay are part of **Parque Nacional Portobelo** *(Portobelo National Park)*, a vast marine and rain-forest reserve contiguous with Chagres National Park. Though several towns lie within the park, and much of its lowlands were deforested years ago, its inaccessible mountains are covered with dense forest that holds plenty of flora and fauna. Extending from offshore coral reefs up to the cloud forest atop 3,212-foot Cerro Brujo, the park comprises an array of ecosystems and is rich in biodiversity. While the coastal area is home to everything from ospreys to sea turtles, the mountains house spider monkeys, brocket deer, harpy eagles, and an array of other endangered wildlife. There is no proper park entrance, but you can explore patches of its forested coast and mangrove estuaries on boat trips from Portobelo, when you might see birds such as the ringed kingfisher and fasciated tiger heron. ⊠*Surrounding Portobelo* ☎*448–2165 or 442–8348* 🖃*Free* ⊗*24 hrs.*

Fuerte San Fernando, one of three **Spanish forts** you can visit at Portobelo, is surrounded by forest and is a good place to see birds. It lies directly across the bay from **Batería Santiago,** on the left as you drive toward town, a large structure with cannons pointed at the entrance to the bay. The youngest of Portobelo's forts, Batería Santiago was built in the 1860s, after Vernon's fateful attack (⇨ "Pirates of the Caribbean" box, *below*). The thick walls are coral, which was cut from the platform reefs that line the coast. Coral was more abundant and easier to cut than the igneous rock found inland, so the Spanish used it for most construction in Portobelo. ■TIP➡**Local boatmen who are usually sitting near the dock next to Batería Santiago can take you across the bay to explore Fuerte San Fernando for $3.** They also offer transportation to several local beaches, as well as a trip into the estuary at the end of the bay.

Portobelo's largest and most impressive fort is **Fuerte San Jerónimo,** at the end of the bay, which is surrounded by the "modern" town. It was built in the 1600s, but was destroyed by Vernon and rebuilt to its current state in 1758. Its large interior courtyard was once a parade ground, but it is now the venue for all annual celebrations involving congo dancers, including New Year's, Carnaval, the Festival de Diablos y Congos (shortly after Carnaval), and the town's patron saint's day (March 20).

Near the entrance to Fuerte San Jerónimo is the **Real Aduana** *(Royal Customs House)* , where servants of the Spanish crown made sure that the king and queen got their cut from every ingot that rolled through town. Built in 1630, the Real Aduana was damaged during pirate attacks and then destroyed by an earthquake in 1882, only to be rebuilt in 1998. It is an interesting example of colonial architecture—note the carved coral columns on the ground floor—and it holds a simple museum

2

with some old coins, cannonballs, and displays on Panamanian folklore. ✉ *Calle de la Aduana* ☎ *No phone* 💲 *$1* ⊙ *Weekdays 8–4, weekends 8:30–3.*

One block east of the Real Aduana is the **Iglesia de San Felipe,** a large white church dating from 1814 that's home to the country's most venerated religious figure: the **Cristo Negro** *(Black Christ)*. According to legend, that statue of a dark-skinned Jesus carrying a cross arrived in Portobelo in the 17th century on a Spanish ship bound for Cartagena, Colombia. Each time the ship tried to leave, it encountered storms and had to return to port, convincing the captain to leave the statue in Portobelo. Another legend has it that in the midst of a cholera epidemic in 1821 parishioners prayed to the

FESTIVAL DEL CRISTO NEGRO

Every October 21, tens of thousands of pilgrims walk or drive to Portobelo to venerate the Iglesia de San Felipe's Black Christ statue. Celebrations begin with an evening mass, followed by a very long procession led by people carrying the statue. Many devotees wear purple robes like the Cristo Negro's; some of them even crawl the last stretch to the church. While it attracts the devout, it's also a party, with drinking and less-than-pious behavior. The road to Portobelo becomes a giant traffic jam (take a boat from a dive center down the road), and ultimately the town is trashed.

Cristo Negro, and the community was spared. The statue spends most of the year to the left of the church's altar, but once a year it's paraded through town in the Festival del Cristo Negro (⇨ *below*). Each year the Cristo Negro is clothed in a new purple robe, donated by somebody who's earned the honor. Many of the robes that have been created for the statue over the past century are on display in the Museo del Cristo Negro *(Black Christ Museum)* in the Iglesia de San Juan, a smaller, 17th-century church next to the Iglesia de San Felipe. ✉ *Calle Principal* ☎ *No phone* 💲 *$1* ⊙ *Weekdays 8–4, weekends 8:30–3.*

WHERE TO STAY & EAT

$–$$$$ ✕ **Restaurante Los Cañones.** This rambling restaurant with tables among palm trees and Caribbean views is one of Panama's most attractive lunch spots. Unfortunately, the food and service fall short of the setting, but not so far that you'd want to scratch it from your list. In good weather, dine at tables edging the sea surrounded by dark boulders and lush foliage. The other option is the open-air restaurant, decorated with shells, buoys, and driftwood, with a decent view of the bay and forested hills. House specialties include *pescado entero* (whole fried red snapper), *langosta al ajillo* (lobster scampi), and *centolla al jengibre* (king crab in a ginger sauce). ✉ *7 km (4 mi) before Portobelo on left* ☎ *448–2980* 🚫 *No credit cards* ⊙ *Closes at 7 PM.*

¢ ✕ 🏨 **Coco Plum Ecolodge.** This place has a great location on the water, but the rooms are set back from the sea in an uninspiring cement building. The owners have tried to compensate with a colorful, playful decor, and satellite TV, but rooms are still dark, and tiny bathrooms have plastic showerheads with the heating element inside them—common in

PIRATES OF THE CARIBBEAN

It has been said that a third of the world's gold passed through Portobelo during the 17th century, and that wealth attracted plenty of pirates. Even before the Spanish founded a town there, the bay of Portobelo was a popular spot for pirates and buccaneers to rest or hide from Spanish galleons. The English navigator and privateer Sir Frances Drake, famous for circumnavigating the globe and capturing many a Spanish treasure, died of dysentery when anchored near the bay in 1596. Legend has it that Drake's men buried him at sea in a lead coffin near what is now known as Drake Island, just east of Portobelo (though why the pirate would have been traveling with a lead coffin begs questioning).

Spanish authorities established the town in Portobelo a year after Drake's demise, and the bay soon turned from a pirates' resting spot to a target. William Parker was the first to attack the Spanish enclave in 1602; he captured significant booty and set a dangerous precedent. Henry Morgan captured the city in 1668 and held it for two weeks, until the Spanish government paid him a hefty ransom. During the interim he tortured prisoners and filled his ships with booty. Morgan was followed by the likes of John Coxon, Edward Cook, and other pirates and privateers. None of them matched Morgan's haul, or his treachery, but together they stole copiously and instilled terror in the local population.

English Admiral Edward Vernon attacked Portobelo with six ships and 2,500 men in 1739, managing to capture the city and destroy its fortresses. Soon afterward, Spain began shipping most of its South American riches around Cape Horn, and Portobelo slipped into obscurity. Only in recent years have foreigners begun descending on the ancient port in growing numbers. The treasures that attract today aren't gold and silver, but rather historic monuments and tropical nature.

the rest of Central America, but a rarity in Panama. Common areas are more appealing: the thatched platform on the dock and the second-floor lounge on the water, with a pool table. Sporting attractions include an on-site dive center, trips to nearby beaches, snorkeling tours, and hikes to a waterfall in the national park. The restaurant, Las Anclas, makes up for its lack of a view with inventive dishes like *langostinos en salsa de piña y jengibre* (prawns in a pineapple-ginger sauce) or *cazuela de mariscos*, a seafood stew in coconut milk. **Pros: Natural setting, outdoor activities. Cons: Small, dark rooms.** ⊠ *5 km (3 mi) before Portobelo on left* ☎ *448–2102* 🖷 *448–2325* ⊕ *www.cocoplum-panama.com* 🛏 *12 rooms* ⚴ *In-room: no a/c (some), no phone. In-hotel: restaurant, bar, diving, no elevator, no-smoking rooms* ⊟ *No credit cards* ⏐◯⏐ *EP.*

¢–$ 🛏 **Scuba Portobelo.** A dive resort owned by Panama's biggest dive company, Scuba Panama, this small place has the best rooms in the Portobelo area, but since it works mostly with tour groups booked out of Panama City, it skimps on services. Accommodations range from a dorm rooms to bungalows; the second-floor "single" rooms—small, but bright and colorful, with ocean views and narrow balconies—are

2

nice for couples. Free-standing *cabañas* (bungalows) are considerably bigger, and cost just $10 more. Large trees shade the ample grounds, and there's a gazebo atop some boulders over the water. The resort has a full dive center with inexpensive trips like snorkeling to Isla Mogotes. The tiny, open-air restaurant serves breakfast and a limited seafood-heavy menu, but there's better food down the road. Rates are slightly lower during the week. **Pros: Great location, inexpensive, scuba diving and snorkeling. Cons: Rooms basic, limited service, dead weekdays.** ⊠*6 km (3 mi) before Portobelo on left* ☎*448–2147* 🖷*261–9586* ⊕*www.scubapanama.com* 🛏*6 rooms, 5 cabañas* ⏃*In-room: no phone, no TV. In-hotel: restaurant, diving, no elevator, no-smoking rooms* ☰*AE, MC, V* ⏃*EP.*

SPORTS & THE OUTDOORS

BEACHES   The easiest beach to visit is **Playa Langosta,** which is about 8 km (5 mi) before Portobelo. You may have that dark-gray beach to yourself during the week, but on weekends and holidays it is usually packed with visitors from Colón and Panama City. There are more isolated beaches to the east of Portobelo that are accessible only by sea; boatmen who hang out at the docks next to the Batería Santiago and Fuerte Jerónimo can take you to one for $20–$30 round-trip. About 20 minutes east of Portobelo by boat, **Playa Huertas** is a long beach backed by tropical vegetation and a good place for swimming. **Playa Blanca** is a small, white-sand beach about 30 minutes by boat east of Portobelo. It has the nicest sand of any beach in the area, but is backed by pasture and homes.

BIRD-   The bird-watching is quite good at the edge of town and around the
WATCHING   ruins. Bird-watchers may want to hire one of the boatmen who hang out around the docks near Batería Santiago and Fuerte San Jerónimo to take them into the estuary behind town, which should cost $20.

HIKING   **Salvaventura** (☎*442–1042*) is a small company, started by José Malet, that offers guided hikes into Portobelo National Park, including one to a small waterfall. Guides don't speak much English, though.

SCUBA DIVING   Miles of coral reefs awash in rainbows of underwater wildlife lie within
& SNORKELING   the northern reaches of **Portobelo National Park,** and dive centers on the road to Portobelo provide easy access to those marine wonders. Though they've suffered some damage from fishermen and erosion, the reefs in the Portobelo area consist of nearly 50 coral species and are inhabited by more than 250 fish species. The underwater fauna ranges from moray eels to colorful butterfly fish, damselfish, trumpet fish, and other reef-dwellers. Popular spots include Buffet Reef, a plane wreck, a shipwreck, and the distant Escribano Bank, east of Isla Grande. Visibility varies according to the sea conditions, but tends to be low from December to April, when high seas can hamper dives. The best conditions are between September and December.

Most boat dives cost less than $50, and snorkeling equipment rentals are a mere $10 per day. PADI certification courses are also available. **Scuba Portobelo** (⊠*6 km [3 mi] before Portobelo on left* ☎*448–2147 or 261–3841*) is a dive center owned by Scuba Panama, the country's oldest dive operator. **Panama Divers** (⊠*Coco Plum Ecolodge, 5 km [3 mi]* *before Portobelo on left* ☎*314–0817 or 448–2102*), a small American-owned company, offers various boat dives, tours, and courses.

TO & FROM AND LOGISTICS

Portobelo is a two-hour drive from Panama City and a mere 40 minutes from Colón. To drive there from Panama City, follow the directions to Colón, but turn right after 60 km (37 mi), at the town of Sabanitas; from there it's 39 km (24 mi) to Portobelo. From Colón, head south toward Panama City for 15 km (9 mi) and turn left at Sabanitas. To get there by bus, take one of the Colón buses that depart from the Allbrook bus terminal every 20 minutes and ask the driver to drop you off in Sabanitas, at the turnoff for Portobelo and Isla Grande. There, catch one of the buses to Portobelo, which pass every hour. There is no reason to go to Colón on your way to Portobelo, unless you take the Panama Canal Railway, in which case hire a taxi or rent a car and drive to Portobelo to avoid hanging out at the Colón bus terminal.

ISLA GRANDE

10- to 20-min boat trip from La Guaira; 25 km (16 mi) east of Portobelo.

Lushly forested hills, palm fronds swaying in the breeze, and glistening aquamarine waters give Isla Grande an idyllic, tropical ambience, but its scarcity of beaches (it has just one decent beach) and crowded, cement-block town make it less attractive than some of the country's other coastal destinations. It's comparable to Bocas del Toro, though smaller and with fewer things to do. If you're spending time in the latter, you can easily skip Isla Grande; it's popular mostly for its proximity to Panama City—just over a two-hour drive.

The island sits just a few hundred meters off the coast in front of the fishing town of **La Guaira,** a 30-minute drive east of Portobelo. Isla Grande (Big Island) is a misnomer, as the island is just 3 mi long. The funky little Afro-Caribbean community along its southern shore has neither roads nor addresses, people come and go by boat, and it takes less than 30 minutes to walk from one end of town to the other. Most of the island is quite precipitous, and hills covered with dense foliage rise up just behind town, thus visits are generally confined to the town, the small beach on the island's western tip ($3 entrance fee), or the north-shore bay where Bananas Village Resort is located.

A nicer beach with better snorkeling can be found on **Isla Mamey** (⇨ Sports & the Outdoors, *below*), a short boat trip away. The main activity on Isla Grande, aside from eating and drinking, is skin diving. Though the reefs here are in bad shape, they have a good variety of fish and other marine life. There are, however, dozens of dive spots within 20 to 60 minutes from the island by boat, including healthy coral reefs, caves, and shipwrecks (⇨ Sports & the Outdoors, *below*).

On weekend and holidays Isla Grande can get crowded, which in Panama means noise and littering. During the week it's a ghost town, and it's sometimes tough to find a meal. Only a few hundred people live on the island, surviving on a mix of fishing, farming on the mainland, and tourism. Despite their relative dependence on tourism, the people of Isla Grande are not terribly friendly. But they do a good job of preparing lobster and other local seafood. Ask at the restaurants in town if they have *fufu,* a seafood soup made with coconut milk, plantains, and jungle tubers such as *ñame.*

WHERE TO STAY & EAT

$–$$ ✕🏨**Bananas Village Resort.** Nestled on the north side of the island in a
★ private cove surrounded by jungle, Bananas is Isla Grande's best hotel
☾ by far. Bright, spacious rooms are in two-story buildings between the gardens and the forest. The ocean views from the hammocks on their balconies alone make the trip worthwhile. Suites, built out over the water, have a more impressive view for just $15 more. Apart from the caged birds, the only disappointment is the tiny beach, which is atop a coral platform, so the water is shallow. A swimming area at the end of the property has a dock and a nearby open-air bar. The use of kayaks and snorkeling equipment is included in the rates, as are volleyball, Ping-Pong, and a saltwater pool. Excursions such as a boat trip to Isla Mamey are extra. Guests arrive and depart by water, but you can also hike the 30-minute cement trail through the forest to town. The open-air restaurant ($–$$$$) serves fresh seafood, pastas, paella, and steaks, with an ocean view. **Pros: Views, quiet, lots of diversions, kid-friendly. Cons: Inconsistent service, relatively expensive tours.** ⊠*North side of Isla Grande* ☎*448–2252 or 263–9510* 🖷*264-7556* ⊕*www.banan-asresort.com* ⊲*28 rooms* ⌂*In-room: no phone, DVD (some), safe. In-hotel: restaurant, bar, pool, beach front, water sports, no elevator, parking, no-smoking rooms* ⊟*AE, DC, MC, V* ⦿*CP.*

$ 🏨**Sister Moon.** These rustic wooden bungalows perched along a steep hillside east of town have great views of the of the sea and mainland, but cheap mattresses and no hot water. They feature colorful tile bathrooms and other artistic touches. The higher ones are more private and have the best views. The open-air restaurant next to a small saltwater pool and stone deck is a great place to hang out and watch the waves crash against the rocks below. This is the closest hotel to the surf break, but the farthest from the town beach. **Pros: Great ocean view, quiet. Cons: Rooms rustic and small, far from beach.** ⊠*Isla Grande, east of town* ☎*448–2182 or 226–9861* 🖷*261–9586* ⊕*www.hotelsister-moon.com* ⊲*13 bungalows* ⌂*In-room: no a/c, no phone, no TV. In-hotel: restaurant, bar, pool, no elevator, public Internet, no-smoking rooms* ⊟*MC, V* ⦿*BP.*

¢ 🏨**Villa en Sueño.** Rooms in this brightly painted hotel in the heart of town are in two cement buildings behind the restaurant of the same name. They are simple, but clean, with cold-water showers, decent beds, and shared porches with hammocks overlooking a small lawn lined with lush gardens. The restaurant in front has an ocean view and is one of the better places to eat in town. The on-site store rents snorkeling equipment and can arrange boat tours. On weekends and holidays the hotel can get pretty crowded, since the hotel rents picnic areas on the grounds, but it's usually dead during the week. **Pros: Central location, near beach, boat tours available, inexpensive. Cons:**

Rooms very basic, little privacy, can be noisy. ⊠*Isla Grande, in front of cross* ☎*448–2964* 🖷*320–6321* ✍*villaen@cwpanama.net* 🛏*16 rooms* ⚒*In-room: no phone, no TV. In-hotel: restaurant, water sports, no elevator, no-smoking rooms* ⊟*AE, MC, V* ⦿*EP.*

SPORTS & THE OUTDOORS

BEACHES The island only has one decent beach, on the grounds of the dilapidated Hotel Isla Grande west of town, which charges nonguests $3. The advantage is that is gets less crowded on weekends, and there is always a cold beer nearby. The nicest beach in the area is on **Isla Mamey**, an excursion offered by the hotels and boatmen.

SCUBA DIVING Isla Grande is surround by reefs, but the coral is in bad shape. The best
& SNORKELING snorkeling is off the island's north side, near the Banana Village Resort. You'll find healthier coral and more fish at **Isla Mamey**, a popular excursion, or farther out on the fringe reefs. Local barrier reefs are home to hundreds of fish and invertebrate species, including barracudas, nurse sharks, and spotted eagle rays. There are also several shipwrecks in the area, one of which dates from the 16th century.

Diving conditions are best during the rainy season, especially from September to December.

The **Isla Grande Dive Center** (☎*6501–4374 or 232–6994*), next to the town dock, offers snorkeling trips to Isla Mamey and other nearby islands, and scuba diving at more than two dozen spots for reasonable prices. If the seas are calm, they can arrange (more-expensive) dives at the Escribano Bank—a long coral reef to the east with some of the best coral formations on the Caribbean coast.

SURFING There is a surf break on the east end island—a left reef break at El Faro—though it's often flat. When it pumps, it is an intermediate to expert spot, since it breaks over a mix of rock and coral. You are most likely to find good waves there between December and April.

TO & FROM AND LOGISTICS

To drive to Isla Grande, follow the directions for Portobelo, but continue through town and veer left at the intersection just after it, following the signs to La Guaria. Buses to La Guaira, the departure point for Isla Grande, leave Sabanitas and Portobelo every hour from 8 to 5. Boatmen are usually waiting at the dock in La Guaira; they charge $2 for the 10-minute trip to the island and $5 to Bananas Village Resort.

SANTA ISABELA

44 km (27 mi) east of Isla Grande, 26 km (16 mi) west of El Porvenir (Kuna Yala).

To the east of the Isla Grande the coast becomes wilder, and the ocean more pristine. Nestled in a remote cove about two-thirds of the way between Isla Grande and the Kuna Indian enclave of El Porvenir (⇨Chapter 6), is one of the country's best eco-lodges, Coral Lodge, which provides access to miles of coral reefs that few divers have seen. Those reefs, known as the Escribano Bank, hold giant sea fans, stag-horn and elkhorn coral, colorful sponges, legions of parrot fish, moray eels, and several sea turtle species. The lodge is near the fishing village of Santa Isabela, which is 16 km (10 mi) from the nearest road, in Miramar, and 29 km (18 mi) by water from the island of El Porvenir, which is reached by daily plane flights. Coral Lodge thus allows you to experience the beauty and culture of the Kuna Yala (San Blas Islands) without having to stay in the rustic lodges of the Kuna Indians.

WHERE TO STAY & EAT

$$$$ ✕🏠**Coral Lodge.** The idyllic cove that Coral Lodge occupies is the stuff
Fodor$Choice of tropical fantasies: emerald waters washing over coral reefs and a
★ golden beach backed by jungle. Miles from the nearest road, halfway between El Porvenir and the village of Miramar, this remote ecolodge combines constant exposure to nature with such creature comforts as air-conditioning and excellent food. Spacious, octagonal bungalows stand over the water atop coral platforms, with waves washing beneath them. A ladder from the wraparound balcony lets you climb into the crystalline sea whenever you feel the urge, and the view of the lagoon and coast is hypnotic. The bungalows are wonderfully designed, with high thatched roofs, cane furniture, and Indonesian art. A walkway connects them to a small beach, the pool, and an open-air restaurant over the water. Snorkeling equipment and kayaks are included in the rates; skin diving, horseback riding, and rain-forest trips are extra. It's quite expensive, but rather than luxury, the Coral Lodge offers exposure to pristine nature with more comfort and better food than you'll get in Kuna Yala (⇨ Porvenir *in* Chapter 6), which is visited as a half-day trip. **Pros: Gorgeous scenery, skin diving, kayaking, good food, friendly. Cons: Expensive, no-see-ums a problem in rainy season, boat rides rough in dry season.** ✉*Santa Isabela, 25 km (16 mi) west of Porvenir by sea* ☎*317–6754 or 202–3795* 📠*Apdo. 0843–02518, Balboa* 🌐*www.corallodge.com* 🛏*8 bungalows* ⚐*In-room: no phone, no TV. In-hotel: restaurant, bar, pool, beachfront, diving, water sports, no elevator, public Internet, no kids under 10, no-smoking rooms* ▭*AE, MC, V* ⊙*FAP.*

THE EASTERN SIERRAS

A large mass of mountains rises up to the northeast of the waterway, and most of the rain that falls on it provides the water used by the canal's locks. The Panamanian government has consequently protected that vast watershed within Parque Nacional Chagres. Chagres is contiguous with Portobelo National Park—the relatively small Sierra Llorona defines the border between the two parks—and its southern border runs through a collection of hills known as Cerro Azul, which is the closest highland area to Panama City. To the east of Parque Nacional Chagres the Serranía de San Blas stretches eastward toward Colombia. That long, narrow mountain range defines the southern border of the *comarca*, or autonomous indigenous territory, of Kuna Yala. The area to the south of it is known as Alto Bayano, and contains the vast Lago Bayano, a hydroelectric reservoir created in the 1970s.

SIERRA LLORONA

80 km (50 mi) north of Panama City, 22 km (14 mi) southeast of Colón.

Sierra Llorona is a small but steep mountain range east of Gatún Lake and southwest of Portobelo that spends much of the year enveloped in clouds, and the abundant waterfalls that result from that rain are the origin of the range's name, which translates as "crybaby sierra." The Sierra stretches southwestward from Portobelo and Chagres national parks to a sparsely populated area where you'll find the family-run Sierra Llorona Lodge, on a 500-acre private reserve that is home to hundreds of bird species and an array of other wildlife. The lodge is well worth spending a night or two at, but day visitors get lunch and a local guide for $35.

WHERE TO STAY

$ ⛰ **Sierra Llorona Panama Lodge.** Birdsong is the Muzak at the Sierra
★ Llorona Lodge, where the chirping plays from sunup to sundown, and the gardens are visited by an array of winged creatures from snowy-bellied hummingbirds to clay-colored robins. The lodge is surrounded by 500 acres of protected rain forest that can be explored on 6 km (4 mi) of trails, but many visitors are happy to sit in the garden and wait for the birds to come to them. The lodge is simple but comfortable, with rooms in the old family home and a nearby wooden building which has small balconies overlooking the woods. Rooms at the ends of that building are brighter, though all are quite spacious. Rooms in the house are farther from the forest, but the bright suite on the second floor, with a Jacuzzi, is worth the extra $20. The restaurant serves a set menu that changes daily. A local guide, who speaks very little English, is included in the rates, but if you want a bilingual birding guide, you'll need to request one when you reserve and pay extra. Massages can be arranged a day in advance. The lodge is short drive up narrow country roads from the Transísmica (see Web site for directions). The lodge can provide transportation. **Pros: Good bird-watching, forest, hiking. Cons: Service inconsistent.** ✉ *Santa Rita Arriba, 4½ km (3 mi) east of Transístmica* ☎ *442–8104* 🖷 *470–0634* ⊕ *www.sierrallorona.com* 🛏 *7 rooms, 1 suite* ♿ *In-room: no a/c, no phone, no TV. In-hotel: restaurant, bicycles, no elevator, laundry service, public Internet, airport shuttle, no-smoking rooms* ☰ *MC, V* ⦿ *BP.*

TO & FROM AND LOGISTICS

It's an easy one-hour drive to Sierra Llorona from Panama City. Follow directions for Colón and turn right shortly before Sabanitas, at a sign for Santa Arriba and Sierra Llorona, from where it's a 4½ km (3 mi) drive up a narrow, windy road. In the rainy season a four-wheel-drive vehicle is recommended for the last stretch. The Sierra Llorona Lodge has detailed instructions on its Web site, and can pick guests up in either Panama City or Colón.

PARQUE NACIONAL CHAGRES (CHAGRES NATIONAL PARK)

40 km (24 mi) north of Panama City.

The mountains to the northeast of the canal form a vast watershed that feeds the Chagres River, which was one of the country's principal waterways until it was damned to create the canal, and is now the source of nearly half of the water used in the locks. To protect the forests that help water percolate into the ground and keep the river running through the dry season, the Panamanian government declared the entire watershed a national park in 1985. It is one of the country's largest parks, covering more than 320,000 acres, and it holds an array of ecosystems and expanses of inaccessible wilderness that is home to spider monkeys, harpy eagles, toucans, tapirs, and other endangered species. The park's northern border, defined by Sierra Llorona, and its southern extreme, in Cerro Azul, are the easiest areas to visit, thanks to paved roads. Most people visit the national park on day tours from Panama City to one of several Emberá Indian villages in it, but you can see more of its forests on a white-water rafting trip down the Chagres River, or by hiking on the trails of Cerro Azul.

All the major tour operators in Panama City offer day trips to **Emberá villages** in the park (⇨ "Tours," *in* Panama City Essentials, Chapter 1). Visiting the villages—relocated here from Alto Bayano three decades ago, when their land was flooded by a hydroelectric project—is an interesting cultural experience, but most itineraries aren't great for seeing wildlife. The Emberás' traditional territory stretches from eastern Panama to northwest Colombia, but the relocated communities live much as their relatives to the east do, in thatched huts with elevated floors and scant walls. Years of exposure to Western society and religion have led most people in the Chagres communities to wear clothes, but they switch to traditional dress when they know a tour is coming. The men wear loincloths and women wrap themselves in bright-color cloth skirts and no tops, sometimes covering their breasts with large necklaces. Men and women often paint their upper bodies with a dye made from mixing the sap of the *jagua* fruit with ashes. The tours are a bit of a show, but they provide an interesting introduction to Emberá culture. (However, if you will be traveling to the Darién or Alto Bayano, you can get a more authentic, if less picturesque, Emberá experience there.) Tours usually include demonstrations of how the Emberá live, a traditional dance, handicraft sales, and optional painting of visitors' arms with *jagua*. (Note the *jagua* tattoos take more than a week to wash off.) The community that receives the most visitors is Parara Puru, because it is accessible year-round. The town of San Juan de Pequiní, farther up river, can be difficult to reach in the dry season, but it is a less scripted trip that includes some exposure to nature. The best trip for nature lovers and adventurers is to Emberá Drua, which only the small companies book, since it entails a boat trip deeper into the park and a tough hike. For those who are up to the hike, this is the most authentic village trip in the Chagres area. ⊠ *Transístmica, Km. 40* ☎ *500–0080* ⊠ *Free* ☉ *Daily 8–5.*

SPORTS & THE OUTDOORS

HIKING   Serious hikers can trek deep into the jungles of Parque Nacional Chagres by following the old **Camino Real** across the mountains to the Caribbean coast. Spanish colonists built the "Royal Road" in the 16th century to carry gold and other goods between Panamá Viejo and the Caribbean port of Nombre de Dios, and most of that route remains surrounded by lush rain forest. Weeklong trips organized by **Ancon Expeditions** (☎269–9415 ⊕www.anconexpeditions.com) includes visits to colonial ruins and an Emberá Indian village, and several nights in tent camps in the national park, plus lots of exposure to tropical nature.

WHITE-WATER   **Aventuras Panama** (☎260–0044 ⊕www.aventuraspanama.com) runs
RAFTING   white-water rafting trips on the Chagres River (class II–III), which flows through the heart of Parque Nacional Chagres. The full-day trip requires no previous rafting experience. It begins with a long drive down dirt roads deep into the national park, followed by a five-hour river trip that includes a picnic lunch. The trip is only available from May to late March; it lasts 11–12 hours and costs $175.

SHOPPING

A big part of a visit to an Emberá village is the opportunity to buy authentic indigenous handicrafts from the artisans themselves. Among the items usually sold are tightly woven baskets and platters, and animal figures carved from *tagua* palm seeds, or *cocobolo* wood.

TO & FROM AND LOGISTICS

The only part of Parque Nacional Chagres that you can easily visit on your own is the Cerro Azul area (⇨*below*). To get deeper into the park, you have to take a tour.

CERRO AZUL

45 km (27 mi) northeast of Panama City.

This highland retreat a short drive east of Panama City offers a bit of relief from the heat, plus hiking trails and some birds than you won't find in the canal area. The altitude is around 2,500 feet above sea level, and when there is a breeze it can be pleasantly cool; you may even need a light jacket if you spend the night. Cerro Azul translates as "blue hill," but the predominant color here is green, since the northern half of these mountains is draped in a blanket of lush forest protected within Parque Nacional Chagres, and the area along the roadways is dominated by Honduran pines that were planted after a U.S. company deforested the hills to create pasture decades ago. The tiny community of Cerro Azul is next to a small lake completely surrounded by homes and fences.

WHERE TO STAY & EAT

¢–$ ✕**La Posada de Ferhisse.** Perched on a hill across the street from the lake, this simple open-air restaurant is the best place to have lunch in Cerro Azul. The menu is predominantly Panamanian, with a few twists, such as the *colombo de pollo* (chicken in a mild curry sauce) and *chilindrín de cordero* (lamb in a tomato and beer sauce). There is a pool below the restaurant that is open to the public for a small fee, and next to that are a few basic, inexpensive rooms for rent. ⊠ *Calle Principal, on right* ☎ *297–0197* ▭ *MC, V.*

$–$$ ⬛ **Hostal Casa de Campo.** Nestled among tall trees in the quiet residential neighborhood of Los Nubes, this small inn is a good spot to relax or watch some birds, but its rooms are a mixed bag. The nicest ones are in the main house—a former vacation home that has been decorated with a pleasant mix of antiques, wicker furniture, and an eclectic collection of art. The Hiedra and Geranios rooms share a large balcony with a hammock, table, and chairs. The bright suite, Orquídeas, is the nicest room of all, with a king bed, plus two singles on request. The other rooms tend to be dark and a bit musty, especially the newer cabañas in the back, which have stone walls and open onto wide covered terraces. In front of the restaurant are a small pool and a Jacuzzi, with a large barbecue that is fired up for weekend lunches. Spa services and yoga are available with reservations, but Panama City's many spas are much better options. Casa de Campo isn't all it could be, but is nevertheless a tranquil, pleasant spot. **Pros: Natural surroundings, nice decor, transport from Panama City. Cons: Some rooms dark, untidy.** ⊠ *Urbanización Los Nubes (turn left after lake)* ☎ *297–0067* ⎙ *226–0336* ⊕ *www.panamacasadecampo.com* ⬡ *10 rooms, 1 suite* ⌂ *In-room: no a/c, no phone, no TV (some). In-hotel: restaurant, bar, pool, no elevator, laundry service, airport shuttle, no-smoking rooms* ▭ *MC, V* ⬤ *EP.*

¢ ⬛ **Cabañas Turismaru.** This is the best option for travelers on a tight budget. Rooms are in cement duplexes with high ceilings, colorful paint jobs, sparse furnishings, and small porches with hammocks. Most overlook the pool, but those in the back—rooms 11 and 12—view some of the verdure and are quieter. There is a small playground, and a restaurant above the lobby that serves basic Panamanian fare. **Pros: Inexpensive. Cons: Very basic.** ⊠ *Calle Prinicpal, across from lake* ☎ *297–0213* ⬡ *12 rooms* ⌂ *In-room: no a/c, no phone. In-hotel: restaurant, pool, no elevator, laundry service, no-smoking rooms* ▭ *No credit cards* ⬤ *EP.*

SPORTS & THE OUTDOORS

HIKING The most accessible hiking trails into the forests of Chagres National Park are beyond the town of Cerro Azul in a large housing development called **Altos de Cerro Azul** (⊠ *Entrance on left a few km after lake* ☎ *279–7189*), owned by the Melo corporation, a Panamanian conglomerate. However, because it is a private, guarded development, you should call ahead to get the name of a salesperson to give the guard, even if you don't look at real estate.

Several kilometers after entering Altos de Cerro Azul there is a small waterfall on the right called **Cascada el Vigia.** Continue on for several kilometers more to a road on the left called El Valle de Alcanzar. Turn left onto it and drive to the end to the entrance to the **Sendero el Patriarca,** a trail that heads about 5 km (3 mi) into the forest to a massive mahogany tree called the Patriarch. If that seems like too long a hike, you can take a shorter trail called **Sendero Romeo y Julieta** that branches off Sendero El Patriarca after about 1 km, and leads to two small lakes another kilometer deeper into the forest. To access a third trail, **Sendero Cantar,** which makes a 2-km (1½-mi) loop through the forest, continue straight at the intersection with El Valle de Alcanzar, and stay on the main road to the far end of the development, veer right after a small lake, and follow Calle Andora to the end. If you get lost, ask somebody to point you in the direction of El Mirador. The dirt road that leaves Calle Andora on the left shortly before the trailhead leads to the **Mirador Vistamar,** a scenic overlook atop a small hill from which you can see most of Parque Nacional Chagres on a clear day, including the forested peaks of Cerro Jefe and Cerro Brewster, and Sierra Llorona in the distance. ■TIP➔ **You should head to the Mirador first, because the earlier you get there, the clearer the view will be.**

HORSEBACK RIDING   **Margo Tours** (☎302–0390 ⊕*www.margotours.com*) offers half-day horseback-riding tours through the pastures and forest of the Haras Orillac Ranch, on the slopes of Cerro Azul.

TO & FROM AND LOGISTICS

It takes less than an hour to drive to Cerro Azul from downtown Panama City. Take the Corredor Sur to Tocumen Airport, turn left before the airport onto the Interamericana (CA1), following the signs to Chepo, and turn left again a few kilometers later, after the Super Xtra. The road will soon begin to climb, passing a large horse statue and some lovely views of Panama City before reaching the small collection of homes and restaurants around the lake that marks the center of Cerro Azul. The entrance to Los Nubes, where Casa de Campo is located, is on the left about a kilometer after the lake, and the entrance to Altos de Cerro Azul is on the left after that. You should be able to hire a taxi to take you to Cerro Azul for $10–$15 per hour. To arrive by bus, catch an eastbound city bus with 4 de diciembré on its windshield (on Calle 50), and get off at the terminal behind the Super Xtra, where buses leave for Cerro Azul every 30 minutes.

ALTO BAYANO

100 km (60 mi) northeast of Panama City.

The Alto Bayano region is dominated by a large reservoir called Lago Bayano, which is surrounded by pastureland, and forests clinging to the upper slopes of the *serranías* (mountain ranges) to the north and south. There are various Emberá Indian villages on the rivers that flow into the lake, and a dirt track heads north from it to the autonomous indigenous territory, or *comarca,* of Kuna Yala, which holds vast expanses of rain forest.

The road that heads north to Kuna Yala, known as the Llano-Cartí Road, leads to the private nature reserve of **Burbayar** (⇨ Where to Stay, *below*), which offers access to lush forests that are home to ocelots, night monkeys, dozens of snakes and frog species, and hundreds of bird species.

The indigenous community of **Unión Emberá**, on the Río Majé in the southeast corner of Lago Bayano, receives a tiny fraction of the visitors that the Emberá communities in Parque Nacional Chagres do. To visit, you can hire a boat (about $50) at the bridge where the Interamericana crosses a sliver of Bayano Lake. The Burbayar nature reserve organizes visits to Unión Emberá as an add-on to overnights at the lodge. An interesting addition to a trip here is a bit of spelunking in La Cueva del Tigre (⇨Sports & the Outdoors, *below*).

WHERE TO STAY

$$$ ▥ **Burbayar Lodge.** Perched on a ridge on the western end of the Ser-
★ ranía de San Blas, surrounded by the forests of the eponymous 150-acre private reserve, Burbayar was created by and for nature lovers. Its cabins overlook the treetops, where you might spot collared aracaris, brown-hooded parrots, or any of the other 320 bird species found in the area. Rare specimens such as the speckled ant shrike and broad-billed sapayoa draw serious birders, but all guests enjoy the abundant hummingbirds, howler monkeys, and other jungle denizens. Nearly 20 km (12 mi) of trails wind through the adjacent forest, which borders the *comarca* Kuna Yala. A day hike takes you to a 220-foot waterfall deep in the jungle. Rooms are comfortably rustic, with thatched roofs, varnished wood, small bathrooms, and balconies with forest views. Meals are served family style on the porch of the main house, and are included in the rates along with a guide, equipment, and transport to and from Panama City. The owner, Ignacio Ruiz, has taken pains to make Burbayar as environmentally friendly as possible. **Pros: Small, surrounded by forest, hiking. Cons: Rustic rooms.** ✉*Camino Llano-Cartí, Km 15* ☎☎390–6674 ⊕*www.burbayar.com* ⇆*6 rooms* ⚿*In-room: no a/c, no phone, no TV. In-hotel: restaurant, no elevator, no-smoking rooms* ▭*MC, V* ⦿*FAP.*

SPORTS & THE OUTDOORS

SPELUNKING **La Cueva del Tigre** *(Jaguar's Cave)* is a large cave with a stream running through it on the southern shore of Bayano Lake. You'll need a good flashlight and a set of clothes and shoes that can get wet to explore the cave, which has waterfall inside it. Boats can be hired (about $50) at the bridge where the Inter-American Highway crosses Bayano Lake—ask them to take you to the village of Pueblo Nuevo de Bayano; from there you can have locals point you in the direction of the cave.

TO & FROM AND LOGISTICS

Alto Bayano lies 100 km (60 mi) east of Panama City, which is reached by driving east on the Corredor Sur and turning left onto the Interamericana (CA1) right before Tocumen Airport. Transportation to and from Burbayar is included for guests of the lodge.

THE CENTRAL PACIFIC ISLANDS

The Gulf of Panama holds more than a dozen islands and countless rocky islets, which include Isla Taboga, a mere 20 km (12 mi) south of Panama City, and the Archipelago de las Perlas (Pearl Islands), which are scattered across the gulf between 60 and 90 km (about 40–60 mi) southeast of the city. Isla Taboga has a historic town lined with vacation homes, whereas the Pearl Islands remain largely undeveloped, with a few fishing villages and vast expanses of rain forest. Only two of the Pearl Islands currently have hotels: Isla Contadora, which has several, as well as dozens of homes, and Isla San José, which has the eco-resort of Hacienda del Mar. The aquamarine waters that wash against the islands hold varied and abundant marine life, especially the sea south of Isla San José, so there are opportunities for sportfishing, skin diving, and whale-watching to complement the beaches.

The islands were inhabited well before the Spaniards arrived in Panama, as petroglyphs found on some of them attest. Isla Taboga became a Spanish stronghold from the start, due to its deep bay, ideal for mooring ships close to shore. The Spanish conquistador Francisco Pizarro defeated the indigenous leader of the Pearl Islands, King Toe, in 1515. Pizarro stole plenty of pearls from Toe's people, and the Spanish government continued to exploit the archipelago's pearl beds for the next two centuries, first with indigenous labor, and later, with African slaves, after disease decimated the indigenous population. Overexploitation exhausted the pearl supply in the 19th century, and since then the archipelago's inhabitants have survived on fishing, tourism, and building vacation homes.

Because the Pearl Archipelago is so extensive, its islands were often the haunt of pirates, who used them as bases from which to attack Spanish galleons carrying South American gold to Panama during the 16th and 17th centuries. More recently, the archipelago has been exploited by a new breed of opportunist: the producers of the *Survivor* television series, who have based several seasons here. Modern-day invaders have discovered that the islands' true treasures are their beaches and ocean views, and their hotel supply will likely expand in the near future.

ISLA TABOGA

20 km (12 mi) south of Panama City.

A pleasant 60-minute ferry ride from the Amador Causeway takes you far from the traffic jams of Panama City to the tranquil isle of Taboga, which has a lovely beach, clear waters, and a funky little fishing village. Since the island lies so close to the city, most people visit on day trips, but it does have hotels, and is worth an overnight.

Dominated by two large hills, Isla Taboga is known as the "Island of Flowers" for the abundant gardens of its small town, **San Pedro**, spread along the steep hillside of its eastern shore. One of the country's oldest towns, San Pedro was founded in 1524, though its whitewashed church is the only surviving structure from the colonial era. The conquistador Francisco Pizarro embarked from Taboga in 1530 on his voyage to crush the Incan empire, and it remained an important port until the 20th century. Because of the extreme variation of Panama's Pacific tides, ships were unable to moor near the coast of Panama, so the deep bay on Taboga's eastern shore was the perfect alternative. The Spanish built a fortress on Taboga in an attempt to defend the bay from pirates, the Pacific Steamship Company was based there during the 19th century, and the French built a sanatorium on the island during their attempt to build a canal. Upon completion of the canal, with its various docks and marinas, Taboga became what it is today, a sleepy fishing village that wakes up on weekends and holidays, when visitors from the capital arrive en masse.

2

Though it has a few historic buildings and ruins in the area of the church, San Pedro is mostly made up of the humble abodes of fishermen and the weekend homes of families from Panama City, which occupy most of the waterfront. There are few vehicles on the island, and most of its streets resemble extra-wide sidewalks. The main road runs along the town beach, Playa Honda, which lines a small bay holding dozens of fishing boats. Many of the bougainvillea-lined streets pass shrines to the Virgen del Carmen, considered the protector of fishermen throughout Latin America, who is celebrated every July 16 here. Near the central plaza stand the ruins of a colonial-era house where French painter Paul Gauguin lived for a while during the 1880s, before continuing westward to Tahiti.

Isla Taboga's main attractions are its two beaches: **Playa Honda,** the beach in front of town, and **Playa Restinga,** a spit of sand that connects Taboga with the tiny island of El Morro, just north of town. At low- or midtide, Playa Restinga is a gorgeous swath of golden sand flanked by calm waters, but at high tide it almost completely disappears. It's often packed on weekends and holidays, when the radios and screaming kids can be a bit too much, but it is practically deserted on most weekdays. For years Playa Restinga was accessible only via the Hotel Taboga, which was demolished in 2005, but a resort planned for that site could eventually restrict access to it. Playa Honda, the beach in front of town, is unfortunately unattractive, a bit rocky, and dirty—you are as likely to see vultures on it as seagulls—though it does retain a bit of sand at high tide. ⚠ **San Pedro's sewage flows untreated into the bay, so swimming at Playa Honda, or even on the south side of Playa Restinga, is not recommended.**

Aside from swimming and sunbathing, Taboga's outdoor options include snorkeling around El Morro, hiking, fishing, or a boat trip around the island. Trails lead to the island's two highest points: Cerro de la Cruz, a hill south of town that is topped with a 20-foot cross, and Cerro Vigia, the mountain behind town. A **wildlife refuge** covers the western half of Isla Taboga and the nearby island of Urabá, which is the best dive spot in the area. One of the best parts of going to Isla Taboga is actually the trip itself, since the ferry passes dozens of massive ships and provides great views of the islands and the city.

The **traditional celebrations** on Isla Taboga are June 29, when the local parishioners celebrate San Pedro's day, and July 16, when the Virgen del Carmen is celebrated with a procession through town and a boat caravan around the island. Taboga is truly a bedroom community of

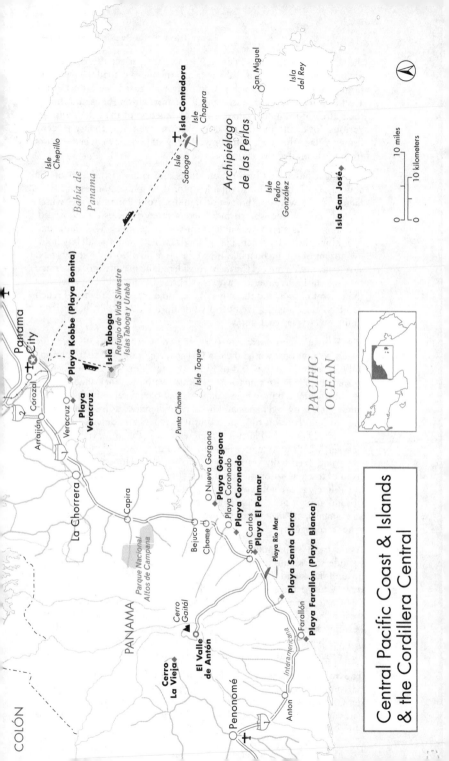

Central Pacific Coast & Islands
& the Cordillera Central

2

Panama City, and it consequently has no pharmacy, and only a very small clinic. ■TIP➜ There is no ATM on Taboga, so stock up on cash before heading there—Isla Perico near the ferry dock on the Amador Causeway has ATMs.

WHERE TO STAY & EAT

$ ✕🏨 **Hotel Vereda Tropical.** Isla Taboga's best hotel, the Vereda Tropical is perched on the hillside overlooking the Bay of Panama. Its best rooms share a view of the town's fishing fleet, cargo ships, and Panama City, which is almost as impressive at night, when the ship lights glow against the dark sea. Rooms have high ceilings, fans, Guatemalan bedspreads, and small bathrooms with colorful tile. The best rooms have French doors that open onto Juliet balconies with ocean views—well worth the extra money, since the cheapest rooms overlook rooftops, and can be noisy. It's well worth eating at the restaurant ($–$$), even if you don't stay here; it's the best kitchen on the island and the terrace view is gorgeous. The eclectic menu includes a good pizza selection, pastas with a choice of about a dozen sauces, lobster served various ways, curried prawns, and *paella*. The house specialty is *corvina* (sea bass) in a coconut milk–passion fruit sauce. **Pros: Great views, good restaurant, short walk to beach. Cons: Staff not friendly, some noise.** ✉*100 meters south of ferry dock* 🕾🕾*250–2154 or 214–2143* ⊕*www. veredatropicalhotel.com* 🛏*12 rooms* ♿*In-room: no a/c (some), no phone. In-hotel: restaurant, no elevator, laundry service, public Internet, no-smoking rooms* ⊟*MC, V* ⦿*CP.*

$ 🏨 **Cerrito Tropical.** Perched at the top of a steep hill at the edge of the forest, this two-story apartment rental has good views, especially from the second-floor balcony. The Canadian owners have two apartments, which are a great deal for two couples or a family, but they can also be split and rented separately, with use of a full kitchen. The rooms are in the back and lack views, but they are spacious, with ceiling fans, private baths, and tiny TVs. People tend to spend most of their time on the wide terraces, with a hammock, table and chairs, and ocean views. **Pros: Great views, quiet. Cons: Far from beach, steep hike.** ✉*6 blocks south of ferry dock* 🕾🕾*215–2436* ⊕*www.cerritotropicalpanama.com* 🛏*5 rooms* ♿*In-room: no phone, Ethernet. In-hotel: no elevator, no-smoking rooms* ⊟*No credit cards* ⦿*CP.*

¢ 🏨 **Cool Hostal.** Isla Taboga's backpacker option, this tiny hostel has two private rooms with two single beds each, as well as a small dorm. In a quiet, shady compound steps from the ferry dock and Playa Restinga, the hostel has a picnic table out front and a kitchen available to guests. **Pros: Cheap, quiet, near beach. Cons: Small beds, foam mattresses, share bath.** ✉*Uphill from ferry dock* 🕾🕾*6596–2545* ✉*luisveron@ hotmail.com* 🛏*2 rooms, 1 dorm* ♿*In-room: no a/c, no phone, no TV, kitchen. In-hotel: no elevator, laundry service, no-smoking rooms* ⊟*No credit cards* ⦿*CP.*

SPORTS & THE OUTDOORS

HIKING Hiking up one of Isla Taboga's two hills is an invigorating effort rewarded by amazing views. The easiest hike is to the top of **Cerro de La Cruz,** the smaller hill south of town that is topped by a 20-foot cross. The trail is reached by following the main street south along the coast and all the way through town until it becomes a dirt road; look for the footpath heading up the hill to the left. Since the hill is almost completely deforested, wear a hat and use sunblock. If you stay on the dirt road, it will take you to the top of **Cerro Vigia,** the highest point on the island, at 1,200 feet. There is a lookout point on the summit, which has the remains of a U.S. Army spotlight installation built during World War II. A nicer, though steeper trail to the top of Cerro Vigia heads through the forest above town. To take that route, go up the street next to Restaurant Acuario, follow the trail into the forest, and when you reach the three crosses follow the road to the summit. ■TIP➔Either hike should be done either early in the morning or later in the afternoon, since it is simply too hot in the middle of the day for such exertion.

SNORKELING   The snorkeling is pretty good around El Morro, where the visibility is best when the tide is coming in. Serious divers head to Isla Urubá, a protected island just south of Taboga. The **Hotel Vereda Tropical** (☎470–1100) rents snorkeling equipment to guests for $8 and can arrange a boat ride around the island for $50 that includes snorkeling at Isla Urubá. Taboga lacks a dive center, but the Panama City–based operator **Scuba Panama** (☎261–3841 ⊕www.scubapanama.com) can arrange diving around Taboga.

TO & FROM AND LOGISTICS

Barcos Calypso Taboga (✉Marina Isla Naos ☎314–1730) has a daily ferry service to Taboga departing from the marina on Isla Naos, on the Amador Causeway. The trip is one hour. It leaves Monday, Wednesday, and Friday at 8:30 and 3; Tuesday and Thursday at 8:30 only; and weekends and holidays at 8, 10:30, and 4. The ferry departs from Taboga from the pier on the west end of town Monday, Wednesday, and Friday at 9:30 and 4:30; Tuesday and Thursday at 4:30; and weekends and holidays at 9, 3, and 5. ■TIP➔On weekends and holidays you should arrive 30 minutes before departure to buy your ticket.

ISLA CONTADORA

70 km (43 mi) southeast of Panama City.

Fodor'sChoice   The resort island of Contadora, a mere 20 minutes from Panama City
★   by plane, has some of the country's nicest beaches. More than a dozen swaths of ivory sand backed by exuberant foliage line Contadora's perimeter, and they lie within walking distance of accommodations to fit any budget. It is a small island, covering less than a square mile, but it can serve as a base for day trips to nearby isles with deserted beaches and snorkeling sites, as well as deep-sea fishing, scuba diving, and whale-watching. There is enough to see and do on Isla Contadora to fill several days, and if all you're looking for in Panama is sun, sea, and sand, you could easily spend a week there.

The Pearl Archipelago's indigenous inhabitants must have had another name for Contadora, but its current name, which translates as "counting isle," was given to it nearly five centuries ago, when it held the offices of the Spanish crown's pearl-diving enterprise. The island was deserted for years after the pearl harvest diminished. The U.S. Army built a small base and airstrip on it during World War II, only to abandon it after the war. Contadora gained its current status as a resort isle in the 1970s, when Panamanian businessman and statesman Gabriel Lewis Galindo, father of the country's current vice president, was stranded on the island during a fishing trip and fell in love with it. He apparently purchased Contadora for $30,000, built roads, and sold coastal property to other wealthy Panamanians. The government then built the massive Hotel Contadora—now privately owned—and the island developed a healthy weekend party scene. Lewis Galindo lent his home to the deposed Shah of Iran on the heels of the Tehran embassy takeover in 1979, as a favor to Jimmy Carter, and the Persian monarch spent some of his last days on the island. Contadora's star faded a bit in the 1980s and '90s, but it has recently undergone a renaissance, with the construction of new accommodations and condominiums.

The island's tiny town center is just to the west of the airstrip, to the north and east of which are its two resort hotels, whereas nearly everything to the west is residential. A series of narrow roads winds through the forests that cover most of the island to the stately vacation homes scattered along its coastline, and an inland neighborhood that has some smaller houses. Interestingly, the mansions tend to be Panamanian vacation homes, whereas the more humble abodes tend to belong to foreigners, many of them permanent residents. In the center of the island are a soccer field, a pond, and a small church; to the north lies Playa Ejecutiva, and to the south Playa Cacique, two of the island's nicest beaches. Contadora is small enough to walk everywhere, but given the tropical heat you may want to rent a golf cart or scooter to get around.

Isla Contadora's main attraction is its selection of **beaches** (⇨ Sports & the Outdoors, *below*), and it has a baker's dozen to choose from, plus those of nearby islands. As idyllic as its beaches may be, there is actually a good bit more to do at Isla Contadora. As you explore the island, you may spot white-tailed deer, agoutis (large brown rodents), and any of dozens of bird species, especially the abundant pelicans. There is decent **snorkeling** (⇨ Sports & the Outdoors, *below*) around its many rocky points, though you'll find even better snorkeling at several nearby islands. Though the water is warm most of the year, high winds from December to April can cool it down significantly. Taking a boat trip to some of the surrounding islands is an excellent way to spend a morning or afternoon, and from June to December, you may see humpback whales on those trips. **Isla Pacheca,** 3 mi north of Contadora, has a lovely white-sand beach and a brown pelican rookery where about 8,000 birds nest, whereas the nearby islets of Pachequilla and Bartolomé have good skin-diving and snorkeling spots. **Isla Mogo Mogo** *(Isla Pájaros)* , 4 mi south of Contadora, on the other side of Isla Chapera, has a sugar-sand beach in a deep cove where snorkelers may find sea stars. Tiny Isla Boyarena, just to the south, has a pale sandbar that becomes a beach at low tide.

Captain Marco (☎6689–4916 *or 6605–5057*) offers popular half-day trips to nearby islands on a 26- or 33-foot boat for just $35 per person. He also offers more expensive sportfishing charters.

WHERE TO STAY & EAT

$$$ ⛺**Contadora Pearl Island.** Long known as the Hotel Contadora, the island's original resort has an enviable location on Playa Larga, but despite changes in management and ongoing renovation it remains an iffy place to book a vacation.

WORD OF MOUTH

We recently stayed at Punta Galeon on Contadora. There is a nice pool where you can relax. There is no snorkeling off the beach—you have to take a boat out. In any case, we found the water too cold to be pleasant and didn't go on a boat trip (except for fishing).

–PlumCreek

The ample selection of games and activities, from Ping-Pong to kayaks, and seemingly inexpensive, all-inclusive rates make it a tempting place to take the kids, but after a few buffet dinners here, moms and dads will likely want to hike up the hill to one of the nearby restaurants. Giant fish tanks with filthy glass and a miserable little zoo with cages that are neither humane nor safe for children who might wander near them are just a couple of this hotel's many infractions. Guest rooms in two-story, wooden buildings are nice enough, with colorful fabrics, large balconies, and a small refrigerator, but most of them overlook the pools or grounds—Blocks 1 and 14 have the best views. The beach is lovely, but when full this place can be noisy, crowded, and you can spend a lot of time waiting for service. **Pros: Great location. Cons: Mediocre food, service often poor, can get crowded and noisy.** ✉*Playa Larga, east end of island* ☎*214-3719 or 250-4033* 🖷*264-1178* ⊕*www.hotel-contadora.com* ⇆*326 rooms, 24 suites* ♿*In-room: safe, In-hotel: 4 restaurants, bars, tennis court, pools, gym, beachfront, water sports, no elevator, children's programs (ages 5–12), laundry service* ▤*AE, DC, MC, V* ❍|*AI.*

$$–$$$$ ✕**El Suizo.** Contadora's best (and most expensive) restaurant offers dishes that you would expect to find at a good restaurant in Switzerland—the chef and owner is Swiss—with some local touches. The ample menu includes beef tenderloin, prawns Provençal, and fish of the day prepared various ways, such as with herbs and butter or smothered in hollandaise sauce. The restaurant is a rustic, open-air affair under a thatch roof with a view of what was once the island's golf course and is now a pasture for its deer herd. ✉*On hill between Punta Galeón and Contadora Pearl Island hotels* ☎*6560-3824* ▤*MC, V.*

$$ ✕⛺**Hotel Punta Galeón.** Spread along a rocky point that juts into the
Fodor'sChoice Pacific on the north side of the island, the Hotel Punta Galeón has a
★ wide wooden boardwalk around its perimeter with captivating views of the surrounding sea and waves crashing against the rocks below. Just behind that boardwalk is a series of low, white-stucco buildings with barrel-tile roofs that hold the well-equipped guest rooms, each with a terrace with a view of the ocean through the foliage. Rooms have a very tropical feel, thanks to bright colors, shells decorating the mirrors, and the scenery visible through the picture window. The grounds and large

poolside deck are shaded by huge trees. The open-air restaurant ($–$$) has sea views and is one of the nicer spots to eat on the island, specializing in fresh seafood such as *corvina al ajillo* (sea bass in a garlic sauce) and *camarones* (shrimp) served half a dozen ways, though they also offer a few meat and vegetarian dishes. **Pros: Great views, attractive rooms, beach, good restaurant. Cons: Low ceilings, terraces not private.** ⊠*North of airstrip, next to Playa Galeón* ☎*214–7869 or 250–4220* ⌂*Torre Universal Local 1, Calle 51 y Av Federico Boyd, Bellvista* 📠*269–8749* ⊕*www.hotelpuntagaleonresort.com* 🛏*48 rooms* ⌂*In-room: safe. In-hotel: restaurant, bar, pool, beachfront, water sports, no elevator, laundry service, public Internet, airport shuttle, no-smoking rooms* ☰*AE, MC, V* ⦿*EP.*

$–$$ ✕🖼 **Villa Romántica.** You can't top this small hotel's location, on a ridge
★ just above stunning Playa Cacique, which means all the rooms are just steps away from the beige sand and turquoise waters. The friendly Austrian owner converted his vacation home into this hotel several years ago, making some questionable interior decorating decisions in the process. The giant hearts and bas-relief Grecian nudes on the walls of rooms and the shiny polyester bedspreads may be too much for some travelers. Rooms are quite varied. The Hawaii 1 and 2 rooms, on the bottom floor of the main building, have king-size beds, sliding-glass doors, and ocean views. The Panama and Castle rooms are similar but less private. Two "Panorama" rooms in the top floor have smaller gable windows with nice views, but they share a bathroom. The "Romantic" rooms, with heart motifs, overlook the gardens and minigolf course, but the suite next door has an ocean-view balcony and a round water bed worthy of real swingers. The restaurant ($$–$$$$) is over the beach and has a good menu that ranges from the traditional chateaubriand and chicken cordon bleu to fish of the day—usually mahimahi—served with a selection of sauces. **Pros: Beachfront, good restaurant, friendly owner. Cons: Some tacky decor.** ⊠*Playa Cacique, 200 meters southwest of church* ☎*250–4067* 📠*250–4184* ⊕*www. villa-romantica.com* 🛏*11 rooms, 1 suite* ⌂*In-room: no phone, safe, Wi-Fi. In-hotel: restaurants, beachfront, no elevator, laundry service, airport shuttle, no-smoking rooms* ☰*AE, MC, V* ⦿*BP.*

$ 🖼 **Contadora Island Inn.** This small B&B in a quiet residential neighborhood a 10-minute walk from the beach has some of the most economical rooms on the island. Occupying adjacent ranch houses with decks and a thatched *rancho* overlooking the forest in back, the rooms don't offer a lot of privacy, but they are bright, clean, and share ample common areas, such as the small TV lounge, front porch, and back deck. Guests can use the kitchen, but the best room, Frigata Magnífica, has its own kitchen. The friendly, helpful owners and staff rent bicycles and scooters, and can book day trips. **Pros: Affordable, quiet, clean. Cons: Not on the beach.** ⊠*Paseo Urraca* ☎*250–4067* 📠*250–4184* ⊕*www. contadoraislandinn.com* 🛏*8 rooms* ⌂*In-room: no phone, safe, no TV. In-hotel: bicycles, no elevator, laundry service, airport shuttle, no-smoking rooms* ☰*MC, V* ⦿*CP.*

$ 🖼 **Perla Real Inn.** This attractive B&B was designed to resemble a Span-
Fodor's Choice ish mission, and the owners paid great attention to detail in the process,
★ importing hand-painted tiles and sinks and getting a local carpenter to

make replicas of furniture in southern California missions. The bright rooms have high ceilings with fans and are tastefully decorated with ceramics and fine Mexican carpets. Suites are double the size, with kitchens and breakfast bars, and cost only $35 more. Rooms open onto a courtyard with a fountain, where they serve the complimentary breakfast. The only drawback is that it isn't on a beach—it is in a residential neighborhood a 10-minute walk from Playas Cacique and Ejecutiva. Nevertheless, the inn is quiet, comfortable, and provides the personalized attention that the big resorts don't offer. The owner and manager can arrange day tours, provide free snorkeling equipment, and will rent you a golf cart at a discount. **Pros: Tasteful, friendly, nice rooms. Cons: Not on the beach.** ⊠ *Paseo Urraca 50* ☎️ *250–4095* ⊠ *Apdo. 0843-03073, Balboa* ⊕ *www.perlareal.com* 🛏 *4 rooms, 2 suites* ♿ *In-room: no phone, refrigerator (some), no TV, Wi-Fi. In-hotel: no elevator, laundry service, airport shuttle, no-smoking rooms* ▤ *MC, V* ¶◉¶ *CP.*

¢ ⛺ **Cabañas Contadora.** Travelers on a budget too tight for Contadora's B&Bs can travel like Panamanians and stay at this simple inn behind the airstrip. Its four basic rooms in a two-story building have fans, cold-water baths, and porches with hammocks overlooking the nearby tarmac, though those on the second floor glimpse the sea. You are pretty much on your own here, and it is a bit of a hike to the store, but there is an inexpensive restaurant nearby and it's a short walk to the beach. **Pros: Inexpensive, near beach. Cons: Very basic rooms, far from town.** ⊠ *Behind airstrip, left on dirt road after church* ☎️ *250–4214 or 674–3839* 🛏 *4 rooms* ♿ *In-room: no a/c, no phone. In-hotel: no elevator, airport shuttle, no-smoking rooms* ▤ *No credit cards* ¶◉¶ *EP.*

SPORTS & THE OUTDOORS

BEACHES Because the Pacific tides are so extreme, beaches change considerably through the course of the day; what is a wide swath of sand at low tide is reduced to a sliver at high tide. Two of the beaches are dominated by the island's biggest hotels, and have bars and thatched umbrellas on them, giving the appearance that they are private, but ■ **TIP**→**all beaches in Panama are public property, so you can use any of them, no matter what hotel you stay in.**

Contadora's longest beach, **Playa Larga,** stretches along the island's eastern end, in front of the lamentably mismanaged Contadora Pearl Island resort. It is a lovely strip of ivory sand, backed by coconut palms and Indian almond trees, but at low tide large rock formations are exposed at either end of it. It is Contadora's busiest beach. **Playa Galeón,** just to the north of the airstrip and east of Punta Galeón, is a small beach in a deep bay that is used by the guests at the Hotel Punta Galeón, so it can also get crowded during high season. It is a good swimming beach, and has decent snorkeling along the rocks of nearby Punta Galeón. One

★ of Contadora's quietest beaches is **Playa Ejecutiva,** a few hundred yards north of the church and soccer field, which is backed by a small forest and has attractive thatched structures where the owners of the nearby

★ homes have occasional beach parties. **Playa Cacique,** on the south side of the island, is its loveliest beach, with pale sand backed by tropical

2

trees and vacation homes and Isla Chapera visible across the turquoise waters. If you walk west on Playa Cacique and around a small bluff, you'll come upon a smaller beach called **Playa Camaron.** Hidden in the island's southeast corner, at the end of the road that runs east from Hotel Villa Romantica, is **Playa Suecas,** Contadora's nude beach—be sure to use plenty of sunscreen on those pale parts!

SKIN DIVING   The reefs around Contadora have much less coral than you find in the Caribbean or the western Pacific, but you can see a lot of fish there, some of which gather in big schools. Isla Pachequilla, a small island near Isla Pacheco, is one of the area's best dive spots, with an array of reef fish, as well rays, moray eels, white-tipped reef sharks, and large schools of jacks. The only problem is visibility, which averages 15 to 30 feet, but sometimes tops 45 feet, especially from June to August, though there is less marine life in the area then. The best diving is in December and January, when there is decent visibility and large numbers of fish; visibility is low from February to April. **Coral Dreams** (⊠ *Main road, across from airstrip* ☎ *6536–1776* ⊕ *www.coral-dreams.com*) offers scuba diving at various dive spots, as well as certification courses and snorkeling excursions.

SPORTFISHING   The fishing around Contadora is quite good, which means you can go out for half a day and stand a decent chance of hooking something. The most common fish in the area are dolphin, jacks, tuna, wahoo, rooster-fish, and—in deeper water—snapper and grouper. Anglers sometimes hook sailfish and marlin in the area, but if it's billfish you're after, you'll want to head for the waters south of Isla Del Rey, which requires a full-day charter.

Captain Marco at **Las Perlas Fishing Charters** (☎ *6689–4916 or 6605– 5057*) has a 26-foot boat with one engine for $250 per half day and $500 per full day, and a 33-foot open-hulled boat with twin 200-hp engines for $450 per half day and $800 for a full day. Rods, tackle, snacks, and beverages are included.

TO & FROM AND LOGISTICS

Panama's domestic airlines Aeroperlas and Air Panama have daily flights to Contadora from Aeropuerto Marcos a Gelabert, commonly called Aeropuerto Albrook. The flight takes 20 minutes and round-trip tickets costs less than $100. **Aeroperlas** (☎ *315–7500* ⊕ *www.aeroperlas.com*) has flights to Contadora every morning and evening, with the exception of Sunday morning, plus a Saturday afternoon flight. **Air Panama** (☎ *316–9000* ⊕ *www.flyairpanama.com*) has a morning flight to Contadora every day but Sunday, and evening flights on Fridays and Sundays.

ISLA SAN JOSÉ

90 km (54 mi) southeast of Panama City.

The southernmost island of the Pearl Archipelago, Isla San José is a remote, 14,000-acre isle that is almost completely covered with rain forest, and is lined with dozens of pristine beaches. Its lush forests are home to white-tailed deer, tamandu anteaters, keel-billed toucans, four species of macaws, and thousands of feral pigs. The ocean that surrounds it teems with an even greater diversity of life, and if you snorkel around the rocky islets off its coast you may see snapper, stingrays, parrot fish, and moorish idols. From June to September you may also spot humpback whales offshore. Head out for some fishing near Isla Galera, 25 mi to the east, and you stand the chance of hooking Pacific sailfish and tuna upwards of 100 pounds. The only wildlife that you won't be able to see are the sand fleas (aka no-see-ums), which can be a plague when the winds die down during the rainy season and are the only drawback of an otherwise enchanting isle.

This entire island belongs to one man: Panamanian pilot and entrepreneur George Novey, who also owns Air Panama. Aside from a landing strip, a small oyster farm, and a series of dirt roads built by the U.S. Army during World War II, its only development is his idyllic Hacienda del Mar, a nature lodge that covers a point on the island's western coast. Before Novey acquired it, Isla San José belonged to Earl Tupper, the inventor of Tupperware, who apparently intended to build a housing development there. Before Tupper bought it, the U.S. Army used the island as a training ground and bombing range, and there could be unexploded ordnance in its forests, though apparently, not near Hacienda del Mar. Nevertheless, it's not a place you want to go bushwhacking, nor would you need to, since you can see plenty of wildlife from its roads and beaches, or even from the porch of your bungalow.

One of Isla San José's big attractions is its beaches (⇨ Sports & Outdoors, *below*), which are lined with jungle and slope into blue-green waters peppered with dark, rocky islets.

WHERE TO STAY & EAT

$$$$ ✕▦**Hacienda del Mar.** Perched on a point overlooking the sea, Hacienda
★ del Mar enjoys breathtaking views of the waves crashing against the surrounding islets, an adjacent beach, and forested coastline. Its comfortably rustic bungalows with large balconies that take advantage of the views are nestled in the forest along the ridge. Cane walls, wood ceilings, and hand-carved furniture are harmonious with the surroundings, though the decorations that adorn the walls are an odd mix of Panamanian handicrafts and New England kitsch. VIP suites have full ocean views, and are quite spacious; smaller junior suites are more private and set back from the point—only No. 14 overlooks the sea. The airy second-floor restaurant ($$–$$$$) has a wide balcony with the best view on the property. The menu is strong on seafood, such as paella and lobster thermidor, and fish of the day (usually mahimahi). The round, stone pool is set at the edge of the point. The dark, air-conditioned bar has the hotel's only TV, plus foosball and pool tables. The hotel rents kayaks and snorkeling equipment, and tours include bird-watching, sportfishing, jet skiing, and mountain biking. **Pros: Gorgeous surroundings, outdoor activities, good food, friendly staff. Cons: Expensive, sand fleas, disappointing breakfasts.** ☎264–1787 or 202–0214, 866/433–5627 in the U.S. 🖷264–1787 ⊕www.haciendadelmar.net ⇥12 bungalows, 2 suites ⚑In-room: no phone, safe, no

TV, refrigerator (some). In-hotel: restaurant, bar, pool, beachfront, water sports, no elevator, laundry service, no-smoking rooms ⊟*AE, DC, MC, V* ⑩⑤*CP.*

SPORTS & THE OUTDOORS

BEACHES The most visited beach on the island is **Playa Arenosa**, an attractive stretch of dark-beige sand just to the north of Hacienda del Mar. The Indian Almond trees that rise up behind that beach are often

WORD OF MOUTH

Hacienda del Mar is a small resort but very nicely done on Isla San José . . . All by itself so you are at the mercy of the hotel for meals—but from what I hear they do a good job so that's not such a big deal.

–AndrewW

populated by macaws, and the rocks that surround the adjacent point are an excellent area for snorkeling at high tide. The hotel has a beach house where they provide chairs and umbrellas, and rent kayaks and snorkeling equipment.

SPORTFISHING The sea southeast of Isla San José has some of Panama's best fishing, since the continental shelf ends nearby. Pacific sailfish and blue and black marlin ply those waters most of the year, but they are tough to catch. Anglers are more likely to get amberjack, tuna, dolphin, wahoo, roosterfish, and mackerel. Fishing charters cost $400 to $750 for a half day, which is usually enough to catch some fish, though billfish are always more of a challenge.

TO & FROM AND LOGISTICS

Air Panama (☎*316–9000* ⊕*www.flyairpanama.com*) has evening flights to Isla San José on Monday, Thursday, Friday, and Sunday, but the hotel sometimes schedules charter flights for other days during the dry season. Because of the flight schedule, visitors usually have to spend a minimum of two nights on Isla San José.

THE CENTRAL PACIFIC COAST

The Central Pacific Coast has Panama's most popular beaches, but it does not have Panama's best beaches, nearly all of which are on islands. Due to the organic matter that washes out of the rivermouths along the coast, its beaches tend to have gray or salt-and-pepper sand. Also, the land behind most coastal beaches is almost completely deforested, so they lack the natural settings of the beaches on Isla Contadora or the islands of other regions. The Central Pacific beaches range from Coronado, lined with vacation homes and with little access for tourists, to Farallón (aka Playa Blanca), which has the country's best all-inclusive resort. Several of the region's beaches attract devoted surfers but are backed by dingy towns with low-budget cement-box accommodations blocks from the beach. Though the Central Pacific beaches are geographically close to Panama City, it actually takes longer to reach most of them than it does to visit the Pacific islands, and in some cases, the Caribbean coast. But if you're a surfer or golfer, they're worth the trip.

PLAYA KOBBE (PLAYA BONITA)

7 km (4 mi) southwest of Panama City.

With 2 km (1 mi) of beige sand washed by relatively clear waters and surrounded by tropical forest, Playa Kobbe is a lovely spot. It is also the closest beach to Panama City, a mere 20 minutes from downtown by car, which could be a problem considering that all the city's sewage goes straight into the sea. Nevertheless, the water off Kobbe Beach *looks* clean, and the Intercontinental hotel management claims that lab tests have deemed the water perfectly safe for swimming. During the 1980s and '90s Kobbe was a popular weekend spot for the capital's residents. Before that, it was sequestered in the U.S. Canal Zone, next to the U.S. Army's Fort Kobbe, and received relatively few visitors. Since 2006, however, it has been dominated by the massive Intercontinental Playa Bonita Resort & Spa, built by local construction and hotel mogul Herman Bern, who also owns the Intercontinental Miramar and Gamboa Rainforest Resort. Since the resort owns all the land around the beach and restricts access to it, it is for all practical purposes private, though under Panamanian law all beaches are public property. The name Playa Bonita (beautiful beach) is a PR invention, but given the resort's stature and plans for a housing development there, it will probably replace Playa Kobbe as the beach's official name.

WHERE TO STAY & EAT

$$$$ 🛏 **Intercontinental Playa Bonita Resort & Spa.** It would be hard not to be
★ impressed by this resort's vast lobby, with its polished marble floor,
🕑 soaring arches, and giant wall of windows providing a panoramic view of the gardens, pool, beach, and blue Pacific. The hotel's design mixes Panamanian and Mediterranean motifs—white walls, orchid displays, Spanish tiles, and Grecian domes—that work together surprisingly well. Its 300 guest rooms are in a series of gleaming white five-story buildings that spread out to the east and west of the lobby like the wings of a giant seagull. They are equipped with the amenities you would expect to find at any luxury hotel, and have large balconies with ocean views. The beach is lined with coconut palms, behind which are two restaurants and a bar, several pools, volleyball courts, kayaks, and four-poster beds for massages. The hotel's vast spa is one of the best in the country. **Pros: Nice beachfront, facilities, spa; near Panama City. Cons: Massive, ocean could be polluted, polyester sheets.** ⊠ *7 km (4 mi) southwest of Panama City* 📞 *211–8600, 877/800–1690 in the U.S.* 📠 *316–1463* ⊕ *www.playabonitapanama.com* ⤏ *272 rooms, 28 suites* ⚘ *In-room: safe, refrigerator, Wi-Fi. In-hotel: 3 restaurants, room service, bars, pools, gym, spa, beachfront, water sports, laundry service, concierge, public Wi-Fi, airport shuttle, parking (no fee), no-smoking rooms* 🖃 *AE, MC, V* ⑂*BP.*

TO & FROM AND LOGISTICS

To drive to Kobbe from Panama City, take the Avenida de los Mártires to the Bridge of the Americas and take the first exit after crossing the canal, turning left and following the signs to the Intercontinental Playa Bonita Resort. A taxi from Panama City should cost $20–$25.

PLAYA VERACRUZ

15 km (9 mi) southwest of Panama City.

Panamanians who want to hit the beach but can't make the long drive over the mountains west of La Chorrera to the Central Pacific's nicest beaches usually pop over the canal to Playa Veracruz. It is a working-class beach, with no hotels and only rustic restaurants called *fondas*. On weekends its long stretch of light-brown sand can get pretty busy with families, groups of young people, and an array of vendors, but during the week you can practically have the beach to yourself. The beach is long and good for strolling, and at low tide you can walk out the spit of sand at the end of the beach to Isla Venado—a tiny, forested island. ⚠ **Head back to town once the sun sets—there have apparently been muggings on the beach at night.**

TO & FROM AND LOGISTICS

To drive to Playa Veracruz from Panama City, take Avenida de los Mártires to the Bridge of the Americas, turn off at the second exit after crossing the canal (Farfán and Veracruz), and follow the road around the abandoned airport to the beach. Buses to Veracruz depart from the Terminal de Buses hourly on weekends. If you go by taxi, you'll want to hire it for your entire trip ($10–$15 per hour) to avoid getting stranded there.

OFF THE BEATEN PATH Though **Parque Nacional Altos de Campana** lies just north of the Carretera Interamericana, a mere 50 km (31 mi) west of Panama City, few people take the time to check out its exuberant forests and breathtaking views. The first national park created in Panama, Altos de Campana protects patches of cloud forest on the peaks of a steep and severely deforested mountain ridge to the southwest of La Chorrera. An excellent destination for hikers, thanks to its refreshingly cool climate and 3 km (2 mi) of trails, Altos de Campana is also home to some interesting birds, such as slaty ant wrens, orange-bellied trogons, and hummingbirds not found in the forests around the canal. The summits of Cerro Campana and Cerro de la Cruz, in particular, have dramatic mountain scenery and amazing views. Panama City–based **Futura Travel** (☎*360–2030* ⊕*www.extremepanama.com*) has half-day hiking tours to Altos de Campana that include an ascent of Cerro de La Cruz. To visit the park on your own take the Carretera Interamericana 47 km (29 mi) west from Panama City, turn right 5 km (3 mi) after Capira, and drive another 5 km (3 mi) up a serpentine, paved road to the ranger station; 3 km (2 mi) beyond that are the radio towers where the trails begin. ■TIP→ **You'll need a 4WD vehicle to drive the rough final few kilometers.** ✉*52 km (32 mi) west of Panama City* ☎*232–7223* ✍*$3.50* ⏱*Daily 7–5.*

PLAYA GORGONA

80 km (48 mi) southwest of Panama City.

Gorgona attracts primarily Panamanians with limited budgets. Its beach is narrow, with dark sand, and the town behind it is depressing. The only reason to stop at Playa Gorgona is to surf, since there is a good break east of town at **Playa Malibu.** That rivermouth break has both lefts and rights, and is best at low and middle tides. ⚠**Theft is a problem here, so park on the beach if you have a 4x4 vehicle, or leave your car unlocked with nothing in it.** Another option is to leave your car at the hotel and pay them guard it, or stay there and walk to Playa Malibu.

WHERE TO STAY & EAT

¢–$ 🏨**Cabañas de Playa Gorgona.** This spartan hotel and restaurant at the east end of Playa Gorgona gets packed with Panamanian families during dry-season weekends and holidays, but is often empty the rest of the time. Despite the dreary cement-box rooms with cold-water showers, it is the best option in town for surfers, since you can hike down the beach to the surf break from here. Rooms have kitchenettes and terraces with plastic tables and chairs. In back, by the beach, are a large restaurant, picnic areas, and two pools that are used by guests and day visitors—keep an eye on your things at the pool. The entire compound is surrounded by a chain-link fence. **Pros: Near beach. Cons: Cold shower, spartan rooms.** ✉*Playa Gongona, east of town* ☎*269–2433* 🛏*43 rooms* ♿*In-room: no phone, kitchen, refrigerator. In-hotel: restaurant, pool, beachfront, no elevator, parking (no fee), no-smoking rooms* 🚫*No credit cards* 🍴*EP.*

TO & FROM AND LOGISTICS

To drive to Playa Gorgona, take the Carretera Interamericana west from Panama City for about one hour. Look for the turnoff to Gorgona on the left just after the tiny town of Chame. Turn left when you get to the town to reach the Cabañas and surf break.

PLAYA CORONADO

84 km (52 mi) southwest of Panama City.

From the capital this is the closest decent Central Pacific beach. Playa Coronado began to develop as a weekend destination for wealthy Panamanians decades ago, and today the coast is almost completely lined with weekend homes, leaving very few spots for nonresidents to get onto the beach. The sand is pale gray with swaths of fine black dirt running through it, which gives it a sort of marble appearance, and though it gets some waves it is usually safe for swimming. The big attraction is an 18-hole golf course designed by Tom and George Fazio, which is part of the Coronado Golf & Beach Resort (⇨*below*). One of the country's best golf destinations, the resort is not fancy, but spacious, with plentiful green areas. It is a time-share, and its golf course and other facilities are also part of a private club, so it gets packed with Panamanian families on weekends and holidays, but is practically dead most weekdays. Foreign tourists are always a minority here, which makes it a good place to experience the real Panama. If you are in Playa Coronado on a Saturday, be sure to catch the **horse and folklore show,** which is free with dinner at **Estribo de Plata** (✉*Calle Principal, on left before resort* ☎*240–4444*), a restaurant at the resort's equestrian center that specializes in grilled meat.

WHERE TO STAY & EAT

¢–$$$ ✕**El Rincon's del Chef.** In a pleasant, colonial-style shopping plaza on the road to Coronado, this Panamanian restaurant belongs to Fernando Paredes, who was the executive chef at the nearby golf resort for years before starting his own place. He changes his menu daily, but it always offers a good mix of meat and seafood dishes with predominantly Panamanian preparation but varied international inspiration. There is invariably *corvina* (sea bass), *langostinos* (prawns), and other seafood served with sauces that range from mushroom to mango. He also serves (rather expensive) grilled USDA beef. The building is right out of the 19th century, with terra-cotta floors, ochre walls, and ceiling fans hung from the high wooden beams beneath the barrel-tile roof. ✉*Beginning of road to Coronado, on right* ☎*240–1941* ▤*MC, V.*

$$$ ☗**Coronado Golf & Beach Resort.** Red-tile roofs, archways, beamed ceil-
☾ ings, and painted tiles reflect a hacienda architectural style at this ram-
bling complex that is both a hotel and a country club. As the name suggests, its main attractions are the 18-hole, par-72 golf course and the nearby beach club, which rents kayaks and Jet Skis. However, it also has an equestrian center, and its extensive, landscaped grounds hold several tennis courts, an Olympic-sized pool, Jacuzzis, and a spa. Spacious guest rooms are in a series of two-story buildings scattered around ample grounds with common gardens, porches, and lawns. All rooms are high-ceiling suites with master bedrooms that can be separated from the living room and have wicker furniture, sofa beds, and big windows with views of the golf course or gardens. "Royal suites" have two bedrooms, two bathrooms, and a large balcony. "Residential suites" have full kitchens to boot. The gourmet restaurant upstairs serves dinner only, the spacious open-air restaurant by the pool is known for its Sunday lunch buffet. The beach is nearly a kilometer (½-mi) away from the rooms and greens, though sporadic transportation shuttles guests there. **Pros: Golf course, spacious rooms, ample facilities. Cons: Not on beach, very busy on weekends.** ✉*Playa Coronado, Calle Principal, left at Brigada de Bomberos* ☎*264–2863 or 240-4444, 866/465–3207 in the U.S.* 🖷*223–8513* ⊕*www.coro-
nadoresort.com* ⬲*77 suites* ⚅*In-room: safe, kitchen (some), refrig-
erator, Wi-Fi. In-hotel: 3 restaurants, bars, golf course, tennis courts, pools, gym, spa, beachfront, water sports, children's programs (ages 4–10), laundry service, public Wi-Fi, airport shuttle, parking (no fee), no-smoking rooms* ▤*AE, DC, MC, V* ⭘|*EP.*

$ ☗**Hotel Gaviota.** This small hotel and day resort at the west end of Playa Coronado sits behind one of the widest parts of the beach, next to a river mouth, which keeps the water murky here during the rainy months. Its large restaurant, pool, and lawn strewn with picnic areas cater to crowds of Panamanians on weekends and holidays, when you can get a $15 day pass that includes lunch, a welcome cocktail, and use of the beach and facilities. The guest rooms are in several buildings set back from the beach, and while they won't win any design awards, they are clean and comfortable, with red-tile floors, wicker furniture, kitchenettes, and covered terraces furnished with plastic chairs and tables. To get here, drive to the end of the main road and turn right at the market. **Pros: Clean, covered terraces. Cons: Murky water in rainy season.** ⊠*Playa Coronado, end of Paseo George Smith* ☎*240–4526 or 224–9056* ☞*9 rooms* ☆*In-room: no phone, kitchen, refrigerator. In-hotel: restaurant, pool, beachfront, no elevator, parking (no fee), no-smoking rooms* ▤*MC, V* ⦿|*EP.*

SPORTS & THE OUTDOORS

GOLF   The **Coronado Golf & Beach Resort** (☎*240–3137*) has an 18-hole, par-72 golf course designed by Tom and George Fazio, which makes it a popular destination for golfers. The course is also open to nonguests, who sometimes drive the hour west of Panama City for a day of golf. The greens fee for 18 holes is $125, which includes golf-cart rental and lunch. They also rent clubs, and have a par-27, 9-hole executive course that is better for beginners and younger golfers. Bilingual golf pros hold classes for golfers of all ages and skill levels.

SHOPPING

The **Centro Artesanal de Coronado** (⊠*Road to Playa Coronado, on right* ☎*No phone*) has a collection of tiny shops in what resembles the central square of a traditional Panamanian village. Each building holds several small shops selling different Panamanian handicrafts, such as hammocks, hats, and jewelry, as well as beach wear. None of the shops accepts credit cards.

TO & FROM AND LOGISTICS

There is no public transportation to Coronado, but the Coronado Golf & Beach Resort provides a shuttle for guests from Panama City for $30, with a two-passenger minimum. It is also an easy drive; take the Carretera Interamericana west from Panama City one hour, and look for the turnoff next to a large shopping center on the left, just after the town of Chame. You'll have to stop at a guardhouse, then look for the golf resort on the left. For Hotel Gaviota, head all the way to where the road veers left, after a tiny supermarket, and turn right onto Paseo George Smith.

PLAYA EL PALMAR

93 km (58 mi) southwest of Panama City.

One of the less attractive beaches on the Central Pacific coast, tiny Playa Palmar is a mecca for surfers, since it has one of the country's most accessible surf breaks and reasonably priced accommodations. Nonsurfers have no reason to stop at El Palmar, and should keep driving to Playa Santa Clara, which has a wider, whiter beach and nicer accommodations.

WHERE TO STAY & EAT

¢–$ 🏠 **Palmar Surf Camp.** The best spot for surfers, around the corner from the breaks, this place has rooms in a two-story building set back from the beach, though close enough to hear the crashing of the waves when the surf is up. Rooms are air-conditioned, with small bathrooms, and either one queen or two single beds. Two suites at the end of the building have kitchenettes, and three beds each. Rooms cost $10 less during the week, which the best time to come if you want to surf without a crowd. Basic meals and cold beers are available beneath a thatch roof just behind the beach. The hotel rents surfboards and kayaks, and gives surfing lessons. **Pros: Activities, near beach, small camping area. Cons: Crowded weekends.** ⊠ *Playa Palmar, just before end of road* ☎*240–8004* ✐*palmarsurfcamp@yahoo.com* ⇨*8 rooms, 2 suites* ⌂*In-room: no phone. In-hotel: restaurant, pool, beachfront, no elevator, parking (no fee), no-smoking rooms* ☰*No credit cards* ⦿*EP.*

SPORTS & THE OUTDOORS

SURFING Waves are the only reason to come to Playa El Palmar, which has two breaks. The beach break has lefts and rights, and can be ridden at any size by surfers with any level of experience, though it tends to close out at lower tides. The right point break nearby is for experienced surfers only, since the wave breaks over a stone platform, and it is only rideable when the tide is high and the swell is big. El Palmar can get crowded on weekends and holidays, especially during the dry season, but the surf is best in the rainy season, when you may have the break to yourself on weekdays.

TO & FROM AND LOGISTICS

To drive to Playa El Palmar, take the Carretera Interamericana west from Panama City for about 90 minutes and look for the entrance on the left after San Carlos. El Palmar is one of the few beaches that you can reach by public transportation. Buses to any of the destinations farther west—Penonomé, Aguadulce, Santiago, or Chitré—can drop you off across the highway from the entrance. From there it is a quarter-mile walk to the beach. Those buses depart from the Terminal de Buses in Albrook every 20 or 30 minutes.

PLAYA SANTA CLARA

112 km (69 mi) southwest of Panama City.

Playa Santa Clara is one of the Central Pacific coast's nicest beaches, with plenty of pale sand and good water for swimming. It is just east of Farallón (Playa Blanca), which has two big, all-inclusive resorts, but Santa Clara's hotels are comparatively small, and cater mostly to Panamanians. On the western end of the beach is the tiny fishing village of Santa Clara, where dozens of small boats are anchored offshore, and visible from the beach is **Isla Farallón,** a giant, pale rock that has decent snorkeling around it. On dry-season weekends and school holidays, Panamanians flock to this beach, which has a couple of restaurants and picnic areas for rent on it, but is quiet any other time.

WHERE TO STAY & EAT

¢–$ ✕▦ **Cabañas Las Veraneras.** The rambling restaurant ($) on the beach
★ is the primary business here, but they also offer economical accommodations. Four rustic rooms above the restaurant, with high thatch roofs and tiny bathrooms, are right on the beach, but unfortunately the restaurant blasts music day and night. Two-story bungalows perched along the ridge behind the restaurant have ocean views and are quieter,

though you'll hear the music on weekend nights. Each has a double bed downstairs and three singles in the loft, and a small porch with hammocks. The quietest rooms are behind the ridge in cement buildings, with air-conditioning, cable TV, and terraces that view a small forest. A large pool nearby is surrounded by a lawn and a small bar open on weekends. The restaurant serves a wide variety of Panamanian food, from *corvina con camarones* (sea bass in shrimp sauce) to *churrasco*, grilled strip sirloin. **Pros: On beach, inexpensive, nice pool. Cons: Mediocre rooms, crowded and loud on weekends/holidays.** ✉*Playa Santa Clara, 2 km south of CA1, veer right at Y, end of road* ☎*993–3313* 🖷*993–2628* 🛏*27 rooms* 🛆*In-room: no a/c (some), no phone. In-hotel: restaurant, bar, beachfront, no elevator, parking (no fee), no-smoking rooms* ▤*AE, MC, V* ⦿*EP.*

$$ 🏨**Las Sirenas.** Families frequent Las Sirenas, since each bungalow can sleep four to six people, albeit some on the foam cushions that serve as couches by day, and it is on a quieter stretch of beach. The nicest of these cement cottages are on a ridge, and have great ocean views past the palm trees, bougainvillea, and other foliage. Decorated in yellow and blue, the bungalows have high ceilings, an air-conditioned bedroom, a well-stocked kitchen, breakfast bar, living room with fans, and a big front terrace with a table, chairs, hammock, and grill. Those down the hill, on the beach, are slightly smaller and not as bright, but are mere steps from the sea; they share a lawn with common grills and a playground. There are restaurants down the road, but this place was designed for people who want to do their own cooking. The shopping center at the entrance to Coronado has a supermarket. **Pros: Nice beach, spacious bungalows. Cons: No pool, no restaurant.** ✉*Playa Santa Clara, 2 km south of CA1, bear left at Y and turn right at end of road* ☎*263–7577 or 993–3235* ⊕*www.lassirenas.com* 🛏*10 rooms* 🛆*In-room: no phone, safe, kitchen, refrigerator, Wi-Fi. In-hotel: beachfront, no elevator, parking (no fee), no-smoking rooms* ▤*MC, V* ⦿*EP.*

¢–$ 🏨**Hotel Vida Abundante.** Set back about 1 km from the beach, this small, American-owned hotel offers Santa Clara's most economical rooms, and is a quiet, Christian alternative to the party atmosphere that dominates the beach on weekends. The hotel's antipartying policy is posted in every room, and Bible scriptures have been written on the walls with markers. The rooms themselves are simple but clean, ranging from small doubles with one queen bed to larger rooms with two or three beds in a house that has a kitchen guests can use. **Pros: Quiet, pool. Cons: No restaurant, far from beach, no booze allowed.** ✉*Playa Santa Clara, 1 km south of CA1, bear right at Y and turn right at end of road* ☎*202–1347* 🛏*9 rooms* 🛆*In-room: no phone, no TV. In-hotel: pool, no elevator, parking (no fee), no-smoking rooms* ▤*AE, MC, V* ⦿*EP.*

TO & FROM AND LOGISTICS

To drive to Playa Santa Clara, take the Carretera Interamericana (CA1) west from Panama City for about 90 minutes and look for the entrance on the left at Santa Clara.

PLAYA FARALLÓN (PLAYA BLANCA)

115 km (71 mi) southwest of Panama City.

For years, few people visited the long stretch of white beach between the fishing villages of Santa Clara and Farallón because it lay beneath a military base used by Panama's national guard. A landing strip built by the U.S. government during World War II bisects the Inter-American Highway at Farallón, and former dictator Manuel Noriega had a weekend home on the coast there, so access to the area was restricted. The base saw heavy fighting during the 1989 U.S. invasion, and for much of the 1990s its buildings, pockmarked with bullet holes, were slowly being covered with jungle. Everything changed at the beginning of the 21st century, when the Colombian hotel chain Decameron opened a massive resort here and began promoting it as "Playa Blanca" (White Beach). Now the area has an 18-hole golf course, a second all-inclusive resort on the other side of the Farallón River, and various housing developments under construction.

WHERE TO STAY & EAT

$$–$$$$ 🖼 **Royal Decameron Beach Resort.** This rambling vacation city is one of
★ Panama's most attractive beach hotels. Its 1,020 rooms are in 50 four-
☾ story buildings scattered along 2 km of beach. Sidewalks and narrow roadways cruised by shuttle buses wind their way between those units through luxuriant grounds shaded by massive tropical trees, which also hold six pools, 11 restaurants, 11 bars, a game room, gym, aquatic center, and legions of beach chairs. The rooms have large bathrooms and balconies or terraces—those that do cost more, and are worth it. Meal options range from massive buffets to restaurants specializing in seafood, Japanese, Thai, and Italian, but the food isn't spectacular. Nor are the nightly shows, performed in an amphitheater below the main restaurant, in which dancers bedazzle vacationers with loud music and lots of hip shaking. The myriad daytime activities include kayaking, paddle-boating, windsurfing, horseback riding, tennis, and volleyball. For a small fee you can rent Jet Skis, play golf, fish, go diving or snorkeling around nearby Farallón Island, or rejuvenate at the spa. Reserve early, since the hotel often fills up. **Pros: Nice beach and grounds, lots of activities, good Web rates. Cons: Mass tourism, mediocre food, lots of lines.** ☎993–2255 or 214–3535, 800/279–3718 in U.S. 📠993–2415 or 214–8059 ⊕*www.decameron. com* 📞*960 rooms, 60 junior suites* ⌂*In-room: safe, refrigerator. In-hotel: 11 restaurants, bars, tennis courts, pools, gym, spa, beachfront, water sports, children's programs (ages 4–12), laundry service, public Internet, airport shuttle, parking (no fee), no-smoking rooms* 🖃*AE, DC, MC, V* ⧀*AI.*

$$$ 🖼 **Playa Blanca Beach Resort.** With fewer than a quarter the number of rooms as the nearby Royal Decameron, Playa Blanca is definitely the lesser beach resort, though it is less a case of "size matters" than of design and location. The resort's Grecian-style white buildings are surrounded by grounds that were clearly bulldozed clean before construction began, because there is little shade to be found outside of the thatch-roof structures that surround the pools. The beach has swaths of black in its white sand, and because the hotel is next to a river mouth, the ocean is often murky there. The bright and spacious rooms are well equipped, with wicker furniture and balconies or terraces; most overlook the pool or grounds—the few that have ocean views are worth the additional $20. Shows are performed nightly by the pool, and there are a tiny discotheque, a gift shop, and an aquatic center that provides free kayaks and pedal boats and sells an array of tours. **Pros: On beach, nice rooms, low-season discounts. Cons: Murky sea, mediocre food, surrounded by construction sites.** ☎*993–2912 or 888/790-5264* 🖷*993–2917* ⊕*www.playablancaresort.com* ⇱*219 rooms, 3 suites* ⌂*In-room: safe. In-hotel: 3 restaurants, bars, tennis court, pools, beachfront, water sports, children's programs (ages 4–12), laundry service, public Internet, airport shuttle, parking (no fee), no-smoking rooms* ▤*AE, DC, MC, V* ⑪*AI.*

SPORTS & THE OUTDOORS

GOLF The Royal Decameron Beach Resort's **Mantaraya Golf Club** (☎*986– 1915*) has an 18-hole, par-72 golf course designed by Randall Thompson that lies just inland from the hotel. Greens fees for 18 holes are $35 weekdays and $60 weekends and holidays. Greens fees for nine holes are $25 weekdays and $40 weekends. Cart rental costs $11 for nine holes and $22 for 18. Club rentals range from $15 to $25, according to their condition.

TO & FROM AND LOGISTICS

To drive to Playa Blanca, take the Carretera Interamericana west from Panama City for about 90 minutes and look for the hotel entrances on the left after Santa Clara—the entrance to the Playa Blanca Beach Resort is 2 km (1 mi) after the entrance to the Royal Decameron and Tucán Country Club; they are well marked. Both resorts provide shuttle services from Tocumen Airport and Panama City hotels for $32.

THE CORDILLERA CENTRAL

Mountains rise up to the north of the Central Pacific coast, offering a refreshing alternative to the hot and deforested lowlands a short drive from the beaches. The massif to the southwest of Panama City is an extinct volcano that was in eruption 5 million years ago, which forms the eastern extreme of the Cordillera Central, the country's longest mountain range. On the eastern slope of that verdant mountain is Parque Nacional Altos de Campana; its western slope holds Cerro de la Vieja. The highest point of the range is Cerro Gaitál, a forested hill more than 3,500 feet above sea level that towers over El Valle de Antón, the ancient volcano's crater. Both Cerro de la Vieja and El Valle de Antón are cool and verdant refuges where you can take a break from the lowland heat, explore the mountain forests, and do a bit of bird-watching and hiking. El Valle is a well-established destination with an array of hotels and restaurants, but Cerro la Vieja, to the northeast of Penonomé, has just one eco-lodge.

EL VALLE DE ANTÓN

125 km (78 mi) southwest of Panama City; 28 km (17 mi) north of Las Uvas: the turnoff from Carretera Interamericana.

A serpentine road winds north from the Carretera Interamericana between Playa Coronado and Playa Farallón to a small, lush mountain valley and the town that is sheltered in it, both called El Valle de Antón, commonly referred to as El Valle (The Valley). That verdant valley has a refreshing climate, an abundance of trees and birds, and an array of outdoor activities. Thanks to its altitude of approximately 2,000 feet above sea level, the temperature in El Valle usually hovers in the 70s, and at night it often dips down into the 60s, which means you may need a light jacket. El Valle has long been a popular weekend and holiday destination for Panama City's wealthier citizens, and the roads to the north and south of its Avenida Principal are lined with comfortable vacation homes with large lawns and gardens. In fact, one of those streets is called Calle de los Milionarios (millionaires' row).

Avenida Principal belies the beauty of El Valle's remote corners, resembling the main drag of any Panamanian town, with ugly Chinese-owned supermarkets and other uninspiring cement-block structures. The attractions for travelers are the flora and fauna of the protected forests north and west of town center, the varied hiking, mountain-biking, and horseback-riding routes, and the colorful crafts market, which is especially lively on weekends. Since El Valle has long been popular with Panamanian tourists, it has developed some touted but tepid attractions that can be skipped, such as its tiny hot springs, Pozos Termales, and the "square trees," or *arboles cuadrados,* behind the old Hotel Campestre.

Bowl-shaped El Valle was the crater of a volcano that went extinct millions of years ago. This is apparent when you view it from the *mirador* (lookout point) on the right as the road begins its descent into town—a worthwhile stop. The former crater's walls have eroded into a series of steep ridges that are covered with either luxuriant vegetation or the pale-green pasture that has replaced it. El Valle's volcanic soil has long made it an important vegetable-farming area, but as outsiders bought up the land on the valley's floor, the farming and ranching moved to its periphery, to the detriment of the native forests. Thankfully, large tracts of wilderness have been protected in the Cerro Gaitál Natural Monument and adjacent Chorro el Macho Ecological Reserve.

NORTH AND WEST OF TOWN

★ El Valle's northern edge is protected within the 827-acre (335-hectare) nature reserve **Monumento Natural Cerro Gaitál** *(Cerro Gaitál Natural Monument),* which covers the hills of Cerro Gaitál, Cerro Pajita, and Cerro Caracoral. Cerro Gaitál is a steep, forest-draped hill that towers over the valley's northern edge, rising to a summit of more than 3,500 feet above sea level. The lush wilderness that covers it is home to more than 300 bird species, including such spectacular creatures as the red-legged honeycreeper, bay-headed tanager, and blue-crowned motmot. It also protects the habitat of the rare golden toad (*Atelo-*

pus zeteki), which has been wiped out in the wild by a fungal disease during the past decade. The bird-watching is best along the edges of that protected area, since its lush foliage provides too many hiding places for those feathered creatures. The areas around El Nispero, Los Mandarinos hotel, and the old Hotel Campestre are excellent for bird-watching. The trail to Cerro Gaitál's summit is on the right just west of Los Mandarinos, and the hike up and back takes two to three hours, depending on how much bird-watching you do. It requires good shoes and decent physical condition, and is best done with a guide. Even if you don't make it to the summit, you should try to climb up to the mirador (lookout point), part of the way up, which provides

> **LEGEND OF THE SLEEPING INDIAN GIRL**
>
> The partially forested ridge on the valley's far western edge is said to resemble the profile of a sleeping woman, and is known locally as the **India Dormida** (sleeping Indian girl). Legend has it that the daughter of Chief Urraca, who led local resistance to Spanish colonization, fell in love with a conquistador, thus betraying her people and the Indian brave who loved her. When the brave committed suicide by throwing himself off a precipice, the girl wandered into the forest and died of grief; her spirit entered the mountain, which now has her form.

a panoramic vista of the valley, the Pacific coast, and, on a clear morning, the Caribbean coast. ⊠ *Take right off Av. Principal at Supermercado Hong Kong, left after 1.2 km, trail on right after entrance to Los Mandarinos* ☏ *No phone* 🏷 *$3.50* 🕙 *Daily 6–6.*

☾ **Fodor'sChoice** ★ El Valle's most user-friendly forest experience is available at the small, private **Refugio Ecológico del Choro Macho** *(Chorro el Macho Ecological Reserve)*, west of Cerro Gaitál. The reserve has well-kept trails, walking sticks, and the option of hiring a guide at the gate. It belongs to Raul Arias, who also owns the adjacent Canopy Lodge, and it contains one of El Valle's major landmarks, **El Choro Macho,** a 115-foot cascade surrounded by lush foliage. You're not allowed to swim beneath the waterfall, but there is a lovely swimming pool fed by river water to the left upon entering the reserve, so bring your bathing suit and a towel. Enter the gate to the left of the main entrance to reach the pool. The refuge has a tour called **Canopy Adventure** (⇨ *Sports & Outdoors, below*), which can take you flying through the treetops and over the waterfall on zip lines strung between platforms high in trees. Most visitors are happy to simply explore the trails that loop through the lush forest past the waterfall and over a small suspension bridge that spans a rocky stream. ⊠ *2½ km (1½ mi) northwest of church, at west end of Av. Principal, on left* ☏ *983–6547* 🏷 *$2.50, guided hike $25* 🕙 *Daily 8–5.*

A short drive to the west of the Mercado (⇨ *below*), at the end of a rough road and trail, is a simple remnant of El Valle's pre-Columbian culture called **Piedra Pintada,** a 15-foot boulder, the underside of which is covered with a bizarre collection of ancient petroglyphs. To get there, turn right at the end of the Avenida Principal and left onto the second

2

road after the bridge, then drive to the end of that road, where a foot path heads to the nearby boulder. Kids sometimes hang out around the rock and explain the significance of the petroglyphs to visitors in Spanish, in hopes of extracting a tip. ⚠ **Cars left at the trailhead have been broken into, so don't leave any valuables in your vehicle, and leave the doors unlocked to avoid broken windows.** ⊠ *End of Calle La Pintada* 📷*No phone* 🎫*Free* 🕙*24 hrs.*

IN TOWN

The town center is basically the area west of the market, where you will find the library and the town church, **Iglesia de San José** (⊠*Av. Prinicpal, on left two blocks after Mercado* 📷*No phone* 🎫*Free* 🕙*Sun. 10–2*), which is more a reference point than a sight. On the other side of an attractive garden to the left of the church is a tiny museum, **Museo del Valle,** which, together with the church, is only open on Sunday. Its meager collection includes some religious statues and pre-Columbian ceramic pieces.

★ One traditional tourist attraction that you will definitely want to check out is the **Mercado,** an open–air bazaar under a high red roof on the left side of the Avenida Principal, two blocks before the church. The market is most interesting on weekends, especially Sunday mornings, when vendors and shoppers arrive from far and wide. Locals go to the market to buy fresh fruit, vegetables, baked goods, and plants. Handicrafts sold here include the *sombrero pintao* (a traditional straw hat), handmade jewelry, soapstone sculptures, and knickknacks such as the various renditions of El Valle's emblematic golden toad. Even if you don't want to buy anything, it's worth checking out, since it is a colorful, festive affair. The shops just to the east of the market have a comparable, if not better selection of handicrafts. ⊠*Av. Prinicpal, on left two blocks before church* 📷*No phone* 🎫*Free* 🕙*Daily 8–6.*

🐣 **El Nispero,** a private zoo and plant nursery, is a good place to take the kids, even though most of the animals are in lamentably small cages. The zoo covers nearly 7 acres at the foot of Cerro Gaitál and is one of the only places you can see the extremely rare golden toad, which has been wiped out in the wild by a fungal disease. Those attractive little yellow-and-black anurans—often mistakenly called frogs—are on display at the **El Valle Amphibian Research Center,** funded by several U.S. zoos. Biologists at the center are studying the fungus that is killing the species (*Batrachochytrium dendrobatidis*), while facilitating the toad's reproduction in a fungus-free environment. The zoo has many other Panamanian species that you are unlikely to see in the wild, such as endangered ocelots and margays (spotted felines), collared peccaries (wild pigs), white-faced capuchin monkeys, tapirs, toucans, parrots, and various macaw species. Exotic species such as Asian golden pheasants and white peacocks run the grounds. Most of the animals at El Nispero are former pets that were donated to the zoo, or confiscated from their owners by government authorities. The tapirs, for example, belonged to former dictator Manuel Noriega. ⊠*Calle Carlos Arosemena, 1½ km (1 mi) north of Av. Principal* 📷*983–6142* 🎫*$2* 🕙*Daily 8–5.*

A small but educational menagerie can be found at the **Serpentario Maravillas Tropicales** *(Tropical Wonders Serpentarium)* , an exhibit of a dozen snake species, frogs, iguanas, tarantulas, and scorpions a couple of blocks north of the Avenida Principal. It belongs to Mario Urriola, one of the valley's top nature guides, who is often on hand to tell about the creatures on display. ⊠ *Off Calle Rana Dorada* ☎ *6569–2676* 🗐 *$2* ⊙ *Daily 8–7.*

WHERE TO STAY & EAT

$$$$
Fodor's Choice
★

🔟 **Canopy Lodge.** Nestled in the forest overlooking the boulder-strewn Guayabo River, this lovely lodge is dedicated to nature in all its glory. Its attractions are honeycreepers, euphonias, hummingbirds and the other 300 bird species found in the surrounding forest. The sister lodge of the Canopy Tower, near Panama City (you get a deal on weeklong packages that combine the two lodges), this place is more attractive and comfortable. Its bright, spacious rooms in a two-story cement building open onto wide balconies that overlook the river and forest. They have two queen beds, sliding screens, and ceiling fans; corner "suites" have king beds and lots of windows. Meals are served family-style in an airy restaurant-lounge with a self-service bar. There is a good natural-history library, but not one TV to be found. Though rates are steep, they include tours led by an expert guide, three meals, and wine with dinner. There is a minimum two-night stay, which is what you need to appreciate this place. **Pros: Gorgeous setting, nice rooms, abundant birds, guide, good food, friendly, quiet. Cons: Expensive, two-night minimum, set meals.** ⊠ *2 km past church on road to Chorro Macho* ☎ *264–5720 or 983–6837, 800/930–3397 in the U.S.* 🖷 *263–2784* 🖃 *Apdo. 0832-2701 WTC, Panama City* ⊕ *www.canopylodge.com* 🖘 *12 rooms* ⚛ *In-room: no a/c, no phone, safe, no TV. In-hotel: restaurant, no elevator, laundry service, parking (no fee), no-smoking rooms* ⊟ *AE, MC, V* ¶⊙¶ *FAP.*

$–$$$
Fodor's Choice
★

✕ **La Casa de Lourdes.** After years of running one of Panama City's most popular restaurants, Golosinas, Lourdes Fabrega de Ward built this elegant place across from her retirement home so that she wouldn't get bored. It now seems unlikely that she will ever retire, since former Golosinas clients and a growing list of new fans pack the place on weekends, drawn by Lourdes' inventive menu and the magical ambience of her Tuscan-style *casa.* Meals are served on a back terrace with views of a garden and nearby Cerro Gaitál framed by high columns, arches, and an elegant lap pool. It is truly a house, and you enter through a spacious living room with couches, a piano, and family photos. The menu changes, but is likely include *yucca* (cassava) croquets with a Thai sauce, blackened *corvina* (sea bass) with a tamarind sauce, and the *Cassoulet de Lulu,* a stew of white beans, lamb, duck, pork, and sausages. Save room for desserts such as the Heart Attack: a chocolate sundae atop a chocolate cake. This place is so special that people have been known to helicopter in from Panama City for lunch. ⊠ *Calle Ciclo, behind Hotel Los Mandarinos, 1.2 km north and 800 meters west of Supermercado Hong Kong* ☎ *983–6450* 🖆 *Reservations essential on weekends* ⊟ *MC, V.*

2

$$ ⚟**Los Mandarinos.** Like its sister restaurant, Casa de Lourdes, this small
★ hotel and spa are built in the Tuscan style—stone and stucco walls, bar-
rel-tile roofs—which the Panamanian owner fell in love with during an
Italian vacation. The style is not entirely incongruous in highland El
Valle, but the architects went overboard on the small Tuscan windows
that shortchange guests on the views. Spring for a superior room or
a suite, which have balconies and big windows. The hotel sits at the
foot of Cerro Gaitál, just steps away from the trail that leads to its
summit, and is the perfect spot for morning walks and bird-watching.
All rooms have high ceilings, paintings by Panama's best artists, and
the same amenities provided by any of the country's top hotels. If you
can afford it, the Gaitál Suite has the best view, and the Honeymoon
Suite, overlooking the valley, is a close second. The spa has an array
of treatments and a Jacuzzi and sundeck on the roof. **Pros: Great loca-
tion, excellent restaurant, well-equipped rooms, friendly staff. Cons:
Standard "executive rooms" lack views.** ⊠*800 meters west of Calle
El Ciclo* ☎☎*983–6645* ⊕*www.lacasadelourdes.com* ⤶*13 rooms, 4
suites* ⌂*In-room: safe, kitchen (some), refrigerator, Wi-Fi. In-hotel:
restaurants, pool, spa, no elevator, laundry service, public Wi-Fi, park-
ing (no fee), no-smoking rooms* ☰*MC, V* ⓞ*BP.*

$–$$ ⚟**The Golden Frog Inn.** One of the best deals in El Valle, this attractive
Fodor'sChoice B&B near Cerro Gaitál has bright rooms surrounded by 2½ acres of
★ gardens and lovely views. Built by a retired sea captain, it now belongs
to another captain, Larry Thormahlen, and his wife Becky, who make
a stay here that much more enjoyable. On their extra-big front porch,
with tables, chairs, and hammocks, they serve complimentary breakfasts and a glass of wine during social hour, when guests gather to
watch the sunset. Another perk is the small pool surrounded by a stone
deck and abundant flowers. Rooms in back have tile floors, wood ceilings, and varied views. The cheapest have two single beds, the slightly
larger No. 6 has a queen bed and more windows, and is nestled against
the forest. The spacious "suites" have big windows, high ceilings, and
private patios, and they don't cost much more; Suite 3 looks out over
the India Dormida. Massages or breakfast can be arranged in your
room. Guests can use a small kitchen by the pool. **Pros: Friendly owners, pool, lovely grounds, great views, quiet. Cons: No bar or restaurant, 2 km from town.** ⊠*1½ km (1 mi) north of Texaco Station, dirt
road on right* ☎*983–6117* ⊕*www.goldenfroginn.com* ⤶*6 rooms*
⌂*In-room: no a/c, no phone, no TV. In-hotel: pool, no elevator, laundry service, public Wi-Fi, parking (no fee), no-smoking rooms* ☰*No
credit cards* ⓞ*BP.*

$–$$ ⚟**Park Eden.** This lovely collection of houses and rooms surrounded
★ by manicured gardens, great trees, and a babbling brook is one of El
☺ Valle's more pleasant spots. Owners Lionel and Monica Alemán transformed their vacation home into a B&B upon retiring, and the accommodations are certainly homey, with frilled curtains and bedspreads,
knickknacks, and cement ducks on the lawn. Ideal for families is either
the two-bedroom Linda Vista cottage with a full kitchen, gas grill, fold-
out couch, and an adjacent room with a bunk bed, or the suites with
three beds. Two rooms in the back of the original home are less expen-

sive: Limoneros, a yellow room, has a lovely private terrace, and the very pink Ma Vie En Rose has a slightly smaller patio. The policy here is to pamper, as is apparent in the sumptuous breakfasts, dinners, and attention provided by the charming, bilingual owners. **Pros: Friendly owners, nice gardens. Cons: Far from center of town.** ⊠ *Calle Espave, 100 meters south of Rincón Vallero* 🏠🏠*983–6167* ⊕*www.parkeden. com* ➡*3 rooms, 2 suites, 1 cottage* ⚒*In-room: no a/c (some), no phone, kitchen (some), refrigerator (some). In-hotel: bicycles, no elevator, laundry service, public Wi-Fi, parking (no fee), no-smoking rooms* ☱*AE, MC, V* ⑩*BP.*

$ ✕🖼**Los Capitanes.** This friendly little hotel on the northern side of the valley is owned by a retired German sea captain, who is usually there to offer advice on what to do during your stay. It is one of El Valle's older hotels, but is well maintained, with verdant grounds bordered by a stream in back. Rooms are rather simple, with red-cement floor and white-stucco walls, cane furniture, and corrugated metal ceilings. The nicest standard rooms are on the left in the back, since they have small terraces from which you can admire Cerro Gaitál. Family suites are spacious, semicircular structures with bedroom lofts, lots of furniture (including rocking chairs), and wraparound balconies with great views. The octagonal restaurant ($–$$) serves good German and Panamanian dishes. The owner extends the Panamanian senior discount to tourists, which is unusual. **Pros: Nice grounds, views, friendly owner, good price. Cons: Average rooms, some dark.** ⊠ *Calle El Ciclo, 0.7 km north of Supermercado Hong Kong* 🏠*983–6080* 🏠*983–6505* ⊕*www.los-capitanes.com* ➡*11 rooms, 4 suites* ⚒*In-room: no a/c, no phone, refrigerator (some). In-hotel: restaurant, room service, bar, no elevator, bicycles, no elevator, laundry service, public Internet, parking (no fee), no-smoking rooms* ☱*AE, MC, V* ⑩*BP.*

$ ✕🖼**Rincón Vallero.** Once the valley's best restaurant and hotel, the
☾ Rincón Vallero has gotten mixed reviews of late. Its rooms, in particular, have been left in the dust by the competition. Still, the open-air restaurant ($–$$) is a wonderful spot, like something out of a fairy tale, with stone floors, lots of plants, a fish pond, and a stream running through it. The selection ranges from traditional Panamanian *sancocho* (chicken soup with tropical tubers) to chicken cordon bleu and filet mignon. Rooms, in the back, open onto a small yard and garden, with a playhouse, swing set, and a tiny pool and Jacuzzi surrounded by a stone terrace. They are a bit cramped and dark, with low, beamed ceilings, but are equipped with such amenities as DVD players and minibars. The suites and junior suites are considerably nicer, with high cane ceilings and big bathrooms. **Pros: Charming restaurant and gardens, nice suites, kid-friendly. Cons: Standard rooms cramped and dark, low ceilings; down rough roads.** ⊠ *Calle Espave, southern end of valley, 1 km from main road; turn left after bridge and veer right at Y* 🏠*983–6175 or 271–5935* 🏠*983–6791* ⊕*www.rinconvallero.com* ➡*13 rooms, 4 suites* ⚒*In-room: safe, DVD. In-hotel: restaurant, room service, no elevator, laundry service, parking (no fee), no-smoking rooms* ☱*AE, MC, V* ⑩*BP.*

2

¢–$ ✕**Bruchetta.** This small Italian restaurant in the corner of what was once the town gas station has a small covered terrace where you can watch the townsfolk roll by. The food is usually quite good, with an ample selection of salads, half a dozen different bruschettas, plenty of pastas, *corvina* (sea bass), salmon, beef tenderloin, and other meats. You can sit in the tiny dining room if it's too cool at night, but the TV is usually blasting there. Service can be slow when it's full. The sister restaurant, Pizzeria Pinocchio's (open Thursday–Sunday), in the same building, serves good, inexpensive pizza. ✉*Av. Principal, 200 meters past market on right* ☎*983–6603* ⊟*No credit cards* ⊘*Closed Mon. and Tues.*

¢–$ ⌂**De Colores.** A short walk from the center of town, these four cement bungalows are good option for travelers on a budget. The bungalows occupy what was once the owner's backyard, and surround a tiny playground, benches, and hammocks. They're a bit cramped, but colorful, with kitchenettes and one or two bedrooms. The furniture is a bit dog-eared, but the Colombian owner is nice, and the location is conveniently central but relatively quiet. **Pros: Friendly owner, central location, garden, inexpensive. Cons: Small bungalows, time-worn furniture.** ✉*Calle El Gaitál, 100 meters north of Av. Principal* ☎*983–6613* ↩*4 bungalows* ⌂*In-room: no a/c, no phone, kitchen, refrigerator. In-hotel: no elevator, laundry service, parking (no fee), no-smoking rooms* ⊟*No credit cards* ⍾*EP.*

¢–$ ✕**La Niña Delia.** The high, thatch roof on the left side of the Avenida Principal as you roll into town marks this spot for inexpensive Panamanian food. Its open-air dining area is rustic by design, with a hedge of foliage around the edges, and woven hats and baskets hanging from the wood columns. Meals include traditional Panamanian breakfast and such favorites as *langostinos a la criolla* (prawns in a tomato sauce) and *lechon* pork roast, but you can also get some international dishes, such as *pollo al limón* (lemon chicken) and filet mignon. The pastas should be avoided. Some of the cheapest rooms in town are rented in the building next door. ✉*Av. Principal, on left 600 meters past Texaco station* ⊟*No credit cards.*

¢ ⌂**Don Pepe.** In a three-story building on Avenida Principal, with a crafts shop and restaurant on the ground floor, this hotel has centrally located, basic accommodation for budget travelers. Rooms are big, with tile floors, fans, so-so beds, and small bathrooms. Get one in back to avoid the street noise; corner rooms have more windows. The restaurant serves decent, inexpensive Panamanian fare, and is one of the first places to open in the morning and last to close at night. **Pros: Inexpensive, big rooms, restaurant, bike rentals. Cons: On busy street, zero decor.** ✉*Av. Principal, half a block before market* ☎*983–6425* ⊟*983–6835* ↩*77 suites* ⌂*In-room: no a/c, no phone. In-hotel: restaurant, bicycles, no elevator, laundry service, parking (no fee), no-smoking rooms* ⊟*MC, V* ⍾*EP.*

SPORTS & THE OUTDOORS

BIKING   Mountain biking is a great way to explore El Valle's side roads, which become rutted, dirt tracks the farther you get from the center of town. Good riding areas include the trail behind the old Hotel Campestre and the dirt roads west of the church. **Don Pepe** (⊠ *Av. Principal, half a block before market* ☎ *983–6425*) rents mountain bikes for $2 per hour and $10 per day.

BIRD-WATCHING   From tiny green hermits to elegant swallow-tailed kites, a remarkable diversity of birds inhabits El Valle's sky and forests. More than 350 bird species have been spotted in the area—compared with 426 species in all of Canada. The best viewing season is October to March, when northern migrants such as the yellow warbler and northern waterthrush boost El Valle's bird diversity. The migrants are especially common in the gardens of the valley's hotels and homes, whereas the forests of Cerro Gaitál and surroundings hold such tropical species as the tody motmot and sun bittern. El Valle's avian rainbow includes five kinds of toucans, six parrot species, and 25 hummingbird species. Though you can only hope to see a fraction of those birds, your chances will be greatly increased if you hire an experienced guide.

The most popular nature guide in El Valle is **Mario Urriola** (☎ *6569–2676*), a biologist who regularly leads visitors on hikes and birding tours, and whose rates are surprisingly inexpensive. El Valle's most experienced guide is **Mario Bernal** (☎ *6693–8213*), who has written a guide to the birds of El Valle. But he is often on the road with a group for Ancón Expeditions. Guests at the **Canopy Lodge** (☎ *264–5720* ⊕ *www.canopylodge.com*) enjoy the services of **Danilo Rodríguez,** who has been birding in El Valle for 15 years.

CANOPY TOUR   Adventure seekers will want to try the **Canopy Adventure** (☎ *983–6547* ⊕ *www.adventure.panamabirding.com*), which takes you flying through the forest canopy and over a 115-foot waterfall via zip-line cables strung between four platforms high in trees. The tour ($52) is in the **Refugio Ecológico del Choro Macho** (⇨ *above*), a private reserve a few kilometers northwest of town. This is more adrenaline rush than nature tour, though you do pass through some gorgeous rain forest scenery. The tour takes 60 to 90 minutes and begins with a 30-minute hike to the first platform.

HIKING   El Valle has enough hiking routes to keep you trekking for days. ▪ **TIP→ Hikes are best done early in the morning, when the air is clearer and the birds are more active.** One of the best trips is the two- to three-hour hike up **Cerro Gaitál,** which passes through lush forest and includes a mirador (lookout point) affording a view of the valley, the Pacific coast, and, on clear days, the Caribbean coast. There is also a trail around the back of Cerro Gaitál that begins just behind the Hotel Campestre, which lacks the scenic views but passes through forest. Another impressive view of El Valle is the one from the **Monte de la Cruz,** a deforested mountain ridge topped by a cement cross on the northwest end of the valley. It is reached by heading up the road to El Chorro Macho until it becomes a dirt road that ascends the slope as a

2

series of switchbacks. The popular hiking route up and along the **India Dormida** ridge on the western end of the valley combines treks through patches of forest with scenic views. The trail up the ridge is reached by heading west of town, turning right after the baseball stadium, and left again at the first road.

Because El Valle's trails are not well marked, you should hire a guide for these hikes. Any of El Valle's hotels can set you up with a hiking guide. Nature guide **Mario Urriola** (☎6569–2676) is a bilingual biologist who regularly leads small groups up Cerro Gaitál, the India Dormida, and other hiking routes.

HORSEBACK RIDING
An inexpensive horseback adventure is available from **Alquiler de Caballos Mitzila** (✉ *Calle El Hato* ☎6646–5813), across from the small church on Calle El Hato, a few blocks before the Hotel Campestre. A horse costs $5 per hour, and each group has to pay an additional $5 per hour for the guide. The most popular ride is around the back of Cerro Gaitil, a loop that takes about four hours to complete, though you can also ride for an hour and then come back on the same route. Neither the owner, Mitzila, nor her guides speak English, so have your hotel receptionist make the arrangements.

SHOPPING

El Valle is known for its Sunday-morning handicrafts market at the **Mercado** (✉ *Av. Prinicpal, on left two blocks before church* ☎No phone), a festive affair that brings together vendors and shoppers from far and wide. A handicrafts selection to rival that at the nearby Mercado is available at **Artesanía Don Pedro** (✉ *Av. Prinicpal, on left 1 block before Mercado* ☎983–6425), open seven days a week.

TO & FROM AND LOGISTICS

El Valle is 125 km (75 mi) southwest from Panama City, about two hours by car, on good roads. To drive, take the Carretera Interamericana west for 98 km (59 mi) to Las Uvas, where you turn right and drive 28 km (17 mi) north on a narrow, winding road. Buses to El Valle depart from the Terminal de Buses in Albrook every hour and cost $4, but they take almost three hours. Taxis hang out at the Mercado during the day, and charge $1–$2 for most trips within the valley.

CERRO LA VIEJA

32 km (20 mi) northeast of Penonomé, 176 km (109 mi) southwest of Panama City.

To the west of El Valle, on the road from Penemomé to Churuquita Grande, stands the impressive forested hill of Cerro la Vieja, with thick foliage clinging to its rocky face. The area around that peak holds a mix of farms and patches of forest, and it has been experiencing a slight ecological recovery in recent years, as local farmers allow regrowth in areas that were deforested decades ago. This is in no small part thanks to the efforts of Alfonso Jaen, who owns the Posada Ecológico Cerro la Vieja, one of the country's first eco-lodges. Guides at that lodge lead visitors through the surrounding countryside, to the summit of Cerro la Vieja, or all the way to El Valle. Because Cerro La Vieja is in a valley between the country's Pacific and Atlantic slopes, it gets more rain than the nearby Pacific lowlands, and thus stays greener during the dry season. It is also home to a good variety of birds, since it lies within the range of Pacific and Caribbean species. Travelers who prefer to take it easy may want to dedicate their stay to the Posada Ecológico's small spa.

WHERE TO STAY & EAT

$ ★ 🔆 **Posada Ecológico Cerro de la Vieja.** The view of Cerro la Vieja from the restaurant, spa, and rooms at this small eco-lodge is alone worth the trip there—the bird-watching, hiking, and inexpensive spa therapies are icing on the cake. The *posada* is perched on a hilltop directly in front of Cerro de la Vieja, with rooms in various buildings spread along the slope amid trees and gardens that attract an array of birds. "Premier" rooms are well worth the top dollar, since they are bright and spacious, and have small balconies with hammocks and views. "Superior" rooms just below them are similar, but not as bright, and have less spectacular views. "Standards," in back, are even darker, and overlook the forest. The panorama is best appreciated from the restaurant, which has a wall of windows, and the spa below it. A lounge next door has pool and Ping-Pong tables, couches, and the hotel's only TV. The lodge offers eight inexpensive guided hikes, most of which can be done on a mule for slightly more money. The Trinidad Spa has a sauna, a hot tub with a view, and affordable massages and beauty treatments. **Pros: Amazing views, nature, hiking, spa. Cons: Standard rooms lack view.** ✉ *Chiguirí, 32 km (20 mi) northeast of Penonomé on road to Churuquita Grande* 🕾🕾*983–8900 or 269–8698* ⊕*www.posadaecologica. com* ➪*18 rooms* &*In-room: no a/c (some), no phone, no TV. In-hotel: restaurant, bar, spa, no elevator, laundry service, public Wi-Fi, parking (no fee), no-smoking rooms* ➡*MC, V* ⦿|*BP.*

SPORTS & THE OUTDOORS

HIKING   Hiking is the specialty at the **Posada Ecológico Cerro de la Vieja** (🕾*983–8900*), where guests choose from eight different guided hikes ranging from the three-hour climb to the summit of Cerro la Vieja to full-day treks deep into the mountains. After the Cerro la Vieja ascent, the most popular hike is the three-hour trek to Tavidá Waterfall and nearby petroglyphs.

TO & FROM AND LOGISTICS

The drive from Panama City to Cerro la Vieja takes about two and a half hours. Drive 144 km (89 mi) west on the Carretera Interamericana to Penonomé, and take the first entrance, which veers right after the Hotel Dos Continentes. Turn right again at the second street and follow the signs to Churuquita Grande and Tambo, for 32 km (20 mi).

THE GOLDEN TOAD

El Valle has long been synonymous with a bright yellow amphibian with black spots called the golden toad (*Atelopus zeteki*), which, together with the harpy eagle, is one of Panama's emblematic animals. The beautiful toads were revered by the area's pre-Columbian inhabitants, who crafted frog-shaped jewelry and ceramic wares. The fascination continues, and you're likely to see images of golden toads on brochures, T-shirts, and an array of knickknacks. Where you won't see them, however, is in El Valle's forests, where they were fairly abundant as recently as the 1980s. The population of the golden toad, which exists only in Panama's Cordillera Central, has plummeted in recent years, due to the spread of a chytrid fungus (*Batrachochytrium dendrobatidis*) that covers the frogs' skin until they suffocate. Scientists have consequently captured toads in the wild and sequestered them in fungus-free environments, such as in the Amphibian Conservation Center at El Nispero zoo, which is one of the only places you can see the golden toad today.

Amphibian populations have declined throughout the mountains of Central America, and around the world, in recent decades, causing considerable alarm in the scientific community. Several scientists who studied climate changes in the Costa Rican mountain community of Monteverde, where another golden toad species went extinct in the 1990s, published a report in the prestigious journal *Nature* claiming that seasonal drought conditions resulting from global warming have weakened frogs' immune systems and made them more susceptible to diseases such as the chytrid fungus. Other scientists studying the fungal disease say that it is working its way eastward through Panama, and worry that tourists may transport the spores. Consequently, if you hike in the forests in western or central Panama you should, before traveling to the eastern half of the country, wash your hiking boots with soap and water and then alcohol to kill any fungus.

THE CANAL & CENTRAL PANAMA ESSENTIALS

Because central Panama's sites and attractions literally surround Panama City, you are rarely more than two or three hours away from the capital. Panama City is consequently the place to go for most major services, such as hospitals, car rentals, banks, mail, and shipping. Some areas, such as the islands, lack ATMs and pharmacies; none of the clinics outside Panama City is suitable for anything beyond first aid.

TRANSPORTATION

BY AIR

The domestic airlines Aeroperlas and Air Panama both have daily 20-minute flights to Isla Contadora. Aeroperlas flies every morning and evening; Air Panama flies every afternoon. Only Air Panama flies to Isla San José, an hour from Panama City; flights are every Monday, Thursday, Friday, and Sunday morning. Both depart from the **Aeropuerto Marcos a Gelabert** ⊠ *Av. Gaillard, Albrook, Panama City* ☎*315–0241.*

Airlines Aeroperlas ☎ 315–7500 ⊕ www.aeroperlas.com. **Air Panama** ☎ 316–9000 ⊕ www.flyairpanama.com.

BY BOAT

For Panama Canal boat trips, see Tours, below. **Barcos Calypso Taboga** (✉ *Marina Isla Naos* ☎ 314–1730) has a daily ferry service from Panama City to Isla Taboga departing from the Marina on Isla Naos, on the Amador Causeway, Monday, Wednesday, and Friday at 8:30 and 3, Tuesday and Thursday at 8:30 only, and weekends and holidays at 8, 10:30, and 4. The ferry departs from Taboga from the pier on the west end of town Monday, Wednesday, and Friday at 9:30 and 4:30, Tuesday and Thursday at 4:30 only, and weekends and holidays at 9, 3, and 5. On weekends and holidays, arrive 30 minutes before departure to buy your ticket.

RIP-CURRENT KNOW-HOW

Though Central Pacific beaches are usually safe for swimming, rip currents (riptides) are a danger on any beach with waves. Even the strongest swimmer can't fight these currents, but almost anyone can escape one. Swim parallel to shore until you feel that you are no longer heading out to sea, then head toward shore. Rip currents aren't wide, and it is always possible to swim out of them; however, you may be far from shore by the time you do, so don't waste energy swimming against the current. Only swim toward shore when you are free of the rip current.

BY BUS

Buses to the Miraflores Locks, Summit, most of the trails into Parque Nacional Soberanía, and Gamboa depart from the **Terminal de Buses SACA** (✉ *Calle 9 de Enero, Plaza Cinco de Mayo, Panama City* ☎ *No phone*), just to the north of Plaza Cinco de Mayo, every 60 to 90 minutes; the trip takes 30 to 40 minutes.

All regional buses depart from the massive **Terminal de Transporte de Albrook** (✉ *Av. Gaillard, Albrook, Panama City* ☎ 232–5803). Buses to Colón and Sabanitas, where you get off to catch the bus to Portobelo and Isla Grande, depart every 20 minutes, and the trip takes 90 minutes. Buses to Penonomé and Santiago, which depart every 30 minutes, will drop you off at the entrances to the Pacific beaches, though most of them are a long hike from the highway. Buses to El Valle de Antón depart every 30 minutes.

BY CAR

Renting a car is an easy way to visit many of the Central Pacific sites, since there are paved roads to just about everything but the islands. Cars can be rented in Panama City and Colón. Rentals usually cost $40–$50 per day, whereas 4WD vehicles cost $60–$70. All major car-rental companies have offices in Panama City (⇨ Essentials, *in* "Panama City" chapter); only Budget and Hertz have offices in Colón.

Car-Rental Agencies Budget ✉ *Colón 2000, Colón* ☎ 441–7161. **Hertz** ✉ *Colón 2000, Colón* ☎ 441–3272.

BY TRAIN

The Panama Canal Railway's commuter train to Colón departs from the train station in Panama City weekdays at 7:15 AM and departs from Colón at 5:15 PM. The trip costs $22 one way, $44 round-trip.

Train Station Information **Panama Canal Railway** ☎ *317–6070*. **Corozal Passenger Station** ✉ *Calle Corozal, Corozal, Panama City* ☎ *317–6070*. **Atlantic Passenger Station** ✉ *Calle Mt. Hope, Mt Hope, Colón* ☎ *No phone.*

CONTACTS & RESOURCES

EMERGENCIES

Ambulance service can be slow in rural areas. There are clinics in some of the rural communities, but they are good for nothing more than first aid. If you suffer an accident, or have medical problems, get to the Hospital Punta Pacífica or Centro Médico Paitilla in Panama City as soon as possible.

Emergency Services **Ambulance** *Alerta* ☎ *263–4522, Cruz Roja* ☎ *228–8127*. **Fire department** ☎ *103*. **National police** ☎ *104*.

Hospitals *See Essentials in "Panama City" chapter.*

PHARMACIES

All branches of Farmacia Rey are in the Supermercado Rey. Colón's branch is open until midnight. The Farmacia Rey in Sabanitas is the closest pharmacy to Portobelo, Isla Grande, and Sierra Llorona. The branch at the entrance to Playa Coronado is the closest pharmacy to the Pacific beaches and El Valle de Antón.

Pharmacies**Farmacia Rey** ✉ *Calle 13, Colón* ☎ *445–0185* ✉ *Transísmica, Sabanitas* ☎ *442–0922* ✉ *Centro Comercial Coronado, Playa Coronado* ☎ *240–1247*.

INTERNET

Most hotels in Central Panama offer Internet access to their guests.

MAIL & SHIPPING

Mail service from rural post offices is quite slow, so if you will be returning to Panama City within less than a week, it is worthwhile to hang onto your cards and letters and mail them from the city. In Central Panama, courier services are only available from Colón and Panama City, where your hotel can arrange a FedEx pick-up. *For post-office and FedEx information, see Essentials in Chapter 1.*

MONEY MATTERS

Credit cards are widely accepted in this region, except for at the smaller restaurants and hotels. ATM distribution is less uniform outside of Panama City, so it is often a good idea to stock up on cash before exploring the Central Pacific's rural reaches. The only ATMs near the Caribbean Coast's attractions are in and around Colón, whereas the eastern sierras and Pacific islands have no ATMs, so get cash before driving east, or boarding the ferry or plane to Islas Taboga, Contadora, or San José. There are ATMs in the Albrook Airport terminal and at the Brisas de Amador shopping center, near the Taboga ferry dock, as well as in the lobby of the Gamboa Rainforest Resort, the Gatún Locks, and in the Super 99 supermarket in Colón 2000. To the west of Panama City, you can find ATMs in the Rey Supermarket at the entrance to Coronado, one block north of the Royal Decameron Beach Resort, in the lobby of the Playa Blanca Resort, on the Avenida Principal of El Valle, and at various banks in Penonomé, near Cerro de la Vieja.

SAFETY

When hiking through the forest, always be careful where you put your hand and where you step, since there are poisonous snakes and sting-ing insects. If you slip on a muddy trail in the rain forest, which hap-pens quite frequently, resist the temptation to grab the nearest branch, because palms with spiny trunks are relatively common. If there are big waves at a beach you visit, don't go in unless you are an expert swim-mer, since waves can create dangerous currents.

TOURS

PANAMA CANAL TOURS **Canal Bay Tours** ⊠*Bahia Balboa Building, next to Nunciatura Punta Pait-illa, Panama City* ☎*209–2009* offers partial- and full-transit tours on one of two ships: the 115-foot *Fantasia del Mar*, which has air-conditioned cabins and a large upper deck, and the 85-foot *Isla Morada*, which has one large covered deck. Partial transits cost $99; full transits are $145. **Pacific Marine Tours** ⊠*Villa Porras and Calle Belén, No. 106, San Francisco, Pan-ama City* ☎*226–8417* ⊕*www.pmatours.net* runs canal transits on the 119-foot *Pacific Queen*, a comfortable ship with air-conditioned cabins and two large decks. Partial transits cost $105, full transits are $165.

OTHER TOURS Most of the major tour operators in Panama City (⇨chapter 1) offer half- or full-day trips to trails in Parque Nacional Soberanía and to Emberá villages in Parque Nacional Charges. **Ancón Expeditions** has an excellent boat tour of Gatún Lake; bird-watching on Pipeline Road; a day trip that combines the Panama Railway with the rain forest and colonial ruins of San Lorenzo; and a weeklong hiking expedition through Parque Nacional Chagres. The white-water outfitter **Aven-turas Panama** offers rafting on the Chagres River, hiking, and visits to Emberá Indian communities in Parque Nacional Chagres. **Margo Tours** offers horseback-riding tours in Cerro Azul. **Futura Travel** has half-day hiking tours to Altos de Campana. **Eco Circuitos** runs a boat trip on Gatún Lake, a morning hike on the Camino de Cruces, and day trips to San Lorenzo, Portobelo, and Parque Nacional Chagres. **Extreme Tours,** in Coronado and Farallón, offers an array of outdoor and marine activities in the Coronado and Playa Blanca areas, includ-ing scuba diving, snorkeling, surfing, and sportfishing.

Tour Companies *See Essentials in Chapter 1 for most tour companies that oper-ate in the Central Pacific region.* **Extreme Tours** ⊠*Playa Coronado* ☎*240–1823 or 6673–0820.*

The Azuero Peninsula & Veraguas

WORD OF MOUTH

"Whether by good planning or luck, the alternating of comfort to more rustic, cities to remote highlands is a great way to see Panama and to make trips like this more interesting."

—Beaker

By David
Dudenhoefer

THE AZUERO PENINSULA AND VERAGUAS constitute the other Panama, or perhaps, the real Panama. This was one of the first areas of the country to be colonized by Spain, and the colonial churches and squares of its historic towns provide perfect backdrops for its frequent folk festivals and religious celebrations. Before the Europeans arrived, the area had well-established indigenous societies, remnants of which can be seen today in museums, local ceramic work, and elements of Panamanian folk music. The region's predominant culture and race is now *mestizo,* a mixture of European and indigenous, whereas the economy is dominated by cattle ranching, a livelihood introduced by Spaniards centuries ago.

Panamanians flock to the Azuero Peninsula for Carnaval and other celebrations, but tourists have largely ignored it—those who do come are usually bound for some of Panama's best surfing beaches. Those beaches are neither as attractive nor as accessible as strands in Central Panama or Bocas del Toro, and are less of a draw for the non-surfing traveler. Nor does the region have lush forests—centuries of colonization have left it predominantly deforested. There are, however, some patches of rare tropical dry forest here, whereas Isla Iguana and Isla de Coiba are surrounded by phenomenal marine life.

The peninsula is Panama's driest region, and is consequently a good place to head during the rainy months, when conditions are optimal for surfing and skin diving. It is always an excellent destination for travelers with a keen interest in culture, especially during festival times, and it is the place to go to stray from the beaten path.

ORIENTATION & PLANNING

ORIENTATION

The Azuero region is usually reached by driving west from Panama City on the Carretera Interamericana (CA1), though it can be easily visited on a drive from Central Panama or the western province of Chiriquí. From the Interamericana, roads head south into the Azuero Peninsula and to Santa Catalina.

PLANNING

WHEN TO GO

Most tourists visit during the December–May dry season, but because this is Panama's driest region, you can also head here in the rainy months and expect less rain than you'll get elsewhere. Serious surfers go to Playas Venao and Santa Catalina between May and January when the waves are biggest and the ocean warmer. The rainy months are also the best time for skin-diving trips to Isla Iguana or Isla de Coiba. Deep-sea fishing is best from January to April, though winds can be problematic. Keep in mind that the peninsula's hotels get packed during Carnaval in mid-February, but it's a fun time to be here.

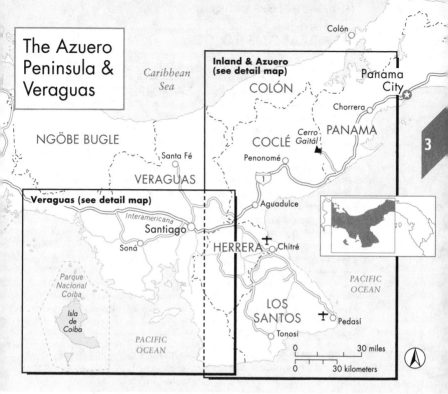

The Azuero Peninsula & Veraguas

Inland & Azuero (see detail map)

Caribbean Sea

Colón

Panama City

COLÓN

Chorrera

NGÖBE BUGLE

Santa Fé

Cerro Gaitál

PANAMA

COCLÉ

Penonomé

VERAGUAS

Veraguas (see detail map)

Interamericana

Santiago

Soná

Aguadulce

HERRERA

Chitré

Parque Nacional Coiba

Isla de Coiba

PACIFIC OCEAN

LOS SANTOS

Pedasí

Tonosí

PACIFIC OCEAN

0   30 miles

0   30 kilometers

GETTING AROUND

This region is best explored by car, though you can visit the main towns by bus. It is possible to fly directly from Panama City to Chitré or Pedasí on the Azuero Peninsula on Friday and Sunday afternoons. In Chitré you can rent a car or get a taxi to a hotel.

WHAT TO DO

SURF, DUDE Playa Venao and Playa Santa Catalina are Panama's two most consistent and biggest surfing spots, with lefts and rights available at both. They are long trips from the capital, and have limited accommodations nearby, but the waves are usually well worth the journey.

DIVE AND SNORKEL Isla de Coiba is considered the best dive spot on Central America's Pacific coast, with hundreds of fish species in remarkable abundance. Certified scuba divers and snorkeling buffs enjoy Isla Iguana, and the cove behind La Playita, next to Playa Venao, also has decent snorkeling.

ATTEND A FESTIVAL The Azuero Peninsula's rich cultural heritage is on display at least once a month at various festivals, religious and otherwise, with music, dancing, masks, and traditional dress.

BE A BEACH BUM The Azuero Peninsula and Veraguas have at least a dozen beaches between them, from seemingly endless Playa Venao to the tiny white-sand beach of Grano de Oro, near Isla de Coiba. Take your pick.

TOP REASONS TO GO

FOLK FESTIVAL
From Guararé's relatively tranquil Mejorana Festival to the unrepentant revelry of Carnaval, the Azuero Peninsula's frequent celebrations are great opportunities to experience the area's vibrant culture.

ISLA IGUANA
One of the oldest and best-developed coral reefs in Panama's Pacific waters and a lovely beach can be found at this small, protected island a short trip from Pedasí. Scuba divers may encounter more than 200 fish species found there, but it's also a great trip for sunbathers.

PLAYA VENAO
One of Panama's best surf spots, Playa Venao has the added attraction of being near patches of tropical dry forest, good snorkeling and sportfishing, as well as the country's most important sea-turtle nesting area.

SANTA CATALINA
This laid-back fishing town at the end of the road is synonymous with great surf, but it is also the gateway to excellent diving and good sportfishing and a nice place to get away from it all.

ISLA DE COIBA
One of Central America's best Pacific dive spots, Isla de Coiba is known for its abundant sharks, vast schools of jacks, and varied reef fish. It is a remote and wild spot that rewards those who make the trip with spectacular natural beauty.

GET OFF THE BEATEN PATH If you want to get far from the resorts and city lights, and feel as if you were the first outsider to visit someplace, head for the narrow roads that wind through the Azuero Peninsula and Veraguas.

RESTAURANTS & CUISINE
The region's dining options are quite limited, but there are a few excellent restaurants, and plenty of mediocre ones. Seafood—especially fresh tuna—is put to great use at the few quality restaurants.

ABOUT THE HOTELS
The Azuero region is short on quality hotels and has nothing even resembling a resort. There are plenty of cheap backpacker places, and a few charming inns that take advantage of the surrounding nature. Hotel prices in the peninsula's towns double during Carnaval, when you should reserve at least a month in advance, and they all increase about 50% for New Year's and Easter week.

WHAT IT COSTS IN U.S. DOLLARS					
	¢	$	$$	$$$	$$$$
RESTAURANTS	under $5	$5–$10	$10–$15	$15–$20	over $20
HOTELS	under $50	$50–$100	$100–$160	$160–$220	over $220

Restaurant prices are per person for a main course at dinner. Hotel prices are for two people in a standard double room, excluding service and 10% tax.

INLAND

The Carretera Interamericana crosses Panama to the north of the Azuero Peninsula, skirting the towns of Penonomé and Santiago, and passing a couple of quick stops that offer introductions to the region's history. Parque Arqueológico El Caño and Natá are just off the highway, making them worthwhile cultural pit stops if you're driving.

PARQUE ARQUEOLÓGICO EL CAÑO

27 km (17 mi) west of Penonomé, 171 km (106 mi) west of Panama City.

One of only two archaeological sites in Panama that are open to the public, El Caño illustrates why so little remains of the country's pre-Columbian jewelry and artwork. The looting of historic treasures in Panama began with the Spanish conquest, and continues today, as grave diggers called *huaceros* raid pre-Columbian sites and sell what they find to private collectors. At El Caño in the 1920s, American adventurer Hyatt Verrill removed 1,000-plus-year-old sculpted figures topping pillars and shipped them to U.S. museums, along with the ceramic pieces and gold jewelry that his crew found at the site. Today a circle of stone slabs is all that's left of the pillars. To make matters worse, most of the valuable pieces held in the site's small museum were stolen in the 1990s—quite possibly by corrupt government officials. The site's museum consequently doesn't have much to see, but the excavated burial pit nearby is worth a look. ✉*3 km (2 mi) north of Carretera Interamericana, veer left at El Caño church* ☎*No phone* ✉*$1* ☉*Tues.–Sat. 9–noon and 1–4, Sun. 9–1.*

TO & FROM

To drive to El Caño from Panama City, head west on the Carretera Interamericana for 171 km (106 mi) and look for the turnoff on the right 27 km (17 mi) after Penonomé.

NATÁ

36 km (22 mi) west of Penonomé, 180 km (112 mi) west of Panama City.

★ One of Panama's oldest inhabited towns, Natá (officially Natá de los Caballeros) has a lovely central plaza with a restored colonial church, and is worth a quick stop on the drive to the Azuero Peninsula or Santa Catalina. Founded in 1522, Natá was a key Spanish outpost in a region dominated by Indian chiefs who organized stiff resistance to colonization. *Caballeros* (knights) were sent to pacify the Indians and construct a Christian enclave here in 1522. The most impressive of Natá's buildings is the ancient **Basílica Menor Santiago Apóstol,** with its high bell tower and wide facade. One of Panama's oldest functioning churches, it was built in the 17th century, and it holds eight colonial altars under its hardwood roof. The church is open only for mass.

A BIT OF HISTORY

While Panama City grew rich from the transport of treasures to and from distant lands between the 16th and 18th centuries, Veraguas and the Azuero Peninsula developed economies based on agriculture and ranching, which have endured the booms and busts of Central Panama. The region had complex indigenous societies when the Spanish conquistadors arrived, as the pre-Columbian ceramic and gold work found here attests. The region's Indians resisted Spanish colonization for the first half of the 16th century, but conquistadors persisted, bolstered by the lure of gold in the mountains. After defeating the local chiefs, the Spaniards brought in African slaves to work the gold mines, and founded towns such as Parita and La Villa de Los Santos to grow food for the mining communities. The Spaniards mined out the region's major gold deposits by the 17th century, but the lowland communities continued to produce meat and produce for Panama City, and cottage industries producing such traditional goods as straw hats and ceramic wares remain to this day.

Recent centuries have seen the expansion of pastureland at the cost of the region's forests, first as a result of the population boost while the Panama Canal was built, and later when the country began exporting beef. The region's people have consequently become as synonymous with deforestation as they are with folklore.

TO & FROM

To drive to Natá from Panama City, head west on the Carretera Interamericana for 180 km (112 mi), and look for the turnoff on the left 36 km (22 mi) after Penonomé.

OFF THE BEATEN PATH

Parque Nacional El Copé, also known as Parque Nacional Omar Torrijos, was created after the Panamanian strongman died when his plane crashed into a mountain here in 1981. Together with the contiguous Parque Nacional Santa Fe, El Copé protects a vast expanse of forest along the Cordillera Central that provides a refuge for such rare endangered animals as the jaguar, tapir, and harpy eagle. Bird-watchers make the long, rough drive up to El Copé to look for such rare species as the red-fronted parrolet and the umbrella bird. The park's misty forests extend from the Pacific slope of the continental divide over to the Caribbean slope, which means it can rain here any time of year—the reason for its vast array of wildlife. Views of the Caribbean forest are amazing, and from the lookout point above the ranger station you can see both the Pacific and Atlantic oceans on a clear morning. The park has several well-marked hiking trails, a small camping area, and a rustic cabin that you can rent for $5. Several families rent rooms in the town of Barrigón, a 60-minute hike from the park. The road to the park is a rough, 4WD track for the last 7 km (4 mi). Bring warm clothes if you overnight here—it cools off considerably. ⊠ *50 km (31 mi) west of Penonomé via El Copé and Barrigón* ☎ *997–7538* ⊠ *$3* ⊙ *Daily 9–5.*

THE AZUERO PENINSULA

The Azuero Peninsula is sometimes called Panama's cultural cradle, due to the folk music and dance performed at its frequent festivals. The relatively dry region is covered with cattle ranches and dotted with tranquil agricultural towns where families chat on the porches of adobe houses and historic churches overlook tidy central plazas. The peninsula is known for maintaining traditions from the colonial era, when Spanish and indigenous customs were melded. These traditions include everything from folk music and dancing to the exquisite, hand-stitched *polleras* (elaborate embroidered dresses) and ubiquitous straw hats. Festivals—ideal opportunities to experience the region's folklore—are celebrated just about every month here.

Deforestation for farming and ranching has been rampant on the peninsula, and little remains of the original wilderness. Nevertheless, the roads are lined with gumbo limbo and Madera negro trees, and streams and gullies are shaded by kapok, guanacaste, and other tropical trees that provide homes for howler monkeys, iguanas, and birds. The long coast holds many beaches, the nicest of which are Playa Venao and the small beach on Isla Iguana, which also protects coral reefs. In addition to its main towns of Chitré, La Villa De Los Santos, Las Tablas, and Pedasí, Azuero has some picturesque villages that are worth checking out, such as Parita and—deep in the peninsula's interior—Pesé, Las Minas, and Ocú.

PARITA

240 km (149 mi) southwest of Panama City, 12 km (7 mi) north of Chitré.

★ One of the most picturesque and best-preserved colonial towns in the peninsula, Parita is just off the Carretera Nacional—the main road into the peninsula—which makes stopping here to admire its lovely central plaza and shady streets practically obligatory. Founded in 1566, it was the first Spanish settlement in the Azuero Peninsula, and it soon became one of the principal suppliers of food for the gold mines in the Cordillera Central. Parita's only monument is its colonial church, the 17th-century **Iglesia de Santo Domingo de Guzmán,** two blocks west of the Carretera Nacional. It holds some elaborately carved wooden altars and statues dating from the 18th century, but is usually closed. The grassy plaza that lies in front of that church is surrounded by long, colorful adobe homes with barrel-tile roofs.

TO & FROM
To reach Parita, and the Azuero Peninsula, drive west from Panama City on the Carretera Interamericana 215 km (129 mi) to the well-marked intersection at Divisa, where you turn south onto the Carretera Nacional. The entrance to Parita is on the right 25 km (16 mi) south of Divisa. You can also take a taxi there from nearby Chitré for $8.

LA ARENA

250 km (155 mi) southwest of Panama City, 10 km (6 mi) south of Parita.

This small, traditional town has been producing pottery since colonial times—and perhaps earlier. Much of the ceramic work replicates pre-Columbian designs, though the local artisans also produce more modern pieces. The town is most famous for its traditional *tinajas,* ceramic jugs or pots used to store water, which make lovely vases but are tough to get home in one piece. The Carretera Nacional runs right through La Arena 2 km (1 mi) before Chitré, and the traffic slows here since the street is lined with shops and pedestrians.

SHOPPING

Shopping is what La Arena is all about, and most of the shops line the Carretera Nacional. At the center of town is a two-story building called the **Mercado de Artesanías** (⊠ *Carretera Nacional, on left* ☎ *No phone*) that holds the stands of various vendors. In addition to ceramics, you'll find hammocks, Carnaval masks, straw hats, and more. Some of the most traditional ceramic work is available at **Cerámica Calderón** (⊠ *Carretera Nacional, on left* ☎ 947–4646).

TO & FROM

To drive to La Arena from Panama City, follow directions for Parita and continue 15 km (9 mi) beyond. It's a five-minute taxi ride ($3) or 15-minute bus trip (25¢) from Chitré to La Arena.

CHITRÉ

252 km (156 mi) southwest of Panama City, 37 km (23 mi) south of Divisa.

Chitré is a rambling town with a compact center that includes a lovely 18th-century church and the region's best museum. Those sites can be visited in an hour's time, but because it has the peninsula's best hotels outside of the beaches on the southern coast, Chitré can be a convenient base from which to visit the area's traditional towns, such as nearby La Villa de los Santos, Parita, Las Minas, Ocú, and Pesé.

The capital of Herrera Province, Chitré is the principal commercial and administrative center for the Azuero Peninsula. Chitré's only landmark to speak of is the lovely **Catedral de San Juan Bautista** (⊠ *Calle Aminta Burgos de Amado* ☎ *No phone*), which was inaugurated in 1910 but was built in the colonial style and has an attractive hardwood interior and stained-glass windows. The area around it is perfect for an afternoon stroll and a cool drink at a restaurant.

Several blocks northwest of the cathedral is a white neoclassical building that holds the provincial museum, which is surprisingly good. The **Museo de Herrera** features pre-Columbian artifacts found in the area, some of which are more than 1,000 years old. There is also a replica of a chief's burial site that was discovered during the colonial era and well chronicled before being looted. Its exhibits on local folklore include

FOLK FESTIVALS

Check www.visitpanama.com for current information.

JANUARY

The first days of January are marked by the **Reyes Magos** celebration in Macaracas, southwest of Chitré. **Patron saint days:** Ocú, January 17–20; Guararé, January 21; La Enea (just north of Las Tablas), January 30.

FEBRUARY

Las Trancas, between Las Tablas and Pedasí, is known for its **Festival de la Candelaria,** a religious celebration with folk music and dance on February 2. Las Tablas is famous for its **Carnaval** festivities (⇨ Las Tablas, *below*), but Chitré, Parita, Ocú, La Villa de Los Santos, and Pedasí also have notable celebrations.

MARCH AND APRIL

Rum-producing Pesé, southwest of Chitré, celebrates the **Festival de la Caña (Sugar Cane Festival)** in March (dates vary). **Semana Santa** is especially picturesque in La Villa de Los Santos, Pesé, and La Arena. The country-fair-like **Feria de Azuero** is held the last week in April in La Villa Los Santos. **Patron saint days:** San José (south of Las Tablas), March 19.

MAY AND JUNE

The week following **Corpus Christi,** held in either May or June, is celebrated in La Villa de Los Santos with dances by *los diablitos* (the little devils; ⇨ "Devilish Celebrations,"

below). The **Festival de Manito,** a major folk-music and dance event, is held in Ocú the last week of June. **Patron saint days:** Chitré, June 24; La Arena, June 29; Monagrillo (just north of Chitré), June 30.

JULY AND AUGUST

Las Tablas's **Festival de la Pollera,** July 21–23, features folk music, dancing, parades, and women in embroidered dresses. Parita celebrates its **foundation day** on August 18. Las Minas comes alive at the end of August for the **Festival de la Flor del Espiritu Santo. Patron saint days:** Las Tablas, July 20; Guararé, July 16; Parita, July 26–August 8; Tonosí, August 18.

SEPTEMBER AND OCTOBER

The **founding of Macaracas,** a small town southwest of Chitré, is fêted on September 12. The folk-music **Festival de la Mejorana** (⇨ Guararé, *below*) takes place the third weekend of September. La Villa de Los Santos, La Arena, and other towns celebrate **Semanas del Campesino** during various weeks from August to October.

NOVEMBER AND DECEMBER

The **founding of Chitré** is celebrated on October 19. La Villa de Los Santos celebrates **El Primer Grito de la Independencia** with folk music and dance on November 10. **Patron saint days:** Pedasí, November 25; Las Minas, December 4.

Carnaval masks, traditional musical instruments such as the mejorana, and lovely embroidered polleras. Unfortunately, the information is all in Spanish. ⊠ *Calle Manuel María Correa and Av. Julio Arjona* ☎ *996–0077* ☜ *$1* ⊙ *Tues.–Sat. 8:30–noon and 1–4, Sun. 9–noon.*

WHERE TO STAY & EAT

¢–$ ✗ **Restaurante DKDAS.** This small, open-air eatery at the edge of town is one of Chitré's most popular restaurants. It is often packed with locals, who head there for inexpensive seafood and grilled meat, such as *filet de res pimienta* (fillet in a pepper sauce) or *langostinos al ajillo* (prawns sautéed with garlic). Everything is served no-frills in a long, bright dining room lined with ferns, which usually has a couple of TVs blasting. The name is pronounced *day*-ka-das. ✉ *Vía Circunvalación, half a block north of Hotel Hong Kong* ☎996–3339 ▭MC, V.

3

$ ✗ 🏨 **Hotel Guaycanes.** Chitré's best hotel is west of town and bears some ↻ resemblance to an American motel. Ample grounds include a small pool, a small park with an artificial lake, and a playground. Rooms, in two-story buildings, are bright, with nice wood furniture and cable TV, but bathrooms are cramped and the mattresses are soft. Second-floor rooms, with small balconies and views of the grounds, are the nicest. A large casino near the parking lot is popular with locals. The attractive, open-air restaurant ($) serves a wide selection of food, from the traditional *arroz con pollo* (rice with chicken) to *corvina thai* (sea bass in a spicy coconut sauce). **Pros: Quiet, spacious grounds, decent restaurant. Cons: Far from town center.** ✉ *Vía Circunvaluación* ☎996–9758 📠996–9759 ⊕*www.losguayacanes.com* 📞*56 rooms, 8 suites* ♨*In-hotel: restaurant, room service, bar, tennis courts, pool, gym, no elevator, laundry service, public Wi-Fi, no-smoking rooms* ▭*AE, MC, V* ⦿*BP.*

¢ ✗ 🏨 **Hotel Rex.** Near the cathedral and a short walk from the museum, ↻ shops, and restaurants, this older place is the best option for budget travelers, or anyone who prefers to stay in the heart of town. The rooms are rudimentary, but have cable TV and air-conditioning—those on the top floor are brighter. There's a small Internet café by the lobby, and a common terrace with a view of the Plaza Central and cathedral. The restaurant (¢–$) downstairs, El Mesón, serves decent Panamanian and international fare and its café seating in front is perfect for people-watching. **Pros: Central location, good restaurant. Cons: Basic rooms.** ✉*Calle Malitón Martín* ☎996–4310 📠996–2391 📞*32 rooms* ♨*In-hotel: restaurant, laundry service, public Internet, no-smoking rooms* ▭*AE, MC, V* ⦿*BP.*

TO & FROM

Via car, head west from Panama City on the Carretera Interamericana 215 km (133 mi) to the well-marked intersection at Divisa; turn south onto the Carretera Nacional. Chitré is 37 km (23 mi) south of Divisa, and the Carretera Nacional continues south of it to nearby La Villa de Los Santos, Las Tablas, and Pedasí. Buses to Chitré depart from Panama City's Albrook Terminal every 30 minutes; the trip is four to five hours. Air Panama has a 30-minute flight to Chitré's small airport from Panama City's Albrook Airport every Friday and Sunday afternoon. Chitré is the only town in the Azuero Peninsula where you can rent a car.

CLOSE UP

Traditional Towns

Chitré is the perfect base from which to explore the peninsula's interior, where narrow roads wind between traditional agricultural towns with adobe homes and ancient churches. The tiny communities of Las Minas, Pesé, and Ocú become packed during annual folk festivals, but for most of the year they are somnolent villages seem hardly touched by the hand of time. You can drive a loop through the most interesting towns in a matter of hours, heading first to Pesé, then to Las Minas, and north to Ocú, where you can continue north to the Carretera Interamericana just west of Divisa, and back to Chitré. The easiest town to visit is **Pesé**, 22 km (14 mi) west of Chitré, which is surrounded by a sea of sugarcane, used by the town's one industry, the rum distillery that produces Seco Herrerano, Panama's most popular booze. The rocket fuel powers the region's folk festivals and keeps its AA chapters running. Witness large quantities being consumed during Pesé's annual Festival de la Caña (Sugar Cane Festival) in March. Thirty-two kilometers (20 mi) southwest of Pesé in the mountains is **Las Minas**, a gold-mining community during the colonial era and now the site of traditional celebrations during the first days of September and on December 4. From Las Minas it's a rough 21-km (13-mi) drive north to **Ocú**, a more developed town that hosts the annual Festival de Manito that attracts musicians and dancers from across the region.

LA VILLA DE LOS SANTOS

256 km (159 mi) southwest of Panama City, 4 km (2 mi) south of Chitré.

Just across the muddy Río La Villa from Chitré is La Villa de Los Santos, which is considerably smaller than its neighbor but more historically significant. When it was founded in 1569 it was one of just two Spanish outposts in an area dominated by hostile Indians. That indigenous population was highly developed, as excavations at the nearby burial site of Cerro Juan Díaz have established, but they were no match for Spanish swords or the old-world diseases.

La Villa's claim to fame in Panama is that it was the first community to express support for Simón Bolívar's South American revolution against Spain. People in the region were fed up with Spanish exploitation, but the politicians in the administrative center of Natá were pro-Spain, and they repressed La Villa's independence movement. The town's most powerful families consequently sent a letter directly to Bolívar on November 10, 1821, expressing their desire to join his recently liberated state of Gran Colombia (modern-day Colombia, Ecuador, and Venezuela). Several weeks later Panama declared its independence from Spain. The drafting of that letter, known as *el Primer Grito de la Independencia*, (the First Shout of Independence), is celebrated every November 10 on La Villa's central plaza with speeches and folk dancing.

Three blocks east of the Carretera Nacional, La Villa's central Plaza Simón Bolívar is surrounded by colonial- and republican-era buildings,

DEVILISH CELEBRATIONS

The Christian holiday of Corpus Christi takes place in either May or June—62 days after Holy Thursday—and has been observed in Europe since the 13th century, but no town celebrates it like La Villa de Los Santos. Despite the fact that its name translates as Village of the Saints, the town celebrates Corpus Christi with traditional dances performed by *los diablitos* (little devils)—men in red and black costumes and demonic papier-mâché masks. Those pagan characters dominate 10 days of ancient rituals and modern revelry that begin the Wednesday before Corpus Christi and culminate with concerts that attract people from across Panama.

The pagan activities peak eight days after the mass of Corpus Christi, when diablitos dance in the streets and groups of adolescents in masks run around trying to scare people. The adult diablitos, who are usually accompanied by musicians, carry inflated, dried cow bladders that they bang with sticks while emitting bizarre groans. Groups of them may go from house to house performing their dances, though rather than candy they're given shots of rum. Though the masks were traditionally made of wood, and first had indigenous, then Chinese motifs—Panama has had a Chinese population since the mid-19th century—they are increasingly influenced by the monsters of Hollywood movies.

the most impressive of which is the town's church. The **Iglesia de San Atanasio** (⌧*Calle José Vallarino* ☎*No phone*), completed in 1773, holds various treasures of colonial art, including a massive mahogany altar covered with gold leaf and nine smaller altars. The church also has an ornate mahogany archway and a large statue of Christ that is paraded through the streets during Semana Santa.

The famous letter to Simón Bolívar was drafted in 1821 in the whitewashed colonial building across from the plaza, now the **Museo de la Nacionalidad** *(Nationhood Museum)*. The colonial-era furniture and sad collection of pre-Columbian pottery within are hardly worth the entrance fee, but the well-preserved building, with its ancient handhewn rafters, adobe walls, and terra-cotta floors, certainly is. ⌧*Calle José Vallarino* ☎*966–8192* 🎫*$1* 🕐*Tues.–Sat. 9–4, Sun. 9–noon.*

TO & FROM

La Villa de Los Santos lies to the east of the Carretera Nacional (Route 2) 4 km (2½ mi) south of Chitré. Driving directions are the same as those for Chitré, only you continue past town and drive over the Río La Villa. The 10-minute taxi trip from Chitré costs $2.

GUARARÉ

277 km (172 mi) southwest of Panama City, 21 km (13 mi) south of Chitré.

It would be quite possible to miss the tiny town of Guararé as you drive from Chitré to Las Tablas. Though it's a sleepy spot most of the year, the town plaza wakes up during the last week of September, when it hosts the **Festival de la Mejorana,** which attracts fans of folk music from around the country. The festival was founded in the 1940s by a local scholar to celebrate and promote the preservation of *la mejorana,* a traditional genre of Panamanian music that is played on small five-string guitar called the *guitarra mejoranera,* (or simply a *mejorana*) and usually accompanied by folk dances. It's less of a party scene than Carnaval or Corpus Christi. September 24 is the town's patron-saint day, with masses and other activities. Other than the Mejorana Festival, there is little reason to stop in Guararé.

> ### A LOCAL SPECIALTY
>
> Las Tablas, Guararé, and the nearby town of La Enea are known for producing some of the country's best *polleras*, the delicately embroidered dresses that are Panama's national costume and worn primarily during folk festivals. They take months to make, which is why they sell for thousands of dollars.

TO & FROM

Most of Guararé lies to the east of the Carretera Nacional, just north of Las Tablas, which is served by buses that depart from Panama City's Albrook Terminal every 30 minutes. Driving directions are the same as those for Chitré, from which you continue south for another 21 km (13 mi).

LAS TABLAS

282 km (175 mi) southwest of Panama City, 30 km (19 mi) south of Chitré.

Though it has fewer than 9,000 inhabitants, Las Tablas is the main commercial center for the southern Azuero Peninsula. Its Carnaval celebrations and its annual Festival de la Pollera (July 21–23) are famous throughout Panama. The latter features folk music, dancing, and the election of a pollera-wearing queen.

Though it was founded in the late 17th century, Las Tablas has few historic monuments. The town is the birthplace of Belisario Porras, one of the founders of the Panamanian republic, who served three presidential terms. The **Museo Belisario Porras,** across from the central plaza (Parque Porras) is his former home and holds a small collection of memorabilia from his life. (⊠ *Av. Belisario Porras at Parque Porras* ☎994–6326 💷*50¢* ⏰*Tues.–Sat. 8–4, Sun. 9–noon*).

West of Parque Porras is **La Iglesia Santa Librada** (⊠ *Calle 8 de Noviembre and Av. Belisario Porras* ☎*No phone*), which has an attractive hardwood interior and an impressive gilt alter with an image of the town's patron saint—the Santa Librada. It is the focus of a major pilgrimage every July 20, just before the annual pollera festival.

Carnaval transforms the normally quiet town of Las Tablas into a wild and colorful place for several days. Locals spend the better part of the year preparing for the four days of competitive events. The town is divided into the Calle Arriba (Upper Street) and Calle Abajo (Lower Street), and each elects its own queen and organizes competing parades. Adding to the festivities are strolling bands called *murgas,* folk-dance performances, fireworks, and water trucks that douse overheated revelers by day. Hotel prices double during Carnaval; reserve at least a month in advance.

3

WHERE TO STAY & EAT

¢–$ ✕ **El Caserón.** This large, bright restaurant on a quiet corner several blocks east of the central plaza has long been considered the best in Las Tablas, but that doesn't say much. They have an extensive menu that includes pizza and Chinese, both of which should be avoided. The best bets are the seafood, such as corvina *al ajillo* (in a garlic sauce) and inexpensive *langostinos* (prawns) or *langosta* (lobster), either of which costs less than $10. If you want meat, order a *filet,* or perhaps *pollo con almendras* (chicken breast with almonds, mushrooms, and ginger). ✉ *Av. Moises Espino and Calle Agustin Batista* ☎ *994–6066* ▭ *No credit cards.*

¢ ✕ **Hotel Manolo.** Also called Hotel Piamonte, this is one of Las Tablas's older hotels. Basic second-floor rooms have tile floors, small bathrooms, and TVs. Most have small windows that open onto the central hallway, so opt for either inexpensive "junior suites," with views of the street, or the quieter and brighter rooms at the back. Popular with locals, the large restaurant (¢–$) serves Chinese and Panamanian food; you're better off ordering the latter, such as corvina *a la plancha* (sautéed), arroz con pollo, or *filet a la parrilla* (grilled tenderloin). **Pros: Inexpensive, central location. Cons: Rooms are nothing special.** ✉ *Carretera Nacional, 1 block east of park* ☎ *994–6372* *17 rooms* *In-hotel: restaurant, no elevator, laundry service, no-smoking rooms* ▭ *AE, MC, V* *EP.*

TO & FROM

Las Tablas lies 26 km (16 mi) south of Chitré via the Carretera Nacional (Route 3), which runs right through the middle of town, turning left (east) at the end of Parque Porras. It takes about four hours to drive to Las Tablas from Panama City, and buses, which depart from Panama City's Albrook Terminal every 40 minutes, take five hours.

PEDASÍ

324 km (201 mi) southwest of Panama City, 42 km (26 mi) south of Las Tablas.

Little Pedasí may make Chitré and Las Tablas look like cities, but it is the tourist center of the Azuero Peninsula due to its proximity to Isla Iguana and Playa Venao. A quiet ranching community with plentiful gardens and a few adobe homes among cement-block buildings, Pedasí is the birthplace of Mireya Moscosa, Panama's only female president (1999–2004). She did a lot for her hometown, which now has a large branch of the Banco Nacional, a refurbished central plaza, and a street sign on every corner.

For travelers, Pedasí is simply a place to sleep, eat, or hit the bank before heading elsewhere. The Carretera Nacional runs right through town, where it is called Avenida Central. Pedasí has a few small hotels, a couple of grocery stores, and, oddly enough, a gourmet restaurant.

The nicest beaches on the mainland around Pedasí are Playa Los Destiladeros, 10 km (6 mi) to the south, and Playa Venao, 35 km (22 mi) to the southwest (⇨ both *below*).

WHERE TO STAY & EAT

$$
Fodor'sChoice
★

✕**Manolo Caracol.** A branch of Panama City's popular restaurant of the same name, this is hands down the best restaurant in the Azuero Peninsula. It lacks the historic charm of the original Manolo Caracol, but follows the same recipe of white walls with artwork, a good all-Spanish wine selection, and a seasonal menu of about 10 items served in five courses. Dishes are made with fresh tuna or mahimahi, or with tender cuts of local beef. In one meal, dishes could range from sashimi to gazpacho to tenderloin in pepper sauce. Owner Manolo Maduño is often here, moving from kitchen to dining area to ensure that every meal is a culinary adventure. ✉*Calle Las Tablas, behind Cantina Central* ☎*995–2810* ▭*MC, V.*

¢

✕**Restaurante Angela.** This small restaurant serves decent Panamanian fare at dirt-cheap prices, but its best asset is the covered terrace. Popular standards on the short menu might include *carne guisada* (stewed beef), *sopa de mariscos* (seafood soup), and *pescado al ajillo* (fish of the day with garlic). For a typical Panamanian breakfast, try *bistec encebollado* (skirt steak smothered in onions), *hojaldre* (deep-fried bread), or *carimañolas* (fried cassava dumplings filled with ground beef). ✉*Av. Central at Calle Estudiante* ☎*995–2207* ▭*No credit cards.*

¢

🏠**Dim's Hostal.** This simple two-story house in the heart of town is Pedasí's best lodging, which isn't saying much. The rooms are rustic but nicely decorated. Aside from the owner's hospitality, this place's best asset is the round, thatched *rancho* in back where complementary breakfast is served, and where guests can hang out during the day in hammocks and chairs in the shade of mango trees. Guests can use the adjacent kitchen. **Pros: Friendly owner, central location. Cons: Very basic rooms, some street noise.** ✉*Av. Central at Calle Estudiante* ☎*995–2303* 📠*995–2509* 🛏*7 rooms* ⚐*In-hotel: no elevator, laundry service, public Internet, no-smoking rooms* ▭*No credit cards* 🍴⃝*BP.*

SPORTS & THE OUTDOORS

DIVING &
SNORKELING

For excellent scuba diving and snorkeling, head to Isla Iguana, a 30-minute boat trip from Playa El Arenal, just east of town. **Buzos de Azuero** (✉*Carretera Nacional, north of town* ☎*995-2405* ⊕*www.dive-n-fishpanama.com*) arranges fishing and scuba-diving trips.

For more information on diving see the Isla Iguana and Playa Venao sections, below.

SPORTFISHING

The ocean east and south of the Azuero Peninsula holds rich fishing waters, and Pedasí is a good place for relatively inexpensive fishing charters. The area is known for its abundant tuna, but it also has plenty of roosterfish, wahoo, dolphinfish, amberjack, and occasional billfish.

Buzos de Azuero (✉ *Carretera Nacional, north of town, Pedasí* ☎*995–2405* ⊕*www.dive-n-fishpanama.com*) charters a 27-foot boat with twin motors and fishing equipment for $300 per day.

TO & FROM

Pedasí lies 74 km (46 mi) south of Chitré via the Carretera Nacional. It takes a little over an hour to drive there. Buses that depart from Panama City's Terminal de Buses every 40 minutes can take four to five hours. Air Panama has three flights a day from Panama City to Pedasí on Wednesdays, Fridays, and Sundays.

ISLA IGUANA

11 km (7 mi) northeast of Pedasí.

Fodor$**Choice**

★ With the only white-sand beach on the Azuero Peninsula and excellent snorkeling and scuba diving less than an hour from Pedasí, Isla Iguana is the Azuero Peninsula's top natural attraction. Less than 1 km long, the island is covered with coconut palms and other tropical vegetation and has two beaches: immaculate **Playa El Cirial,** nearly 250 meters (800 feet) in length, and the tiny Playita del Faro, on the other side of the island's thin middle. The largest coral reef in the Gulf of Panama, at nearly 99 acres, surrounds Isla Iguana. The reef is composed of 14 coral species; some colonies are more than 800 years old. More than 200 species of invertebrates and at least 350 fish, including parrot fish, black-and white-tipped reef sharks, puffer fish, and 16 eel species inhabit the reef. The island itself is inhabited by crabs and black iguanas and has a rookery used by more than 5,000 magnificent frigate birds. Both island and reef are protected within the **Reserva de Vida Silvestre Isla Iguana.**

Considering Isla Iguana's natural treasures, it's hard to believe that the U.S. Air Force used the island as a bombing range during World War II. Some unexploded bombs were detonated when it became a wildlife refuge, but ⚠ **there may be still-unexploded shells buried in the sand, so stick to the trail when crossing the island between beaches.** In the middle of the trail is a lighthouse with views of the bomb craters.

The National Environment Authority (ANAM) charges a $3 admission fee to visit the island; you can camp next to the ANAM station for $10. Fishing is prohibited in the reserve, as is removing anything from the reef, or island. For more information, go to the Web site of the non-profit Fundación Isla Iguana (⊕ *www.islaiguana.com*).

SPORTS & THE OUTDOORS

SCUBA DIVING & SNORKELING Isla Iguana is a great place for snorkeling—the reef begins just a short swim from the island's beaches—and also has plenty for scuba divers to explore. Visibility is best and waters are calmest and warmest April to December. January through March, strong winds can make boating dangerous and the water gets quite cool.

Buzos de Azuero (✉ *Carretera Nacional, north of town, Pedasí* ☎*995–2405* ⊕*www.dive-n-fishpanama.com*), run by Canadian dive master Jeremy Mitchell, arranges day trips from Pedasí for snorkeling or scuba diving. They rent snorkeling gear for $10, scuba gear with two tanks for $35, and can arrange a boat to the island for up to six people for about $50.

TO & FROM

Isla Iguana is reached from Playa El Arenal, a beach just east of Pedasí, via a 20- to 30-minute boat ride, which can be arranged by Buzos de Azuero (⇨ *above*).

PLAYA LOS DESTILADEROS

334 km (208 mi) southwest of Panama City, 10 km (6 mi) south of Pedasí.

This beach in the Azuero Peninsula's southeast corner isn't the region's nicest, given its dark sand and abundant rocks, but it has the peninsula's two best hotels. It is an attractive enough spot, with a swath of brown sand backed by hills covered with a mix of pastures, patches of forest, and scattered vacation homes. Rough seas often make for dangerous swimming here at high tide, but at low tide offshore rocks tend to break the force of the waves, creating some small pools for safe swimming. The best beach for swimming in the area is **Puerto Escondido**, a few miles north. Los Destiladeros is the most comfortable and expensive base for trips to Isla Iguana and Playa Venao, thanks to the two good hotels. The surrounding countryside is excellent for walking or horseback riding.

WHERE TO STAY & EAT

$$$–$$$$
★
╳🏠**Villa Camilla.** On a forested ridge overlooking the ocean, this palatial boutique hotel—built as a showcase for the adjacent residential community—blurs the lines between nature and dwelling, with earth-toned polished cement, varnished hardwoods, tropical foliage, and abundant birdsong. Spacious guest rooms have high ceilings, large bathrooms, and modern amenities. Prix-fixe meals ($$$$) are served either by the pool or in the dining room-cum-library. (A full meal plan is $50 per person per day.) The hotel is a five-minute walk from the beach. The main drawback is that the management is more concerned with selling real estate than catering to vacationers. **Pros: Gorgeous design, great views, good food. Cons: Weekend rates nearly double midweek rates, built to sell real estate.** ⊠*On right before beach* 🏠🏠*232–6721 or 6678–8555* ⊕*www.azueros.com* ➥*3 rooms, 4 suites* ⌂*In-room: no phone, safe. In-hotel: restaurant, pool, no elevator, beachfront, public Wi-Fi, no-smoking rooms* ═*MC, V* ⍢*EP.*

$–$$$
Fodor's Choice
★
╳🏠**Posada Los Destiladeros.** This funky little lodge right on Playa Desiladeros has tropical gardens and views of the surf breaking over the rocks. The central wooden restaurant ($$) with a terrace and sea views, serves good French cuisine, mostly fresh seafood, on its ever-changing prix-fixe menu. Rooms, surrounding the gardens, a shallow pool, and several sun decks, are nature-inspired, with plenty of bamboo, terra-cotta, stonework, wooden sinks, high sloping ceilings, and terraces. The nicest rooms are the Viginia and the smaller Bouboulina on the beach. The spacious, thatched A-frames in back (Izania and

Azuero's Tropical Dry Forest

CLOSE UP

Centuries ago, this region was largely covered with tropical dry forest, but that wilderness has been reduced to tiny remnants everywhere but in the mountains of the Azuero Peninsula's remote southwest corner and on Isla de Coiba. That endangered ecosystem is different from what you'll find in central and eastern Panama, or along the Caribbean coast. It is less diverse than the country's more humid forests, because fewer plants can endure the region's severe dry season, but it contains some species that you won't find in other parts of the country, such as the rare painted parakeet and the endemic Veraguan mango hummingbird.

The Azuero Peninsula is Panama's driest region, and gets virtually no rain from December to May, when the pastures turn brown and most trees drop their foliage. From May to December, however, Pacific storms regularly drench the peninsula, and the trees burst into lush foliage.

The region's marked seasons make it easier to grow many food crops and maintain pasture, which appealed to Spanish colonists. They cut significant forest during the colonial era, but it wasn't until after World War II, when international banks promoted ranching in Latin America to meet the growing demand for hamburgers in the United States, that deforestation became rampant in the region. In the1980s the Panamanian government finally began protecting the region's dwindling forests, but by then its original wilderness had receded to tiny remnants.

The region's remaining tropical dry-forest patches hold some interesting flora and fauna. Kapok, gumbo limbo, and spiny cedar trees are common here, and in the dry season you may see the rose and yellow flowers of the Tabebuia trees, or various orchid species. You may also catch sight of riverside wrens, brown jays, black iguanas, or howler monkeys in the branches of those trees. While Panama's underfunded National Environment Authority (ANAM) struggles to enforce the laws governing the protected areas on the western side of the Azuero Peninsula, organizations and landowners in its eastern half are focusing on ecological restoration, reforesting former pastureland and protecting existing forest.

Ariel) are also nice, though more rustic. Less-expensive rooms behind the restaurant are a bit dark. The posada also sells real estate. **Pros: Gorgeous views, nice rooms, good food. Cons: Cheapest rooms dark.** ⊠ *On beach, left at end of Rd.* 🖼995–2771 *or 6673–9262* 🖂*Apdo. 0816-02847* ⊕*www.panamabambu.net* ☎*10 rooms* ⚐*In-room: no TV (some), kitchen (some). In-hotel: no elevator, public Wi-Fi, parking (no fee), no-smoking rooms* ☰*MC, V* ⦿*CP.*

SPORTS & THE OUTDOORS

HORSEBACK
RIDING
The hills around Playa Destiladero hold a mix of pasture, patches of tropical dry forest, and stunning ocean views, which make the area perfect for horseback riding. Both **Villa Camilla** and the **Posada Los Destiladeros** rent horses to their guests. Ride first thing in the morning or in the late afternoon to see birds.

TO & FROM

By car, follow the Carretera Nacional through Pedasí, and turn left 3 km (2 mi) south of town. That road quickly loses its pavement, but is in good condition for the entire 7 km (4 mi) to the beach. Air Panama has flights from Panama City to Pedasí on Friday and Sunday afternoons, and the hotels at Los Destiladeros can arrange an airport pickup.

PLAYA VENAO (PLAYA VENADO)

358 km (222 mi) southwest of Panama City, 34 km (21 mi) southwest of Pedasí.

Fodor'sChoice Long a mecca for surfers, the 2-mi-long pale-brown Playa Venao, in a
★ deep, half-moon bay surrounded by largely deforested hills, has some of Panama's most consistent surf, and what could be the country's best beach break. The center of the beach is consistently pounded by surf, creating dangerous swimming conditions, but the western and eastern extremes are protected within the curved ends of the bay, and thus have calm water, especially the eastern end. Other outdoor options include snorkeling, horseback riding, fishing, or a trip to the turtle-nesting beaches of Isla Cañas.

Playa Venao is off the beaten track, with no stores or ATMs and neither phone lines nor cell-phone coverage—which means you need to leave messages or e-mail reservations well ahead of time—and only one hotel accepts credit cards. All services are in Pedasí.

About 4 km (2½ mi) before Playa Venao on the road from Pedasí (on the left) is the tiny fishing community of **El Ciruelo,** the embarkation point for local sportfishing charters and snorkeling trips. A couple of kilometers west of El Ciruelo is the **Laboratorio Achotines** (☎ *995–8166* ⊕ *www.iattc.org*), a research center where biologists are studying the reproductive cycles of yellowfin tuna. You can take a guided tour of its 130-acre protected tropical dry forest, where you might see monkeys and other wildlife, by reserving at least one day in advance.

Fodor'sChoice Just past the Laboratorio Achotines, in a bay east of Playa Venado, is
★ lovely **La Playita,** a safe swimming beach with the area's best snorkeling along its rocky edges. Though a "resort" on the beach rents a few rooms, most people visit La Playita on day trips. It has a decent restaurant; it gets packed during the holidays.

Just west of La Playita, the first entrance to Playa Venao on the left leads to Villa Marina, the best swimming area, protected behind forested **El Morro** island. At low tide you can walk out to the island. About a mile west of the beach's first entrance is the main entrance, next to a colorful bus stop, which is where you'll find the surf break and an open-air restaurant, Jardin Vista Hermosa. On holidays and dry-season weekends there is usually a small tent city on the beach near the surf break. Campers use the restaurant's bathrooms and showers for a small fee. ⚠ **If there are waves, this area can develop dangerous rip currents, so don't swim there if the sea is rough.** There is another, steep entrance to the beach on Playa Venao's western end, a safe place to swim.

A few kilometers to the west of Playa Madroño is the town of Cañas, where boats embark to cross the estuary to Isla Cañas.

WHERE TO STAY & EAT

$ ✕🍴 **La Playita Resort.** With dino-
☺ saur statues decorating the lawn,
★ pet macaws flying about, and tame emus wandering the grounds, La Playita is certainly unique. Owner Lester Knight may be eccentric, but while his neighbors chop trees down, he plants them, and most of his 15-acre property is covered with forest. The beige beach is in

> **WHAT'S IN A NAME?**
>
> Playa Venao appears as Playa Venado on some maps and signs. *Venado* is Spanish for deer, which is what the beach was named for, but the Panamanian pronunciation is vehn-*ow*, thus Venao has come to be accepted as the name of the beach. Unfortunately, the deer for which the beach was named were hunted to extinction here years ago.

a deep, protected bay, making it perfect for swimming and snorkeling. Overlooking the beach is a large, thatched restaurant specializing in fresh seafood, such as *corvina al ajillo* (sea bass with garlic) and *langostinos a la criolla* (prawns in a tomato sauce). Rooms, in two cement buildings set back from the beach, are simple, with tile floors, nice woodwork, and small terraces with hammocks. Rooms 1 and 2 are the most private. Although you'll have the place to yourself most weekdays, on weekends between Christmas and Easter you'll share it with more than 100 often-boisterous Panamanian day visitors. **Pros: Great beach, forest, friendly, good food. Cons: Packed most weekends and holidays.** ✉*La Playita, 2 km (1 mi) east of Playa Venao* ☎*996-6727 or 6639-2968* ⊕*www.playitaresort.com* 🛏*5 rooms* ♿*In-room: no phone, no TV. In-hotel: 2 restaurants, bar, beachfront, water sports, no elevator, no-smoking rooms* ▤*No credit cards* ⊙*BP.*

$$ 🍴 **Villa Marina.** At the eastern end of Playa Venao—the safest swimming area—this colonial-hacienda-inspired lodge is on a 160-acre ranch. Older rooms have high ceilings and porticos with hammocks overlooking a small courtyard with a fountain. Newer rooms are bright and spacious and have ocean views, but are less attractive. Prix-fixe meals ($$) are served family-style in a traditional ranch house or on the porch with a view of the sea. The hotel has great potential, but falls short on many details. Nevertheless, it's the only place in Playa Venao that takes credit cards or that has Internet and satellite TV. Horseback riding, fishing, and hiking trips can be arranged. **Pros: Beachfront location, nice design, friendly. Cons: Loosely managed.** ✉*First entrance to Playa Venao* ☎*211-2277 or 6673-9455* ⊕*www.playavenado.com* 🛏*9 rooms* ♿*In-room: no phone, safe. In-hotel: restaurant, bar, pool, no elevator, beachfront, water sports, laundry service, public Wi-Fi, no-smoking rooms* ▤*MC, V* ⊙*EP.*

¢–$$ 🍴 **Eco Venao.** This laid-back lodge up the hill from Playa Venao is part
★ of a project to reforest 300 acres of pastureland, funded in part by tourism earnings. It is largely self-service, with kitchens and no restaurant (groceries are in Pedasí). Three gorgeous houses with high ceilings, polished cement walls, and lovely woodwork—made from fallen trees—are perched on ridges with great views. Each house has two

bedrooms with private bathrooms and a kitchen and living room. You can rent a house, or just one room. Rustic thatch-roof *cabañas* (cabins) in the forest share a small bathhouse. They have one double bed, fans, mosquito nets, and a loft with a mattress. Even cheaper are tiny doubles behind the dorm, with shared bathrooms. The lodge rents surfboards, kayaks, and snorkeling equipment and can arrange horseback riding or hiking tours. **Pros: Great views, lovely design, eco-friendly. Cons: No restaurant, off the beach.** ⊠*Playa Venao, on right after bus stop* ☎202–0530 ⊕*www.venao.com* 📮2 rooms, 2 cabins, 3 houses ⌂*In-room: no a/c, no phone, kitchen (some), no TV. In-hotel: water sports, no elevator* ▭*No credit cards* ⦿*EP.*

$ 🏨 **Sereia do Mar.** Perched above the sea in the fishing village just east of Playa Venao, this is a convenient hotel for anglers, but also a decent base for surfing and other activities. Simple rooms have high ceilings, red-tile floors, and two queen beds each. They open onto a long covered terrace with hammocks and chairs and ocean views, where breakfast is served. There is a rustic bar under a thatch roof next door. **Pros: Reasonable rates, nice view, sportfishing. Cons: No restaurant, several miles from beach.** ⊠*El Ciruelo, 4 km (2½ mi) east of Playa Venao* ☎6716–8301 or 6524–9421 I*neni_panama@hotmail.com* 📮4 rooms ⌂*In-room: no phone, no TV. In-hotel: bar, no elevator, water sports, public Wi-Fi, no-smoking rooms* ▭*No credit cards* ⦿*BP.*

SPORTS & THE OUTDOORS

HORSEBACK RIDING   The hills around Playa Venado have some excellent horseback routes. **Villa Marina** (☎211–2277 or 6673–9455) offers horseback riding on the beach or on the surrounding ranch. **Eco Venao** (☎202–0530) has a horseback tour of their vast property.

SCUBA DIVING & SNORKELING   The coast and islets around Playa Venao hold rocky reefs with sparse coral formations that are frequented by an array of fish. The **Islas Frailes,** two islets to the south of Playa Venado, have more, and bigger, fish. From June to October you may also see humpback whales in the sea south of Playa Venao.

Experienced divers can arrange boat dives at Islas Frailes with **Buzos de Azuero** (⊠*Calle Principal, Pedasí* ☎995–2405 ⊕*www.dive-n-fish-panama.com*). The boat to Islas Frailes costs $100.

The hotel **Sereia do Mar** (⊠*El Ciruelo* ☎6716–8301 or 6524–9421) rents snorkeling equipment and can provide transportation to nearby Isla La Monja, which is a good skin-diving spot when the sea is calm. **La Playita Resort** (☎996–6727 or 6639–2968 ⊕*www.playitaresort.com*) rents snorkeling equipment for exploring the deep bay it sits on.

SPORTFISHING   It is no coincidence that the Inter-American Tropical Tuna Commission has its research center next to Playa Venao. The ocean here holds plenty of tuna, as well as dolphinfish, roosterfish, wahoo, and other sport fish. Some of the area's best fishing is around the **Islas Frailes,** just to the south of Playa Venado. Sportfishing charters can be arranged through the hotel **Sereia do Mar** (⊠*El Ciruelo* ☎6716–8301 or 6524–9421 ✉ *neni_panama@hotmail.com*). A day of fishing in the hotel's 30-foot boat with twin 70-hp motors costs $400. Less expensive ($30 per hour) inshore fishing is available at **La Playita Resort** (☎996–6727 or 6639–2968 ⊕*www.playitaresort.com*), but they only have a 16-foot boat with a 40-hp motor, so don't go out far on a rough day.

Pedasí-based **Buzos de Azuero** (✉*Calle Principal, north of town, Pedasí* ☎995–2405 ⊕*www.dive-n-fishpanama.com*) charters a 27-foot boat with twin motors with tackle for $300 per day.

SURFING **Playa Venao** is one of the country's most popular surf spots. It is one of the few good beach breaks in the country—popular with experts and novices alike. On weekends and holidays it's crowded, but it's usually not bad during the week. Breaks are a good mix of lefts and rights, but the waves are only decent from mid- to high tide and below 6 feet—beyond that they close out.

When Playa Venao is crowded, or at lower tides, you can drive a couple of miles to the west, over the ridge, and hike 20 minutes to **Playa Madroño**, a left beach break that is best near low to medium tide and tends to be bigger than Playa Venao. If you've got the time, and a 4WD vehicle, you can drive to **Playa Cambutal**, south of Tonosí, about 90 minutes from Playa Venado, which has point breaks and beach breaks. Waves are often bigger than at Playa Venado, and great when the swell gets overhead. The surf tends to be good here from March to November, though it's best from August through October. Eco Venao and La Playita Resort rent surfboards.

TO & FROM
By car, follow the Carretera Nacional through Pedasí and drive southwest on a windy road for 34 km (21 mi). There is just one bus per day between Venao and Pedasí, but taxis in Pedasí will make the 20-minute trip for $15. Air Panama has flights from Panama City to Pedasí on Friday and Sunday afternoons.

VERAGUAS

The only Panamanian province with coastline on both oceans, Veraguas was named by Christopher Columbus, who sailed along its Caribbean coast on his fourth voyage to the Americas. The name is likely a contraction of *verdes aguas* (green waters), referring to the coastal jungle reflected in the sea. Traveling along the province's coast or islands during the rainy season, you may experience that green-water effect.

Few tourists visit Veraguas, and those who do head for its remote Pacific coast and Isla de Coiba for world-class scuba diving and surfing. Playa Santa Catalina, which has one of the country's best surf breaks, is currently the only spot in the province with any semblance of a tourist industry, catering primarily to surfers on tight budgets. Santa Catalina and Isla de Coiba are well off the beaten track.

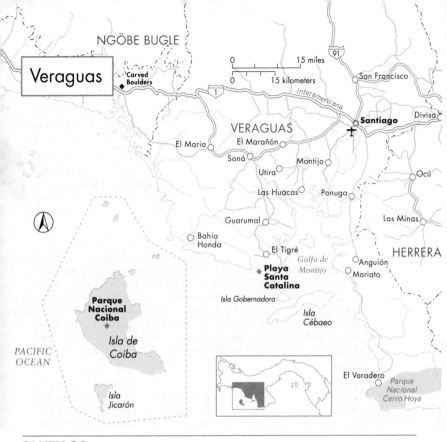

SANTIAGO

250 km (155 mi) southwest of Panama City, 190 km (118 mi) east of David.

The provincial capital, Santiago is usually nothing more than a pit stop between Panama City and the westernmost province of Chiriquí, Playa Santa Catalina, or Isla de Coiba. With a population of 33,000, Santiago is little more than a large town, but as the commercial and administrative center for a large ranching and farming area, it's considered one of Panama's principal cities. Though founded in the colonial era, Santiago has very little historic architecture and lacks charm. Its main street, Avenida Central, runs southwest from the highway to the Plaza Central. An attractive, white, 19th-century church, the **Catedral Santiago Apóstol** (⊠*North side of plaza* 🕾*No phone*), dominates the Plaza Central. It is the focus of a small religious festival the last week of July. Turn left at the church to head to Playa Santa Catalina.

WHERE TO STAY & EAT

¢ 🏨 **Hotel La Hacienda.** If you get stuck spending a night in Santiago, this large hotel on the Carretera Interamericana a few kilometers west of town is your best option. The two-story, white-stucco building has tile floors, lots of wide arches, and a large interior garden. Rooms are bright and decorated with colorful Mexican art. They have cable TV and small bathrooms, and the hotel's ample facilities include a nice pool, a tiny gym, a playground, and a bar. The restaurant serves a mix of Mexican and Panamanian dishes. **Pros: Reasonable rates, decent rooms, nice pool. Cons: Mediocre restaurant, on the highway.** ⊠ *Inter-American Hwy, 3 km (2 mi) west of Santiago, Uvito exit* ☎ *958–8580* 🖶 *958–8579* ➟ *56 rooms* ⚴ *In-hotel: restaurant, room service, bar, pool, gym, public Internet no-smoking rooms* ▤ *MC, V* ⏃ *BP.*

TO & FROM

To drive to Santiago from Panama City, head west on the Carretera Interamericana 250 km (155 mi), and look for the Avenida Central on the left. The road to Playa Santa Catalina is on the left at the Plaza Central. Direct buses to Santiago depart from Panama City's Albrook Terminal every hour and take four hours. Buses also run every 90 minutes between Santiago and David, in Chiriquí Province.

OFF THE BEATEN PATH

If you've got an hour to spare, consider making the 20-minute drive north to the tiny town of San Francisco, known for the colonial art in its historic church, the **Iglesia de San Francisco de Asis.** Built in the early 1700s, that stout stone structure doesn't look like much from the outside, but it holds some lovely baroque altars. San Francisco was one of the first Spanish settlements in western Panama, and played an important role in their struggle to subjugate the Indians and convert them to Christianity. By 1756 the town had a population of 2,277, which is about how many people live there today. It was largely indigenous artisans that built the eight altars with local hardwoods, under the supervision of Franciscan monks. The ornate main altar, which consists of more than 400 pieces of colorfully painted tropical cedar, is an impressive example of colonial art. The road to San Francisco (and, ultimately, Santa Fe) heads north from the Carretera Interamericana just west of the turnoff for Avenida Central and is paved for the entire 17 km (11 mi).

PLAYA SANTA CATALINA

360 km (223 mi) southwest of Panama City, 110 km (68 mi) southwest of Santiago.

Fodor'sChoice
★

Literally at the end of the road, the tiny fishing village of Santa Catalina sits near some of the best surfing spots in the country, and is the closest port to Isla de Coiba, Panama's top dive destination. For years, the only people who visited Playa Santa Catalina were adventurous surfers who made the long trip here on rough roads and slept in rustic rooms for the pleasure of riding La Punta, a right point break. The roads and accommodations are better now, and a dive center has opened. For the moment, Santa Catalina remains a quiet beach town with little to offer other than ocean views through the palm fronds, friendly locals, cheap seafood, and amazing surf and diving.

WHERE TO STAY & EAT

¢–$$ ★ **Jammin Pizza.** Surprisingly good pizza is served at this small, Italian-owned open-air restaurant a short walk from the beach. The thin pies baked in a wood-burning brick oven would be popular in Panama City, but they taste that much better served at the edge of civilization. On holidays and dry-season weekends the place can get packed, and stays open late as locals and visitors top off their dinners with cold beers and good music. ✉ *Road to El Estero, first right* ☎ *No phone* ▭ *No credit cards.*

¢ **Oasis Surf Camp.** This rustic, Italian-owned lodge is right on Playa Santa Catalina, amid the coconut palms mere steps from the surf. Most rooms are basically cement boxes with beds, a fan, and a bathroom with a cold-water shower—the additional $10 for air-conditioning and hot water is well worth it. But you can hear the waves and the rustling of palm fronds at night, and when you step out your door you're on the beach. A nearby open-air restaurant ($–$$) serves three meals a day and becomes a bar at night. Surfing lessons are given on the nearby beach break—the only place in Santa Catalina where novices can surf without risking their lives. The lodge rents boards. Camping is allowed for a small fee, and it's a zoo during the holidays. **Pros: On the beach, laid-back atmosphere, good food. Cons: Very basic rooms.** ✉ *Playa Catalina* ☎ *6588–7077* 🌐 *www.oasissurfcamp.com* *10 rooms* *In-room: no a/c (some), no phone, no TV. In-hotel: restaurant, water sports, no elevator, no-smoking rooms* ▭ *No credit cards* *EP.*

¢–$ **Punta Brava Lodge.** On a grassy ridge overlooking the sea, Punta Brava is owned by veteran Panamanian surfer José Crespo, and is the perfect spot for surfers, right behind the point break. José rents surfboards, but he also organizes fishing and island-hopping trips in his 25- and 27-foot boats. The lodge has the best accommodations in town—rooms range from basic crash pads with fans and cold-water showers to air-conditioned bungalows with two queen beds, a TV and DVD player, and a small refrigerator. Midpriced rooms are in a two-story building with a long balcony and a wide, covered terrace with an ocean view. An open-air bar-restaurant serves decent food, including pasta and seafood. This is the only hotel in Santa Catalina with satellite phones and Internet connection. **Pros: Ocean view, near surf break. Cons: Rough access road, 5 minutes from beach.** ✉ *Down dirt road on left before beach* ☎ *6614-3868 or 6618–9362* 🌐 *www.puntabrava.com* *11 rooms* *In-room: No phone, refrigerator (some). In-hotel: restaurant, water sports, no elevator, public Internet, no-smoking rooms* ▭ *No credit cards* *EP.*

SPORTS & THE OUTDOORS

SCUBA DIVING & SNORKELING

Playa Santa Catalina is the closest embarkation point to Isla de Coiba (⇨ *below*), which has Panama's best skin diving, but there are numerous other spots nearby. Visibility and sea conditions can change from one day to the next, but in general the diving is better during the rainy season than during the dry season. Many of the dive spots around Isla de Coiba require ocean-diving experience, but some dive spots closer to town are appropriate for novices, or for snorkeling. Within an hour of Santa Catalina are dive sites such as **Punta Pargo,** and **Palo Grande,** where you might see moray eels, parrot fish, various types of puffers, and big schools of jacks, among other things. If you can afford a trip to Isla de Coiba, a 90-minute boat trip away, you can expect to see an even greater variety and amount of marine life, including lots of sharks, and with luck, manta rays, or whale sharks. Isla de Coiba is best done as an overnight.

Scuba Coiba (✉ *Calle Principal, near beach* ☎ *202–2171* ⊕ *www.scubacoiba.com*) is the only dive operator in Santa Catalina. Started in 2005 by Australian expat Herbie Sunk, the company offers boat dives at dozens of spots near Santa Catalina and multiday trips to Isla de Coiba with overnights in the ANAM cabins there. They also offer PADI certification courses and snorkeling/beach trips to nearby islands.

SURFING Santa Catalina's legendary point break, known simply as **La Punta**, is one of the country's best. The waves break over a rock platform in front of a point just east of town, forming both lefts and rights, though the rights are more hollow, and longer. It is best surfed from mid- to high tide, and usually needs a 4- to 5-foot swell to break. When a good swell rolls in, the faces can get as big as 15 to 20 feet. An alternative to La Punta that can be surfed at low to mid-tide is the nearby beach break at **Playa Santa Catalina**, which is usually smaller and less treacherous than the point break, so it is better for surfers who are out of practice. If La Punta is too small, or crowded, you can hike 30 minutes west of town, past the beach, to another point called **Punta Brava**, where a fast left tubes over a rocky bottom. The waves here are often bigger than at La Punta, but it can only be surfed from low to medium tide. An excellent alternative to the coastal breaks is **Isla Cebaco**, a 90-minute boat ride from Santa Catalina, which has both a beach break and point break. Those breaks are usually noticeably bigger than at Santa Catalina. The trip there costs $15–$30.

Panama Surf Tours (☎ *6671–7777* ⊕ *www.panamasurftours.com*), run by longtime resident Kenny Myers, has a rustic lodge near the break and offers five- and eight-day guided surfing packages that include transportation to and from Playa Santa Catalina and a guide. They also offer lessons.

TO & FROM

It takes about six hours to drive to Santa Catalina from Panama City, driving west on the Carretera Interamericana to Santiago, and then southwest, via Soná, the 110 km (68 mi) to Playa Santa Catalina. In Santiago, turn left at the church and follow the signs to Soná, which is 50 km (31 mi) southwest of Santiago. The turnoff for Santa Catalina is shortly before Soná, by the Shell gas station. From there, it is another 45 km (28 mi) to the village of El Tigre, where you have to make another left, and at the next town, Hicaco, turn right at the police station. The main road ends at the beach, but the Punta Brava Lodge and other hotels are up a rough dirt road on the left before the beach.

PARQUE NACIONAL COIBA

50 km (31 mi) southwest of Santa Catalina.

Fodor'sChoice Remote and wild Isla de Coiba, Panama's largest island, has the coun-
★   try's best skin diving, world-class fishing, and palm-lined beaches.
About 80% of the island is covered with tropical dry forest, home for
an array of wildlife, including the scarlet macaw. But it is the ocean that
holds the big attractions: Parque Nacional Coiba is one of the world's
largest marine parks, and a UNESCO World Heritage Site.

For the better part of the 20th century, however, Isla de Coiba was a
penal colony, where as many as 3,000 criminals once toiled on farms
carved out of the dry forest, growing food for the country's entire
prison system. The Panamanian government declared the island a
national park in 1991, but it took more than a decade to relocate the
prisoners. In 2004 the prison was finally shut down, and the park was
significantly expanded to include nine more islands, 28 islets, and vast
expanses of ocean to the north and south of Coiba. Parque Nacional
Coiba now protects 667,493 acres of sea and islands, of which Isla de
Coiba constitutes about 120,000 acres.

The marine life of the park is as impressive as that of the Galapagos.
The extensive and healthy reefs are home to comical frog fish, sleek
rays, and massive groupers. The national park holds more than more
than 4,000 acres of reef composed of two-dozen different types of coral
and is home to 760 fish species. The park's waters are also visited by
22 species of whale and dolphin, including killer whales and humpback
whales, which are fairly common there from July to September.

The wildlife on Coiba doesn't compare to that on the Galapagos, but
its forests are home to howler monkeys, agoutis (large rodents), and
150 bird species, including the endemic Coiba spinetail, the rare crested
eagle, and the country's biggest population of endangered scarlet
macaws. Several trails wind through the island's forests; the **Sendero de
los Monos** (Monkey Trail), a short boat trip from the ranger station, is
the most popular. The island's extensive mangrove swamps are inhabited by crocodiles, and sea turtles nest on some beaches from April to
September. The most popular beach in the park is on the tiny **Granito
de Oro** (Gold Nugget) island, where white sand is backed by lush foliage, and good snorkeling lies a short swim away. It's a popular stop
with small cruise ships from December to May, so local tour operators
often avoid it during those months.

Options for visiting Isla de Coiba range from a day trip out of Playa
Santa Catalina to one-week tours, or cruises that include lodging on a
ship, or in the National Environment Authority (ANAM) accommodations ($18 per bed; five beds per building) in air-conditioned cement
buildings near the ranger station. There is a communal kitchen; you
have to bring your food. There is also space for 15 campers ($10 per
two-person tent). Reserve at least a month ahead of time during the dry
season. ☎998–4271 or 998–0615 🖃$10.

SPORTS & THE OUTDOORS

SCUBA DIVING
& SNORKELING

Isla de Coiba has Panama's best skin diving, and some of the best diving in Central America, with vast reefs inhabited by hundreds of species and jaw-dropping schools of fish. On any given dive there you may see spotted eagle rays, white-tip reef sharks, sea turtles, giant snapper and grouper, moray eels, stargazers, frog fish, pipefish, angelfish, and Moorish idols. The reefs hold plenty of invertebrates, whereas offshore pinnacles attract big schools of jacks, Pacific spadefish, and other species.

Among the park's best dive spots are **Santa Cruz,** a vast coral garden teeming with reef fish; **Mali Mali,** a submerged rock formation that is a cleaning station for large fish; **La Viuda,** a massive rock between Islas de Coiba and Canales that attracts major schools of fish; and **Frijoles,** submerged rocks where divers often see sharks, large eels, and manta rays. Many of the dive spots around Isla de Coiba require a bit of ocean diving experience, but there also dive spots that are appropriate for novices, and good snorkeling areas. Visibility can change from one day to the next, but in general it is better during the rainy season, when it averages 70 feet and the sea is warmer. Surface water temperatures average in the low 80s, but thermoclines in the depths can be in the mid-70s, and upwelling from February to April brings colder water and lower visibility—down to 20 feet—but more fish.

Ecocircuitos (☎314–0068 ⊕www.coibadventure.com), based in Panama City, has a one-week snorkeling and hiking tour to Isla de Coiba with overnights in the ANAM cabins and in Santa Catalina. The **M/V** *Coral Star* (☎866/924–2837 in U.S. ⊕www.coralstar.com), a 115-foot yacht based in David, has one-week cruises to Isla de Coiba and surroundings that can include sportfishing, skin diving, snorkeling, and sea kayaking. **Panama Divers** (☎314–0817 or 448–2102 ⊕www.panamadivers.com) offers relatively inexpensive diving tours to Isla de Coiba for small groups that include overnights in the ANAM cabins. **Panama Diving Tours** (☎6671–2112 ⊕www.panamadivingtours.com) offers one-week diving cruises to Isla de Coiba on their boat, the **M/V** *Balboa Explorer.* **Scuba Coiba** (☎202–2171 ⊕www.scubacoiba.com), in Santa Catalina, are the local experts, offering boat dives at dozens of spots in the park on trips with overnights in the ANAM cabins.

SPORTFISHING

Catch-and-release fishing is permitted inside Coiba National Park, but the fishing is just as good outside the park. Blue marlin, black marlin, and Pacific sailfish run here in significant numbers from December to April, with January to March being the peak months. The area also holds legions of wahoo, dolphinfish, and tuna, which often run bigger than 200 pounds. The fishing is less spectacular from April to December, but there are still plenty of roosterfish, mackerel, amberjack, snapper, and grouper. Some of the area's best fishing is around **Isla Montousa** and the **Hannibal Banks,** which are 65–80 km (40–50 mi) west of Isla de Coiba. The sea south of **Isla Jicarón** and **Isla Jicarita,** 10 km (7 mi) south of Isla de Coiba, also has good fishing.

Captain Tom Yust's **Coiba Adventure Sportfishing** (☎ *999–8108, 800/800–0907 in the U.S.* ⊕ *www.coibadventure.com*) runs fishing tours of the waters around Isla de Coiba on a 31-foot Bertram, or a Mako 221, with overnights at the ANAM cabins. The **M/V** *Coral Star* (☎ *866/924–2837 in the U.S.* ⊕ *www.coralstar.com*) is a 115-foot ship that runs Saturday-to-Saturday cruises to Isla de Coiba and surroundings with sportfishing from 22-foot launches. **Panama Yacht Tours** (☎ *263–5044* ⊕ *www.panamayachtours.com*) offers fishing tours to the waters around Isla de Coiba. **Pesca Panama** (☎ *6614–5850, 800/946–3473 in the U.S.* ⊕ *www.pescapanama.com*) offers one-week fishing tours to the waters west of Isla de Coiba with overnights on a barge near David.

TO & FROM

Most people visit Isla de Coiba on fishing, diving, or nature tours offered by the companies listed above. It is possible to organize your own trip, in which case you would hire a boat in Playa Santa Catalina. Most fishermen there charge about $200 for a day trip to Isla de Coiba, and more if they must stay overnight on the island.

AZUERO & VERAGUAS ESSENTIALS

TRANSPORTATION

BY AIR

The domestic airline Air Panama has afternoon flights to Chitré and Pedasí on Wednesday, Friday, and Sunday. Flights depart from Panama City's Albrook Airport *(⇨ Chapter 1)*, from Chitré's **Aeropuerto Capitan Alonso Valderrama** (⊠ *Road to Playa El Agallito, Chitré* ☎ *996–4432*), and from Pedasí from an airstrip east of town on the road to Playa el Bajadero.

Airlines **Air Panama** (☎ *316–9000* ⊕ *www.flyairpanama.com*)

BY BOAT

Various companies offer cruises to Isla de Coiba departing from David, in Chiriquí Province (⇨ Isla de Coiba, *above,* and David, *in* Chapter 4).

BY CAR

All of this region's towns can be reached in a standard vehicle except for Parque Nacional El Copé and Playa Santa Catalina, which require four-wheel drive. Cars can be rented in Chitré and Santiago.

Car-Rental Agencies **Budget** (⊠ *Via Carmelo Spadafora, Chitré* ☎ *996–0027, 263–8777 reservations* ⊠ *Hotel Galeria, Carretera Interamericana, Santiago* ☎ *998–1731, 263–8777 reservations*). **Hertz** (⊠ *Aeropuerto Capitan Alonso Valderrama, Chitré* ☎ *996–2256, 260–2111 reservations*).

CONTACTS & RESOURCES

EMERGENCIES

As far as medical care goes, this is one of Panama's more isolated regions, with local clinics and hospitals below the international standards of Panama City's major clinics. If you have health problems in most of the Azuero Peninsula, you'll want to head to Chitré. From Santa Catalina, you should head to Santiago. Some emergency numbers are different for these two regions.

Pharmacies tend to open from 8 AM until between 7 and 9 PM. If you need medication late at night, go to the provincial hospital.

Emergency Services **National police** (☎ 998–4387 in Herrera and Los Santos provinces, 996–4333 in Veraguas Province). **Fire department** (☎ 103). **Ambulance** (☎ 996–7446 in Azuero Peninsula, 958–7979 in Veraguas).

Hospitals **Hospital General Cecilio A Castillero** (✉ Av. Carmelo Spadafora, Chitré ☎ 996–4444). **Hospital Luis Chico Fabrega** (✉ San Antoni, Santiago ☎ 999–3070).

Pharmacies **Farmacia La Placita** (✉ Av. Central, Santiago ☎ 998–4465). **Farmacia Las Tablas** (✉ Calle Bolívar, Las Tablas ☎ 994–6936). **Farmacia Marquisa** (✉ Av. Carmelo Spadafora, Chitré ☎ 996–4193). **Farmacia Vega** (✉ Carretera Interamericana, Natá ☎ 993–5573).

INTERNET

Biznet Center (✉ Av. Herrera, Chitré ☎ 996–2956). **Generación Web** (✉ Calle 8 de Nov., Las Tablas ☎ 994–0438). **VIP Planet Internet Café** (✉ Av. Central at Calle 5, Santiago ☎ 998–3518).

MONEY MATTERS

ATM machines that accept international credit and debit cards can be found at the branches of major banks in Chitré, Las Tablas, Pedasí, and Santiago. The closest ATMs to Playa Venao or Santa Catalina are at the Banco Nacional in Pedasí or Soná.

ATMs **Banistmo** (✉ Av. Pérez, Chitré ☎ 996–0666 ⊠ Calle 8 de Nov. and Av. Belisario Porras, Las Tablas ☎ 994–7241 ⊠ Av. Central, Santiago ☎ 998–3651). **Banco Nacional** (✉ Calle Principal, Pedasí ☎ 995–2257 ⊠ Av. Central, at Calle 3, Santiago ☎ 998–4117 ⊠ Av. Principal, Soná ☎ 998–8361).

SAFETY

Most of this region's beaches get big waves, and some have rocks, which can be very dangerous. When hiking through the forest, always be careful where you put your hand, since many of the dry forest plants have thorns, and there are many creatures that bite or sting.

TOURS

Ecocircuitos (☎ 314–0068 ⊕ www.coibadventure.com) has a weeklong snorkeling and hiking tour to Isla de Coiba that includes several nights in Santa Catalina, and a one-week luxury tour to the Azuero Peninsula that includes several nights at Villa Camilla. Seven-day cruises to the Isla de Coiba region on the 115-foot yacht **M/V** *Coral Star*

Folklore Fanatics

The Azuero Peninsula has been called Panama's cultural cradle, but its rich cultural heritage is by no means dormant, like some babe who's been rocked to sleep—rather, it is wide awake and impatiently awaiting the next folk festival. In these seemingly somnolent ranching towns folk music and dancing aren't mere cultural artifacts, they are the way people celebrate life, and there are plenty of folks in the region who celebrate as often as possible.

Panama is a land of many cultures. You may experience indigenous or Afro-Caribbean folklore elsewhere in Panama, but the predominant culture in the Azuero Peninsula is *mestizo*, the mixture of European and indigenous races and traditions, which happens to be the folk tradition with which the majority of Panamanians identify. The mestizo culture is consequently considered the national culture, and you may see it on display throughout the country, but because the Azuero Peninsula was one of the first regions to be colonized, and has been a bit of a backwater since the colonial era, it has maintained more of the old traditions.

The best way to experience Panama's rich cultural heritage is to attend one of the Azuero Peninsula's frequent *ferias*, or festivals, of which there are usually a couple every month. These celebrations range from relatively solemn religious feasts in which icons are paraded through town to the pagan antics of *los diablitos* (the little devils) that animate the streets during Corpus Christi, but they invariably include plenty of folk music and dancing.

The frequency of folkloric celebrations in the Azuero Peninsula means that there should be one that coincides with your vacation, and this chapter has an extensive list of them. But since some celebrations change dates from year to year, you should check the Web site of the **Panama Tourist Bureau (IPAT)** (⊕ *www.visitpanama. com*) for up-to-date information on fairs and festivals. Those with a keen interest in the subject should also check out the site **Folklore Panama Típico** (⊕ *www.folklore.panamatipico. com*).

Before you go exploring the world of Panamanian folklore, however, you should be familiar with its basic components:

Pollera. Panama's national dress, the *pollera* is a derivation of formal dresses worn by Spanish women in centuries of yore. Consisting of a white blouse and dress with elaborate embroidery, often in red or blue thread, they can take months to sew, and consequently can cost thousands of dollars. They also are often worn with thousands of dollars in gold jewelry. The best opportunity for admiring polleras is during the Festival de la Pollera in Las Tablas in late July.

Sombrero Pintao. The real Panama hat, these tightly woven straw hats have dark brown patterns woven into them, hence their name, which translates as "painted hat." They are national dress as well, since the majority of men in the countryside wear them everywhere but in church and bed. They are as practical as the pollera is extravagant, since they save necks and faces from being toasted by the tropical sun.

Música Folclórica. The pulse of any traditional celebration, this rhythmic acoustic music is performed by small

groups with an accordion, two different types of drums, and a *churuca*—a serrated gourd or metal cylinder that is scraped with a stick. It is the music that most folk dances are performed to, with the exception of the *mejorana*, a more subdued kind of folk music played on a five-string guitar called the *guitarra mejoranera* and accompanied by different folk dances. *Tamborito*, on the other hand, is a drum-based music accompanied by a call and response similar to that of traditional African music.

Máscaras. Masks form an important part of Carnaval and Corpus Christi celebrations, but Panamanian devil masks have evolved significantly in recent decades. The traditional Panamanian devil mask bears some resemblance to the masks of Chinese New Year parades, and are similar to those used in the Peruvian highlands. Some of the most colorful characters of Panamanian folklore are *los diablitos* (the little devils), who dance in the streets of La Villa de Los Santos during Corpus Christi celebrations.

Those pagan characters wear diabolical papier-mâché masks and red-and-black striped jump suits. They often carry inflated, dried cow bladders, which they hit with sticks while emitting long guttural shouts. To witness a group of men performing this ritual is to get an idea of just how seriously Panamanians take their folklore.

(☎866/924–2837 *in U.S.* ⊕*www.coralstar.com*) can include hiking, bird-watching, sportfishing, skin diving, snorkeling, and sea kayaking. **Panama Private Tours** (☎263–6873 ⊕*www.panamaprivatetours.com*), in Panama City, runs a surfing tour to Playa Venao, Santa Catalina, and surrounding breaks. **Panama Surf Tours** (☎6671–7777 ⊕*www.panama-surftours.com*), owned by longtime Panama resident and surfing expert Kenny Myers, runs multiday tours to Santa Catalina that include visits to breaks that few people get to. Accommodation is in a small lodge in Santa Catalina.

Panama Yacht Tours (☎263–5044 ⊕*www.panamayachtours.com*), in Panama City, offers fishing tours to the waters around Isla de Coiba. **Panama Divers** (☎314–0817 *or* 448–2102 ⊕*www.panamadivers. com*), a small company owned by two Americans, runs inexpensive diving tours to Isla de Coiba for small groups that include overnights in the ANAM cabins on the island. **Panama Diving Tours** (☎6671–2112 ⊕*www.panamadivingtours.com*) offers one-week diving cruises to the waters around Isla de Coiba on a live-aboard boat. Captain Tom Yust of **Coiba Adventure Sportfishing** (☎999–8108, 800/800–0907 *in the U.S.* ⊕*www.coibadventure.com*), in David, offers fishing tours of the waters around Isla de Coiba on a 31-foot Bertram or a Mako 221.

VISITOR INFORMATION

Chitré, Pedasí, and Santiago have **IPAT** offices, open weekdays 8:30–4:30 and weekends 8:30–1:30.

Information **IPAT** (✉ *Calle 19 de Octubre, Chitré* ☎*974–4532* ✉ *Carretera Nacional, north end of town, Pedasí* ☎*995–2339* ✉ *Av. Central, Santiago* ☎*998–3929*).

Chiriquí Province

WORD OF MOUTH

"We loved the Chiriquí area . . . Great hiking up there in the mountains, rolling farmland, coffee plantations, volcanoes, etc."

—glover

"La Amistad is a beautiful area. I have never seen anything so lush, moist and green."

–Suzie2

By David
Dudenhoefer

PANAMA'S SOUTHWEST PROVINCE OF CHIRIQUÍ contains the country's most varied scenery. Landscapes that evoke different continents—from the alpine peak of Volcán Barú to the palm-lined beaches of Parque Nacional Golfo de Chiriquí—lie mere hours apart. The diverse environments provide conditions for world-class sportfishing, bird-watching, skin diving, river rafting, horseback riding, hiking, and surfing, making Chiriquí an ideal destination for nature lovers.

The Cordillera de Talamanca, which extends from Costa Rica into Panama, defines northern Chiriquí. Lush cloud forest covers its upper slopes, and the valleys that flank Volcán Barú—an extinct volcano and Panama's highest peak—have cool mountain climates and unforgettable scenery. Those valleys hold the towns of Boquete, Bambito, and Cerro Punta, which are popular with bird-watchers, rafters, and hikers, and have captivating landscapes and charming restaurants and inns.

The lowlands to the south of the Cordillera are less impressive—hot and almost completely deforested—and become brown and dusty in the dry season. To the south lies the Golfo de Chiriquí, with dozens of pristine islands and countless acres of coral reef awash with rainbows of marine life. Those waters also offer world-class surfing and sportfishing that few have sampled. The tiny fishing port of Boca Chica provides convenient access to the gulf's treasures, whereas the isolated lodges of Cala Mia, Islas Secas, and Moro Negrito are in the gulf itself.

Chiricanos, or residents of Chiriquí, fly their red-and-green provincial flag with more vigor than the national banner. The province's population is almost as varied as its landscapes; the majority is mestizo—a mix of European and indigenous bloodlines—with a sprinkling of Asian immigrants. The Ngöbe-Buglé (aka Guaymí), the country's largest indigenous group, have been in this region since long before Chiriquí or Panama existed. Though most Ngöbe-Buglé live in the tribe's *comarca* (autonomous indigenous territory) northeast of Chiriquí, you find them in Boquete, Cerro Punta, and David. Ngöbe-Buglé women are recognized by their colorful traditional dresses.

ORIENTATION & PLANNING

ORIENTATION

Most travelers arrive by plane in the provincial capital of David, centrally located in the lowlands, no more than two hours from most of Chiriquí's attractions. The Carretera Interamericana (CA1) skirts David's northern edge, where it is a four-line highway lined with gas stations, shopping plazas, and fast-food restaurants. It becomes a two-lane road east of town, where it leads to the town of Chiriquí and to the turnoff for Boca Chica, the gateway to Parque Nacional Marino Golfo de Chiriquí. A 30-minute drive southwest of David takes you to Playa Barqueta; a 40-minute drive north takes you to Boquete. Concepción is a short drive west of David on CA1, and there the road veers north to

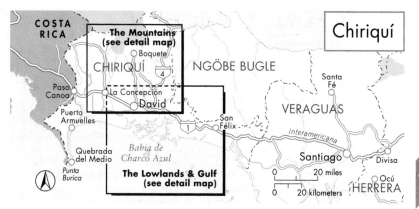

Volcán, Bambito, and Cerro Punta. The first of these is near the base of Barú Volcano; the latter two are nestled along that mountain's western slope. If you continue west on CA1 you'll reach the border with Costa Rica at Paso Canoa in 15 minutes.

PLANNING

WHEN TO GO

The December-to-May dry season is the most popular time to visit Chiriquí, since days tend to be sunny in the lowlands. From December to March the valleys of Cerro Punta and Boquete can be cool and windy, and may get light rain; trade winds push clouds over the mountains creating a misty condition known as *bajareque.* In March and April the mountain valleys are warm and sunny, whereas the lowlands become increasingly dry and brown. It rains just about every day from May to mid-July, but from mid-July to mid-September you can get several sunny days in a row. From mid-September to mid-December it rains almost daily. Boquete's Feria de Flores, the annual flower festival, is the third week of January, and includes folk dancing and indigenous handicrafts, but also excessive drinking and blasting music; the town's Expo Orquideas in mid-April is more pleasant. The water in the Golfo de Chiriquí is clearest for scuba diving and snorkeling from December to July, whereas the surf is best from July to December.

GETTING AROUND

Driving is the easiest way to explore the spread-out mountain regions (you can rent a car in David), especially around Boquete. But renting isn't obligatory; there's frequent bus service to the mountain towns and convenient taxi service in the towns. In fact, if you want to hike the Sendero los Quetzales, it's best to hire a taxi in Cerro Punta to take you to the trailhead. It takes about 90 minutes to drive from David to Boca Chica, but if you spend a few nights there you may want to arrange a taxi or boat transfer from David through your hotel. The remote lodges in the Golfo de Chiriquí arrange transport as part of their packages.

TOP REASONS TO GO

MISTY MOUNTAINS
The upper slopes of the Cordillera de Talamanca are draped with lush cloud forest and usually enveloped in mist. Much of that forest is protected within La Amistad and Barú Volcano National Parks, home to a wealth of wildlife, which can be explored via hiking trails.

TEEMING SEA
The Golfo de Chiriquí is home to an amazing array of fish, ranging from colorful king angelfish to the mighty black marlin, making the province an ideal destination for skin divers and sportfishers alike.

BIRDS IN THE BUSH
The mountains of Chiriquí are a must-visit for bird-watchers since they hold species found nowhere else in Panama, such as the resplendent quetzal and long-tailed silky flycatcher. From November to April, northern migrants push the count to over 500 species.

PRISTINE ISLANDS
Between Parque Nacional Marino Golfo de Chiriquí and the Islas Secas, the sea here brims with uninhabited islands: think palm-lined beaches, crystalline waters, and coral reefs a mere swim from shore.

FARMING COMMUNITIES
The mountain communities of Boquete, Bambito, and Cerro Punta are surrounded by gorgeous scenery, and are distinguished by charming wooden houses, exuberant flower gardens, cozy restaurants, and hotels that combine all of the above.

WHAT TO DO

TAKE A HIKE The Talamanca Mountains have plenty of hiking routes, the most famous of which are the Sendero los Quetzales, between Cerro Punta and Boquete, and the grueling climb to the summit of Barú Volcano.

PADDLE THE RAPIDS The boulder-strewn streams that begin in the cloud forests feed into the Chiriquí and Chiriquí Viejo rivers, two of the country's best white-water rafting routes, which flow through rain forests and rock canyons.

VISIT NEPTUNE Golfo de Chiriquí waters around the Islas Secas and Islas Ladrones offer amazing skin diving, with hundreds of fish and invertebrate species ranging from octopi to whale sharks. Parque Nacional Marino Golfo de Chiriquí, on the other hand, offers excellent snorkeling.

HOOK A WHOPPER The Golfo de Chiriquí has some of the country's best fishing, especially from January to April, when massive black and blue marlin, sailfish, and tuna reign. You can hook feisty roosterfish, wahoo, amberjacks, mackerel, snapper, grouper, and other fighters year-round.

EXPERIENCE COFFEE Boquete produces some of the world's best coffee on beautiful farms where the coffee bushes are shaded by massive tropical trees. Coffee tours provide an interesting introduction to the production of that aromatic bean, and the farms are great spots for bird-watching.

RESTAURANTS & CUISINE
You can get a good meal almost anywhere in the province, but Boquete has its best restaurant selection. The specialty in the mountains is local farm-raised trout, but because the Gulf of Chiriquí has such great fish-

A BIT OF HISTORY

Though conquistadors first visited the region in the 16th century, founding a few outposts that were soon abandoned or destroyed, Chiriquí remained the realm of indigenous chiefdoms for most of the colonial era. According to Spanish chroniclers, the region was divided among various indigenous ethnicities, which conquistadors collectively dubbed the Guaymí—a name that persists to this day. Though they founded David and a few neighboring towns in the early 17th century, the Spaniards remained a minority in the region until the 19th century. They introduced cattle early in the conquest; as ranching took hold the area's forests receded, and the Indians retreated into the mountains they now call home. The trend continues to this day; pasture is the province's predominant landscape.

Originally considered part of Veraguas, the province of Chiriquí wasn't created until 1849, when it had just 16,000 inhabitants. Because nearly all the buildings were made of wood or adobe, hardly a structure survives from the colonial era. Chiriquí didn't really start to grow till the late 19th and early 20th centuries, when ranches and banana and sugar plantations completely covered the lowlands and European immigrants began moving into the mountain valleys, where they took advantage of the rich volcanic soil to produce coffee, fruit, and vegetables. With agricultural expansion, indigenous territory shrank; the majority of Chiriquí's Indians now live in the mountains in what was once the province's northeast corner, though many also work on farms in Boquete and Cerro Punta. The 21st century brought a real-estate boom as foreigners were drawn to the mountain valleys' spring-like climate and to the beautiful coast.

ing, seafood is also a good bet. Chiriquí is cattle country, so you'll also find plenty of beef on the menu, and while not as tender as corn-fed beef, the fillets and sirloins are quite good.

ABOUT THE HOTELS

Accommodations in Chiriquí range from Boquete's affordable B&Bs to the luxury ecolodge on the Islas Secas, where the rates are twice those of any other hotel in the country. The province has some of Panama's best small lodges, many surrounded by tropical nature.

PAYING

The accepted currency is the U.S. dollar, which is often called the balboa, in reference to the long defunct national currency. Credit cards are widely accepted and ATM machines are all over, including in the lobbies of large hotels and at gas stations and supermarkets.

WHAT IT COSTS					
	¢	$	$$	$$$	$$$$
RESTAURANTS	under $5	$5–$10	$10–$15	$15–$20	over $20
HOTELS	under $50	$50–$100	$100–$160	$160–$220	over $220

Restaurant prices are per person for a main course at dinner. Hotel prices are for two people in a standard double room, excluding service and 10% tax.

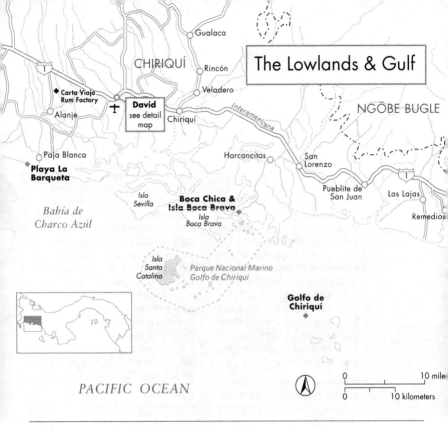

THE LOWLANDS AND GULF

The torrid lowlands that spread out around David are almost all pasture, and the small towns there are home to the province's traditional Chiricano cowboy culture. You'll drive past these towns on your way to the more attractive valleys or beaches, but there is little reason to stop in any of them. The vast Golfo de Chiriquí holds dozens of islands, coral reefs, world-class surf breaks and sportfishing; although David can serve as a base for gulf trips, it's more easily explored from Boca Chica, Boca Brava, the Islas Secas, or Moro Negrito.

DAVID

440 km (274 mi) west of Panama City, 53 km (33 mi) east of Paso Canoa.

With almost 80,000 inhabitants, this provincial capital is Panama's second-largest city, yet it has almost nothing to offer travelers. The expansive town has zero zoning—businesses are scattered among the houses—and an equal amount of charm. David is the commercial and administrative center for a province of about 370,000, and consequently has plenty of banks, car-rental agencies, and other services. Many shops are concentrated in the streets and avenues around its central plaza; newer shopping centers line the roads around its periphery.

Though founded in the 17th century, David has almost no historic buildings or attractions. The central plaza, **Parque Cervantes**, was renovated in 2007, but is surrounded by some uninspiring architecture, including the very unattractive **Iglesia de la Sagrada Familia**, built in the early 20th century. Add oppressive heat, and you have enough reasons to avoid David, but since it's

> ### TAKE A DIP
>
> If the heat is too much, head to **Balenario Mojagua**, a popular river swimming hole with a small waterfall and tropical foliage. It can be busy on weekends and holidays when *pindín* or *reggaetón* music blasts from the open-air bar, but tends to be dead at other times. ⊠ *Road to Boquete, 4 km (2 mi) north of David* ☎ *No phone* 💲$1 ⊙ *Daily 9–6.*

the regional transportation hub, many visitors must spend a night here at the beginning or end of their time in Chiriquí. It also serves as a departure point for skin diving or sportfishing excursions, and can be a convenient base for hiking the Sendero Los Quetzales, since you can bus to Cerro Punta in the morning, hike to Boquete, and bus back to David in the evening.

David is a grid of *avenidas* running north–south, and *calles* running east–west. Avenida Central and Calle Central cross near the heart of town; the rest of the calles are lettered (Calle A, etc.), followed by either Norte or Sur (North or South), whereas the avenidas are numbered and Este or Oeste (East or West). A recent administration changed many street names, but locals still use the old ones.

The **Museo José de Obaldía** is in one of David's only historic structures, a 19th-century wooden building that was once the home of José de Obaldía, who was instrumental in the creation of Chiriquí Province in 1849. Its small array of pre-Columbian and colonial items includes 19th-century swords and indigenous *metates*—three-legged stone tables used for grinding corn. ⊠ *Av. 8 Este and Calle Aristides Romero (Calle A Norte)* ☎ *774–1851* 💲$1 ⊙ *Tues.–Sat. 8:30–4:30.*

If you're in Chiriquí during the third week of March you can check out the **Feria Internacional de David.** It's like a county fair with lots of cows and commercial exhibits, but with folk music and dancing, too.

WHERE TO STAY & EAT

¢–$$ ✕ **Pizzería Gran Hotel Nacional.** This simple place serves 17 kinds of good pizza, as well as mediocre pastas, many meat and seafood dishes, and inexpensive, three-course lunch specials. The decor is limited to vibrant tablecloths and tacky art, but the place is clean, bright, and air-conditioned. ⊠ *Gran Hotel Nacional, Calle Pérez Balladares (Calle Central) at Av. 9 de Enero (Av. Central)* ☎ *775–1042* ▭ *AE, MC, V.*

¢–$$ ✕ **Restaurante Steakhouse.** Though at the edge of town across from the *estadio* (stadium), this popular spot is worth the $2 taxi ride. It's a Chinese restaurant, but true to the name, its extensive menu includes lots of grilled items. The spacious dining room has a high ceiling, huge

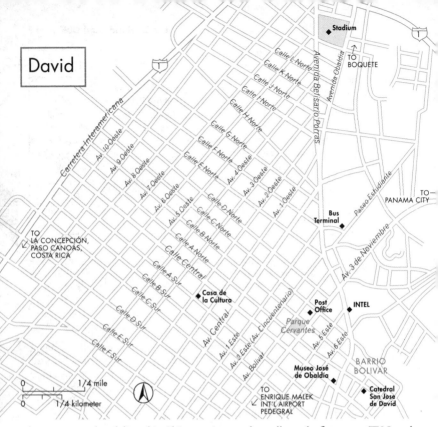

chandeliers, big Chinese prints on the walls, and a flat-screen TV. Locals pack in to feast on *chiau jiam ja* (spicy shrimp in fried noodles), *king tung* (pork ribs with sweet-and-sour sauce), and *langosta estilo cantonés* (lobster medallions stir-fried with vegetables). ⊠ *Calle Alberto Osorio at Av. 7 Oeste* ☎ *775–3385* ▤ *MC, V* ☉ *Closed Sun.*

$ ✕▥**Gran Hotel Nacional.** The best hotel in town, this 1950s two-story complex with a colonial Spanish motif was remodeled in the 1990s. Rooms are spacious but the decor's dated. Front rooms have views of the large trees that shade the parking area; rooms near the lobby have Wi-Fi. The small pool area's gardens and lawn may be the most pleasant spots in David. There's an in-house movie theater and casino; its three restaurants include a pizzeria (⇨ *above*) and the open-air Barbacoa, which serves a small dinner selection of meat and seafood. **Pros: Pool, quiet, spacious rooms, central location, decent restaurants. Cons: Unfriendly receptionists.** ⊠ *Calle Pérez Balladares (Calle Central) and Av. 9 de Enero (Av. Central)* ☎ *775–1042* 🖷 *775–7729* ⊕ *www.hotel-nacionalpanama.com* ▱ *73 rooms, 2 suites* ⌂ *In-room: safe. In-hotel: 3 restaurants, room service, bar, pool, laundry service, public Wi-Fi, parking (no fee), no-smoking rooms* ▤ *AE, MC, V* ▯❶ *EP.*

¢–$ ▥**Hotel Castilla.** This three-story building kitty-corner from Parque Cervantes has basic rooms with good beds and small desks at a reasonable price. Interior rooms are dark, but corner junior suites have big windows and a private balcony, albeit overlooking busy streets. This place is nothing fancy, but well located and a good value. Pros: Central location, competitive rates. Cons: Interior rooms dark, junior suites can be noisy. ⊠ *Calle Aristides Romero (Calle A Norte) at Calle Bolívar (Calle 3 Este)* ☎774–5236 ⊟774–5246 ✐*castilladavi@cwpanama. net* ⊷*62 rooms, 6 suites* ⇘*In-room: refrigerator (some). In-hotel: restaurant, bar, public Internet, laundry service, parking (no fee), no-smoking rooms* ⊟*AE, MC, V* ⦿*EP.*

NIGHTLIFE & THE ARTS

The **Fiesta Casino** (⊠ *Calle Pérez Balladares [Calle Central] and Av. 9 de Enero [Av. Central]* ☎775–6534), across the street from the Hotel Nacional, is a popular, though smoky, spot that includes a small sports bar called Salsa Bar. The **Cine Alhambra** (⊠ *Calle Pérez Balladares [Calle Central] and Av. 9 de Enero [Av. Central]* ☎775–1042), David's main movie theater, is part of the Hotel Nacional.

SPORTS & THE OUTDOORS

HIKING David is a convenient base from which to hike the **Sendero Los Quetzales**
★ (⇨Cerro Punta, *below*), an all-day adventure through the cloud forest on the north slope of Volcán Barú, the country's highest peak, between the mountain valleys of Cerro Punta and Boquete. Watch for the rare resplendent quetzal and dozens of other birds. Tours with David-based guide **Yania Massiel de Bradford** (☎775–9649 *or 6709–8204*) include transportation from David to Cerro Punta, a guided hike (3–4 hours) to Boquete, and transportation back to David, all for $30–$65, depending on the number of hikers. Bring sunblock, plenty of water, food, and warm, waterproof clothing, since it can get quite cool on the trail, and is often raining when David is hot and sunny.

SCUBA DIVING The excellent dive spots around Islas Ladrones and Islas Secas (⇨Golfo
& SNORKELING de Chiriquí, *below*) are two hours from David, and within just one hour are the islands of the Parque Nacional Marino Golfo de Chiriquí (⇨box, *below*), with decent diving and snorkeling.

Day trips to the spots in the Gulf of Chiriquí with **Scuba Charters** (☎6536–0483) depart from Pedregal Marina, 10 minutes south of David, as do overnight excursions to Isla Coiba (⇨chapter 3).

SPORTFISHING The Gulf of Chiriquí has great fishing within hours of David's Pedregal Marina. Cast for amberjack, mackerel, tuna, wahoo, roosterfish, and seasonal billfish. The **M/V** *Coral Star* (☎866/924–2837 *in U.S.* ⊕*www. coralstar.com*), a 115-foot live-aboard, runs weeklong fishing cruises to the Gulf of Chiriquí and Isla Coiba. **Pesca Panama** (☎6614–5850 *in Panama, 800/946–3473 in the U.S.* ⊕*www.pescapanama.com*) has one-week fishing tours west of the Golfo de Chiriquí with overnights on a barge, or day charters out of Pedregal on 27-foot boats.

TO & FROM

The 440-km (274-mi) drive between David and Panama City takes six to seven hours—an easy trip on the Carretera Interamericana (CA1) that can be done in a day. However, because there are plenty of flights and rental-car companies in David, it isn't worth doing unless you visit the Azuero Peninsula or Santa Catalina en route, since the scenery consists primarily of pastures and ugly towns.

Domestic airlines Aeroperlas and Air Panama have half a dozen flights a day between David and Panama City; there is a flight between David and Bocas del Toro most mornings; and Air Panama has three flights a week between David and San José, Costa Rica.

Buses between David and Panama City depart hourly during the day, and direct, overnight buses depart at 10:45 PM and midnight. The trip usually takes eight hours, with a meal stop in Santiago. A couple of buses depart each morning for the nine-hour trip to San José, Costa Rica, which is a rough way to spend a day. From David, buses depart every 20 minutes for the 53-km (33-mi) trip to Paso Canoas, the Costa Rica border post, where hourly buses leave for Golfito. Buses also depart from David for Boquete or Cerro Punta every 30 minutes.

PLAYA LA BARQUETA

26 km (16 mi) southwest of David.

Playa La Barquete, the closest beach to David, is a long ribbon of dark-gray sand that's popular with local surfers. The area behind the beach is deforested, and the sea is often murky due to a nearby mangrove estuary. Nonetheless, it's a pleasant spot to spend a day or two. La Barqueta has the province's only beach resort and several vacation homes and condos, but most of the beach is backed by scrubby vegetation; you can stroll for miles without seeing a soul (except during holidays). The beach is public, but a day pass ($45) from the resort, Hotel Las Olas, includes pool and bar access and lunch. There's also a simple restaurant (not part of the resort) with inexpensive Panamanian fare. ⚠ **La Barqueta's sand can get hot enough to burn your feet, and if the sea is rough there's a risk of rip currents, so don't go in any deeper than your waist.** Five sea-turtle species nest on Playa la Barqueta, and 14 km (8½ mi) of the beach's eastern half is within the **Refugio de Vida Silvestre Playa de la Barqueta Agrícola** (*Playa La Barqueta Agricultural Wildlife Refuge* ☎6716–8301 or 6524–9421). From June to November, olive ridley, hawksbill, loggerhead, and green sea turtles nest on the beach; massive leatherback turtles and olive ridleys nest from November to March. The marine reptiles crawl onto the beach at night and bury their eggs in the sand; two months later eggs hatch and baby turtles dig their way out and scurry to the sea. The best time to look for nesting turtles is high tide, preferably when the moon is a mere crescent, though you may find hatchlings on the beach any afternoon from August to January. To look for nesting turtles, you must pay an admission fee ($3.50) and get a permit during the day at the ranger station just east of the Las Olas Beach Resort.

WHERE TO STAY & EAT

$$$ 🖫 **Las Olas Beach Resort.** The only hotel on Playa La Barqueta, this small resort sits right behind the beach. Second-floor rooms have the best views, but ground-floor rooms are just steps away from the surf.

Rooms are modestly sized with one king or two queen beds. Though no Central Panama resort, Las Olas has ample diversions, including two pools, massage, volleyball, boogie boards, and horseback riding. It can also be a base for sportfishing or skin-diving charters, white-water rafting, or day trips to Cerro Punta and Boquete. The all-inclusive meal rate is usually the best deal. Discount rates outside of high season can be a bargain. **Pros: Beachfront, wildlife refuge, ample facilities. Cons: Mediocre beach, can be dead during low season.** ⊠*Playa La Barqueta* ☎772–3000 ⊞772–3619 ⊕*www.lasolasresort.com* ⌖48 *rooms* ⌂*In-room: safe. In-hotel: 2 restaurants, room service, bar, pools, gym, beachfront, water sports, no elevator, laundry service, public Internet, no-smoking rooms* ▤*AE, MC, V* ⏀*EP.*

SPORTS & THE OUTDOORS

SURFING Playa La Barqueta has the best surf near David, with various beach breaks. Serious surfers will want to go west of La Barqueta to **Playa Sandía,** due south of Santo Tomás, which has a beach break and a long right in front of the estuary at the west end of the beach. Few surfers get to isolated **Punta Burica,** a three-hour trip down the beach south from Puerto Armuelles. It's only accessible at low tide and with a 4WD vehicle. A rustic, American-owned lodge called the **Mono Feliz** (☎6595–0388 *or* 6574–4386 ✉*monofeliz@hotmail.com*) offers inexpensive lodging and basic meals there.

TO & FROM

The 26-km (16-mi) drive southwest from David to Playa La Barqueta has a few turns, but they are all well marked with signs for Las Olas. Take Avenida 9 de Enero south, across Calle F Sur, and follow the signs. Few buses make the trip, so you have to drive or take a taxi.

BOCA CHICA & ISLA BOCA BRAVA

54 km (32 mi) southeast of David.

Long a sleepy fishing port at the end of a bone-rattling road, Boca Chica now has a paved road and a small selection of hotels that serve the islands of Parque Nacional Marino Golfo de Chiriquí. The town is on a peninsula overlooking the nearby island of Boca Brava. Together, Boca Chica and Isla Boca Brava define the eastern edge of a mangrove estuary that extends all the way to Playa La Barqueta.

Isla Boca Brava, across the channel from Boca Chica, is mostly covered with forest and is home to howler monkeys, but neither the island nor the mainland has nice beaches, and the ocean is usually murky because of the estuary. The attractions are beyond Boca Brava on the uninhabited islands of the Parque Nacional Marino Golfo de Chiriquí (⇨*below*), a 40-minute boat ride away. Beyond them lie world-class sportfishing and diving around the Islas Ladrones and Islas Secas.

WHERE TO STAY & EAT

$$$$ ⊞**Panama Big Game Fishing Club.** This small lodge on Boca Brava, just across the channel from Boca Chica, is all about sportfishing. Customized three- to six-day packages include daily fishing, all meals and

beverages, and in-country transportation. You can access the waters around the Islas Ladrones, Islas Montuosos, and the Hannibal Bank for some of Panama's best fishing. Accommodations are in two- to six-person cement bungalows nestled in the rain forest, whereas meals are served family style in a circular building at the top of the hill, decorated with the obligatory mounted fish. **Pros: Small, great fishing, good food. Cons: No pool, nothing for non-fishers, bugs can be a problem.** ⊠*Isla Boca Brava* ☎*6674–4824, 866/281–1225 in the U.S.* ⊟*305/653–2322 in the U.S.* ⊕*www.panamabiggamefishingclub.com* ⇦*3 bungalows* ᗢ*In-room: no phone, safe. In-hotel: restaurants, bar, water sports, no elevator, laundry service, public Wi-Fi, no-smoking rooms* ⊟*AE, MC, V* ⦿*FAP.*

$$$
Fodor's Choice
★

Cala Mia. Bungalows at this Boca Brava eco-lodge are tastefully decorated and have terraces with couches, hammocks, and tree-shrouded water views. The restaurant ($$) at the end of the point has walls of windows, and specializes in fresh seafood and vegetables from the hotel's organic farm. Three-course dinners change nightly. A suspension bridge leads to an islet with a massage and yoga gazebo. Activities include sea kayaking, excursions to nearby islands, snorkeling, scuba diving, and horseback riding. Ocean-view bungalows are better ventilated than bay-view ones. Most electricity is solar (meaning no a/c), garbage is recycled or composted for farm use, and 5% of earnings goes to projects for indigenous communities. **Pros: Gorgeous design and location, trips to islands, natural food, friendly. Cons: Isolated, no-see-ums can be a problem.** ⊠*Isla Boca Brava* ☎*6747–0011* ⊡*Entrega General, Horconcito, San Lorenzo, Chiriquí* ⊕*www.boutiquehotelcalamia.com* ⇦*11 bungalows* ᗢ*In-room: no a/c, safe, no TV. In-hotel: restaurant, room service, bar, pool, beachfront, water sports, no elevator, laundry service, no-smoking rooms* ⊟*MC, V* ⦿*BP.*

$$
★

Gone Fishing. Though fishing is an option, this is really a luxury B&B that offers various activities. The name reflects the attitude of the owners, Bruce and Donna, who retired to Boca Chica from South Florida. Rooms are well equipped and have themed murals. It's family-oriented with ample grounds, a large pool, and the best view in town. Bruce's boats are docked below for his next fishing trip, but he'll take you island-hopping and can arrange scuba diving. Meals are served on a wide terrace with a view; guests can use the kitchen. At this writing there are plans to expand into a full hotel. **Pros: Friendly, great view, nice pool. Cons: Bugs can be a problem.** ⊠*Boca Chica, on left before town* ☎*6573–0151* ⊕*www.gonefishingpanama.com* ⇦*4 rooms* ᗢ*In-room: no phone, safe. In-hotel: restaurant, pool, water sports, no elevator, laundry service, no-smoking rooms* ⊟*MC, V* ⦿*BP.*

$$
★

Seagull Cove Lodge. This hillside hotel belongs to a Spanish-Italian couple; the decor is Mediterranean, as is the cuisine served in the large restaurant. The bungalows have high ceilings, hand-painted ceramic sinks, and barrel-tile roofs. They are well equipped with satellite TV and other amenities, but their best selling points are the terrace views of the forest and bay. There is a tiny pool, and a long stairway leads past the bungalows to a sliver of beach and a dock where you can leave for island trips. The restaurant ($$–$$$$) has the best view on the property, and serves light lunches and a dinner menu that's strong on fresh pasta and seafood. **Pros: Well-equipped bungalows, great views, good food, friendly. Cons: Steep stairs, small grounds, bugs can be a problem.** ⊠ *Boca Chica, on left just before town* ☎ *6611–7574* ⊕ *www. seagullcovelodge.com* ↙ *5 bungalows* ⚷ *In-room: no phone, safe. In-hotel: restaurant, bar, pool, water sports, no elevator, laundry service, no kids under 10, no-smoking rooms* ⊟ *MC, V* ¶⊙ *EP.*

¢ ⬛ **Hotel Boca Brava.** Across the channel from Boca Chica, this lodge belongs to a retired German architect, though you wouldn't guess it from uninspiring white rooms with foam mattresses on cement platforms. Rooms are scattered around the forested grounds; the best have glimpses of ocean, a/c, and TV. Four without a/c cost half as much and share a bathhouse. The restaurant at the end of the point serves a good selection of seafood and meat and can get busy on weekends; the kitchen closes early. The lodge rents kayaks and snorkeling equipment and has island excursions. The nearest beach is a mile via forest trail. **Pros: Inexpensive, decent restaurant. Cons: Very basic rooms, bugs can be a problem.** ⊠ *Isla Boca Brava* ☎ *6588–7775* ↙ *11 rooms* ⚷ *In-room: no phone, no a/c (some), no TV (some). In-hotel: restaurant, bar, water sports, no elevator, no-smoking rooms* ⊟ *No credit cards.*

SPORTS & THE OUTDOORS

SCUBA DIVING & SNORKELING
Boca Chica is the most convenient base for scuba-diving and snorkeling trips to Parque Nacional Marino Golfo de Chiriquí (⇨ *below*) and to Islas Ladrones and Islas Secas (⇨ *below*).

Caros Spragge at **Buzos Boca Brava** (⊠ *Boca Chica* ☎ *775–3185 or 6600–6191* ⊕ *www.scubadiving-panama.com*) offers day trips to either the Islas Ladrones or Islas Secas and overnight trips with lodging on board that combine the two, or can include Isla Coiba (⇨ chapter 3).

SPORTFISHING
The Gulf has superb fishing, especially around the Islas Montuosos and the Hannibal Bank. The best is for black marlin and sailfish from January to April. Find huge yellowfin tuna from March to May, and dolphin (the fish, not the mammal) abound from November to January. From July to January it's roosterfish and wahoo; catch amberjacks, mackerel, snapper, and grouper year-round. **Panama Big Game Fishing Club** (⇨ Where to Stay & Eat, *above*) includes daily fishing trips to the gulf's best spots in their rates. **Gone Fishing** (⇨ Where to Stay & Eat, *above*) offers deep-sea charters or less-expensive inshore fishing.

TO & FROM

The Panama Big Game Fishing Club and Cala Mia have boat transport (40 minutes) for guests from Pedregal. It's more expensive than by land, but more pleasant and half the time. It takes about 90 minutes to drive from David to Boca Chica; go east on the Carretera Interamericana (CA1) for 39 km (24 mi), then turn right at the intersection for Horconcitos. From David's airport, turn left onto Avenida Reed Gray, then left onto Calle F Sur at the police station, and right onto the Interamericana. Follow the signs in Horconcitos, after which the road improves. Most hotels arrange transfers from the David airport.

GOLFO DE CHIRIQUÍ ISLANDS

The vast Gulf of Chiriquí holds dozens of uninhabited islands surrounded by healthy coral formations and excellent conditions for surfing, diving, and fishing. You can base yourself in the Boca Chica/Boca Brava area (⇨*above*) to explore these islands, but there are also two gulf-island resorts that provide more immediate access. Isla Ensenada, in the gulf's northeast corner, is near five of the country's best and most remote breaks, accessed from the Morro Negrito Surf Camp. The beautiful, remote **Islas Secas** (Dry Islands), a 16-isle archipelago 35 km (21 mi) from the coast, has one luxury eco-lodge, but can be visited from Boca Chica or Boca Brava. On the southern edge of the gulf are the **Islas Ladrones**, with fantastic scuba diving and angling.

The 14,740 hectares (36,400 acres) of the **Parque Nacional Marino Golfo de Chiriquí** *(Chiriquí Marine National Park)* include more than 20 islands—all but one of which are uninhabited. The islands' beaches are the nicest in Chiriquí Province, with pale sand, clear waters, tropical dry forest, and colorful reef fish just a shell's toss from shore. The loveliest are the palm-lined strands of **Isla Parida** (the largest in the archipelago), **Isla San José, Isla Gamez,** and **Isla Bolaños,** where the sand is snow-white. Various species of sea turtle nest on the islands' beaches, and the water holds hundreds of species including lobsters, moray eels, and schools of parrot fish. You may also see frigate birds, brown pelicans, and green iguanas. Dolphins sometimes cruise the park's waters, and from August to October you may spot humpback whales. There are no facilities; visit on day trips from Boca Chica, 30 to 60 minutes away, depending on the island. ✉*12 km (7 mi) southwest of Boca Chica* ☎*774–6671 or 774–6671* 🎫*$3.50* ⏲*Daily 8–6.*

WHERE TO STAY

$$$$ ★ **Islas Secas Resort.** Constant exposure to nature, gourmet food, spa services, and other pampering are what you get at this luxury eco-lodge on the Islas Secas. To limit environmental impact, accommodations are in seven spacious *yurts* (round tents of Mongolian origin), with a hot-water bath, minibar, and other amenities. Meals are served in an open-air restaurant overlooking a cove. Snorkeling, scuba diving, surfing, use of catamarans and kayaks, and light-tackle fishing are included, as are meals and drinks; deep-sea fishing and spa services are extra. The downside is rates are more than double those of any other hotel in Panama. During the dry season you are flown directly from Panama City to a landing strip on the island, which takes one hour, but from May to December you have to take a commercial flight to David, then a two-hour boat trip. **Pros: Gorgeous, remote location, excellent skin diving, gourmet food. Cons: Extremely expensive.** ✉*Islas Secas* ☎*805/729–2737 in the U.S.* 🌐*www.islassecas.com* *11 rooms* *In-room: no a/c, no phone, safe, no TV. In-hotel: restaurant, room service, spa, beachfront, diving, water sports, no elevator, laundry service, public Internet, no-smoking rooms* 💳*AE, MC, V* *FAP.*

$$$ **Morro Negrito Surf Camp.** California surfer Steve Thompson built this comfortably rustic lodge on a coastal island in the gulf's northeast corner, near five excellent breaks that are usually ridden only by the

two-dozen surfers the camp accommodates. The lodge rents boards and provides transportation to nearby breaks and also offers inshore fishing, snorkeling, horseback riding, hiking, bird-watching, and massages. A one-week package ($600 at this writing) is usually required, but if you are in the area and e-mail them, they may have room for two nights or more. Rooms have tile floors, basic beds with mosquito nets, lots of windows, and fans. Hearty meals are served family style, and there's a small bar, a Ping-Pong table, horseshoes, basketball, and lots of hammocks. The camp has low environmental impact—solar and wind energy, recycling—and supports a local student scholarship fund. Pros: Great waves with few surfers. Cons: Basic rooms, shared bathrooms, cold-water showers, bugs can be a problem. ⊠ *Isla Ensenada* ☎ *202–9131, 760/632–8014 in U.S.* ⊕ *www.panamasurfcamp.com* ⌁ *12 rooms, 1 with bath* ⚒ *In-room: no a/c, no phone, no TV. In-hotel: restaurant, water sports, no elevator, laundry service, public Internet, no-smoking rooms* ⊟ *V, MC* ⊺*FAP.*

4

SPORTS & THE OUTDOORS

SCUBA DIVING & SNORKELING The Islas Secas and Islas Ladrones are surrounded by excellent skin-diving waters, with visibility averaging 70 feet and healthy coral formations surrounded by hundreds of fish species and comparable invertebrate diversity. You might see various species of eel, shark, sea stars, and angelfish, elegant Moorish idols, frog fish, and sea turtles.

The **Islas Secas Resort** (⇨ *above*) lies in the middle of the archipelago's coral gardens, and daily scuba dives and snorkeling are included in the rates. Those islands can also be visited on day trips from the Morro Negrito Surf Camp or the Boca Chica/Boca Brava lodges. **Buzos Boca Brava** (☎ *775–3185 or 6600–6191* ⊕ *www.scubadiving-panama.com*) offers day trips and overnights to the Islas Secas out of Boca Chica.

SURFING The Golfo de Chiriquí has some undervisited, remote surf breaks. Surfing is best from June to December when waves consistently break overhead, and faces sometimes reach 20 feet; there are often 4- to 5-foot swells during the dry season too. The most impressive wave in the gulf is called **The Point,** a tubular reef break that has surfers booking weeks at the Morro Negrito Surf Camp year after year. Advanced surfers enjoy the rush of **Nestles,** a big reef break in front of Isla Silva de Afuera. **The Sandbar,** a long break that has both lefts and rights, is popular with intermediate surfers and beginners. Intermediate and advanced surfers enjoy **P Land,** a left reef break on Isla Silva de Afuera, year-round. The most convenient wave for guests at the Morro Negrito Surf Camp is **Emily,** a left that breaks over the reef right in front of the camp.

TO & FROM

Transportation to Golfo de Chiriquí lodges is provided. The Parque Nacional Marino Golfo de Chiriquí, Islas Secas, and Islas Ladrones can be visited on day trips from Boca Chica and Boca Brava via boat.

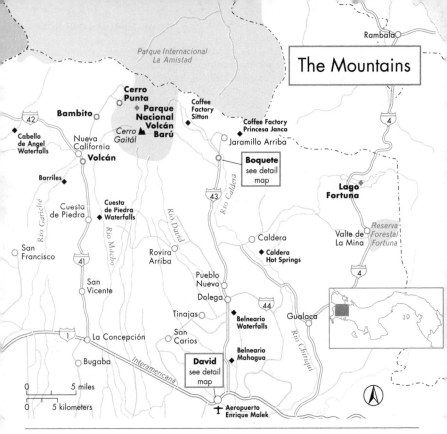

The Mountains

THE MOUNTAINS

Nestled in the Cordillera de Talamanca, which towers along the province's northern edge, are the lush mountain valleys of Boquete, Cerro Punta, and Bambito, each with unique scenery. To the east of Boquete a road winds over the Cordillera near Lago Fortuna, an area that also has excellent hiking and amazing vistas. The mountain range's upper slopes are covered with lush cloud forest, which is kept wet by the mist that the trade winds regularly push over the continental divide. That mist not only keeps the landscape green, it creates the perfect conditions for rainbows, common sights during the afternoon. Mountain streams feed half a dozen rafting rivers in the Cordillera, and its abundant forests are excellent areas for bird-watching, hiking, horseback riding, or a canopy tour. And all travelers enjoy the area's captivating beauty, abundant flowers, and charming restaurants and inns.

BOQUETE

★ *38 km (24 mi) north of David.*

This pleasant town sits at 3,878 feet above sea level in the always springlike valley of the Río Caldera. The surrounding mountains are covered with forest and shade coffee farms, where coffee bushes grow amidst tropical trees. It's superb for bird-watching, and the roads and trails can be explored on foot, horseback, mountain bike, or four wheels. Boquete's main landmark is the country's highest mountain, **Volcán Barú,** an extinct volcano that towers over the valley's western edge. Much of Volcán Barú's green mantle of cloud forest is protected within Parque Nacional Volcán Barú. The rough road to Barú's summit begins just west of Boquete's commercial center, but its forests can also be explored on trails in the Alto Quiel area northwest of town.

Though the surrounding countryside holds most of Boquete's attractions, the town itself is quite nice, with tidy wooden houses and prolific flower gardens. Fewer than 30,000 people live there, most of them scattered around the valley. The town center is thus sparsely populated, with a simple *parque central* (central park), officially the Parque de las Madres, surrounded by shops, the town hall, and roads lined with patches of pink impatiens and the pale trumpetlike flowers of the deadly nightshade. Streams meander through town, and the Río Caldera flows through a wide swath of boulders along its eastern edge.

Unlike most Panamanian towns, Boquete was settled by European and North American immigrants at the beginning of the 20th century. This lineage is visible in everything from the architecture to the faces of many residents. There are also plenty of Ngöbe-Buglé Indians in Boquete who migrate there from the northeast of Chiriquí to work in the orange and coffee harvests. Recently the valley has become popular with U.S. retirees, drawn by the climate and beauty.

➊ If you're driving, stop at the **CEFATI Information Center,** on the right as you climb the hill into town. They offer free information on local sights and services, but the main reason to stop is to admire the view of the Boquete Valley. The building also has a small café and gift shop. ⊠ *Av. Central, 1 km (½ mi) south of town* ☎ *720–4060* ☺ *Daily 9–5.*

➋ Two blocks east of the parque central is the **Feria** (⊠ *Follow Calle 4 Sur, along park's southern side, go over bridge across Río Caldera, Feria on east side of bridge*), the fairgrounds where the Feria de las Flores (Flower Fair) is held for 10 days in mid-January, and the smaller Expo Orquídeas (Orchid Fair) is held in mid-April. During the interim, the fairgrounds are open to anyone who wants to admire their flower beds.

➌ A few blocks north of the parque central, Avenida Central veers left at a Y in the road. Just past the Y is **Mi Jardín es Su Jardín** *(My Garden Is Your Garden)*, a garden surrounding an eccentric Panamanian's vacation home. Cement paths wind past vibrant flower beds and bizarre statues of animals and cartoon characters, which make this place a minor monument to kitsch. ⊠ *Av. Central ½ km (¼ mi) north of park, on right* ☎ *No phone* ⊠ *Free* ☺ *Daily 9–5.*

➍ The Ruiz family has been growing coffee in Boquete since the late 1800s, and their **Café Ruiz** coffee-roasting and packaging plant just north of Mi Jardín es Su Jardín offers a 15-minute tour that includes

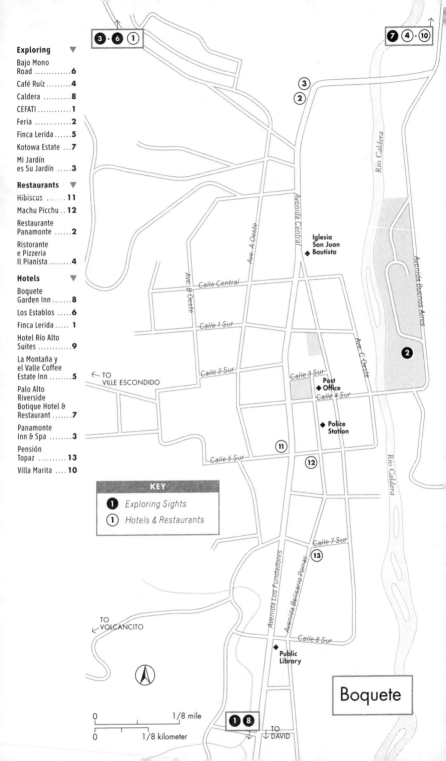

a taste of the coffee on sale here. A full tour visits the family farm and processing plant in the mountains above town. Because it has plenty of trees and uses few chemicals, the farm is a good place to see birds. Do the tour in the morning between October and May, during harvest. Reserve a tour by phone or via the Web site. ⊠ *Av. Central, ½ km (¼ mi) north of park, on right* ☎ *720–1000* ⊕ *www.caferuiz.com* ⊠ *Plant tour $4, full tour $15* ⊙ *Mon.–Sat. 8–11:30 and 1:30–4.*

❺ On the eastern slope of Volcán Barú, at an altitude of 4,800 feet above **FodorśChoice** sea level, the **Finca Lerida** coffee farm has nearly 500 hectares of bird-★ filled cloud forest. The farm is recommended in *A Guide to the Birds of Panama* as the place to see quetzals, and you're practically guaranteed to see them here from February to June. You may also see silver-throated tanagers, collared trogons, clorophonias, and about 150 other bird species. The farm's resident guide can take you along its 8 km (5 mi) of hiking trails, one of which leads to a small waterfall, but you can also explore them on your own. The guide is invaluable if you're looking for quetzals. If owner John Collins is available, you can get a coffee tour from a native English speaker who grew up on the farm. The farm has a moderately priced restaurant with a great view that serves Panamanian food, homemade desserts, and fresh-roasted coffee. ⊠ *7 km (4 mi) northwest of second Y, via Callejón Seco, Alto Quiel* ☎ *720–2285* ⊕ *www.fincalerida.com* ⊠ *$10, coffee tour $25, guided hike or bird-watching $35* ⊙ *Daily 9–5.*

❻ The **Bajo Mono road,** near San Ramón, leads to the trailhead for the ★ **Sendero Los Quetzales** (⇨ *Cerro Punta, below*), which winds its way through the forest between Cerro Punta and Boquete. Start that hike in Cerro Punta, though; it's all uphill from Boquete. Head to Bajo Mono to look for quetzals and hundreds of other bird species; the best area for bird-watching is the beginning of the Sendero Los Quetzales, above the Alto Chiquero ranger station. Two other good hiking trails head off of the Bajo Mono road: the **Sendero Culebra,** on the right 1½ km (1 mi) up the road to Alto Chiquero, and **Pipeline Road,** a gravel track on the left that leads to a canyon and waterfall.

❼ **Kotowa Estate,** in the hills of Palo Alto, has belonged to the MacIntyre family for three generations. They produce one of Boquete's best coffees and own a small chain of coffee shops. The farm still has the original coffee mill. A Dutch couple, Hans and Terry van der Vooren, runs tours here that provide a close look at the cultivation, harvest, and processing of coffee. Go during the October-to-May harvest, and reserve for the tour a day in advance for free transport from your hotel. ⊠ *Palo Alto* ☎ *720–3852 or 6634–4698* ⊕ *www.coffeeadventures.net* ⊠ *Tour $22* ⊙ *Tour daily at 9 AM by reservation.*

❽ Half an hour south of Boquete is the small village of **Caldera,** known for its hot springs (Los Pazos) and pre-Columbian petroglyphs. Los Pazos are next to the Caldera River, at the end of a rough road on the right after town, which requires 4WD. Before the turnoff for Los Pozos is the Piedra Pintada (Painted Rock), behind the Jardín La Fortuna, a large boulder with pre-Columbian petroglyphs scrawled into its side.

CLOSE UP

The Quetzal and the Cloud Forest

Some people travel to Boquete specifically to see a resplendent quetzal (*Pharomachrus mocinno*), and if you're lucky enough to spot a male quetzal in flight, its iridescent colors flashing and long tail feathers streaming behind it, you'll quickly understand why. The resplendent quetzal is one of the world's most beautiful birds, a flying jewel with an emerald-green back and wings, ruby-red belly, and golden-green crest. Though a mature bird stands just 14 inches tall, male quetzals have two- to three-foot tail feathers that float behind them as they fly, giving the impression of an airborne snake, or a tiny dragon. Quetzals, which live only in cloud forests from western Panama to southern Mexico, occupied an important place in ancient Maya and Aztec cosmology. The Aztecs associated the bird with Quetzalcoatl, one of their most important deities, who was known as the Plumed Serpent. The chiefs of those cultures wore headdresses of quetzal tail feathers—Montezuma's is on display in Mexico City's anthropology museum—but the feathers were plucked from live birds that were then released, since it was a crime to kill a quetzal in those pre-Columbian societies.

The quetzal is the national bird of Guatemala, where the currency is named for it, but destruction of its cloud forest habitat has made the bird extremely rare there, and throughout its range. Quetzals abound in the forests above Boquete, which is one of the best places in the world to see the bird. That said, it is not easy to see a quetzal, since they spend most of their time sitting on branches in the shade of the cloud forest, where their green feathers blend in perfectly

with the lush surroundings. You will consequently want to hire a local birding guide who can take you to spots where they commonly feed, or reproduce during the February to June nesting season.

In January the quetzal's slightly melancholy song becomes more common in the forests above Boquete, as the mating season begins. Female quetzals aren't as spectacular as males, and look more like trogons—the quetzal is a member of the trogon family—since they lack the long tail feathers and crimson breast. Interestingly, they have black beaks, whereas the male's beak is light brown. The females' lack of adornment doesn't discourage males from courting them energetically. Lucky is the bird-watcher who witnesses the aerial mating dance that males perform for females, flying high and then plummeting in front of them, iridescent tail feathers streaming behind.

Once a match is made, the quetzal couple digs, or finds a cavity in a rotting tree trunk and she lays two pale blue eggs, which they take turns incubating for several weeks. They guard their nest tirelessly, since various animals prey on quetzal eggs and chicks, especially the emerald toucanet, a common cloud-forest bird. Quetzals feed their chicks insects, frogs, lizards, and fruit, but the primary food for adults is *aguacatillo*, the pecan-size fruit of several trees in the avocado family. Those fruits have very large pits that are too big to pass through the quetzal's digestive tract—they can barely get them past their beaks—so the birds simply keep the fruit in their stomach for awhile, digesting the pulp, and then

vomit the seed up, often far from the tree it came from. The quetzal thus distributes aguacatillo seeds around the forest, so the bird and tree are interdependent, which leads biologists to believe they evolved together. As destruction of the region's cloud forests continues, and climate change leaves many cloud-forest regions drier than they should be, the quetzal and the agaucatillo tree are increasingly endangered. Thanks to the amount of protected cloud forest around Boquete, though, both species should remain abundant there for many years, hopefully generations.

Even if you have little interest in birdwatching, taking a tour to Finca Lerida, or one of the other spots above Boquete where quetzals are common, is highly recommended. Even if you don't catch a glimpse of the legendary resplendent quetzal, you're bound to see dozens of other spectacular birds, and the quetzal's cloud-forest habitat is a magically beautiful ecosystem. If you travel to Cana, in Panama's eastern Darién Province, you may be fortunate enough to also see a golden-headed quetzal, which is native to South America, but is found in the mountains of the Darién. Such a quetzal double-header is only possible in Panama, and is just one of the countless examples of why this country such an amazing place for nature lovers.

Both sites can be visited on a tour offered by Boquete's bird-watching and hiking guides (⇨ *below*).

WHERE TO STAY & EAT

Hotels in Boquete don't have air-conditioning—the town's spring-like climate makes it unnecessary. Theft has been a problem at some Boquete hotels, so lock your valuables in a safe if you can.

> **A GOOD DRIVE**
>
> Just north of Café Ruiz there's a second Y in Avenida Central. The right fork heads to the farms and scenic overlooks of Alto Lino, looping back to Boquete via Palo Alto. Veer left there to reach yet another Y that marks the beginning of a second, longer loop (30 minutes) that winds through the farming areas of Alto Quiel, Bajo Mono, and San Ramón, passing forest and more great views. Both loops are well worth driving.

$-$$$ ✗**Hibiscus.** In the Plaza Los Establos shopping center, this small restaurant doesn't have the best ambience but fills up with people who appreciate good food. Chef Cristophe Giroud serves traditional French cuisine, including escargots and chicken cordon bleu, but has organized much of the menu into two lists: one list of meats and seafood, and a separate list of sauces, so you can have your *corvina* (sea bass) or fillet with a béarnaise sauce, a bordelaise sauce, or a blue-cheese sauce, etc. The delicacies also include fresh trout in a papillote, shrimp flambé with bourbon, and lobster medallions and tomatoes au gratin. Giroud's smaller El Café next door serves a comparably delicious selection of breakfasts. ✉ *Plaza Los Establos, Av. Central, one block south of park* ☎ *720–2652* ▭ *MC, V* ☼ *Closed Sun.*

$-$$ ✗**Machu Picchu.** The local branch of Panama City's most popular Peruvian restaurant serves the same selection of spicy delicacies. The dining room is a bit plain, despite paintings of Peruvian landscapes and colorful woven tablecloths, but you can't go wrong with such classics as ceviche, *ají de gallina* (chicken in a chili cream sauce), *seco de res* (Peruvian stewed beef), and *sudado de mero* (grouper in a spicy soup). Be careful with their *ají* hot sauce; it's practically caustic. ✉ *Av. Belisario Porras, behind Banco Nacional* ☎ *720–1520* ▭ *AE, MC, V.*

$-$$ ✗**Palo Alto Riverside Restaurant.** This place's greatest selling point is its view of the Palo Alto River and forest beyond it. If the weather is nice, you may want to sit outside near the riverbank, though the spacious walls of windows let you enjoy the scenery from inside too. The food is tasty and inventive, though service can be slow. Starters range from seafood crepes and creamy chicken soup to spicy-sour butterfly shrimp on a nest of wontons. Entrées worth sinking your teeth into include steamed trout in a black-bean sauce, tenderloin with a Cognac-and-green-pepper sauce, baby back ribs, and steamed salmon with a caviar-hollandaise sauce. ✉ *Right at first Y north of town, left after bridge, then 1½ km (1 mi) on left, Palo Alto* ☎ *720–1076* ▭ *MC, V.*

$-$$ ✗**Restaurante Panamonte.** Though Boquete's first hotel now faces stiff

Fodor'sChoice
★

competition, its charming restaurant remains one of the best in town, if not the country. Inventive dishes are based on traditional Panamanian cuisine like pumpkin soup, shrimp-and-plantain croquettes, mountain trout sautéed with almonds, and grilled beef tenderloin topped with a three-pepper sauce. It's served in a historic European atmosphere that's hardly changed over the past century. Sunday brunch is popular, and on weekdays the three-course prix-fixe lunches are a deal. Service is friendly, but can be slow. ⊠*Panamonte Inn and Spa, right at first Y north of town, on left* ☎*720–1324* ✆*Apdo 0413–3086, Boquete, Chiriquí* ☰*AE, MC, V* ⊗*Closed 10* AM*–noon and 2:30–6.*

$–$$ ✕**Ristorante e Pizzería Il Pianista.** There is something European about the stone building that houses this restaurant a short drive northeast of town, and Chef Giovanni Santoro completes the illusion with his authentic Italian cuisine. The small dining room is on the ground floor overlooking a stream surrounded by trees and impatiens. The menu includes fresh pastas such as vegetable lasagna and fettuccine *del Chef* (with prawn-and-mushroom cream sauce) or *napolitano* (with tomato-clam sauce). Other specialties include *trucha al forno* (trout baked with tomatoes and mushrooms) and *calamares rellenos* (squid stuffed with tomatoes, cheese, and pine nuts). You can also build your own pizza or calzone. ⊠*Right at first Y north of town, left after the bridge, 3½ km (2 mi) north on right, Arc Iris* ☎*720–2728* ✆*Giovanni Santoro, Entrega General, Boquete, Chiriquí* ☰*No credit cards* ⊗*Closed Mon.*

FodorsChoice ★

$$–$$$$ ▦**Los Establos.** This small, Spanish-style inn with a stirring view of Volcán Barú started out as a horse stable, hence its name, and each room is named after a horse. Standard rooms are dark but nicely decorated and have small terraces. Only the Solita room has a volcano view, since the breakfast room–bar takes up most of that side of the building. Double-sized suites on the second floor have great views but are much more expensive. Rates include beer and wine in the evening. The 12-acre grounds have a wide lawn and a coffee farm. **Pros: Volcano view, nice decor, ample grounds, lovely lounge and porch. Cons: Most standard rooms lack views, a bit dark, no kids, expensive.** ⊠*2 km (1 mi) northeast of town, right at first Y north of town, left after bridge, then first right, Jaramillo Arriba* ☎☎*720–2685* ⊕*www.losestablos. net* ⌸*5 rooms, 2 suites* ⚐*In-room: no a/c, safe, Wi-Fi. In-hotel: restaurant, no elevator, laundry service, airport shuttle, no kids under 14, no-smoking rooms* ☰*AE, MC, V* ◧|*BP.*

$$$ ✕▦**Palo Alto Riverside Boutique Hotel.** This large yellow house with a wide front lawn looks like something you'd expect to see in New England. In it are six luxurious suites and a cozy lounge with a stone fireplace, Panamanian art, and a view of the Río Palo Alto. Elegant guest rooms have high ceilings and handsome hardwood furniture, one king or two queen beds with Egyptian cotton linens, and appliances like satellite TV and a boom box. A few rooms also have lofts with two single beds. Only the master and bonsai suites have river views, but there is a stone terrace overlooking the river where you can eat breakfast. The Palo Alto Riverside Restaurant (⇨*above*) is next door. **Pros: Luxurious rooms, lovely lounge, nice riverside location, great restaurant. Cons: Grounds a bit barren, service inconsistent.** ⊠*Right at first Y north of town, left after bridge, then 1½ km (1 mi) on the left, Palo Alto* ☎☎*720–1076* ⊕*www.paloaltoriverside.com* ⌸*5 suites, 1 master suite* ⚐*In-room: refrigerator, DVD, Wi-Fi. In-hotel: restaurant, no* *elevator, laundry service, concierge, public Wi-Fi, airport shuttle, no-smoking rooms* ▭*AE, MC, V* ⦿*CP.*

$–$$ ✕▦**Panamonte Inn & Spa.** Opened in 1914, the Panamonte was long Boquete's only tourist hotel, and over the decades it has hosted the likes of Teddy Roosevelt, Charles Lindbergh, and Ingrid Bergman. You haven't been to Boquete unless you at least stop by the restaurant (⇨*above*) and wander the hotel's charming gardens, but staying at the historic inn isn't for everyone. The honeymoon suite and Quetzal I room are bright and pleasant, but some standard rooms are cramped, and the Fresal annex has historic mustiness. Though much less charming, the newer cement *cabañas* in the garden offer more room and privacy and have front porches. The cozy bar is a great spot to hang out, and the hotel has a small spa and arranges day tours. **Pros: Charming, timeless, nice gardens, great restaurant and bar. Cons: Some rooms small, musty, or both; near a busy road.** ⊠*Right at first Y north of town, on left* ☎*720–1324* 🖷*720–2055* ⊕*www.panamonteinnand-spa.com* ⤳*11 rooms, 1 suite, 4 cabañas, 1 apartment* ⌂*In-room: safe, Wi-Fi. In-hotel: restaurant, bar, spa, no elevator, laundry service, public Wi-Fi, airport shuttle, no-smoking rooms* ▭*AE, MC, V* ⦿*EP.*

$–$$$ ▦**Finca Lerida.** This working coffee farm on the eastern slope of Volcán
Fodor'sChoice Barú above Boquete has almost 500 acres of bird-replete cloud forest.
★ The hotel has a resident nature guide and tours. Rooms are either in the newer mountainside "eco-lodge" or in the original farmhouse "B&B." Eco-lodge rooms are bright and spacious with hardwood floors, high, sloping ceilings, one king or two queen beds, and picture windows with panoramic views, but immediate surroundings are a bit bare. They share a large lounge with a fireplace, self-service bar, and library. The small restaurant has views and serves hearty lunches and dinners. B&B rooms are smaller, older, and less expensive, but have character, and the house is surrounded by big trees and gardens—great for bird-watching. Kids under 10 aren't allowed in the B&B. **Pros: Gorgeous views, nice rooms, bird-watching, cloud forest, guide, coffee tour. Cons: Eco-lodge lacks greenery nearby, isolated.** ⊠*7 km (4 mi) northwest of Av. Central, turn left at second Y, entrance on left, Callejón Seco, Alto Quiel* ☎🖷*720–2285* ⊠*John Collins, Entrega General, Boquete, Chiriquí* ⊕*www.fincalerida.com* ⤳*16 rooms* ⌂*In-room: no a/c, no phone, no TV. In-hotel: restaurant, bar, no elevator, laundry service, public Internet, no-smoking rooms* ▭*AE, MC, V* ⦿*BP.*

$$ ▦**La Montaña y el Valle Coffee Estate Inn.** These charming bungalows
Fodor'sChoice on a 6-acre shade coffee farm offer peace, privacy, plentiful birdlife
★ and one of Boquete's best views. Each unit has a kitchenette, sitting room with dining table, and large bedrooms. Big windows and ample balconies with lounge chairs frame Volcán Barú and the valley below. Use the footpaths and benches in the tropical gardens, coffee plants, and forest patches to spot the 130 avian species here. You can have a delicious dinner served by candlelight in your bungalow some nights, though you need to order in the morning. Friendly Canadian owners Barry and Jane sell crafts and coffee and will help you plan your time in Boquete. Reserve well ahead of time. **Pros: Great views, lovely grounds, bird-watching, helpful owners, gourmet dinners. Cons: Often full, two-**

night minimum stay, no kids. ✉ 1½ km (1 mi) northeast of town; right at first Y, first right north of bridge, just past El Explorador, Jaramillo Arriba 🖀 720–2211 ⊕ www.coffeeestateinn.com ⇌ 3 bungalows ♨ In-room: no a/c, no phone, kitchen, Wi-Fi. In-hotel: room service, no elevator, laundry service, concierge, airport shuttle, public Internet, no kids under 14, no-smoking rooms ☰ MC, V ⌾ CP.

$–$$ 🖭**Hotel Río Alto Suites.** This small collection of two-story buildings has
★ lush gardens, tall trees, and the rocky Río Palo Alto nearby. Rooms are ideal for couples, with one queen and a roll-out bed; suites with several beds and full kitchens work well for families. All rooms have a cluttering array of appliances, and their decor is a bit tacky—lots of gold and shiny polyester—but they open onto enclosed terraces with great views of the surrounding verdure. Second-floor rooms have high ceilings and the best views. There are several patios in the gardens and a gas grill for guest use. **Pros: Lush grounds, great views, nice terraces, good value. Cons: Rooms a bit cluttered and tacky.** ✉ Left at first Y, 2½ km (1½ mi) north of bridge, on left, Palo Alto 🖀 720–2278 ⊕ www.boqueteparadise.com ⇌ 8 rooms, 3 suites ♨ In-room: no a/c, no phone, refrigerator, Wi-Fi. In-hotel: no elevator, laundry service, airport shuttle, no-smoking rooms ☰ AE, MC, V ⌾ BP.

$ 🖭**Boquete Garden Inn.** As the name suggests, this small hotel's grounds hold plenty of flowers, as well as trees and a few boulders. The nicest area is behind the rooms, along the Río Palo Alto, where a gazebo bar overlooks the swift-running waters and forest beyond. Guests gather here nightly for cocktail hour at 6 PM—the first beer or wine is on the house. Rooms are in two-story cement buildings, one to a floor, but they have small windows (in bare stucco walls) so you don't see much of the surrounding greenery. They have kitchenettes in a corner, and most have a double bed plus a single or a bunk bed. The staff will arrange day trips. **Pros: Lovely grounds on river, friendly, spacious rooms, good value. Cons: Rooms lack personality, limited views.** ✉ Right at first Y north of town, 1½ km (1 mi) north of bridge over Río Caldera, Palo Alto 🖀 720–2376 ⊕ www.boquetegardeninn.com ⇌ 10 rooms ♨ In-room: no phone, safe, kitchen (some), refrigerator. In-hotel: no elevator, laundry service, public Internet ☰ AE, MC, V ⌾ CP.

¢–$ 🖭**Villa Marita.** On a ridge a five-minute drive north of Boquete, these
★ yellow cabañas (bungalows) with bay windows and terraces share a gorgeous view of the valley, volcano, and nearby coffee farms. Each has two simple, bright rooms: a bedroom with one queen or two single beds, and a smaller sitting area with a couch that can double as a bed. Three smaller rooms in back lack the view, but cost less. The main building has a lounge with a long porch where a $4 breakfast buffet is served; a deck has a grill for guest use. Owner Rodrigo Marciacq arranges hiking and horseback tours. **Pros: Great views, ample grounds, friendly, helpful owner, a bargain. Cons: Mediocre rooms, no restaurant, far from town.** ✉ 4 km (2½ mi) north of Boquete, left at first Y, right at second Y, Alto Lino 🖀 720–2165 🖨 720–2164 ⊕ www.villamarita.com ⇌ 3 rooms, 7 bungalows ♨ In-room: no a/c, no phone, refrigerator (some), Wi-Fi. In-hotel: no elevator, laundry service, public Internet, no-smoking rooms ☰ AE, MC, V ⌾ EP.

¢ ⚏ **Pensión Topaz.** This small, German-owned lodge near the parque central has several different room types and one of Boquete's only swimming pools. The brightest rooms are in a two-story cement building behind the house; the biggest ones are across from the tiny pool, in a low building with a covered terrace. They're all clean, well decorated, and have firm beds. A couple of tiny, dirt-cheap singles share a bathroom. Hearty breakfasts are a few dollars extra. **Pros: Quiet, yard, pool, nice rooms, good value. Cons: Big rooms a bit dark.** ⊠*Calle 6 Sur and Av. Belisario Porras, behind Texaco station* ☎*720–1005* ⇦*8 rooms, 6 with bath* ⚏*In room: no a/c, no phone, no TV. In-hotel: pool, no elevator, no-smoking rooms* ▤*No credit cards* ⎜⊘*EP.*

NIGHTLIFE & THE ARTS

The most pleasant place in Boquete for a quiet cocktail is the bar in the **Panamonte Inn and Spa** (⊠*Right at first Y north of town, on left* ☎*720–1324*), which has a terrace hemmed by gardens, a big fireplace, and lots of couches and cane chairs. The hip crowd hangs at **Zanzibar** (⊠*Av. Central, 2 blocks north of church* ☎*No phone*), an attractive lounge with an odd African decor and comfy chairs.

SPORTS & THE OUTDOORS

BIRD-
WATCHING

Boquete is bird-watchers heaven and diversity tops 400 species during the dry season. The mountain forests shelter emerald toucanets, collared redstarts, sulfur-winged parakeets, a dozen hummingbird species, and the resplendent quetzal. Even the gardens of homes and hotels offer decent birding; they're the best places to see migrant birds wintering in Boquete, from Tennessee warblers to the Baltimore orioles. The less accessible upper slopes of Volcán Barú are home to rare species like the volcano junco and volcano hummingbird.

One of the best places to see the quetzal and other cloud-forest birds is **Finca Lerida** (⇨*above*), a short drive north of town in Alto Quiel. Another good place to see quetzals is the **Bajo Mono** (⇨*above*), just up the road from Finca Lerida. One great birding area that few people get to is **Finca El Oasis,** above the ANAM ranger station on the road to the summit of Volcán Barú, a 90-minute drive from Boquete on a rough, 4WD-only road, which has plenty of quetzals and others.

Quetzals are hard to spot, and bird-watching in general is difficult in a cloud-forest environment; even experienced birders should hire a local guide, at least for the first day. **Santiago (Chago) Caballero** (☎*6626–2200*) is considered the best guide in Boquete, and can practically guarantee you'll see quetzals from February to June, when they nest. Santiago's son **Cesar Caballero** is the resident guide at Finca Lerida. **Eduardo Serrano** (☎*6504–6658*) is a bird-watching and hiking guide who speaks some English and can customize day trips to suit your interests. **Hans van der Vooren** (☎*720–3852 or 6634–4698*), who runs coffee tours at the Kotowa Estate, also offers bird-watching tours.

CANOPY TOUR

A canopy tour involves gliding along cables, to which you're attached via a harness, strung between platforms in the high branches of tropical trees. The sensation is that of flying through the treetops, and provides a bird's-eye view of the cloud forest. **Boquete Tree Trek** (⊠*Plaza Los*

Establos, Av. Central ☎720–1635 ⊕*www.aventurist.com*) has trained guides that provide instruction and accompany groups through the tour ($60), which lasts about three hours. Prohibited from canopy tours are children under six and anyone weighing more than 250 pounds.

HIKING ★ Boquete is a great place for hiking, with countless farm roads and footpaths in and around the valley. The most popular hike here is the 9-km (5-mi) **Sendero Los Quetzales** (⇨Cerro Punta, *below*). The forest here is a breeding area for quetzals, and holds many other birds and animals. It's best to go from Cerro to Boquete, since the reverse trip is completely uphill. For a day trip from Boquete, pay someone to drive you to El Respingo and pick you up at Alto Chiquero four hours later, or pay them to drop off your 4WD vehicle at Alto Chiquero. **Daniel Higgins** (☎6617–0570) regularly drops people and cars off for this hike.

The summit hike to **Volcán Barú** in Parque Nacional Volcán Barú (⇨*below*) is more demanding than the Sendero Los Quetzales as it's uphill and very steep. You can drive your 4WD vehicle to, or arrange for a ride to and from, the ANAM ranger station, 14 km (8½ mi) from the summit, above which the road is so rough that only high-suspension trucks can ascend it. Some people begin hiking around midnight in order to summit at sunrise, when you might see both the Atlantic and Pacific oceans, weather permitting. (You can always see the Pacific.) Bring at least three liters of water, snacks, sunblock, a hat, and warm, waterproof clothing; ⚠ **the weather can change drastically within minutes near the top, where it freezes regularly during the dry season—hypothermia is a real risk if you're caught in a storm.** The **Bajo Mono** area, near Alto Quiel, has shorter trails into the park that can be explored in a matter of hours. The **Pipeline Road,** a dirt track that heads off of the main road to the left, leads into a forested canyon with a waterfall. The **Sendero Culebra** trailhead is on the right from the road to Alto Chiquiero about 1.4 km from the Bajo Mono road.

Feliciano González (☎6624–9940, *or 6632–8645* ⊕*www.geocities.com/ boquete_tours*) has been guiding hikers through Boquete's mountains for two decades. In addition to tours of the Sendero Los Quezales and to the summit of Volcán Barú, he has a six-hour hike on the Sendero El Pianista through primary forest along the continental divide. Tours are $20–$50 per person. **Eduardo Serrano** (☎6504–6658) can drop people off and pick them up on either end of the Sendero los Quetzales, or arrange a guided hike of any of the valley's other hiking routes. **Aventurist** (✉*Plaza Los Establos, Av. Central* ☎720–1635 ⊕*www.aventurist. com*), which owns Boquete Tree Trek, has a four-hour hike ($25) in its private reserve, which holds waterfalls and wildlife.

HORSEBACK RIDING There are some excellent horseback-riding routes in the mountains around Boquete that include panoramic views and exposure to abundant birdlife. Eduardo Cano at **Boquete Tours** (☎720–1750) can arrange inexpensive horseback tours, as well as a guided hike down the Sendero Los Quetzales or a Volcán Barú ascent.

MOUNTAIN
BIKING

Aventurist (*Boquete Tree Trek* ⊠*Plaza Los Establos, Av. Central* ☎720–1635 ⊕*www.aventurist.com*) runs a three-hour bike tour ($25) through the mountains north of Boquete that is mostly downhill.

WHITE-WATER
RAFTING

Chiriquí has Panama's best white-water rafting, with many rivers to choose from during the rainy season (June–November). ■TIP→Only one river—Río Chiriquí Viejo—is navigable during the December–May dry season.

The **Río Chiriquí Viejo** is considered Panama's best white-water river, since it churns its way through pristine rain forest and an impressive canyon. It has two rafting routes, the harder of which is the Class III–IV Palón section, which requires previous experience and can become too dangerous to navigate during the rainiest months. The easier, Class II–III Sabo section is good for beginners. Chiriquí Viejo is a three-hour drive from Boquete each way, which makes for a long day. Unfortunately, it's threatened by government plans to dam it for a hydroelectric project. The **Río Estí** is a fun Class II–III river fit for beginners that is closer to Boquete (a 90-minute drive). It doubles as a good wildlife-watching trip. The **Río Chiriquí** is a fun Class III river with one Class IV rapid; it's a 90-minute drive from Boquete and appropriate for beginners. The **Río Gariche** is one of several Class II–III rivers near Boquete, and is a great trip for seeing wildlife. The **Río Dolega** is a fun Class II–III river near Boquete and suitable for beginners.

Chiriquí River Rafting (⊠*Av. Central, across from park* ☎720–1505 ⊕*www.panama-rafting.com*), founded in the early 1990s by Hector Sanchez, makes safety and eco-friendliness a priority. They offer trips on all area rivers ($60–$105); Río Chiriquí Viejo is the most expensive. **Panama Rafters** (⊠*Av. Central, 2 blocks north of park* ☎720–2712 ⊕*www.panamarafters.com*) is a small, American-owned company that only runs rafting trips on the Chiriquí Viejo; trips cost $75–$90, depending on the section. They have kayaking trips on other rivers.

SHOPPING

The small shop at **CEFATI** (⊠*Av. Central, 1 km (½ mi) south of town* ☎720–4060) has a good selection of indigenous handicrafts such as Emberá woven bowls and Ngöbe-Buglé *chacaras* (colorful woven jute bags). **Folklorica** (⊠*Av. Central, 2 blocks north of church* ☎720–2368) has an eclectic mix of antiques, ceramics, jewelry, and handicrafts. **Souvenirs Cacique** (⊠*Av. Central, at park* ☎No phone) sells everything from handicrafts to T-shirts.

TO & FROM

It's an easy 45-minute drive to Boquete from David, where you follow Avenida Obaldía north across the highway, and continue straight. From David's airport, turn left onto Avenida Reed Gray, then left onto Calle F Sur at the police station and right onto the two-lane Interamericana (CA1); get into the left lane and watch for the turnoff for Boquete. Buses depart from David's terminal on Avenida del Estudiante every 30 minutes and take 60–90 minutes to reach Boquete. From Boquete, catch the bus to David on Avenida Central anywhere south of the parque central. The trip costs $1.60. If you bus from Cerro

Punta, Paso Canoas, or Bocas del Toro, you'll need to change to the Boquete bus in David. **Boquete Shuttle Service** (☎720–1635) runs direct transfers between hotels in Boquete and David's airport for $10.

Boquete's local transportation is via vans that depart regularly from Avenida Central just north of the parque central for either the Alto Quiel/Bajo Mono loop or the Alto Lino/Palo Alto loop. They pick up and drop off passengers anywhere en route for $1. Taxis wait around

WORD OF MOUTH

After Boca del Toro, we hired a driver to take us up to Boquette. A beautiful area. We were able to do a coffee tour, lots of hiking, and birding. We had a driver take us to the airport but we missed our flight, so we got to experience the bus. Also very easy and doable. It was a wonderful trip.

–ttraveler

4

the parque central and charge $1–$5 for valley trips. **Daniel Higgins** (☎6617–0570) is an English-speaking driver who'll take you to David, Boca Chica, or Cerro Punta. He can also drive you to or from Almirante, the gateway to Bocas del Toro, for $120; it's a beautiful drive.

PARQUE NACIONAL VOLCÁN BARÚ

★ *15 km (9 mi) west of Boquete.*

Towering 11,450 feet above sea level, Barú Volcano is literally Chiriquí's biggest attraction, and Panama's highest peak to boot. The massive extinct volcano is visible from David, and is the predominant landmark in Boquete and Volcán, but Bambito and Cerro Punto are tucked so tightly into its slopes that you can hardly see it from there. The upper slopes, summit, and northern side of the volcano are protected within Barú Volcano National Park, which covers more than 14,000 hectares (35,000 acres) and extends northward to connect with the larger Parque Internacional La Amistad. The vast expanse of protected wilderness is home to everything from cougars to howler monkeys and more than 250 bird species. You might see white hawks, black guans, violet sabrewings, sulfur-winged parakeets, resplendent quetzals, and rare three-wattled bellbirds in the park's cloud forests. The volcano's craggy summit, on the other hand, is covered with a scrubby high-altitude ecosystem known as *páramo,* a collection of shrubs and grasses common in the Andes. There you may spot the rare volcano junco, a small gray bird that lives on the highest peaks of the Cordillera de Talamanca. The summit is also topped by radio towers and a cement bunker, and unfortunately many of its boulders are covered with graffiti.

Several paths penetrate the park's wilderness, including two trails to the summit. The main road to the summit begins in Boquete, across from the church, and is paved for the first 7 km (4 mi), where it passes a series of homes and farms, after which it becomes increasingly rough and rocky. You pay the park fee at the ANAM ranger station 15 km (9 mi) from town, which takes about 90 minutes to reach in a 4WD vehicle. Park your vehicle at the station, since the road above it can only be ascended in trucks with super-high suspension. From here it's a steep 14-km (8½-mi) hike to the summit. The other trail to the summit begins 7 km (4 mi) north of Volcán and ascends the volcano's more deforested western slope, a grueling trek only recommended for serious athletes. Another popular trail into the park is the **Sendero Los Quetzales** (⇨Cerro Punta, *below*), which has excellent bird-watching.

For information about hiking in Parque Nacional Volcán Barú, see Hiking in Boquete, above. ☎774–6671 or 775–2055 ✍$3.50.

TO & FROM
You can drive to the park's entrances in a 4WD vehicle, or hire a 4WD taxi to drop you off and pick you up.

VOLCÁN

60 km (36 mi) northwest of David, 16 km (10 mi) south of Cerro Punta.

A breezy little town, Volcán has the best view of Volcán Barú, several miles northeast. The town, also known as Hato de Volcán, is a dreary succession of restaurants, banks, and other businesses spread along a north-south route, from which roads to east and west lead to residential areas. This is where residents of Bambito and Cerro Punta come to shop and pay bills. As you drive north from the Interamericana the road descends onto a plain and heads into the center of Volcán, where the town's one stoplight marks the right turn for Bambito and Cerro Punta; the road continues northwest to Río Sereno.

Bambito and Cerro Punta are more attractive and have the area's best hotels, so there is little reason to stay in Volcán except that it's much warmer than Cerro Punta, which can get cool at night between December and March; it's also convenient for summiting Barú Volcano via the southern route or bird-watching at Finca Hartmann. It is also a convenient base for white-water rafting on the Río Chiriquí Viejo, since you can join rafting trips in Concepción, 33 km (21 mi) south.

★ One of Panama's most important archaeological sites, and its most visitor-friendly by far, **Sitio Barriles** *(Barrels Site)* is a collection of abandoned digs and pre-Columbian artifacts on a private farm 6 km (3½ mi) south of Volcán. The site was discovered in 1947 by the farm's owner, who found cylindrical stone carvings that resembled barrels. Subsequent digs unearthed hundreds of artifacts, the most important of which have been taken to other museums, but many are displayed in the small museum on-site. Sitio Barriles was the main town of an agricultural society that farmed the surrounding plains from AD 300 to 600, though archaeologists know very little about their culture. They left behind an interesting collection of volcanic-stone carvings, ceramic wares, tools, jewelry, and other artifacts. The farm's current owners, José Luis and Edna Landau, manage it under an agreement with the National Culture Institute. Edna, who speaks some English, usually leads visitors on a 45-minute tour. The turnoff for Sitio Barriles is west of the road to Bambito, on the left one block after the road to the airstrip, and is marked Cazán. ⊠ *Road to Cazán, 6 km (3½ mi) south of Volcán* ☎ *771–4281 or 6575–1828* ✉ *$6* ⊙ *Daily 8–5.*

La Torcaza Estate, a large coffee farm near the Lagunas de Volcán, has a coffee tour of the farming and processing of their high-quality beans; it ends with a cupping. Do the tour during the October–March harvest. They also offer horseback-riding tours of the farm and nearby lakes. ⊠ *Vía Aeropuerto, 2 km (1 mi) south of Volcán* ☎ *771–4306* ✉ *$10* ⊙ *Mon.–Sat. 8–noon and 1–5; tours by appointment or upon arrival.*

Lagunas de Volcán, two protected lakes with adjacent forest near Volcán's old airstrip, are visited by a mix of migratory and native birds, making this a decent stop for bird-watchers. You may spot a least grebe, purple gallinule, or, during the dry season, migrants such as the black-and-white warbler. **Western Wind Ventures** (☎ *771–5094 or 6704–4251*) runs canoeing and bird-watching tours of the lakes. Though the lakes are just 2 km (1 mi) south of town, the road gets quiet rough as you approach them, so you'll need 4WD or you'll have to hike the last stretch. ⊠ *Vía Aeropuerto, 2 km (1 mi) south of Volcán, turn left at Agroquimicos Volcán* ☎ *775–2055* ⊙ *Daily 6–6.*

WHERE TO STAY & EAT

$ ✕ **Restaurante Acropolis.** George Babos's story is similar to that of many of Panama's hotel and restaurant owners. After years on ships, he married a Panamanian and settled in the mountains. Many locals still have trouble with the concept of Greek food, but travelers are happy to sample his authentic moussaka, souvlaki, and *pasitiso* (Greek lasagna). The small restaurant in a former home set back from the main road is decorated with photos of Greece. By day, the nicest place to sit is on the narrow front terrace, which has a great view of Volcán Barú. There is some Panamanian food, but order something like *corvina santorini* (baked sea bass with dill sauce). Save room for their killer baklava. George rents a few inexpensive cabañas in town. ⊠ *1½ km (1 mi) north of turnoff for Bambito, on left after Delta station* ☎ *771–5184* ✉ *No credit cards* ⊙ *Closed Mon.*

$ ⛺ **Hotel Dos Ríos.** Volcán's biggest hotel, the Dos Ríos is an original two-story wooden building fronted by a newer cement lobby. The L-shaped structure encloses a lush yard with a playground and footbridges over a stream. Most rooms have wooden floors that could use refinishing and colorful murals of tropical nature. The "suites" are the nicest rooms with lots of windows and small balconies with views of the gardens and Volcán Barú. The cement casitas are cramped and dark. A restaurant in front serves Italian cuisine; the bar next door is a bit ugly but has large windows with volcano views. **Pros: Best in town, good volcano views. Cons: Time-worn, most rooms mediocre.** ⊠ *Road to Río Sereno, 2½ km (1½ mi) north of turnoff for Bambito* ☎ *771–5555* ☎ *771–5794* ⊕ *www.dosrios.com.pa* ⇆ *16 rooms, 2 bungalows* ♿ *In-room: no a/ c. In-hotel: restaurant, room service, bar, no elevator, laundry service, public Internet, no-smoking rooms* ✉ *AE, MC, V* ⦿ *CP.*

SPORTS & THE OUTDOORS

HIKING   Volcán is a popular departure point for summit hikes of **Volcán Barú** (⇨ Parque Nacional Volcán Barú, *above*) via the southern route, though the Hotel Bambito is just as close to that trailhead. Though not a technical climb, that trail is more demanding than hiking up from the ANAM station above Boquete. The trail begins at the foot of the volcano, at the end of a rough road 7 km (4 mi) east of Volcán. Hire a guide for the hike; volcano's base has various confusing trails on it. Start before dawn to ensure you return before dark (the hike up and back takes about 12 hours). Pack several liters of water, food for a day, warm, waterproof clothing, sunscreen, and a hat.

~~Western Wind Ventures~~ (☎771–5049 *or* 6704–4251 ⊕ *naturaltour.tri-pod.com/index.html*) offers hiking tours up Volcán Barú, on the Send-ero Los Quetzales, and into Parque Internacional La Amistad, as well as visits to the Lagunas de Volcán and Macho del Monte. **Arturo Rivera** (☎771–5917 *or* 6690–6632 ⊕ *www.volcantourism.com*) can guide hikers up Volcán Barú, down the Sendero Los Quetzales, or into Parque Internacional La Amistad. He also offers tours of Lagunas de Volcán, Macho del Monte, and horseback riding.

TO & FROM

Because Volcán's attractions are so spread out, it's best to drive there. From David, head west 22 km (14 mi) on the CA1 to Concepción, where you turn right after the Shell station and drive north 33 km (21 mi) through the mountains to Volcán. Buses depart from David's terminal for Volcán ($2) every 30 minutes during the day.

OFF THE
BEATEN
PATH

Finca Hartmann. The combination of forest and shaded coffee bushes at this gourmet coffee farm 27 km (16 mi) west of Volcán makes it one of the country's best bird-watching spots. The farm borders Parque Internacional La Amistad, so it's home to an array of wildlife ranging from hummingbirds to collared peccaries. To date, 282 avian species have been identified here, including the brown-hooded parrot, collared trogon, golden-browed chlorophonia, and king vulture. They also have a coffee tour, which is most interesting during the October–April harvest. Rustic accommodations are available for overnights. Getting here is half the fun, since the road winds through amazing scenery. ✉ *Road to Río Sereno, 27 km (16 mi) west of Volcán, up gravel road on right 300 yards after gas station, Santa Clara* ☎ *775–5223* ⊕ *www.finca-hartmann.com* 🎫 *$10* ⊙ *Mon.–Sat. 6–6.*

BAMBITO

★   *7 km (4 mi) north of Volcán, 8 km (4½ mi) south of Cerro Punta.*

Rather than a town, Bambito is a series of farms and houses scattered along the serpentine Río Chiriquí Viejo valley on the western slope of Volcán Barú, between Volcán and Cerro Punta. Since the people who live in the valley do their shopping in nearby Volcán, it has almost no stores or other businesses—just a few hotels—so it lacks the kinds of architectural eyesores that dominate most Panamanian towns.

The valley's scenery seems to grow more impressive with each hairpin turn. As you drive northeast from Volcán, ever closer to the volcano, you suddenly enter the narrow valley and are surrounded by tall trees and sheer rock walls adorned with bromeliads and other foliage. Even if your destination is Cerro Punta, make a few stops to admire the suspension bridges spanning the boulder-strewn river, lush forest clinging to hillsides, wildflowers, and neat wooden farmhouses. Small farms line the road, and several roadside stands sell vegetables, fruit preserves, and *batidos,* fresh fruit smoothies. From December to April, the trade winds whip down the valley, keeping it cool, but it's still warmer than Cerro Punta. Bambito's forests and farms are full of birds, and Volcán's guides can help with bird-watching there.

WHERE TO STAY & EAT

¢–$$ ✕**Parrillada Estilo Argentino.** If you're in the mood for beef, this is the
★   place to go. The owner, Chef Fernando Aristizabal, serves the best beef in Chiriquí, charcoal grilled with a baked potato and a salad. He also offers *cordero asado* (grilled lamb), *corvina*, *langostinos* (prawns), and chicken cordon bleu. Fresh herbs are from his organic garden, and a good wine selection accompanies dishes. The dining area is furnished with rustic pine tables and chairs, but is a bit dark and cramped; you may want to sit out front. ⊠*Road to Cerro Punta, just south of Hotel Bambito* ☎771–5368 ⊟*No credit cards.*

$$ ✕🏨**Hotel Bambito.** This alpine-style resort overlooks sheer rock faces
☾   and lush slopes across a wide lawn with fountains. Built in the early 1980s, it's a bit timeworn, and they have a hard time keeping the windows clean, but rooms are spacious and the ample facilities are family friendly. The hotel has the only pool in this area, as well as a Jacuzzi and sauna. You can fish in the trout ponds, hike a forest trail, go horseback riding, and take day tours. Rooms have hardwood floors and picture windows that let in the verdant view. Junior suites have balconies, and master suites have bedroom lofts. Las Truchas restaurant ($$–$$$) next door specializes in fresh trout, but offers everything from pastas to chateaubriand. **Pros: Lovely setting, big rooms, covered pool, good restaurant, activities. Cons: Decor dated, close to road.** ⊠*Road to Cerro Punta on right, beginning of valley* ☎771–4265 📠771–4207 ⊕*www.hotelbambito.com* ⇆*33 rooms, 10 suites* ♿*In-room: no a/c, refrigerator, Ethernet (some). In-hotel: restaurant, bar, room service, tennis courts, pool, no elevator, laundry service, airport shuttle, no-smoking rooms* ⊟*AE, MC, V* ⍵*BP.*

$–$$ ✕🏨**El Manatial Spa & Resort.** The setting here is idyllic: massive trees
★   shade the wooden buildings and lawns, the Río Chiriquí Viejo is a
☾   stone's toss away, and everything is hemmed by dense forest. Rooms have hardwood floors, big windows, and porches with hammocks or plastic chairs and tables. Suites are bigger and brighter; those up the hill offer more privacy and nicer views. The vast property includes 400 acres of forest, part of which can be explored on a 2-km hiking trail, and the list of activities includes mountain biking, horseback riding, river tubing, and a zip-line canopy tour. Spa treatments are reasonably priced. The restaurant (¢–$$$) serves good Italian food, including pizza, and fresh trout prepared several ways; its walls of windows

246 <   **Chiriquí Province**

let you admire the surrounding verdure. **Pros: Surrounded by nature, activities. Cons: Standard rooms mediocre.** ✉ *Road to Cerro Punta, on left after Hotel Bambito* ☎771–5126 ▤771–5127 ⤷10 *rooms, 10 suites* ♿ *In-room: no a/c. In-hotel: restaurant, bar, spa, no elevator, laundry service, no-smoking rooms* ▤*AE, MC, V* ⍥*BP.*

TO & FROM

Bambito is reached by turning right at the main intersection in Volcán. The hotels and restaurants are scattered along the road once it enters the valley. Buses head up and down the valley every 30 minutes, and will pick you up and drop you off anywhere.

CERRO PUNTA

★ *75 km (45 mi) northwest of David, 15 km (9 mi) north of Volcán.*

This bowl-shaped highland valley northwest of Volcán Barú holds some splendid bucolic scenery, and is bordered by vast expanses of wilderness that invite bird-watchers, hikers, and nature lovers. A patchwork of vegetable farms covers the valley's undulant floor and clings to the steep slopes that surround it, and ridges are topped with dark cloud forest and rocky crags. The eastern side of the valley holds the large Harras Cerro Punta ranch, where thoroughbred racehorses graze. East of the ranch, a steep slope rises up into a wedge of granite for which the valley was named—*cerro punta* means "pointy hill." That eastern ridge, part of the country's continental divide, is often enveloped in clouds that the trade winds push against it. That mist, which locals call *bajareque,* often engulfs the valley then retreats back to the mountaintops. The results are frequent fleeting rain showers that keep the valley green year-round, and an inordinate number of rainbows.

The road that winds up through Bambito bursts into the expansive Cerro Punta just west of a few shops, restaurants, and a gas station next to an intersection that marks the beginning of a loop through the valley. If you head straight at that intersection, you soon pass the road and El Respingo, where the Sendero Los Quetzales begins. Shortly after that is Guadelupe, a small collection of farms including Los Quetzales Lodge and Spa and the orchid farm of Finca Dracula. If you turn left at the intersection, you reach the road to Las Nubes—the entrance to Parque Internacional La Amistad—more quickly, but the whole loop takes only 15 minutes to drive either way. If you take any of the side roads that head into the mountains from the loop, you quickly come upon patches of forest with plenty of birds.

Cerro Punta is the highest inhabited area in Panama, nearly 6,000 feet above sea level. It can get chilly when the sun goes down or behind the clouds, though it is usually warm enough for shorts and T-shirts by day. From December to March the temperature sometimes drops down to almost 4°C (40°F) at night, so you'll want to bring warm clothes and a waterproof jacket, as well as sturdy boots for the slippery mountain trails. Insects aren't a problem here, but the sun is intense, so use sunblock or wear a hat when you aren't in the woods.

★ The most popular hike in Cerro Punta is the **Sendero Los Quetzales,** a footpath through Parque Nacional Volcán Barú that ends in the mountains above Boquete (you can hike it in reverse, but it's entirely uphill). The trail begins at the ANAM station in El Respingo, east of town, where you pay the $3.50 park admission fee. From there it's a 9-km (5-mi) downhill hike to Alto Chiquero, a short drive from Boquete. The trail winds through the cloud forest and follows the Río Caldera, crossing it several times en route. You might see quetzals, emerald toucanets, collared redstarts, coatis, and other wildlife on the hike, which takes most people 3–4 hours. ■ TIP→ Because the trail is not well marked, hire a guide or join an organized tour; the area's bird-watching guides (⇨ *below*) regularly use the trail. Pack a lunch, lots of water, and rain gear, and wear sturdy waterproof boots. It's possible to hike first thing in the morning and return to Cerro Punta (via bus or taxi) by evening, but it takes 4–5 hours to bus from Boquete to Cerro Punta. The best option is to have your bags transferred to a Boquete hotel and end there for the night. Hire a taxi in Cerro Punta to drop you off at El Respingo, which should cost $15, and arrange for a Boquete taxi to pick you up in Alto Chiquero. Otherwise, walk 90 minutes from the end of the trail through farmland to Bajo Mono, where you can catch public transportation to Boquete.

★ **Los Quetzales Lodge and Spa** has a 400-hectare (988-acre) private reserve inside Parque Nacional Volcán Barú, a 20-minute drive, or 30-minute hike from the lodge. The reserve has well-maintained trails through the cloud forest, one of which leads to a small waterfall, and all of which pass moss-laden scenery. It is home to more than 100 bird species, including the resplendent quetzal and 10 kinds of hummingbirds. You must be accompanied by one of the reserve's (non-English-speaking) guides. Guests of the lodge are transported to the reserve every morning (at a mutually agreed-upon time) for $5; nonguests pay a $20 shared fee for transport, but it's an easy 30-minute hike. ⊠ *3 km (2 mi) east of Guadelupe* ☎ *771–2182* ⊕ *www.losquetzales.com* 🖳 *Free for guests, nonguests $5; guide $10 per hour* ☉ *Daily 6–6.*

★ Anyone with the slightest interest in orchids should visit **Finca Drácula,** which has one of Latin America's largest orchid collections. The farm's name is taken from a local orchid, which has a dark red flower. The main business here is reproducing orchids for export, but workers also give 40-minute tours, though in limited English. The farm has 2,700 orchid species from Panama and around the world, as well as a laboratory where plants are reproduced using micropropagation methods. If you don't have a 4WD vehicle, walk 20 minutes from Guadelupe to get here. ⊠ *Road to Los Quetzales reserve, 1 km east of Guadelupe* ☎ *721–2070* 🖳 *$10* ☉ *Daily 8–noon and 1–5.*

Fodor'sChoice **Parque Internacional La Amistad** (PILA) stretches from the peaks above
★ Cerro Punta down to the remote hills of Bocas del Toro Province, comprising more than 200,000 hectares (more than 500,000 acres) of remote wilderness. It protects a succession of forest types that together hold most of the country's endangered animals, including jaguars and tapirs, and some 400 bird species, from the rare umbrellabird to the

harpy eagle. The name La Amistad—Spanish for "friendship"—refers to the park's binational status; Panama's park is contiguous with Costa Rica's Parque Internacional La Amistad, which is slightly smaller than its Panamanian twin and harder to reach. UNESCO has declared it a World Heritage site, and it forms the core of La Amistad Biosphere Reserve, a vast array of parks and indigenous reserves that stretch over much of the Cordillera de Talamanca in Panama and Costa Rica to cover 1.1 million hectares (2.7 million acres) of wilderness.

Cerro Punta provides the most convenient access to the park entrance and ANAM ranger station at Las Nubes, a 15-minute drive from town up a dirt road; several trails start here. You might see any of more than 150 bird species and mammals such as the coati and olingo. If you don't go with a guide, one of the (non-English-speaking) rangers may accompany you on the trails. An excellent bird-watching trail is the **Sendero el Retonio,** a 2-km (1-mi) loop over easy terrain that includes cloud forest and a stand of bamboo. If you have a few hours, hike the **Sendero La Cascada,** a 4-km (2-mi) trail to a ridge with views of the valley and a spectacular waterfall. To reach the park, drive around the loop to the intersection near Entre Ríos, on the northern end of the valley, and follow the road all the way to the park, veering left after you drive through the gate. The last stretch is fit only for 4WD vehicles; a Cerro Punta taxi will drop you there for $10. ⊠ *Las Nubes, 5 km (3 mi) north of Cerro Punta* ☎*775–2055* ⊡*$3.50* ⊙*Daily 7–4.*

WHERE TO STAY & EAT

¢–$$ ✕🏨 **Los Quetzales Lodge and Spa.** This ecolodge owned by activist Car-
★ los Alfaro has accommodations ranging from backpacker dorms to
☻ private cabins in the cloud forest. Rooms in wooden buildings have polished hardwood, photos of local birds, and original art. Standards are slightly cramped, but junior suites are spacious and bright, with wood stoves and kitchenettes; larger master suites also have balconies. Room 21, by the river, is our favorite. At night guests gather in the lounge with wood stoves, couches, and computers. The restaurant ($–$$) serves good pizza, pastas, soups, fresh trout, and organic salads. Bicycles and horseback riding are available; jeeps transport guests to the reserve each morning for a guided hike. Three cabins in the reserve itself lack electricity, but have gas stoves and lanterns. Cabins 2 and 3 are gorgeous, perfect for constant exposure to nature. Fresh trout is available; otherwise, you bring food to cook for yourself. Cabin 1, a cement duplex near the edge of the forest, is much less attractive. **Pros: Private forest reserve, good restaurant and lounge, lots of activities. Cons: Most rooms far from reserve, service sometimes deficient.** ⊠*Guadelupe* ☎*771–2182* ⊟*771–2226* ⊕*www.losquetzales.com* ⤶*8 rooms, 4 junior suites, 2 suites, 3 cabins, 2 dormitories* ⊘*In-room: no a/c, refrigerator (some), no TV. In-hotel: restaurant, room service, bar, spa, bicycles, no elevator, laundry service, public Internet, airport shuttle, no-smoking rooms* ⊟*AE, MC, V.*

$ 🏨**Cielito Sur.** The best thing about this B&B is the service provided by
FodorsChoice its Canadian owners, Janet and Glenn Lee. They rent mountain bikes,
★ prepare box lunches, and organize tours ranging from bird-watching

to a guided hike on the Sendero Los Quetzales with luggage transfer to your hotel in Boquete. Then there's its tranquil location at the forest edge, where a stream runs through the gardens and birdsong plays from sunrise to sunset. Spacious, well-equipped guest rooms are decorated with indigenous Panamanian crafts. Brighter end rooms are worth the extra $10. Guests share a cozy lounge with a fireplace, DVD, stereo, and computer, as well as a wide covered terrace with rocking chairs for watching the hummingbirds. You might end up skipping lunch after the magnificent breakfasts. **Pros: Quiet, near nature, great breakfasts, helpful owners, nice rooms. Cons: No restaurant, often full.** ⊠ *4 km (2½ mi) south of Cerro Punta center, Nueva Suiza* ☎ *771–2038 or 5502–3008* ⊕ *www.cielitosur.com* ⊃ *4 rooms* ⌂ *In-room: no a/c, no phone, refrigerator (some), Wi-Fi. In-hotel: bicycles, no elevator, laundry service, public Internet, airport shuttle, no kids under 12, no-smoking rooms* ☰ *AE, MC, V* ¶⊙¶ *BP.*

SPORTS & THE OUTDOORS

BIRD-WATCHING The valley's feathered creatures are most easily spotted around its edges, especially near streams and along the trails that head into the nearby national parks. A good guide can significantly increase the number of species you see. **Ito Santamaría** (☎ *6591–1621*), who lives in Guadelupe, is Cerro Punta's best bird-watching guide, and the only one who speaks English. The private nature reserve of **Los Quetzales Lodge and Spa** (☎ *771–2182* ⊕ *www.losquetzales.com*) has guides who speak little English but are good at spotting birds, especially quetzals. **Western Wind Ventures** (☎ *771–5049 or 6704–4251* ⊕ *naturaltour.tripod.com/index. html*), a Volcán-based company, arranges birding hikes on the Sendero Los Quetzales or in Parque Internacional La Amistad.

HIKING Between La Amistad and Volcán Barú national parks, there are enough trails around Cerro Punta to keep you hiking for several days. The area's bird-watching guides are familiar with all the local trails and are happy to guide hikers. Wherever you hike, be sure to pack plenty of water, sunscreen, a hat, and warm, waterproof clothing, even if it's sunny, since the temperature can plummet when a storm rolls in.

TO & FROM

Reach Cerro Punta by turning right at Volcán's main intersection. Buses come and go every 30 minutes, and let you on and off anywhere.

LAGO FORTUNA AREA

60 km (36 mi) northeast of David.

The road over the eastern end of the Cordillera de Talamanca that connects the provinces of Chiriquí and Bocas del Toro passes breathtaking views and a large hydroelectric reservoir called Lago Fortuna. The dense forests around Lago Fortuna hold a wealth of birdlife, including such species as black guans, swallow-tailed kites, barbets, euphonias, and various types of hummingbird. The peaks to the south of the man-made lake are traversed by trails with gorgeous views. Most people simply drive through this area, or bypass it by taking one of the quick flights between Chiriquí and Bocas del Toro, but if you take the time to explore its often misty landscapes, you'll be happy you strayed from beaten path.

The road to Lago Fortuna and Bocas del Toro begins 12 km (7½ mi) east of David on the Interamericana, at a tiny town called Chiriquí, from where it heads north via Gualaca, after which it becomes increasingly steep. After climbing past amazing views of mountainsides and the Chiriquí plains, you reach the tiny outpost of Los Planes Continue 3½ km (2 mi) beyond its entrance for **Finca Suiza**, a private reserve with 20 hours worth of hiking trails. The trails are well marked, have benches for resting, and lead to waterfalls, lookout points, and a patch of cloud forest. Children under 12 aren't allowed on the trails. ⌂*Los Planes* ☎*6615–3774* ⌂*$8* ☉*Nov.–May and July and Aug., daily 6–6.*

WHERE TO STAY & EAT

$ ⬚**Finca Suiza.** This simple, remote lodge is in a private reserve atop the Cordillera de Talamanca. Swiss expats Herbert Brulmann and Monika Kohler have converted part of their home into three guest rooms and a dining room with a stone fireplace. The rooms are bright and spacious, with big baths, two single beds, and walls decorated with Monika's nature photos. They open onto a terrace with rocking chairs and a small lawn hemmed by bougainvillea. Monika prepares three-course dinners ($14) with ingredients from the organic garden; they also make sandwiches for hikes. Pros: Quiet, close to nature, good hiking, great views. Cons: Remote, few amenities, can be cold, windy. ⌂*Hornito* ☎*6615–3774* ⌂*3 rooms* ⌂*In-room: no a/c, no phone, no TV. In-hotel: no elevator, laundry service, no kids under 12, no-smoking rooms* ⬚*No credit cards* ⦿*EP.*

TO & FROM

To drive from David, head east on the Interamericana 12 km (7½ mi) to Chiriquí, where you turn left and drive through Gualaca, then up the slopes toward Chiriquí Grande and Changuinola. Buses to Changuinola depart from David every 60 minutes and can drop you off at either Finca La Suiza or Lago Fortuna.

CHIRIQUÍ PROVINCE ESSENTIALS

TRANSPORTATION

BY AIR

The easiest way to reach Chiriquí is by plane. There are half a dozen daily flights between Panama City and David's **Aeropuerto Enrique Malek** (⌂*Av. Reed Gray, 5 km [3 mi] south of town* ☎*721–1072*). Aeroperlas and Air Panama have daily flights between Panama City and David. Aeroperlas has one flight between David and Bocas del Toro on weekdays. Air Panama has direct flights between David and San José, Costa Rica, three days a week.

Airlines Aeroperlas (☎*315-7500 or 721-1230* ⊕*www.aeroperlas.com*). **Air Panama** ☎*316-9000 or 721-0841* ⊕*www.flyairpanama.com.*

BY BUS

Padafont has hourly buses between Panama City's Albrook Terminal and David from 6 AM to 8 PM and direct buses at 10:45 PM and midnight. The trip takes about 8 hours, with a meal stop in Santiago. Small buses to Boquete, Volcán, Cerro Punta, and Paso Canoa, the border post with Costa Rica, depart every 20–30 minutes during the day.

Bus Information Padafont ☎774–2974. **Terminal de Buses** Piquera ✉Av. del Estudiante, just east of where Av. Obaldía and Av. 2 Este intersect, east side of town, David.

BY CAR

A car is the best way to explore Chiriquí; roads are in good repair and relatively well marked. Most major rental companies have offices in David. Avenida Obaldía heads straight north out of David to Boquete, no turns required. All other areas are reached via the Carretera Interamericana (CA1), which skirts David to the north and east. To reach CA1 from David's airport, turn left onto Avenida Reed Gray, then left onto Calle F Sur at the police station, 1½ km north of which you'll reach the two-lane CA1. All rental agencies in David offer 4WD vehicles and less expensive standards (sufficient for most trips).

Car-Rental Agencies Alamo ✉Enrique Malek Airport, David ☎721–0101 or 236–5777. **Avis** ✉Enrique Malek Airport, David ☎721–0884 or 278–9444. **Budget** ✉Enrique Malek Airport, David ☎775–5597 or 263–8777. **Hertz** ✉Av. 20, at Calle F Sur, David ☎775–8471 or 301–2611. **National** ✉Enrique Malek Airport, David ☎721–0974 or 265–2222. **Thrifty** ✉Enrique Malek Airport, David ☎721–2477 or 204–9555.

CONTACTS & RESOURCES

EMERGENCIES

If you have a medical emergency in Chiriquí, head straight to David, which has a modern hospital. Boquete and Volcán have ambulances, and there are police stations in every town.

Emergency Services Ambulance ☎775–4221 in David, 720–1356 in Boquete, 771–4283 in Volcán. **Fire** ☎103. **Police** ☎104.

Hospital Hospital Chiriquí ✉Calle Central and Av. 3 Oeste, David ☎775–2161.

INTERNET

Most hotels in the region have Internet access for guests; some even have Wi-Fi. If yours doesn't, there's usually an Internet café nearby.

MAIL & SHIPPING

The best places to post mail from are Cotel offices in David or Boquete, which are open Monday–Saturday 8 to 5. The only courier service in these parts is DHL, which can pick up from David hotels.

Courier Services DHL ✉Av. Domingo Díaz, David ☎774–1000.

Post Office Cotel ✉Av. 4 Este, at Calle C Norte, David ☎775–4136 ✉Av. Belisario Porras, east of park, Boquete ☎720–1265.

MONEY MATTERS

There are ATMs all over David, in front of banks and in the big super-markets, pharmacies, and gas stations, though they tend to be concentrated around the central plaza and along the Interamericana. There are also ATMs at the banks in the centers of Boquete and Volcán.

ATMs BBVA ⊠ *Av. 3 de Noviembre at Calle Pérez, David* ☎ *775–4136.* **Banco Nacional** ⊠ *Calle B Norte, across from Parque Cervantes, David* ☎ *775–6011* ⊠ *Av. Central, Boquete* ☎ *720–2776.* **Banistmo** ⊠ *Av. Central, Boquete* ☎ *720–1790* ⊠ *Calle Central, Volcán* ☎ *771–4711.*

SAFETY

Aside from the usual dangers associated with scuba diving and surfing, the province's big dangers are sunburn and hypothermia on the heights of Volcán Barú. If you hike to the summit of Barú, take warm, water-proof clothing, even in the dry season, since the weather can change radically near the peak within an hour. If you get wet and the temperature plummets, hypothermia can be a danger.

TELEPHONES

For international calls, buy a Telechip or Claro phone card at most supermarkets or convenience stores. Use them at pay phones or at most hotel phones. Dial ☎ 106 for international operator assistance.

TOURS

Chiriquí has plenty of tour options, most of which can be set up through your hotel. *See the Sports & Outdoors sections in this chapter for specialized tour guides and operators.* Boquete and Cerro Punta are included in country tours offered by Ancon Expeditions and Eco-circuitos, which are led by experienced bird-watching guides. Small, Maine-based tour operator Venture Outside offers various inexpensive adventure tourism packages concentrated on Chiriquí.

Tour-Operator Recommendations Ancon Expeditions ☎ *269–9415* ⊕ *www.anconexpeditions.com.* **Ecocircuitos,** ☎ *720–1560 or 314–0068* ⊕ *www.ecocircuitos.com.* **Venture Outside** ☎ *720–1505, 207/846–0637 in the U.S.* ⊕ *www.ventureoutside.org.*

VISITOR INFORMATION

People at the IPAT's regional office (open weekdays 8:30–4:30) in David are nice, but not very helpful. The CEFATI visitor center (open daily 9–5), on the southern end of Boquete, does a better job.

Tourist Information IPAT ⊠ *Av. Domingo Díaz, across from Cable & Wireless, David* ☎ *775–4120* ⊕ *www.chiriqui.org.* **CEFATI** ⊠ *Av. Central, 1 km [½ mi] south of town* ☎ *720–4060* ⊕ *boquete.chiriqui.org.*

Bocas del Toro Archipelago

WORD OF MOUTH

"[Bocas del Toro] is the real Gold Coast on the Isthmus of Panama. You get a real feel for the Spanish Main, which is alive and well in the Province of Bocas del Toro. For those of you that have never been there, you need to go there *now*!"

—cmcfong

"The first day in Bocas seemed like we knew everyone—it didn't matter if they were locals or gringos. Everyone said hi/hello/*bueno*. . . . We were planning to only stay in the Bocas region for a few days, but those plans went up in smoke after about two days in Bocas."

—mike & beth

By David
Dudenhoefer

WITH ITS TURQUOISE WATERS, SUGAR-SAND beaches, and funky island towns, the relatively isolated archipelago of Bocas del Toro has the same attractions as major Caribbean destinations with a fraction of the crowds and development. Add to this the flora and fauna of its super-lush forests and the culture of the province's indigenous majority, and you've got St. Thomas-plus, at half the price.

As you fly over the archipelago, you see brown blotches of coral reefs scattered across the sea between islands. Below the surface is a kaleidoscope of corals, sponges, fish, and invertebrates. The crystalline waters that hold those coral gardens wash against half a dozen beaches ranging from forest-hemmed Red Frog Beach to the ivory sands of the Cayos Zapatillas, where lanky coconut palms stretch out over the tide line. The islands have a dozen surf spots—from fun beach breaks to challenging tubes over coral reefs—and trails into the jungle where you might see monkeys, toucans, and colorful poison dart frogs.

The eponymous provincial capital of Bocas del Toro has an ample selection of affordable hotels and good restaurants, and on any given morning dozens of boats depart from it carrying visitors to nearby beaches, reefs, and rain forests. You can soak up local culture at the colorful little town of Old Bank, or at indigenous villages on Isla Bastimentos. The islands' original inhabitants, Ngöbe-Buglé Indians, live in villages scattered around the province, but the population in the archipelago's main towns is a mix of Afro-Caribbean, Hispanic, and Chinese—all proud *bocatoreños,* as the local people and culture are called. Most townspeople are as comfortable speaking English as Spanish, but prefer to speak the local dialect, called Guari-Guari, which is a patois English with traces of Spanish and the indigenous tongue Ngöbere.

Whether you prefer diving, kayaking, surfing, hiking, bird-watching, partying, or swaying in a hammock cooled by an ocean breeze, the Bocas del Toro archipelago can keep you busy—or lazy—for days on end. The province incorporates a large piece of the Panamanian mainland, but it is mostly covered with banana farms and a few farm-worker towns. The Cordillera de Talamanca towers to the south of the archipelago, and is covered with largely inaccessible wilderness, but if you travel by land between Bocas del Toro and Chiriquí, you can get a good look at its vast, unexplored jungle. Otherwise, you'll want to stick with the islands, which have plenty of sultry rain forest to complement their sand, sea, and sun.

The only caveat is that those rain forests are the result of copious and frequent rain, which has ruined more than a few vacations. It rains an average of two out of three days in Bocas del Toro, and while downpours are often over in a matter of hours, an entire week of rain isn't out of the question. Outside of March, September, and October, don't book your entire vacation here, since the likelihood of getting sunny days elsewhere in Panama is greater. But don't let the rain scare you away, because when it's sunny, Bocas del Toro is simply amazing.

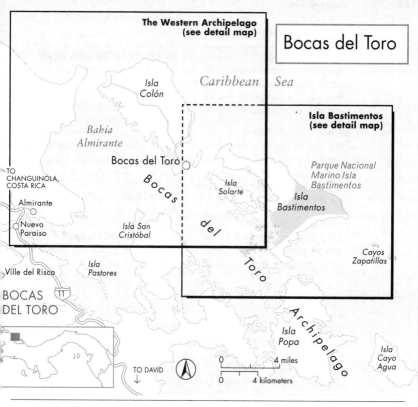

ORIENTATION & PLANNING

ORIENTATION

The Bocas del Toro Archipelago represents a small portion of the large and wild province of the same name, yet it holds virtually all of its attractions. Those islands are scattered across a shallow gulf between banana-dominated lowlands and the rugged Peninsula Valiente. Tourism is centered around Bocas del Toro town, which occupies a spit of land on the southern tip of Isla Colón, the westernmost island. That small town has a tiny airport on its western edge that most visitors fly in and out of, whereas regular water taxis and a ferry ply the waters between it and the mainland port of Almirante, from which roads lead to east to Chiriquí and west to banana farms and the Costa Rican border. To the east of Isla Colón are several other islands with communities and isolated hotels—Islas Carenero, Solarte, and Bastimentos—and by day, private boats and water taxis travel regularly between the islands. The eastern half of Isla Bastimentos is a wild and beautiful area that is partially protected within Parque Nacional Marino Isla Bastimentos, as are the two idyllic isles of Cayos Zapatillas, to the southeast of it.

TOP REASONS TO GO

IDYLLIC ISLANDS

Jungle-hemmed beaches, coconut palms growing in pale sand, emerald waters . . . the archipelago has the stuff of tropical fantasies.

FUNKY BOCAS TOWN

The offbeat, colorful town of Bocas offers a mix of historic architecture, mellow locals, good food, nightlife, and abundant views of the surrounding sea and islands.

NEPTUNE'S GARDENS

The submarine wonders—from the sponge-studded reef beneath Hospital Point to the seemingly endless

coral gardens of the Cayos Zapatillas—can keep you diving for days.

THE JUNGLE

Though the sea and sand are the big attractions, the rain forests that cover much of the archipelago are home to everything from howler monkeys to tiny poison dart frogs, as well as hundreds of bird species.

CARIBBEAN CULTURES

Bocas del Toro's mix of Afro-Caribbean, Panamanian, and indigenous Ngöbe-Buglé cultures adds layers to the islands' personality, making it interesting as well as beautiful.

PLANNING

WHEN TO GO

The big drawback of Bocas del Toro is the rain. It sometimes rains for days on end, and it can do so at just about any time of year. Statistically, March is the sunniest month. September and October are the next-driest months, and May and June tend to be nice as well. Since May, June, and (especially) September and October are the rainiest months in the rest of Panama, Bocas del Toro is the place to be at those times. December is the wettest month, and July and August are right behind it, though it tends to be sunny about a third of the time then. December, July, and August are, however, good months for surfing in the archipelago but the worst months for diving. In January and February the odds of enjoying sunny days are about fifty-fifty. The annual *feria* (fair) in mid-September is party time in Bocas town. Many of the outlying lodges and some restaurants close during May and June.

GETTING AROUND

Getting around in Bocas del Toro usually means getting into a boat, so it's the last place you want to bring a rental car. Several water-taxi companies make hourly trips between Bocas del Toro and the mainland. Mainland ports are at Almirante, the gateway for travel between the islands and Chiriquí, and Finca 60, for people heading to or from Costa Rica. You can also take a water taxi between the islands, but if you head to Islas Carenero or Bastimentos, it can be less expensive to do as the locals do, and travel with boatmen who wait at the dock next to Farmacia Rosa Blanca. Most boat trips cost between $2 and $20, though the farthest lodges are more expensive to reach. Share taxis run along the main streets in Bocas, and charge 50 cents. A bus travels five times daily between the town of Bocas and Boca del Drago, on the other end of Isla Colón.

A BIT OF HISTORY

The archipelago of Bocas del Toro was "discovered," or at least visited, by Christopher Columbus in 1502, when he sailed through the area on his fourth voyage to the Americas. Centuries later the islands of Isla Colón and Isla Cristobal were named for the Italian explorer, who is called Cristobal Colón in Spanish. A few conquistadores ventured into the province after Columbus, but were discouraged by its impenetrable jungles and lack of gold. The Spanish crown virtually ignored the region, leaving it to the indigenous inhabitants and French and English buccaneers, who rested there between raids. During the early 19th century Afro-Caribbean turtle hunters from the English-speaking islands of San Andrés and Providencia began visiting the archipelago, where they built seasonal camps. In 1826 some of them brought their families and established the town of Bocas del Toro, which remained a fishing and turtle-hunting village for decades.

In the 1880s the province was transformed as American companies began cultivating bananas on the mainland, and established their offices in Bocas del Toro town. Laborers were brought in from Jamaica, Europeans arrived following the collapse of the French canal effort, large wooden buildings were erected, and the local economy burgeoned. By the time Panama declared independence from Colombia in 1903, Bocas del Toro was a prosperous, cosmopolitan town with several English-language newspapers and U.S., British, German, and French consulates. But a decade later a fungal disease decimated the banana farms, which were abandoned, and new farms were established inland. When the disease returned in the 1930s, the United Fruit Company, the province's main employer, pulled up stakes and moved its Panama operations to Chiriquí, which sent the local economy into a tailspin. The company returned to the province in the 1950s with a new name, Chiquita, using pesticides to keep the fungi at bay, but it established its offices on the mainland.

It wasn't until the 1990s that significant numbers of foreigners began visiting the archipelago and tourism revenue began to lift it out of poverty. The 21st century brought a real-estate boom, with foreigners snatching up land and driving prices up by hundreds of percent, while wages hardly rose. Thanks to tourism, Bocas del Toro has become a relatively prosperous community, where once-scarce jobs are now abundant, but real-estate development has left many locals unable to afford land in their own community.

WHAT TO DO

SUBMERGE Anyone, whether an experienced scuba diver or a first-time snorkeler, can explore the archipelago's abundant submarine wonders.

BEACHCOMB Bocas del Toro has half a dozen beaches ranging from the golden sands of Bluff to the ivory Cayos Zapatillas, and they are rarely crowded.

EXPLORE FOREST TRAILS The islands are covered with lush rain forest that can be explored via various jungle trails.

VISIT FLIPPER   The calm waters of Laguna Boca-torito are a popular spot with dolphins, and a trip to see them is often part of excursions to the archipelago's top sites.

RIDE THE   Bocas del Toro has an array of
WAVE   surf spots ranging from fun beach breaks to gnarly reef breaks, making it a great destination for wave riders.

> **WORD OF MOUTH**
>
> "You can drive [from Panama City] to Almirante and park the car in a fenced, locked, and guarded yard while in the islands. Catch a water taxi to Isla Colón and then go from there to wherever you want to. The road over is very good, relatively new."   –AndrewW

RESTAURANTS & CUISINE

The town of Bocas del Toro has an ample restaurant selection, with such surprising options as Thai and Indian cuisine to complement the traditional seafood. Like everything in Bocas, dining is casual, and most restaurants are on the water. Local specialties include lobster, whole-fried snapper, octopus, and shrimp served with *patacones* (fried plantain slices) or *yuca frita* (fried cassava strips).

ABOUT THE HOTELS

Accommodations here range from rooms in traditional wooden buildings in town to rustic but enchanting bungalows nestled in the wilderness of Isla Bastimentos. All of them have private baths, and all but the ecolodges have air-conditioning. Although Bocas del Toro town has an array of budget and moderately priced hotels, the out-of-town lodges tend to be rather expensive, though hardly luxurious. Other advantages of staying in town are local color and the selection of restaurants, shops, and nightlife. The downside is noise from neighbors and revelers, which is a problem at most in-town hotels. Lodges outside town provide more natural, tranquil settings. You can get information on Bocas lodging on the Bocas Web site (⊕*www.bocas.com*). ■TIP➔**A good option is to divide your stay between a hotel in town and a one on the outer islands.**

WHAT IT COSTS IN U.S. DOLLARS					
	¢	$	$$	$$$	$$$$
RESTAURANTS	under $5	$5–$10	$10–$15	$15–$20	over $20
HOTELS	under $50	$50–$100	$100–$160	$160–$220	over $220

Restaurant prices are per person for a main course at dinner. Hotel prices are for two people in a standard double room, excluding service and 10% tax.

THE WESTERN ARCHIPELAGO

The westernmost island in the archipelago, Isla Colón is also the most developed, with a road running across it and the provincial capital occupying a peninsula on its southern tip. Across a channel from that urbanized headland is the smaller Isla Carenero, which together with the town of Bocas was one of the first places in the archipelago to be settled by people other than Indians. Boats travel between the two

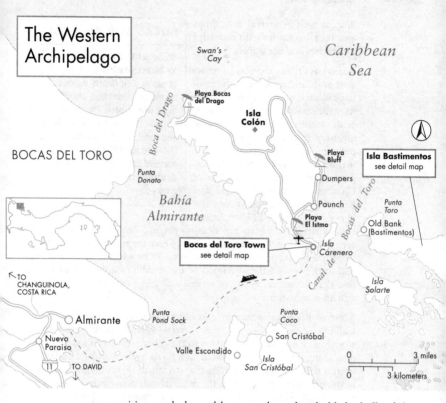

communities regularly, and between them they hold the bulk of the archipelago's residents and most of its hotels and restaurants. Isla Solarte, farther to the east, is more sparsely populated, with a few homes near its western extreme. Most travelers stay in Bocas del Toro town and make day trips to the other islands, beaches, and dive spots.

BOCAS DEL TORO TOWN

550 km (341 mi) northwest of Panama City, 170 km (105 mi) north of David.

The town of Bocas del Toro, which the locals simply call Bocas, sits on a little headland connected to the island's main bulk by a narrow isthmus. The western half of that headland is covered by a mangrove swamp, but the eastern half holds a neat grid packed with homes, businesses, and government offices. The town is surrounded by water on three sides, which means it has plenty of ocean views, but the nearest beach, on the isthmus that connects it to Isla Colón, is not nice. In order to play in the surf and sand you either have to boat to Isla Bastimentos or take a bike, taxi, bus, or boat to one of the beaches on Isla Colón. Luckily, Bocas has an abundance of boatmen eager to show you paradise, as well as several dive shops and tour operators with day trips to beaches and coral reefs.

Bocas has little in the way of museums and landmarks, but the laid-back town is worth exploring, with its wide streets, weathered Caribbean architecture, and plentiful greenery. It is home to an interesting sampling of humanity, with a majority of Afro-Caribbean or Hispanic extraction, a fair number of Chinese, some Ngöbe-Buglé and Kuna Indians, and a growing number of European and North American expatriates. There are domino-playing fishermen, Rastafarian artisans, and South American surfers. There seem to be a fair number of people for whom doing nothing seems to be a full-time occupation, and in the heat of the afternoon or the middle of a downpour you'll find that Bocas has plenty of spots to do just that, with a cool drink and an ocean view.

> ### BOCAS BY BIKE
>
> Bocas del Toro is a perfect town for biking, which a good way to get to Bluff Beach. Various businesses rent bikes, among them **Bocas Bicis** (⌧ *North end of Calle 3, at Av. F* ☎*6446–0787*) and **Land, Sea & Air Adventures** (⌧ *Road to Bluff Beach, 2 km north of Bocas* ☎*6684–4418* ⊕ *www.land-sea-air-adventures. com*).

Most of Bocas's restaurants and other businesses are located along Calle 3, sometimes called Main Street—a wide, north-south track stretching from one end of town to the other (seven blocks) and running along the sea for its southern half. Boats to the mainland and other islands depart from docks along that stretch, as do tours bound for fun in the sun, while people from the other islands arrive here to shop and run errands. Halfway up Calle 3, Calle 1 branches off it to the right, passing various hotels and restaurants built over the water.

① Two blocks east of Calle 3 on the right is the local office of the Panamanian Tourism Bureau, **IPAT** (⌧ *Calle 1, next to Policía Nacional* ⊕ *www.visitpanama.com* ☎*757–9642*), housed in a large Caribbean-style building on the water. It has an information desk, a museum on the second floor with information about the area's ecology and history, and a small café in back. It's open weekdays 8:30–4:30.

② **Parque Simón Bolívar** (⌧ *Calle 3, at Av. Central*) is a large park shaded by mango trees and royal palms near the north end of Calle 3. Children play here and locals chat on its cement benches in the evening. North of the park stands the **Palacio Municipal,** a large cement building that houses various government offices. Three blocks north of the park, Calle 3 ends at Avenida Norte, which runs west to the isthmus that connects the town to Isla Colón and across the island. If you turn right onto Avenida Norte and walk two blocks to the island's northeast corner, you find the fire station, which holds a couple of antique fire engines.

③ **Playa Bocas** (⌧ *Av. Norte, 1 km northwest of Calle 3*) stretches along the narrow isthmus that connects the town to Isla Colón, overlooking tranquil Bahia Chitre (Sand Flea Bay). It is a mediocre beach, but will

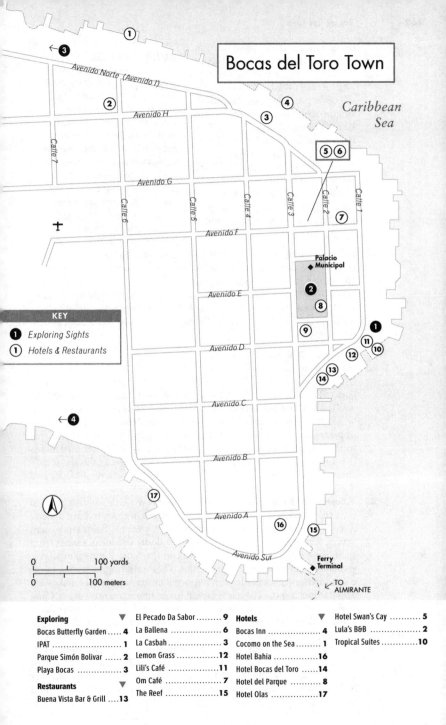

Bocas del Toro Town

Caribbean Sea

Avenido Norte (Avenido 1)

Avenido H

Avenido G

Avenido F

Avenido E

Avenido D

Avenido C

Avenido B

Avenido A

Avenido Sur

Calle 7

Calle 6

Calle 5

Calle 4

Calle 3

Calle 2

Calle 1

Palacio Municipal

Ferry Terminal

→ TO ALMIRANTE

KEY

1 *Exploring Sights*

① *Hotels & Restaurants*

0   100 yards

0   100 meters

Exploring ▼

Bocas Butterfly Garden **4**

IPAT **1**

Parque Simón Bolívar **2**

Playa Bocas **3**

Restaurants ▼

Buena Vista Bar & Grill **13**

El Pecado Da Sabor **9**

La Ballena **6**

La Casbah **3**

Lemon Grass **12**

Lili's Café **11**

Om Café **7**

The Reef **15**

Hotels ▼

Bocas Inn **4**

Cocomo on the Sea **1**

Hotel Bahia **16**

Hotel Bocas del Toro **14**

Hotel del Parque **8**

Hotel Olas **17**

Hotel Swan's Cay **5**

Lula's B&B **2**

Tropical Suites **10**

do in a pinch. If you have the time and energy, rent a bike and make the rough 40-minute ride out to Bluff Beach (⇨Isla Colón, *below*), which is gorgeous. The dozens of simple structures that line Bocas Beach are transformed into exhibits, restaurants, and beer shacks during the annual **Feria del Mar** *(Sea Fair)* , during the second or third week in September. The normally deserted beach becomes packed with locals and visitors who enjoy folk dances, a boat race, and a beauty contest.

> **HURRICANE SEASON?**
>
> Bocas del Toro gets plenty of rain, and tropical storms sometimes blow in from the Caribbean. Panama is generally considered to be below the hurricane belt, but there's no guarantee that hurricanes will stick to their assigned area. You can take comfort in the fact, however, that Bocas hasn't been hit by a hurricane in recent history. The most recent natural disaster to affect the area was a 7.2 earthquake in 1991 that damaged many buildings.

❹ A few minutes west of town by boat is the **Bocas Butterfly Garden** (✉ *Macca Hill, near Bocas Marina* ☎ *757–9008 or 6671–4724* ⊕ *www.bocasbutterflygarden.com* ✉ *$5* ⊗ *Mon. and Wed.–Sat. 9–3, Sun. 9–noon*), where a dozen native butterfly species inhabit a screened flyway and a trail leads through a small forest reserve.

WHERE TO STAY & EAT

$–$$$ ✕**La Ballena.** Nestled in a cement building just behind the Palacio Municipal, on one of Bocas's many somnolent side streets, La Ballena ("The Whale") has a colorful interior with wine bottles lining the walls. The nicest place to sit is at the plastic tables on the street in front, which is cooler by night. The Italian owner offers an ample selection of pizzas, salads, Italian pasta, Cuban beer, and fresh Panamanian seafood. Specialties include penne *con langosta* (with lobster medallions in a tomato sauce), fusilli *al Gorgonzola,* and chicken marsala. It isn't cheap, but it's good, and stays open late. ✉ *Av. F, between Calles 2 and 3* ☎ *757–9088* ▤ *AE, MC, V.*

$–$$$ ✕**Buena Vista Bar & Grill.** The back deck of this wooden building perched
★ over the water is one of the pleasantest places in town to have a meal, since it overlooks the sea and nearby Isla Carenero. Boats zip by and waves wash against the pilings under the floor. The menu ranges from such gringo standards as T-bone steak to the more daring jambalaya, enchiladas, and ginger-orange shrimp. Their selection of salads, burgers, and sandwiches made with imported meats and cheeses makes it a popular lunch spot. The bar is famed for its frozen margaritas. ✉ *Calle 1, half a block east of Calle 3* ☎ *757–9035* ▤ *MC, V* ⊗ *Closed Tues.*

$–$$$ ✕**Lemon Grass.** This restaurant's location on the second floor on an old
Fodor'sChoice wooden building over the water gives it a great view of the turquoise
★ sea and nearby islands. Tables sit beneath a battery of ceiling fans. The English owner worked in Southeast Asia before landing in Bocas, where the sea provides the perfect ingredients for his Asian recipes that include the likes of spicy crab cakes, steak teriyaki, various curries, and fish-and-chips. The changing dessert selection could include such deca-

dent inventions as Oreo-Baileys cheesecake and a cappuccino tiramisu sundae. ⊠ *Calle 2, above Starfleet Scuba* ☎757–9630 ⊟ *No credit cards* ⊘ *Closed Thurs. No lunch Sat.*

$–$$ ✗**La Casbah.** To say that this tiny roadside eatery doesn't look like much ★ is an understatement. With digs like these, you have to stay on top of your kitchen to compete with restaurants on the water, and the Belgian chef does just that. His global menu hops from falafel to gazpacho to shrimp in a Sambuca cream sauce. Daily specials are a good bet, or you can stick with such local favorites as pork loin in a Marsala sauce or fish of the day in a coconut sauce. ⊠ *Av. Norte, between Calles 3 and 4* ☎6477–4727 ⊟ *No credit cards* ⊘ *Closed Sun. and Mon. No lunch.*

$–$$ ✗**Om Café.** You can get authentic Indian cuisine in Bocas del Toro at ★ this cozy café atop a surf shop. Owner Sunanda Mehra is a Torontonian of Punjabi descent who raided her aunt's cookbook before running off to Panama. You can savor such improbable delicacies as her prawn vindaloo, *palaak paneer* (fresh cheese in a spinach sauce), chicken tandoori, or any of half-dozen vegetable dishes. In the morning, treat yourself to an Indian breakfast, which includes vindaloo eggs in a roti wrap and *chana bhatura* (garbanzo curry with fried bread), accompanied by a refreshing fruit *lassi* (yogurt smoothie). ⊠ *Av. F at Calle 2* ☎6624–0898 ⊟ *No credit cards* ⊘ *Closed Wed. and May–June. No lunch.*

$–$$ ✗**El Pecado Da Sabor.** Occupying the second floor of one of the oldest **Fodor'sChoice** buildings in town, half a block south of Parque Bolívar, this place— ★ whose name translates as "The Sin Adds Flavor"—is one of Bocas's best. "The sin" might refer to gluttony—a temptation when faced with tuna fried in a crunchy herb breading or beef tenderloin with a creamy Dijon mustard sauce. Certainly, the food is sinfully good, and the colorful decor includes Christmas lights, candles, and giant devil masks left over from Carnaval celebrations. The nicest seating is on the wraparound balcony overlooking Calle 3, though you can feel it vibrate every time somebody moves. The waitstaff is friendly and attentive. ⊠ *Calle 3, just south of Parque Bolívar* ☎6597–0296 ⊟ *No credit cards* ⊘ *Closed Sun. and May–June. No lunch.*

¢–$$ ✗**Lili's Café.** A fun spot for breakfast or a light lunch with an ocean view, Lili's is at the back of a building over the water at the south end of Calle 1, with seating limited to long bar and a few tables on the deck. Order and pay at the window, then wait for Lili and company to deliver one of their creative breakfast items, sandwiches made with home-baked bread, or something along the lines of vegetarian quiche. You can get sandwiches to go, and there are daily lunch specials. Unless it's a daily special, this isn't a good place for seafood. You can spice up your vittles with Lili's Killin' Me Man sauce, sold by the bottle. ⊠ *Calle 1, next to Tropical Suites* ☎6560–8777 ⊟ *No credit cards.*

¢–$$ ✗**The Reef.** Though slightly out of the way, at the southern end of Calle ★ 3, this traditional *bocatoreño* restaurant has a pleasant open-air setting over the water and serves fresh seafood at lower prices than the more centrally located places do. It is consequently a popular spot with locals. Fresh delicacies include whole fried red snapper, garlic prawns, a hearty seafood soup, and *parrillada de mariscos* (a seafood mixed grill for two). It has one of the best views in town, and its minimal decoration includes a couple of dugout canoes hanging from the rafters. It occupies a corner of what was once the United Fruit Company dock, where most of the town's able-bodied men once gathered each morning to catch boats to the banana plantations on the mainland. ⊠ *Calle 3, across from Hotel Bahia* ☎*No phone* ⊟*No credit cards.*

> ### CONSERVING WATER
>
> As unlikely as it may seem in a place where it rains as much as it does in Bocas del Toro, the town suffers periodic water shortages, since it has outgrown its decades-old water system. The best hotels have massive water tanks to ensure they don't run out, but do your part, and conserve water. ■TIP→ The tap water in Bocas isn't potable, so drink bottled or filtered water.

$$–$$$ **Tropical Suites.** The spacious rooms evoke Florida condos, with
☺
Fodor'sChoice their tropical colors, tile floors,
★ ceiling fans, and sliding glass doors opening onto balconies, half with ocean views. Each room has a queen bed, cable TV, a kitchenette with breakfast bar, and a large bathroom with a Jacuzzi tub. The hotel is built over the water, and there's a floating plastic dock in back with a swimming area, though the water here is not that clean. Pay the extra money for an ocean-view room—they're nicer and quieter. It is conveniently close to most restaurants and bars. **Pros: Nice, spacious rooms, great ocean views. Cons: Expensive, can be noisy.** ⊠*South end of Calle 1* ☎*757–9081* 🖷*757–9080* ⊕*www.tropical-suites.com* ➪*20 suites* ☾*In-room: safe, kitchen, Wi-Fi. In-hotel: laundry facilities, no-smoking rooms* ⊟*AE, MC, V* ⽥*EP.*

$–$$$ **Hotel Bocas del Toro.** Guest rooms in this attractive wooden hotel on
Fodor'sChoice the water could be on a yacht, with their polished hardwoods and nau-
★ tical decor, and it's no coincidence—it was made by a boat builder. The current owner, Carla Rankin, runs it like a cruise ship, with what could be the most helpful staff in town. Rooms vary in size and price, but have cable TV, nice bathrooms, botanical prints on the walls, and blue and white fabrics to complement the dark wood. Town-view rooms can be noisy at night; more expensive ocean-view rooms are quieter. The open-air restaurant serves a good mix of Panamanian and international fare, with an ocean view. Day trips can be arranged. **Pros: On water, nice rooms, friendly staff. Cons: Expensive, street noise at night.** ⊠*Calle 2, next to Hotel Limbo* ☎*757–9771* 🖷*757–9018* ⊕*www. hotelbocasdeltoro.com* ➪*10 rooms, 1 suite* ☾*In-room: safes, Wi-Fi (some). In-hotel: restaurant, bar, water sports, no elevator, laundry service, no-smoking rooms* ⊟*AE, MC, V* ⽥*BP.*

$–$$ **Hotel Swan's Cay.** This two-story wooden complex behind the Palacio
☺ Municipal fits into Bocas well enough, but inside the lobby feels like Old Europe. The Italian owners seem as out of place as the decor, and if you get one of them to smile, congratulations. Still, their rambling hotel has its selling points, mainly the oceanfront pool, one block behind the hotel, with a small bar beside it. Rooms, with wall-to-wall carpeting, imported furniture, and cable TV, are a mixed bag: some are bright, some are dark, and some are musty. Ask for one with a balcony. A large

restaurant serves good pastas and pizzas. **Pros: Reasonable rates, pool by the sea, restaurant. Cons: Unfriendly, incongruous decor.** ✉ *Calle 3, between Avs. F and G* ☎ *757–9090* 🖷 *757–9027* ⊕ *www.swanscayhotel.com* 🛏 *44 rooms, 2 suites* ⚒ *In-room: refrigerator (some). In-hotel: 2 restaurants, bars, pools, no elevator, laundry service, no-smoking rooms* ☰ *AE, MC, V* ⚏ *EP.*

$ ⭐   🛏 **Bocas Inn.** This small lodge in an older wooden building over the water has a great location at the end of Calle 3, and is buffered from the street by a large garden, so it's relatively quiet. It has a lovely second-floor balcony and large, open-air restaurant with plenty of hammocks and chairs from which to contemplate the sea. Most guest rooms are on the second floor of the main building; they have varnished hardwood floors, colorful tile bathrooms, and either one queen or two single beds. The Zapatilla and Escudo rooms, which open onto the common porch with an ocean view, are well worth the extra $10. The rooms over the office, Cristobal and Carenero, are too close to the street. **Pros: Great views, friendly, good breakfasts. Cons: No TV, no Internet.** ✉ *Av. Norte just west of Calle 3* ☎ *757–9600* ⊕ *www.anconexpeditions. com* 🛏 *7 rooms* ⚒ *In-room: no phone, no TV. In-hotel: restaurant, no elevator, laundry service, no-smoking rooms* ☰ *AE, MC, V* ⚏ *BP.*

$ ⭐   🛏 **Cocomo on the Sea.** This homey waterfront hotel has plenty of common areas for enjoying the ocean view or the small tropical garden. Rooms are small but cozy, with hardwood floors, white walls decorated with *molas* (cloth pictures), and colorful Guatemalan bedspreads. They all have air-conditioning, but also have ceiling fans and lots of windows letting in the ocean breeze. The breeziest spot is the wide porch over the water, with a couch and hammocks, where the sumptuous breakfasts are served. Kayaks are available for paddling to Isla Carenero. The friendly American owner, Douglas Ruscher, is happy to give travel advice. **Pros: Great view and common areas, friendly owner, good breakfasts. Cons: Noisy neighbors, no TV, no Internet.** ✉ *Av. Norte, at Calle 6* ☎ *757–9259* ⊕ *www.panamainfo.com/cocomo* 🛏 *4 rooms* ⚒ *In-room: no phone, no TV. In-hotel: water sports, no elevator, laundry service, no kids under 8, no-smoking rooms* ☰ *MC, V* ⚏ *BP.*

$ ⭐   🛏 **Hotel Bahia.** This two-story wooden building was the headquarters of the United Fruit Company in the 1930s. The top floor served as guest rooms and still has the original veranda overlooking the bay, where mint juleps were probably the order of the hot tropical days. The spacious rooms have been completely refurbished, with shiny hardwood floors, double beds, cable TV, air-conditioning, and small tile bathrooms. Deluxe rooms have queen beds, and two of them have small balconies. The art is tacky and the only decent view is from the veranda, but this could be the quietest hotel in town. **Pros: Quiet, good value, comfortable. Cons: Off water, small windows.** ✉ *Southern end of Calle 3* ☎ *757–9626* 🖷 *757–9692* ⊕ *www.hotelbahia.biz* 🛏 *20 rooms* ⚒ *In-room: no phone, safes (some), Wi-Fi. In-hotel: no elevator, laundry service, airport shuttle, no-smoking rooms* ☰ *AE, MC, V* ⚏ *BP.*

¢–$ **Lula's B&B.** Across the street from the water and a short walk from the center of town, this small B&B offers simple accommodations and a hearty breakfast. Run by a friendly couple from Atlanta, who bought the property from Lula a few years back, the lodge has a nice veranda on the second floor with a sea view over rooftops and a self-service bar. Rooms are behind it, and have wood floors, air-conditioning, small bathrooms, and a nautical decor. Breakfasts are served in a big common area with a computer in one corner. **Pros: Inexpensive, nice veranda, good breakfasts. Cons: Rooms pretty basic.** ⊠ *Av. Norte, at Calle 6* 🕾757–9057 ⊕*www.lulabb.com* ↩*6 rooms* ⚿*In-room: no phone, no TV, Wi-Fi. In-hotel: no elevator, public Internet, no-smoking rooms* 🟰*MC, V* ⓘ❘*BP.*

¢   **Hotel Olas.** Hidden at the south end of town, this large wooden hotel
Fodor's Choice   built over the water is one of the best deals in Bocas, comparable to
★   more centrally located inns that charge twice as much. It has an open-air restaurant and bar on a deck in back with a great view of the sea and mainland, where a hearty breakfast is served. Guest rooms are slightly cramped, but comfortable enough, with lots of wood, a small TV (with cable), and air-conditioning. Those at the end have nice views. Affordable boat excursions depart from the floating platform at the back of the restaurant. **Pros: Inexpensive, on water, restaurant, quiet. Cons: Rooms smallish.** ⊠ *Av. Sur, at Calle 5* 🕾757–9930 ⊕*www. hotelolas.com* ↩*24 rooms* ⚿*In-room: no phone, Wi-Fi. In-hotel: restaurant, bar, water sports, no elevator, laundry service, public Internet, no-smoking rooms* 🟰*No credit cards* ⓘ❘*BP.*

¢   **Hotel del Parque.** Hidden behind lush gardens at the southeast cor-
★   ner of Parque Bolívar, this small family-run hotel is a short walk from most restaurants and businesses, yet is far enough from the main drag to be tranquil. It's as close as you'll come to staying with a local family, since the owners, Luis and Magally Mou, live there. Rooms have big, screened windows, air-conditioning, ceiling fans, cable TV, small bathrooms, and foam mattresses. You can hang out in a hammock on the veranda overlooking the park or on the patio in the back garden. Guests are welcome to use the kitchen, and there's always free fruit and coffee available. **Pros: Inexpensive, central location, nice veranda, kitchen. Cons: Soft beds, street noise.** ⊠ *Calle 2, at Parque Bolívar* 🕾757–9008 ✎*delparque35@hotmail.com* ↩*8 rooms* ⚿*In-room: no phone. In-hotel: no elevator, public Internet, no-smoking rooms* 🟰*MC, V* ⓘ❘*EP.*

NIGHTLIFE & THE ARTS

Bocas livens up when the sun goes down, since the temperature becomes more conducive to movement. The decks of the town's various waterfront restaurants are pleasant spots to enjoy a quiet drink and conversation. **Lemon Grass** (⊠ *Calle 2, above Starfleet Scuba* 🕾757–9630) sometimes has live music on weekends. **Barco Hundido** (*Sunken Ship* ⊠*Calle 1, at Av. H* 🕾757–9695) is a funky, open-air affair with tropical gardens and wooden platforms over the water around a small shipwreck, which is lit at night so you can watch the fish. Watch your step—more than one partier has danced into the water here. **Iguana Surf Club** (⊠ *Calle 2, next to Starfleet Scuba* 🕾*No phone*), in a wooden building over the water, is owned by local surfers. It's popular with younger travelers and locals, which is a problem for the nearby hotels. **El Tablón** (*The Plank* ⊠*Av. Norte, at Calle 4* ☎*No phone*) is a large wooden bar on the north end of town with pirate paraphernalia, lots of barrels, and a couple of foosball tables.

WORD OF MOUTH

"We spent every evening in town, walking, having a drink, dining, using the Internet, making calls, just hanging out. It never seemed loud. Very relaxed atmosphere."

–shillmac.

SPORTS & THE OUTDOORS

SCUBA DIVING & SNORKELING
Bocas is a fun town, but it is primarily a base for exploring the wonders of the surrounding archipelago, the most impressive being the acres of colorful coral reef. More than a dozen dive spots are within five minutes to one hour by boat from Bocas, which has several good dive centers and dozens of boatmen offering inexpensive excursions that combine snorkeling with beach time. Excursions usually cost $10–$30, depending on the destination and number of passengers, and depart at 8 or 9 AM. You can guarantee a low rate for everyone if you organize a small group. Two-tank boat dives cost $50–$80, depending on distance.

Bocas Water Sports (⊠*Calle 3, 1 block south of Parque Bolívar* ☎*757–9541* ⊕*www.bocaswatersports.com*) is the town's original dive shop and maintains the best reputation. They offer scuba diving at a dozen sites, and have enriched air nitrox and certification courses. They also have daily snorkeling tours to the Cayos Zapatillas and other spots, waterskiing, and snorkeling-equipment and kayak rentals. **Starfleet Scuba** (⊠*Calle 2, next to Buena Vista* ☎*757–9630* ⊕*www.starfleet-scuba.com*) offers various two-tank boat dives and snorkeling excursions, and has inexpensive certification courses. **Boteros Bocatoreños** (⊠*Calle 3, across from Hotel Bahia* ☎*757–9760*) is an association of local boatmen who run inexpensive day trips to the archipelago's most popular spots. **J&J Transparente Boat Tours** (⊠*Calle 3, 1 block south of Parque Bolívar* ☎*757–9915*) has various day trips that combine snorkeling with beach time.

SURFING
Bocas is a short boat ride from the breaks on Islas Colón, Carenero, and Bastimentos, which makes it a great base for surfers. **Del Toro Surf** (☎*6570–8277*), run by an Argentine surfer named Javier, offers surf tours, boat transportation to nearby breaks, and surfing lessons. **Mondo Taitu** (⊠*Av. G, at Calle 5* ☎*757–9425*), on the north side of town, rents surfboards. **Tropix** (⊠*Calle 3, across from park* ☎*757–9415*), one of Bocas's two surf shops, is a good place to get advice, wax, or a board. **Flow** (⊠*Av. A, at Calle 2* ☎*757–9696*) is a large surf shop underneath Om Café that sells boards and provides information about nearby breaks.

HORSEBACK RIDING
Hacienda del Toro (☎*757–9158 or 6612–9159* ⊕*www.haciendadel-toro.com*) has horseback-riding tours ($25) at a ranch and rain-forest reserve on Isla Cristobal, a short boat trip from Bocas.

UNDER THE SEA

For many a traveler, the submarine wonders of Bocas del Toro's extensive coral reefs are the number-one reason to visit. Though Bocas lacks the spectacular schools of fish you see at Panama's top Pacific dive sites of Isla de Coiba and Islas Secas, it has greater coral diversity and hundreds of fish and invertebrate species. You can see dozens of colorful coral and sponge species, and such delicate reef denizens as bristle sea stars, peppermint shrimp, anemones, and sea horses. You may also spot spiny lobsters, moray eels, damselfish, angelfish, spiny puffers, spotted eagle rays, and hundreds of other creatures. Visibility varies, but the water is always warm. The best diving conditions are usually in March and between September and November.

The closest dive spot to town is **Hospital Point,** where an impressive coral and sponge garden extends down a steep wall into the blue depths, which can be appreciated both by snorkelers and scuba divers who can descend the wall. **Olas Chicas,** on the north shore of Isla

Bastimentos, is a good snorkeling spot, with coral, sponges, and sea fans clinging to volcanic rocks off the beach. **Cristobal Light,** 5 km (3 mi) southeast of Bocas town, is a good spot for snorkeling and scuba, with a coral garden spread across a platform some 15 feet below the surface. The most popular snorkeling spot in the archipelago is **Crawl Cay** (*Coral Cay*), an extensive reef on the east side of Isla Bastimentos, which has plenty of coral and invertebrates, but fewer fish than the nearby Cayos Zapatillas. The most famous snorkeling and scuba spot in the archipelago is **Cayos Zapatillas,** and for good reason; the two idyllic islands are surrounded by more than 1,000 acres of coral reef that is inhabited by an array of marine life. While the area around the islands offers excellent shallow snorkeling, the barrier reef has some good scuba spots, including caves, though the sea is often too rough to dive there. The most spectacular dive site in the archipelago is **Tiger Rock,** east of the Cayos Zapatillas, which offers a deep dive along an impressive wall.

SHOPPING

Artesanías Bri Bri (⊠ *Calle 3, at Av B* ☎ *No phone*) sells indigenous handicrafts, such as the jute bags made by local Ngöbe-Buglé Indians. **Flow** (⊠ *Av. A, at Calle 2* ☎ 757–9696), the surf shop underneath Om Café, sells some indigenous handicrafts in addition to surf wear.

TO & FROM

Most people fly to Bocas del Toro from Panama City; Aeroperlas and Air Panama have flights every morning and afternoon. Those airlines also have flights every morning between Bocas and David. Costa Rican airline Nature Air has afternoon flights between Bocas and Limón or San José in Costa Rica. Bocas del Toro is too far from Panama City to reach by land in one shot, but if you're in Chiriquí you can bus or taxi to Almirante (3 hours), where water taxis depart to Bocas every 30–60 minutes from 6 AM to 6 PM. Hourly water taxis also travel between Bocas and Finca 60, a banana farm 20 minutes by taxi from the border with Costa Rica.

ISLA COLÓN

172 km (107 mi) north of David, 2 km (1 mi) north of Bocas.

Though it is the most populated and developed island in the archipelago, Isla Colón is still a wild and beautiful place, with just two dirt roads, two lovely beaches, and significant swaths of tropical forest. The road from Bocas heads north along the isthmus that connects it to Isla Colón, where it is soon enters the forest. About 3 km (2 mi) north of town there's a fork in the road where the left branch leads across the island to the beach and community of Bocas del Drago, and the right branch leads to the surf spots of Paunch and Dumpers and beautiful Bluff Beach.

The nicest and biggest beach on Isla Colón is **Bluff Beach** *(Playa Bluff)*, a 3-km (2-mi) stretch of golden sand backed by tropical vegetation and washed by aquamarine waters. It's a great place to spend a day, or even an hour, but it has neither restaurants nor shops nearby, so pack water and snacks. When the waves are big, Playa Bluff has a beach break right on shore, but it can also develop rip currents, so swimmers beware. When the sea is calm it's an excellent swimming beach, and the rocky points at either end of it have decent snorkeling. Massive leatherback sea turtles nest here from April to September, when a local group runs night tours to look for them. If you're lucky, you may find baby turtles on the beach between June and December.

Boca del Drago (⊠ *14 km [9 mi] northwest of Bocas town*) is a tiny fishing community in the northwest corner of the island that overlooks the mainland across a channel of the same name. It has a narrow beach lined with coconut palms and other foliage that is much smaller than Bluff, but the water there is almost always calm, which makes for good swimming and snorkeling. There are often starfish in the shallows, and the rocks farther out hold coral formations. It's a popular destination for boat tours, but can also be reached by a bus that makes the 40-minute trip from Bocas several times a day. A small restaurant on the beach serves decent seafood and always has plenty of cold beer. Halfway across the island, at the village of Colonia Santeña, is **La Gruta** (*The Grotto* ⊠ *7 km [4 mi] north of Bocas, Colonia Santeña*), a bat-filled cave with a stream running out of it, surrounded by ferns and other foliage. Two statues of the Virgin Mary guard its entrance.

Swan's Cay (*Isla de los Pájaros* ⊠ *5 km [3 mi] northeast of Boca del Drago*) is a rocky islet off the north coast of Isla Colón that is commonly visited on boat tours to Boca del Drago. The swan it was named for is actually the red-billed tropicbird, an elegant white seabird with a long tail and bright-red bill that nests on the island in significant numbers. The rugged island is draped with lush foliage and has a narrow, natural arch in the middle of it that boatmen can slip through when the seas are calm. The surrounding ocean is a good scuba-diving area.

WHERE TO STAY & EAT

$$$$ ⊞**Punta Caracol Acqua Lodge.** This collection of spacious bungalows above the turquoise shallows off Isla Colón's western coast is both gorgeous and innovative. The hotel consists of nine wooden *cabañas* (bungalows) perched over the ocean atop pilings and connected to one another, the restaurant, and the mainland by wooden walkways. Each cabaña has a living room downstairs that opens onto a wide porch with lounge chairs and a ladder down to the crystalline waters. Bedroom lofts hold a king bed or two twins with mosquito nets. The ecolodge uses only solar energy, has its own sewage-treatment plant, and protects 60 hectares (148 acres) of rain-forest and mangrove-forest reserve. The downside is that it can be very hot at night, and insects and water shortages are sometimes a problem. Snorkeling, kayaks, breakfast, and dinner by candlelight are included in the rates, but the food is mediocre. It is accessible only by a 15-minute boat trip from town. **Pros: Gorgeous setting, charming rooms, ecofriendly. Cons: Overpriced, mediocre food, rooms can be hot, sometimes buggy.** ⊠ *10 km (6 mi) northwest of Bocas town* ☎ *6612–1088 or 6676–7186* ⊕ *www.puntacaracol.com* ↩ *8 cabañas, 1 suite* ⅏ *In-room: no a/c, no phone, safe, no TV. In-hotel: restaurant, bar, diving, water sports, no elevator, laundry service, airport shuttle, no-smoking rooms* ⊟ *AE, MC, V* Ⅷ *MAP.*

$$ ⊞**Playa Mango Resort.** Just north of the isthmus that connects Bocas
♻ to Isla Colón, on tranquil Sand Flea Bay, this place is far enough from town to be quiet but close enough to pop in for a meal or shopping. It is near the Paunch surf break, and a short bike ride from Bluff Beach. The array of activities includes skin diving, kayaking, horseback riding, jungle tours, waterskiing, ATV tours, and jet-skiing. The rooms, in two-story cement buildings, don't win any decorating awards, but they're comfortable and well equipped with a queen or two single beds, a tiny kitchenette, DVD player, air-conditioning, and ceiling fans. They surround a pool and grounds shaded by tropical trees with hammocks. **Pros: On water, quiet, pool, abundant diversions. Cons: Lousy beach, functional decor, bugs sometimes a problem.** ⊠ *4 km (2 mi) north of Bocas* ☎ *6684–4824 or 305/720–2565* ↩ *15 rooms* ⅏ *In-room: no phone, kitchen, Wi-Fi. In-hotel: restaurant, room service, bar, pool, beachfront, diving, water sports, bicycles, no elevator, laundry service, public Internet, no-smoking rooms* ⊟ *No credit cards* ⅧBP.

SPORTS & THE OUTDOORS

SCUBA DIVING   Isla Colón doesn't have great diving, but it does have good snorkel-
& SNORKELING   ing, mostly along the west side of the island, which has scattered reefs along the mangrove islets, one of the best of which is in front of the Punta Caracol Aqualodge. Excursions to Boca del Drago and Swan's Cay also include snorkeling.

Land Sea Air Adventures (⊠ *2 km north of Bocas* ☎ *6684–4418* ⊕ *www. land-sea-air-adventures.com*), based at the Playa Mango Resort, offers snorkeling excursions, scuba diving, and scuba certification courses. **Barco Hundido** (⊠ *Calle 1, at Av Central* ☎ *757–9695*) offers snorkeling excursions along the reefs and mangroves west of Isla Colón.

PANAMA'S SEA TURTLES

Sea turtles have long been common in the archipelago, where they graze on sea-grass beds by day, and lay their eggs on its beaches by night. Bocas del Toro has a relatively healthy turtle population, which makes it a good place to see those endangered reptiles and an important place for their conservation. Divers may come upon a turtle near one of the reefs, or you can look for them at the night on Playa Bluff. Four turtle species feed in the archipelago's waters, but only leatherback and hawksbill turtles nest here in significant numbers.

Hawksbills are the most beautiful marine turtles, thanks to their shiny marbled shells, which have also been their undoing—hawksbills have been hunted for their shells for centuries. Leatherbacks, on the other hand, have smooth, black carapaces that only a mother turtle could love. They are the largest of the sea turtles, and among the largest reptiles in the world, weighing more than half a ton.

From April to September, female turtles crawl slowly onto beaches in the darkness of night to bury their eggs in the sand. Hawksbills lay about 150 eggs the size of Ping-Pong balls, whereas leatherbacks lay fewer, but larger, elongated eggs. Two months later, eggs hatch and babies dig their way out of the sand, and scurry toward the surf; that is, if nests survive. The area's inhabitants have long eaten turtle eggs, and hunted green turtles for their meat, which is a delicacy. In fact, the town of Bocas was founded by Afro-Caribbean turtle hunters from the island of San Andrés, who were drawn to the area by its abundant hawksbill turtles. The scenario is common throughout the tropics, which is why sea-turtle species are endangered. Thankfully, the locals stopped hunting hawksbills years ago, and fewer people are collecting eggs. Other threats to adult turtles include drowning in fishing nets or long lines; leatherbacks sometimes choke on plastic bags, which resemble their favorite food: jellyfish.

The nesting beaches of Playa Larga, on Isla Bastimentos, and the Cayos Zapatillas, are protected within a national park. Members of **Grupo Ecológico Bluff** (☎ 6714–9162) transplant eggs from nests on Playa Bluff to a hatchery that they guard, to ensure their survival. They also lead tours to look for nesting turtles at night, and the money tourists pay them supports their efforts.

SURFING There are three good surf breaks on Isla Colón, all of them 5–7 km (3–4 mi) from Bocas. The best months for surfing are November to March, though there are often good swells in July and August. When it pumps, the waves have five- to nine-foot faces, and the reef breaks are hollow. They all require intermediate or expert skills. September and October tend to be the flattest months. There are waves about half the time the rest of the year. **Paunch** is a reef break 5 km (3 mi) north of town, around the bend from the Playa Mango Resort, that you have to walk over a coral platform to reach. The best way to get there from town is by boat. It breaks mostly left, and is for intermediate to expert surfers. **Dumpers** is an excellent left reef break on the point north of Paunch, 7 km (4 mi) north of town. It is a quick, hollow wave that gets dangerous when big. **Bluff Beach** has a powerful beach break close to shore when there's a good swell.

TURTLE-
WATCHING

Playa Bluff is a nesting beach for the rare leatherback turtle from April to September, when night tours are led there by members of the Grupo Ecológico Bluff, who are mostly Ngöbe-Buglé Indians. The three-hour tours start at 9 PM and are arranged by **Suite Hotel Costes** (⊠ *Calle 3* ☎ *757–9848*); they cost $10, plus $40 for transportation, split by the group. Wear long pants and shoes, and bring a flashlight and insect repellent.

WORD OF MOUTH

"I highly recommend staying on Carenero Island—there are no cars or roads, only palm trees and sandy grounds and it is 5 minutes by water taxi from Bocas town. There are several great restaurants and tiki bars over the water."

–smgapp.

TO & FROM
Avenida G leads north from Bocas town over the isthmus to Isla Colón, where the road soon forks. Veer right for Bluff Beach and the surf breaks of Paunch and Dumpers, which can be reached in about 30 minutes on a very rough road by bicycle, or in an hour on foot. A taxi takes about 40 minutes, and costs $20. A boat to Paunch or Dumpers from Bocas town should cost $10. Bocas del Drago is accessible by boat, taxi, or bus. On weekdays buses depart from Parque Bolívar for Bocas del Drago at 6:45, 10, 12, 3, and 6, returning 40 minutes later. The trip costs $2. Taxis charge $20, but the boat trip is the same price, and includes Swan's Cay. **Edgar Trotman** (☎ *6631–0120*) is a taxi driver who can provide transportation to the island's sites.

ISLA CARENERO

½ km (¼ mi) east of Bocas Town.

Just east of Bocas—practically swimming distance—is a long, forested island called Isla Carenero (Careening Cay), the southern end of which holds a mix of fishermen's shacks, the large homes of foreigners, a few hotels, restaurants, and a small marina. Staying here is a quieter and more natural alternative to sleeping in town. The island's name comes from the practice of using its narrow beach and shallows to pull ships onto their sides—careening—in order to scrape and repair their hulls. That beach is now dotted with homes and other buildings perched over the water on pilings. Since the island lacks a sewage system, swimming isn't recommended. The eastern side of the island has a rocky coast, but is more forested and sparsely populated, whereas its northern half holds only a handful of foreign-owned homes and a popular surf break known simply as Carenero.

WHERE TO STAY & EAT

$ **Blue Marlin Resort.** "Resort" is a misnomer, but this small inn and
★ restaurant on Isla Carenero's rocky eastern coast is the place to head
☺ for a good meal with an ocean view or a quiet room at a reasonable price. The hotel consists of just two rooms on the bottom floor of a

building at the edge of the forest, mere steps from the sea. They have queen beds and lots of hardwoods, and bright sitting rooms with wet bars where you can put a mattress on the floor. The nearby Pickled Parrot restaurant ($–$$$) sits over the water, where you can enjoy the view of Islas Bastimentos and Solarte across the water or watch TV. The menu includes burgers, fresh snapper, "firecracker shrimp" (sautéed in a spicy sauce), and blackened chicken. The friendly American-Panamanian owners can arrange inexpensive day trips. Snorkeling equipment and kayaks are available for guest use, and it's a 10-minute walk from the Carenero surf break. **Pros: Casual, comfortable atmosphere. Cons: Basic accommodations.** ⊠*Southeast side of island* ☎*757–9093* ⊕*www.bocasbluemarlin.com* ⇆*2 rooms* ♿*In-room: no phone, no TV, refrigerator, Wi-Fi. In-hotel: restaurant, bar, water sports, no elevator* ▭*AE, MC, V* ⑩*EP.*

LAGUNA BOCATORITO
Sheltered between the islands and the mainland on the southern end of the gulf is Laguna Bocatorito, a large lagoon frequented by schools of bottlenose dolphins. Hidden behind a mess of mangrove islets, it is a lovely area where the cetaceans play in tranquil waters. Independent boatmen and tour operators in Bocas include a quick visit to Bocatorito in day tours to the archipelago's other attractions, often referring to it as "Dolphin Bay." There is no guarantee you'll see dolphins, but most people do; they tend to be more abundant between December and March and June to August.

$$ ⛱**Casa Acuario.** The view from the rooms in this two-story building
★ over the water on the south side of Isla Carenero is of turquoise waters, boats, and the occasional seabird. The building has four spacious, airy rooms with wooden floors, walls, and ceilings, cane furniture, and several big windows. They open onto wraparound balconies with memorable views, and are equipped with air-conditioning, ceiling fans, and satellite TV. Inexpensive breakfasts are served on a deck in back. The owners are proprietors of J&J Boat Tours, so transport to nearby Isla Colón is never more than a phone call away. **Pros: Great views, nice rooms. Cons: Somewhat remote.** ⊠*Southern side of island* ☎*757–9565* ⊕*www.bocas.com/casa-acuario.htm* ⇆*4 rooms* ♿*In-room: no phone, Wi-Fi. In-hotel: no elevator, no-smoking rooms* ▭*No credit cards* ⑩*EP.*

SPORTS & THE OUTDOORS

SURFING The left reef break on the northeast side of Carenero is very popular, since it is the closest break to Bocas and can be reached by an inexpensive, five-minute boat ride. There is also a small beach break on the northern end of the island for less experienced surfers.

TO & FROM

Independent boatmen and the water-taxi companies in Bocas provide transportation across the channel between Carenero and town for $1.

ISLA SOLARTE

3 km (2 mi) east of Bocas Town.

Isla Solarte (called Cayo Nancy on some maps) is a long, forested island that is home to scattered Ngöbe-Buglé families and a handful of foreigners. The most visited part of it is Hospital Point, its western tip, which lies just across the deep channel to the east of Isla Carenero. The ocean around that point is one of the archipelago's most accessible dive sites, appropriate for both scuba and skin diving. It is named for a former hospital that was built to quarantine yellow fever patients during Bocas del Toro's banana heyday. There are a few homes behind that point, but most of the rest of the island is covered with rain forest.

WHERE TO STAY

$$
★
Garden of Eden. Rooms in this small lodge on a knoll in the mangroves of northern Isla Solarte overlook a soothing natural panorama of glassy waters and bright green foliage. The owners, from the Florida Keys, built three wooden rooms next to their home that have plenty of windows to take advantage of the view and breeze (they have fans, too). The "suite," below the poolside rooms, is worth the extra bucks, since it is more private. Breakfast is served beneath a thatch roof next to the pool, as is a small-but-succulent selection of lunch and dinner items ranging from barbecued ribs to grilled lobster tail. The surrounding sea is too murky and muddy for swimming, but you can paddle kayaks through the mangroves or cross the bay to Red Frog Beach, a mile away. Tours are arranged, as are daily trips to town (no nighttime trips). **Pros: Great views, spacious rooms, pool, friendly. Cons: No beach, isolated, small grounds.** ⊠*North side of island* ☎*700–0352 or 6487–4332* ⊕*www.gardenofedenbocaspanama.com* ⬅*2 rooms, 1 suite* ⬇*In-room: no a/c, no phone, no TV, Wi-Fi. In-hotel: restaurant, pool, water sports, no elevator* ▭*AE, MC, V.*

TO & FROM

Independent boatmen and water-taxi companies in Bocas can take you snorkeling at Hospital Point, a good excursion if you're short of time. The Garden of Eden lodge arranges transportation for guests.

ISLA BASTIMENTOS

Isla Bastimentos covers 52 square km (20 square mi) of varied landscapes including lush tropical forest, mangrove estuaries, a lake, and several of the archipelago's nicest beaches. It also has several Afro-Caribbean and Ngöbe-Buglé indigenous communities, and some excellent snorkeling and surfing spots. Old Bank, the archipelago's second-largest town, overlooks a cove on the island's western tip. A 2-km (1-mi) trail leads north from there to a gorgeous swath of sand called Wizard's Beach. The island's northern coast holds four beaches separated by rocky points, the longest of which, Playa Larga, lies within Parque Nacional Marino Isla Bastimentos, which also protects a swath of rain forest and the nearby islands of Cayos Zapatillas. Bastimentos's southern side is lined with mangrove forests and dozens of mangrove

MANGROVE FORESTS

As you zip across the glassy waters between the islands, you can admire the bright green foliage of mangroves lining the emerald sea. Most of the coastal forest on Bocas del Toro's islands and the bulk of its countless islets are dominated by the red mangrove, an unusual tree with long, red stilt roots that prop it up in the shallows, and which thrives in saltwater—poison for most trees. Together with the black and white mangroves and various other plants, the red mangrove forms coastal forests in estuaries and on islets throughout the tropics. Mangrove estuaries are eerily beautiful ecosystems spread between the land and the sea, and if you look closely at one you may see barnacles and algae growing on the mangroves' tubular roots, and crabs, shrimp, or small fish around them. Dozens of commercially important fish and seafood species spend the early stages of their lives in the mangroves, which make them a vital component of the ocean's complex web of life. They can also harbor legions of mosquitoes and no-see-ums, so bring your insect repellent if you're going to explore a mangrove estuary.

islets. There you'll find the indigenous community of Bahia Honda, and the beginning of a trail across the island to the second beach, known as Red Frog Beach.

The island's long southeast coast is more distant and remote, taking 40 minutes to reach from Bocas by boat. It lies near the archipelago's best skin-diving spots—Crawl Cay and Cayos Zapatillas—and is backed by thick jungle that is home to an array of wildlife and a small Ngöbe-Buglé community called Salt Creek. A narrow, forest-lined beach stretches along the coast near Old Point, the island's northeast tip. The coast's southern point, Macca Bite, is hemmed by mangroves, perfect for kayak exploration, and is next to the archipelago's most popular snorkeling spot, Crawl Cay. A short boat ride to the east of either point takes you to the bleached sand and vast coral gardens of the paradisiacal Cayos Zapatillas. There is enough to see and do in the area that you could spend a week boating, swimming, hiking, and paddling past its natural treasures.

OLD BANK (BASTIMENTOS)

4 km (2½ mi) east of Bocas.

Spread along a bay on the island's western tip, between the ocean and forested hills, is a colorful collection of simple wooden buildings known as Old Bank, or Bastimentos town. It is a predominantly Afro-Caribbean community where Guari-Guari—a mix of patois English and the indigenous tongue of Ngöbere—is the lingua franca. Most people live in elevated wooden houses, some awfully rudimentary, that line sidewalks and dirt paths instead of streets. It's a poor, but friendly and crowded place where children play in the dugout canoes pulled up on shore, families chat in the shade beneath their homes, and men play dominoes at the local bars. Most of Old Bank's men work on the

Caribbean Sea

Punta Toro

Playa Primera

Isla Carenero

Old Bank (Bastimentos)

Playa Segunda

Playa Primera

Red Frog Beach

Bocas del Toro

Red Frog Beach & Bahia Honda

Parque Nacional Marino Isla Bastimentos

Isla Solarte

Isla Bastimentos

Playa Larga

Quebrada de Sal

Playa Vieja

Old Point (Punta Vieja)

Cayos Zapatillas

Cayo Crawl

Macca Bite

Isla Popa

0   2 miles

0   2 kilometers

banana farms or port on the mainland, commuting via a company boat. Old Bank is the home of an authentic calypso band with a not-too-original name—the Beach Boys—who rock the town on Monday nights: Blue Mondays. Old Bank doesn't have a proper sewage system, so swimming in the bay in front of it is not recommended, even though the local kids do; head to one of the nearby beaches instead.

A 20-minute hike north of Old Bank on a trail through cow pastures and forest patches takes you to **Wizard's Beach** *(First Beach)*, a splendid swath of pale sand hemmed by lush vegetation. The wide, beige beach extends into turquoise shallows that are perfect for swimming when the sea is calm, and there are large coral reefs around the points on either end of the beach. When the ocean is rough, however, this beach can develop strong rip currents that make swimming dangerous. Surfers enjoy the beach break, but when the swell gets really big, it closes out and is dangerous for surfers too. The trail to Wizard Beach starts at the east edge of town, just past the soccer field; it is sometimes muddy. On the east end of the beach, another footpath leads into the forest to Red Frog Beach, less than 1 km (½ mi) away.

WHERE TO STAY & EAT

¢–$$ ✕ **Roots.** Perched over the sea near the center of Old Bank, this rustic,
★ open-air restaurant is known for serving authentic *bocatoreña* food.
House specialties include Caribbean chicken (in a mildly spicy sauce),
fresh lobster, shrimp, and conch, listed as "snail" on the menu. They
are served with a hearty mix of coconut rice, red beans, and a sim-
ple cabbage salad. The ambience is equally authentic, with tables and
chairs made from tree trunks and branches beneath a thatched roof.
✉ *On the water east of police post* ☎ *6473–5111* ▭ *No credit cards*
⊘ *Closed Tues.*

¢ 🖼 **Hotel Caribbean View.** The accommodations here may be too basic
for many travelers, but the view over the water is priceless. The hotel
is a two-story, Caribbean-style building perched over the sea near the
east end of town. Rooms are small, but bright and clean, with lots of
varnished wood and a tiny tile bathroom. The best ones, in the back on
the second floor, have private balconies and air-conditioning. There's
a small restaurant on the back porch, and the owners can arrange day
tours. Pros: Great view. Cons: Very basic accommodations. ✉ *East
end of town* ☎ *757–9442* ✐ *hotelcaribbeanview@yahoo.com* ⇆ *11
rooms* ◊ *In-room: no phone, no a/c (some). In-hotel: restaurant, no
elevator, no-smoking rooms* ▭ *No credit cards* ⚹ *EP.*

5

SPORTS & THE OUTDOORS

SCUBA DIVING & SNORKELING Old Bank lies closer to most of the archipelago's dive spots than Bocas
does, and the local dive operator is less expensive than the dive shops
in town, which makes it an attractive departure point for scuba div-
ing or snorkeling excursions. **Dive Panama** (☎ *6567–1812*) is a small,
Dutch-owned outfitter in Old Bank that offers inexpensive boat dives,
snorkeling excursions, and PADI certification courses.

SURFING The north coast of Isla Bastimentos has half a dozen surf breaks, some
of which are very hard to reach. **Wizard's Beach** has a fun beach break
when the waves are small, but when the swell is big, the beach and
nearby point break develop serious currents and require experience.
Silverbacks is an experts-only reef break in front of the point west of
Wizard's Beach that is the only place to surf when a big swell hits. A
few times a year it gets over 10 feet high, and it can be surfed when the
swell reaches 20 feet, which happens now and then.

TO & FROM

Small boats regularly carry people between the towns of Bocas and
Old Bank during the day, leaving Bocas from the dock next to the
Farmacia Rosa Blanca and Bastimentos from the Muelle Municipal
(the long dock in the middle of town). The trip takes 10 minutes and
costs $2 each way.

RED FROG BEACH AND BAHIA HONDA

8 km (5 mi) east of Bocas, 4 km (2½ mi) east of Old Bank.

A couple of miles east of Old Bank, Isla Basitimentos gets narrow—a mere ½ km (¼ mi) wide—and the sea to the south of it is dotted with mangrove islets. Here you'll find a small dock that marks the entrance to a footpath across the island to Red Frog Beach, one of the loveliest spots in the archipelago, with its golden sand shaded by tropical trees. East of the beach, the island becomes wide again, and is largely covered with lush rain forest that is home to everything from mealy parrots to white-faced capuchin monkeys, and countless tiny, bright-red poison dart frogs. The scattered homes of Ngöbe-Buglé Indians line the bay to the south, known as Bahia Honda, where an indigenous organization has cut a trail through the forest and built a rustic restaurant for tourists. To the east of there is Parque Nacional Marino Isla Bastimentos, and to the south a narrow channel through the mangroves that is the main route to the island's eastern coast and the Cayos Zapatillas.

Relative accessibility—a five-minute walk from a dock—and remarkable natural beauty have combined to make **Red Frog Beach** *(Dreffe Beach)* one of the most popular spots in Bocas del Toro. The beach is almost a mile long, with golden sand backed by coconut palms, Indian almond trees, and other tropical greenery. It's the perfect spot for lounging on the sand, playing in the sea, and admiring the amazing scenery. Unfortunately, the area's pristine beauty is threatened by U.S. developers, who are selling lots and condos and bulldozing roads nearby. A tiny, rustic bar behind the beach sells basic Panamanian lunches and rents snorkeling equipment. ⚠ **Red Frog is usually a good swimming beach, but when the surf is up, rip currents can make it dangerous, so don't go in past your waist if the waves are big.** When the sea is calm, you can snorkel over the large coral reef off the point on the west end of the beach. To escape the crowd, hike around the point on Red Frog Beach's eastern end to **Polo's Beach,** named for a hermit who lived there for years until he sold his land to developers. Serious skin divers should check out the big reef around the island northeast of this beach. The owner of the dock and the land that the trail crosses charges $3 to enter Red Frog Beach.

About 20 Ngöbe-Buglé Indian homes are scattered around **Bahia Honda,** and a group of indigenous families runs a rustic restaurant just to the east of the dock for Red Frog Beach. They offer a half-day tour that includes a boat ride through the mangroves to a hiking trail and, for those who are up to it, exploration of a cave with a stream running out of it and plenty of bats clinging to the stalactite-laden ceiling. The adventure also includes a simple lunch, a weaving demonstration, and a chance to purchase handicrafts such as *chácaras* (colorful woven jute bags). Contact La Loma Jungle Lodge (☎6619–5364 or 6592–5162) a day in advance to arrange a tour.

WHERE TO STAY & EAT

$$$ ✕⊞ **La Loma Jungle Lodge.** The tastefully rustic bungalows at this ecolodge
Fodor'sChoice are perched along a hillside in the rain forest, with 180-degree views
★ of tropical nature. Oropendolas sing in the treetops, hummingbirds flit
about, and those little red frogs are everywhere. The idealistic young
owners designed the lodge to limit negative environmental impacts—
with wood from fallen trees and solar and kerosene lamps—and to
benefit their Ngöbe-Buglé neighbors. It sits in a 20-hectare (49-acre)
private forest reserve with a botanical garden and organic farm, where
they grow some of the food used in sumptuous Panamanian dinners.
Spacious bungalows are open on three sides, though canvas curtains
can be drawn when it's rainy or windy. Bungalows have good beds with
mosquito nets, homemade furniture, hammocks, and big bathrooms.
Meals, jungle hikes, dugout canoes, and transport to Red Frog Beach
are included in the rates, plus they have inexpensive day tours. **Pros:
In jungle, friendly, conscientious, near beach, good tours. Cons: Very
rustic, steep climbs to rooms.** ⊠ *Bahia Honda* ☎ *6619–5364 or 6592–
5162* ⊕ *www.thejunglelodge.com* ☞ *3 bungalows* ⟳ *In-room: no a/c,
no phone, safe, no TV. In-hotel: restaurant, no elevator, no-smoking
rooms* ⊟ *No credit cards* ℻*FAP.*

TO & FROM

Most day tours to Crawl Cay include a stop at Red Frog Beach. Boat
operators in Bocas and Old Bank will drop you off for $3–$5 one way,
and will pick you up at a specified time. It is possible to hike between
Old Bank and Red Frog Beach, which are about 4 km (2 mi) apart.
Footpaths through the forest connect Red Frog to Wizard Beach, which
is a short hike from Old Bank.

MACCA BITE

20 km (12 mi) southeast of Bocas.

The southernmost point on Isla Bastimento has an odd name, and its
origin is as mysterious as Bocas del Toro's, though the theory is that
wild macaws once lived there (there are now tame ones at the epony-
mous lodge). That hilly headland hemmed by mangroves and draped
with lush rain forest is a mere 30 minutes from Bocas by boat, yet it
feels like the end of the world. Far from the nearest road or streetlight,
it is a place where Mother Nature still reigns, where dolphins swim and
monkeys roam. The point has two lodges on it that provide constant
exposure to nature—one at the edge of the sea, and one at the top of
the hill—as well as restaurants that can reward you with a cold beer
and fresh seafood after a hard morning of snorkeling.

Just east of Macca Bite is **Crawl Cay** *(Coral Cay),* a large coral reef
that's between 15 and 35 feet deep. The submarine garden holds an
impressive array of coral heads, colorful sponges, large sea fans, and
hundreds of small reef fish. It is an excellent spot for inexperienced
skin divers, who can simply float over it and watch the show, but it
also has enough marine life in and around its innumerable crannies to
entertain experienced divers. It is also in a sheltered enough location

that the water there is usually calm and clear, even when the sea is too rough for diving at the Cayos Zapatillas. The nearby Crawl Cay Restaurant and competitors serve cold drinks and fresh seafood on decks built over the water—order your food before you go snorkeling to avoid a long wait.

WHERE TO STAY & EAT

$$$$
Fodor'sChoice
★

Tranquilo Bay. This all-inclusive jungle lodge is geared toward active travelers—you can kayak, snorkel, hike, surf, or fish, or just stroll the beach and lounge in a hammock, all amid amazing scenery. The young American owners offer three-, four-, or seven-night stays in well-equipped bungalows spread along a forested ridge with panoramic ocean and island views. They are spacious and comfortable, with two queen beds, large bathrooms, air-conditioning, and wraparound porches; four view the sea, two the forest. Just behind is the lodge's 50-hectare (125-acre) rain-forest reserve, bordering the national park. Daily tours head to spots such as the Cayos Zapatillas, Indian villages, various reefs, and remote isles and beaches. Meals and cocktails are served in a lovely dining-living room in the main building. **Pros: Varied activities, wild surroundings, nice rooms, good food, friendly, well organized. Cons: Expensive, remote.** ⊠ *Macca Bite* ☎ *380–0721 or 713/589-6952 in U.S.* ⊕ *www.tranquilobay.com* ⌁6 *bungalows* ⌂ *In-room: no phone, no TV. In-hotel: restaurant, bar, water sports, no elevator, laundry service, public Internet, no-smoking rooms* ⊟*AE, MC, V* ⊗ *Closed May and June* ❤*AI*.

$$–$$$
Fodor'sChoice
★

Hotel Macca Bite. Perched over the water at the edge of the point, between the mangroves and the sea, this comfortable hotel has inspiring views of crystalline waters dotted with coral heads, the ocean horizon, and nearby Isla Popa. Colorful rooms are in two-story wooden buildings with varnished wood floors, two queen beds, and nice tile baths. The "suites" are bigger, with high ceilings and more furniture. All rooms open onto wide porches perched over the water and are perfect for watching the needlefish, puffers, and pelicans. What distinguishes this place from comparable lodges is local ownership and amenities such as air-conditioning and satellite TV. A small, open-air restaurant over the water serves mostly fresh seafood. Behind it are a garden and a patch of forest with tame macaws and monkeys. You can rent snorkeling equipment and kayaks, and take tours to nearby Cayos Zapatillas and other spots. **Pros: On the water, great view, well-equipped rooms, snorkeling, excursions. Cons: Remote, occasional no-see-ums.** ⊠ *Crawl Cay* ☎ *6673–5155 or 264–5255* ⊕ *www.hotelmaccabite.com* ⌁8 *room, 3 suites* ⌂ *In-hotel: restaurant, water sports, no elevator, no-smoking rooms* ⊟*AE, MC, V* ❤*MAP*.

SPORTS & THE OUTDOORS

The Macca Bite lodges lie near some of the archipelago's best dive spots, and offer daily snorkeling excursions and kayaking. Tranquilo Bay also offers jungle hiking, sportfishing, and surfing.

TO & FROM

Tranquilo Bay provides free transportation from and to Bocas on Wednesday and Saturday, but charges $100 for the trip on other days. Hotel Macca Bite charges $50 for round-trip transportation. Rates are per trip, not per passenger.

OLD POINT (PUNTA VIEJA)

8 km (5 mi) northeast of Macca Bite, 28 km (17 mi) southeast of Bocas.

The northeast point of Isla Bastimentos, known as Old Point, is covered with jungle and surrounded by coral reefs. It probably looks about the same as it did when Christopher Columbus sailed through the archipelago five centuries ago, aside from the small hotels nestled in the forest. And yet it's just a 40-minute boat ride from the ATMs and Internet cafés of Bocas. It is thus an easy place to get away from it all and immerse yourself in nature at its finest. A narrow beach lines the coast between Old Point and Salt Creek, and it is backed by exuberant tropical flora where birdsong complements the lapping of the waves against the sand. The ocean bottom here is a bit mucky, but the water is usually calm, and there are coral reefs in the deeper water near the point. A couple of trails lead into the rain forest, one to the nicer, wider beach of Playa Larga, on the island's northern shore. At the southern end of the beach a trail leads to the Ngöbe-Buglé Indian village of **Salt Creek,** where you can see how the locals live, snap a few photos, or buy indigenous handicrafts such as dyed jute bags called *chácaras.*

WHERE TO STAY & EAT

$$-$$$$
Fodor'sChoice
★

Al Natural. This rustic ecolodge offers intimate contact with nature, with only solar lighting, propane hot-water showers, and ocean breezes in lieu of fans. Bungalows, nestled in the forest behind the beach, are surprisingly exposed, with hardly a wall to them, just mosquito nets, and canvas curtains you can pull shut to protect from wind and rain. The result is a panorama of tropical greenery and turquoise waters visible from bed. It's Mies van der Rohe—the Bauhaus architect who said "less is more"—meets Robinson Crusoe, with lacquered hardwoods, thatch roofs, and tiny bathrooms. You can stroll the beach, swim in the shallows, or kayak out to the coral reef; all-inclusive packages that include trips to Salt Creek and the Cayos Zapatillas are recommended. Meals are served in a two-story, rustic restaurant, and the dinners are excellent Caribbean-Continental concoctions. The second night is less expensive. **Pros: Jungle, beach, tranquillity, good food, friendly. Cons: Rustic, few diversions, breakfast and lunch are light.** ⊠ *Old Point* ☎ *757–9004, 6496–0776, or 6640–6935* ⊕ *www.bocas.com/alnatura. htm* ⏎ *6 bungalows* ⌂ *In-room: no a/c, no phone, no TV. In-hotel: restaurant, beachfront, water sports, no elevator, no-smoking rooms* ⊟ *No credit cards* ⊗ *Closed May and June* ⎟⊙⎟ *FAP.*

TO & FROM

Transportation to Al Natural is included in rates. Boatmen in Bocas charge about $60–$80 for a trip to Old Point.

PARQUE NACIONAL MARINO ISLA BASTIMENTOS

8 km (5 mi) southeast of Old Point, 34 km (22 mi) southeast of Bocas.

★ About one third of Isla Bastimentos and the two Cayos Zapatillas, to the southeast, lie within **Parque Nacional Marino Isla Bastimentos** (*Bastimentos Island National Marine Park*). The park's 13,226 hectares (32,668 acres) comprise an array of ecosystems ranging from sea-grass beds to rain forest, and include some spectacular and ecologically important areas. A few of these are a large lake on Bastimentos, the vast expanses of coral reef to the north and east of the island, and the beaches of Playa Larga and Cayos Zapatillas, which are nesting areas for several sea-turtle species. **Playa Larga** is a long, pristine beach on the northern coast of Isla Bastimentos that is remote enough that few people make it there. It is nearly impossible to visit it at night, when turtles nest, which makes Playa Bluff a better option for turtle-watching. Playa Larga is most easily visited from Old Point, where a trail leads through the forest to that seemingly endless ribbon of windswept sand. Much of the park is almost inaccessible, especially the island's forested interior, but you can see most of its flora and fauna in the private reserves of adjacent jungle lodges.

Most people experience the park's reefs at **Cayos Zapatillas,** two cays southeast of Bastimentos that are the park's crown jewels. Their name translates as "Slipper Cays," which is may be due to their shoelike shapes. Those small, elongated isles with ivory sand shaded by coconut palms have the kind of picture-perfect tropical scenery that northern travel companies put in their brochures. But the Cayos' most impressive scenery is actually in the surrounding ocean, which holds 500 hectares (1,235 acres) of protected coral reef ranging from a shallow platform around the islands to steep walls pocked with caves. Scuba divers can explore the reef's outer expanses, but snorkelers can enjoy views of the shallow platform adorned with some impressive coral formations. The park tends to have more fish than Crawl Cay and other unprotected dive spots, and divers can expect to see tiny angelfish, parrot fish, squirrelfish, octopi, eels, stingrays, and countless other marine creatures. But when seas are rough, as they often are between December and March, skin diving is limited to the leeward side of the island, making Crawl Cay a more attractive dive spot then. There is a ranger station on the island, and a small nature trail through the forest. Bring sunblock, insect repellent, a hat, a towel, water, and snorkeling gear. ☏758–6822 🖾$10 ⊗*Daily 6–6.*

BOCAS DEL TORO ARCHIPELAGO ESSENTIALS

TRANSPORTATION

BY AIR

Because it is relatively remote, most people travel to and from Bocas del Toro by plane. The Aeropuerto Internacional Bocas del Toro, archipelago's tiny airport, is five blocks from the center of Bocas, at the west

COSTA RICA BORDER CROSSING

Bocas del Toro lies geographically close to the Costa Rican beach towns of Puerto Viejo and Cahuita, but traveling between the two isn't as easy as it could be. It usually takes 4 to 5 hours to make the trip by land, but can take longer, due to infrequent bus service from the Costa Rican border post of Sixaola. From Bocas, take a water taxi to Finca 60, where share taxis frequently leave on the 20-minute trip to Guayabito, on the border with Costa Rica. It takes about 30 minutes to cross the border, which includes walking across the Sixaola River on an old railroad bridge. After that you have to wait for the next bus to Limón, or San José, all of which stop at Puerto Viejo (2 hours) and Cahuita (2½ hours). It is quicker, though considerably more expensive, to take a Nature Air flight to Limón, and hire a taxi to take you to Cahuita or Puerto Viejo, a 60- or 80-minute trip south.

end of Avenida E. Domestic carriers Aeroperlas and Air Panama have three daily flights each between Bocas del Toro and Panama City, and one morning flight between Bocas del Toro and David. Costa Rican airline Nature Air has daily afternoon flights between Bocas and the nearby port of Limón, and San José.

Carriers Aeroperlas ☎315-7500 or 721-1230 ⊕www.aeroperlas.com. **Air Panama** ☎316-9000 or 721-0841 ⊕www.flyairpanama.com. **Nature Air** ☎506/299-6000 in Costa Rica, 800/235-9272 in the U.S. ⊕www.natureair.com.

BY BOAT & FERRY

Boats are the most common means of transport in Bocas del Toro, and the town of Bocas has several water-taxi companies and dozens of boatmen who provide transportation between Islas Colón, Carenero, and Bastimentos, as well as day tours. The water-taxi companies Bocas Marine & Tours, Jam Pan Tours, and Taxi 25 have hourly trips between Bocas and Almirante ($3), where you can catch a bus to David, and slightly less frequent trips between Bocas and Finca 60 ($7), a short taxi ride from the Costa Rican border. It takes 20 minutes to reach Almirante and 40 minutes to reach Finca 60, with departures from 6 AM to 6 PM. Jam Pan also provides transport to the other islands, as do independent boatmen who depart from the dock next to the Farmacia Rosa Blanca, on Calle 3 in Bocas. The fare to Carenero is $1, to Old Bank, $2.

A car is of little use in Bocas del Toro, but there is a car ferry, run by Trasbordadores Marinos, that travels between Almirante and Bocas every day but Sunday, departing from Almirante at 8 AM and Bocas at 4 PM. The trip takes an hour and costs $15–$30, according to the size of the vehicle.

Boat & Ferry Information Bocas Marine & Tours ✉Calle 3, at Av. C ☎757-9033. **Jam Pan Tours** ✉Calle 2, at Av D ☎757-9619. **Taxi 25** ✉Calle 1, at Av. Central ☎757-9028. **Trasbordadores Marinos** ✉Town port, Almirante ☎6615-6674.

BY BUS & TAXI

Transporte Boca del Drago has a small bus that travels the length of Isla Colón, from Bocas del Toro to Bocas del Drago, five times daily on weekdays. The bus departs from Bocas's Parque Bolívar at 6:45, 10, noon, 3, and 6, and departs from the restaurant at Bocas del Drago 45 minutes later. Share taxis run up and down Bocas's main streets, charging 50¢ for most trips in town. Taxi driver Edgar Trotman will take you anywhere on the island for $20.

Bocas del Toro is too far from Panama City to travel by land, but if you're in Chiriquí you can bus or taxi from David or Boquete to Almirante (3 hours), where water taxis depart for Bocas every hour. Buses to David depart from Almirante every hour from the bus station on the other side of the train tracks from the water-taxi offices and charge $5. Boquete-based taxi driver Daniel Higgins provides transportation between Boquete and Almirante for $120, though you may get a better price from the taxis that hang out at the bus station in Almirante. Share taxis travel between the water-taxi station in Finca 60 and the border with Costa Rica; the 20-minute trip costs $3.

Bus & Taxi Information **Almirante Bus** ☎ *774–0585.* **Daniel Higgins** ☎ *6617–0570.* **Edgar Trotman** ☎ *6631–0120.* **Transporte Boca del Drago** ☎ *774–9065.*

CONTACTS & RESOURCES

EMERGENCIES

The clinic in Bocas is good only for first aid. If you have a serious medical problem, you should get on the next flight to Panama City or David.

Emergency Services **Fire** ☎ *757–9274 in Bocas del Toro.* **Police** ☎ *757–9217 in Bocas del Toro.*

Hospital **Hospital de Bocas del Toro** ✉ *Av. G and Calle 10, Bocas del Toro* ☎ *757–9201.*

Pharmacy **Farmacia Rosa Blanca** ✉ *Calle 3 and Av. B, Bocas del Toro* ☎ *757–9101.*

MONEY MATTERS

There are two ATMs in Bocas: at the Banco Nacional de Panama and on Calle 1, next to the Policía Nacional. They give cash withdrawals from Visa, MasterCard, and Cirrus- and Plus-affiliated debit cards and credit cards.

ATMs **Banco Nacional** ✉ *Av. E and Calle 4, Bocas del Toro* ☎ *757–9230.* **HBSC ATM** ✉ *Calle 1, at Av. Central, Bocas del Toro* ☎ *997–0608.*

SAFETY

Bocas is a safe town, but it has acquired a few sidewalk hustlers and drug dealers in recent years and has a growing drug problem, so don't wander its side streets late at night. The main dangers in the archipelago, however, are sunburn and bug bites. Take a hat, sunscreen, and insect repellent. Drowning is also a real danger, so don't swim at the beaches if the waves are big, unless you are an experienced surfer, and don't let a boatman take you into rough water in a dugout canoe.

TOURS

Three dive shops and two dozen local fishermen offer one-day excursions to spots such as Bocatorito, Crawl Cay, Cayos Zapatillas, Boca del Drago, and Swans Cay, which cost $17–$25, depending on the destination. Bocas Water Sports is the leading dive operator, but also offers snorkeling excursions, waterskiing, kayak rentals, and snorkeling-equipment rentals. Starfleet Scuba has diving and snorkeling excursions. Land, Sea & Air Adventures offers scuba diving, snorkeling, waterskiing, and glass-bottom kayak tours, as well as snorkeling-equipment rental. J&J Transparente Tours specializes in snorkeling excursions to the most popular spots. Boteros Bocatoreños offers day trips to the archipelago's most popular spots. Always confirm that there are life vests on board before you set out. Most hotels can arrange day trips for their guests. Hacienda del Toro offers horseback-riding tours on Isla Cristobal for $25. Transporte Boca del Drago has a day tour ($35) that includes a drive across the island, a boat trip to Swan's Cay, lunch, and snorkeling equipment. Javier, at Del Toro Surf, can organize surf tours, lessons, or transportation to breaks.

Tour-Operator Recommendations **Bocas Water Sports** ✉ *Calle 3, 1 block south of Parque Bolívar, Bocas del Toro* ☎ *757-9541* ⊕ *www.bocaswatersports. com.* **Boteros Bocatoreños** ✉ *Calle 3, across from Hotel Bahia Bocas del Toro* ☎ *757-9760.* **Del Toro Surf** ✉ *Old Bank, Isla Bastimentos* ☎ *6570-8277.* **Hacienda del Toro** ✉ *Isla San Cristobal* ☎ *757-9158 or 6612-9159* ⊕ *www. haciendadeltoro.com.* **J&J Transparente Tours** ✉ *Calle 3, 1 block south of Parque Bolívar, Bocas del Toro* ☎ *757-9915.* **Land, Sea & Air Adventures** ✉ *2 km north of Bocas, Bocas del Toro* ☎ *6684-4418* ⊕ *www.land-sea-air-adventures.com.* **Starfleet Scuba** ✉ *Calle 2, next to Buena Vista, Bocas del Toro* ☎ *757-9630* ⊕ *www.starfleetscuba.com.* **Transporte Boca del Drago** ✉ *East side of Parque Bolívar, Bocas del Toro* ☎ *757-9065.*

Eastern Panama

WITH KUNA YALA (SAN BLAS ISLANDS) & THE DARIÉN

WORD OF MOUTH

"We arrived by canoe and were greeted by about a hundred villagers, excited to see us and show us their island . . . It was the most incredible experience for all of us to witness firsthand their lifestyle and feel so welcomed."

—sactomama

"Darién is a wild, wonderful, and remote spot. We were sorry to leave."

—glover

By David
Dudenhoefer

THE EASTERN PROVINCES OF KUNA Yala and the Darién are Panama at its most pristine, with spectacular scenery, wildlife, and indigenous cultures that have barely changed since the first Spanish explorers arrived here more than five centuries ago. The region's riveting tropical nature ranges from the colorful diversity of Caribbean coral reefs to amazing birdlife of the rain forest. The traditional Kuna, Emberá, and Wounaan communities that live here offer a fascinating alternative to the modern world. The combination of nature and culture provides the ingredients for unforgettable journeys, on which you might imagine you've traveled back in time or perhaps to the very ends of the Earth. Yet most of the region's lodges lie within a 60-minute flight from Panama City, which is often followed by a dugout canoe trip over aquamarine waters or up a jungle-shaded river. And the flights themselves take you over vast expanses of pure jungle. When it comes to Kuna Yala and the Darién, more than in any other part of Panama, the adventure begins the moment you board your flight.

Nevertheless, true adventure has its price, and it's not for everyone. This region's remarkable but remote attractions lie far from the nearest paved road, convenience store, or ATM, and may require that you put up with conditions you wouldn't stand for at home. Tours and accommodations can be quite expensive; for the cost of a suite in Panama City you may have to settle for a thatched hut with a shared bathroom. You may also have to deal with insects or less-than-fantastic food, but the prize is exposure to extraordinary wildlife, splendid scenery, and unique indigenous cultures. Your adventure may include boat trips to breathtaking islands, jungle hikes, snorkeling over coral reefs, or witnessing ancient rituals. And at night you'll hear only the calls of jungle critters or the slosh of waves against coral.

6

ORIENTATION & PLANNING

ORIENTATION

Kuna Yala stretches along Panama's northeast coast from the Central Caribbean eastward to the border with Colombia, comprising everything from forested mountains to the sea beyond the San Blas Islands. The entire province was once called San Blas, but it is known now by it's indigenous name, Kuna Yala, which translates as "Land of the Kuna." Only one road penetrates the otherwise isolated province, a dirt track called the Camino Llano-Cartí that traverses its western end. The eastern half of the narrow indigenous territory borders the vast Darién province, the southern half of which holds Parque Nacional Darién, various smaller reserves, and two *comarcas* (indigenous territories). The Carretera Interamericana (Inter-American Highway) is a rutted, muddy track in the Darién, where it dead-ends at a frontier town called Yaviza, beyond which there are virtually no roads. Most travelers consequently fly in and out of both regions. There are daily flights to Kuna Yala and twice-weekly flights to the Darién.

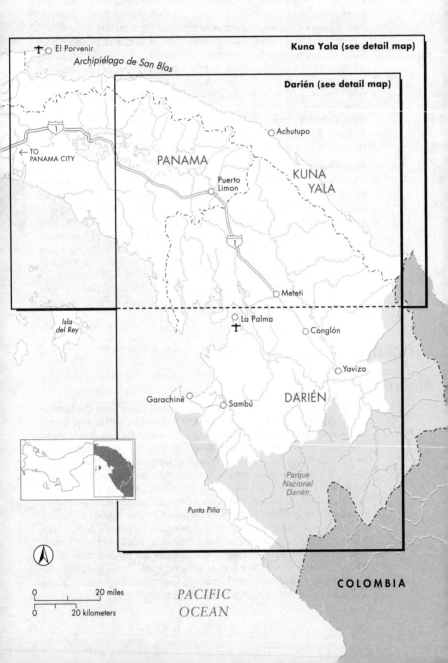

Eastern Panama

Caribbean
Sea

Kuna Yala (see detail map)

El Porvenir

Archipiélago de San Blas

Darién (see detail map)

Achutupo

PANAMA

← TO
PANAMA CITY

Puerto
Limon

KUNA
YALA

Meteti

Isla
del Rey

La Palma

Conglón

Yaviza

Garachiné

Sambú

DARIÉN

Parque
Nacional
Darién

Punta Piña

COLOMBIA

0   20 miles

0   20 kilometers

PACIFIC
OCEAN

TOP REASONS TO GO

INDIGENOUS CULTURES
Eastern Panama's Kuna, Emberá, and Wounaan Indian villages are amazingly traditional, colorful places that provide visitors with unforgettable, cross-cultural experiences.

SAN BLAS ISLANDS
The islands of Kuna Yala have ivory beaches shaded by coconut palms and washed by turquoise waters—scenery fit for the covers of travel magazines or the daydreams of snowbound accountants.

OCEAN TREASURES
Kuna Yala's crystalline sea holds countless coral reefs awash with living rainbows of fish and invertebrates, whereas the white-sand shallows of its islands are idyllic spots for a tranquil swim.

SPECTACULAR WILDLIFE
The eastern provinces' lush rain forests, mangrove swamps, and cloud forests together hold more about 500 bird species, and everything from crocodiles to capuchin monkeys.

FABULOUS FISHING
More than 250 sportfishing records have been set in the sea south of the Darién, which you can troll out of one of the world's best fishing lodges.

6

PLANNING

WHEN TO GO

It rains almost every afternoon from May to January in the Darién, though the rain lets up a bit in July and August. Most people consequently visit the region from January to May. Kuna Yala has similar seasons, though it gets less rain in September and October, and more in December and January. The sea tends to be rough here from January to April. The best diving months are August to November, when the seas tend to be calm and visibility is better.

GETTING AROUND

Motorized dugouts are the most common form of transportation in Kuna Yala and the Darién, where most people travel via jungle rivers. Some of the better lodges in Kuna Yala transport guests in small fiberglass boats, whereas the Tropic Star fishing lodge, in the southwest Darién, uses more seaworthy vessels. Most people simply fly in and out of Kuna Yala or the Darién, but you can charter a boat for longer trips in either of them. That can be expensive, and you'll need to speak Spanish or travel with a guide. The only way to travel directly between the two provinces is to spend a week hiking through the jungle.

WHAT TO DO

EXPLORE THE JUNGLE Whether you hike to a waterfall in the hills of Kuna Yala or climb to a Darién cloud forest, a trip into the inland of eastern Panama will reveal tropical nature in all its glory.

CONTEMPLATE A REEF The undersea scenery that awaits you in Kuna Yala includes colorful coral and sponge gardens where parrot fish, rays, and snappers swim past gently swaying sea fans.

A BIT OF HISTORY

The first European to visit this part of Panama was Rodrigo de Bastidas, a Spanish explorer who sailed along the San Blas Islands in 1501. The following year Christopher Columbus made it to the coast near El Porvenir on his final voyage to the Americas. In 1510 conquistador Vasco Nuñez de Balboa founded the first Spanish town in Central America, Santa María la Antigua del Darién, in a bay on the eastern end of Kuna Yala. Three years later Balboa departed from Santa María with a group of men to look for a sea that the Indians had told him lay to the south. After hiking through the Darién jungle for several weeks, Balboa reached the Gulf of San Miguel, where he became the first European to lay eyes on an ocean he dubbed "Pacific," referring to the gulf's calm waters. Shortly thereafter the Spaniards discovered gold in the mountains of the Darién; mines here became so productive that Spain soon brought in African slaves, as the region's indigenous population succumbed to old-world diseases and inhumane working conditions. Santa María was abandoned by the middle of the 16th century, when central Panama replaced the Darién as the focus of Spanish colonization, but Spain continued to exploit the region's gold mines for centuries.

When the conquistadors first arrived in Panama, the Kuna Indians lived in the jungles of northern Colombia, but in the 16th century they began moving up the coast into present-day Panama, where they eventually established their villages in the San Blas Islands. During the 17th and 18th centuries the Kuna allied themselves with French and English pirates, providing them safe harbor and food in exchange for protection from Spain. Kuna warriors often joined the pirates on raids of Spanish gold mines and ports. The Spaniards never subjugated the Kuna, who lived independently until the early 20th century, when the new Republic of Panama government tried to establish a military presence in the San Blas Islands. In 1925 the Kuna rebelled against the Panamanians, killing or capturing all government officials in their territory in what the Kuna call the Revolución de Tule. Subsequent negotiations led to the eventual creation of the Comarca Kuna Yala, an independent territory governed by the Congreso General Kuna, a democratic congress of Kuna chiefs. Decades later the Kuna model was copied by the Emberá and Wounaan Indians, who now share two *comarcas* in the eastern and western lowlands of the Darién, though they gained their autonomy through political pressure, rather than revolution.

VISIT A VILLAGE Many of this region's indigenous communities welcome tourists, and visiting one of them is exactly the kind of adventure that foreign travel should be.

SPOT NEW SPECIES The forests of Parque Nacional Darién are home to such rare and beautiful birds as the great green macaw, golden-headed quetzal, king vulture, and harpy eagle.

HOOK A
MONSTER

Guests at the Tropic Star Lodge regularly hook marlin weighing more than 300 pounds, tuna bigger than 200 pounds, and hard-fighting Pacific sailfish.

RESTAURANTS & CUISINE

This isn't the part of Panama you head to for epicurean delights. You can count on fresh seafood in Kuna Yala—and little else. If you don't eat seafood, you should mention it when you reserve and again when you arrive. Establishments usually offer lobster, except in March and April, when lobstering is prohibited. There aren't any restaurants to speak of in these provinces, so most all hotels include three meals in their rates.

ABOUT THE HOTELS

Most accommodations in this part of Panama range from comfortably

ENDS OF THE EARTH

Kuna Yala and the Darién may have pristine nature and traditional cultures, but both provinces lack ATMs and pharmacies, and they have only rudimentary clinics, simple stores, and few phones. While many Darién lodges have bilingual guides, few Kuna lodges have English speakers, though you can hire a guide in Panama City to accompany you. To visit Kuna Yala you must take a flight that leaves at 6 AM—at least they serve you breakfast when you arrive. Guides are essential for the forests and indigenous villages. Bring plenty of sunblock, insect repellent, water bottles, and, in the Darién, hiking boots.

6

rustic to downright primitive. Only Kuna Indians are allowed to own businesses in Kuna Yala, so lodges are pretty basic—no hot water, no air-conditioning, and only a few hours of electricity at night—but some of those thatched bungalows have priceless ocean views. There are a few nice Kuna lodges, but the less expensive ones tend to be dirty and serve lamentable food, which is why few are listed in this book. Only two Kuna lodges accept credit cards, and since most lack offices, the owners may meet guests at Albrook Airport the morning they fly to Kuna Yala to collect payment. The alternative is to visit Kuna Yala on a day trip and sleep at Coral Lodge, 26 km (16 mi) away, which has most of the comforts of home (⇨ *Santa Isabela in "The Canal & Central Panama" chapter)*. The lodging situation in the Darién ranges from refurbished Emberá Indian huts to the spacious, air-conditioned rooms at Tropic Star. One characteristic all lodges in this region share is that they are quite expensive for what you get, but rooms come with three meals, guided tours, and transportation, not to mention an unforgettable adventure. Rates usually drop by 10% for stays of two nights or more.

PAYING

The accepted currency is the U.S. dollar, which is often called the balboa, in reference to the long defunct national currency. Credit cards are not widely accepted and there are no ATM machines in this part of Panama.

WHAT IT COSTS IN U.S. DOLLARS					
	¢	$	$$	$$$	$$$$
RESTAURANTS	under $5	$5–$10	$10–$15	$15–$20	over $20
HOTELS	under $50	$50–$100	$100–$160	$160–$220	over $220

Restaurant prices are per person for a main course at dinner. Hotel prices are for two people in a standard double room, excluding service and 10% tax.

KUNA YALA (SAN BLAS)

The San Blas Archipelago and surrounding sea are the main attractions in Kuna Yala—an indigenous *comarca* (autonomous territory) stretching more than 200 km (120 mi) along Panama's northeast coast—but the traditional culture of the Kuna Indians is a close second. The comarca is composed of a thin strip of land dominated by a mountain range called the Serranía de San Blas and the more than 350 San Blas Islands that dot the coastal waters. Called the province of San Blas until Kuna leaders pushed the government to recognize their name for the area, Kuna Yala is a lush and stunning region of forest-cloaked mountains, white-sand beaches, vibrant coral reefs, and timeless villages. Your trip there can consequently combine time on heavenly islands, jungle hiking, handicraft shopping, and exposure to a proud and beautiful indigenous people.

With coral reefs surrounding nearly every island, snorkeling is practically obligatory in the archipelago. Most lodges include the use of snorkeling equipment in their rates, and all of them provide daily trips to beaches with reefs nearby. You don't need to swim to appreciate the area's beauty, though, since the scenery topside is just as impressive; coconut groves shade ivory sand, dugout canoes with lateen sails ply turquoise waters, and cane huts with thatched roofs make up island villages. Kuna Yala's greatest beauty, however, may be in the traditional dress of its women, whose striking clothing includes hand-stitched *molas* (appliqué fabric pictures), colorful skirts and scarves, and intricate beadwork on their calves and forearms. The Kuna's rich cultural heritage is apparent in everything from that traditional dress to the regular town meetings, when villagers gather in a thatched town hall as their *sahila* (chief) sings the songs of their oral history and religion.

EL PORVENIR

95 km (60 mi) northeast of Panama City.

The small island of El Porvenir, on the western end of Kuna Yala, is the most popular gateway into the indigenous territory, as it lies near a dozen other isles scattered around a deep bay. It is the official capital of Kuna Yala, though the indigenous government is decentralized and meets on other islands. El Porvenir is practically uninhabited, but has a police station, government offices, and an airstrip (no airport). Daily flights land here around 6:30 AM, when representatives of lodges on

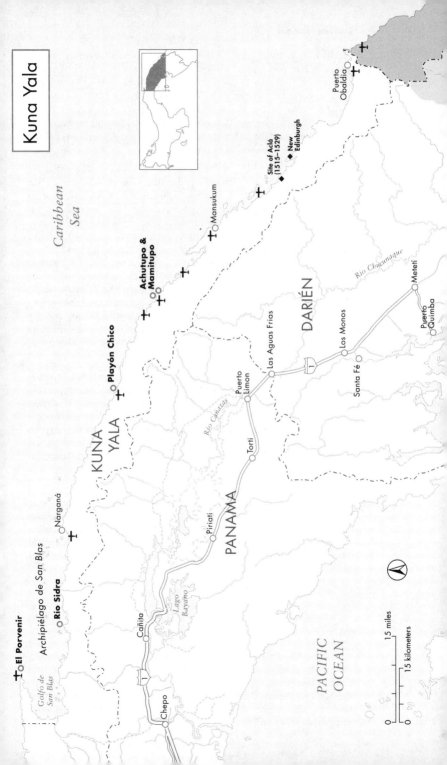

Kuna Yala

Caribbean
Sea

Puerto
Obaldía

Site of Acla
(1515–1529)
New
Edinburgh

Mansukum

Achutupo &
Mamitupo

Playón Chico

Río Chucunaque

DARIÉN

Metetí

Puerto
Quimba

Las Aguas Frías

Los Monos

Puerto
Limón

Santa Fé

KUNA
YALA

Nargana

Río Cañazas

Torti

Río Sidra

Archipiélago de San Blas

Priatí

PANAMA

El Porvenir

Golfo de
San Blas

Lago
Bayano

Cañita

Chepo

PACIFIC
OCEAN

15 miles

15 kilometers

nearby islands await guests. The island also has a rudimentary hotel, a decent beach, and a small museum, but for most travelers it is simply a place to get on and off the plane. El Porvenir has one of Kuna Yala's two museums, the **Museo de la Nación Kuna** (Kuna Nation Museum) (⊠ *El Porvenir* 🕾 *No phone* 🖼 *$1* ⊙ *Daily 8–4*), which is run by the Congreso Kuna. The simple museum housed in a cement building with a thatch roof near the police station has basic exhibits on Kuna culture and livelihood.

Several islands near El Porvenir hold crowded Kuna villages that are interesting places to visit, but the rudimentary hotels on them are the equivalent of backpackers' hostels. Kuna communities have neither sewage systems nor garbage collection, so the water around them is unsafe for swimming. A short boat trip beyond them takes you to uninhabited, white-sand cays shaded by coconut palms that are the area's big attractions. Those idyllic isles hold superb snorkeling, and two of them have rustic lodges that are the area's best options. This part of Kuna Yala has the highest concentration of islands, and receives more visitors than any other area, including seasonal visits by cruise ships. The people on these islands have seen a lot of tourists, and they consequently tend to greet you with the Kuna equivalent of "Come, buy my molas," or by setting their kids up for a $1 photo—the favorite pose is with a parakeet on their head. Don't be offended: it's always good-natured, and they truly need the money.

Just south of El Porvenir is the smaller island of **Wichub Huala,** which is packed with a mix of thatch-roof huts and cement buildings separated by narrow sand paths. As you explore this tiny island you can expect plenty of women to try to sell you handicrafts. The Hotel Anai occupies a small compound on the south side of the island. Just to the south of Wichub Huala is the slightly larger island of **Nalunega,** which has a comparable collection of huts and cement structures, including the archipelago's original lodge, the dilapidated Hotel San Blas.

Deep in the bay to the south of El Porvenir are the adjacent isles of **Cartí Suitupo,** where cruise ships often call, so they hold a collection of refreshment stands and plenty of handicraft hawkers. The main attraction here is the small **Museo Kuna** (Kuna Museum) (⊠ *Cartí Suitupo* 🕾 *No phone* 🖼 *$2* ⊙ *Daily 8–4*), a family-run museum in a typical Kuna home. The English-speaking guide provides detailed explanations of Kuna life and culture.

★ The most popular destinations are the uninhabited or sparsely inhabited islands to the east of the bay, which are perfect for snorkeling, swimming, and lounging. Most lodges near El Porvenir offer trips to **Isla Perro** (Dog Island), with a palm-lined beach and just one resident family. Just off the beach in shallow water lies a sunken metal boat that is home to hundreds of colorful tropical fish. It's a perfect snorkeling spot, with enough marine life to please experienced divers; just beyond it is large coral reef. The owners of the island charge $1 to visit it; they sell soft drinks, shells, and molas. There are several other islands near Isla Perro which also cost $1, such as Isla Pelicano, with similar bleached beaches and coral reefs offshore, but fewer visitors.

THE INDOMITABLE KUNA

Kuna Yala is home to approximately 50,000 Kuna Indians, who live in some 50 villages on islands and, in a few cases, the coast. The name Kuna Yala means "Land of the Kuna" in their language, and the Kuna have been living here for about four centuries, after migrating north from South America. The Kuna—sometimes spelled Cuna—are a fiercely independent people who were never conquered by Spain and who managed to wrest their autonomy from the Panamanian government more than 80 years ago. They call anyone who's not Kuna (including Panamanians) a *waga* (foreigner); wagas are not allowed to own either property or businesses in Kuna Yala. The province is ruled by a congress of chiefs, or *sahilas*, from each island, called the Congreso General Kuna, which sets the local law and works for the preservation of Kuna culture. But the chiefs also recognize the value of modern education, which is why the Congreso provides scholarships for Kuna Yala's best and brightest to study in Panama City. There are plenty of Kuna teachers, lawyers, and other professionals. Tens of thousands of Kuna live and work in Panama City, but they must continue to pay taxes to the comarca government; if they don't, they can be prohibited from leaving the Kuna Yala the next time they visit their families.

Most Kuna are hard-working fishermen and farmers who are happy to share their traditions with visitors. The province is very poor, and tourism dollars are an important supplement to the local income, which is based on the sale of coconuts, lobster, and other seafood. It is, however, very important to respect their laws and customs: avoid especially rudeness or nude sunbathing. Everyone is subject to Kuna law while in the province, and when the chiefs feel their people's interests are threatened, they quickly assemble the warriors, as they did when they rebelled against Panamanian authorities in 1925. Their independence and defense of tradition is exemplary among the region's indigenous nations—they are even more noteworthy when you consider that the Kuna are the second-smallest race of people in the world after the pigmies. So what, you may ask, do these diminutive warriors do for entertainment? They play basketball. It's the Kuna's favorite sport, and nearly every island has a basketball court.

WHERE TO STAY & EAT

Hotels here don't match the comfort and service levels offered farther east, but they are worth considering due to their proximity to Isla Perro and similar islands. They are expensive for rustic rooms with cold-water showers and nary a fan, but rates include three meals, transfers, daily tours to nearby villages and islands, and snorkeling equipment. Electricity comes from generators that run a few hours each night.

$$$ 　Cabañas **Coco Blanco.** Located on a splendid island about the size

Fodor'sChoice of a football field, called Ogobsibudup, this small lodge belongs to

★ the Sanchez family, who have four thatched *cabañas* on a stretch of lawn next to a sugar-sand beach. Each of those bungalows has cane walls, a wood floor, a tiny bathroom, and double or single beds. It's a gorgeous setting, and they do a better job than most of keeping rooms clean and insect-free. An Italian chef helped the Sanchez family improve the food, so you can expect it to be a notch above that of the competition. Hammocks are strung between palms, coral heads lie submerged offshore, and a long sandbar connects Ogobsibudup to a nearby island that you can wade to at low tide. The only problem is the staff don't speak English, but a cousin, Nelson Sanchez, does, and he can accompany tourists for about half what tour companies charge. **Pros: Great beach, clean, friendly, good food. Cons: Rustic, no English spoken.** ✉*Ogobsibudup* ☎*6715–2223 or 6700–9427* 🏠*Familia Sanchez, Ogobsibudup, Entrega General, El Porvenir cabanascocoblanco@yahoo.it* ⤴*4 bungalows* ⌂*In-room: no a/c, no phone, no TV. In-hotel: restaurant, beachfront, water sports, no elevator, no-smoking rooms* ▭*No credit cards* 🍽*FAP.*

> ### BRING SMALL CHANGE
>
> You may want to start stocking up on small bills a couple of days before you head to Kuna Yala or the Darién, because there is plenty to buy in the indigenous villages and an inevitable shortage of change. Even the lodges have trouble breaking big bills when you pay for drinks and other incidentals. Many people charge $1 to take their photo, especially in Kuna Yala. This may seem obnoxious, but for most of these people it is one of the only ways they can earn desperately needed cash. You should consequently try to spread your purchases and photo dollars around.

$$$ 🏨**Walidup Lodge.** This tiny hotel sits on a sparsely inhabited island 30 minutes east of El Porvenir by boat. The island is lovely, with an ivory beach and healthy coral reefs, with several comparable isles nearby. The elevated *cabañas* have cane walls, thatch roofs, rudimentary bathrooms, and small porches with ocean views. Decent meals are served in an open-air restaurant nearby, and the lodge provides snorkeling equipment and electricity for a few hours at night. It belongs to same owner as Kuna Niskua, which has serious problems with cleanliness and food, but Walidup seems to be better managed. **Pros: Great beach, reef, private bungalows. Cons: Rustic, no English spoken, rough boat trip.** ✉*Isla Walidup, east of El Porvenir* ☎*259–3471 or 6537–3071* ⊕*www.kunaniskua.com* ⤴*4 bungalows* ⌂*In-room: no a/c, no phone, no TV. In-hotel: restaurant, beachfront, water sports, no elevator, no-smoking rooms* ▭*No credit cards* 🍽*FAP.*

$ 🏨**Hotel El Porvenir.** This simple hotel next to the runway on El Porvenir is the best option for budget travelers. The rooms, in two cement buildings, are not at all spotless, but they have private bathrooms and tile floors. The advantages of staying here rather than the nearby islands are that the manager speaks some English, there's a beach with relatively clean water, it's quiet, and you can sleep a little later the day you fly out, since the runway is right there. **Pros: Beach, quiet. Cons: Basic, dark rooms, soft beds.** ✉*El Porvenir* ☎*221–1397 or 6653–7766* 📧*hotelporvenir@hotmail.com* ⤴*14 rooms* ⌂*In-room: no a/c, no phone, no TV. In-hotel: restaurant, beachfront, water sports, no elevator, no-smoking rooms* ▭*No credit cards* 🍽*FAP.*

SPORTS & THE OUTDOORS

All hotels include snorkeling equipment in their rates, but it isn't always in good shape. Walidup and Coco Blanco have fairly healthy reefs nearby, but the reefs near El Porvenir have been destroyed. The best dive spot in the area is **Isla Perro,** which has a shallow wreck surrounded by tropical fish. The healthiest reefs and other marine life in Kuna Yala are in the **Cayos Holandeses,** 30 km (19 mi) east of El Porvenir. You can hire a boat to take you there for $100–$120.

SHOPPING

Wherever you go in this area, somebody will try to sell you molas, shells, or other handicrafts. Molas usually cost $8 to $20; the Kuna are happy to barter.

UNDERWATER KUNA YALA

Scuba diving is illegal in Kuna Yala, but snorkeling is permitted, and the abundance of shallow, protected reefs makes it a world-class skin-diving area. Most of the more than 350 San Blas Islands have coral reefs nearby with massive brain, stag-horn, and other coral formations, as well as dozens of colorful sponge species, anemones, and sea fans. Hundreds of fish species inhabit the underwater gardens, including damselfish, angelfish, barracudas, eels, cornet fish, puffers, and nurse sharks. Conditions are best between August and November.

TO & FROM

Both Air Panama and Aeroperlas offer daily flights to El Porvenir, departing from Panama City's Albrook Airport at 6 AM and returning at 6:35 AM. There are no airline offices in Kuna Yala, so if you arrive by boat, or road, and want to fly out, you can board any flight if they have empty seats and purchase your ticket upon arrival in Panama City. El Porvenir is one part of Kuna Yala that you can reach by land via the Llano-Cartí road; it's a four-hour trip from Panama City to where you catch a boat to the islands; buses make the trip daily (⇨ *Essentials below*). Cartí is an hour from the Burbayar ecolodge, which drops guests off at the end of the road for a small fee (⇨ *Alto Bayano in "Central Panama" chapter*).

RÍO SIDRA

99 km (62 mi) northeast of Panama City, 19 km (12 mi) southeast of El Porvenir.

The first airstrip to the east of Porvenir is on the mainland near the islands of Río Sidra, Isla Maquina, and Isla Ratón. Río Sidra is the largest of those communities, and is a good place to see how the Kuna live, but the real attraction is on and around the sparsely populated islands farther out at sea. Those enchanting isles have immaculate beaches washed by crystalline waters and rustic lodges nestled amid coconut groves. The lodges are alternatives to accommodations near El Porvenir, since they are just as close to Isla Perro and have enough coral reefs nearby keep you snorkeling for days.

Isla Maquina, 10 minutes west of Río Sidra by boat, is the best community to visit in this area, since it is both more traditional and less cramped than nearby isles. The women here are known for producing quality molas, and the island gets few visitors, so it's a good place to shop. The **Río Masargandi,** a small river that flows out of the mountains near Río Sidra, provides access to the rain forest and a 30-foot waterfall. Local lodges offer half-day trips to the mainland for an additional charge. ⚠ They are best done early in the morning, to see wildlife; slather yourself with insect repellent.

WHERE TO STAY & EAT

None of the accommodations near Río Sidra offer private baths, and the bungalows are mini versions of the homes the Kuna have been living in for generations, with sand floors, cane walls, and thatch roofs. Those who can do without comforts are rewarded with phenomenal scenery and great diving.

$$$ 🛏 **Kuanidup.** This lodge on the charming little private island of Kuanidup has a small beach, hammocks strung between palm trees, and a
★ row of thatch huts. It's a good spots for snorkelers, since it is encircled by a coral reef teaming with life, but the accommodations are super rustic. The tiny huts with sand floors barely have enough room to walk around the bed, and they are so close to each other that there is little privacy. Everyone shares a few basic bathrooms in a cement building, which can get crowded when the hotel is full. The payoff is the island's beach and reef, and trips to nearby Isla Perro and Kuna communities. The food is okay, but their rack rate is high for what you get. They may give a discount rate if you book direct, or stay more than two nights. **Pros: Lovely island, great snorkeling, pristine area. Cons: Tiny, rustic rooms, shared bathrooms, can get crowded, no English spoken.** ✉ *Kuanidup, near Río Sidra* ☎ *6656–4673 or 6635–6737* ✍ *kuani9@ hotmail.com* 🛏 *10 huts* � *In-room: no a/c, no phone, no TV. In-hotel: restaurant, beachfront, water sports, no elevator, no-smoking rooms* ▤ *No credit cards* ⊙ *FAP.*

$ 🛏 **Cabañas Narasgandup.** Though quite rustic, this lodge has a great setting, and is one of the best deals in Kuna Yala. Its *cabañas* are traditional Kuna huts with foam mattresses on hewn-wood beds. Guests share typical Kuna bathrooms, with a barrel of water and a bowl to splash water on yourself instead of a shower, though there are flush toilets and septic tanks. The good news is that the huts are on a beautiful white-sand beach with clean water and coral reefs nearby. The owner, Ausberto, takes guests to Isla Perro and nearby communities, and has optional trips to a waterfall or a Kuna burial ground at an additional charge. **Pros: Great beach, friendly service, day trips. Cons: Very rustic, no English spoken.** ✉ *Ogobsibudup* ☎ *256–6239 or 6537–3071* ✍ *narasgandup@hotmail.com* 🛏 *6 bungalows* ☐ *In-room: no a/c, no phone, no TV. In-hotel: restaurant, beachfront, water sports, no elevator, no-smoking rooms* ▤ *No credit cards* ⊙ *FAP.*

SPORTS & THE OUTDOORS

The lodges near Río Sidra have good snorkeling nearby, and are just as close to Isla Perro (⇨ *El Porvenir above*) as the lodges near El Porvenir. They are considerably closer to the Cayos Holandeses, the best dive spot in the archipelago, though a boat there costs $80–$100.

TO & FROM AND LOGISTICS

Air Panama and Aeroperlas offer daily flights to Río Sidra's airstrip, on the mainland, departing from Panama City's Albrook Airport at 6 AM and returning at 6:45 AM. Río Sidra is usually the second stop, after Porvenir, so be sure to get off at the right airstrip. Río Sidra can also be reached by land, via the Llano-Cartí road (⇨ *To & From in "El Porvenir"*).

PLAYÓN CHICO

150 km (93 mi) northeast of Panama City.

This community of about 3,000 people lies just offshore, with a wooden footbridge connecting it to the mainland, where the town schools and landing strip are located. Most homes in Playón Chico are traditional thatched buildings, with small gardens shaded by breadfruit, mango, or citrus trees. There are a few cement structures scattered around the island, and the obligatory basketball court near the bridge. It was an important area in the 1925 revolution that led to Kuna autonomy, since it held one of the Panama military outposts that were captured by Kuna warriors. You may consequently see the Kuna flag displayed here, which is orange and yellow with a swastika—a traditional Kuna symbol—in the middle of it.

The lowlands around the landing strip hold the farms of local families, but a nearby hill is topped with the burial ground that resembles a small village. The Kuna bury family members together under thatched shelters complete with the tools and utensils that their spirits require to survive. Forested mountains stand beyond the farmland with trails leading to a waterfall. Insect repellent is essential on the mainland due to sand fleas. There are various uninhabited islands in the area that local lodges take guests to, but they aren't as nice the cays on the archipelago's western end.

WHERE TO STAY & EAT

$$$$ **Sapibenega.** With spacious rooms perched over the sea on a private
★ island surrounded by coral reefs, this is one of the better hotels in Kuna Yala. The only problem is that rooms are in wooden duplexes divided by cane walls that only go halfway up to the roof, so you can hear everything that happens next door. If you don't have noisy neighbors, the accommodations are nice, with good beds and large balconies over the sea. The hotel's kitchen is one of the best in Kuna Yala, and it's the only place with a real bar. Meals are served in a thatched gazebo over the water with a wonderful view of the mainland, or next to the open-air bar on the island. There's decent snorkeling around the island, and the lodge offers trips to beaches and healthier reefs,

as well as tours to Playón Chico, the burial ground, or the waterfall and jungle. **Pros: Big rooms, decent food, roomy island, good tours. Cons: Rooms lack privacy, no beach on island, little English spoken.** ✉*Playón Chico* ☎*215–1406 or 6676–5548* ⊕*www.sapibenega. com* 🛏*6 rooms* 🔑*In-room: no a/ c, no phone, no TV. In-hotel: restaurant, bar, water sports, no elevator, no-smoking rooms* ▭*MC, V* ❤*FAP.*

$$ 📷**Yandup.** With two kinds of wooden bungalows spread across a grassy island near the coast, Yandup is one of Kuna Yala's better deals. The nicest bungalows are octagonal structures over the water with high thatch roofs, basic bathrooms, and narrow porches. Two smaller bungalows in the middle of the island share a bathroom, and cost $40

> ### THE MOLA
>
> The Kuna are famous for their *molas:* fabric pictures—mostly geometric patterns, and, of late, animals—made using a reverse appliqué technique. Kuna women wear these designs on their blouses, but they are also used to decorate everything from purses to pillows to hot pads. Mola production is a major source of income in Kuna Yala, and you'll often see women sewing them as they chat with neighbors. Expect to pay $20 or more for a well-made mola. The most popular way to display them is framed on the wall; get this done in Panama City and it will cost you a fraction of what it would at home.

less. There's a small beach on a corner of the island with a reef nearby. Yandup offers the best selection of tours to the mainland and has one of the few English-speaking guides in Kuna Yala. Snorkeling equipment is not provided. The hotel occasionally has problems with sand fleas, so bring insect repellent. **Pros: Good rates, friendly guide, small beach. Cons: Sand fleas a problem April through December.** ✉*Playón Chico* ☎*261–7229 or 220–0467* ⊕*www.yandupisland.com* 🛏*10 bungalows* 🔑*In-room: no a/c, no phone, no TV. In-hotel: restaurant, no elevator, no-smoking rooms* ▭*No credit cards* ❤*FAP.*

SHOPPING
It would be a crime to visit Kuna Yala and not buy molas. Women usually set up shop outside their homes when tourists arrive in Playón Chico. Bring plenty of small bills and try to buy from various vendors, to benefit as many families as possible.

TO & FROM AND LOGISTICS
Both Air Panama and Aeroperlas offer daily flights to Playón Chico airstrip, departing from Panama City's Albrook Airport at 6 AM and returning at 7 AM.

ACHUTUPO & MAMITUPO

190 km (118 mi) northeast of Panama City.

Achutupo and Mamitupo are two medium-size communities on islands near the mainland in the eastern half of Kuna Yala. Their claim to fame is the fact that two of the best lodges in the archipelago are on private islands nearby. Since this is the most distant area that you can visit in Kuna Yala, it is the best destination if you're especially interested in Kuna culture or want to buy handicrafts. The people here see fewer tourists, and are thus more receptive to visitors. Though there are various uninhabited islands and plenty of coral near Achutupo, the beaches and diving aren't quite as spectacular as what you find around Isla Perro. It's possible to hike into the rain forest to a waterfall on the mainland (bring insect repellent). A tour to the local burial ground is another interesting option, especially early in the morning, when you may see Kuna women leaving gifts of food for their ancestors.

A short trip to the west of Achutupo is the rarely visited island community of **Aligandi,** which played an important role in the Kuna revolt of 1925. You'll see the orange-and-yellow Kuna flag displayed here, as well as a statue of the local revolutionary Simral Colman, one of the architects of the autonomous Kuna state.

WHERE TO STAY & EAT

$$$$
Fodor's Choice
★
Uaguinega *(Dolphin Island Lodge).* The best bungalows at this friendly lodge on a small island across a channel from Achutupo offer the nicest rooms in Kuna Yala. They have spacious, private bathrooms, high thatch roofs, and roomy back porches with splendid ocean views. Keep in mind when you are booking that the older, standard rooms lack the view and are slightly cramped; ask for a "junior suite." Those comfortable bungalows are spread along the shore of the grassy island with hammocks strung between palm trees. The only drawbacks are that the island lacks a beach and snorkeling isn't recommended there because of pollution from nearby Achutupo. However, excursions to nearby islands provide beach and snorkeling time, and the tour of Achutupo in English is excellent. Hikes into the forest and to a waterfall are an additional charge. **Pros: Spacious bungalows, friendly staff, good food. Cons: No beach, several subpar rooms.** ⊠*Achutupo* ☎*263–7780, or 263–1500* ✉*Apdo. 0823–00287, Panama City* ⊕*www.uaguinega. com* ⇱*17 bungalows, 3 rooms* ⚲*In-room: no a/c, no phone, no TV. In-hotel: restaurant, water sports, no elevator, public Internet, no-smoking rooms* ⊟*MC, V* ⏐⊙*FAP.*

$$$
★
Dadibe Lodge. This hotel occupies a tiny island that's hardly bigger than a basketball court: it must have looked like the ones in comics of castaways before locals undertook the construction of three thatched bungalows and an open-air restaurant on either side of it. The little island is little more than a swath of pale sand shaded by a dozen coconut palms with hammocks strung between them. The rooms are simple but comfortable, with two queen beds, cane walls, a tiny bathroom, and a balcony. You'll be lulled to sleep by the sound of soft waves washing beneath the floorboards. It's a great place to do nothing, but you can rent snorkeling equipment and take tours to nearby islands and the community of Aligandi, which few tourists visit. The guide here speaks decent English. **Pros: Beach, excursions, friendly. Cons: Tiny, remote island.** ⊠*Isla Dadibe* ☎*6500–2418, or 6487–6239* ⊕*www. dadibelodge.com* ⇱*3 huts* ⚲*In-room: no a/c, no phone, no TV. In-hotel: restaurant, beachfront, water sports, no elevator, no-smoking rooms* ⊟*No credit cards* ⏐⊙*FAP.*

SHOPPING

Shopping is inevitable here, since the streets of Achutupo and Aligandi fill with mola hawkers whenever tourists arrive. You can barter, but try to buy from various vendors so your money benefits more families. In addition to molas, you can often purchase beadwork, wood carvings, or shells.

TO & FROM AND LOGISTICS

Both Air Panama and Aeroperlas have daily flights to the area from Panama City's Albrook Airport. Air Panama flies to the airstrip at Mamitupo, and Aeroperlas flies to nearby Achutupo. Both depart from Albrook at 6 AM and return at 7 AM.

THE DARIÉN

The easternmost province of the Darién is Panama's wildest, least accessible region, home to extraordinary flora, fauna, and indigenous communities. Its remote eastern and southern extremes are dominated by mountain ranges cloaked with dense jungle, whereas its lowlands are drained by serpentine rivers that flow into the Pacific Ocean at the Golfo de San Miguel. Much of its wilderness is sequestered within Parque Nacional Darién and several nearby protected areas. Those preserves hold imposing, primeval forests dominated by massive tropical trees such as mahogany, strangler fig, and barrel-trunked *cuipos*. They are home to an array of wildlife that includes more than 450 bird species and everything from boa constrictors to strange and wonderful butterflies. While most of that wilderness is inaccessible, there are a half dozen spots that provide easy access to the region's wonders, the best of which are the field stations in Parque Nacional Darién and the Reserva Natural Punta Patiño.

The Darién is a lush and rainy region with muddy rivers lined with the tangled roots of mangroves and thick swaths of elephant grass. Flocks of macaws often pass noisily overhead, and the most popular form of transportation is the dugout canoe. The province's main rivers are dotted with dozens of Emberá and Wounaan Indian villages that probably look much as the region's towns did when Balboa hiked across the isthmus five centuries ago. Villages such as Mogue and La Marea are set up to receive visitors: a day or two spent in these communities can be an unforgettable experience. The Darién has Panama's best bird-watching and best sportfishing, but it is also a good destination for anyone interested in tropical nature and traditional cultures, or travelers who simply want to stray from the beaten path.

PARQUE NACIONAL DARIÉN

265 km (164 mi) southeast of Panama City.

Parque Nacional Darién (Darién National Park) stretches along the border of Colombia from Kuna Yala to the Pacific Ocean, covering 579,000 hectares—more than 1.4 million acres—of wilderness that is

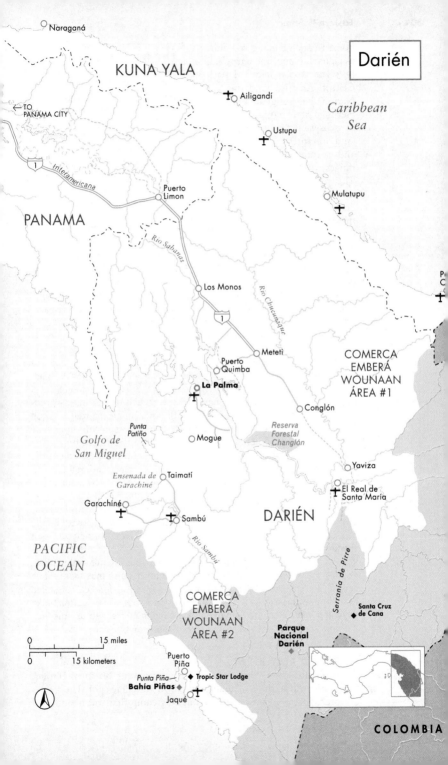

home to such endangered animals as jaguars, tapirs, and harpy eagles. It is the largest national park in Central America, and the United Nations has designated it a World Heritage site. It comprises a mosaic of ecosystems that includes lowland rain forest, jungle-lined rivers, and several *serranías* (mountain ranges) topped with cloud forests. The park's wildlife consequently ranges from vine snakes to brocket deer, and includes such creatures as the great green macaw and golden-headed quetzal among its nearly 500 bird species.

Fodor'sChoice
★
Despite its ample natural assets, few people make it to Parque Nacional Darién, which is remote and expensive to visit. The easiest and safest way to see the park is by taking a charter flight to **Santa Cruz de Cana,** usually called Cana, a former mining camp on the eastern slope of the Pirre Mountain Range that was converted to a field station by Ancón Expeditions in the 1990s. That rustic lodge is surrounded by pristine forest that is home to such spectacular birds as the crested guan and the blue and gold macaw, plus various species of monkeys and plenty of other jungle denizens. Ancón Expeditions also has a tent camp in the cloud forest a four-hour hike uphill from Cana, where guests usually spend a night. The only other part of the park that accommodates visitors is on the west side of the Pirre Mountain Range, at the **Estación Pirre,** a ranger station 14 km (8 mi) south of the town of El Real. El Real can be reached by commercial flights from Panama City, but from there it's a long hike, or a combination of a dugout trip and a hike during the rainy season, to the Pirre Station. The National Environment Authority, ANAM, rents bunks at the ranger station for $10 a night, but you have to bring your own sheets and towels, and register in El Real before hiking in. ■ TIP→ **Hiring a guide is recommended for this trip, since trails are not well marked, nobody speaks English, and the forest has plenty of poisonous snakes.** The ecotourism company **Advantage Tours** (⇨ *Essentials below*) can organize four-day hiking tours to Estación Pirre for about $750. ⚠ **Don't hike any deeper into the park than the area around the Pirre, because the border area can be unsafe.** ⊠ *14 km (8 mi) south of El Real* ☎ *299–6530* ☜ *$3.50*

THE DARIÉN GAP

The impenetrable jungle that covers the eastern and southern Darién occupies the only gap in the Pan-American Highway, which would otherwise run continuously from Alaska to Tierra del Fuego. The United States began promoting and underwriting that regional road system in the 1940s, but they asked Panama to leave the Darién Gap intact to help prevent foot-and-mouth disease from spreading north from South America. That disease was eradicated in Colombia decades ago, but Panama is in no hurry to complete a road into a neighboring country with numerous armed groups and drug traffickers.

WHERE TO STAY & EAT

$$$$
★
🏨 **Cana Field Station.** Nestled in the forest of Parque Nacional Darién, this rustic field station is Panama's top bird-watching spot. The rooms are pretty basic—it's a refurbished mining camp that was abandoned

THE EMBERÁ & WOUNAAN

The Darién is the territory of the Emberá and Wounaan Indians, two tribes with similar customs and languages that once fought one another but that now share an indigenous government that administers two *comarcas* (autonomous territories). Both groups have been called Chocó Indians, because their people also live in the Chocó region of northwest Colombia; groups migrated from there into eastern Panama generations ago. There are 10,000–15,000 Emberá and Wounaan living in remote villages scattered along the Darién's rivers, where they farm, fish, and hunt in nearby forests. Their traditional dress is a loincloth for men and a colorful skirt and necklaces for women. They often paint their upper bodies with a black dye made from juice of the *jagua* plant mixed with charcoal. However, the influence of Christian missionaries has led most Indians to abandon traditional dress. Various villages regularly receive tourists, for whom they put on the traditional costume. Their handicrafts include animal figures carved from *cocobolo* wood or the seed of the *jagua* palm, and lovely rattan baskets and platters dyed with natural colors.

early in the 20th century—with screened windows, battery-powered lights, and two single beds. Guests share several bathrooms, and the lodge generates electricity for a few hours in the morning and at night. The reward for roughing it is constant exposure to nature and access to rare wildlife. The lodge can only be visited on five- or eight-day packages that include charter flights from Panama City, daily tours led by expert birding guides, and hearty meals served family-style. Guests need to be in decent shape. **Pros: In jungle, great birding, expert guides. Cons: Rustic, isolated, expensive.** ⊠ *Santa Cruz de Cana* ☏ *269–9415* ⊕ *www.Anconexpeditions.com* 🛏 *12 rooms* ⚘ *In-room: no a/c, no phone, no TV; In-hotel: restaurant, no elevator, no-smoking rooms* ⊟ *MC, V* ⚑ *FAP.*

SPORTS & THE OUTDOORS

Santa Cruz de Cana is Panama's top birding spot, with more than 400 species, many of which are found nowhere else in the country. Those feathered creatures include four kinds of macaw, six parrot species, about two dozen types of hummingbirds, and such rare species as the blue-fronted parrolet, orange-breasted falcon, and golden-headed quetzal. The field station's experienced guides, well-maintained trails, and cloud-forest camp facilitate seeing as many species as possible during your stay.

TO & FROM AND LOGISTICS

The only way in and out of Santa Cruz de Cana is on charter flights arranged by Ancón Expeditions that depart twice a week from Panama City's Albrook Airport.

LA PALMA

176 km (109 mi) southeast of Panama City.

La Palma is the capital of the Darién, and is the perfect illustration of just how undeveloped this province is. Situated at the end of a peninsula where the Tuira River flows into the Golfo de San Miguel, La Palma has just one commercial street with a handful of government offices, some basic restaurants, and a couple of rustic hotels. La Palma itself has little to offer visitors, but because it has one of the Darién's few airstrips, it is the point of access for the private nature reserve of Punta Patiño and nearby Emberá villages. The closest attraction to La Palma is **Fuerte de Boca Chica,** the ruins of a Spanish fortress built in the 18th century to defend the gold mines upriver from pirates. It's a five-minute boat ride from the town dock, where a boat can usually be hired for $10–$15. A fascinating option for adventurous travelers is to

★ spend a few nights in the Emberá village of **La Marea,** a 48-km (30-mi) boat ride southeast of La Palma. **Advantage Tours** (⇨ *Essentials below)* offers four-day tours to La Marea that include nights in rustic accommodations and hiking tours into the nearby rain forest to look for wildlife such as blue-and-gold macaws and harpy eagles. You can get a

★ quicker look at Emberá life at the village of **Mogue,** on a bank of a river of the same name, about 30 km (19 mi) southwest of La Palma. That trip takes you up a winding river through a thick forest to a traditional Emberá community; you can include a hike to the nearby rain forest, which has plenty of wildlife. A boat from La Palma to Mogue costs $100–$200, depending on group size. The tour company **Eco Circiutos** (⇨ *Essentials below)* has a three-day tour to Mogue with overnights in traditional Emberá dwellings.

The most comfortable accommodations near La Palma are in the **Reserva Natural Punta Patiño,** a private nature reserve 32 km (20 mi) southwest of town managed by ANCÓN, the country's biggest conservation group. A former ranch in the midst of ecological restoration, the reserve consists of 26,000 hectares (65,000 acres) of mature forest and former pastureland. It is home to crab-eating raccoons, crocodiles, capybaras (the world's largest rodent), and hundreds of bird species, ranging from the delicate mangrove swallow to the mighty harpy eagle. Ancón Expeditions offers three- and four-day tours at the Punta Patiño Lodge, on the north end of the reserve.

WHERE TO STAY & EAT

$$$$ ⛺ **Punta Patiño Lodge.** This ecolodge inside the Reserva Natural Punta
★ Patiño sits on a hill with views of secondary forest and the sea. Its wooden bungalows are the Darién's nicest accommodations, with private (cold-water) baths, air-conditioning, and balconies with hammocks that are good bird-watching platforms. Hearty meals are served family-style in the old ranch house, which has a small bar. Ancón Expeditions offers three- and four-night packages at the lodge that include transportation, guided hikes, a boat trip to Mogue, access to beaches, and optional horseback riding. **Pros: Nice rooms. Cons: Quite secluded.** ✉*Punta Patiño* ☎*269–9415* ⊕*www.Anconexpeditions.com* ⤳*10*

bungalows &In-room: no phone, no TV; In-hotel: restaurant, bar, no
elevator, no-smoking rooms ☰MC, V ☯Closed Oct. and Nov.

¢ 🖻 **Baiquirú Bagará.** The best accommodations in La Palma, which isn't
saying much, are at the back of the long wooden building over the
water. The rooms are basic, with ceiling fans; several rooms have large
windows and balconies with views of the bay. Half of them share common bathrooms; those with private baths also have air-conditioning.
Pros: Nice views. Cons: Some rooms lack private bath. ⊠*La Palma,
Calle Principal* ☎299–6224 ☷12 rooms &In-room: no a/c (some),
no phone, no TV. In-hotel: no elevator, laundry service, no-smoking
rooms ☰No credit cards.

TO & FROM AND LOGISTICS

Flying is the easiest way to reach La Palma, and Air Panama flies
there on Monday and Friday mornings, departing from Panama City's
Albrook Airport at 10:45 AM and returning at 11:25.

BAHÍA PIÑAS

230 km (143 mi) southeast of Panama City.

Nestled in the southwest corner of the Darién, just north of the Jaque
River, lies remote and beautiful Bahía Piñas, a deep bay with a rocky
coastline where mountains are covered with virgin rain forest and the
aquamarine sea teems with an array of marine life. In fact, it's the
marine life that draws most people to Piñas Bay, since the quality of
its fishing is legendary, with more than 250 world fishing records set
in the surrounding waters. Zane Grey fished in the area in the 1950s,
and John Wayne and Lee Marvin hooked plenty of billfish here in the
'60s. Since then, thousands of anglers have followed in their wake,
heading out to Zane Grey Reef in search of sailfish and blue, black,
and striped marlin.

Within the bay is the town of Piñas, home to an indigenous community
that has traditionally farmed and fished—though most now work at
the nearby Tropic Star Lodge. That fishing lodge is not only the local
employer but also a benefactor: it makes donations to the local schools
and clinic, and ensures that the surrounding area will remain wild by
protecting a vast expanse of jungle. The lodge's owners also started a
conservation organization, Conomar, which successfully lobbied the
Panamanian government to ban commercial fishing within 20 mi of
the coast near Piñas, which should help to protect the country's best
fishing for many years.

WHERE TO STAY & EAT

$$$$ ╳🖻 **Tropic Star Lodge.** The Tropic Star Lodge offers access to world-class
Fodor'sChoice sportfishing in a comfortable, friendly atmosphere. Built in the 1960s
★ by a Texas millionaire, Tropic Star has since evolved into one of the
world's great fishing lodges. Daily fishing on the lodge's 31-foot Ber-
trams are included in package rates, as are three meals per day. Hiking,
kayaking, and massages are also available. Spacious, air-conditioned
guestrooms have two double beds or one king bed, large baths, and a

porch with views of Piñas Bay. No TVs or phones disturb the tranquillity. Hearty meals, which always include fresh seafood, are served in the air-conditioned restaurant or by the pool. A minimum one-week stay is required during the high season from December to March, but three- and four-night packages are available the rest of the year, when limited nonfishing packages are available for travelers interested in the tropical nature that surrounds the lodge. **Pros: Lots to do. Cons: Expensive if you're not fishing.** ☒*Piñas Bay* ☎*232–8375, 800/682–3424 in the U.S.* ✆*635 N. Rio Grande Ave., Orlando, FL 32805* ⊕*www.tropicstar.com* ⮐*18 rooms* ♿*In-room: safe, no phone, no TV. In-hotel: restaurant, room service, bar, pool, beachfront, water sports, no elevator, laundry service, public Internet, no-smoking rooms* ▭*AE, MC, V* ☾*Closed Oct. and Nov.*

SPORTS & THE OUTDOORS

The ocean around Piñas Bay has Panama's best fishing, with sailfish and blue and black marlin biting most of the year. Black marlin average 300 to 400 pounds in the area (and sometimes top 1,000 pounds); tuna weighing between 100 and 200 pounds are common. December through February are the best months for black marlin—many people book their weeks at the Tropic Star Lodge for then years in advance. The marlin fishing drops off in March, improving again from May to September. Sailfish are common in the area from April to September. Fishing at Tropic Star is catch-and-release for billfish, whereas eating fish such as tuna and dolphin are served for dinner. There are plenty of big tuna and dolphin in the area, and smaller fighters such as roosterfish, wahoo, and mackerel inshore, where you can also troll deep for snapper and grouper.

TO & FROM AND LOGISTICS

Flights to Bahía Piñas depart from Panama City's Albrook Airport in the morning (times vary), and are included in the Tropic Star Lodge packages, as is transportation in Panama City.

EASTERN PANAMA ESSENTIALS

TRANSPORTATION

BY AIR

The only way to get to most parts of Kuna Yala and the Darién is to fly. The domestic airlines Air Panama and Aeroperlas offer daily flights to half a dozen airstrips in Kuna Yala that depart at 6 AM and return between 35 and 75 minutes later. ■TIP➔**Flights often land at several airstrips, so make sure you get off at the correct one!** Air Panama has flights to La Palma and El Real on Monday and Friday mornings. Charter flights to Santa Cruz de Cana and Bahía Piñas are arranged by lodges based in those locations. There are no airline offices in these regions, and no airports in Kuna Yala—only simple airstrips. El Real, Santa Cruz, and Bahía Piña have similar setups, but La Palma has a tiny airport: **Aeropuerto Ramon Xatruch** ☒*2 km [1.2 mi] south of La Palma* ☎*299–6217.*

Airlines **Aeroperlas** ☎315–7500 ⊕ www.aeroperlas.com. **Air Panama** ☎316–9000 ⊕ www.flyairpanama.com.

BY BOAT

Boat transportation is included in the rates of all Kuna Yala hotels and lodges near La Palma. Private boats can be hired at Kuna Yala lodges for special trips, such as to Cayos Holandeses or to nearby areas, but those trips can cost $100–$200. Boats can also be hired through the Hotel Baquirú Bagará in La Palma for trips to nearby Emberá communities for $100–$200.

BY BUS

The only part of Kuna Yala that can be reached by road is the western El Porvenir area, via the rough Llano–Cartí road. **Denesio Ramos** (☎6695–3229) runs a simple bus service to Cartí, where boats can be hired to lodges near El Porvenir and Río Sidra, departing from Panama City's Plaza Cinco de Mayo daily at 5 AM and returning at 10 AM. Several buses depart from Panama City's Albrook Bus Terminal every morning for Yavisa, where boats can be hired to El Real, but it's a rough 10- to 12-hour trip, and neither town has a decent hotel.

CONTACTS & RESOURCES

EMERGENCIES & TELEPHONE NUMBERS

Hotels near El Porvenir have cell-phone reception, but all other areas of Kuna Yala have only pay phones—usually two per island. The larger islands have police stations with radios to call Panama City for help in an emergency and tiny centros de salud (health centers) that can provide first aid. ■TIP→ **You should fly to Panama City if you have serious health problems in either Kuna Yala or the Darién.** La Palma has the Darién's only hospital, the small Hospital San José La Palma. Lodges in Santa Cruz de Cana and Bahía Piñas have satellite phones to call Panama City for an air ambulance in case of emergencies.

Emergency Services **Ambulance** *La Palma* ☎299–6219. **National police** *La Palma* ☎299–6200.

Hospitals **Hospital San José La Palma** ✉*Calle Principal, La Palma* ☎299–6219.

INTERNET

The only place in Kuna Yala with Internet access is Uaguinega (Dolphin Island Lodge). In the Darién, the Tropic Star Lodge has Internet access.

MAIL & SHIPPING

If you write postcards or letters in this region, you would be wise to mail them when you get back to Panama City. There are no courier services here.

Post Office **Correo Nacional (COTEL)** ✉*El Porvenir* ☎*No phone.* **COTEL** ✉*Calle Principal, La Palma* ☎299–6208.

MONEY MATTERS

There are no ATMs in this part of Panama, so bring all the money you'll need during your trip. Stock up on small bills in Panama City, since the indigenous vendors, and even some hotels, are usually short on change.

SAFETY

Visiting Parque Nacional Darién without a guide is not advisable. The area near the border of Colombia is dangerous, as armed guerrilla groups have been known to slip into Panamanian territory; some hikers were kidnapped there years ago. When hiking through the forest, be careful where you put your hands and feet, since there are plenty of palms with spiny trunks, some stinging insects, and the occasional poisonous snake.

TOURS

The outdoor outfitter **Xtrop** offers three- and six-night sea-kayak tours of Kuna Yala that include camping on uninhabited islands. The small **AAA Ecotravel** can arrange custom tours to Kuna Yala. The French company **San Blas Sailing** offers four-day to three-week cruises on large sailboats that visit such hard-to-reach areas as the Cayos Holandeses. **Ancón Expeditions** has two field stations deep in the Darién: Punta Patiño, near La Palma, and Santa Cruz de Cana, at the edge of Parque Nacional Darién. They also offer a two-week, trans-Darién hiking expedition through the jungle for true adventurers. **Advantage Panama** offers short tours to a rustic lodge in the Emberá village of La Marea, near La Palma, and the Chucanti Field Station, in the mountains north of the Golfo de San Miguel. **Eco Circuitos Panama** leads hiking and kayaking tours to Kuna Yala and a three-day Darién adventure with nights at the Emberá village of Mogue. **Exotic Adventures** organizes trips to Kuna Yala and expeditions to Wounaan and Emberá Villages in remote areas of the Darién that few outsiders have seen.

Tour Companies Advantage Panama ☎ *223–9283 or 6676-2466* ⊕ *www.advantagepanama.com.* **Ancón Expeditions** ☎ *269-9415* ⊕ *www.Ancónexpeditions.com.* **AAA Ecotravel** ☎ *263-8918 or 263-0953* ⊕ *www.aaaecotravel.com.* **Eco Circuitos Panama** ☎ *314-0068* ⊕ *www.ecocircuitos.com.* **Exotic Adventures** ☎ *223–9283 or 6733-6068* ⊕ *www.panamaexoticsadventures.com.* **San Blas Sailing** ☎ *260-0044* ⊕ *www.xtrop.com.* **Xtrop** ☎ *317-1279* ⊕ *www.xtrop.com.*

Outdoor & Learning Vacations

7

WORD OF MOUTH

"Panama is a gloriously beautiful country. It has a mix of cultures, pristine beaches, fantastic birding and wildlife viewing opportunities, fabulous jungles and more."

—cmcfong

PLANNING YOUR ADVENTURE

CHOOSING A TRIP

With hundreds of choices for special-interest trips to Central America, there are a number of factors to keep in mind when deciding which company and package will be right for you.

How strenuous do you want your trip to be? Adventure vacations are commonly split into "soft" and "hard" adventures. Hard adventures, such as strenuous treks (often at high altitudes) or Class IV or V rafting, generally require excellent physical conditioning and previous experience. Most hiking, biking, canoeing/kayaking, and similar soft adventures can be enjoyed by persons of all ages who are in good health and are accustomed to a reasonable amount of exercise. A little honesty goes a long way—recognize your own level of physical fitness and discuss it with the tour operator before signing on.

How far off the beaten path do you want to go? Depending on your tour operator and itinerary, you'll often have a choice between relatively easy travel and comfortable accommodations or more strenuous daily activities accompanied by overnights spent in basic lodgings or at campsites. Ask yourself if it's the *reality* or the *image* of roughing it that appeals to you. Be honest, and go with a company that can provide what you're looking for.

Is sensitivity to the environment important to you? If so, determine if it is equally important to your operator. Does the company protect the fragile environments you'll be visiting? Are some of the company's profits designated for conservation efforts or put back into the communities visited? Does it encourage indigenous people to dress up (or dress down) so that your group can get great photos, or does it respect their cultures as they are? Many of the companies included in this chapter are actively involved in environmental conservation and projects with indigenous communities. Their business' future depends on keeping this fragile ecological and cultural mix alive.

Are there hidden costs? Make sure you know what is and is not included in basic trip costs when comparing companies. International airfare is usually extra. Sometimes domestic flights in-country are too. Is trip insurance required, and if so, is it included? Are airport transfers included? Visa fees? Departure taxes? Gratuities? Although some travelers prefer the option of an excursion or free time, many, especially those visiting a destination for the first time, want to see as much as possible. Paying extra for a number of excursions can significantly increase the total cost of the trip. Many factors affect the price, and the trip that looks cheapest in the brochure could well turn out to be the most expensive. Don't assume that roughing it will save you money, as prices rise when limited access and a lack of essential supplies on-site require costly special arrangements.

MONEY MATTERS

Tours in Central America can be found at all price points, but local operators are usually the best deal. Tours that are run by local people are generally cheaper, and also give the greatest monetary benefit to the local economy. These types of tours are not always listed in guidebooks or on the Internet, so often they have to be found in person or by word of mouth. You really have to do your research on every operator, no matter the cost, to be sure you are getting exactly what you need out of them. The payoff in terms of price and quality of experience can be great if you find the right match for your needs.

On the other end of the spectrum, the large (often international) tour agencies such as Abercrombie & Kent, G.A.P. Adventures, International Expeditions and others are generally the most expensive; however, they provide the greatest range of itinerary choices and highest quality of services. If you are a traveler who likes to have every creature comfort provided for, look for tour operators more toward this end of the spectrum.

LODGING

The cost of lodging can vary greatly within Panama. Independent travelers tend to favor budget hotels and hostels costing little more than a few dollars a night, whereas luxurious five-star hotels geared to package tourists are becoming as common as howler monkeys. Your preference will help determine what type of tour operator is best for you. Most multiday tours include lodging, often at a discounted rate, and they generally have options that accommodate most budgets through a number of hotels. On the other hand, many hotels have their own tour agency or will sell tours at a discounted rate to particular agencies. You can book through either one—it just depends on the specific tours and hotels that interest you. Considering the small size of most Central American countries, most sights can be seen on a one-day tour, which allows you to leave your luggage at the hotel for less hassle.

EQUIPMENT

Good gear is essential: sturdy shoes, a small flashlight or headlamp, rain gear, mosquito protection, and medicine are all things you should bring with you no matter what kind of tour you're taking. Tour operators can generally provide equipment, but the quality of this equipment can vary. If you're using provided equipment, ask your operator for a written statement of the gear to be used. When you arrive, check that your expectations have been met, and complain if they haven't. Prices on equipment purchased in Central America tend to be significantly more expensive (roughly 20% to 40% higher) than in North America or Europe. If you prefer or require a specific brand of equipment, bringing your own is a good idea. Airlines accommodate most types of equipment and will likely have packing suggestions if you call ahead. For instance, most bicycle shops can take apart and box up your bike for plane transport. Shipping equipment to Central America tends to be expensive, and if you're not using an agency such as FedEx or DHL (actually, even if you are!) expect the unexpected.

ADVENTURE & LEARNING VACATIONS

ADVENTURE TOURS

MULTISPORT

Season: Year-round
Locations: Central Panama, Veraguas, Chiriquí, Bocas del Toro, San Blas, Bocas del Toro, Chagres National Park
Cost: From $1,245 for eight days from Panama City for package tours; from $180 to $700 for daily
Tour Operators: G.A.P. Adventures, Explorers' Corner, Mountain Travel Sobek, Journeys Latin America, Seakunga, BikeHike Adventures, Coral Lodge, Futura Travel, Islas Secas, Tranquilo Bay, Venture Outside

Hordes of kayak-toting adventure companies recently made their way to Panama from Costa Rica and have opened up a whole new frontier of Central America touring. Explorers' Corner has 10-day kayaking trips led by two Kuna Yala guides that take you camping in San Blas for a total of 96 to 129 km (60 to 80 mi) of paddling, while Mountain Travel Sobek makes almost the same trip in nine days. G.A.P. Adventures' eight-day Kayak Panama samples the best of the Caribbean coast with five days exploring San Blas and another few days inland hiking and rafting around the Mamoni river basin. Similarly, Seakunga Adventures' eight-day kayaking trip centers on San Blas, but adds rafting and hiking in Chagres National Park. For a bit more of a challenge, Journeys Latin Americas' Camino Real Trek takes you from the Pacific to the Caribbean, an 80 km (50 mi) transcontinental trek in the footsteps of Spanish conquistadors, with time to stop in Chagres National Park, Panama City, and Portobelo.

The companies Bikehike Adventures, Futura Travel, and Venture Outside run 1- to 2-week tours that combine biking, hiking, rafting, snorkeling, kayaking, and other sports. The high-end eco-lodges Coral Lodge, Islas Secas, and Tranquilo Bay offers packages that include skin diving, fishing, and other activities in pristine areas.

BIKING

Season: Year-round
Locations: Central Panama, Chiriquí
Cost: $25 for a half-day tour, $233 per day for country tour
Tour Operators: Bikehike Adventures, Venture Outside

Panama has mountain-biking potential, but few companies offer biking tours. Bikes can be rented in Panama City, El Valle de Antón, Boquete, and Bocas del Toro. The companies Bikehike Adventures and Venture Outside run 9- to 14-day tours that combine mountain biking with kayaking, hiking, rafting, snorkeling, and other outdoor activities.

KAYAKING

Season: Year-round
Locations: Central Panama, Chiriquí, Bocas del Toro, Kuna Yala
Cost: $75 to $185 per day
Tour Operators: Panama Rafters, Venture Outside, Xtrop

Many coastal hotels have sit-on-top kayaks available for their guests, but serious kayakers should consider taking a tour with the outfitter Xtrop, which offers a sunset paddle on the canal, day trips down the lower Chagres River, and multiday sea-kayak tours of Kuna Yala. The U.S. organization Venture Outside has programs that combine sea kayaking with other outdoor activities; one includes kayaking in both oceans. Panama Rafters provides support for experienced white-water kayakers who want to paddle the rivers of Chiriquí province.

WHITE-WATER RAFTING

Season: May to March
Locations: Central Panama, Chiriquí
Cost: $70–$175
Tour Operators: Aventuras Panama, Chiriquí River Rafting, Panama Rafters

Panama has spectacular white-water rafting, with warm-water rivers that flow through stretches of rain forest. Most of the country's rivers are only high enough for rafting between July and December, but the two best ones, the Río Chagres and Río Chiriquí Viejo, can usually be navigated through March. The Chagres is a Class II–III river near Panama City that requires no rafting experience and flows through pristine rain forest. One- and two-day Chagres trips are run by Aventuras Panama. The Chiriquí Viejo is a wilder river that flows through some of the country's most beautiful scenery, with lush forests, canyons, and a waterfall, but it requires prior rafting experience during the rainy months. Panama Rafters and Chiriquí River Rafting run trips on the river. Chiriquí River Rafting also runs trips on the Estí (Class II/III), Gariche (Class II/III), Dolega (Class II/III), and Chiriquí (Class III) rivers between June and November.

BEACHES & OCEAN SPORTS

BEACHES

Season: Year-round
Locations: Bocas del Toro, San Blas, Veraguas
Cost: from $1,295 for seven days from Panama City
Tour Operators: Adventure Life, G.A.P. Adventures, Journeys Latin America, Seakunga, Costa Rica Expeditions, Willie's Tours, Wildland Adventures

Escape the crowds on Panama's Caribbean coast where many spots are only reachable by boat or charter jet. The San Blas Islands are some of the cleanest and most serene islands in the world and are home to the Kuna Yala Indians. There are just a few small guesthouses here, but the waters are crystal clear and the marine life is abundant. Every tour operator in the country will be able to arrange kayaking or sailing trips. For something more special, the Punta Caracol resort in the Bocas del Toro archipelago offers affordable overwater bungalows.

CLOSE UP

Tour Operators

Abercrombie & Kent ⊠ *1520 Kensington Rd., Oak Brook, IL 59801* ☎ *630/954-2944 or 800/323-7308* ⊕ *www.abercrombiekent.com.*

Adventure Life ⊠ *1655 S. 3rd St. W, Suite 1, Missoula, MT 59801* ☎ *800/344-6118* ⊕ *www.adventure life.com.*

AmeriSpan ⊠ *117 S. 17th Street, Suite 1401, Philadelphia, PA 19103* ☎ *215/751-1100* ⊕ *www.amerispan. com.*

Bikehike Adventures ☎ *888/805-0061 in the U.S., 0808/234-1403 in the U.K.* ⊕ *www.bikehike.com.*

Costa Rica Expeditions ⊠ *Box 25216, SJO 235, Miami, FL 33102* ☎ *506/710-8016* ⊕ *www.costarica expeditions.com.*

Cruise West ☎ *888/851-8133 in the U.S.* ⊕ *www.cruisewest.com.*

Emerald Planet ⊠ *1706 Constitution Ct., Fort Collins, CO 80526* ☎ *888/883-0736* ⊕ *www.emerald planet.com.*

Exotic Birding ☎ *877/247-3371 in the U.S.* ⊕ *www.exoticbirding.com.*

Explorers' Corner ⊠ *1865 Solano Ave., PMB 926, Berkeley, CA 94707* ☎ *510/559-8099* ⊕ *www.explorers corner.com.*

Field Guides ☎ *800/728-4953 in the U.S.* ⊕ *www.fieldguides.com.*

G.A.P. Adventures ⊠ *E. 19 Charlotte St., Toronto, Ontario M5V 2H5* ☎ *416/260-0999 or 800/465-5600* ⊕ *www.gapadventures.com.*

Geographic Expeditions ⊠ *1008 General Kennedy Ave., Box 29902, San Francisco, C A94129* ☎ *415/922-0448 or 800/777-8183* ⊕ *www.geoex.com.*

International Expeditions ⊠ *One Environs Park, Helena, AL 35080* ☎ *800/633-4734 or 205/428-1700* ⊕ *www.ietravel.com.*

Journeys Latin America ⊠ *12 & 13 Heathfield Terr., Chiswick, London, UK W4 4JE* ☎ *020/8747-8315* ⊕ *www. journeylatinamerica.co.uk.*

Linblad Expeditions ☎ *800/397-3348 in the U.S.* ⊕ *www.expeditions.com.*

Mesoamerican Ecotourism Alliance (MEA) ⊠ *4076 Crystal Ct., Boulder, CO 80304* ☎ *800/682-0584 or 303/440-3362* ⊕ *www.travelwithmea.org.*

Mountain Travel Sobek ⊠ *1266 66th St., Suite 4, Emeryville, CA 94608* ☎ *800/682-0584 or 888/687-6235* ⊕ *www.mtsobek.com.*

M/V Coral Star ☎ *866/924-2837 in U.S.* ⊕ *www.coralstar.com.*

Pesca Panama ☎ *6614-5850, or 800/946-3473 in the U.S.* ⊕ *www. pescapanama.com.*

Seabourn ☎ *800/929-9391 in the U.S.* ⊕ *www.seabourn.com.*

Seakunga Adventures ⊠ *908-1112 W. Pender St., Vancouver, British Columbia V6E 2S1* ☎ *800/781-2269 or 604/893-8668* ⊕ *www.seakunga.com.*

Tauck ☎ *800/788-7885 in the U.S.* ⊕ *www.tauck.com.*

Venture Outside ☎ *207/846-0637 in the U.S.* ⊕ *www.ventureoutside.org.*

Victor Emanuel Adventure Tours (VENT) ☎ *800/328-8368 in the U.S.* ⊕ *www.ventbird.com.*

Wildland Adventures ⊠ *3516 N.E. 155th St., Beulah, WA 98155* ☎ *800/345-4453 or 206/365-0686* ⊕ *www.wildland.com.*

Willie's Tours ☎ *506/843-4700* ⊕ *www.willies-costarica-tours.com.*

PANAMA-BASED

Advantage Panama ✉ *Llanos de Curundú, Panama City* ☏ *223–9283 or 6676–2466* ⊕ *www.advantagepanama.com.*

Ancon Expeditions ✉ *Calle Elvira Mendez, Edificio El Dorado No. 3, Panama City* ☏ *269–9415* ⊕ *www.anconexpeditions.com.*

Aventuras Panama ✉ *El Dorado, Panama City* ☏ *260–0044* ⊕ *www.aventuraspanama.com.*

Bocas Water Sports ✉ *Calle 3, Bocas del Toro* ☏ *757–9541* ⊕ *www.bocaswatersports.com.*

Boquete Tree Trek ✉ *Plaza Los Establos, Av. Central, Boquete* ☏ *720–1635* ⊕ *www.aventurist.com.*

Buzos Boca Brava ✉ *Marina, Boca Chica* ☏ *775–3185 or 6600–6191* ⊕ *www.scubadiving-panama.com.*

Buzos de Azuero ✉ *Calle Principal, Pedasí* ☏ *995–2405* ⊕ *www.dive-n-fishpanama.com.*

Canal Bay Tours ✉ *Bahia Balboa Building, Panama City* ☏ *209–2009* ⊕ *www.canalandbaytours.com.*

Canopy Adventure ✉ *Calle a la Mesa, El Valle de Antón* ☏ *983–6547* ⊕ *www.adventure.panamabirding.com.*

Chiriquí River Rafting ✉ *Av. Central, Boquete* ☏ *720–1505* ⊕ *www.panama-rafting.com.*

Coiba Adventure Sportfishing ✉ *Pedregal, David* ☏ *999–8108, 800/800–0907 in the U.S.* ⊕ *www.coibadventure.com.*

Coral Dreams ✉ *Aeropuerto, Contadora* ☏ *6536–1776* ⊕ *www.coraldreams.com.*

Dive Panama ✉ *Old Bank, Bocas del Toro* ☏ *6567–1812.*

Del Toro Surf ✉ *Bocas del Toro* ☏ *6570–8277.*

Eco Circuitos Panama ✉ *Calle Amador, Panama City* ☏ *314–0068* ⊕ *www.ecocircuitos.com.*

Futura Travel ✉ *Centro Comercial Camino de Cruces, Panama City* ☏ *360–2030* ⊕ *www.extremepanama.com.*

Golf in Panama ✉ *Balboa, Panama City* ☏ *305/735—8054 in U.S.* ⊕ *www.golfinpanama.com.*

Isla Grande Dive Center ✉ *Isla Grande* ☏ *6501–4374 or 232–6994.*

Land Sea Air Adventures ✉ *Playa de Bocas, Bocas del Toro* ☏ *6684–4418* ⊕ *www.land-sea-air-adventures.com.*

Las Perlas Fishing Charters ✉ *Hotel Contadora, Contadora* ☏ *6689–4916*

Margo Tours ✉ *Calle 50, Panama City* ☏ *302–0390* ⊕ *www.margotours.com.*

Nattur Panama ✉ *Colón* ☏ *442–1340* ⊕ *natturpanama.com.*

Pacific Marine Tours ✉ *San Francisco, Panama City* ☏ *226–8417* ⊕ *www.pmatours.net.*

Panama Audubon Society ✉ *Altos de Curundú, Panama City* ☏ *232–5977* ⊕ *www.panamaaudubon.org*

Panama Birding ✉ *Clayton, Panama City* ☏ *264–5720, 800/930–3397 in U.S.* ⊕ *www.panamabirding.com.* **Panama Canal Fishing** ✉ *Clayton, Panama City* ☏ *315–1905 or 6699–0507* ⊕ *www.panamacanalfishing.com.*

Panama Divers ✉ *Portobelo, Central Panama* ☏ *314–0817 or 448–2102.*

Panama Fishing & Catching ✉ *Panama City* ☏ *6622–0212* ⊕ *www.panamafishingandcatching.com.*

Continued on page 318

Tour Operators

Panama Rafters ✉ *Av. Central, Boquete* ☎ *720–2712* ⊕ *www. panamarafters.com.*

Panama Surf ✉ *El Dorad, Panama City* ☎ *279–0108, 805/617–4612 in U.S.* ⊕ *www.panama-surf.com).*

Panama Surf Tours ✉ *Panama City* ☎ *6671–7777* ⊕ *www.panamasurf tours.com.*

Panoramic Panama ✉ *Quarry Heights, Panama City* ☎ *314–1417* ⊕ *www.panoramicpanama.com.*
Pesantez Tours ✉ *Plaza Balboa, Panama City* ☎ *223–5374.*

San Blas Sailing ✉ *Balboa, Panama City* ☎ *314–1800* ⊕ *sanblassailing.com.*

Scuba Coiba ✉ *Santa Catalina, Veraguas* ☎ *202–2171* ⊕ *www.scuba coiba.com.*

Scuba Panama ✉ *El Dorado, Panama City* ☎ *261–3841.*

Starfleet Scuba ✉ *Bocas del Toro* ☎ *757–9630* ⊕ *www.starfleetscuba. com.*

Xtrop ✉ *Balboa, Panama City* ☎ *317– 1279* ⊕ *www.xtrop.com.*

LODGES & RESORTS
Burbayar Lodge ✉ *Alto Bayano, Central Panama* ☎ *390–6674* ⊕ *www. burbayar.com.*

Coral Lodge ✉ *Satna Isabell, Central Panama* ☎ *317–6754 or 202–3795* ⊕ *www.corallodge.com.*

Coronado Golf & Beach Resort ✉ *Coronado, Central Panama* ☎ *240– 3137* ⊕ *www.coronadoresort.com.*

Finca Lérida ✉ *Alto Quiel, Boquete, Chiriquí* ☎ *720–2285* ⊕ *www. fincalerida.com.*

Gone Fishing ✉ *Boca Chica, Chiriquí* ☎ *6573–0151* ⊕ *www.gonefishing panama.com*

Hacienda del Mar ☎ *264–1787, 866/433–5627 in U.S.* ⊕ *www. haciendadelmar.net.*

Hacienda del Toro ☎ *757–9158 or 6612–9159* ⊕ *www.haciendadeltoro.com.*

Islas Secas Resort ✉ *Islas Secas, Chiriquí* ☎ *805/729–2737 in the U.S.* ⊕ *www.islassecas.com*

Los Quetzales Lodge and Spa ✉ *Cerro Punta, Chiriquí* ☎ *771–2182* 🖷 *771–2226* ⊕ *www.losquetzales.com*

Morro Negrito Surf Camp ✉ *Isla Ensenada, Chiriquí* ☎ *202–9131, 760/632–8014 in U.S.* ⊕ *www.panama surfcamp.com.*

Panama Big Game Fishing Club ✉ *Isla Boca Brava, Chiriquí* ☎ *6674– 4824, 866/281–1225 in the U.S.* 🖷 *305/653–2322 in the U.S.* ⊕ *www. panamabiggamefishingclub.com.*

Posada Ecológico Cerro de la Vieja ✉ *Churuguí Grande, Central Panama* ☎ *983–8900* ⊕ *www.posadaecologica. com.*

Sierra Llorona Panama Lodge ✉ *Sierra Llorona, Central Panama* ☎ *442–8104* ⊕ *www.sierrallorona.com.*

Tranquilo Bay ✉ *Isla Bastimen- tos, Bocas del Toro* ☎ *380–0721 or 713/589-6952 in U.S.* ⊕ *www. tranquilobay.com*

Tropic Star Lodge. ✉ *Piñas Bay, Darién* ☎ *232–8375, 800/682–3424 in the U.S.* ⊕ *www.tropicstar.com.*

CRUISING
Season: Year-round; more options December–May
Locations: Panama Canal, Gulf of Chiriquí, San Blas Islands
Cost: From $90 for a half-day canal transit to $900 per day for luxury cruises
Tour Operators: Canal & Bay Tours, Cruise West, Linblad Expeditions, MV *Coral Star*, Pacific Marine Tours, San Blas Cruises, Seabourn, Tauck, Windjammer

Cruise ships regularly transit the Panama Canal, but most provide little exposure to the country's natural and cultural wonders. The exceptions are companies running cruises on smaller ships that include stops at uninhabited islands and indigenous villages. Tauck Tours offers an 11-day Panama Canal and Costa Rica cruise that combines a canal transit with visits to indigenous villages and Pacific islands. Linblad Expeditions runs 8-day cruises that transit the canal and stop at natural sites such as Isla de Coiba and parks in Costa Rica. Seabourn runs two-week luxury cruises that combine Panama with Costa Rica and Belize. Cruise West runs less expensive 10-day tours that visit parks and villages in Panama and Costa Rica, but don't transit the canal.

You can take advantage of less expensive cruising options in Panama, such as weekly partial transits of the canal, or monthly full transits, for a fraction of what a day on a cruise ship costs. Canal & Bay Tours and Pacific Marine Tours offer canal cruises every Saturday year-round, with additional cruises on Thursday and Friday from January to April. The 115-foot MV *Coral Star* runs one-week cruises to Isla de Coiba and surroundings that can include sportfishing, skin diving, snorkeling, hiking, and sea kayaking. Windjammer runs one-week sailing cruises of the Central Caribbean coast and Kuna Yala. San Blas Sailing offers 4-day to 3-week sailing cruises to Kuna Yala that visit such remote and pristine areas as the Cayos Holandeses.

DIVING
Season: Year-round (conditions vary by region)
Locations: Central Caribbean, Gulf of Panama, Isla Iguana, Isla Coiba, Gulf of Chiriquí, Bocas del Toro, San Blas Islands
Cost: From $50 for two-tank boat dive to $440 per day for Isla Coiba dive cruise
Tour Operators: Bocas Water Sports, Buzos Boca Brava, Buzos de Azuero, Coral Dreams, Coral Lodge, Dive Panama, Islas Secas Resort, Land Sea Air Adventures, MV *Coral Star*, Isla Grande Divers, Panama Divers, Panama Diving Tours, San Blas Cruises, Scuba Coiba, Scuba Panama, Starfleet Scuba, Windjammer

Panama has some of the best diving in the Caribbean and eastern Pacific, and is the only country in the world where you can dive both the Pacific and the Atlantic on the same day. The country's most impressive dive destination is remote Isla de Coiba, part of a Pacific marine national park that protects thousands of acres of reef and more than 700 fish species. The 115-foot MV *Coral Star* has one-week dive cruises to the island, whereas Scuba Coiba and Panama Divers offer less expensive trips that include nights in rustic rooms on the island. The country's second-best dive region is the Golfo de Chiriquí, which holds the spectacular Islas Secas, Islas Ladrones, and Parque Nacional Marino Golfo de Chiriquí. Diving here is available at the Islas Secas Resort, or on less expensive trips with Buzos Boca Brava, in Boca Chica, or Panama Diving Tours, in David. Another impressive spot is Isla Iguana, on the east coast of the Azuero Peninsula, where Buzos de Azuero offers inexpensive scuba and skin-diving trips. More accessible sites in the Golfo de Panama can be explored from Isla Contadora with Coral Dreams, or out of Panama City with Scuba Panama, which also offers diving in the Panama Canal and a two-oceans-in-one-day dive trip.

Whereas Panama's Pacific dives offer encounters with schools of big fish, the Caribbean has more coral and sponge diversity, and warmer water. The most accessible Caribbean diving areas are Portobelo and Isla Grande, about two hours from Panama City, where Panama Divers, Scuba Panama, and the Isla Grande Dive Center provide access to miles of barrier reef, sunken ships, and a plane wreck. The most pristine reefs are found in the Escribano Bank, which you can dive out of Coral Lodge, in Santa Isabel. To the east of there lie the San Blas Islands of Kuna Yala, where scuba diving is prohibited. Indigenous lodges include snorkeling trips in their rates, but skin divers can visit more pristine reefs and islands on cruises with San Blas Sailing, or Windjammer. Panama's other important Caribbean region is Bocas del Toro, which has dozens of dive spots near an array of accommodations. The dive operators Bocas Watersports, Dive Panama, Land and Sea Adventures, and Starfleet Scuba offer dives at impressive spots such as the Cayos Zapatillas and Tiger Rock.

FISHING

Season: Year-round (best from January to March)
Locations: The Darién, Gulf of Panama, Azuero Peninsula, Chiriquí, Gatún Lake
Cost: From $300 per day for Gatún Lake to $1,000 per day for fishing cruises, or lodge packages
Tour Operators: Buzos de Azuero, Coiba Adventure Fishing, Gone Fishing, Hacienda del Mar, Islas Secas Resort, Land Sea Air Adventures, Las Perlas Fishing Charters, MV *Coral Star*, Panama Big Game Fishing Club, Panama Canal Fishing, Panama Fishing and Catching, Pesca Panama, Tropic Star Lodge

Popular legend has it that Panama means "abundance of fish" in a native language. Though the Caribbean fishing is average, Panama's Pacific waters have some of the best fishing in the western hemisphere, if not the world, with massive blue and black marlin, Pacific sailfish, tuna, wahoo, dolphin, roosterfish, mackerel, and other fighters in good supply. The country's top fishing spot is remote Bahía Piñas, where the Tropic Star Lodge provides comfortable access to phenomenal fishing. More than 250 world fishing records have been set there, and black marlin average 300 to 400 pounds, whereas tuna between 100 and 200 pounds are regularly hooked. The Golfo de Chiriquí, to the west, is a close second, with lots of marlin, sailfish, and other big fighters near the Hannibal Banks, Isla Montuosa, and Isla de Coiba, where catch-and-release fishing is permitted. Those waters can be fished from the 115-foot MV *Coral Star*, or out of lodges with Gone Fishing, Panama Big Game Fishing Club, Pesca Panama, and Coiba Adventure Fishing. Between those two regions lie the Pearl Islands, where good angling is accessible from Hacienda del Mar, on Isla San José, and Isla Contadora, where Las Perlas Fishing Charters offers affordable trips. Panama Fishing and Catching has charters in the Gulf of Panama and Pacific estuaries out of Panama City. Buzo de Azuero, in Pedasí, has inexpensive charters on the Azuero Peninsula's "Tuna Coast." The best months for marlin are December through March, whereas Pacific sailfish run from April to July. Tuna and other fish are most abundant from December to April. A less expensive alternative to deep-sea fishing is light-tackle angling on Gatún Lake, in the Panama Canal, which has lots of feisty peacock bass, snook, and tarpon. Panama Canal Fishing can guarantee you'll catch plenty of fish there year-round, and has family packages.

SURFING

Season: Year-round
Locations: Central Pacific, Azuero Peninsula, Veraguas, Chiriquí, Bocas del Toro
Cost: $75–$100 per day
Tour Operators: Casa Cayuco, Del Toro Surf Tours, Morro Negrito Surf Camp, Panama Surf, Panama Surf Tours

Though it doesn't have as many breaks as nearby Costa Rica, Panama has world-class surf, and several companies offer access to remote breaks that few people get to. Most of Panama's surf spots are reef breaks, which makes it a better destination for experienced surfers than novices, but the country's surf companies offer lessons at its beaches and less treacherous reef breaks. Though there are a few breaks in Central Panama, most notably at Isla Grande and Playa El Palmar, the country's best surf is at Playa Venao, on the Azuero Peninsula, and Santa Catalina, to the west of it. The best Pacific surfing is from June to December, when the waves regularly break overhead, whereas the Caribbean tends to get its best surf from November to March and July and August.

Because most of Panama's breaks are quite remote, often requiring a boat to reach, surf tours are an excellent option. Panama Surf Tours, run by long-time resident Kenny Myers, has a rustic lodge in Santa Catalina and offers guided trips to the country's best spots. Panama Surf, which is run by several Panamanian surfers, provides a comparable selection of surfing package tours. The Morro Negrito Surf Camp, on an island in the Golfo de Chiriquí, provides access to five isolated breaks that hardly anyone rides. There are several beaks in Bocas del Toro, some of which are a mere 10-minute boat ride from the town of Bocas. The local outfitter Del Toro Surf can provide transport to surf breaks and arrange inexpensive packages in Bocas del Toro, whereas the rustic Casa Cayuco lodge provides access to isolated breaks that few surfers get to.

ECOTOURISM

HIKING & WALKING

Season: Year-round
Locations: Central Panama, Chiriquí, the Darién
Cost: $30 to $175 per day for expeditions
Tour Operators: Advantage Panama, Ancon Expeditions, Burbayar, Eco Circuitos Panama, Finca Lérida, Finca Suiza, Futura Travel, International Expeditions, Los Quetzales Lodge and Spa, Panoramic Panama, Panama Birding, Pesantez Tours, Posada Ecológico Cerro de la Vieja, Sierra Llorona Panama Lodge

Hiking and walking are a big part of exploring Panama's forests, and the options for getting into the country's woods range from an early-morning hike through Panama City's Parque Natural Metropolitano to a two-week trek through the jungles of the Darién. All the country's nature-tour operators offer guided hikes and bird-watching trips in parks near Panama City, but only Ancon Expeditions and Eco Circuitos Panama offer multiday trips that include camping in indigenous communities and the rain forest. Ancon Expeditions' Trans-Darién Explorer and Camino Real treks are the most challenging and adventurous expeditions available, but there are plenty of shorter hikes through pristine forest. For forest hikes intermixed with bird-watching, a canal transit and an introduction to the Emberá Indians, try International Expeditions. Various lodges with private reserves and trail systems serve as excellent bases for day hikes, such as Burbayar, Finca Lérida, Los Quetzales Lodge, Posada Ecológica Cerro de la Vieja, Sierra Llorona Panama Lodge, and lodges run by Ancón Expeditions and Panama Birding. Some of the most popular trails are in the mountains, namely in El Valle de Antón and Chiriqui's Volcán Barú and La Amistad national parks, near Boquete and Cerro Punta.

BIRD-WATCHING

Season: Year-round (more species October–March)
Locations: Central Panama, Chiriquí, the Darién
Cost: From $80 for a day tour to $380 per day for package tour
Tour Operators: Advantage Panama, Ancon Expeditions, Eco Circuitos Panama, Exotic Birding, Field Guides, Nattur Panama, Panama Audubon Society, Panama Birding, Panoramic Panama, Pesantez Tours, VENT

With more than 960 bird species in an area smaller than South Carolina, Panama is a bird-watchers Valhalla. It is not only home to such rare and spectacular species as the blue and gold macaw, resplendent quetzal, and harpy eagle, it is a place where you can witness natural phenomena such as hawk and vulture migrations, or island rookeries where tens of thousands of seabirds gather. The best months for birding are October to April, when northern migrants boost the local population, so you might spot an emerald toucanet and a Baltimore oriole in the same tree.

There are birds everywhere in Panama, but the best birding regions are Central Panama, the mountains of western Chiriquí Province, and the jungles of the Darién. Central Panama has excellent lodges in the middle of the wilderness, such as Birding Panama's Canopy Tower and Canopy Lodge, the Sierra Llorona Panama Lodge, and the Burbayar. The mountain valleys of Boquete and Cerro Punta, in Chiriquí, have many birds you won't find in other parts of the country, including the resplendent quetzal, which you might see at Finca Lérida, Finca Hartmann, and Los Quetzales Lodge. The easternmost province of the Darién has Panama's most impressive bird diversity, including four macaw species, half a dozen parrot species, and harpy eagles, but it is a most expensive area to visit. The country's best birding is found at Ancon Expeditions' Cana Field Station.

Ancon Expeditions has excellent guides and a "birds of Panama" tour that is comprehensive and affordable. Advantage Panama, Eco Circuitos, and Nattur Panama offer comparable trips. Panama Birding has the country's best birding lodges and good guides. Panoramic Panama and Pesantez Tours specialize in shorter trips. Field Guides and Exotic Birding sell Ancon Expeditions' tours, but send an expert guide along, whereas VENT does the same using Panama Birding's lodges. The Panama Audubon Society also offers inexpensive weekend excursions that are open to foreigners. There are also a few good independent birding guides in El Valle de Antón, Boquete, and Cerro Punta.

CANOPY TOURS
Season: Year-round
Locations: El Valle de Antón and Boquete
Cost: $50–$60 for two-hour tour
Tour Operators: Boquete Tree Trek, Canopy Adventure

Panama's canopy tours can send you gliding through the forest canopy on zip-line cables strung between platforms high in trees, using harnesses attached to pulleys. The tours are adrenaline rushes that provide bird's-eye views of the jungle. Though several hotels have "canopy tours" that take people gliding over hotel grounds, there are only two canopy tours in mature forests: Canopy Adventure, in El Valle de Antón, and Boquete Tree Trek, in Chiriquí.

CULTURAL TOURISM

Season: Year-round
Locations: San Blas Islands
Cost: from $545 for three days from Panama City
Tour Operator: Journeys Latin America

Journeys Latin America offers a three-day trip to the San Blas Islands, where you'll flit between islands in traditional dugout canoes and stay in thatched huts belonging to the Kuna Yala Indians. If you're lucky, you'll be taken to the communal houses of the Sahilas, or chief, where local laws, which are completely autonomous from Panama, are made.

VOLUNTEER VACATIONS

Season: Year-round
Locations: San Lorenzo National Park
Cost: from $1,499 for seven days from Panama City
Tour Operator: Emerald Planet

Emerald Planet's focus is the Panamanian community of Achiote. You will help the villagers attract ecotourists, who generally stop just short of this village, while also helping villagers to preserve their traditions. The project is in conjunction with the Conway School of Landscape Design and the Massachusetts Audubon Society. Days are divided between volunteering and diverse ecotours in San Lorenzo National Park, where single-day bird counts have exceeded 300 species.

UNDERSTANDING PANAMA

PANAMA AT A GLANCE

FAST FACTS

Name in local language: Panamá (stress last syllable)

Capital: Panama City (local name: Panamá)

National anthem: Himno Nacional

Type of government: Constitutional democracy

Population: 3.2 million (2007 est.)

Median age: 26

Life expectancy: 75

Ethnic groups: Mestizo (mixed indigenous and Spanish) 70%, black 14%, white 10%, indigenous 6%.

Major languages: Spanish (official), English (14%), indigenous tongues.

Religion: Roman Catholic 85%, Protestant 15%

Internet domain: .pa

"I don't want to go into history; I want to go into the Canal Zone"
—General Omar Torrijos (Panamanian strongman, in 1970s)

GEOGRAPHY & ENVIRONMENT

Longitude: 80 00 West °

Latitude: 9 00 North °

Land area: 78,200 square km (slightly smaller than South Carolina)

Terrain: Five mountain ranges, highest point 3,475 meters above sea level, most coastal areas flat, 2,490 km of coastline

Islands: More than 1,600

Natural hazards: Rip currents present a danger on beaches with waves; poisonous snakes and insects are what you'll need to watch out for in the forests; and Portuguese man-of-wars are a slight worry in the waters of the Caribbean Sea.

PANAMA ONLINE

- *www.visitpanama.com*
- *www.panamatours.com*
- *www.pancanal.com*
- *www.focuspublicationsint.com*

BOOKS & MOVIES

Historical Books. *The Path Between the Seas,* by David McCullough, chronicles the conception and construction of the Panama Canal. *The History of Panama,* by Robert C. Harding, is a relatively up-to-date overview with information on developments since the 1989 U.S. invasion. *The Sack of Panama,* by Peter Earle, tells the story of pirate Henry Morgan's razing of Panamá Viejo. *Divorcing the Dictator: America's Bungled Affair with Noriega,* by Fredrick Kempe, is a fascinating tale of Manuel Noriega's rise to power, with the help of the U.S. military and CIA, and the crisis that led to the U.S. invasion of Panama in 1989. *The Panama Canal: The Crisis in Historical Perspective,* written by Walter LaFeber in 1989, examines the canal's history with a critical perspective of U.S.-Panama relations on the eve of the U.S. invasion.

Photography Books. *Images of an Age: Panama and the Building of the Canal,* by William Friar, offers an overview of the canal's construction and operation accompanied by historic and contemporary photos. *Portrait of the Panama Canal,* by Jerome D. Laval, is a collection of historic photos taken during canal construction, accompanied by explanatory text.

Novels. *The Tailor of Panama* is a sly and entertaining John le Carré novel set in the city by the canal. Though it can be hard to find, Graham Greene's *Getting to Know the General* is a fascinating portrait of General Omar Torrijos and Panama in the 1970s. *Cup of Gold,* John Steinbeck's first novel, is historical fiction about Henry Morgan and the invasion of Panamá Viejo.

Children's Books. *Panama Canal: The Story of how a Jungle was Conquered and the World Made Smaller,* written by Elizabeth Mann and illustrated by Fernando Rangel, uses colorful pictures to explain the canal's construction for kids twelve and over. Fully illustrated *Panama,* by Dana Meachen Rau, introduces the country to readers ages eight to ten and. *Into Wild Panama,* by Elaine Pasco and Jeff Corwin, a spin-off of Jeff Corwin's *Animal Planet* show, is aimed at readers aged eight to twelve.

Nature & Wildlife. *A Guide to the Birds of Panama,* by Robert S. Ridgely and John A. Gwynne, is a field guide with good color illustrations and detailed descriptions. *Field Guide to the Orchids of Costa Rica and Panama,* by Robert L Dressler, calls out a significant sampling of Panama's orchid species. *Neotropical Rainforest Mammals,* by Louise Emmons, has color illustrations and distribution maps that include all the mammals found in Panama's forests. *A Day on Barro Colorado Island,* written by Marina Wong and Jorge Ventocilla, and published by the Smithsonian Tropical Research Institute (STRI), is a handy little guide to the plants and animals common to the rain forests of the canal area. You can pick it up at STRI bookstores on Cerro Ancón or Barro Colorado.

Movies. The film version of *The Tailor of Panama* was directed by John Boorman and stars Pierce Brosnan, Dylan Baker, and Jamie Lee Curtis. It's an entertaining story, with nice shots of Panama City and the canal. *Nova: A Man, a Plan, a Canal–Panama,* is a 60-minute documentary on the canal's construction. It was produced in 1987, and narrated by David McCullough, who wrote the seminal book on the subject. *Biography–Manuel Noriega: Rise and Fall of Panama's Strongman* chronicles Noriega's rise from a nobody in Panama's national guard and fall to America's number one enemy. *The Panama Deception* is an award-winning documentary released in 1992 that is highly critical of George H.W. Bush's invasion of Panama and of the U.S. media's coverage of it.

CHRONOLOGY

2000 BC Indigenous societies farm and produce pottery in Panama's Pacific lowlands.

AD 500 The region's varied indigenous nations are capable of creating complex ceramic and gold work.

1501 Rodrigo de Bastidas leads the first group of Europeans to visit Panama, sailing along what is now the Caribbean coast of the Darién and Kuna Yala.

1502 Christopher Columbus sails along Panama's western Caribbean coast, from Bocas del Toro to Kuna Yala, on his fourth and final voyage to the Americas.

1510 The town of Santa María de La Antigua del Darién, the first Spanish settlement on the American mainland, is founded in what is now eastern Kuna Yala.

1513 Vasco Nuñez de Balboa leads an expedition through the Darién jungle to the Gulf of San Miguel, where he is the first European to see the Pacific Ocean.

1514 Spain's King Ferdinand sends 22 vessels and 1,500 men, led by Pedrarias Davila, to establish a major Spanish presence in Panama.

1519 Pedrarias Davila moves the Spanish settlement from Santa María to the site of a Pacific Coast fishing village—now known as Panamá Viejo.

1532 After various attempts, Francisco Pizarro defeats Incan forces and captures the emperor of the Andes, the Incan king Atahualpa, whom he ransoms for tons of gold and silver, then murders. Pizarro sails to Panama with his booty, establishing the country's role as a vital link between Spain and the mineral-rich Andes.

1597 Spain moves its Caribbean port in Panama from Nombre de Dios to Portobelo after repeated pirate attacks. Panamá Viejo is one of the wealthiest cities in the western hemisphere.

1671 Henry Morgan, who had captured Portobelo several years earlier, marches an army across the isthmus and sacks Panamá Viejo. Spanish authorities subsequently move the city to what is now Panama City's Casco Viejo.

1739 Due to frequent pirate attacks, Spain begins shipping its South American gold and silver around Cape Horn instead of moving it through Panama, marking the end of Panama's glory days.

1821 Panama gains independence from Spain and becomes a province of Colombia.

1849 The California Gold Rush inspires Americans to travel from the east coast to the west, but because of the dangers of crossing Indian territory, most opt for steamship travel via Central America. U.S. investors decide to built a railroad in Panama to facilitate the trip.

1855   The Panama Railroad Company begins service between Aspinwall (Colón) and Panama City. The railway transports more than $700 million of California gold before completion of the U.S. Transcontinental Railroad, in 1869, makes it obsolete.

1882   A French company led by Fernando de Lesseps, who built the Suez Canal, launches an attempt to build an interoceanic canal in Panama. Nearly 20,000 workers die from tropical diseases before the enterprise goes bankrupt in 1889.

1903   With encouragement and military support from the administration of U.S. President Teddy Roosevelt, a group of influential Panamanians declares its country's independence from Colombia on November 3. They promptly sign a treaty ceding control of a 10- by 50-mi strip of land to the United States for canal construction.

1904   The American construction effort begins with a sanitation campaign led by Dr. William Gorgas. The campaign's mission is to eliminate the tropical diseases that killed so many workers in the French attempt.

1914   After a decade of work and the deaths of 5,500 workers, the first ship, the SS *Ancon*, transits the Panama Canal on August 15.

1964   After years of rising tensions and protests, a Panamanian student march in the U.S. Canal Zone is fired upon by U.S. troops, sparking riots that leave dozens dead and hundreds injured.

1968   Panama's National Guard deposes president Arnulfo Arias. Colonel Omar Torrijos soon becomes the country's de facto leader. Torrijos promotes himself to general, institutes broad social improvements, and launches a campaign to reclaim the canal for Panama.

1977   General Torrijos and President Jimmy Carter sign a treaty for the reversion of the canal, U.S. military bases, and other U.S. properties to the Panamanian government by December 31, 1999.

1981   Torrijos dies in a plane crash in the mountains of central Panama. His head of security, Manuel Noriega, soon gains control of the country.

1989   Amid growing charges of drug- and arms-trafficking ties, Noriega rigs presidential elections, then violently cracks down on protesters. Within a year President George H.W. Bush orders an invasion of Panama that results in massive destruction and thousands of deaths, and is followed by widespread looting.

1990   The government of Guillermo Endara begins rebuilding areas destroyed by the invasion and strengthening the country's democratic institutions.

1999   In compliance with the 1977 treaty, the United States cedes control of the canal and its other Panama properties on December 31.

2004   Martín Torrijos, the son of Omar Torrijos, is elected president of Panama and begins serving a five-year term.

MENU GUIDE

Panama's varied restaurant selection offers everything from crepes to curries, but most Panamanians stick to a simple diet of *arroz* (rice), *lentejas* (lentils), or *porotos* (red beans), and either a meat or seafood entrée. Panamanian food is neither spicy nor terribly exciting, but chefs at the better restaurants take advantage of the country's varied ingredients, especially fresh seafood, to create delicious innovations on traditional culinary themes.

SPANISH	ENGLISH

GENERAL DINING

Almuerzo	Lunch
Arroz	Rice
Carne	Meat (beef)
Cena	Dinner
Desayuno	Breakfast
Ensalada	Salad
Mariscos	Seafood
Pescado	Fish
Plato del día	Daily lunch special
Pollo	Chicken
Puerco	Pork
Servicio	Service (tip)
Sopa	Soup

ESPECIALIDADES (SPECIALTIES)

A la criolla	Onion and tomato Creole sauce that meat and seafood are sautéed in
Atún	Tuna
Bistec encebollado	Skirt steak smothered in onions (typical breakfast)
Camarones	Shrimp
Cambute	Conch
Carimañolas	Fried cassava dumplings stuffed with ground beef
Cazuela de mariscos	Seafood stew
Ceviche	Fish marinated in lime juice, served with chopped onion and garlic

Dorado	Mahimahi (dolphin)
Empanadas	Pastry turnovers filled with meat, or fruit
Hojaldre	Deep fried bread
Langosta	Lobster
Palmitos	Hearts of palm
Patacones	Deep fried, smashed plantain disks
Ropa Vieja	Stringy stewed beef in a red sauce
Sancocho	Chicken soup with tropical tubers
Tasajo	Aged beef strip sautéed in a sauce

POSTRES (DESSERTS) & DULCES (SWEETS)

Cajeta	Molasses-flavored fudge
Dulce de leche	Thick syrup of boiled milk and sugar
Flan	Crème caramel
Tres leches	Sponge cake soaked in condensed, evaporated, and fresh milk

FRUTAS (FRUITS)

Aguacate	Avocado
Fresa	Strawberry
Granadilla	Passion fruit
Guayaba	Guava
Melon	Cantaloupe
Piña	Pineapple
Pipa	Green coconut, for drinking
Sandia	Watermelon

BEBIDAS (BEVERAGES)

Batido	Fruit shake made with milk (con leche) or water (con agua)
Café con leche	Coffee with milk
Café negro	Black coffee
Cerveza	Beer
Chicha	Tropical fruit drink with ice and sugar
Vino (blanco, tinto)	Wine (white, red)

Panama
Essentials

PLANNING TOOLS, EXPERT INSIGHT,
GREAT CONTACTS

There are planners and there are those who, excuse the pun, fly by the seat of their pants. We happily place ourselves among the planners. Our writers and editors try to anticipate all the issues you may face before and during any journey, and then they do their research. This section is the product of their efforts. Use it to get excited about your trip to Panama, to inform your travel planning, or to guide you on the road should the seat of your pants start to feel threadbare.

GETTING STARTED

We're really proud of our Web site: Fodors.com is a great place to begin any journey. Scan the Wire section for suggested itineraries, travel deals, restaurant and hotel openings, and other up-to-the-minute info. Check out Booking to research prices and book plane tickets, hotel rooms, rental cars, and vacation packages. Head to Talk for on-the-ground pointers from travelers who frequent our message boards. You can also link to loads of other travel-related resources.

▮ RESOURCES

ONLINE TRAVEL TOOLS

All About Panama **Explore Panama** (⊕ *www.explorepanama.com*) is one-stop shopping for Panama Tourism 101. Packed with maps, listings, and advice, **Panama Info** (⊕ *www.panamainfo.com*) is an excellent resource if you're traveling— or moving—to Panama. **Panama Canal Authority** (⊕ *www.pancanal.com*) has history, photos and even live Webcasts of Panama's most famous feature. Part online newspaper, part travel guide, **Panama Guide** (⊕ *www.panama-guide.com*) has lots of up-to-date information about what's going on in Panama. **The Panama Report** (⊕ *www.thepanamareport.com*) is full of amusing and helpful articles about travel and life in Panama, as well as lots of investment sales pitches.

Back to Nature **Panama Audubon Society** (⊕ *www.panamaaudubon.org*) promotes bird-watching and bird protection in Panama.

Culture & Entertainment **Hasta Tarde** (⊕ *www.hastatarde.com*) has comprehensive listings of Panama's cultural goings-on; nightlife features heavily. **Museo de Arte Contemporáneo** (⊕ *www.macpanama.org*) is Panama City's contemporary arts museum.

INSPIRATION

David McCullough's book *The Path Between the Seas* is a history of the Panama Canal. Ulrich Keller's *The Building of the Panama Canal in Historic Photographs* lets you see the process. Ovidio Díz Espino chronicles the dealings surrounding the canal in *How Wall Street Created a Nation: J.P. Morgan, Teddy Roosevelt, and the Panama Canal*. The U.S. invasion of Panama is the focus of Kevin Buckley's *Panama* and John Lindsay-Poland's *Emperors in the Jungle: The Hidden History of the U.S. in Panama*. *The Tailor of Panama* by John LeCarré is a page-turning adventure novel that hinges around the return of the canal to Panama. The book was made into film shot in Panama and starring Pierce Brosnan.

Currency Conversion **Google** (⊕ *www.google.com*) does currency conversion. Just type in the amount you want to convert and an explanation of how you want it converted (e.g., "14 Swiss francs in dollars"), and then voilà. **Oanda.com** (⊕ *www.oanda.com*) also allows you to print out a handy table with the current day's conversion rates. **XE.com** (⊕ *www.xe.com*) is a good currency conversion Web site.

Safety **Transportation Security Administration** (*TSA;* ⊕ *www.tsa.gov*).

Time Zones **Timeanddate.com** (⊕ *www.timeanddate.com/worldclock*) can help you figure out the correct time anywhere.

Weather **Accuweather.com** (⊕ *www.accuweather.com*) is an independent weather-forecasting service with good coverage of hurricanes. **Weather.com** (⊕ *www.weather.com*) is the Web site for the Weather Channel.

VISITOR INFORMATION

The Instituto Panameño de Turismo (Panamanian Tourism Institute, IPAT) is Panama's official tourism organization. Its bilingual Web site is an excellent pretrip planning resource: there are overviews of Panama's regions and links to tour operators and hotels.

IPAT has 15 offices around Panama, open weekdays 8–5. The English-speaking staff at IPAT's offices is friendly and helpful. Their resources—mostly Panama City brochures—tend to plug local tour companies rather than aid independent touring.

Other resources include *The Visitor,* a small, free paper that can be found at most hotels and travel agencies, and *Panama Planner* an excellent tourism magazine, available at large hotels.

Contacts Instituto Panameño de Turismo (IPAT) ☎800/962–1526 in the U.S., 507/526–7000 in Panama ⊕www.visitpanama.com.

■ THINGS TO CONSIDER

GOVERNMENT ADVISORIES

As different countries have different world views, look at travel advisories from a range of governments to get more of a sense of what's going on out there. And be sure to parse the language carefully. For example, a warning to "avoid all travel" carries more weight than one urging you to "avoid nonessential travel," and both are much stronger than a plea to "exercise caution." A U.S. government travel warning is more permanent (though not necessarily more serious) than a so-called public announcement, which carries an expiration date.

■TIP→ Consider registering online with the State Department (https://travelregistration.state.gov/ibrs/), so the government will know to look for you should a crisis occur in the country you're visiting.

The U.S. Department of State's Web site has more than just travel warnings

WORD OF MOUTH

"Bocas is very laid back, and light clothes and sandals is the order of the day. You might want a rain jacket or poncho as it can rain in Bocas . . . Panama City is more formal: shorts and sandals are for the weekends at the beach not for town (that's the thinking of the locals anyway) so a pair of lightweight long pants and sneakers will be more comfortable in the city. Even I wear shorts, but really only on the weekends when popping to the supermarket, etc."

—AndrewW

and advisories. The consular information sheets issued for every country have general safety tips, entry requirements (though be sure to verify these with the country's embassy), and other useful details.

Most government advisories warn against independent travel to the Darién region, which borders Colombia. Its dense rain forest has long made it the ideal hideout for Colombian guerrillas and paramilitary forces, and drug smuggling gangs from both countries. Going with an organized tour group is the safe option.

General Information & Warnings U.S. Department of State (⊕www.travel.state. gov).

GEAR

They don't call Panama City "the Miami of the South" for nothing: looks (and being looked at) are important here, and city-slicker locals aren't impressed by sloppy appearances. Think capri pants, skirts, or khakis for urban sightseeing, with something a little dressier for eating out at night. Shorts, T-shirts, tank tops and bikinis are all acceptable at the beach or farther afield. Leave flashy jewelry behind—it only makes you a target.

"Insect repellent, sunscreen, sunglasses" is your packing mantra; long-sleeve shirts and long pants also help protect your skin from the relentless sun and ferocious mosquitoes. Panama's rainy season lasts from mid-April to December, and rain is common at other times, too, so a foldable umbrella or waterproof is a must. So are sturdy walking boots if you're planning any serious hiking, otherwise sneakers or flats are fine. A handbag-size flashlight is also very useful: blackouts are more common than at home.

In the Darién, a camping mosquito net is invaluable when staying at places with no screens in the windows (or no windows at all). A water purifier and lots of plastic bags are also helpful in the jungle. So much for packing light.

Tissues and antibacterial hand wipes make trips to public toilets a bit pleasanter. Finding your preferred brands of condoms and tampons in Panama can be hit and miss, so bring necessary supplies of both. All the familiar toiletry brands are widely available.

PASSPORTS & VISAS

Technically, all visitors to Panama should obtain tourist visas, which are issued by consulates and embassies throughout Central and North America; they are valid for 90 days, and cost $10. However, if you are staying for less than 30 days, you can purchase a tourist card ($5) on arrival.

■TIP➡ Before your trip, make two copies of your passport's data page (one for someone at home and another for you to carry separately). Or scan the page and e-mail it to someone at home and/or yourself.

If you decide to prolong your stay once in Panama, you can extend your tourist card for another 30 days by going to the closest *Oficina de Migración* (Immigration Office). There are offices in Panama City, David, Santiago, and Chitré; most are open 7:30–3:30. You need to show your return air ticket and photocopies of the photograph page of your passport, and the page with your Panama entry stamp.

Visa extensions cost $10 and the process takes at least two hours.

Info **Consulate of Panama in Washington D.C.** (☎202/483–1407 ⊕www.embassyofpanama.org). **Oficina de Migración** (for visa extension ✉Av. Cuba and Calle 28, Panama City ☎507/507–1800 ⊕www.migracion.gob.pa/eng/).

U.S. Passport Information **U.S. Department of State** (☎877/487–2778 ⊕http://travel.state.gov/passport).

U.S. Passport & Visa Expediters **A. Briggs Passport & Visa Expediters** (☎800/806–0581 or 202/338–0111 ⊕www.abriggs.com). **American Passport Express** (☎800/455–5166 or 800/841–6778 ⊕www.americanpassport.com). **Passport Express** (☎800/362–8196 ⊕www.passportexpress.com). **Travel Document Systems** (☎800/874–5100 or 202/638–3800 ⊕www.traveldocs.com). **Travel the World Visas** (☎866/886–8472 or 301/495–7700 ⊕www.world-visa.com).

GENERAL REQUIREMENTS FOR PANAMA	
Passport	Must be valid for 6 months after date of arrival
Visa	90-day visa ($10) issued by embassy or 30-day tourist card issued on arrival ($5)
Vaccinations	None required; yellow fever recommended for outside Canal Zone; antimalarial medication recommended in Darién, San Blas, Bocas del Toro
Driving	U.S. driver's license accepted; CDW is compulsory on car rentals and will be included in the quoted price
Departure Tax	US$20, payable in cash only

SHOTS & MEDICATIONS

If you're traveling anywhere outside the Canal Zone, you need a yellow fever vaccination. Remember to keep the certificate and carry it with you, as you may be asked to show it when entering another country after leaving Panama.

Malaria is prevalent in the Darién, San Blas, and Bocas del Toro regions—both Panama City and the Canal Zone are free from risk. Another mosquito-borne disease, dengue, is also rife, particularly on the Pacific coast. The best way to prevent both is to avoid being bitten: cover up your arms and legs and use ample repellent, preferably one containing DEET. The CDC recommends mefloquine, proguanil, or doxycycline as preventative antimalarials for adults and infants in Panama. To be effective, the weekly doses must start a week before you travel and continue four weeks after your return. There is no preventive medication for dengue.

For more information see Health in On the Ground in Panama, below.

Health Warnings National Centers for Disease Control & Prevention (CDC ☎877/394–8747 international travelers' health line ⊕www.cdc.gov/travel). **World Health Organization** (WHO ⊕www.who.int).

TRIP INSURANCE

What kind of coverage do you honestly need? Do you even need trip insurance at all? Take a deep breath and read on.

We believe that comprehensive trip insurance is especially valuable if you're booking a very expensive or complicated trip (particularly to an isolated region) or if you're booking far in advance. Who knows what could happen six months down the road? But whether or not you get insurance has more to do with how comfortable you are assuming all that risk yourself.

Comprehensive travel policies typically cover trip-cancellation and interruption, letting you cancel or cut your trip short because of a personal emergency, illness, or, in some cases, acts of terrorism in your destination. Such policies also cover evac-

WORD OF MOUTH

"Love the Darién, but use Ultrathon there (in addition to mosquitos, there are swarming Africanized bees) and [in] Aligandi."

—mikemo

uation and medical care. Some also cover you for trip delays because of bad weather or mechanical problems as well as for lost or delayed baggage. Another type of coverage to look for is financial default—that is, when your trip is disrupted because a tour operator, airline, or cruise line goes out of business. Generally you must buy this when you book your trip or shortly thereafter, and it's only available to you if your operator isn't on a list of excluded companies.

If you're going abroad, consider buying medical-only coverage at the very least. Neither Medicare nor some private insurers cover medical expenses anywhere outside of the United States (including time aboard a cruise ship, even if it leaves from a U.S. port). Medical-only policies typically reimburse you for medical care (excluding that related to pre-existing conditions) and hospitalization abroad, and provide for evacuation. You still have to pay the bills and await reimbursement from the insurer, though.

■TIP➔ Medical staff at Panamanian public hospitals are well-trained and professional. However, hospitals are underfunded and often lack supplies: as a rule, you're best going to a private clinic, which means medical insurance is a must.

Expect comprehensive travel insurance policies to cost about 4% to 7% or 8% of the total price of your trip (it's more like 8%–12% if you're over age 70). A medical-only policy may or may not be cheaper than a comprehensive policy. Always read the fine print of your policy to make sure that you are covered for the

Trip Insurance Resources

INSURANCE COMPARISON SITES		
Insure My Trip.com	800/487-4722	www.insuremytrip.com.
Square Mouth.com	800/240-0369 or 727/490-5803	www.squaremouth.com.
COMPREHENSIVE TRAVEL INSURERS		
Access America	800/729-6021	www.accessamerica.com.
CSA Travel Protection	800/873-9855	www.csatravelprotection.com.
HTH Worldwide	610/254-8700 or 888/243-2358	www.hthworldwide.com.
Travelex Insurance	800/228-9792	www.travelex-insurance.com.
Travel Guard International	715/345-0505 or 800/826-4919	www.travelguard.com.
Travel Insured International	800/243-3174	www.travelinsured.com.
MEDICAL-ONLY INSURERS		
International Medical Group	800/628-4664	www.imglobal.com.
International SOS		www.internationalsos.com.
Wallach & Company	540/687-3166 or 800/237-6615	www.wallach.com.

risks that are of most concern to you. Compare several policies to make sure you're getting the best price and range of coverage available.

■ TIP→ OK. You know you can save a bundle on trips to warm-weather destinations by traveling in rainy season. But there's also a chance that a severe storm will disrupt your plans. The solution? Look for hotels and resorts that offer storm/hurricane guarantees. Although they rarely allow refunds, most guarantees do let you rebook later if a storm strikes.

BOOKING YOUR TRIP

Unless your cousin is a travel agent, you're probably among the millions of people who make most of their travel arrangements online.

But have you ever wondered just what the differences are between an online travel agent (a Web site through which you make reservations instead of going directly to the airline, hotel, or car-rental company), a discounter (a firm that does a high volume of business with a hotel chain or airline and accordingly gets good prices), a wholesaler (one that makes cheap reservations in bulk and then re-sells them to people like you), and an aggregator (one that compares all the offerings so you don't have to)?

Is it truly better to book directly on an airline or hotel Web site? And when does a real live travel agent come in handy?

▌ ONLINE

You really have to shop around. A travel wholesaler such as Hotels.com or Hotel-Club.net can be a source of good rates, as can discounters such as Hotwire or Priceline, particularly if you can bid for your hotel room or airfare. Indeed, such sites sometimes have deals that are unavailable elsewhere. They do, however, tend to work only with hotel chains (which makes them just plain useless for getting hotel reservations outside of major cities) or big airlines (so that often leaves out upstarts like jetBlue and some foreign carriers like Air India).

Also, with discounters and wholesalers you must generally prepay, and everything is nonrefundable. And before you fork over the dough, be sure to check the terms and conditions, so you know what a given company will do for you if there's a problem and what you'll have to deal with on your own.

▌TIP➜ **To be absolutely sure everything was processed correctly, confirm reservations made through online travel agents, discounters, and wholesalers directly with your hotel before leaving home.**

Booking engines like Expedia, Travelocity, and Orbitz are actually travel agents, albeit high-volume, online ones. And airline travel packagers like American Airlines Vacations and Virgin Vacations—well, they're travel agents, too. But they may still not work with all the world's hotels.

An aggregator site will search many sites and pull the best prices for airfares, hotels, and rental cars from them. Most aggregators compare the major travel-booking sites such as Expedia, Travelocity, and Orbitz; some also look at airline Web sites, though rarely the sites of smaller budget airlines. Some aggregators also compare other travel products, including complex packages—a good thing, as you can sometimes get the best overall deal by booking an air-and-hotel package.

▌ WITH A TRAVEL AGENT

There's little reason for using a travel agent if you're only visiting Panama City and the Canal Zone: booking hotels, tours, and activities by yourself is straightforward. Farther afield, a travel agent can be useful to help pack lots into a short trip, though with a little bit more effort you can probably arrange the same activities alone. Ancon Expeditions and Panama Pete Adventures are both Panama-based travel agents with outstanding reputations.

If you use an agent—brick-and-mortar or virtual—you'll pay a fee for the service. And know that the service you get from some online agents isn't comprehensive. For example Expedia and Travelocity don't search for prices on budget airlines

Online Booking Resources

AGGREGATORS		
Kayak	www.kayak.com	looks at cruises and vacation packages.
Mobissimo	www.mobissimo.com	examines airfare, hotels, cars, and tons of activities.
Qixo	www.qixo.com	compares cruises, vacation packages, and even travel insurance.
Sidestep	www.sidestep.com	compares vacation packages and lists travel deals and some activities.
BOOKING ENGINES		
Cheap Tickets	www.cheaptickets.com	discounter.
Expedia	www.expedia.com	large online agency that charges a booking fee for airline tickets.
Hotwire	www.hotwire.com	discounter.
Onetravel.com	www.onetravel.com	discounter for hotels, car rentals, airfares, and packages.
Priceline.com	www.priceline.com	discounter that also allows bidding.
Travel.com	www.travel.com	allows you to compare its rates with those of other booking engines.
Travelocity	www.travelocity.com	charges a booking fee for airline tickets, but promises good problem resolution.
ONLINE ACCOMMODATIONS		
Hotelbook.com	www.hotelbook.com	focuses on independent hotels worldwide.
Hotel Club	www.hotelclub.net	good for major cities and some resort areas.
Hotels.com	www.hotels.com	big Expedia-owned wholesaler that offers rooms in hotels all over the world.
Quikbook	www.quikbook.com	offers "pay when you stay" reservations that allow you to settle your bill when you check out, not when you book; best for trips to U.S. and Canadian cities.

like jetBlue, Southwest, or small foreign carriers. That said, some agents (online or not) *do* have access to fares that are difficult to find otherwise, and the savings can more than make up for any surcharge.

A knowledgeable brick-and-mortar travel agent can be a godsend if you're booking a cruise, a package trip that's not available to you directly, an air pass, or a complicated itinerary including several overseas flights. What's more, travel agents that specialize in a destination may have exclusive access to certain deals and insider information on things such as charter flights. Agents who specialize in types of travelers (senior citizens, gays and lesbians, naturists) or types of trips (cruises, luxury travel, safaris) can also be invaluable.

■TIP→ **Remember that Expedia, Travelocity, and Orbitz are travel agents, not just booking engines. To resolve any problems with a reservation made through these companies, contact them first.**

Agent Resources **American Society of Travel Agents** (☎703/739-2782 ⊕www. travelsense.org). **Ancon Expeditions** (☎507/269-9415 ⊕www.anconexpeditions. com). **Panama Pete Adventures**

(☎877/726–6222 ⊕www.panamapete
adventures.com).

■ ACCOMMODATIONS

Be it a 900-room behemoth or a bijoux
B&B, a five-star chain dripping luxury
or a one-off hostel packed with travelers,
Panama has plenty of lodging options.
"Hotel" isn't the only tag you'll find
on accommodation: *hospedaje, pensión, casa de huespedes,* and *posada* also
denote somewhere to stay. There are no
hard-and-fast rules as to what each name
means, though hotels and *posadas* tend
to be higher-end places, whereas *hosped-
ajes, pensiones,* and *casas de huespedes*
are sometimes smaller and family run.
Breakfast isn't always included in the
room price.

The usual big international chain hotels
have rooms and facilities equal to those
at home, but usually lack a sense of place.
If five-star luxury isn't your top priority,
the best deals are undoubtedly with midrange local hotels. Granted, there's no
gym or conference center, but comfortable rooms with private bathrooms, hot
water, and much more local character
often come at a fraction of the cost of a
big chain.

Lodges—both eco- and not-quite-so—are
the thing in San Blas and El Darién. Some
are incredibly luxurious, others more
back-to-nature; all are way off the beaten
path, so plan on staying a few nights to
offset travel time.

Most hotels and other lodgings require
you to give your credit-card details before
they will confirm your reservation. If you
don't feel comfortable e-mailing this
information, ask if you can fax it (some
places even prefer faxes). However you
book, get confirmation in writing and
have a copy of it handy at check-in.

Be sure you understand the hotel's cancellation policy. Some places allow you
to cancel without any kind of penalty—

even if you prepaid to secure a discounted
rate—if you cancel at least 24 hours in
advance. Others require you to cancel a
week in advance or penalize you the cost
of one night. Small inns and B&Bs are
most likely to require you to cancel far
in advance. Most hotels allow children
under a certain age to stay in their par-
ents' room at no extra charge, but others
charge for them as extra adults; find out
the cutoff age for discounts.

■TIP➡Assume that hotels operate on the
European Plan (EP, no meals) unless we
specify that they use the Breakfast Plan (BP,
with full breakfast), Continental Plan (CP,
Continental breakfast), Full American Plan
(FAP, all meals), Modified American Plan
(MAP, breakfast and dinner) or are all-inclu-
sive (AI, all meals and most activities).

*See Orientation & Planning at the begin-
ning of each chapter for price charts.*

APARTMENT & HOUSE RENTALS

Short-term furnished rentals aren't common in Panama. Ah! Panamá has a reasonable selection of luxurious properties,
with prices starting at $2,000 a week.
Away.com has rentals in its hotel section. Sublet.com and Vacation Rentals
By Owner deal with more modest apartments, often as cheap as $700 a week.

BED & BREAKFASTS

The Panamanian definition of B&B might
not coincide with yours: the term is frequently extended to luxury hotels that
happen to include breakfast in their price.
Indeed, these make up most of the pick-
ings at Bed & Breakfast.com, BnB Finder,
and Bed & Breakfast Inns Online. The
longer lists at Ah! Panamá and A Thousand Inns include both these and home-
lier midrange establishments. For cheap,
family-run places, try Traveller's Point.

Reservation Services A Thousand Inns
(⊕www.1000inns.com). **Ah! Panamá**
(⊕www.ahpanama.com/travel_and_tourism/
bed_and_breakfast). **Bed & Breakfast.com**
(☎512/322–2710 or 800/462–2632 ⊕www.
bedandbreakfast.com) also sends out an online

Online Booking Resources

CONTACTS		
Ah! Panamá	www.ahpanama/travel_and_tourism	
Away.com	www.away.com	
Sublet.com	www.sublet.com	
Vacation Rentals By Owner	www.vrbo.com	
Villas International	www.villasintl.com	415/499–9490 or 800/221–2260

newsletter. **Bed & Breakfast Inns Online** (☎615/868–1946 or 800/215–7365 ⊕www.bbonline.com). **BnB Finder.com** (☎212/432–7693 or 888/547–8226 ⊕www.bnbfinder.com). **Travellers' Point** (⊕www.travellerspoint.com).

HOSTELS

Hostels offer bare-bones lodging at low, low prices—often in shared dorm rooms with shared baths—to people of all ages, though the primary market is young travelers, especially students. Most hostels serve breakfast; dinner and/or shared cooking facilities may also be available. In some hostels you aren't allowed to be in your room during the day, and there may be a curfew at night. Nevertheless, hostels provide a sense of community, with public rooms where travelers often gather to share stories. Many hostels are affiliated with Hostelling International (HI), an umbrella group of hostel associations with some 4,500 member properties in more than 70 countries. Other hostels are completely independent and may be nothing more than a really cheap hotel.

Membership in any HI association, open to travelers of all ages, allows you to stay in HI-affiliated hostels at member rates. One-year membership is about $28 for adults; hostels charge about $10–$30 per night. Members have priority if the hostel is full; they're also eligible for discounts around the world, even on rail and bus travel in some countries.

Panama is an established stop along the gringo trail and has a good selection of cheap, shared accommodation in small B&B-style hotels and in hostels. Budget

lodging terminology varies: hostel, *hostal* and *la casa de . . .* are commonplace names, and some places are just listed as a hotel or *pensión*. Most establishments have a choice of shared dorms or private rooms. Bathrooms are usually communal.

Staff in most Panamanian hostels are young, enthusiastic, and knowledgeable, and can usually inform you about Spanish classes and excursions—many have in-house travel agencies. Hostels proper do tend to cater to party animals—a family-run hotel might be quieter.

Panama has no HI affiliates, but Traveller's Point and Hostel World have ample listings and booking services. Try to sort out your first nights in advance, then get recommendations from fellow travelers for your next port of call.

Information **Hostels.com** (⊕www.hostels.com). **Hostel World.com** (⊕www.hostelworld.com). **Travellers' Point** (⊕www.travellerspoint.com).

ECOLODGES

In addition to hotels and hostels, Panama does a brisk trade in so-called eco-lodges, most of which are in the Darién and San Blas. If you are seriously interested in sustainable accommodation, it pays to do your research. The term "ecolodge" is used freely, sometimes simply to describe a property in a rural or jungle location rather than somewhere that is truly sustainable. The International Ecotourism Society has online resources to help you pick somewhere really green. Responsible

Travel is an online travel agency for ethical holidays.

Information International Ecotourism Society (⊕ www.ecotourism.org). **Responsible Travel** (⊕ www.responsibletravel.com).

∎ AIRLINE TICKETS

Most domestic airline tickets are electronic; international tickets may be either electronic or paper. With an e-ticket the only thing you receive is an e-mailed receipt citing your itinerary and reservation and ticket numbers.

The greatest advantage of an e-ticket is that if you lose your receipt, you can simply print out another copy or ask the airline to do it for you at check-in. You usually pay a surcharge (up to $50) to get a paper ticket, if you can get one at all.

The sole advantage of a paper ticket is that it may be easier to endorse over to another airline if your flight is canceled and the airline with which you booked can't accommodate you on another flight.

∎TIP➔ Discount air passes that let you travel economically in a country or region must often be purchased before you leave home. In some cases you can only get them through a travel agent.

CHARTER FLIGHTS

Charter companies rent aircraft and offer regularly scheduled flights (usually nonstops). Charter flights are generally cheaper than flights on regular airlines, and they often leave from and travel to a wider variety of airports. For example, you could have a nonstop flight from Columbus, Ohio, to Punta Cana, Dominican Republic, or from Chicago to Dubrovnik, Croatia.

You don't, however, have the same protections as with regular airlines. If a charter can't take off for mechanical or other reasons, there usually isn't another plane to take its place. If not enough seats are sold, the flight may be canceled. And if

a company goes out of business, you're out of luck (unless, of course, you have insurance with financial default coverage; ➪ *Trip Insurance under Things to Consider in Getting Started, above*).

Air Transat runs charter services to Panama City from Montréal and Toronto's Pearson Airport and sometimes has good deals for last-minute flights.

Charter Companies Air Transat (☎ 866/847–1112 ⊕ www.airtransat.ca).

∎ RENTAL CARS

When you reserve a car, ask about cancellation penalties, taxes, drop-off charges (if you're planning to pick up the car in one city and leave it in another), and surcharges (for being under or over a certain age, for additional drivers, or for driving across state or country borders or beyond a specific distance from your point of rental). All these things can add substantially to your costs. Request car seats and extras such as GPS when you book.

Rates are sometimes—but not always—better if you book in advance or reserve through a rental agency's Web site. There are other reasons to book ahead, though: for popular destinations, during busy times of the year, or to ensure that you get certain types of cars (vans, SUVs, exotic sports cars).

∎TIP➔ Make sure that a confirmed reservation guarantees you a car. Agencies sometimes overbook, particularly for busy weekends and holiday periods.

In Panama City taking taxis is cheaper and much less stressful than driving. Outside the city a car can be a real asset to your trip. You don't have to worry about unreliable bus schedules, you can control your itinerary and pace of travel, and you can head off to explore on a whim. Driving standards are a little more erratic than in the United States, but you should be fine if you keep your eyes open, maintain your distance, and assume that other

Car-Rental Resources

AUTOMOBILE ASSOCIATIONS		
U.S.: American Automobile Association (AAA)	315/797–5000	www.aaa.com
		most contact with the organization is through state and regional members.
National Automobile Club	650/294–7000	www.thenac.com
		membership is open to California residents only.
MAJOR AGENCIES		
Alamo	800/522–9696	www.alamo.com.
Avis	800/331–1084	www.avis.com.
Budget	800/472–3325	www.budget.com.
Dollar	866/700–9904	www.dollarpanama.com.
Hertz	800/654–3001	www.hertz.com.
National Car Rental	800/227–7368	www.nationalcar.com.
Thrifty	800/847–4389	www.thrifty.com.

drivers will make unexpected maneuvers. Wearing a seatbelt is compulsory, though many locals flout the rule.

The roads in urban areas and between big cities are generally paved, in reasonable condition, and easily navigable by a regular car. A 4WD (*doble tracción* or *cuatro por cuatro*) is only necessary for exploring the Darién. Many rental agencies prefer—or even stipulate—that you park your car in guarded lots or hotels with private parking, not on the street.

Compact cars like a Kia Pianto, Ford Fiesta, or VW Fox start at around $32 a day; for $40–$50 you can rent a Mitsubishi Lancer, a VW Golf, or a Polo. 4WD pickups start at $70 a day, though for a 4WD with a full cabin you pay up to $120. International agencies sometimes have cheaper per-day rates, but locals undercut them on longer rentals. Stick shift is the norm in Panama, so check with the rental agency if you only drive automatics.

Rental-car companies routinely accept driver's licenses from the United States, Canada, and most European countries. Most agencies require a major credit card for a deposit, and some require that you be over 25, or charge extra insurance if you're not.

CAR-RENTAL INSURANCE

Everyone who rents a car wonders whether the insurance that the rental companies offer is worth the expense. No one—including us—has a simple answer. It all depends on how much regular insurance you have, how comfortable you are with risk, and whether or not money is an issue.

If you own a car, your personal auto insurance may cover a rental to some degree, though not all policies protect you abroad; always read your policy's fine print. Some credit cards offer CDW coverage, but it's usually supplemental to your own insurance and rarely covers SUVs, minivans, luxury models, and the like. If your coverage is secondary, you may still be liable for loss-of-use costs from the car-rental company. But no credit-card insurance is valid unless you use that card for *all* transactions, from reserving to paying the final bill. All companies exclude car rental in some countries, so be sure to find out about the destination to which you are traveling.

TIP→ Diners Club offers primary CDW coverage on all rentals reserved and paid for with the card. This means that Diners Club's company—not your own car insurance—pays in case of an accident. It *doesn't* mean your car-insurance company won't raise your rates once it discovers you had an accident.

In most cases it's cheaper to add a supplemental CDW plan to your comprehensive travel-insurance policy (⇨ *Trip Insurance under Things to Consider in Getting Started, above*) than to purchase it from a rental company. That said, you don't want to pay for a supplement if you're required to buy insurance from the rental company.

Panamanian car-rental agencies require collision insurance (CDW), which also covers you if the car is stolen. You have to pay extra (between $12–$18 per day) for this, unless you pay with a major credit card that covers the CDW. Ask your credit-card company whether your card is suitable, or else you may end up paying for CDW separately. Many rental companies also insist on third-party insurance (insurance covering injuries caused by you), which costs $6–$10 per day if you purchase your CDW from the rental company, and double that if CDW is covered by your credit card. There's generally also a deductible (around $2,000) you have to pay regardless of where your CDW comes from, so consider adding on the extra fee to reduce your liability: it's often as low as $6 a day.

TIP→ Rental companies in Panama only accept insurance purchased from them or provided by your credit-card company. Other third-party insurers are not valid.

■ VACATION PACKAGES

There's no real reason to visit Panama on a package tour—in fact, doing so will probably cost you considerably more. If you like having everything prebooked, consider hunting for flights yourself (the cheapest deals are often online) and getting a Panama-based agent to arrange accommodation and internal travel. *See With a Travel Agent, under Booking Your Trip, above.*

Packages *are not* guided excursions. Packages combine airfare, accommodations, and perhaps a rental car or other extras (theater tickets, boat trips, reserved entry to popular museums, transit passes), but they let you do your own thing.

Packages will definitely save you time. In Panama, they can occasionally save you money, but—and this is a really big "but"—you should price each part of the package separately to be sure. And be aware that prices advertised on Web sites and in newspapers rarely include service charges or taxes, which can up your costs by hundreds of dollars.

TIP→ Some packages and cruises are sold only through travel agents. Don't always assume that you can get the best deal by booking everything yourself.

Each year consumers are stranded or lose their money when packagers—even large ones with excellent reputations—go out of business. How can you protect yourself?

First, always pay with a credit card; if you have a problem, your credit-card company may help you resolve it. Second, buy trip insurance that covers default. Third, choose a company that belongs to the United States Tour Operators Association, whose members must set aside funds to cover defaults. Finally, choose a company that also participates in the Tour Operator Program of the American Society of Travel Agents (ASTA), which will act as mediator in any disputes.

You can also check on the operator's reputation among travelers by posting an inquiry on Fodors.com forums.

Organizations **American Society of Travel Agents** (ASTA ☎703/739–2782 or 800/965–2782 ⊕www.astanet.com). **United**

States Tour Operators Association (USTOA ☎ 212/599–6599 ⊕ www.ustoa.com).

❚ GUIDED TOURS

Guided tours are a good option when you don't want to do it all yourself. You travel along with a group (sometimes large, sometimes small), stay in prebooked hotels, eat with your fellow travelers (the cost of meals sometimes included in the price of your tour, sometimes not), and follow a schedule.

But not all guided tours are an if-it's-Tuesday-this-must-be-Belgium experience. A knowledgeable guide can take you places that you might never discover on your own, and you may be pushed to see more than you would have otherwise. Tours aren't for everyone, but they can be just the thing for trips to places where making travel arrangements is difficult or time-consuming (particularly when you don't speak the language).

Whenever you book a guided tour, find out what's included and what isn't. A "land-only" tour includes all your travel (by bus, in most cases) in the destination, but not necessarily your flights to and from or even within it. Also, in most cases prices in tour brochures don't include fees and taxes. And remember that you'll be expected to tip your guide (in cash) at the end of the tour.

Panama has some very professional guides and travel professionals who will take you just about anywhere you want to go or customize a trip for you. Ancon Expeditions has some of the country's best eco-adventure trips, as well as terrific day trips, and educational volunteering opportunities.

Overseas Adventure Travel keeps tour groups small and has excellent guides. Five days in Panama is an optional extension to its Costa Rican and Route of the Maya trips. Abercrombie and Kent places the emphasis on luxury: its 10-day Tailor Made Panama is a private guided tour.

Responsible Travel is a British company that specializes in ethical tourism. It runs Panama trips lasting 10–15 days and also has a trip combining Panama and Costa Rica. Certified by the International Ecotourism Society, Tropical Nature Tours has two Panama tours with an ecological focus; one is aimed at families. Wildland Adventures prides itself on culturally and ecologically sensitive trips. Its Panama tours include a family-oriented package and the 10-day Panama Discovery tour, which takes in a variety of ecosystems.

You combine touring with hiking, snorkeling, and white-water rafting on The World Outdoors's eight-day Panama Multi-Sport holiday. Adrenaline is also a top priority with BikeHike Adventures: the Panama Rumble in the Jungle includes biking, rafting, zip-line tours, and snorkeling. The Adventure Center's trips usually involve a little bit of action (rafting, hiking, or cycling) as well as more standard touring. It has a general-purpose two-week Panama tour, a kayaking tour, and multicountry Central America tours; the longest lasts 60 days.

Recommended Companies **Abercrombie and Kent** (☎ 800/554–7016 ⊕ www. abercrombiekent.com). **Adventure Center** (☎ 800/228–8747 ⊕ www.adventurecenter. com). **Ancon Expeditions** (☎ 507/269–9415 ⊕ www.anconexpeditions.com). **BikeHike Adventures** (☎ 888/805–0061 ⊕ www. bikehike.com). **Overseas Adventure Travel** (☎ 800/493–6824 ⊕ www.oattravel.com). **Responsible Travel** (☎ 44/1273/600030 ⊕ www.responsibletravel.com). **Tropical Nature Tours** (☎ 877/827–8350 ⊕ www. tropicalnaturetours.com). **Wildland Adventures** (☎ 800/645–4453 ⊕ www.wildland. com). **The World Outdoors** (☎ 800/488–8483 ⊕ www.theworldoutdoors.com).

SPECIAL-INTEREST TOURS

BIRD-WATCHING
Tropical Nature Tours runs an eight-day bird-watching tour to Panama. You visit several different national parks on Advantage Panama's 10-day birding tour.

EcoCircuitos Panama also takes you bird-watching to various parts of the country.

Contacts Advantage Panama (⊕www.advantagepanama.com). **EcoCircuitos Panama** (☎507/6681–4800 ⊕www.ecocircuitos.com). **Tropical Nature Tours** (☎877/827–8350 ⊕www.tropicalnaturetours.com).

CULTURE

Expediciones Tropicales specialize in visits to Panama's Kuna people. You can spend several days immersed in the culture of indigenous people on one of Eco-Circuitos Panama's cultural trips.

Contacts EcoCircuitos Panama (☎507/6681–4800 ⊕www.ecocircuitos.com). **Expediciones Tropicales** (☎507/317–1279 ⊕www.xtrop.com).

ECOTOURS

Local tour operator Advantage Panama runs an 8-day rain-forest tour and the longer Isthmian Explorer, which visits a wider variety of ecosystems. Ancon Expeditions is another local company with an excellent track record. There's two weeks' worth of animal-watching on the Panama Wildlife Tour run by British company Reef and Rainforest.

Contacts Advantage Panama (⊕www.advantagepanama.com). **Ancon Expeditions** (☎507/269–9415 ⊕www.anconexpeditions.com). **Reef and Rainforest** (☎44/1803/866–965 ⊕www.reefandrainforest.co.uk).

FISHING

Panama Travel Experts has good sport-fishing tours.

Contacts Panama Travel Experts (☎507/265–5323 ⊕www.panamatravelexperts.com).

FLIGHTSEEING

Helipan Corp operates helicopter tours of the Panama Canal, Panama City, and Taboga Island.

Contacts Helipan Corp (☎507/315–0452 ⊕www.helipan.com).

HIKING

Both Wildland Adventures and Responsible Travel run two-week trekking holidays in the Darién region. EcoCircuitos Panama has a large selection of hiking trips: one is a weeklong crossing of the isthmus from the Caribbean to the Pacific.

Contacts EcoCircuitos Panama (☎507/6681–4800 ⊕www.ecocircuitos.com). **Responsible Travel** (☎44/1273/600030 ⊕www.responsibletravel.com). **Wildland Adventures** (☎800/645–4453 ⊕www.wildland.com).

LANGUAGE PROGRAMS

Short Spanish immersion courses are one of the programs run by EcoCircuitos Panama. Alternatively, you can combine studying Spanish with classes giving insight into local business etiquette.

Contacts EcoCircuitos Panama (☎507/6681–4800 ⊕www.ecocircuitos.com).

VOLUNTEER PROGRAMS

Responsible Travel's 2–10 week conservation projects help save leatherback turtles. Helping a community in the Darién with its organic farm is one of the volunteer holidays that EcoCircuitos Panama coordinates.

Contacts EcoCircuitos Panama (☎507/6681–4800 ⊕www.ecocircuitos.com). **Responsible Travel** (☎44/1273/600–030 ⊕www.responsibletravel.com).

▌ CRUISES

Crossing from the Pacific to the Caribbean through the 80 km (50 mi) of the Panama Canal is one of the world's must-do voyages. Indeed, a huge number of companies offer Panama Canal cruises. The ports of call and the style of cruising you like are what should guide your choice. Note that some cruise companies visit Panama without actually cruising the canal.

Celebrity Cruises has 18 Panama Canal cruises; they leave from San Diego, San Francisco, and Fort Lauderdale, last around two weeks, and call at various Mexican ports. Cunard's *Queen Mary* docks in Cristobal but doesn't go through the canal on its 14-night Panama and the Caribbean cruise. Crystal Cruises dock in Panama or transiting the canal; many also call at Mexican, Costa Rican, and Caribbean ports.

On Disney Cruise Line you can go through the canal in either direction, and also visit Aruba and Mexican beaches. In addition to basic canal cruises, Holland America has cruises that travel from Panama to Brazil (including a cruise up the Amazon), or to Cartagena in Colombia. Starting ports include New York, Los Angeles, Fort Lauderdale, Seattle, and Vancouver. Oceania Cruises' *Regatta* stops in Grand Cayman, Colombia, Guatemala, Costa Rica, and Mexico on its voyage between Miami and Los Angeles. With Norwegian Cruise Line you can traverse the canal on a Miami–Los Angeles cruise, or continue down the western coast to Santiago in Chile.

Four Princess Cruise ships go through the Canal—one sails from Tahiti to Fort Lauderdale. Regent Seven Seas' *Voyager* and *Mariner* both sail between Fort Lauderdale and Los Angeles or San Diego. Most of Royal Caribbean International's Panama cruises include other Central American ports. You can cruise the Canal on *Seabourn Legend*; the two-week voyage also stops at Belize, Costa Rica, Honduras, and Nicaragua. Silversea's 14- and 15-night Fort Lauderdale–Los Angeles Canal cruises take in Santa Marta and Cartagena in Colombia, Puerto Quetzal in Guatemala, and Acapulco and Puerto Vallarta in Mexico.

If you prefer sails to motors, *S.V. Mandarlay,* one of Windjammer Barefoot Cruises' sailboats, does a six-day trip around Panama's San Blas islands, leaving from Portobello and finishing in Colón. Windstar Cruises is another sail-powered option:

its Panama Canal cruise starts in Costa Rica, and also calls at port in Colombia, Aruba, Curacao, Venezuela, and Grenada before finishing in Barbados.

Cruise Lines Celebrity Cruises (☎800/647–2251 ⊕www.celebrity.com). **Crystal Cruises** (☎310/785–9300 or 800/446–6620 ⊕www.crystalcruises.com). **Cunard Line** (☎661/753–1000 or 800/728–6273 ⊕www.cunard.com). **Disney Cruise Line** (☎407/566–3500 or 800/951–3532 ⊕www.disneycruise.com). **Holland America Line** (☎206/281–3535 or 877/932–4259 ⊕www.hollandamerica.com). **Norwegian Cruise Line** (☎305/436–4000 or 800/327–7030 ⊕www.ncl.com). **Oceania Cruises** (☎305/514–2300 or 800/531–5658 ⊕www.oceaniacruises.com). **Princess Cruises** (☎661/753–0000 or 800/774–6237 ⊕www.princess.com). **Regent Seven Seas Cruises** (☎954/776–6123 or 800/477–7500 ⊕www.rssc.com). **Royal Caribbean International** (☎305/539–6000 or 800/327–6700 ⊕www.royalcaribbean.com). **Seabourn Cruise Line** (☎305/463–3000 or 800/929–9391 ⊕www.seabourn.com). **Silversea Cruises** (☎954/522–4477 or 800/722–9955 ⊕www.silversea.com). **Windjammer Barefoot Cruises** (☎305/672–6453 or 800/327–2601 ⊕www.windjammer.com). **Windstar Cruises** (☎206/281–3535 or 800/258–7245 ⊕www.windstarcruises.com).

TRANSPORTATION

Panama is the southernmost part of an isthmus that stretches between Colombia and Costa Rica, making it a kind of bridge between Central and South America. Although Panama is a relatively small, narrow swath of land, it nonetheless has hundreds of miles of Pacific and Caribbean coastline. The 80-km-long (50-mi-long) Panama Canal, which runs north-south across the center of the country, connects these two oceans. The band of land it passes through is known as the Canal Zone; beautiful national rain forest parks make up much of it. A mountain range, usually referred to as the Cordillera Central, forms a topographical backbone along the entire length of the country.

Panama is divided into nine provinces and three semi-autonomous indigenous *comarcas*, or counties. Somewhat confusingly, the capital, Panama City, the province containing it, *and* the country itself are all known in Spanish simply as "Panamá." Panama City is on the Pacific coast, just east of the canal. It is the commercial, political, and cultural hub of the region, and more than 60% of the country's population lives in or near it. Colón, the run-down town at the Caribbean end of the canal, is known for its duty-free zone and high crime rate.

To the east, the Carretera Panamericana heads toward the Darién province, home to a vast, near-impenetrable jungle, which creates the only break in the whole highway. The road starts again on the other side of the Colombian border and continues to Patagonia. The Darién region takes up most of southeastern Panama; it contains some of the world's best-preserved rain forest, but is also home to Colombian guerrillas and paramilitary groups.

North of the Darién is Kuna Yala comarca, which stretches along Panama's Caribbean coast between Panama province and Colombia. A coral atoll known as the San Blas Islands lies off this coast. Home to the indigenous Kuna people, San Blas is only accessible by light airplane or boat. A larger group of islands—the Perlas Archipelago—lies off Panama's Pacific coast, in the Gulf of Panama.

The Carretera Panamericana (Panamerican Highway) runs west from Panama City to Costa Rica (and eventually to Alaska). It passes through Penonomé and Santiago, two regional hubs, on the way. Halfway along this stretch, the Azuero Peninsula juts out into the Pacific; area coral reefs are prime diving sites.

Two provinces border Costa Rica: Chiriquí, to the south, and Bocas del Toro, to the north. Cloud forests and extinct volcanoes are what draw visitors to Chiriquí; its capital, David, is popular with expats and retirees. The main attraction in Bocas del Toro is the eponymous archipelago lying off its coast. Rain forests, unspoiled beaches, mangrove swamps, and yet more coral reefs have made this Panama's ecotourism capital. You can reach Bocas by land from Chiriquí, by light airplane, and by boat.

TRAVEL TIMES FROM PANAMA CITY		
To	By Air	By Bus
Colón	¼ hour	½ hour
David	1 hour	6 hours
Bocas del Toro	1 hour	12 hours (to Almirante)
Chitré	½ hour	4 hours
Las Tablas	N/A	4½ hours
San Blas	½ hour	N/A
La Palma (Darién)	1½ hours	N/A

■ TIP→ **Ask the local tourist board about hotel and local transportation packages that include tickets to major museum exhibits or other special events.**

▍BY AIR

All scheduled international flights land at Panama City's Aeropuerto Internacional de Tocumen. From New York or Chicago flying time is about 5 hours; from Miami 2¾ hours; from L.A. 5½ hours; and from Dallas or Houston 4¼ hours. Flights from Toronto via Newark take 9 hours, or 7 hours via Miami.

Airlines & Airports Airline and Airport Links.com (⊕ www.airlineandairportlinks.com) has links to many of the world's airlines and airports.

Airline Security Issues Transportation Security Administration (⊕ www.tsa.gov) has answers for almost every question that might come up.

AIRPORTS

Panama's main air hub is Aeropuerto Internacional de Tocumen (PTY), about 26 km (15 mi) northeast of Panama City. All scheduled international flights land here. The passenger terminal was completely overhauled in 2006 and is now a pleasant glass-walled construction. There's an abundance of shops—most sell luxury clothing and electronics—but only one snack bar and a couple of food carts, so don't plan on much more than a coffee and sandwich. Tocumen also has a tourist-information booth, an ATM, 24-hour luggage storage, car-rental agencies, and a telephone and Internet center. Arrival and departure formalities are usually efficient, and there is a $20 departure tax.

Domestic flights operate out of Aeropuerto Paitilla–Marcos A. Gelabert (PAC), more commonly known as Albrook Airport, after the U.S. military base that once stood here. Albrook has a tourist-information stand, an ATM, and some car-rental offices.

Airport Information Aeropuerto Internacional de Tocumen (☎238–2761 ⊕www. tocumenpanama.aero). **Aeropuerto Paitilla–Marcos A. Gelabert** (Albrook Airport ☎No phone).

GROUND TRANSPORTATION

Taxis are the quickest way into Panama City from Tocumen Airport. The fare is a flat $25, an expensive ride for Panama, so it's worth finding out if your hotel has a shuttle service. Sharing the ride with strangers is commonplace, and the tourist-information booth often helps travelers club together. The trip can take between 30 and 60 minutes, depending on traffic, and whether the driver takes the Corredor Sur toll road, which is quicker but costs an extra $2.50. Note that taxis are often scarce late at night.

Public buses run frequently between Tocumen and the terminal north of Plaza Cinco de Mayo, but it can be a hassle to hoist your luggage onto them. They cost 70¢ and take 45 to 60 minutes.

The 15-minute taxi ride from Albrook Airport to the city center costs $2–$3. The bus to Plaza Cinco de Mayo costs 25¢ and takes 25 minutes.

TRANSFERS BETWEEN AIRPORTS

A taxi ride between Tocumen and Albrook airports is usually a $25 flat fare, though if you're catching the cab at Albrook you might be able to negotiate a cheaper price. The trip takes about 30 minutes. Alternatively, buses to both airports start and finish at Plaza Cinco de Mayo, but the trip could end up taking a couple of hours.

FLIGHTS

Copa, a Continental partner, is Panama's flagship carrier. It operates direct flights to New York JFK, Los Angeles, Miami, Washington Dulles, and Orlando. Copa also flies to many Central and South American cities. You can fly to Panama from Houston and Newark on Continental; from Atlanta on Delta; and from Miami on American and Iberia. Charter company Air Transat has flights from Montréal and Toronto, but only during some months of the year.

Aeroperlas and Air Panama are Panama's main two domestic carriers and serve destinations all over the country, including San Blas, Bocas del Toro, David, and the Darién. Domestic flights usually cost $60–$110 round-trip; you can buy tickets directly through the airline or with a travel agent. Sometimes buying your flight at the airport just before you travel is cheaper.

Airline Contacts American Airlines (☎800/433–7300 in North America, 507/269–6022 in Panama ⊕www.aa.com). **Continental Airlines** (☎800/231–0856 in North America, 507/265–0040 in Panama ⊕www.continental. com). **Copa** (☎507/227–5000 in Panama ⊕www.copaair.com)."<!–Central and South America–>**Delta Airlines** (☎800/241–4141 in North America, 507/263–3802 in Panama ⊕www.delta.com). **Iberia** (☎800/722–4642 in North America, 507/227–3966 in Panama ⊕www.iberia.com).

Domestic Carriers Aeroperlas (☎507/315–7500 in Panama ⊕www.aeroperlas.com). **Air Panama** (☎507/316–9000 in Panama ⊕www.flyairpanama.com).

▌BY BOAT

For information about Panama Canal boat trips, see "The Canal & Central Panama Essentials" in Chapter 2. Arriving in Panama by boat is increasingly popular. Private sailing boats operate between Cartagena in Colombia and San Blas or Portobelo, on Panama's Caribbean coast. The few operators cater mainly to backpackers and sometimes expect passengers to help with cooking, cleaning, or sailing. Zuly's and Mamallena, two hostels in Panama City, have ties with reputable sailboat captains and act as booking intermediaries. The trip can take up to five days (you stop at islands in San Blas) and costs $250–$300, including all food.

Within Panama, boats are the only way to get between points in the archipelagos of San Blas and Bocas del Toro and much of the Darién. There are regular, inexpensive water-taxi services connecting the city of Almirante with Bocas del Toro.

> **THE MATTER OF METERS**
>
> In directions and addresses in Panama, "100 meters" almost always means one block, regardless of actual measurements. Likewise, 200 meters is two blocks and 50 meters is half a block.

In the Darién, water taxis run between Puerto Quimba and La Palma. To get farther afield, people wind their way up narrow waterways in dugouts with outboard motors. Rides can be expensive ($60–$200), especially when traveling alone, so you're often better off going with a tour company.

Information Mamallena (☎507/6538–9745 ⊕www.mamallena.com). **Zuly's Independent Backpacker** (☎507/269–2665 ⊕www.geo cities.com/zulys_independent_backpacker).

▌BY BUS

ARRIVING & DEPARTING
You can reach Panama by bus from Costa Rica. Most services cross the border at Paso Canoas. The Darién jungle causes a gap in the Panamerican Highway, meaning bus travel to Colombia is impossible.

Popular with budget travelers, Ticabus is an international bus company connecting all of Central America. A bus leaves Panama City daily at 11 AM and takes 16 hours (direct) to get to San José in Costa Rica. One-way tickets cost $25. Ticabus continues to Nicaragua, Honduras, Guatemala, and Mexico. The buses are usually clean, air-conditioned, and comfortable.

Costa Rican company Panaline has daily services between San José and Panama City. The trip costs $50 one way; buses leave Panama at midday, and take 16 hours.

International Bus Companies Panaline (☎507/314–6383 ⊕www.panalinecr.com). **Ticabus** (☎507/314–6385 ⊕www.ticabus. com).

GETTING AROUND PANAMA

Getting around Panama by bus is comfortable, cheap, and straightforward. Panama City is the main transport hub. Services to towns all over the country (and to the rest of Central America) leave from a huge building in Albrook—half terminal and half mall, it has shops, ATMs, Internet access, and restaurants. To get to smaller cities and beaches, you need to catch minibuses out of regional transit hubs.

Long-distance buses are usually clean and punctual, and the only real annoyance is the occasional blaring radio. The most comfortable buses are those running between Panama City and David. Routes are operated by many different bus companies, and there's no centralized timetable service. The best way to get departure times is to call the bus company or go to the terminal. Similarly, rates are not set in stone, but you can estimate $1–$2 per hour of travel.

For bus company and terminal information, see the Essentials section in each destination chapter.

▍BY CAR

Panama is probably the best Central American country to drive in, and driving is a great way to see the country. The Panamerican Highway takes you to or near most towns in the country, and with a car you can also visit small villages and explore remote areas more easily. Even secondary roads are well signposted and in reasonable condition.

True, Panamanian drivers can be a little aggressive, but they're not much worse than New Yorkers or Angelinos. All the same, you're best saving the car for outside Panama City: traffic jams and lack of safe parking can make downtown driving very stressful.

WORD OF MOUTH

"If you are in the city, I would avoid a car—people drive crazy . . . and traffic can be a nightmare, so to save the added stress, pay the very low fare of a taxi driver. It's $1.25–$5 to almost anywhere in the city, $1.25–$1.50 around the city, and $5 to get to the outer part of the city, Causeway, etc. If you are outside the city, traveling [by] car would be great. If driving up towards Boquete, there are places to stop and see along the highway, endless beaches, fun local giftshops and ceramic shops, etc."

—maui206

GASOLINE

There are plenty of gas stations in and near towns in Panama, and along the Panamerican Highway. Most are open 24 hours. On long trips fill your tank whenever you can, even if you've still got gas left, as the next station could be a long way away. An attendant always pumps the gas and doesn't expect a tip, though a small one is always appreciated. Both cash and credit cards are usually accepted.

Most rental cars run on premium unleaded gas, which costs about $2.80 a gallon.

PARKING

On-street parking generally isn't a good idea in Panama City, as car theft is common. Instead, park in a guarded parking lot—many hotels have them. Note that many rental agencies insist you follow this rule.

ROAD CONDITIONS

The Panamerican Highway is paved along its entire length in Panama, and most secondary roads are paved, too. However, maintenance isn't always a regular process, so worn, pockmarked—or even potholed—surfaces are commonplace. Turnoffs are often sharp, and mountain roads can have terrifying hairpin bends.

In and around Panama City traffic is heavy. The mostly two-lane road from

Panama City to the town of Colón is a nightmare between 8 and 9 in the morning and 5 to 6 in the afternoon because of rush-hour traffic. Two highways going north and south out of the city somewhat alleviate the congestion.

Turnoffs and distances are usually clearly signposted. Be especially watchful at traffic lights, as crossing on yellow (or even red) lights is common practice.

FROM PANAMA CITY	
To	Distance
Colón	89 km (55 mi)
Penonomé	150 km (93 mi)
Santiago	252 km (157 mi)
David	486 km (302 mi)
Boquete	515 km (320 mi)
Costa Rican Border	592 km (368 mi)

ROADSIDE EMERGENCIES

Panama has no private roadside assistance clubs—ask rental agencies carefully about what you should do if you break down. If you have an accident, you are legally obliged to stay by your vehicle until the police arrive, which could take a long time. You can also call the transport police or, if you're near Panama City, the tourist police.

Emergency Services **National police** (☎104). **Tourist police** (☎211–30448). **Transport police** (☎211–7000).

RULES OF THE ROAD

Drivers in Panama stick to the right, as in the United States. You cannot turn right on a red light. Seat belts are required, and the law is now enforced. Locals take speed-limit signs, the ban on driving with cell phones, and drinking and driving lightly, so drive very defensively. As you approach small towns, watch out for *topes,* the local (Central American) name for speed bumps.

Driving into Panama from Costa Rica is common practice. As well as car ownership papers, ID, and insurance, the only thing you'll need at the border is a lot of patience.

▌BY TRAIN

Panama's only train service is the Panama Canal Railway, which operates between Panama City and Colón on weekdays. Tracks run alongside the canal itself and over causeways in Lago Gatún. The hour-long trip costs $22 each way; trains leave Panama City at 7:15 AM and Colón at 5:15 PM. You can buy tickets at the station before you leave.

Information **Panama Canal Railway** (☎507/317–6070 ⊕www.panarail.com).

ON THE GROUND

▌BUSINESS SERVICES & FACILITIES

In Panama City the Ocean Business Center provides secretarial services, meeting and conference facilities, and office rentals. Regus is an international company that offers similar facilities in two Panama City office blocks. Contact SOS for translating and secretarial services. For printing, photocopying, and fax services, head to a branch of Mail Boxes, Etc.

ATLAPA is Panama's flagship convention center. It's a massive, government-owned complex right in Panama City; IPAT, the tourist office, runs it.

Contacts ATLAPA Convention Center (☎226–7000 ⊕www.atlapa.gob.pa). **Mail Boxes, Etc.** (☎302–4162 ⊕www.mbe. com). **Ocean Business Center** (☎340–0200 ⊕www.oceanbusinesscenter.com). **Regus** (☎888/271–4615 from the U.S. ⊕www. regus.com). **SOS** (☎264–2073 ⊕www. serviofionline.com).

▌COMMUNICATIONS

INTERNET

Internet access is widely available. Most midrange and top-end hotels in big cities have some kind of in-room access (often Wi-Fi) but you need to have a laptop. Computers for guest use are unusual in this kind of establishment, although hostels often have a PC or two for guests.

Panama has a dazzling selection of cyber-cafés. In big cities it's hard to walk more than a block without tripping over one, and even remote locations usually have at least one. Rates usually range from 50¢ to $1 an hour. Broadband connections are common, and you can expect speeds on par with those in the United States. Many cybercafés also have Internet phone services.

Contacts Cybercafes (⊕www.cybercafes. com) lists over 4,000 Internet cafés worldwide.

PHONES

The good news is that you can now make a direct-dial telephone call from virtually any point on earth. The bad news? You can't always do so cheaply. Calling from a hotel is almost always the most expensive option; hotels usually add huge surcharges to all calls, particularly international ones. In some countries you can phone from call centers or even the post office. Calling cards usually keep costs to a minimum, but only if you purchase them locally. And then there are mobile phones (⇨below), which are sometimes more prevalent—particularly in the developing world—than landlines; as expensive as mobile phone calls can be, they are still usually a much cheaper option than calling from your hotel.

The country code for Panama is 507. To call Panama from the United States, dial the international access code (011) followed by the country code (507), and the 7-digit phone number, in that order. Note that cell phones have 8 digits. Panama does not use area codes. To make **collect or calling-card calls,** dial 106 from any phone in Panama and an English-speaking operator will connect you.

CALLING WITHIN PANAMA

Panama's telephone system, operated by Cable and Wireless, is cheap and highly efficient. You can make local and long-distance calls from your hotel—usually with a surcharge—and from any public phone box. All local phone numbers have seven digits, except for cell phones, which have eight digits and start with a six.

The bright blue public phone boxes all take phone cards and some also accept coins; you insert coins or your card first, and then dial. You can also use prepaid calling cards from them free of charge.

Standard local calls cost 10¢ a minute, less with a prepaid calling card (⇨ "Calling Cards," *below*) such as ClaroCOM. For **local directory assistance** (in Spanish), dial 102.

CALLING OUTSIDE PANAMA

To make international calls from Panama, dial 00, then the country code, area code and number. The country code for the United States is 1.

Many cybercafés have Internet phone services: rates are usually cheap (they're always posted outside the shop), but communication quality can vary. You can also make international calls from pay phones using a prepaid card such as ClaroCOM. Dialing the international operator lets you make collect international calls. It's possible to use AT&T, Sprint, and MCI services from Panama, but using a prepaid card is cheaper.

Access Codes AT&T (☎109). **MCI** (☎108). **Sprint** (☎115).

CALLING CARDS

ClaroCOM are by far the best prepaid calling cards, and can be used to make local and international calls from any telephone in Panama. Calls both within Panama and to the United States cost 5¢ a minute; cards come in denominations of $3, $5, $10, and $20. To use them, you dial a free local access number, enter your PIN number and the number you want to call. You can buy cards from Claro-COM's Web site, or from supermarkets, drugstores, and pharmacies all over the country. Ask for *una tarjeta telefónica prepaga.*

Calling Card Information ClaroCOM (☎200–0100 ⊕www.clarocom.com).

MOBILE PHONES

If you have a multiband phone (some countries use frequencies different from what's used in the United States) and your service provider uses the world-standard GSM network (as do T-Mobile, Cingular, and Verizon), you can probably use

your phone abroad. Roaming fees can be steep, however: 99¢ a minute is considered reasonable. And overseas you normally pay the toll charges for incoming calls. It's almost always cheaper to send a text message than to make a call, since text messages have a very low set fee (often less than 5¢).

■TIP➜ If you travel internationally frequently, save one of your old mobile phones or buy a cheap one on the Internet; ask your cell phone company to unlock it for you, and take it with you as a travel phone, buying a new SIM card with pay-as-you-go service in each destination.

Mobile phones are immensely popular in Panama. If you have an unlocked tri-band phone and intend to call local numbers, it makes sense to buy a prepaid Panamanian SIM card on arrival—rates will be much better than using your U.S. network. Alternatively, you can buy a cheap handset in Panama for about $25.

There are two main mobile-phone companies in Panama: Movistar, owned by Telefónica, and Cable and Wireless. Their prices are similar but Cable and Wireless is said to have better coverage in farther-flung areas of the country. You only pay for outgoing calls, which cost between 5¢ and 50¢ a minute. You can buy a SIM card (*tarjeta SIM*) from any outlet of either company; pay-as-you-go cards (*tarjeta prepaga para celular*) to charge your account are available from supermarkets, drugstores, gas stations, and kiosks.

You can also rent from companies like CellRent, or from top-end hotels. A basic phone costs $5 a day, but you have to pay for incoming and outgoing calls, and for theft insurance, so buying a phone might be cheaper.

Contacts Cellular Abroad (☎800/287–5072 ⊕www.cellularabroad.com) rents and sells GMS phones and sells SIM cards that work in many countries. **Mobal** (☎888/888–9162 ⊕www.mobalrental.com) rents mobiles and sells GSM phones (starting at $49) that operate in 140 countries. Per-call rates vary. **Planet Fone** (☎888/988–4777 ⊕www.planetfone. com) rents cell phones, but the per-minute rates are expensive.

■ CUSTOMS & DUTIES

You're always allowed to bring goods of a certain value back home without having to pay any duty or import tax. But there's a limit on the amount of tobacco and liquor you can bring back duty-free, and some countries have separate limits for perfumes; for exact figures, check with your customs department.

You may import 500 cigarettes (or 500 grams of tobacco or 50 cigars) and three bottles of alcohol duty-free. Panamanian customs can be very strict; even if you are only making an airline connection, make sure your papers are in order. Prescription drugs should always be accompanied by a doctor's authorization. When departing the country by land, travelers are not allowed to export any duty-free items. Duty-free items, by law, have to be shipped to a foreign address if the buyer is departing from the country by land.

U.S. Information U.S. Customs and Border Protection (⊕www.cbp.gov).

■ EATING OUT

Panama's cosmopolitan history is reflected in its food. Panama City has a great range of restaurants serving both local and international fare. Among the latter, Greek, Chinese, Italian, and American eateries are the most common. Fast-food outlets abound—some are names you'll recognize, others are local chains.

Traditional Panamanian food is often referred to as *comida típica*. As you'd expect in a country with so much coastline, seafood plays a big part in local dishes. *Corvina* (sea bass) is a favorite, as are prawns, which are one of the countries top export items. Another standout

WORD OF MOUTH

"I now have an 10-year-old daughter who when served her whole red snapper simply looked at her father and said "Papa, can I eat the eyeballs?" lol."

—faithie

dish is *ceviche,* chilled marinated seafood "cooked" using lime juice.

Chicken is the most common meat in Panama. It's the main ingredient, along with yucca, in *sancocho,* robust soup bursting with *culantro,* a powerful local version of cilantro. Rice and beans are as much a staple here as in the rest of Central America, but are supplemented by yucca and plantains. Caribbean flavors like lime and coconut milk are common on the northern coast.

Popular snacks include tamales, ground maize stuffed with meat and cooked wrapped inside a banana leaf, and Panama-style tortillas: deep-fried burger-sized patties of corn dough, often topped or filled with cheese. Follow them with Panama's version of flan (akin to crème caramel), the most popular local dessert.

Panama has a fabulous range of tropical fruits, but they're usually sold as a juice or shake (either with milk or with water; ask if you don't want extra sugar added). Forget about cutting down your cholesterol while you're in Panama: deep-frying is a way of life here. Goodies to go out of the way for include *patacones* (twice-fried rounds of plantain) and *hojaldras* (deep-fried flaky dough).

Panamanians might not eat huge quantities of meat, but somehow shredded chicken, ground beef, ham, or meat stock manages to make its way into most dishes, so truly vegetarian options are limited. Remember that in Spanish *carne* (meat) usually refers to red meat, so don't be surprised to get fish or chicken if you ask for something "*sin carne*" (without meat).

LOCAL DO'S & TABOOS

Customs of the Country. Most Panamanians—especially those living in and around Panama City—are open-minded and cosmopolitan, and there are few taboos to worry about when interacting with them. Some locals feel animosity towards the United States over the canal, but are usually happy to discuss this and other political issues.

Punctuality is a flexible issue in Panama, and you shouldn't be offended if local friends or acquaintances arrive late—even very late—for meetings or meals. You as a foreigner will generally be expected to be punctual, however. Buses and airplanes usually run to schedule.

In Panama it is acceptable to make a quick hiss or whistle to get someone's attention—you may find that you even take up the habit yourself, particularly with waiters. You also may hear men catcall women in this way, which, unfortunately, is not considered terribly rude either.

Panama has a large indigenous population, many of whom conserve traditional lifestyles and habits. Some communities, such as the Kuna in San Blas, are very used to interacting with visitors, but peoples in more remote areas have less contact with outsiders and so might be less at ease around visitors, or less welcoming. Always ask for permission when taking photographs of people or events.

Greetings. Like most Latin Americans, Panamanians are a demonstrative lot and greet each other enthusiastically in social situations. Women often greet each other with one kiss on the cheek. Among men, hand-shaking is the norm, sometimes accompanied by a friendly back-slap; closer acquaintances go in for big bear hugs.

The use of formal salutations (*buenos días*, *buenas tardes*, and *buenas noches*) is common in business meetings and among older people. The formal "you" form, *usted,* is also common in such situations.

Out on the Town. Alcohol—especially beer—plays a big part in Panamanian social life. But while men drink on par with North Americans, women tend to drink much less, if at all. Smoking is prohibited on public transport and in some enclosed public spaces.

Public displays of affection are fine between heterosexual couples in Panama, but expect conservative—or even aggressive—reactions to same-sex couples.

People usually dress up a little to go out for dinner, to the theater, or even the cinema, but keep their really fancy gear for special occasions. If you're invited to someone's house for dinner, take along a bottle of wine or some chocolates.

Language. Try to learn a little of the local language. You need not strive for fluency; even just mastering a few basic words and terms is bound to make chatting with the locals more rewarding.

Spanish is the official language of Panama. English is also widely spoken, especially near the Canal Zone, and some of Panama's indigenous communities speak their own languages. Panamanian Spanish sounds more like Cuban Spanish than Mexican, and can take a while to get your ear around. Locals often aspirate, rather than pronounce, the *s* at the end of words or syllables. Even though many people—especially those who work in the tourist business—speak English, attempts to use Spanish are usually appreciated.

A phrasebook and language-tape set can help get you started.

Fodor's Spanish for Travelers (available at bookstores everywhere) is excellent.

MEALS & MEALTIMES

A typical Panamanian breakfast (*desayuno*) consists of fried tortillas or hojaldras, washed down with coffee. Most hotels catering to foreigners also offer fruit, toast, and cereal, and you can expect breakfast buffets at five-star hotels.

Lunch (*comida* or *almuerzo*) is the main meal, and thus the longest, running from noon to 2 or 3. Many restaurants do set-price meals of two or three courses at lunch. In Panamanian homes dinner is often merely a light snack eaten around 9 PM. If you're eating out, dinner is just as big a deal as in the United States, but is usually served until 10:30 PM.

Unless otherwise noted, the restaurants listed in this guide are open daily for lunch and dinner.

PAYING

In restaurants with waiter service you pay the check (*la cuenta*) at the end of the meal. In fast-food restaurants and at food stands, you generally pay up front. Credit cards are accepted in more expensive restaurants, but it's always a good idea to check before you order, especially as some establishments only accept one kind of credit card.

For guidelines on tipping see Tipping below.

See Orientation & Planning at the beginning of each chapter for price charts.

RESERVATIONS & DRESS

Regardless of where you are, it's a good idea to make a reservation if you can. In some places (Hong Kong, for example), it's expected. We only mention them specifically when reservations are essential (there's no other way you'll ever get a table) or when they are not accepted. For popular restaurants, book as far ahead as you can (often 30 days), and reconfirm as soon as you arrive. (Large parties should always call ahead to check the reservations policy.) We mention dress only

WORD OF MOUTH

Was the service stellar or not up to snuff? Did the food give you shivers of delight or leave you cold? Did the prices and portions make you happy or sad? Rate restaurants and write your own reviews in Travel Ratings or start a discussion about your favorite places in Travel Talk on www.fodors.com. Your comments might even appear in our books. Yes, you, too, can be a correspondent!

when men are required to wear a jacket or a jacket and tie.

WINES, BEER & SPIRITS

Alcohol is available in just about every restaurant in Panama, though cheaper places have limited selections.

For meals and light drinking, beer—usually lager—is the local favorite. Good brands made in Panama include Balboa, Atlas, Panamá, and Soberana, but North American and European brands are also widely available. For more serious drinking, Panamanians reach for a bottle of *seco*, a fierce white rum that gets you under the table in no time.

Wine still isn't a big thing in Panama, but most decent restaurants have imported bottles from the United States or Chile and Argentina. Imported liquor is also easy to find in supermarkets.

▌ELECTRICITY

You won't need a converter or adapter, as the electrical current in Panama is 110 volts, the same as in the United States. Outlets take either plugs with two flat prongs or two flat prongs with a circular grounded prong.

Don't use 110-volt outlets marked FOR SHAVERS ONLY for high-wattage appliances such as hair-dryers.

▌EMERGENCIES

Dial 104 for **police** and 103 for **fire**.

In a medical or dental emergency, ask your hotel staff for information on and directions to the nearest private hospital or clinic. Taxi drivers should also know how to find one, and taking a taxi is often quicker than an ambulance. There is no centralized ambulance service, so if you do need an ambulance, call for one from the hospital you want to go to; alternatively, you can call the Red Cross or SEMM, a private ambulance service. Many private medical insurers provide online lists of hospitals and clinics in different towns. It's a good idea to print out a copy of these before you travel.

For theft, wallet loss, small road accidents, and minor emergencies, contact the nearest police station. Expect all dealings with the police to be a bureaucratic business—it's probably only worth bothering if you need the report for insurance claims.

Most embassies in the capital open at 8:30 and close by noon.

The Hospital Nacional is an excellent private hospital with English-speaking doctors, a 24-hour emergency room, and specialists in many areas. The Centro Médico Paitilla is the country's best, and most expensive, hospital. The Clínica Bella Vista is a private clinic with English-speaking doctors. To take advantage of Panama's state-run healthcare, head to the public Hospital Santo Tomás.

Pack a basic first-aid kit, especially if you're venturing into more remote areas. If you'll be carrying any medication, bring your doctor's contact information and prescription authorizations. Getting your prescription filled in Panama might be problematic, so bring enough medication for your entire trip.

Two chains of 24-hour supermarket/pharmacies—Arrocha and Rey—have numerous branches.

Embassies U.S. Embassy (✉Calle 37 and Av. Balboa ☎507/263–6011 or 507/207–7000).

General Emergency Contacts Ambulance (Red Cross ☎507/315–1388). **Ambulance** (SEMM ☎507/264–4122). **Fire department** (☎103). **National police** (☎104).

Hospitals & Clinics Clínica Bella Vista (✉Av. Perú and Calle 38, Calidonia, Panama City ☎507/227–1266). **Centro Médico Paitilla** (✉Av. Balboa and Calle 53, Punto Paitilla, Panama City ☎507/265–8800). **Hospital Nacional** (✉Av. Cuba and Calles 38 and 39, Calidonia, Panama City ☎507/207–8100). **Hospital Santo Tomás** (✉Av. Balboa at Calle 34 Este, Calidonia, Panama City ☎507/227–4122 ⊕www.hst.sld.pa).

▌HEALTH

The most common types of illnesses are caused by contaminated food and water. Especially in developing countries, drink only bottled, boiled, or purified water and drinks; don't drink from public fountains or use ice. You should even consider using bottled water to brush your teeth. Make sure food has been thoroughly cooked and is served to you fresh and hot; avoid vegetables and fruits that you haven't washed (in bottled or purified water) or peeled yourself. If you have problems, mild cases of traveler's diarrhea may respond to Imodium (known generically as loperamide) or Pepto-Bismol. Be sure to drink plenty of fluids; if you can't keep fluids down, seek medical help immediately.

Infectious diseases can be airborne or passed via mosquitoes and ticks and through direct or indirect physical contact with animals or people. Some, including Norwalk-like viruses that affect your digestive tract, can be passed along through contaminated food. If you are traveling in an area where malaria is prevalent, use a repellant containing DEET and take malaria-prevention medication before, during, and after your trip as directed by your physician.

GETTING STARTED / BOOKING YOUR TRIP / TRANSPORTATION / **ON THE GROUND**

Condoms can help prevent most sexually transmitted diseases, but they aren't absolutely reliable and their quality varies from country to country. Speak with your physician and/or check the CDC or World Health Organization Web sites for health alerts, particularly if you're pregnant, traveling with children, or have a chronic illness.

For information on travel insurance, shots and medications, and medical-assistance companies see Shots & Medications under Things to Consider in Getting Started, above.

SPECIFIC ISSUES IN PANAMA

It's safe to drink tap water and have ice in your drinks in urban areas, but stick to bottled water in rural areas.

Two mosquito-borne diseases are prevalent in Panama: dengue fever (especially in Bocas del Toro) and malaria (in the Darién, Bocas del Toro, and San Blas). Prevention is better than a cure: cover up your arms and legs and use a strong insect repellent containing a high concentration of DEET. Don't hang around outside at sunset, and sleep under a mosquito net in jungle areas. Preventive antimalarial medication may also be necessary: consult your doctor well before you travel. There are no preventive drugs for dengue.

Sunburn and sunstroke are potential health hazards when visiting Panama. Stay out of the sun at midday and use plenty of high-SPF-factor sunscreen when on the beach or hiking. You can buy well-known brands in most Panamanian pharmacies. Protect your eyes with good-quality sun glasses, and bear in mind that you'll burn more easily at higher altitudes and in the water.

OVER-THE-COUNTER REMEDIES

In Panama *farmacias* (drugstores) sell a wide range of medications over the counter, including some, but not all, drugs that would require a prescription in the United States. Familiar brands are easy to find, otherwise ask for what you want with the generic name. Note that acetaminophen—or Tylenol—is called *paracetomol* in Spanish. Farmacia Rey and Farmacia Arrocha are two local drugstore chains with branches all over the country, many of which are open 24 hours.

Information Farmacia Arrocha (⊕www. arrocha.com). **Farmacia Rey** (⊕www.smrey. com/smr/_farmacia/farmacia.asp).

❚ HOURS OF OPERATION

Businesses and government offices typically open weekdays between 8 and 9 AM and close between 4 and 6 PM; many keep these hours on Saturdays too. Banks open between 8 AM and 3 PM, but ATMs are usually open 24 hours. Standard hours for shops are 9 AM–6 PM. Restaurants are generally open until 10:30 PM, as dinner in Panama is eaten later than in the rest of Central America.

HOLIDAYS

Panama's national holidays for 2008 and 2009 are as follows: Año Nuevo (New Year's Day), January 1; Día de los Mártires (Martyrs' Day), January 9; Martes de Carnaval (Carnival Tuesday), February 5, 2008 and February 24, 2009; Viernes Santo (Good Friday), March 20, 2008 and April 9, 2009; Día del Trabajado (Labor Day), May 1; Día de los Difuntos (All Souls' Day), November 2; Día de la Independencia (Independence Day from Colombia), November 3; Primer Grito de la Independencia (First Cry of Independence), November 10; Día de la Emancipación (Emancipation Day from Spain), November 28; Dí de la Madre (Mother's Day), December 8; Navidad (Christmas), December 25.

Each region also has its own holidays, and many towns have saint's days.

▌ MAIL

Panama's national mail system is called Correo Nacional, or COTEL. There are branches in most cities and towns; standard opening hours are 7 AM to 5 or 6 PM. It's best to send mail from big cities—the more remote the origin of your letter, the better the chances of it getting lost. An airmail letter to the United States costs 35¢ and takes a week or two to arrive if posted from Panama City.

You can receive mail by Entrega General (general delivery) at most post offices. Letters should be addressed as follows: [Name on your passport], Entrega General, [city], [province], República de Panamá. There's a Panama City, Florida, so be sure to include the "República de Panamá." Note that for letters to Panama City you also need to include the city zone.

Airbox is a private mail company with both incoming and outgoing services to and from the United States. Their standard charge for sending documents is $3.50.

Information Airbox (☎269-9774 ⊕www.airbox.com.pa). **Correo Nacional** (☎212-7600 ⊕www.correos.gob.pa).

SHIPPING PACKAGES

Sending packages home through COTEL, the Panamanian mail system, isn't always reliable, so it's worth paying the extra for recorded delivery (*correo registrado*). Most packages take anywhere from a week to a month to arrive in the United States. Many stores—particularly upmarket ones—can ship your purchases for you, for a price. Valuable items are best sent with private express services. International couriers operating in Panama include DHL and Federal Express—overnight delivery for a 1-kg (2.2-pound) package starts at about $100. Sending a 1-kg package to the United States with Airbox costs $8.75 and takes two to three days.

Express Services Airbox (☎269-9774 ⊕www.airbox.com.pa). **DHL Worldwide Express** (☎271-3451 ⊕www.dhl.com). **Federal Express** (☎271-3838 ⊕www.fedex.com).

▌ MONEY

Although Panama is more expensive than the rest of Central America, prices still compare favorably to those back home. Midrange hotels and restaurants where locals eat are excellent value. Rooms at first-class hotels and meals at the best restaurants, however, approach those in the United States. Trips into remote parts of the country and adventure travel are also relatively expensive.

You can plan your trip around ATMs—cash is king for day-to-day dealings—and credit cards (for bigger spending). U.S. dollars are the local currency; changing any other currency can be problematic. Traveler's checks are useful only as a reserve.

Using large bills is often a problem in Panama, even in big shops or expensive restaurants. Trying to pay for a $3 purchase with a twenty may get you dirty looks, or just a straight "no." Have plenty of ones and fives at hand. Shop owners are wary of forged bills, and may record the serial number of $50 or $100 bills, along with your name and passport number.

SAMPLE COSTS	
Item	Average Cost
cup of coffee	$1.25
glass of wine	$3
glass of beer	$1.50
sandwich	$3
1-mi taxi ride in Panama City	$2
museum admission	free–$3

Prices throughout this guide are given for adults. Substantially reduced fees are almost always available for children, students, and senior citizens.

ATMS & BANKS

Your own bank will probably charge a fee for using ATMs abroad; the foreign bank you use may also charge a fee. Nevertheless, extracting funds as you need them is a safer option than carrying around a large amount of cash.

■ TIP→ **PIN numbers with more than four digits are not recognized at ATMs in many countries. If yours has five or more, remember to change it before you leave.**

ATMs—known locally as *cajeros automáticos*—are extremely common in Panama. In big cities even supermarkets and department stores usually have their own ATM. On-screen instructions appear automatically in English. Using large bills can be tricky in Panama, so try to withdraw smaller bills (ask for $90 rather than $100, for example). Make withdrawals from ATMs in daylight, rather than at night.

The main ATM network, which accepts cards with both Cirrus and Plus symbols, is called Sistema Clave. Its Web site lists ATM locations all over the country. Major banks in Panama include Banistmo, Banco General, and Banco Continental. Many international banks also have branches in Panama City.

Information **Sistema Clave** (⊕ www.sclave. com).

CREDIT CARDS

Throughout this guide, the following abbreviations are used: **AE,** American Express; **DC,** Diners Club; **MC,** MasterCard; and **V,** Visa.

It's a good idea to inform your credit-card company before you travel, especially if you're going abroad and don't travel internationally very often. Otherwise, the credit-card company might put a hold on your card owing to unusual activity—not a good thing halfway through your trip. Record all your credit-card numbers—as

well as the phone numbers to call if your cards are lost or stolen—in a safe place, so you're prepared should something go wrong. Both MasterCard and Visa have general numbers you can call (collect if you're abroad) if your card is lost, but you're better off calling the number of your issuing bank, since MasterCard and Visa usually just transfer you to your bank; your bank's number is usually printed on your card.

If you plan to use your credit card for cash advances, you'll need to apply for a PIN at least two weeks before your trip. Although it's usually cheaper (and safer) to use a credit card abroad for large purchases (so you can cancel payments or be reimbursed if there's a problem), note that some credit-card companies *and* the banks that issue them add substantial percentages to all foreign transactions, whether they're in a foreign currency or not. Check on these fees before leaving home, so there won't be any surprises when you get the bill.

Credit cards are widely accepted in Panama's urban areas. Visa is the most popular, followed by MasterCard and American Express. If possible, bring more than one credit card, as smaller establishments sometimes accept only one type. In small towns only top-end hotels and restaurants take plastic.

Reporting Lost Cards **American Express** (☎800/528–4800 in the U.S. or 336/393–1111 collect from abroad ⊕ www.american express.com). **Diners Club** (☎800/234–6377 in the U.S. or 303/799–1504 collect from abroad ⊕ www.dinersclub.com). **MasterCard** (☎800/627–8372 in the U.S. or 636/722–7111 collect from abroad ⊕ www.mastercard. com). **Visa** (☎800/847–2911 in the U.S. or 410/581–9994 collect from abroad ⊕ www. visa.com).

CURRENCY & EXCHANGE

Panama's national currency is the U.S. dollar. Don't get confused if you see prices expressed in *balboas*: it's just the local name for the dollar. All bills come in standard American denominations, although Panama also mints its own version of nickels, dimes, and quarters. If you get stuck with these at the end of the trip, you can use them in parking meters, ticket machines, and phones back home. Try to avoid coming to Panama with other currencies, as the exchange rates are generally unfavorable.

■TIP➔ Even if a currency-exchange booth has a sign promising no commission, rest assured that there's some kind of huge, hidden fee. (Oh … that's right. The sign didn't say no *fee*.). And as for rates, you're almost always better off getting foreign currency at an ATM or exchanging money at a bank.

TRAVELER'S CHECKS & CARDS

Some consider this the currency of the cave man, and it's true that fewer establishments accept traveler's checks these days. Nevertheless, they're a cheap and secure way to carry extra money, particularly on trips to urban areas. Both Citibank (under the Visa brand) and American Express issue traveler's checks in the United States, but Amex is better known and more widely accepted; you can also avoid hefty surcharges by cashing Amex checks at Amex offices. Whatever you do, keep track of all the serial numbers in case the checks are lost or stolen.

U.S.-dollar American Express traveler's checks are the easiest to change in Panama. By all means take some along as an emergency option, but plan your trip around cash, ATMs, and credit cards—you'll save a whole lot of time and headaches, not to mention commission charges.

American Express now offers a stored-value card called a Travelers Cheque Card, which you can use wherever American Express credit cards are accepted, including ATMs. The card can carry a minimum of $300 and a maximum of $2,700, and it's a very safe way to carry your funds. Although you can get replace-

ment funds in 24 hours if your card is lost or stolen, it doesn't really strike us as a very good deal. In addition to a high initial cost ($14.95 to set up the card, plus $5 each time you "reload"), you still have to pay a 2% fee for each purchase in a foreign currency (similar to that of any credit card). Further, each time you use the card in an ATM you pay a transaction fee of $2.50 on top of the 2% transaction fee for the conversion—add it all up and it can be considerably more than you would pay when simply using your own ATM card. Regular traveler's checks are just as secure and cost less.

Contacts American Express (☎888/412–6945 in the U.S., 801/945–9450 collect outside of the U.S. to add value or speak to customer service ⊕www.americanexpress.com).

▌ RESTROOMS

Restrooms in Panama use Western-style toilets. Cleanliness standards vary widely, especially in public facilities such as bus and gas stations. Toilet paper isn't guaranteed, so carry tissues in your day pack. Antibacterial hand wipes—for sanitizing you or the facilities—are also useful.

Find a Loo The Bathroom Diaries (⊕www.thebathroomdiaries.com) is flush with unsanitized info on restrooms the world over—each one located, reviewed, and rated.

▌ SAFETY

As Latin American countries go, Panama is relatively safe. In most of the country crime against tourists is usually limited to pickpocketing and bag-snatching. Taking a few simple precautions is usually enough to keep you from being a target.

In urban areas attitude is essential. Strive to look aware and purposeful at all times. Look at maps before you go outside, not on a street corner; and keep a firm hold on your purse. At night exercise the same kind of caution you would in any big American city and stay in well-lit areas with plenty of people around. Ask hotel or restaurant staff to call you a taxi at night, rather than flagging one down. If you're driving, park in guarded lots, never on the street; and remove the front of the stereo if that's possible.

In Panama City, the Casco Viejo has a sketchy reputation after dark. It's also best to steer clear of the neighborhoods of El Chorrillo, Calidonia, and El Marañón, where muggings are commonplace. Finally, local drivers are a danger to pedestrians in all the city's neighborhoods, so look twice (or thrice) before crossing the street.

Two places in the country are blots on Panama's safety reputation. The city of Colón is a hot spot for violent crime, and most locals warn against wandering its streets alone. Bordering Colombia, the Darién Province is a largely impenetrable jungle far from the reach of the law. Colombian guerrillas or paramilitary forces have kidnapped tourists crossing the border overland. Drug traffickers ply the region, and the small boats running between the two countries on both the Caribbean and the Pacific are often involved in smuggling. Visiting the Darién on an organized tour is the smart choice.

The most important advice we can give you is that in the unlikely event of being mugged or robbed, do not put up a struggle. Nearly all physical attacks on tourists are the direct result of their resisting would-be pickpockets or muggers. Comply with demands, hand over your stuff, and try to get the situation over with as quickly as possible—then let your travel insurance take care of it.

Report any crimes to the nearest police station. In Panama City you can also ask English-speaking tourist police (identifiable by a white armband) for help. Panamanian police are usually helpful when dealing with foreigners. However, their resources are limited: they'll happily provide you with reports for insurance claims, but tracking down your stolen goods is pretty unlikely.

In Panama you're legally obliged to carry ID—preferably your passport—with you at all times. If you prefer to keep your passport safe, laminate a color copy of the photo page and carry that, together with your driver's license or other photo ID. You may be asked for proof of your identity when dealing with the police.

■ TIP → Distribute your cash, credit cards, I.D.s, and other valuables between a deep front pocket, an inside jacket or vest pocket, and a hidden money pouch. Don't reach for the money pouch once you're in public.

▌ TAXES

Panama has a value added sales tax (IVA) of 5%–10%, which is usually included in the displayed price. Hotels also have a 10% tax. Visitors departing by air are charged an exit tax of $20, though this is sometimes included in your ticket.

▌ TIME

Panama is 5 hours behind GMT, the same as U.S. Eastern Standard Time. Panama does not observe Daylight Savings.

▌ TIPPING

In Panama tipping is a question of rewarding good service rather than an obligation. Restaurant bills don't include gratuities; adding 10% is customary. Bellhops and maids expect tips only in more expensive hotels, and $1–$2 per bag is the norm. You should also give a tip of up to $10 per day to tour guides. Rounding up taxi fares is a way of showing your appreciation to the driver, but it's not expected.

INDEX

PHOTO CREDITS

8, José Fuste Raga/age fotostock. 9 (left), Humberto Olarte Cupas/Alamy. 9 (right),
Sergio Pitamitz/age fotostock. 12, Ken Welsh/age fotostock. 13, ImageState/Alamy.
14, Robert Harding Picture Library Ltd/Alamy. 15, David Tipling/Alamy. 20, Dixon
Hamby/Alamy. **Chapter 1: Panama City:** 35, Julio Etchart/Alamy. 87, Craig Lovell/Eagle
Visions Photography/Alamy. **Chapter 2: The Canal & Central Panama:** 112, Popperfoto/
Alamy. **Chapter 3: The Azuero Peninsula & Veraguas:** 211, M. Timothy O'Keefe/Alamy.
Chapter 4: Chiriquí Province: 233, Andoni Canela/age fotostock.

NOTES

NOTES

NOTES

NOTES

NOTES

NOTES

NOTES

NOTES

NOTES

NOTES

NOTES

ABOUT OUR WRITER

Freelance writer David Dudenhoefer grew up in Chicago's North Shore and South Florida. After studying biology at the University of Colorado, he worked as a journalist and naturalist tour guide in Costa Rica. He first visited Panama in 1992. After a week in the country, he was already planning his next trip there. He returned to Panama frequently during the next decade to report on everything from politics to the environment for various publications, spending plenty of time in the country's forests, mountains, and indigenous communities. He also returned to the States to get an M.A. at the University of Illinois at Chicago (UIC), and spent a couple of years traveling, writing, and taking photos in Latin America and Asia.

David has contributed to eight Fodor's guides since 1991. To research this book, David returned to towns he'd first visited more than a decade earlier, which had gone from having several hotels to several dozen, and headed into areas that have only recently begun receiving tourists. By the time he was done, he was as impressed as ever with Panama, and just as on his first visit to the country, he was planning his next trip there before he'd even left. Despite Panama's impressive natural and cultural attractions, which surpass those of neighboring Costa Rica, memories of political strife in the late 1980s long hindered tourism there, and David would like to change that. David lives in Lima, Peru, with his wife María Angélica Vega and his stepchildren, Marcel and Isabelle.